Understanding Canton

Studies on Contemporary China

The Contemporary China Institute at the School of Oriental and African Studies (University of London) has, since its establishment in 1968, been an international centre for research and publications on China. *Studies on Contemporary China*, which is edited at the Institute, seeks to maintain and extend that tradition by making available the best work of scholars and China specialists throughout the world. It embraces a wide variety of subjects relating to Nationalist and Communist China, including social, political, and economic change, intellectual and cultural developments, foreign relations, and national security.

Understanding Canton

Rethinking Popular Culture in the Republican Period

VIRGIL K.Y. HO

Division of Humanities
Hong Kong University of Science and Technology

OXFORD
UNIVERSITY PRESS

OXFORD
UNIVERSITY PRESS

Great Clarendon Street, Oxford OX2 6DP

Oxford University Press is a department of the University of Oxford.
It furthers the University's objective of excellence in research, scholarship,
and education by publishing worldwide in

Oxford New York

Auckland Cape Town Dar es Salaam Hong Kong Karachi
Kuala Lumpur Madrid Melbourne Mexico City Nairobi
New Delhi Shanghai Taipei Toronto

With offices in

Argentina Austria Brazil Chile Czech Republic France Greece
Guatemala Hungary Italy Japan Poland Portugal Singapore
South Korea Switzerland Thailand Turkey Ukraine Vietnam

Oxford is a registered trade mark of Oxford University Press
in the UK and in certain other countries

Published in the United States
by Oxford University Press Inc., New York

First published 2005

British Library Cataloguing in Publication Data

Data available

Library of Congress Cataloging in Publication Data

Data available

Typeset by Newgen Imaging Systems (P) Ltd., Chennai, India
Printed in Great Britain
on acid-free paper by
Biddles Ltd., King's Lynn

ISBN 0–19–928271–4 978–0–19–928271–5

1 3 5 7 9 10 8 6 4 2

Acknowledgements

I COULD never have completed this study without the truly kind support, generous assistance, and much-needed encouragement of my mentor Professor Mark Elvin. His thought-provoking comments on the earlier versions of this manuscript helped to improve its conceptual clarity, historical accuracy, and analytical depth. Professor Göran Aijmer of Gothenburg University in Sweden is another mine of intellectual stimulation that I have greatly benefited from. His useful comments on earlier drafts of some of the chapters of this monograph, and his insightful, often witty, remarks about Chinese society and culture, helped broaden my views and knowledge on the subject, as much as remind me of the complexity of social events and human action.

During my archival researches in Hong Kong and Canton between 1985 and 1993, I was more than fortunate to be offered the invaluable help of Dr Ming K. Chan at the History Department of Hong Kong University, and Professor T'an Ti-hua at Chung-shan University. Only through their recommendations could my work at the different libraries and archives in their city be smoothly accomplished. Their assistance and support was indispensable.

During the final stage of writing of this monograph, Professor Frank Dikötter kindly provided me with not only perceptive comments on some of the chapters, but also much-appreciated encouragement and technical assistance. Special thanks also go to Professor Geremie Barmé who has kindly given his permission to reproduce some of the materials that had appeared in *East Asian History*.

I owe a great debt of gratitude to the John Swire & Sons/Cathay Pacific Scholarship, which granted me the opportunity of pursuing my post-graduate study at St Antony's College in Oxford. Colleagues and staff at the Division of Humanities, Hong Kong University of Science and Technology, and Jennifer Wilkinson, Jenni Craig, Carol Bestley, Sylvia Jaffrey, Mick Belson, Arthur Attwell of Oxford University Press, have been very helpful during the final stage of preparing the manuscript.

I am also indebted to many friends for their intellectual stimulation as well as their much-needed emotional support and encouragement during the long, and at times frustrating, process of research and writing. They are the Elvins (Dian, John, Charles), Ivana Kawikova, Mok King-fai, Yong Juquan, Virginia Unkefer, Motono Eiichi, Lo Ju-jung, Yap Kai-chung, Christian Henriot, Sebastian Tse, Kenneth Law, Jane Chan, Irene Chiu, Vivien and Peter So, and Steven Kwong.

I would like to dedicate this book to the sweet memories of my parents, Bing-chung and Sau-wan, my two aunts, Lee Ho and Lee Pien, and uncle Chow Chi-wong. It was their views of life, sense of humour, thoughts and sentiments that aroused my initial curiosity to learn more about the social and mental history of modern Cantonese. I wish they all had lived to see today. Special thanks must be given to all my siblings, in particular my eldest sister, Mary, whose moral, and at times financial, support helped to raise my spirits again when I was low. The final stage of revising the manuscript of this book was marked by two tragic events that have shattered my life and made a deep impact on my view towards human existence. The loss of my most beloved young nephew Derek to the senseless SARS virus, and the death of my eldest brother, Wai-ming, remind me of the fragility of life and the irreplaceable value of love. Last but not least, I could hardly have finished revising this book on time without the patience and support of my wife Monica and our cheerful daughter Athena. To them I must also dedicate this book.

Contents

List of Plates viii

Introduction 1

1. City versus Countryside: The Growth of an Urban Identity and its Meanings in Canton 9
2. The Limits of Hatred: Popular Attitudes Towards the West in Republican Canton 49
3. The 'Problem' of Opium Smoking in Canton 95
4. Gambling in Canton: Myth and Reality of a Calamity 156
5. The Worlds of Prostitution in the Early Republic 226
6. Cantonese Opera as a Mirror of Society 301

Conclusion 354

Endnotes 364

Abbreviations 431

Selected Western and Japanese Language References 433

Selected Chinese Language References 447

Glossary 470

Index 475

List of Plates

(between pages 264–265)

1. The Waterfront of Canton in the 1930s.
2. Modern buildings in the commercial heart of the 1930s Canton.
3. Respect the clothes, not their owner.
4. The Quaker Oats: Superiority of Western Culture in the Popular Minds.
5. A different Person Before and After.
6. The Only One Who is Insightful.
7. The Dream of Mr Ho: Favourable Attitude Towards Prostitution.
8. Spiritual Training for the Inmates of Canton Addiction Termination Hospital.
9. A Gambling Den in Canton.
10. A Gambling-House in Macao.
11. A Row of 'Flower Boats' on the Pearl River in Canton.
12. A 'Flower Boat' in Canton.
13. Hua Tsai, a High-class Prostitute in the 1920s.
14. 'Yellow Rose', a Popular 'Dance Girl' in the Early 1930s.
15. An Anti-Prostitution Processsion in Canton.
16. The Influential Cantonese Opera Singer and Actress Li Hsüeh-fang.
17. The Legendary Ma Shih-ts'êng.
18. The Legendary Hsüeh Chüeh-hsien.

Introduction

With an administrative area of about 57,100 acres and a population of over one million, Canton was the largest city solely administered by the Chinese, and undoubtedly the most important metropolis in South China in the 1920s and 1930s.[1] To most foreign travellers to the city, Canton was both exciting and bustling. As one American traveller vividly recorded of the busy waterfront of Canton in the mid-1920s, 'all the rank and file and chaos of Chinese life stretching as far as the eye can see and farther than the ears can hear or the nose protest down the wide street between the more or less foreign face of the city and the river with its even more crowded streets of boats' (Franck 1925: 223). Being the heart of South China's commerce and economy, Canton, like Shanghai, was a city packed with intense human activities.

In a somewhat contradictory way, Cantonese of this period took pride in the city's past as well as its present. In both official literature and unofficial guides to the city, Canton was popularly introduced as the 'City of the Rams', or the 'City of the Immortals', or 'Grain City'. All these 'courtesy names' have their origin in one 'beautiful legend' dated back to the remote days of the Chou Dynasty which 'is indeed most cherished by the people of the city', as one unofficial guide book wrote in 1936 (Ng 1936: 1). In the eyes of its people, therefore, the glorious past of the city rendered its modern-day prosperity and development even more respectable and reputable. As early as 1922, Canton had already been praised for its commitment to municipal reform and its many accomplishments (Li 1922). By the mid-1930s, Canton was no longer just the highly regarded capital city of the 'New Kwangtung', wherein the transformation of southern China was said to have first been launched, but a modern metropolis that had accomplished many commendable changes that were believed to have brought about modernization not only to the cityscape, but also to many aspects of urban life and culture (Lee 1936). Meanwhile, however, some old customs and traditions persisted and thrived in harmony along with the new and Western ideas in Canton. Adjacent to skyscrapers were humble traditional houses with tiled roofs, automobiles operated side by side with rickshaws, and narrow tortuous lanes were interwoven with wide asphalt roads (Ng 1936; Murayama 1941: 8–12, 31–2, 40–69). Canton was a city of contrasts; contrast in terms not only of architecture or the means of transport, but also more importantly of human experiences, emotions, feelings, attitudes, and perceptions.

This book aims at presenting a 'thicker' glimpse of perceptions of realities—and the realities themselves—that prevailed in the dynamic city of Canton during the 1920s and 1930s. It is not a sociological inquiry into the notion of social perception,[2] nor a historical account of urban or municipal development of this city, which have been well studied by many scholars,[3] nor an overall survey and analysis of Cantonese popular culture, nor a comprehensive social history of Republican Canton—topics that deserve much more space and research. It also does not intend to seek any paradigmatic access that might enable us to read the Cantonese mind and character, or to define their patterns and systems of thought—both are highly problematic subjects hard to accomplish without biased generalizations. What it does modestly attempt is the study of certain specific aspects of life in Republican Canton, and especially the popular attitudes towards them, as a way to tell the story of the city and the life of its people from a different point of view—an approach that resembles, on a much humbler scale, that of Theodore Zeldin (1979) in his monumental works on modern France.[4] These attitudes, being the cognitive product of the Cantonese themselves, embodied personal views and reflected social and cultural values relative to the specific phenomena discussed in this book. They are rich sources of information about the citizens' life and representations of their thought. They also provide a socio-cultural historian with materials to study the processes by which meanings were constructed into social phenomena and historical events. I hope, moreover, by underlining the coexistence of contradictory views of one and the same social phenomenon, and by an awareness of alternatives to a given belief system, to demonstrate the inherently complex and unmonolithic nature of life in a Republican Chinese city. Perceptions of realities, like realities themselves, are full of incongruities, ambiguities, and even contradictions.[5] These imperfect perceptions of realities, however, must not be simply dismissed as totally wrong or erroneous because they still represent different possible ways that socio-cultural events are perceived and understood. They are not necessarily wrong; but they are also by no means the *only* way that people's perceptions of and attitudes towards socio-cultural phenomena are structured and defined. To paraphrase Roger Chartier (1988: 13–14), 'history is turning to [study] practices that give meaning to the world in plural and even contradictory ways'. Alternatives were, and are, there. They coexist and sometimes compete with each other. In both ways, these bundles of alternatives become a dynamic force in history and society.

One does not need much specialized historical knowledge to be aware that life and reality in the past, as it is in the present, could well be complex. It is, however, quite a different matter to substantiate this awareness with appropriate and convincing examples drawn from history. One of the major purposes of this work is to provide substantial examples that help unveil the complexity of history and to offer alternative ways to construe the past events and human experiences in the context of this southern Chinese city. This book contains six chapters that are structurally and thematically independent of each other. Instead of locking the focus onto one single aspect of social reality or onto the entire society, each chapter deals with one specific social phenomenon in Canton in this period: changing social perceptions of the city and the countryside; popular views of the West; gambling and its social, cultural, and political meanings; the extent of the 'problem' of opium smoking, and the habit's social and political functions; contradictory social perceptions of prostitution, and the diversity of experiences of prostitutes; the popularity of Cantonese opera and its social implications. This multi-focal approach is preferred over the alternatives because it is able to show the richness of peoples' lives in former times and their cultures from more than one aspect of social reality, by which the inherent complexity of this city and its human components can be adequately outlined and better appreciated.

Cantonese perceptions of the city and the countryside are studied in Chapter 1. One of the reasons for including this aspect of urban experience in the present study is the commonness of the discourse as seen from contemporary sources. The living conditions in metropolitan Canton, as compared with those of the countryside, were a much-discussed issue in local intellectual circles. Writing of different kinds, such as short stories, travelogues, prose pieces, novels, poems, and so on, which examined the situation and the fate of urbanity and rurality in this part of China, are abundant in local highbrow magazines and student journals. Such concern was also shared by many residents, other than those men of letters, whose opinions might not be adequately represented in intellectual writings, but reflected, sometimes only indirectly, from popular materials. Popularity to such an extent was a sign of the seriousness of this phenomenon, and a study of this common concern about the city and the countryside throws light on our understanding of the mentality and self-realization of this group of urbanites. These perceptions also help us to understand the growth of city identity among the inhabitants of Canton, and the cultural relationship between city and countryside. In spite of the fact that the countryside and its intrinsically idyllic values and way of life were by and large idealized in traditional Chinese orthodox thinking and ideology, the socio-cultural relations between city and countryside remained ambiguous, rather than one-sidedly anti-urban.[6] There was indeed an alternative set of values that recognized the city's social and cultural importance. By the 1930s, with the continuous growth of Canton into a modern metropolis, this cultural ambiguity, though it persisted, had apparently turned to the advantage of the city. More and more Cantonese openly pronounced their culturally superior identity as urbanites. The city's socio-cultural functions were imbued with new symbolic meanings. And urban values were increasingly idealized at the expense of the countryside. The rise of the city became an irreversible cultural process in the modern history of China; its socio-cultural consequences are still being vividly felt today.

Due to its alleged contribution to the success of the modern Chinese revolution at its various stages, Canton was, and still is, generally hailed as 'the cradle of the Chinese Revolution'. Cantonese were, and still are, unduly praised for their patriotic stance and acts of bravery in withstanding the encroachment of the foreign powers. Anti-imperialism, and to some extent anti-foreignism, was upheld as official foreign policy by the Republican government in Canton. Anti-foreign messages permeated most official publications and much unofficial literature as well. Occasionally, the general public did respond enthusiastically to the emotional appeal for patriotism. The aim of Chapter 2 is to penetrate the façade of anti-foreign rhetoric in order to obtain a better glimpse of how 'anti-foreign' anti-foreignism was. This chapter also intends to draw attention to a much neglected issue in the history of Sino-Western cultural relations in the Republican period: the existence of an explicitly pro-Western mentality among the inhabitants of Canton and, apparently, of other treaty-port cities as well. This pro-Western mode of thinking found its expression in numerous political, social, and cultural facets of life in Republican Canton—the cityscape, fashion, notions of beauty, the lifestyle, public entertainment, political campaigns, and so on. A group of iconoclastic young intellectuals even put forward their high regard for Western values and culture and preached for the total Westernization of, initially, Cantonese society, and then of the whole of China.

This second chapter, for all that, is not intended to discredit or repudiate the 'revolutionary' reputation or the contribution of Canton and its people; many remained sincerely patriotic and devoted to the cause of the National Revolution. Instead, it tries only to unveil the simple historical fact that Cantonese in this period were capable of unduly admiring their Western 'enemies', as much as of hating them. The common people in this city were not all anti-foreign revolutionary heroes; there was no short supply of citizens who were unpretentiously practical and openly unequivocal in their attitudes toward the West, which was admired and followed as a model of modernity and an antidote to China's problems. By outlining this pro-Western mentality, the over-boosted image of the revolutionary Cantonese, as long propagated in Chinese Communist rhetoric and history textbooks, is demythologized. This uncommon view of the common people helps redress the romanticized lore of their historic contributions to the making of modern Canton.

Chapters 3 to 5 deal with the 'problems' of opium-smoking, gambling, and prostitution in Canton, respectively. These chapters, however, are not a general history of these 'profligate' pastimes in this city, although the situation of these 'vices' is also discussed. One of the major purposes of all these chapters is to open up the official and aristocratic presumptions about such 'vices' in order to deconstruct their politicized views and representations and analyse their ideological motives. Attention is also drawn to the fact that there were indeed highly favourable popular views of these 'vices' as acceptable forms of pastime, and why there was no shortage of patrons of these amusements despite all the official outcry against them.

It is not surprising to find that in all official and civilian literature, opium was denounced as the root of China's long list of chronic national problems. Since opium was an emotionally loaded and politically sensitive subject, official views of the harmful impact of opium smoking on Chinese society, though sensationally exaggerated, were rarely questioned, still less challenged. And the extent of the problem of opium consumption was also purposely overstated by every new administration in order to discredit the public image of its predecessor. All official anti-opium campaigns were political sham and no more than half-heartedly implemented. A substantial opium revenue continued to be happily utilized by the government, despite its anti-opium stance, for financing the administration as well as the province's many modernization projects.

There was also the element of class in the official view of opium consumption. Lower-class opium addicts were victimized and criminalized as a threat to the social and political order of the country. And it was this group of opium addicts who were ordered to be registered and forced to undergo perfunctorily administered medical and psychological treatment in a prison-like institution in Canton. Opium addiction by upper-class citizens, though by no means uncommon, was by and large accepted as socially harmless and hence left alone. It is also true that not every Cantonese considered opium-smoking as vicious or pernicious. People consumed opium for their own reasons; and none seems to perceive it in the same politicized way as in the official rhetoric or in moral tracts.

One historian quite rightly observes that Asian historians, the Marxist ones too, failed to approach the question of opium seriously (Trocki 1990: 5–6). But in place of 'for reasons that are not clear', as the same historian alleges, there are political and moral reasons for such avoidance. Chinese Marxist historians, and to some extent their Nationalist counterparts as well, are nurtured on the official orthodox view of the perniciousness of opium and its devastating effect for modern Chinese history. Any attempt to reappraise the issue of opium for this history in ways that deviate from that standpoint inevitably arouses bitter criticism from 'conscientious' colleagues, from patriotic laymen, and, above all, from the watchful Party. Moreover, most Chinese historians are burdened by a patriotic duty of renouncing opium and its negative effect on China, a view that they have been taught and has been reaffirmed since primary-school days. This is highly problematic because numerous findings on opium smoking in other countries all indicate the inadequacy of such a moralized view of the issue. The social and cultural impact of opium smoking was a lot more complex than our history textbooks tell us. It is about time to put aside the old moral and nationalistic stance and to try to look at the problem from another angle that will unearth a much-neglected, but no less real, picture of opium smoking in this period.

Gambling was an equally emotionally charged subject in Canton. Official rhetoric and moral tracts concentrated on 'reporting' the harmful effects of gambling: the degraded health it brought, the sensational cases of bankruptcy, the breaking up of otherwise happy families, the uncontrollable spread of crime. Even the economic output of the country was said to be threatened. The images of gambling and gamblers were stigmatized socially. This deterministic view does little to explain why gambling nonetheless remained so popular in Canton during this period. In fact, such sensational accusations about gambling provide us with no more than a fraction of the true picture of the 'vice' and its impact on the society. Surprisingly, gambling was not only widely enjoyed and favourably accepted, but was also a major source of revenue for the Canton government. Moreover, many Cantonese found in gambling a unique source of hope that they could turn to in an age of political turmoil and economic uncertainty. Gambling never lacked its better social function and meaning.

In Chapter 5, on prostitution, the main concern is to explore the actual extent of the problem, to report conventional attitudes towards prostitutes, and to unveil the alternative social images of this group of unfortunate women in Republican Canton. As to the extent of the problem, reliable official statistics on prostitution are extremely difficult to obtain, and those available are seemingly not comprehensive enough. Nevertheless, the sketchy sources available suggest that the problem of prostitution, considered as a social issue, had been improving in Republican Canton, rather than deteriorating as most moralists alleged. Most contemporary writers on the subject tended to presume that the problem of prostitution would only be aggravated with the gradual shattering of traditional mores and values in an increasingly 'modernized' Canton. The 'past' was idealized and the 'present' stigmatized.

For their own ideological reasons, many moralist writers liked to portray prostitutes as helplessly exploited and physically weak or dilapidated women living in the most pitiable condition of permanent dire poverty. But this was only a part of the picture. Being a prostitute was a disgrace. It did not, however, follow that all prostitutes must thus live a miserable life. There were in fact some prostitutes in Canton who were not only rich but leading a highly luxurious and comfortable life, of a kind denied to most Chinese women in this period. If they were lucky, they would marry into a respectable and wealthy family as concubine, or, in some cases, even as first wife. Mistreatment by aggressive madams, though it undoubtedly existed, was certainly not every prostitute's experience. Moreover, prostitutes did know how to defend themselves quite effectively and, when necessary, how to fight back. It is also important to note that not everyone saw prostitution as a sinful pastime. In the minds of many Cantonese, brothel-going, like opium smoking and gambling, with some kind of self-restraint, could be 'transformed' into an enjoyable and morally acceptable form of entertainment.

Not everyone who patronized establishments of vice was rich, as brothels, opium dens, and gaming-houses were much divided in classes and charges. On the other hand, such forms of pastime, vices though they might be, were by no means inexpensive. The participation of those who could afford to patronize the higher-class houses of such pleasures further helped keep up the image of these vices as some sort of gentlemanly pursuit. Since only the better-off citizens could afford to indulge in them, the social respectability of these vices, as of their practitioners, remained high in the thinking of ordinary folk. As an old Cantonese saying explicitly states: 'One who indulges in brothel-going and gambling is a smart chap; [and] an addict of [expensive] imported opium is a first[-class] [i.e. wealthy] fellow.'[7] It is this popular perception of these vices, which were ignored and played down by contemporary intellectuals and officials, that this chapter aims to explore and deliberate.

The 1920s and 1930s saw one of the most innovative periods in the history of Cantonese opera. A long list of changes, both technical and structural, were experimented with or introduced into the theatre. In Chapter 6, these aspects of change in contemporary opera are examined. The history of Cantonese opera in this period provides an interesting case study of cultural modernization in Republican Canton. Such aesthetical and structural changes revealed the social trend of, or the popular craze for, modernizing the city and its culture. But it is wrong to assume that modernization was nothing but Westernization. The cultural influence of the West on this process was strong, but by no means exclusive or dominant. Modernization in Cantonese opera also meant reinterpretation, and reintroduction of some old theatrical traditions. Therefore, like many other aspects of life in Canton in this period, Cantonese opera was characterized by cultural incongruities and anachronisms, in the form of mixtures of Chinese and Western, of modern and traditional elements.

Moreover, the sharp criticism of the 'new' opera by some intellectuals can be interpreted as a popular fear, in one section of society, of the fast pace of change in the city, and its allegedly polluting impact on cultural life and social values. To them, this form of genuinely 'mass opera', which in many aspects went against their conception and ideal of mass entertainment, had to be denounced and suppressed. And their dream came true in 1949, when the new regime eventually had the contemporary Cantonese opera thoroughly 'reformed' and ideologically cleansed. Modernization was never without its opponents.

Other aspects of life in this city were also reflected through the theatre world. It was in this period that Cantonese opera reached its maturity as a regional form of performing art or popular entertainment. This may be linked with the rise of a 'Kwangtung awareness', a mode of thought that became immensely popular among the Cantonese, especially since Canton was hailed as 'the cradle of the Chinese National Revolution' in official propaganda. Hence, the trend of vernacularization in Cantonese opera was a sign of this emerging regional consciousness.

The same chapter also shows how the cultural elite failed to impose its aesthetic values, and hence its dominance, or hegemony (to borrow Gramsci's term), on the increasingly commercialized and popularized contemporary opera. By analysing the reasons behind its unprecedented popularity, we may be able to learn more about the tastes of the general audiences, and through them, glimpse popular values and mentalities. The remarkable improvement in the social position of opera singers pointed to an important shift in contemporary cultural values and social attitudes, not only with regard to the popular opera profession itself, but also to popular culture generally. Last but not least, the amelioration of women's social position in Canton was also vividly reflected in the opera world. Cantonese opera was a mirror of the contemporary urban society of Canton.

Initially, this research project, in addition to its presently discussed six aspects of life, planned to include four more on crime and public security, education and student culture, merchant organizations, and the life of workers. Due to space limitations, however, they have been excluded from the present work. (Also excluded are maps of Canton and its adjacent areas, for which readers are welcomed to request from the author). But space is only one of the considerations involved. The six aspects of life in Republican Canton discussed in this book are chosen from an awareness that they are more misrepresented than the other four in contemporary perceptions and literature, and that they have been misunderstood by historians. Hence they needed to be reassessed and better understood from a more fitting historical perspective.

The socio-cultural history of urban Republican China is a massive field of inquiry that offers numerous possibilities. These six chapters represent only a limited effort to tackle some of the issues within this vast subject. I hope that they will improve our understanding of life and culture in the Canton of this period and stimulate further intellectual discussion on the socio-cultural history of urban Republican China.

REFERENCES

Burke, Peter (1986), 'Strengths and Weaknesses of the History of Mentalities', *History of European Ideas*, 7/5.

Chartier, Roger (1988), *Cultural History: Between Practices and Representations* (Cambridge: Polity; Oxford: Basil Blackwell).

Ch'êng Hao (1985), *Kuang-chou kang shih* (Peking: Hai-yang ch'u-pan-shê).

Franck, Harry (1925), *Roving Through Southern China* (New York: The Century Co.).

Lee, Bing-shuey Edward (1936), *Modern Canton* (Shanghai: Kelly & Walsh).

Levine, Donald N. (1985), *The Flight from Ambiguity* (Chicago: University of Chicago Press).

Li Tsung-huang (1922), *Hsin Kuang-tung kuan-ch'a chi* (Shanghai: Shang-wu yin-shu-kuan).

Liao Shu-lun (1948) (ed.), *Kuang-chou ta kuan* (Canton: T'ien nan ch'u-pan-shê).

Murayama Shigeru (1941), *Kanton sa dan* (Osaka: Ki bunku).

Ng, Yong-sang (Wu Yang-shêng) (1936), *Canton: City of the Rams* (Canton: M. S. Cheung).

Rowe, William T. (1984), *Hankow: Commerce and Society in a Chinese City, 1796–1895* (Stanford: Stanford University Press).

Tajfel, Henri (1972), 'Social Perception', in David L. Sill (ed.), *International Encyclopedia of the Social Sciences* (New York: Macmillan), xi.

Trocki, Carl A. (1990), *Opium and Empire: Chinese Society in Colonial Singapore, 1800–1910* (Ithaca, NY: Cornell University Press).

Vogel, Ezra (1969), *Canton Under Communism: Programs and Politics in a Provincial City, 1948–1968* (Cambridge, Mass.: Harvard University Press).

Yeung, Wing-yu Hans (1998), 'Guangzhou, 1800–1925: The Urban Evolution of a Chinese Provincial Capital' (unpublished Ph.D. dissertation, University of Hong Kong).

Zeldin, Theodore (1979), *France 1848–1945. Ambition and Love* (Oxford: Oxford University Press).

1

City versus Countryside: The Growth of an Urban Identity and its Meanings in Canton

Some historians take far too simple a view of the formulations of Chinese attitudes towards the city and the countryside in imperial and early modern times. The socio-cultural role played by the city in Chinese history is so underestimated that urban values are said to be insignificant in their impact on intellectual thinking and the commoners' mind. In this chapter, what would seem to be a flawed judgement will be critically examined. By the middle of the Republican era, popular perceptions of the city were markedly departing from their old-time ambiguity. City life and values had become more than ever overtly championed, which added to the long list of cultural characteristics as another sign of Chinese 'modernity'.

1. WAS THERE AN ABSENCE OF URBAN IDENTITY IN TRADITIONAL CHINA?

In arguing the view that there was no single great city that symbolized China for the Chinese, F. W. Mote (1977: 102) states that Chinese civilization 'has not granted the same importance to typically urban activities that other civilizations have'. Etienne Balazs (1964: 66, 78) argues that the absence of an urban class comparable to the Western bourgeoisie arrested the development of towns in traditional China. Mark Elvin (1973: 177–8) attributes that to the institutional and legal limitations inherent in Chinese cities, and to a late-imperial process of 'urban devolution' generated by an increase in the relative importance of middle-sized urban centres or market towns, which had lessened the contrast between the big cities and the countryside (see also Elvin 1978: 85–7).[1] He also argues that the image of the city as the administrative seat of the government and tax-collecting agents often led it to being feared—and hated—by the peasants (ibid. 87). Chang Chak-yan opines, rather unconvincingly, that the Legalist ideology of ruralism (which should be more appropriately termed 'physiocratic militarism') and its economic system, which was first implemented by the rulers of the state of Ch'in during the 'Warring States' period, and then by many leaders in the different dynasties, uprooted the 'model of urbanism and its market society'. He also argues that all 'peasant rebellions' (as they are somewhat misleadingly and indifferently called) since the Chou Dynasty onward were conscious reactions of rural peasant forces against the cities, whose expanding market structure threatened the economic interests and the egalitarian ideology of the peasants (Chang 1976: 7–10, 75–84, 118–20, 310–13, 336–45).

In the view of Rhoads Murphey (1984: 190–4), the primary concern and responsibility of imperial Chinese officials was to ensure the orderliness and the productivity of the countryside, because 'it was this which sustained the empire, its power, its cultural grandeur, and its bureaucratic structures.' The functional significance of the agricultural countryside had seemingly enhanced also its cultural importace at the expense of the city. According to Murphey (ibid.):

> Urban élites were drawn in the first instance, in each new generation, as much from the countryside as from the cities, and retain a close tie with their rural origins.... There was no denigration of rural circumstances and values, but rather, on the part of many of the urban élite, a longing for the countryside, to which they would retreat whenever they could, and to which they almost invariably retired.... The rural sector was recognized as the source of at least as much wisdom and virtues as the city.... The great sages did not live in cities, nor did the happiest people. The Chinese version of the good and the true had a strongly rural, and even anti-urban bias.[2]

Classical literature and poetry have also been said to be mostly devoted to depicting the tranquillity of nature and the simplicity of life in the countryside, though this is a serious oversimplification of complex tradition. Country people are said to be better attuned to the world of nature and its rhythm, and thus better able to understand the universe and man's place in it. In Confucian logic, this gave the rural people an upright moral character and a simple goodness that were denied to their urban countrymen. In Murphey's view (1982: 192), city life, which stood for physical comfort and materialistic richness, could not establish a legitimate position in the orthodox Confucian philosophy that emphasized frugality and character cultivation—values that were largely identified with the rural culture.

Such an anti-urban attitude seemed to have exerted a certain degree of influence on the mindset of those men of literature in the imperial period who had written about cities. For instance, authors of some of the extant travelogues on imperial Kwangtung were seemingly more attracted by the countryside (such as its wonderful landscape, famous historic and scenic spots, exotic plants and flowers, and wildlife) than by things urban. The city also had its peculiar curiosities. But fortuitously or not, all somehow stumble into the category of things improper or lewd, such as gambling and prostitution.[3]

Although the city might not play the important role in pre-modern Chinese history that its European counterparts did, its favourable contributions to the shaping of Chinese civilization should not be underestimated. Mote (1977: 117) himself also admits that: 'The concentration of people and wealth, and the possibilities for division of labour and specialization, enabled cities to support some cultural activities that were not possible in the countryside.' These 'cultural activities' could be innovative and far-reaching as well: realism was introduced into popular novel; innovations were made in painting and poetry; distinctive architectural forms were built, and so on (Skinner 1977: 268–9). The view that the most commonly adopted motif in classical literature and poetry was the appraisal of nature and the idyll is over-simple. In pre-Han classical poetry, Nature is generally adopted only as a setting for, or responses to, human emotion and action. It is not until the Han Dynasty that descriptive *fu* came nearer to pure description of nature. Nature itself as a topic starts with poets during the Nan-Pei Dynasties. Poems in the T'ang Dynasty reveal a balance between scenery (*ching*) and human emotion (*ch'ing*); and pure 'Nature' poetry ends with the Wei Dynasty. In traditional Chinese painting, the city was never a negligible motif, as the well-known *Ch'ing-ming shang-ho t'u* (Going up the river at Ch'ing-ming festival time), which is a vivid portrayal of city life in a southern Sung town, reveals. Nor does traditional Chinese landscape painting depict only pure Nature. Life, in the forms of travellers, hermits, fishermen, or of animals or insects, is always represented in landscape painting.[4] The collapse of the ward system (*fang li*) in late-T'ang big cities, an institution for urban control in use probably since the Han times, boosted to a further extent urban economic and cultural activities. By the Six Dynasties, it was clear to such big urban centres as Yang-chou that its vigorous commercial activities, concentration of affluent or official families, non-agricultural land use, dominance of brick buildings and the fashion of erecting luxury mansions by the rich, proliferation of Buddhist institutions, and so on, had already distinguished themselves from the countryside culturally, economically, and socially (Liu Shu-fên 1992: 81–134). When Etienne Balazs (1964: 66) writes that 'there is almost no literature on Chinese towns at all', he is probably referring to the Chinese literary scene before the late-T'ang and Sung Dynasties. By Sung, a whole genre of vernacular literature (*shih-ching wên-hsüeh*) had emerged which was devoted to representing lives and cultures of the urban dwellers. The fact that many of these creative works are set in the city indicated to the rising cultural significance of city as distinct geo-cultural space in the minds of contemporary scholar-literati (P'ang Tê-hsin 1974: ch. 1). In respect of education, the city had also made its indispensable contributions. Government schools were built mostly in cities. Private *shu-yüan* (academies), though originally located in rural settings, were eventually moved into, or near, the cities (Grimm 1977: 476–87).[5]

It might be true that there was still no well-articulated, anti-rural system of thought in the minds of urbanites, but that probably could not prevent or stop urban dwellers, whose lifestyle and socio-cultural milieu were so shaped by a distinct mode of culture, from being aware of their distinctive urban, and materially superior, identity.[6] Although the Chinese intellectual tradition demonstrates an ideological tendency towards the idealization of what might be termed the rural idyll, it is necessary to be sceptical as regards the view that this ideal was sincerely shared and practised by the literati and the elite. Officials continued to rule from the city, with power delegated to local gentry on rural matters.[7] With the relative safety it provided, the greater variety of entertainments it offered, the incessant activities in the streets and markets, the pleasures, the luxury, the lures of the town were seemingly irresistible to patricians and plebeians alike.[8] Discrepancy between ideal and reality was a matter of fact. For instance, in the 1946 edition of a village gazetteer, the city was stigmatized as a source of 'tens of thousands of kinds of evils', while village life was idealized as tranquil, compassionate, altruistic, virtuous, orderly, honest, and joyful.[9] However, behind this factitious rhetoric of idyllic life was the reality of the out-migration of the local elites from the same area to towns during the same period (Siu 1989: 54–5).[10] Although some of these rural emigrants might claim not to intend to settle in the city or abroad, it is highly likely that a considerable number of them might have changed their minds in the course of time. But this was not a recent phenomenon in the history of China. On late-Ming Su-chou, Susuma Fuma (1993) writes that the general tendency of this period of social transformation was from rural to city residential landlords. An estimated 70-plus per cent of Su-chou's population was a privileged section composed of upper classes, degree graduates, unranked official functionaries, and so on. Han Ta-ch'êng's (1991) research into the social structure in Ming cities shows the trend on the part of wealthy denizens and the political elite towards residence in a city. This concentration of a strong consumer class in Su-chou, which was made possible by the commercialization of agriculture in the region and by the high intensity of trading and commercial activities in the city and its adjacent areas, helped reinforce the attractiveness of Su-chou as a haven of comfortable and luxurious living in central China. In the eyes of the people, Su-chou, by the time of the late Ming, had already become a symbol of quality, esteem, and respectability; merchandise produced in the city was all generally perceived to be of the highest quality and henceforth much sought after by people all over the empire (Ts'ai Jên-chien 1987). It is, therefore, reasonable to assume that a considerable portion of the urban elite might maintain strong ties with their native villages, and might visit there occasionally, but it is doubtful if they would contemplate abandoning their relative security and comfortable lavish lifestyle in the city, and resettling permanently in the countryside.[11]

Nevertheless, in Rhoads Murphey's (1974) view, the cultural ideal of the idyll survived the challenge of the treaty-ports. The treaty-port city is alleged to be detested by the Chinese as a negative, and hence undesirable, form of living environment identified closely with social inequalities, racial discrimination, and economic exploitation.

The socio-cultural history of Republican Canton, however, shows us a somewhat different story. With the importation of foreign goods, technology, ideas, and values, the character of the city, and the lifestyle and mentality of its citizens, were greatly, though gradually, transformed. The city assumed a new cultural significance that was more articulately expressed, in contrast to the subtle and ambivalent cultural position it had occupied in imperial times. The acceleration of rural migration to Canton had not only stimulated the growth of the city,[12] but might also have reinforced the urban identity, as much as the pride, of the urban Cantonese. The 'realities' of incessant economic deprivation, social disorder, and political disturbances in the countryside in this period, though not necessarily as bad as it was conventionally assumed, brought about a gradual decline in the popularity of the orthodox cultural ideal of the rural idyll.[13] A more distinct, explicit, and elaborate set of urban values had taken over from the displaced rural values in the city.[14] The ascendancy of the social and cultural position of the city at the expense of the countryside signified the surfacing of a 'new' pattern of disharmonic, and even antagonistic, cultural relations between big-city dwellers and village rustics.

Nobody knows quite when this process of cultural transvaluation started in Canton, though the fall of Imperial China greatly accelerated it. By the late 1920s, more and more Cantonese perceived their city in terms of an aloof superiority, because of their more refined qualities of life, greater variety of entertainments, and better public security, in comparison with the countryside which was widely believed to be disorderly and backward. The magnification of this attitude and perception reflected not only on how the urbanites of this metropolis were trying to redefine and reassert their geo-cultural identity and importance by boosting the achievements and contributions of the modern city to the 'progress' of human civilization, but also signified the gradual dismantling of China's age-old Confucian ideological foundation and its subsequent replacement with a hybrid modern culture that was created and re-created relentlessly in and by the city.

2. *PERCEPTIONS OF THE CITY IN CONTEMPORARY CANTONESE WRITINGS*

Tranquil Countryside and Hellish City?

By the late 1920s, the concept of good and bad, as seen in contemporary Cantonese literature, no longer assumed the simple anti-urban bias that Rhoads Murphey has suggested. It remained true, however, that some writers preferred to see the modern city as a bogey threatening the moral souls of its inhabitants, and causing environmental pollution, social inequalities, the collapse of traditional moral codes, and the demise of simple and harmonious human relations.[15] Village life was still often believed to be conducive to one's spiritual existence due to its proximity to nature, and to its simple, altruistic, and moral way of life.

In the prose-piece 'Wo ti kuo-ch'ü' (My Past), the harsh living conditions in Canton evoke in its author beautiful memories of the countryside that he and his family have left to look for a better life in the city. After their arrival in Canton, they earned their living by peddling. But the heavy taxation imposed by the government, together with extortion by local bullies, made life extremely difficult for them. The social realities of poverty and exploitation have shattered the dream he once entertained about the city. In retrospect, the author misses the happy life he led in his native village:

> When I was at the age of seventeen, I was still living a holy life in the village. Every morning after breakfast, I . . . picked up the plough and walked straight to the field in happy mood . . . During breaks, we usually sat on the field and ate crunchy raw sweet-potatoes . . . after that [we] ran to the clear pool at the periphery of the field, and drank until we felt satisfied . . . After dinner, [we] usually joined the village elders by the riverside behind the bushes to chat about everything . . . and even sang folk songs which had been passed down to us from our ancestors. How amazingly happy that [life] was! (Tsai Liang 1934)

To him, the contrast between the city and the countryside is absolute. Hard manual work in the field was given a virtuous and sacred meaning, in sharp contrast with his miserable life in Canton. Village life is so idealized that it symbolizes tranquillity (moon, riverside, regular gathering in the evening), fraternity (congregating with the village elders), orderliness (the daily life-cycle in the fields), and harmony with nature (eating raw sweet-potatoes and drinking water from a fresh pool).

In the essay 'Pieh liao, wo ti ku hsiang' (Good-bye, My Beloved Native Village: Fei Fei 1933: ii. 80–1), the author, a student staying in Canton, sadly misses life in her village. The beautiful scenery, the lovely hills, the wildflowers, and the woods, are all lingering memories of nature to which her emotions are still attached. Her native village was a paradise on earth where people ate fruits directly from the trees, where the laughter of children was sweeter, and where she and her kinsfolk used to sing and dance. In stark contrast, the city is described as devoid of any comparable happiness, and, instead, as full of traps that cause people terrible trouble. Canton is a place that makes her weep.

In 'Ch'ün pien jên yü' (The Story of the Petticoat's Hem Man: Yün An 1933: ii. 15–20), lavishly luxurious city life is denounced as superficial and joyless. The hero has lived happily in the countryside until he moves to work in the city as a successful journalist, where he later marries a beautiful girl from a respectable family. The lavish lifestyle of his city wife brings him no happier life, but drains his wealth. She spends most of her time attending parties, while he spends his on work. At the end of the story, he uses up all his savings to buy off a blackmailer who threatens to publish the anti-government writings of his student days. As a result, he goes bankrupt, with no sympathy from his wife who continues to spend recklessly. One evening, after a serious quarrel, he has a strange dream. In this, he meets the old fisherman and his beautiful young daughter whom he often visited in his village in the past. They are still living happily as before in the countryside. When the old fisherman sees the sadness in the man's face, he consoles him by teaching him how to live a happy life, a message that is the moral of this story:

> [Water] is clear in the mountain. But once it flows out of it, it becomes muddy . . . Moreover, in the world of vexations, one's true nature is readily and profoundly polluted

> by the easy and sensually exciting life [in the city]... The gay quarters, where lights are red and wines are green, will have fallen into pieces of rubble before long; [and] those beautifully painted and perfumed faces will become skeletons [of dead bodies] in the near future. [But] rivers and sky are [always] as beautiful as a painting. The breeze and the moonlight [always] embrace every one of us.

True happiness, as this suggests, can be only found in the countryside, in nature.

The city was also believed to be particularly dangerous for young people. According to a short article contributed to a popular newspaper in Canton, the city, which was described as the hub of greed and love of money, could easily erode the moral integrity of all those youngsters who came from 'sublime and beautiful villages'. For a village man spending time in the city, the author of this article argued, the greatest moral threat was not the temptation of money, but the carnal trap of lust. Once a young man from the country was bewitched by one of these sexually alluring 'modern ladies', whom the city bred in abundant supply, his youth would be certainly wasted, together with his intelligence and an otherwise happy future life. The author also stated that he had witnessed numerous tragedies in which some young men who went to receive their education in a big city had eventually accomplished nothing in their studies. Instead, they embarked on a life of total dissipation that resulted in suicide because of love-sickness, or, in some cases, broken relationships with their wives left behind in the villages. 'Ridiculous occurrences' like these could only be found in the city (Wei 1934: 3).

To some writers, the romantic countryside is the antithesis of the polluted city. On a train journey to Kowloon, a student records her feelings of delight when she sees all the 'tall buildings and dirty air' of Canton disappearing behind her. The countryside is another world. Distant hills, like those she has seen in paintings, rise and fall. The sky is dotted by a few flying birds that hover restlessly above. The misty, rainy weather enhances the beauty of the scenery. Occasionally, her train passes by waterfalls that make a tinkling sound that is part of the music of nature. The gentle waving of the grass, blown by the wind, brings peace to the author's spirit, and comforts her (Ch'en Pei-ying 1934, iv. 151).

One's native village is sometimes seen as possessing a unique ability to soothe and protect one's spirit. In the short story 'Mi-mang chung' (In Loss: Hsiao Ling 1930: 39–56), the heroine Ching Ying is the victim of an unhappy marriage in the city, a social phenomenon, though hardly new or exclusively urban, which was increasingly identified with modern city life.[16] After long and serious thought, Ching Ying decides to separate from her husband just a few months after their marriage, an act that shatters her romantic dream about modern marriage. The ordeal has led her into a state of loneliness, helplessness, and sadness that she has never experienced before. She is profoundly psychologically battered, disillusioned, and depressed.

Such an agony prompts her to embark on an escapist journey back to her native village. The train journey, with its metaphorical therapeutic function, evokes in her sweet memories of her happy student days, when she commuted to school with her classmates. As the train is approaching her destination, the healing effect of the countryside surges up: 'When the locomotive reduces its speed and slowly approaches the station of [her] native village, every [bit of the ordeal] in her mind-and-heart is completely gone. Her heart jumps vigorously, like a child excited by a strong but simple mirth.' The reunion with her family is a joyful one. 'Everyone [at home] wears an excited smile. Ching Ying also cannot stop smiling.' In order not to disappoint her family, she lies to them about how happy life was after her marriage. Nonetheless, she has found a truly comfortable and happy refuge at her native home. In a letter to a close friend, she states that 'an over-night journey has brought me to another world. Here is [filled with] happiness and felicity . . . I still feel as if I were rushing suddenly from a deep dark room into a sunlit [open place].' To Ching Ying, her native village is a seed-bed of warmth and happiness: 'Life at home is permeated everywhere with ease and joy, as if one's heart is warmly embraced by [a thick layer of] velvet. Sometimes, Ching Ying looks as if she has [totally] dissolved herself into this ambience of joy, with all her misery vanished from her mind.' The parental affection and familial warmth heal her psychological wound. She regains her lost confidence in love. Her view of her family has also substantially changed from that of an oppressive social unit into a source of love, warmth, trust—all that she failed to achieve in her marriage. The therapeutic functions of the countryside for hard-pressed city-dwellers are implied, though idealized.

Some Cantonese writers endow women bred in the countryside with sublime qualities. Country girls are idealized not only in their physical charm, but also in their spiritual purity and innocence—qualities allegedly absent from city girls. In the short story 'Chih-fên yü-shêng' (The Remainder of the Life of a Feminine Beauty; Ling 1933: 5–12), T'ien Hsin, the male protagonist, is a playboy from a big city before he meets Chuan Hsiung in the countryside. T'ien Hsin is infatuated by Chuan Hsiung's idyllic naturalness, simplicity of character, and faithfulness to him. No girls in Canton are comparable to her:

> [Knowing Chuan Hsiung] is the happiest thing he has experienced for years. In retrospect, he realizes how his delicate heart has been broken into pieces; leaving on it a deep scar [by his unhappy love affairs with girls from the city]. Although good wines and attractive women are never in short supply [in the city], none of them are sincere about love . . . Moreover, these women . . . treat love as a plaything for children . . . The countryside is the only place where he can look for a sincere lover.

The anti-urban bias is explicit.[17]

The charming heroine Lady Hsiang in another short story (Hsing 1933: 25–35) is also a country girl. She possesses all the best qualities of a natural beauty such as can be found, allegedly, only in rural girls—eyebrows like willow-leaves, a high-bridged and slightly rounded nose, a light complexion, and deep dark eyes. However, the idyllic qualities symbolized by Hsiang are soon ruined by her scheming cousin, Lieh Jên, from the city. He is bewitched by Hsiang. As soon as Lieh has seduced Hsiang, he abandons her with a baby in the womb. After this,

Hsiang lives a miserable life under strong social pressure from both her family and the community. At the end of the story, she takes her own life. A tragic outcome of the symbolic rapine inflicted by the 'city' on the innocent 'countryside'.

In 'Ch'ang t'u' (The Long Journey), Chang Tzu-p'ing (1930: ii. 208–345) shows how the materialistic culture of modern city corrupts the spirit and the bodies of its inhabitants. In the city, the inhabitants are described as hypocritical, suspicious, mercenary, and covetous. Lust has replaced love and affection, corrupted bureaucracy has replaced revolutionary idealism. Spiritual corruption is externalized as a concomitant physical corruption. The protagonist's sister, once the beauty-queen in her village, is portrayed as a pale and zombie-like woman whose heavy make-up fails to conceal her physical degradation. At the end of the story, the protagonist is as degraded as her sister. The countryside is no ideal place to live (since it was poverty and paternal abuses that induced them to migrate to the city in the first place), but in other respects the city is even worse.

Such corrupting influence of the big city was particularly dangerous to young and innocent girls from the countryside. In a true story published in the supplement of a popular newspaper (Wu Lang 1936), its author described what had happened to a schoolgirl called Li Min. Min grew up and received her junior high-school education in a small town. Once she had accompanied her father on a business trip to Canton, where she instantly fell in love with its bustling life and materialistic prosperity. From that day on she implored her father to allow her to live in Canton. Her wish came true some years later when she was admitted into a boarding-school in Canton. Less than a year after Li Min had moved to Canton, the author wrote, she took up 'the fashion of freedom', lost her virginity, and became promiscuous. Her father was saddened by this and decided to have her allowance stopped. Unrepentantly, she took up with a married civil servant who kept her as a mistress, but eventually abandoned her. Feeling hopeless, Min returned home and begged tearfully for her parents' forgiveness. Loose morals and abuse of an individual's freedom were, in the view of this concerned author, predators behind the façade of prosperity in Canton.

The emotional value of the city is questioned, but not the reality of its existence and its socio-cultural position. This was best reflected in a lengthy article, 'Ts'un-chü sou chih' (A Miscellany Relating to Life in the Country; Chü Hsiang 1935), written with the aim of glorifying the physical and spiritual advantages of country life. It describes in detail the pleasures of living in the countryside in all four seasons. Its author, with the symbolically meaningful pseudonym Chü Hsiang (lit. 'frost resistant'), taught his or her readers to learn how to prepare and appreciate simple and yet nutritious and refreshing vegetarian dishes whose ingredients all come from the garden or backyard of one's country home, how to enjoy the God-given beauty of Nature, to nourish one's spirit through gardening or working in the fields, to keep oneself attached to Nature by growing one's own food, brewing wine, raising fish, and so on.

It was only by living in, or very close to, the country that the health of a man or woman's body and soul could be nourished and maintained in sound condition. To add authority to his or her idea about all the benefits of living in the country, Chü Hsiang cited quite substantially from the classics and from a number of old masters' works from the medieval Chinese literary world, especially those of the famous Su T'ung-p'o, Tu Fu, and T'ao Ching-chieh, and claimed that what he or she advocated was neither anything new nor unrealistic, but was indeed old wisdom and a lifestyle that had been actively practised by the wisest of the wise over centuries. At the end of the essay, however, the author disclosed his or her real intention of publishing it:

> The objective of this paper is [to redress the serious problem of] a deformed development of the city [in China] in recent times and the decline of the villages as villagers are abandoning their homes steadily and congregating in increasing number in the city. Those beautiful things and sceneries that I wrote about in this paper, therefore, are intended to arouse the interest of the city people and to lure them to return to live in the countryside. It is hoped that, by doing so, the city and the country can once again resettle into a balanced condition, which is also one of the best ways to help raise the rural productivity... (ibid. 1/5: 89–92; 1/6: 90–3)

All these jeremiads, including the anti-urban writings mentioned earlier, seemingly aim at reminding their urban readers of the ugly side of city life, and, by contrast, of the sweetness and simplicity of country existence. Although sublime spirituality, health, sincerity, and true love might be difficult to find in the modern city, none of these Cantonese writers share the Spenglerian sense of hopeless despair as regards the metropolis;[18] and although the emotional functions of the countryside are fulsomely upheld, no writer advocates transplantation of rural values and culture to the city as a remedy for urban social problems. Not every one appreciated a big city such as Canton, as corroborated by the examples cited above. But there were also very few local Cantonese who hated Canton so much that they would take pleasure in, or even advocated, the physical destruction of the city as a way of expunging all the evils associated with modern urbanism from the face of China.[19] The City, Canton in this case, was an object for criticism, but not, surely, extermination.

Wonderful City and Hellish Countryside

In his study on popular fiction in early Republican Shanghai, Perry Link (1981: 202–3, 235–9) points out that in contemporary popular 'fiction for comfort', rural life and its innate idyllic values are deliberately idealized (though obviously contrary to the real situation in the countryside, which its readers were aware of) in order to provide 'the comfort of knowing about a reliable fallback position from the uncertainties of urban life'. His study, however, mentions little about anti-countryside values in the contemporary literary scene in Shanghai. He interprets such anti-countryside satirical fiction as 'The Countrymen Revisits

Shanghai' more as a kind of 'soft' fiction whose aim to give its readers 'the comfort of feeling superior', than as a reflection of any anti-countryside attitude on the part of the urbanites. Chang Ying-chin (Zhang Yingjin 1996: 16–20) argues in his study on the culture of the city in modern China that Chinese writers and intellectuals during the early and mid-Republican periods generally held ambivalent attitudes towards the city and the country; and this ambivalence was largely due to their predominantly rural background and their distinct 'peasant consciousness'. Their urban sojourns brought self-realization, disillusionment, and alienation from the city and urban culture, which, in turn, had driven them closer to a voluntary identification with rural culture. The urban–rural problematic of the early Republic was eventually displaced by a new political structure, inaugurated by Mao Tse-tung with his famous speeches on literature and art in Yenan, in which urban discourses were subordinate to rural discourses. Chang's observation certainly helps us to understand better the tensions inside the minds of these 'intellectualised urban country folk'; their anti-countryside voices were, at most, ambivalent. His findings, however, may only speak for this group of well-known and 'intellectualised' writers; one will question, almost naturally, how widely were these attitudes and views shared by other lesser- or even least-known, writers or intellectuals. Moreover, although the idea about the dissolution of the 'old' city–country ambivalence and its replacement with a largely leftist, politicized, and ideologically clear-cut rural mode of social realism since the 1940s may speak perhaps for the literary scene in those 'liberated' areas, there was yet little evidence to show that such a 'predominant' trend in the leftist camp of the intellectual and literary world was dominating enough to extinguish all previous cultural envy of the city within both the intellectual and less scholarly mindscape, not even during the 1940s.

The situation in Canton, however, was more complicated and somewhat different, in that contemptuous views of the countryside and its values were often explicitly and loudly proclaimed. In addition to the 'idyllic fictions' that Perry Link mentions, Cantonese readers apparently also sought comfort from fiction and essays that depicted the cruel realities of life in the 'bankrupted countryside' as much as the manifold superiority of the city. The city was closely identified with modernity, material progress, freedom to love, democracy, modern education, and science.

In an anthology of some forty short stories, pieces of prose and poems composed by students at two Canton middle schools on topics relating to their feeling towards their native villages, only about a quarter of them show any appreciation of life in their villages.[20] Among this group, only a few poeticize or idealize peasant life and the countryside. Although many of these forty young writers complain about the difficulty of human relations in a complex society such as Canton, and miss the simple and professedly friendly alternative of the village, they are also concerned about the alarming way in which socio-economic and political order is deteriorating in the countryside.[21] None of them advocates the restoration of the idyllic values of earlier rural culture as a means to win back the countryside. Instead, some of them criticized the villagers for causing devastation to their own villages. These rural descendants have lost faith in the rural world.

The disruption of public order in the countryside was in fact caused by many factors, with misconduct by the soldiery being an important one. This is the theme of a short story called 'Shui ti tsui-kuo' (Whose Guilt?; Chou Chung 1934). The story begins with a description of a community of villagers who are joyfully preparing for the Chinese New Year celebration. Then a newspaper report tells of the 'triumphant return' of Colonel Hu T'u (a pun on the Chinese words for 'stupidity') and his troops from a military campaign against the bandits. Village elders deride this news:

> Damn it! Who will care whether it was the bandits or [the Communist] armies whom he has exterminated. However that may be, he will only ruin us, the people! The year before last, [he] fought a few battles with the Communist bandits in which he suffered heavy loss while the Communist bandits did not even lose one single horse or man! . . . Last time when he arrived in this village after his defeat, the village was so badly disturbed that even chickens and dogs could not live peacefully. (Ibid. 31)

A temporary disruption of the normal way of life in the village is expected. This time, however, the pranks played by two villagers on each other caused an even bigger tragedy. Ah Ken and Tso Tso are good friends. Tso Tso is a cheerful character who enjoys playing pranks on other villagers; Ah Ken's stoic character induces every villager to make fun of him. Shortly before the arrival of Colonel Hu, Tso Tso has played a prank on Ah Ken by pasting on his back a piece of paper with the characters for 'eunuch' written on it, confirming his own role as prankster for the villagers. This time, unfortunately, Ah Ken loses his usual patience. He swears to take revenge. A little while later, he writes on a piece of paper the characters for 'Communist' and surreptitiously pastes it on Tso Tso's back.

Colonel Hu finally arrives in the village. The newspaper report, however, is a deception because his troops have been badly defeated by the rebels. Thus, when the village head asks Hu to deliver a discourse on his glorious campaign, the embarrassed Colonel thinks that the welcoming party is making a mockery of his humiliating defeat. Before he bursts out in anger, Hu notices the red paper stuck on the back of Tso Tso. Although knowing that this is a joke played on an innocent man, Colonel Hu is in no mood to let his conscience override his determination to sacrifice Tso Tso and so redeem his military defeat before his superiors in Canton. Accordingly, Tso Tso is arrested as a Communist captured during the battle. The wife of Tso Tso, when pleading for her husband's release, is shot dead by Hu. The doomed Tso Tso is later publicly executed in Canton together with other captives (ibid. 30–46).

The threat of misconduct by the soldiery was no fiction: newspaper reports of it were frequent. Illegal abduction of peasants for military service, the looting of villages, racketeering, and the illegal imposition of surtaxes upon villages, were not uncommon in the countryside of Republican Kwangtung, nor indeed in Canton.[22]

In the short story 'Huo-yen Shan' (The Hill in Flame; Chou Hsing 1934: 47–58), life in the countryside is no longer depicted as poetically beautiful, or transcendentally enlightening. Exploitation by landlords, widespread impoverishment, and peasant selfishness are attributed to the breakdown of human relations between the villagers of Ho Ning ('tranquillity') and Yung Hua ('forever prosperity'), which are geographically separated by the 'Hill in Flame'. The hill possesses a rich resource of grass that has been enjoyed in common by villagers of both settlements, until the day when a tacit agreement is reached between the village headmen stipulating that the hill will be closed both to cattle and to haymakers. In future, hay on that hill is to be mowed and sold in the market, and the profit evenly shared by the headmen of the two villages. However, since cattle-rearing is the Ho Ning villagers' major means of livelihood, and since the inhabitants of Yung Hua rely upon the hay as their only source of fuel, this ban threatens the very existence of the villagers.

Sporadic violations of the ban are thus inevitable. Later, an extreme shortage of fuel in the depths of winter leads to a major defiance against the ban by a group of women from Yung Hua village under the leadership of Ah Tso Ma. Cowherds and haymakers flock to the hill. Their defiance is answered by police intervention summoned by the village headmen, which, however, still fails to stop the belligerent villagers. Eventually the headmen yield; and the ban is lifted. But before long a serious dispute breaks out between the two settlements when some haymakers cross the tacitly accepted boundary of the area assigned to their village and go to the other side of the hill to collect hay. The dispute is ended in a bloody vendetta in which Ah Tso Ma and some cowherds are brutally killed. After the vendetta, the villagers believe that the hill is cursed, and none dare set foot on it again. The story exposes the ugly side of life in rural Kwangtung. Instead of harmonious and simple human relations, one finds here only selfishness, covetousness, collective violence, and distrust.

A travelogue records the author's striking impression of her native village which she has not seen for a decade. She is shocked by the breakdown of traditional virtue, values, lifestyle, and order. Her native village has become infested with gambling-houses, which are protected by the local authorities blinded by greed for revenue. Farmers and local merchants indulge in gambling to the point at which fields are deserted and village shops closed.[23] Opium-smoking is widespread. The number of young addicts in the village is increasing rapidly, while local officials are uninterested in its suppression. Violent crime has become a daily event. An entire village could be plundered by bandits in daytime. During the author's short stay, one of her neighbours is stabbed to death by his nephew after the latter's demand for money from the victim to pay off his debt incurred by gambling and opium-smoking has been refused. News about indebted gamblers committing suicide, about indebted peasants forced to leave the lands they till, is heard time after time: 'Living in such a horrific environment, I longed to run away from this native village of mine immediately. There was nothing here that I wanted to hear or see! In the end, we packed our luggage and rushed back to Canton' (Liang Yün-chiao 1934: 99–101). Life in the countryside has become so demoralized and corrupted that Canton, by comparison, was a haven for decent and righteous living.

In 'Ai chih wei ch'ou shen hsu kuo' (The Unfulfilled Will; Chieh 1933: 64–70), the elopement of Piao Lung from his native village, in order to escape from an arranged marriage imposed on him, and to pursue his love for his girlfriend in Canton, is an act full of symbolism. The countryside is berated as a crucible of patriarchalism, parental authoritarianism, and small-mindedness. Freedom to love, one of the many individual freedoms that the city promises, can only be realized in the city.

The city's assimilating power was strong. Contemporary literature tells us that some rural visitors there are quick to identify themselves with the city and subsequently adopt a discriminatory attitude towards the countryside whence they have come. This theme is vividly shown in the short story 'The Question of Braids' (Pien ti wen-t'i; Tu Chuan 1934, 82–92). Accompanied by her mother, the young girl protagonist visits her aunt in Canton. This is her first visit there. Like every woman in her village, she is wearing long braids. The night before they set off, the girl asks her mother why her aunt has never visited them in their village. Her mother's answer hints at the unequal socio-economic position between city and countryside and how it can affect the confidence and self-awareness of rural people:

> Oh you foolish child! Do you think that your aunt dislikes the comfortable and free life in the city? If we have the chance to live there for three to five years, we shall certainly also forget everything here. Over there [in the city], there are all sorts of spectacular things to see, [interesting] things to play with. Let me tell you something about their foods and clothing. Sparkling silk-pieces are the clothes that they wear; fresh fish and meats are the foods that they eat. How can you expect them to live such a thrifty, meagre life as that of a village like ours! You should have seen your cousins. Compared with you, they are just like [angels] from Heaven, whereas you are from the soil! (Ibid. 83)

Psychological debasement of one's rural identity as such is also reflected in the mother's great efforts at making her little daughter look proper and tidy—a means to appease the child's aunt, as much as to modify her appearance in order to justify her place in the city.

In Canton, this little girl learns that her braids are very unfashionable, and that they make her a laughing-stock for naughty boys who regard them as a stigma of rustic backwardness. To keep the little girl from further harassment, her aunt has the braids cut off. With the passing of this physical symbol, the little girl lives happily in Canton until she leaves. She is amazed by how easily a person can be 'modernized'.

One month later they return to their native village. For the first time in her life, this little girl realizes that her village is a filthy place full of idle slovens:

> Scenes of my native village reappear gradually before my naked eyes. The market is revoltingly dirty. The unpaved lanes are full of shabby-looking rustics. We have only been

away for thirty days, [but] it seems that I have been away for thirty years. Everything looks so unfamiliar to me! I suspect that this place is a deep dark hell, and my mother and I are zombies! (ibid. 91)

After returning home, the little girl's short hair in turn becomes the laughing-stock of the villagers. The more she tries to defend her modern hair-style, the more resentful criticism she receives: 'Go and look at yourself in mirror! City girls look far more elegant than you do! Shameless creature!' (ibid. 92).

The story shows the incompatibility of city and countryside cultures and values. The adoption of urban culture and attitudes by this young girl indicates the author's favourable view of the intrinsic values of the urban lifestyle and its progressive meanings. The concept of good and bad is no longer imbued with an anti-urban bias. Instead, rustic obstinacy and ignorance are ridiculed.[24] The materially inferior conditions in the countryside further inflate the public image of Canton in the eyes of the country people.

The deterioration in living conditions in the countryside contributed to the decline of popular faith in the values of the rustic way of life. Apparently, some writers still believed in the intrinsic noble values and sublimity of the countryside. But many more adopted a contemptuous attitude towards rural culture and values which they saw as increasingly synonymous with obstinate resistance to change, parochialism, familial authoritarianism, slovenliness, and backwardness. A distinctive system of urban values was firmly established and adopted by the citizens. The concept of goodness became so transformed that more and more urban values were injected into it. Even the concept of an ideal husband changed so that it could include such urban criteria as a university degree and a fashionable appearance.[25] The traditional prerequisites for a 'gentleman' (*chün tzu*), such as moral virtues, delicacy, and a good knowledge of the Chinese classics, were seemingly relegated to secondary importance in Canton's modern model of the ideal man.

3. THE URBAN IMAGE OF RURAL BACKWARDNESS

In contemporary literature, the public image of the countryside plummeted. In real-life terms, the materially inferior conditions of living (where these were observable) in such rural communities as Chiu-fêng-huang on the island of Ho-nan, on the south bank of the Pearl River, and Sha-nan in suburban Canton, which were geographically close enough to Canton for people to come across, helped to reinforce the unpleasant image of the countryside in the minds of urban Cantonese.

By the early nineteenth century, Chiu-fêng-huang was one of thirty-three villages on the island of Ho-nan. Tea had been among the main agricultural products which brought wealth and fame to these villages (Ch'ü Ta-chün 1974: ii. 384). But by the late 1920s, the good old days for this village had gone. A social survey conducted by Lingnan University into this village revealed a very gloomy picture of the community. Poverty had forced many young men to leave the village and search for jobs in Canton or elsewhere (Wu and Huang 1935: 106–7). 'Outsiders' then moved into the village because of its proximity to Lingnan University, where most of them worked as minor staff. These newcomers did not, however, bring about any improvement in the village's economic conditions, since most of them only stayed there because they were too poor to afford better quarters in Canton (ibid. 96–7).[26]

Of the total 748 inhabitants in the village, about a hundred were farmers. Of these, only seven were owner-farmers, with sixty-nine tenant-farmers. Together they ploughed barely fifty mou of land. Such scarcity of resources was said to have reduced the standard of living of most peasant families to the level of sub-subsistence (ibid. 109–19).[27]

In marked contrast to the 150-foot wide carriageways and multistorey concrete buildings of Canton, worn-out narrow alleys and filthy dilapidated houses were common sights in Chiu-fêng-huang and Sha-nan. The stone-paved pedestrian walks of Chiu-fêng-huang were said to be often befouled with animal dung and the refuse casually dumped by every household.[28] In both communities, poor ventilation, inadequate lighting, and greasy and dusty floors rendered most residential houses dark and stinking. In contrast to a general belief in the physical robustness of country folk, the surveys show that the physical health of most villagers was far from being satisfactory. In Sha-nan, almost 20 per cent of the villagers suffered from eye disease, beri-beri, tapeworm, or skin trouble. Poverty was said to be the major reason for the lack of nutritious food in village diet; and the absence of tap-water supply for its poor hygiene. A single suit of clothes, in one extreme case, was said to have been worn by an old lady for decades without being changed. It was not uncommon for the whole family to share a single piece of towel (Wu Jui-lin 1934: 77–80, 113; Wu and Huang 1935: 154–5).

In both communities, the high rate of illiteracy and poor educational facilities were seen as sign of the cultural deprivation of the countryside. The literacy rate of the total population in Chiu-fêng-huang and Sha-nan was 11 and 28 per cent respectively (Wu Jui-lin 1934: 76; Wu and Huang 1935: 110).[29] In Chiu-fêng-huang, only about 10 per cent of school-age children received a formal education at the village school, which was poorly equipped; and truancy was common (Wu and Huang 1935: 131–40). The two primary schools in Sha-nan were also poorly attended since most parents were said either to be indifferent to their children's education, or to prefer them to work and earn money for their families (Wu Jui-lin 1934: 58, 81–2, 133).

Meanwhile, the urbanites were eagerly boasting of Canton's image as the cultural centre of modern Kwangtung. In official publications, plans and reports on the expansion and modernization of education in Canton were always included (Lee 1936: ch. 4; Kuang-chou nien chien 1935: ii. ch. 12; *HCLCCN* 1934: 146–77). Official and unofficial guides alike proudly presented their readers with photographs of modern school buildings in Canton (Kuo 1924; *Kuang-chou chih-nan* 1934: ch. 5; Lee 1936: ch. 4), even though the city's illiteracy rate was by no means low.[30] There was no official plan to redeem any rural communities, though they were allegedly 'at the brink of bankruptcy'. Schools there were run only by voluntary agencies; public health utilities were non-existent.[31] The 'progressive' municipal government of Canton, though seemingly successful in modernizing the city, had abandoned its 'rural affines'.

In fact, this kind of social survey is only partially successful in accomplishing its original aim, which was to provide objective descriptions of these rural communities. It is simply, but crucially, because the researchers, most of them seemingly students of urban origin, apparently superimposed a strong, anti-rural, bigoted view upon their analyses and observations. Working with the presumption that village life was impoverished and pathetic, these researchers were instructed to assume a 'sympathetic attitude' towards their informants (Wu and Huang 1935: 94). As a result, social surveys as such became a pompous, though perhaps subconscious, attempt by these urbanites to reaffirm their contemptuous preconceptions and presumptions about the rural world. Field investigations became exercises in collecting 'evidence' to illustrate preconceived pessimistic ideas about 'the bankruptcy of the countryside', even though real life might suggest it was otherwise.[32]

For example, on the issue of family income, despite the fact that most families lived with an income surplus, the report preferred to conclude that '[On the whole], its (Chiu-fêng-huang's) economic conditions are not [so bad that the villagers] cannot make ends meet. However, it is certain that it is an impoverished community in which its standards of living have reached rock-bottom' (ibid. 118–19).

As a matter of fact, the average amount of gross monthly income for a randomly surveyed 100 households in this settlement (with an average of four persons per household) was about 53 yüan, which by no means indicated dire straits (ibid. 112).[33] In a survey of urban workers' families in Canton conducted by the Sun Yat-sen University in the same period, nearly 40 per cent of the 243 families interviewed (with an average of four persons per family) earned between 11 and 40 yüan per month (Huang Yin-p'u 1934: 57). Moreover, there is strong reason to believe that the villagers were misrepresenting the real figure of their families' income, which might have been even higher because of remittances from agnatic relatives who worked in the cities.[34] In spite of this, our researchers continued to indulge their use of the phrase 'the bankruptcy of the countryside' (*nung-ts'un p'o-chan*), and reiterated the assertion that the falling farming population in these villages, as elsewhere throughout China, could only exacerbate the collapse of the rural economy, resulting in the impoverishment of the population (Wu and Huang 1935: 95, 109, 127–9).[35]

Likewise, the countryside was also looked down upon as the stronghold of 'backward' customs and values. The inferior social position of women in these two rural communities was criticized. In Sha-nan, women were allowed to take only low-paid jobs of socially inferior status (Wu Jui-lin 1934: 42–4). Education was not considered as essential for women, and hence most of them above 20 years of age were illiterate in Sha-nan (ibid. 90). Arranged marriage, which was commonly practised in both communities, was seen as another illustration of the 'bondage' imposed on these rural women. Writing in an essentially contemptuous tone, the report stated that 'since Sha-nan is a conservative and backward society', their concept of marriage, which was nothing more than perpetuating the patrilineal line, and their form of it, which was 'blind marriage', were hence both 'definitely backward' (ibid. 82).

The practice of 'marriage resistance' by some Kwangtung women was strongly criticized by the authorities as 'barbaric acts' damaging morality and disrupting social order (*FSKKTK* 1930: 243). In Chiu-fêng-huang, two 'spinsterhood houses' (*ku-p'o wu*) provided residences to nearly thirty young girls who had pledged to stay together to avoid marriage. Our sociologists, however, were uninterested both in studying this unique pattern of marriage, and in the existence of a favourable popular attitude (even among some Kwangtung men) towards the practice of spinsterhood and delayed transfer marriage.[36] Instead, in an arbitrary manner, they subscribed to the orthodox prejudicial view of the phenomenon by stating that these 'spinsters' were unmarriageable because they were ugly, of bad character, carriers of hereditary disease, or lesbians (Wu and Huang 1935: 150).

On the issue of religious belief, the report pompously stated: 'Blinded as they are by the traditional mode of thinking, the residents of Chiu-fêng-huang Village still retain that primitive and naive form of belief—polytheism' (ibid. 156). And on the situation of popular religion in Sha-nan: 'their ignorance and stupidity costs them [not only] their ability to understand all natural phenomena in this universe, but also to apprehend what proper religious belief is . . . Since their concept of ghost and god is [as primitive as] this, their attitudes towards worship are hence clearly nonsensical and blind.' The polytheism that these villages were practising was ridiculed as nothing but a 'naive and disgraceful' form of superstition that could hardly be regarded as religion. Instead of revering God, these rural people were said to bribe their deities for protection and blessing. They worshipped only out of fear of ghosts and deities. Although they were poor, they reportedly 'wasted' a considerable portion of their income on preparing the celebrations of religious festivals, or on patronizing *feng-shui* masters or spirit-rappers for advice on 'superstitious matters' (ibid. 154–8; Wu Jui-lin 1934: 137–43). Similar phenomena, however, were by no means non-existent or even concealed in Canton.[37]

In Sha-nan, the report also stated, there was no facility for any kind of 'proper and righteous' (*chêng-tang*) entertainment. 'Tedious and stressful' work provided these villagers with no other chances of entertainment than the few religious festivals in which they could escape briefly from their monotonous work and boring life (Wu Jui-lin 1934: 102). The report on Chiu-fêng-huang was even more explicit in its bigoted opinion:

> Those poor village residents who even face great difficulty in solving all the carnal problems, how then can they ever ask for anything more than having their stomachs filled and their bodies warmly clothed? Every day, they busy themselves with work... hence they have very little recreation. Moreover, poverty and poor intellect hamper them from asking for any superior and righteous [forms] of entertainment.

Therefore, to the dismay of our researchers, villagers in both communities were found spending their leisure time on gambling, gossiping, and opium-smoking, while only a handful played a musical instrument or sang folk songs (ibid. 102–5; Wu and Huang 1935: 150–4).

Similar characteristics filled the report of another, though comparatively less well-researched, social survey conducted and written by one single researcher from Lingnan University. The community under study, namely Hsin-fêng-huang, was located not far away from Chiu-fêng-huang, and was the home of about 200 households with a population of 587 people. In this report the investigator, due to a lack of time and resources, on the whole presented only a general picture of this community and its residents. Within this general portrayal of the village were some relatively prominent features that he hopes his readers will notice. These included the presence of seven opium smoking-rooms and one gambling house in this community, which, the investigator sighed, was an alarming number disproportionate to the small size and population of this village and also a sign of the state of demoralization, perversion, and decadence in this community; these places of ill repute, no wonder, were the first establishments the author mentioned in his report on shops and commercial activities in this village (Wang Chiu-hsing 1937: 81–3). The demographic imbalance between males and females was another feature that worried the investigator and was, therefore, described at length. Although without any supportive evidence from his fieldwork in this village, the fact that there were 314 males and 273 females in Hsin-fêng-huang alone was taken by him as concrete evidence corroborating a list of sociological theories that explain the gruesome phenomenon of the mistreatment of women by men in China. Such an imbalance was blamed on a combination of factors: marriage for girls at the early age of puberty contributed to higher rates of premature mortality of females, who died of tuberculosis, respiratory diseases, or ovary trouble (a claim that was professedly based on the finding of scientific research on female mortality rates in Punjab); widespread female infanticide; and a general lack of care for girls by their parents who, as a result of age-old prejudice against females, rarely spent any money on treating a sick girl but simply let her die. Although he added that female infanticide was not found in Hsin-fêng-huang, he was convinced that the other aforementioned factors did hold true and explained the dreadful conditions suffered by women in the countryside (ibid. 83–4). The interesting and important thing about this 'finding' was that the researcher did not even bother to test the validity of those horrific theories about sex imbalance on his surveyed community; and not even one single case from Hsin-fêng-huang was cited to substantiate his argument about the causes of this unpleasant phenomenon there. The investigator also explored at some length the conditions of the village school in Hsin-fêng-huang. The organization, the funding, and the operation of the school were described and explained in part. His depiction sounded complimentary only until the end:

> Judging by the terms of reference of the School Board and its headmaster, the Hsin-fêng-huang Primary School should be a well-established school with a sound organization. But the reality tells us that those directors of the School Board are merely villagers who know barely little about education principles. And how about its headmaster? [He is] only a loafer too! Its teachers are even worse. I remember when I met them during the early phase of my research, one of the teachers was clad in sloppy clothes, wearing a pair of slippers, and smoking a cigarette in his mouth, and talking casually with me while grading [his students'] assignments; he just looked like a ne'er-do-well.... (ibid. 89)

The report then goes on to describe the communal religious activities and the state of public security in this village. In the concluding remarks, the investigator wrote that this village, in comparison with its neighbouring village, Chiu-fêng-huang, was enjoying some degree of materialistic superiority and, henceforth, 'progress'. In spite of this, the researcher still chose to conclude his survey by giving a highly pessimistic view of the seriousness of the problem of rural bankruptcy, even though the findings in the report did not clearly point in that direction. This, however, corroborates what he described in the introductory note as his mission of writing his report: to provide a realistic picture on the distressful situation and conditions in rural China, where economic bankruptcy, depopulation, demoralization, and prevalence of old feudal practices contributed to the 'internal collapse' and impoverishment of Chinese villages (ibid. 81–2, 92).

The factual findings of these rural researches, for all our criticism of them, are by no means negligible. First, they reveal the underlying discriminatory attitude of many of these rural reformers towards the country folks and the rural culture, despite their apparent good faith and enthusiasm in undertaking their reforming work in the villages.[38] Secondly, they show, in a sensational way, how different the realities were between Canton and its rural periphery,[39] and how this phenomenon could further polarize the cultural identity and the public images of the city and of the countryside. However, the prejudiced anti-rural mentality of their authors poses serious doubts about the objectivity of their overall perspective, observations, and interpretations. These reports seemingly reaffirm, and then reinforce, the derogatory and pitiful urban image of the countryside. Once again, they illustrate the preconceived ideas about rural poverty and total backwardness. To borrow loosely from Foucault, the countryside is objectified through the 'dividing practices' of the dominant groups of power and knowledge (Rainbow 1987: 7–8).

Not all these supposedly intellectual writings hide the prejudice of their urban-based authors against the countryside as discreetly as these social surveys did; some of them are straightforward and blunt. Fêng Rui, for example, was a case in point.[40] In 1928, Fêng Rui, a young American-trained Cantonese agriculturalist, who was then a professor at the Nanking University and an active rural reconstructor in Hupeh Ting Hsien, wrote an essay entitled 'Hsiang-tsun shê-hui hsin-li fen-hsi' (Analysing the Psychology of the Village Society), which was aimed to help comrades in the rural reconstruction movement to develop a better understanding of 'the psychology of Chinese rural society' and the roots of some of its problems. He mentioned in this essay some commendable psychological traits among the country people, such as strong commitment to morality and religious belief (which professedly could help them distance themselves from improper behaviour or beliefs), perseverance and tolerance (which, as it was claimed, helped bring down the incidence of collective violence in the countryside), individuality as a result of the sparse pattern of habitation (which was believed to be conducive to the breeding of new thoughts), and remarkable communal cohesion, which was the outcome of tight kinship and loyalty (which would be beneficial to the building up of a strong social organization and henceforth a society). In the opinion of Fêng, however, the presence of these positive psychological traits was not enough to transform villages and villagers in China from a generally pathetic state of backwardness into a realm of scientific rationality and modern public-mindedness. Fêng cited various reasons for the problems of this peasant mentality in China and for helping to perpetuate it.

First of all, in Fêng's view, the physical nature of farming work prevented Chinese peasants from developing a healthy mental state of mind. Persistent and heavy physical demands from toiling on the land were said to have turned peasants into strong beings with well-developed limbs; but the drawback was a serious underuse of their 'brains' (*nao chin*), which in return was taking toll on the mental vigour of the peasants who displayed commonly such psychological traits as stupidity, inertia, strong reluctance to change, depression, apathy, indolence, and vulgarity. Moreover, since farming was such a physically stressful and bitter job, Chinese peasants all disliked working in the fields and tended to run away from it whenever given the chance; the thought of leading an easy and comfortable life in the city also emerged as a consequence. Secondly, Fêng believed that peasants were prone to believe in luck and to let chance to take control of their lives. Psychological dependence on chance as such, which was a direct result of their lack of scientific knowledge to help them better comprehend such physical or natural phenomena as changes in weather and fluctuation in grain prices, only fostered superstition, complacency, and difficulty in persevering among the peasants. Thirdly, despite many peasants disliking the menial and physical nature of farming, most were not able to leave their villages for a better and more comfortable job in the city. These people were forced by circumstances to remain in the countryside where they neither gained any satisfaction from working the fields nor showed any respect for their jobs. Under these conditions, these unhappy peasants, Fêng argued, had all become aimless, hopeless, and despondent; all these outcomes exerted negative impact on the social psychology. Fourthly, the calendars of work and facets of life for a peasant family were so heavily dominated by norms and customs with 'superstitious' overtones that Chinese peasants had developed another unhealthy psychological trait—they submitted themselves to the rule of these superstitious customs and often behaved in ways that contradicted their conscience and rational thinking. Fifthly, the general pattern of habitation in Chinese villages—close association with the same kinship group but segregation from other kinship communities—caused serious lack of the spirit of togetherness and cohesion beyond one's own family group. Chinese rural society was basically atomistic in nature, which, Fêng opined, helped explain country people's many unwelcome psychological attributes: strong resistance to change; unquestioned observance of old customs and norms; excessive confidence in oneself; weakness in understanding the concepts of collectivity and civility; uncooperativeness; disobedience to the law; poor ability in comprehending the acts and thoughts of others; difficulty in leading a decent, hygienic lifestyle; selfishness; lack of goals for life; cruelty; ruthlessness; dullness; taking great pleasure in gossip and smearing others; and distrusting the rules of any sound organization or good leader (Fêng Rui 1928: 208–12). All these 'psychological traits', in the view of Fêng, were unique to the country folks in China; and their existence had been seriously inhibiting China's peasantry and countryside from embarking onto the road of 'progressive' and 'modern' socio-cultural development. Although Fêng himself did not support the idea of cultural borrowing from modern urban centres by the peasants, a phenomenon that was said to be gaining momentum at the time of his writing, he, on the other hand, hardly questioned the superiority of those comparable urban social organizations and cultural, or 'psychological' (in his words), traits that had enabled the modern Chinese cities and their citizens to travel on a different path to modernity. The modern city and its cultures were, beyond doubt, more advanced and hence better (ibid. 214).

4. *THE CULT OF THE CITY*

The Rural Peril

In both fiction and reality, the deteriorating economic conditions in the countryside reduced the social status and respectability of the peasantry in the eyes of urban Cantonese. To town folk, the growing awareness of their distinctive urban identity was increasingly manifested in their contempt and distrust of the rural inhabitants.

Such anti-rural sentiment was revealed in a directive issued by the Public Safety Bureau, a set of working guidelines for policemen on how to intensify public vigilance in times of emergency. This stipulated that travellers and pedlars from the rural districts around Canton must be thoroughly searched for illegal possession of weaponry. Special attention should also be drawn to visitors from the countryside who were not employed in 'decent jobs' ('I-chiu-erh-liu nien tung-fang-ling' 1927: 2.2, 18 August).

The call for special attention to rural migrants probably arose from a prejudicial fear of 'outsiders'. In 1929, of 309 criminals convicted in Canton, more than 10 per cent were specified as *wai shêng jên* (persons from other provinces). Although this figure was not alarmingly high, it was probably already enough to arouse the suspicion of the Cantonese, and reaffirm their prejudice against the 'hicks' from other provinces (Kuang-chou-shih shih-chêng-fu 1929: 104). The countryside on the outskirts of Canton was also commonly believed to be a dangerous area best avoided; these rural places were reportedly full of vices, such as covert prostitution, and, worst of all, practically run by bandits and gangsters (Ai-k'o-ssu 1928: 8). Moreover, the presence of a visibly large number of young bumpkins in Canton, who flocked there looking for jobs or sought refuge whenever natural disaster or war broke out in the countryside,[41] further helped intensify this fear of the 'rural peril'. Since Canton was not an inexpensive place for these impoverished visitors, some of them resorted to begging, and slept out on the streets.[42] To the people who put 'face' before anything else, this was a shameful act that not only damaged the dignified image of the city, but also discredited the already tainted image of the rustics[43]—an image that once it was formed and had taken hold, proved almost ineradicable.[44]

The tendency of the Cantonese to identify *ch'êng wai* (outside the city) with *wai shêng* (outside the province) signified the extension of this anti-rural mode of thinking as much as their almost paranoid desire to safeguard their urban identity. Anyone from places other than Canton, probably with the exception of Shanghai, Hong Kong, and Western or Japanese metropolises, was almost bound to be discriminatorily labelled as *wai* (alien) in a negative sense. The commonly used term for the rustics, *hsiang-hsia lao* (country bumpkins) has strongly insulting overtones. *Hsiang*, the countryside, was conceived as *hsia*, below, with a strong implication of being inferior compared with the city; and the term *lao* was generally used of any men in a socially low-status occupation.

Such contempt was also expressed in social language. One of the most popular proverbs in the 1920s displays a clearly contemptuous attitude towards the country people. *Hsiang-hsia lao chu ch'êng, ku-ling ching-kuai* (Behaving as oafishly as country bumpkins out on the town), implies the existence of innately inferior behavioural and cultural traits in country people (*HTJP* 1927: 4.4, 5 July). At least one piece of vernacular 'dragon-boat song' (*lung-chou ko*) ridicules the ignorance of the rustics with respect to things 'modern' in Canton. This song is an adaptation from a newspaper report that mocked the naive response of a country person on seeing a Western thriller film, his first motion picture. The writer's facetious contempt was explicit: 'As expected, it is a stupid hick, [which can be told] by the kind of clothing he is wearing. He is an ignorant man with an ignorant mind, talking to those who sit next to him about the story of the movie' (ibid. 2.2, 24–25 August). This rural visitor thought that what he was watching on the screen were real events actually taking place. When the hero's life was threatened in the film by a large, fierce panther, this poor countryman could not control his excitement and screamed out for someone to help the hero. As a result, the showing was forced to stop. The man was taken away by police, and later released. An account such as this was detrimental to the public image of the rustics in Canton.[45]

Country people's unfamiliarity with things urban was always good for a laugh, and became a popular subject for banter. The amusing experience of a country person with a water tobacco-pipe in the city is the plot of a humorous prose-piece showing the 'stupid' and yet laudable demeanour of rustics in the city. A countryman visits a friend at his city home. He is being served a water tobacco-pipe. Being entirely ignorant of what it is, he lights the pipe, and slurps up the whole can of water that is meant to be used for filtering the nicotine. After he has finished, he tells his friend jauntily: 'City men are really civilized. [A] small tea-pot which will be heated [automatically] when being lighted is [something] really convenient. However, too many tea-leaves have been used [in my last pot because that tasted of] bitterness [that] is difficult to be rid of' (ibid. 1928: 4.4, 9 June). Such mockery of the unsophisticatedness of the country people seems to reaffirm the easy urban assumption of their cultural backwardness, as much as to reinforce the city's own swaggering sense of superiority.

Sometimes, there was even no need for an excuse for being prejudicial against those country bumpkins, as in the case of the outrageous mistreatment experienced by a disabled countrywoman in Canton. One afternoon in a small alley, a newspaper reporter was attracted to the thunderous noise of handclapping and laughter from a crowd of over a hundred men and women. On closer inspection, he realized that the excited crowd had surrounded a dumb and lame woman. Although this woman was not able to speak, the spectators, including the reporter himself, were certain about her rural identity as judged by the outfit she was wearing. She had become a focal point of ridicule for no better reason than the way she was dressed and her grave difficulty in communicating with those people who had her encircled—she was seemingly trying to ask for directions or assistance. At the height of this display of humiliation, a lout ran up to her and poured a bucket of water over her head and then told her that it was urine that she was now soaked with. Utterly infuriated, the countrywoman, limping, tried to run after him, the sight of which turned out to be even more amusing to the already uproarious onlookers who awarded the prankster a round of applause. The crowd dispersed only after the local police had taken the poor woman away (*KPP* 1928: 8, 23 March). Throughout this report, not a word of protest was voiced against this cruel act of mockery of a cripple. Instead, the incident was happily described as another typical and laughable case of a 'country bumpkin in town'. Public humiliation of the countryfolk by their city 'superiors' was seemingly accepted as a matter of course.

The 'rustics' were also sometimes believed to be so unsophisticated that they were totally ignorant of national politics, now increasingly identified with the city. In the heydays of the Nationalist revolution during the mid-1920s, when the subject of causing revolution was winning a considerable number of supporters in cities such as Canton, many nationalistic intellectuals were getting indignant at the countryfolk who were assumed to be innately weak in patriotic feelings. The supplements of the local *Republican Daily News* in this period had published articles, and letters from the readers, that aired their contempt concerning the political indifference assumed to be shared by all the countryfolk in China.

On the occasion of the Double-Tenth celebration in 1926, for example, a journalist recorded a short conversation between two 'come-to-town' country people, who are watching the memorial parade. One of them asks if it is a fancy-dress carnival. The other replies: 'This is quite likely some sort of birthday celebration for a deity. Can't you see all those red and green flags in their hands? The characters on them must be read as something like "Welcome to Your Excellency" '. After the parade, they shout to each other that the show was very spectacular and wonder if there will be another one the next day (*KCMKJP* 1926: 4, 10 October). In a special newspaper issue commemorating the sixteenth anniversary of the Double-Tenth, a contributor wrote bluntly that the symbolic meanings of the date 'Double-Tenth' were never understood by the village people living in the countryside and that was also the reason why the occasion was never seen celebrated outside the city (Ju Shih 1927: 3.4).

In another context, a Cantonese wrote to a local newspaper about what he had seen and heard, in shock. He recorded that one day when a mass demonstration was under way in the city of Canton commemorating the Shameen Incident (23 June 1925), many participants were enthusiastically distributing political pamphlets to the passers-by, and had nearly lost their voices by repeatedly shouting slogans that called for unity among the Chinese people to stop the invasion of China by the British. At one point, this angry writer stated, he and his friends overheard the conversations of two women, who both looked to him like unmistakable 'country bumpkins'. These women talked merrily: 'I cannot care less about what they say on the subject of the fall of this country. If [our enemies] invade and capture the provincial capital, I shall of course run away from here and go back to my native village for shelter!' These comments aroused a deep sense of sadness within the author. By the time he decided to scold these countrywomen, they had already disappeared into the crowd (Mo Yin-chih 1925: 9).

In another piece of writing contributed to this newspaper's supplement, its author wrote about what he knew of the quality of education in a village school. In his visits, the author noticed that the school placed heavy emphasis on teaching Confucian classics to its students. The reason, as this author understood, was that Confucian classics were strongly believed by the teachers to be an effective antidote to the growing problem of demoralization among students, who were under the bad influence of Westernization, and to the trend of students' radical activism, which was manifested in the outbreak of countless incidents of anti-imperialist demonstration. At school, neither teachers nor students were allowed to utter anything concerned with the issue of anti-imperialism; offenders would be publicly rebuked by the principal and avoided by other staff and their peers. The school principal demanded that everyone besides the teachers wait on him like servants; they were even asked to prepare opium and smoking paraphernalia for him. It was a school, in the critical eyes of this author, that shamelessly propagated foreign imperialism in China (Hsin Yin 1925: 9).

Thus the countrypeople were mocked for their lack of political consciousness and for ignorance of national affairs. Underneath these scornful criticisms was not only an open contempt for the socio-political backwardness of the countryside, but also a reaffirmation of the superiority of the city in the sense that it was the nursery of modern nationalism and hence held the hope of China's future.

Canton as a Showpiece of Modernity

Meanwhile, in contrast, the KMT (Kuomintang) authorities assiduously propagated the image of Canton as 'the birth-place and the base of the [national] revolution' (*kê-ming t'sê-yüan-ti*). A contemporary politician described Canton as the model city of Kwangtung, and Kwangtung as the model province of China from which the spirit of the Chinese revolution emanated (Li 1922: 1–4).[46] Such a biased view of this city was often quoted in political speeches, official publications, and party rhetoric throughout the Republican era.[47]

Moreover, the authorities were also keen on 'planting' politically symbolic artefacts and monuments throughout the city as a means to legitimize its position, and also to strengthen its professed image as the base of the Chinese revolution. On the small hill to the north of the city, and on the site of a deconsecrated temple, was built the cenotaph-like Sun Yat-sen Monument. It rises about 120 feet above the top of the hill, and is the city's highest landmark. A large area in front of the monument was levelled in order to make it visible from most parts of the city (Ng 1936: 45–6). The most publicized piece of political architecture in the 1930s was the Sun Yat-sen Memorial Hall, which was said to be the 'no. 1 view of Canton'. This huge auditorium, with a capacity of 10,000 seats, was situated at the centre of the city, and cost $3.6 million to build (ibid. 45; Lee 1936: 132). Furthermore, bronze statues of deceased revolutionary heroes were installed in some of the most prestigious public parks (*Kuang-chou chih-nan* 1934: 167–70; *HCLCCN* 1934: 298). Together with other revolutionary monuments scattered around the city, these served as visual reminders of the role of Canton in China's Republican revolution.[48] To further highlight the political and cultural importance of this city, the local authorities invested huge sums of money in building two iron river bridges in Canton, which were the first of its kind constructed solely by the Chinese in south China. In addition, Canton Municipal Government had also built for itself a Western-style palatial office building, which was criticized by a concerned young middle-school student as the most lavish municipal government house in the whole of

China (Ch'i Chih-t'ang 1934: 366–7). In its quest for political legitimacy and popular respect and support, local authorities in Canton had been anxiously planting politically symbolic architectures in the city. Canton was granted an unprecedented, and idealized, ideological importance and historical status. The cultural and political distance between Canton and the countryside was thus further widened.

With the popular tendency to identify the city with modernity, a Canton resident took pride in his citizenship. Parks and widened carriageways were some of the more important urban symbols that helped build this modern image of the city. Intensive construction of public parks and wide carriageways had begun with the establishment of the municipal government in 1921 (*HCLCCN* 1934: 57–9, 296–300). The emphasis on urban parks may have been inspired by the influential trend of urban planning in Europe and the United States between 1910 and 1920, which advocated that parks could exert on the urban masses a 'harmonizing and refining influence' that would subsequently 'provide the foundation stone of an even more close-knit and harmonious moral order' in the city.[49] In Canton, as in 'the civilized countries in Europe and America', parks were officially given an ethical value as an important means of 'healthy recreation' to improve the morality of the citizens (ibid. 179). Sometimes it was hyped as a moral antidote to a whole range of social vices from prostitution to gambling (Li 1922: 19). But, more practically, parks were said to be built for 'delighting [a citizen's] spirit, [and] refreshing the air [in the city]' (*HCLCCN* 1934: 296). The concept of the park was not an expression of the rural–urban continuum. Instead, it may be interpreted as an urban attempt to capture the ambience of the countryside by reconstructing an artificial natural area for town-dwellers to enjoy. Parkland may thus be seen as a perverted, but idealized, form of nature built exclusively for the service of the city, a symbolic act that expresses the city's immense transformative power and domination over the countryside.

Narrow streets were among the first things that struck nineteenth-century travellers to Canton (Turner 1982: 22–3). In spite of their practical value in providing shade to passers-by during the long, hot summer, these narrow lanes had been gradually relegated to being seen as a stigma of backwardness. Hence, during this period, it was generally believed that widened carriageways like those in the big Western cities were an essential feature of a modern and 'civilized' city, such as Canton was thought to be (Liu Tsai-su 1926: 107–8). The technocrats took great pride in the so-called 'model carriageways'—150-foot, tree-lined, tarmac-paved roadways with concrete pavements (Li 1922: 20–1). So did the citizens. In a pictorial guide of Canton, widened carriageways are one of the main motifs. The caption to one panoramic photograph of the city reveals this sense of civic pride:

> Canton is the only city in the world where ancient and modern civilization meet today... In some places [in Canton], however, one may dine in restaurants with every comfort found in up-to-date hotels in London, Paris, or New York; ride on automobiles;

look over the carriageway of 150-feet wide from roof-top gardens of the many modern hotels and buildings. (Kuo 1924)

Another writer states that:

To come to a full appraisal of the achievement of construction work in Canton city, then one has to look further than what meets the eyes. There are today some 300,000 feet of fine motor roads in the city, but 20 years ago, not a single street was wider than twenty feet or so... they call forth nothing less than the highest praise. (Ng 1936: 81–2)

Since its establishment in 1921 and up until 1934, the Canton Municipal Government had built approximately 400,000 feet of concrete carriageway, of which about three-quarters was in the city and the rest in the suburban area (*HCLCCN* 1934: 59). An intercity bias in such infrastructural development may also have helped stimulate the growth of urban identity, as a result of greater mobility within the city.

Modern architecture and cityscape were equally important symbols fostering civic awareness and augmenting urban identity (Lynch 1985: 1–2 and esp. ch. 3; Lethaby 1922: 1–2). By the late 1920s, Western architectural styles and forms of buildings—urban artefacts that were unknown in the nearby rural area—had already become a visual identity-symbol of Canton. High-rise buildings, which symbolized the achievement of modern technology and human ability to conquer 'space', were objects of great appreciation there.

Until 1940 the tallest building in Canton was the twelve-storeyed Sun Company Building (*Ta-hsin kung-ssu*). Within it was a department store, a hotel, a bank, a restaurant and a roof-top amusement park. The building occupied a significant psychological position, both good and bad, in the thinking of contemporary Cantonese. To some, it stood for a modern urban lifestyle that was increasingly stigmatized as mercenary, lavishly consumerist, hedonistic, and creating moral turpitude. In Chang Tzu-p'ing's 'Ch'ang-t'u' (1930: ii. 294–5), the lure of the great variety of imported luxury goods on sale in this building's store, the expensive Western cuisines served in its restaurant, and the Hollywood romance movies shown at its roof-top park, are seen as traps of modern urban materialism that subsequently corrupt, both spiritually and physically, the protagonists in the story. Its roof-top amusement park was regarded by some contemporary writers as a cauldron of social vices. Among its regulars were prostitutes who solicited customers, licentious young wastrels who hunted for innocent girls, and ne'er-do-wells who came for the opera shows by all-female troupes (I Hsaio 1922: 1–2).[50]

On the other hand, these trenchant, and perhaps also rhetorical, comments tell further how popular this place was. Its popularity may also have reflected the surge of a new urban youth culture that was made up of a consumer culture and a cult of things 'modern'. To some, this building, being one of the best in Canton, was a symbol of prosperity and modernity, may be even a landmark of the successful channelling of human resources to the building of a new era.[51] In the nostalgic words of one writer, it was the 'most impressive building in Canton' in terms of height, modern architectural style, and facilities.[52]

In a contemporary pictorial on Canton, the picture of the Bund, where most of the city's modern high-rise buildings were situated, significantly occupies the first page.[53] Moreover, a large proportion of its one hundred selected photographs is devoted to showing the Western-style modern high-rise buildings, government offices, and multi-storey buildings on the campuses of prestigious local schools and universities, the busy street-life, and newly constructed wide carriageways. There are only six photographs of Canton's countryside. Among these few, one shows a very narrow village road in the interior of Kwangtung, probably intended to provide a visual contrast with the 150-foot 'model carriageways' in the city. Another is of a village where a farmer is seen ploughing the field with a buffalo, and readers are asked to 'note the uniform size and design of the farm houses', seemingly intended to be contrasted with the great varieties of architectural styles in the modern multi-storey buildings of Canton (Kuo 1924). The photographs are so selectively chosen by the author as to mirror the popular perception of the geo-cultural contrast between city and countryside. Modern urban architecture helped foster civic loyalty and pride among the Cantonese.

The motifs of the illustrations in the official *Kuang-chou chih-nan* (*Guide to Canton*; 1934) display a similar 'cult' of modern buildings. Nearly all the illustrations are photographs of modern multi-storey government buildings, universities and prestigious high-school buildings, and busy street scenes with high-rise buildings to left and right. Not one photograph is of the suburban area, let alone the rural periphery. The vast countryside at the outer boundary of Canton is seemingly considered unfit to form a part of the commonly accepted image of modern Canton.

Multi-storey buildings proliferated in Republican Canton. They were a means both to ease the scarcity of living-space in the crowded city (Canton had a population of almost 1 million by 1930), and to show off individual wealth. In Hsi-kuan, the residential area for rich businessmen and the upper classes, the once dominant traditional-style single-storey mansions (Ch'ü Ta-chün 1974: ii. 469) were eventually replaced by modern Western-style multi-storey buildings, which the modern bourgeoisie conceived of as more appropriate for their progressive outlook. In Tung-shan and Hsiao-pei, the newly developed residential areas in suburban Canton, there were also 'hundreds of modern houses' that were mostly two-storey villas, and three- or four-storey Western-style buildings (Ng 1936: 7–8).[54] In the countryside, there was a trend on the part of well-to-do rural families to imitate this urban architectural form. Remittances by Chinese abroad facilitated this (Ch'en 1939: 106–11).[55] It was an indication of the process of changing values expressed through architecture, from a traditional rural to a modern and Western orientation. Multi-storey buildings had become an ostensible symbol of social status in the new era.[56] No wonder that in the visualized dream of a bride-to-be as depicted in one contemporary satirical cartoon, a comfortable life in a modern high-rise apartment, plus car and diamond ring, are the things that she eagerly dreams of achieving in her future marriage (*Pan-chiao man-hua* 1932: 6).

The identification of material progress and modernity with modern high-rise buildings is also to be seen in the advertisements for certain locally made medicines. Drawings using such advertising motifs may have been intended to create an impression that these medicines were as scientifically advanced as modern city architecture; or that they were taken by 'sophisticated citizens' of a modern city—since urban people trusted these drugs, they must be reliable and good.[57]

It seems that the public image of Canton in this period was mostly so constructed that those districts with identifiable high-rise buildings were subconsciously conceived by its citizens as being the essential Canton, the city. Apparently the demarcation line was sharply drawn between high-rise buildings and all their related symbolism of modernity on the one hand, and a visibly different countryside with all its implications of inferiority on the other. This consolidation of urban identity in Republican Canton was therefore by and large the result of a mental process of perception-construction based on contrasting realities between city and countryside.

Pride of the City Dwellers

The cultural superiority of the city was commonly accepted. In an essay published in a school magazine, the young Cantonese author tried to compare urban with rural women, in accordance with her perceptions of their differences. In her mind, city women already enjoy 'the fruits of the women's liberation movement'. They are not only able to afford a far better material life in the city, but are also given the chance to receive modern education, to choose their occupations, and to select their spouses. In a condescending tone, she aired her disappointment at the indifference of urbanites to the suffering of women in the countryside, where they are said to be still enslaved by inviolable social customs and many forms of physical and psychological oppression (Ho Chin-hsing 1934: 20–1). In another context, when analysing at length the causes of the insurmountable problem of gambling in Kwangtung, the editor-in-chief of a popular local newspaper wrote that the situation was a lot worse in the countryside and the hinterland than in the city for the important reason of the serious shortage of 'decent entertainment' in the former. In the city, the editor explained, one could easily spend the day visiting an amusement park or a public park, watching a movie, or even strolling along its tarmac streets; but there was only gambling available in the remotely located county towns and in the country (*CTKL* 1936: 164–9). Although a similar problem existed in most cities in Kwangtung, this journalist seemed unwilling to study that, and his unsubstantiated criticism of countrypeople reminds us of the contemptuous urban intellectuals from the Lingnan University and their dislike of the countryside.

The city people were also believed to be more sophisticated and refined. In respect of contemporary Cantonese opera, the distinctions between 'Canton-Hong Kong troupes' (*Shêng Kang pan*), who performed almost exclusively in Canton and Hong Kong, and 'countryside troupes' (*lo-hsiang pan*) who played anywhere except the aforesaid two cities, were markedly clear as to their social status, aesthetic quality and reputation, and commercial successfulness—in favour, naturally, of the former. According to a contemporary opera critic, the *lo-hsiang pan* (translatable literally and symbolically as 'troupes that travel down to the countryside') were 'conservative' (*shou-chiu p'ai*), in respect of theatrical technique, while *Shêng Kang pan* were 'Europeanized and Americanized' (*Ou Mi p'ai*) and hence progressive and modern. New and original scripts, characterized by their modern setting of plots and wider use of modern Western musical instruments and costumes, were generally performed by the latter. In contrast, 'countryside troupes', because of their less-sophisticated rural audiences, were said to be able to perform only traditional popular but prosaic and familiar scripts (Ch'in 1931: 66).

The attraction of city life was recognized by all walks of life, including, sometimes, the unlikely ones. For example, when a 'retiring' prostitute was looking for her ideal man to marry, she listed as one of her seven requests that she would not marry any man who would require her to move to live in a village (*Chu-kiang hsing-ch'i hua pao* 3, 1927: 20).

This almost structuralistic view of the cultural superiority of city people is vividly revealed in an article published in an official daily. The author of the article compared the intellectual differences between children in the city and the countryside. As a result of the more favourable socio-cultural circumstances provided by the city, urban children were, our author opined, much stronger in their intellectual power, analytical ability, and sensitivity than their counterparts in the countryside. Moreover, they were also superior in concentration, richer in imagination and aesthetical sense, more articulate, more sociable, and even more aware of cleanliness than the country children. In contrast, the author told us, the country boys and girls were not only slower to respond, poorer in intellect and powers of observation, but were also less articulate and imaginative, had weaker concentration and memory, were less sociable, and lacked cleanliness. The city children even looked nicer and more refined while the young people in the countryside were described as dirty, ugly, and wild. The cultural power of the city was nearly absolute (*KCMKJP* 1929: 12, 5 Nov.).

It is not surprising, therefore, to find that local editors in Canton in this period seemed eager to publish news, in a narrative style they enjoyed, about how country visitors fell prey to the city tricksters. For example, there was a report about two well-to-do brothers from the country, one a widower, the other a bachelor, who were both eager to marry a woman from Canton. After a long search with the help of a go-between, two young widows in Canton were identified as possible candidates. In their first meeting in a restaurant, the brothers were instantly bewitched and decided to marry them right away, the same evening. To show their sincerity, the two brothers lost no time in paying these widows a handsome amount of betrothal money. The women received the money happily, but soon excused themselves from the party on the pretext that it was not safe to have so much cash in hand and that they preferred to convert the money into gold accessories. This pair of young widows, of course, never returned, and neither did the go-between. In the narrative of the reporter, what made the scam succeed was because its victims were 'fools from the countryside' whose 'stupid character and unsophisticated sensibility' was said to be leading them into a state of uncontrollable obsession with modern women in the city. It was the stupidity of these country bumpkins, interestingly, rather than the swindlers, that had become the focal point of criticism in this narrative (*YHP* 1934: 6, 2 July). In another context, another widower from the countryside was eager to find himself a new wife from the big city. Under the arrangement of a go-between, he met a young, beautiful widow in Canton, with whom he was instantly bewitched. Without giving a second thought, this 'stupid countryman', in the parlance of the reporter, 'whose mind was blocked by lustful desire so much so that his soul has left his body', paid in full the sum of betrothal money this widow had demanded and agreed to wait for her in Canton for a few days to let her prepare for moving with him to his village. The new bride, of course, never showed up after this 'fruitful' first meeting (*KHP* 1921: 8, 5 August). An interesting common point about these accounts is that their reporters apparently did not express much sympathy for the victims in these swindling incidents, who were just 'country bumpkins', but took pleasure in writing about their stupidity and naivety. Such narratives of prejudice seemed to suggest that the victims deserved the way they had been mistreated in the city; these misdeeds were not denounced in a way that one would expect from news reports of this kind, nor were the con-artists criticized for the scam they had committed. Rather, it was the 'stupidity' and the unsophistication of the countryfolk that became, ironically, the focal point of these reports, which were written in light-hearted rather than solemn and admonishing language. News as such seemed to be symbolic announcements to their urban readers about the triumph of urban sophistication over rural ignorance and stupidity.

Contemporary literature shows that there was concern about problems of human relations and mass poverty in the city. However, compared with the intellectuals' response in the West, such 'fear of the city' in Republican Canton was significantly weaker. Occasionally, one might come across a pessimist like Liu Yao-hsin (1935: 69–72) who warned that the city, being a foreign enclave and the agent of foreign economic imperialism, had become a destructive force that was undermining China's national economy, as well as social order in the city. And yet his view was by no means a critique of the socio-cultural position of the city. True pessimists such as Oswald Spengler were seemingly rare in Canton (Hall 1984: 19–25; Lees 1985: 6–12, and chs. 5–8).

In contrast, the optimists appear to have been numerous. In the mid-1930s, there arose in Canton a group of academics who tried to redefine the position of the countryside in contemporary Chinese culture. They advocated the total Westernization of Chinese culture, beginning from Canton, the city highly regarded as the beachhead of modernization and Westernization. Ch'en Hsü-ching, a leading advocate of the idea, repudiated the Rural Reform School's belief that the countryside was the cradle and the source of Chinese culture. A catalogue of examples was cited to support their view that the city did play an important role in the shaping of Chinese culture. Liang Shou-ming's idea of salvaging China by means of reviving and restoring the traditional countryside culture was denounced as both unfeasible and unwanted, on the grounds that China's idyllic values and village culture were in every way inferior to its modern urban counterparts.[58] In Ch'en's opinion, the 'spirit of the village' (*hsiang-ts'un ching-shen*), which stood only for ardent conservatism and obstinate resistance to change, was accountable for Chinese cultural backwardness and national weakness. For two thousand years China had paid heavily for upholding this 'countryside spirit', her knowledge, technology, commerce, and industry being stagnant as a result. By contrast, all the prerequisites for a strong new China were deemed to lie exclusively in the city. City culture, allegedly synonymous with the 'cream' of modern Western civilization, was upheld as the model that should be followed by the countryside in immediately achieving the modernization (by means of wholesale Westernization) of China.

With all its symbolism of material progress, industrialization, science, and democracy, the city became the promise of modernity. Rustics were expected to be admirers of the city and things urban. In Ch'en's view, the old but still apt proverb 'one will die with regret if one has never been to the capital city' (pu tao ching-ch'êng chung chien ku), means something more than mere curiosity about a distant place.[59] It implies rural recognition and envy of the city's symbolic superiority. Ch'en (*CPHH* ii. 122–38) further berates the backwardness of the Chinese countryside as a shameful sight that threatens the international name and image of China.

By the late 1920s, many rural inhabitants had seemingly cast a vote of no confidence in the countryside by emigrating from their villages to the city. A decade earlier, one politician noted that since the building of modern carriageways and other municipal projects, a substantial number of village people, tempted by the city's improvements and booming economy, had moved to Canton (Ch'en Hsü-ching 1935: 122–38).[60] According to some later official statistics, since the 1930s there was close on a monthly four-digit inflow of people into Canton (probably gross inflow, but no details are given), save for brief drops in July 1931 and June 1933 (*Kuang-chou nien-chien* 1935: 36–9). The provincial government even had to reiterate its order to stop the heads of some county governments from residing in Canton, which was seriously disrupting their proper work of administration (*HTJP* 1927: 3.3, 24 Oct.).[61] The countryside values, culture, and lifestyle were no longer the model the urbanites were looking for, but vice versa. The trend of rural migration into Canton, which was effectively stopped during the first three decades of the Communist rule, has been clearly re-emerging since the inauguration of the current 'liberal era' in 1979.[62]

The full emergence of an overtly pro-city popular mentality was a milestone in modern China's socio-cultural and intellectual history. On the ideological level, the traditional preferential attitudes towards countryside values and culture met an unprecedented challenge. Although nostalgic perceptions of the countryside still lingered, the foundation for the cult of the city had already been firmly laid. Contemporary literature disclosing the unhappy side of urban life seemed powerless to deter the urbanites from taking pride in their city, to rid the rural villagers of their obsession with the city whose lures of material comfort and economic opportunity were unknown out there. The rural–urban continuum, though it existed, appeared weakened and under constant pressure in Canton.[63] There, the cult of the city was also one of many expressions of the cult of things Western, and hence modern. And the physical transformation of the cityscape of Republican Canton might be interpreted as a collective effort to construct the Western image of a modern and cultured city on Chinese soil.

In the first three decades of Communist rule, the Chinese government tried high-handedly, though without much long-term success, to return the cultural and material centre of gravity back from the city to the countryside.[64] In present-day China, living in big cities is a privilege, and 'sending down' to the village is equivalent to a punishment (Murphey 1984: 199–202).[65]

A city household status is the dream shared by millions of peasant families living in the poverty-stricken countryside,[66] a dream to be materialized by all possible means (Potter and Potter 1990: 322).[67] Since the 1980s, with further uneven development totally favouring Canton, the 'cult of Canton' seems to have reached its apogee. Unlike the pro-city literature of the 1920s and 1930s, which lacked the intellectual clarity, depth, and sophistication of its Western counterparts,[68] present-day publications on this subject appear more lucid and confident in asserting the total superiority of Canton.[69]

In short, despite the fact that the position of the city in classical Chinese ideology might be low and hence relatively neglected in traditional literati's discourses, the actual socio-cultural significance and importance of the city in pre-Republican China was indisputable. In the case of Canton, the rising importance of both the image and the reality of the city, as well as the esteem of its citizens, signalled an ideological reorientation in the minds of the people in this part of China since the early Republic. By the end of the Republican era, the old ambivalent cultural relations between city and countryside were gradually redefined as the result of a cumulative process that gave its first sign of full eruption during the 1920s and 1930s. Since then, the conflict has been more open and has followed a path of increasingly permanent divergence that will cost the country dear.

REFERENCES

Ai-k'o-ssu (1928), 'Li Wan Hsün yüeh chi', *Kung-p'ing pao*, (*KPP*), 20 June.

Alitto, Guy S. (1979), *The Last Confucian: Liang Shou-ming and the Chinese Dilemma of Modernity* (Berkeley: University of California Press).

Balazs, Etienne (1964), *Chinese Civilization and Bureaucracy* (New Haven, Conn.: Yale University Press).

Beattie, John, *Other Cultures* (London: Routledge & Kegan Paul, 1969).

Chan, Anita, Unger, Jonathan, and Madsen, Richard (1984), *Chen Village* (Berkeley: University of California Press).

Chang Chak-yan, (1976), ' "Ruralia" vs "Urbania" in Chinese Political_Thought' (unpublished Ph.D. dissertation, State University of New York at Binghamton).

Chang Hsin-tai (1898), 'Yüeh yu hsiao chih', in Wang Hsi-pu (ed.), *Hsiao-fang-hu-chai yü-ti ts'ung Ch'ao* (Shanghai: Chu i t'ang), ix.

Chang Tzu-p'ing (1928), 'Kung-tsai wei-yüan', *Tzu-p'ing hsiao-shuo hsüan* (Shanghai: Hsien-tai shu-chü), i.

—— (1930), 'Ch'angt'u', *Tzu-p'ing hsiao-shuo hsüan* (Shanghai: Hsien-tai shu-chü), ii.

Ch'ao-lien hsiang chih (1946), ed. Lo Tzu-chün (Hong Kong: n.p.).

Ch'en Chao-yü (1937), *Kuang-tung t'ang-yeh yü Fêng Rui* (n.p., n.p.).

Ch'en Han-seng (1936), *Agrarian Problems in Southernmost China* (Shanghai: Kelly & Walsh).

Ch'en Hsü-ching (1935), 'Hsiang-ts'un wên-hua yü ch'êng-shih wên-hua', in Fêng En-yung (ed.), *Ch'üan-pên hsi-hua yen-lun su-chi* (*CPHH*) (Canton: Ling-nan ta-hsüeh hsüeh-sheng tzu-chih hui ch'u-pan-shê), ii.

Ch'en Pei-ying (1934), 'Hsiang-kang lü-hsing chih', *Kuang-tung hsüeh-shêng* (*KTHS*) 4.

Ch'en Ta (1939), *Emigrant Communities in South China: A Study of Overseas Migration and its Influence on Standards of Living and Social Change*, ed. Bruno Lasker (Shanghai: Kelly & Walsh).

Ch'i Chih-t'ang (1934), 'Kuang-chou shih ti tai chien-chu', *Shêng-li I-chung hsüeh-shêng jih-chi hsüan* (Canton: Kuang-tung Shêng-li I-chung).

Chieh (1933), 'Ai chih wei ch'ou shen hsu kuo', *KTHS* 2.

Chin Wên-huan et al. (1992), 'Kuang-tung shêng 16 hsien shih chih-li tsan-chi tiao-cha ti tzu-liao fên-his chi fang-tsan chien-i', in Kuang-tung hsin-li hsüeh-hui (ed.), *Kuang-tung hsin-li hsüeh tsung-hêng* (Canton: Hua-nan li-kung ta-hsüeh ch'u-pan-shê).

Chin-tai Kuang-chou k'ou-an ching-chi shê-hui kai-k'uang: Yüeh hai-kuan pao-kao hui tsi (1996) (*YHKPK*), ed. Kuang-chou-shih ti-fang-chih pien-hsüan wei-yüan-hui pan-kung-shih and Kuang-chou hai-kuan-chih pien-hs'üan wei-yüan-hui (Canton: Chi-nan ta-hsüeh ch'u-pah-shê).

Ch'in Ch'in (1931), 'Yüeh-chü chih chin hsi kuan', *Hsi ch'uan* 1.

Chin-tu kai lan (*CTKL*) (1936), ed. Kuang-tung-shêng chin-tu wei-yüan-hui.

Chou Ch'ih-shih (1969), 'Yang-chêng ku ch'ao', in Shen Yün-lung (ed.), *Chin-tai Chung-kuo shih liao ts'ung k'an* (Taipei: Wên hai shu-chü). First published 1806.

Chou Chung (1934), 'Shui ti tsui-kuo', *KTHS* 4.

Cho Yu (1928), 'Shang-hai ti lai hsin', in Kuang-chou wên-hsüeh-hui (ed.), *Ying shih* (Canton: Yüeh Kang shou k'uang ch'u-pan pu).

Chou Hsing (1934), 'Huo-yen Shan', *KTHS* 4.

Chü Hsiang (1935), 'Ts'un-chü sou chih', in *Hsien-tai shêng-chan tsa-chih* 1/5: 89–92, 1/6: 90–3.

Chu-kiang hsing-ch'i hua pao (1927), 3.

Ch'ü Ta-chün (1974), *Kuang-tung hsin-yü*, 2 vols. (Hong Kong: Chung-hua shu-chü). First published 1700.

Ch'ü Ying-chieh (1991), *Shêng-Ch'in tu-ch'êng fu-yüan yen-chiu* (Harbin: Hêh-long-kiang jên-min ch'u-pan-shê).

Elvin, Mark (1973), *The Pattern of the Chinese Past* (Stanford: Stanford University Press).

——(1978), 'Chinese Cities since the Sung Dynasty', in P. Abrams and E. Wrigley (eds.), *Towns and Societies* (Cambridge: Cambridge University Press).

——(1991), 'The Crisis of Absurdity: Reflections on *Tides in the Human Sea*' (unpublished paper).

——and Skinner, G. William (1974) (eds.), *The Chinese City Between Two Worlds* (Stanford: Stanford University Press).

Faure, David (1989), *The Rural Economy of Pre-Liberation China: Trade Expansion and Peasant Livelihood in Jiangsu and Guangdong* (Hong Kong: Oxford University Press).

Fei Fei (1933), 'Pieh liao, wo ti ku-hsiang', *I-shê ch'i k'an* 2.

Fei Hsiao-tung (1948), *Hsiang-tu chung-chien* (Shanghai: Kuan-cha shê).

Fêng Rui (1928), 'Hsiang-tsun shê-hui hsin-li chih fen-hsi', in *Shê-hui-hsüeh chieh* (Peking) 1/2, June.

Fêng-su kai-kê wei-yüan-hui (1930) (ed.), *Fêng-su kai-kê ts'ung k'an* (*FSKKTK*) (Canton: Kuang-chou-tê-pieh-shih tang-pu hsüan-ch'uan-pu).

Freedman, Maurice (1971), *Chinese Lineage and Society: Fukien and Kwangtung* (London: The Athlone Press).

——(1979), *The Study of Chinese Family: Essays by Maurice Freedman*, ed. and intro. G. William Skinner (Stanford: Stanford University Press).

Fuma, Susuma (1993), 'Late Ming Urban Reform in Hangzhou', in Linda Cooke Johnson (ed.), *Cities of Jiangnan in Late Imperial China* (Albany: State University of New York).

Galbiati, Fernando (1984), *P'eng P'ai and the Hai-lu-feng Soviet* (Stanford: Stanford University Press).

Gernet, Jacques (1962), *Daily Life in China on the Eve of the Mongol Invasion, 1250–1276.* Trans. H. W. Wright (Stanford: Stanford University Press).

Grimm, Tilemann (1977), 'Academies and Urban Systems in Kwangtung', in William Skinner (ed.), *The City in Late Imperial China* (Stanford: Stanford University Press).

Hall, Peter (1984), 'Metropolis', in A. Sutcliffe (ed.), *Metropolis* (Chicago: University of Chicago Press).

Han Ta-ch'êng (1991), *Ming-tai ch'êng-shih yen-chiu* (Peking: Chung-kuo jên-min ta-hsüeh ch'u-pan-shê).

Ho Chin-hsing (1934), 'Nung-ts'un fu-nü yü ch'êng-shih fu-nü', *I-shê ch'i k'an*, 2–3.

'Hsiang-jên k'ou chung ti hsiang-shih-chieh' (1926), *Kuang-chou min-kuo jih-pao*, (*KCMKJP*), 10 October.

Hsiao Ling (1930), 'Mi-mang chung', in *Wan jên tsa chih* 1/1, April.

Hsin Yin (1925), 'Hsüan-ch'uan ti-kuo chu-i ti hsüeh-hsiao', *KCMKJP* 13 July.

Hsing Chuang (1933), 'Hsiang ku-liang, *Kuang-chou li-pai-liu* (*KCLPL*) (Canton: Kuang-chou li-pai-liu shê), iv.

'Hsiung-t'i chiu-ma ch'êng-hun tuo pien-chü' (1934), *Yüeh hua pao* (*YHP*), 2 July.

Hua-tzu jih-pao (*HTJP*) (1911) (Hong Kong), 15 November; (1912), 25 June; (1923), 22 April; (1927), 10 June, 5 July, 17, 24–5 August, 24 October; (1928), 9 June.

Huang Nai-ch'ao and Ho Wên-kuang (1987), *Kuang-chou jên: tso-jih yü chin-jih* (Canton: Kuang-chou wên-hua ch'u-pan-shê).

Huang P'o-yüan et al. (1992), 'Mi-hsin fan-tsui chih hsin-li p'ou-hsi', in Kuang-tung hsin-li hsüeh-hui (ed.), *Kuang-tung hsin-li-hsüeh tsung-hêng* (Canton: Hua-nan li-kung ta-hsüeh ch'u-pan-shê).

Huang Tsun-shêng (1941), *Ling-nan min hsin yü Ling-nan wên-hua* (Canton: Min-tsu wên-hua ch'u-pan-shê).

Huang Yin-p'u (1934), *Kuang-chou kung-jên chia-t'ing chih yen-chiu* (Canton: Kuo-li Chung-shan ta hsüeh ching-chi tiao-ch'a ch'u).

'I-chiu-erh-liu nien tung-fang-ling' (1927), *HTJP*, 18 August.

I Hsiao (*c.*1922), 'So-yeh fu', *Hsi-chü shih-chieh* 1/3, sect. *Yu-chi wên-chang*.

I Li (1990), *Yü-hai yü shen-ên* (Canton: Hu-nan wên-i ch'u-pan-shê).

Johnson, David (1985), 'Communication, Class, and Consciousness', in David Johnson, Andrew Nathan, and Evelyn Rawski (eds.), *Popular Culture in Late Imperial China* (Berkeley: University of California).

Ju Shih, 'Shuang-shih tzu-hsing ti ch'i-tzu' *HTJP*, 1927: 10 October.

Kuang-chou chih-nan (1934) (Canton: Kuang-chou shih-chêng-fu).

KCMKJP (1926), 6 November; (1929), 5 November.

Kuang-chou nien-chien pien tsuan wei-yüan-hui (1935) (ed.), *Kuang-chou nien-chien*, 2 vols. (Canton: Kuang-chou nien-chien pien tsuan wei-yüan-hui).

Kuang-chou shih-chêng-fu (1934) (ed.), *Kuang-chou shih chih po-yin-t'ai* (Canton: Kuang-chou shih-chêng-fu).

Kuang-chou shih-chêng-fu hsin chu lo-ch'êng chi-nien tê-k'an (1934) (*HCLCCN*), ed. Kuang-chou shih-chêng-fu (Canton: Kuang-chou shih-chêng-fu).

Kuang-chou shih shih-chêng-fu (1929), *Kuang-chou shih shih-chêng-fu t'ung-chi nien-chien. Ti i hui* (Canton: Kuang-chou shih shih-chêng-fu).

Kuang-chou-shih êrh-shih-i-nien jên-k'ou tiao-ch'a pao kao (1932), ed. Kuang-chou-shih jên-k'ou tiao-ch'a wei-yüan-hui mi-shu ch'u (Canton: Kunag-chou-shih jên-k'ou tiao-ch'a wei-yüan-hui).

Kulp, Daniel Harrison, II (1925), *Country Life in South China: The Sociology of Familism, i. Phenix Village, Kwangtung, China* (New York: Teacher College of Columbia University).

Kuang-tung shêng-chêng-fu ts'ai-chêng-t'ing and Kuang-tung ts'ai-chêng tê-pai-yüan kung-chü (1934) (eds.), *Kuang-tung shêng ts'ai-chêng chi shih*, 3 vols. (Canton: Kuang-tung-shêng chêng-fu ts'ai-chêng-t'ing).

KPP Kung-p'ing pao (1924–1949) (Canton: Kuang-chou Kung-ping pao shê).

KHP Kuo hua pao (1921), 5 August.

Kuo Wên-fang (1924), *Modern Canton Illustrated*, 2nd edn. (Canton: The China Photo-Engraving Co.).

Lee, Bing-shuey Edward (1936), *Modern Canton* (Shanghai: Kelly & Walsh).

Lees, Andrew (1984), 'The Metropolis and the Intellectual', in Anthony Sutcliffe (ed.), *Metropolis: 1890–1940* (Chicago: University of Chicago Press).

——(1985), *Cities Perceived: Urban Societies in European and American Thought* (Manchester: Manchester University Press).

Lethaby, W. R. (1922), *Form in Civilization* (Oxford: Clarendon Press).

Lewis, John Wilson (1971), 'Introduction: Order and Modernization in the Chinese City', in id. (ed.), *The City in Communist China* (Stanford: Stanford University Press).

Li T'iao-yüan (1937), 'Nan Yüeh pi chi', in Wang Yün-wu (ed.), *Ts'ung-shu chi-ch'êng* (Shanghai: Shang-wu yin shu kuan). First published in 1778,

Li Tsung-huang (1922), *Hsin Kuang-tung kuan-ch'a chi* (Shanghai: Shang-wu yin shu kuan).

Liang Yün-chiao (1934), 'Ai wo ku-hsiang', *KTHS* 4.

Ling Hsiao-shêng (1933), 'Chih-fên yü shêng', *Kuang-chou li-pai liu* (*KCLPL*) (Canton: Kuang-chou li-pai-liu shê), iv.

Link, Perry (1981), *Mandarin Ducks and Butterflies: Popular Fiction in Early Twentieth-Century Chinese Cities* (Berkeley: University of California Press).

Liu Shu-fên (1992), *Liu-chao ti ch'êng-shih yü shê-hui* (Taipei: Hsüeh-shêng shu-chü).

Liu Tsai-su (1926), *Kuang-chou kuai-lan* (Shanghai: Shih-chich shu chü).

Liu Yao-hsin (1935), 'Chung-kuo tu-shih shê-hui ti wei-chi', *Shê-hui yen-chui ch'i-k'an* 1/1.

Lynch, Kevin (1985), *The Image of the City* (Cambridge, Mass.: MIT).

Ma Ya-ko (James Laidlaw Maxwell) (1934), *Kuang-chou Ho-nan wei-shêng kung-tso chi-hua* (Honan Island Health Scheme) (Canton: Kuang-tung chia-ting wei-shêng ts'u-chin hui).

Mo Yin-chih (1925), 'Yu fu', *KCMKJP*, 9 July.

Mosher, Steven W. (1983), *Broken Earth* (New York: Free Press).

Mote, F. W. (1977), 'The Transformation of Nanking', in G. William Skinner (ed.), *The City in Late Imperial China* (Stanford: Stanford University Press).

Mumford, Lewis (1938), *The Culture of Cities* (New York: Harcourt Brace Jovanovich).

Murphey, Rhoads (1974), 'The Treaty Ports in China's Modernization', in Mark Elvin and G. William Skinner (eds.), *The Chinese City Between Two Worlds* (Stanford: Stanford University Press).

——(1984), 'City as a Mirror of Society: China, Tradition and Transformation', in J. A. Agnew, J. Mercer, and D. E. Sosher, *The City in Cultural Context* (Boston: Allen & Unwin).

Ng Yong-sang (Wu Yang-shêng) (1936), *Canton: City of the Rams* (Canton: M. S. Cheung).

Ou-yang Shan (1948), 'Tsai shen ching li', *Shih-pai ti shih-pai chê* (Shanghai: Chiao-fêng ch'u-pan-shê).

Pa Pên, 'San-shih nien', in Kuang-tung chung-hsüeh hsüeh-shêng tzu-chih-hui (1933) (ed.), *KTHS* 2 (Canton).

——(1934) (ed.), *KTHS* 4 (Canton).

Pahl, R. E. (1968), 'The Rural–Urban Continuum', in id. (ed.), *Readings in Urban Sociology* (Oxford: Pergamon).

P'ang Tê-hsin (1974), *Ts'ung hua-pên chi i-hua-pên so chien chih Sung-tai liang ching shi-min shêng-huo* (Hong Kong: Lung-mêng shu-tien).

Parish, William L., and Whyte, Martin K. (1978), *Village and Family in Communist China* (Chicago: University of Chicago Press).

Potter, J. M., and Potter, S. H. (1990), *China's Peasants: The Anthropology of a Revolution* (Cambridge: Cambridge University Press).

Rainbow, Paul (1987) (ed.), *The Foucault Reader* (Harmondsworth: Peregrine Books).

Rawski, Evelyn S. (1979), *Education and Popular Literacy in Ch'ing China* (Ann Arbor: University of Michigan Press).

Siu, Helen F. (1989), *Agents and Victims in South China* (New Haven, Conn.: Yale University Press).

Skinner, G. William (1977), 'Introduction: Urban and Rural in Chinese Society', in id. (ed.), *The City in Late Imperial China* (Stanford: Stanford University Press).

Stapleton, Kristin (2000), *Civilizing Chengdu: Chinese Urban Reform, 1895–1937* (Cambridge, Mass.: Harvard University Press).

Stockard, Janice E. (1989), *Daughters of the Canton Delta: Marriage Patterns and Economic Strategies in South China, 1860–1930* (Stanford: Stanford University Press).

T'an Jen-chiu (1932), *Chung-kuo ti li-hun yen-chiu* (Shanghai: Chung-hua Chi-tu chiao nü ch'ing-nien hui ch'üan kuo hsieh hui).

Têng Tuan-pên (1986), *Ling-nan chang-ku* (Canton: Kung-tung lü-yu ch'u-pan-shê).

Têng Yen-ch'ao et al. (1988), *Kuang-chou-jên ti shêng-huo fang-shih* (Hai-k'ou: Hai-nan jên-min ch'u-pan-shê).

Tien Chung-chi and Sun Chang-hsi (1984), *Chung-kuo hsien-tai hsiao-shuo shih* (Tsi-nan: Shan-tung wên-i ch'u-pan-shê).

Topley, Marjorie (1975), 'Marriage Resistance in Rural Kwangtung', in Marjorie Wolf and Roxane Witke (eds.), *Women in Chinese Society* (Stanford: Stanford University Press).

Ts'ai Jên-chien (1987) (ed.), *Tien-kung k'ai-wu* (Taipei: Shih-pao wên-hua ch'u-pan ch'i-yeh you-hsien kung-ssu).

Tsai Liang (1934), 'Wo ti kuo-ch'ü', *KTHS* 4.

Tsin, Michael (1999), *Nation, Governance, and Modernity in China* (Stanford: Stanford University Press).

—— (2000), 'Canton Remapped', in Joseph Esherick (ed.), *Remaking the Chinese City* (Honolulu: University of Hawaii Press).

Tu Chuan (1934), 'Pien ti wen-t'i', *KTHS* 4.

'Tu-shih ti i wan' (1935), *Jên chien shih* 35: 39–41, September.

Turims, Edward, and Kelly, David (1985) (eds.) *Unreal City* (Manchester: Manchester University Press).

Turner, J. A. (1982), *Kwangtung or Five Years in South China* (Hong Kong: Oxford University Press).

Tzu Yün (1936), 'Kê-ming t'sê-yüan-ti', *Ta-chung shêng-huo* 1/10.

US Department of Commerce (1926) (ed.), *China: A Commercial and Industrial Handbook* (Washington, DC: US Dept. of Commerce).

Wang Chiu-hsing (1937), 'Hsin-fêng-huang tsun kai-k'uang tiao-cha', *Nan fêng* 1/4–5.

Watt, John R. (1977), 'The Yamen and Urban Administration', in William Skinner (ed.), *The City in Late Imperial China* (Stanford: Stanford University Press).

Wei (1934), 'Ch'ing-nien mên ti hsien-ching', *YHP*, 23 September.

Wu Jui-lin (1934), 'Sha-nan tan-min tiao-ch'a pao-kao', in *Ling-nan hsüeh-pao* 3/1.

—— and Huang En-lin (1935), 'Chiu-fêng-huang ts'un tiao-ch'a pao-kao', *Ling-nan hsüeh-pao* 4/3.

Wu Lang (1936), 'I-ko nü hsüeh-shêng', *YHP*, 7 November.

Yang, C. K. (1959), *A Chinese Village in Early Communist Transition* (Cambridge, Mass.: MIT).

YHP Yüeh hua pao.

Yün An (1933), 'Ch'ün pien jên yü', in *Kuang-chou li-pai-liu* (*KCLPL*) (Canton: Kuang-chou li-pai-liu shê), iv.

Zhang, Yingjin (1996), *The City in Modern Chinese Literature and Film* (Stanford: Stanford University Press).

2

The Limits of Hatred: Popular Attitudes Towards the West in Republican Canton

1. *HOW ANTI-FOREIGN WAS ANTI-FOREIGNISM?*

Anti-foreignism is sometimes too simply defined as a kind of collective, spontaneous, and belligerent mass sentiment against foreign countries (Liao Kuang-sheng 1986: 2, 3, 8–10). The terms 'anti-imperialism' and 'anti-foreignism', despite their obvious theoretical disparity, tend to be casually and indiscriminately used by provocative rhetoricians as much as by some sinologists. Foreigners, however, were not always regarded as 'imperialists'; nor was everything foreign automatically stigmatized as imperialistic, and hence rejected. In the cultural context, anti-foreignism in Canton in this period was not yet a well-defined ideology, nor a unified movement. With their focus locked on the bellicose side of the history of Sino-foreign relations, and on the officially manipulated political campaigns against imperialist Powers, some scholars have tended to foster a false impression that the Chinese attitude towards foreigners was always hostile and negative.[1]

On the failure of an identity crisis to emerge in China after her encounter with the West, Rhoads Murphey (1974: 32–3, 56) writes:

> The Western challenge merely reinforced existing Sinocentric pride . . . all foreigners could with some reason be dismissed as barbarians . . . the strong sense of cultural continuity and identity prevented any surrender . . . And the confrontation with the West heightened the Chinese sense of identity rather than destroying it, in part because the treaty ports had so little cultural impact. . . . To China, foreign had come to mean inferior. . . . China was in danger, but not Chineseness.

As a result, foreigners were believed to have aroused resentment rather than admiration among the Chinese.

Somewhat carelessly, the anthropologists Robert Redfield and Milton Singer choose modern Canton as an example to show the limits of the common view about the city as centres of cultural diffusion and progress:

> We may see Canton . . . as a centre for the diffusion of Western culture into the 'East'. We may also see these cities . . . beginning as minor outliers of Oriental civilizations and then

> attracting both foreign and also uprooted native peoples... and becoming at last not so much a centre for the introduction of Western ways as a centre for nativistic and independence movements to get rid of Western control and dominance. (Redfield and Singer 1969: 231–2)

Canton is mistakenly perceived as the epitome of Chinese xenophobia.

Although Canton was the first Chinese city to taste the bitterness of military defeat by the Westerners, and its subsequent economico-political encounter with them was not always happy, it would be a mistake to conclude that the Cantonese attitude towards the West must have been negative through and through and uncompromisingly hostile. The San-yüan-li Incident (1840), and the Canton-Hong Kong strike and boycott (1925–6), may at different times have exerted some impact on the general feeling towards the West. But it is questionable whether these events 'radicalized' the people's minds or 'converted' them to an anti-foreign creed.

The popular Cantonese attitude towards the West was in fact more complicated and ambiguous. Different sorts of attitudes, contradictory or complementary to each other, could exist in the same geographical domain at the same time within the same community of people. Cantonese in this period were pragmatic enough to differentiate 'foreign' from 'imperialist'—practical borrowing from rhetorical denunciation.[2] Foreign imperialism never ceased to be seen as a threat to China's security and economic interests. However, to many Cantonese, foreign material progress, lifestyles, and cultural achievements were something to be admired and, if possible, emulated. 'Foreign' had come to mean 'superior', instead of 'inferior' as Murphey suggests.

2. *SHAMEEN AND HONG KONG: AN ALTERNATIVE SYMBOL*

Shameen

The burning down of the Canton Factories site during the Second Opium War in 1856, and the indemnity subsequently paid by the Ch'ing court to the British authorities for the cost of building afresh on a new site for the same purpose, made possible the creation of Shameen from a piece of sand-bar into a modern and Europeanized 'fine place' (Smith 1939: 8). Although Shameen was not any fenced-off foreign concession, the foreign residents there consciously turned the island into an 'autonomous' area set apart from the rest of Canton. It was only connected to the Chinese city of Canton by two guarded stone bridges. Shameen Municipal Council, with members elected from among the Land Renters, had been running the island since the early 1870s (ibid. 16). Public amenities were built for the exclusive use of its residents.[3] It was a semi-banned place to the Chinese, since they were required to produce a permit issued by the Shameen Municipal Council to gain entry to the island, and they were forbidden to travel on certain parts of Shameen. Chinese were said to be consistently prohibited from renting any premises or dwelling there;[4] and the gates to the island were normally kept open to Chinese until midnight only.[5]

This overcautious policy as put into effect against the native population provided a convenient target for accusations by fanatics against the foreign Shameen inhabitants. During the turbulent mid-1920s, especially after the outbreak of the Shakee Incident in June 1925, Shameen was increasingly stigmatized by the jingoists as a symbol of foreign imperialism in southern China. The Canton authorities also helped internalize the stigma of Shameen by renaming the Shakee Road, where the shooting incident of 23 June 1925 took place, 'June 23rd Road' and erecting a monument there. This tainted image of Shameen often appeared in the work of the patriotic writers.[6] Visiting Shameen during an anti-Japanese boycott, one such writer was perplexed by the fact that a number of Cantonese pedlars were smuggling Japanese goods out of the settlement for sale in local markets. This activity reminded him of the limited receptivity of the ideology of national revolution by the multitudes. His deep hatred of Shameen and its symbolic meaning was clear: 'Whenever one sets foot on this island branded with a shameful mark, who, except those Chinese collaborators, would not be inflamed in his heart with anger and hatred? Who would not spell out a curse on the force which occupies this piece of sand-bar?' (Chin Wei 1936: 13.4–5).

The popular attitude towards Shameen, however, was far from being only hostile. To the rich, Shameen stood for security and stability. Falling under the military umbrella of the Powers, Shameen became a refuge for the rich in times of political turmoil. In June 1925, for instance, a large number of wealthy families flocked to Shameen where they spent several nights in the open air while awaiting a berth on the next steamship to Hong Kong (Waln 1933: 215). During the Central Bank crises in August 1927 and mid-1928, many Cantonese merchants, bankers, and businessmen hurriedly took their money with them to Shameen in order to escape the extortionate measure of 'compulsory lending', a racketeering expedient often used by the KMT in tiding over financial crises.[7] Contemporary Cantonese novels also relate that most of the wealthy Cantonese deposited their money in the foreign banks in Shameen.

To some, Shameen was simply a source of livelihood. As we shall see later in this chapter, local pedlars and boat-people were anxious to trade with the foreign community in Shameen, at great risk to their own lives, even at the peak of the anti-British boycott in 1925–6, as well as during the anti-Japanese boycott in 1935.

The physical beauty and orderliness of Shameen, due mainly to the extensive planting of trees, the keeping of lawns, and the proliferation of European architecture, won admiration from the general public in Canton (ibid. 186). The 'Europeanized' ambience was so tranquil and peaceful that all contemporary guide books on Canton, both in English and Chinese, strongly recommended to their readers a walk on the island in order to appreciate in full the beauty of the city of Canton (Liao Shu-lun 1948: 26–7; Liu Tsai-su 1926: 8; Huang Ming-hui 1936: 32–3; Ng Yong-sang 1936). This advice was apparently also eagerly taken by local Cantonese. A travelogue has recorded that 'thousands of other Celestials find some excuse to enter Shameen, some merely to report the wonders of the foreigners' ways of living to their open-mouthed villages' (Franck 1925: 226). Even a professedly patriotic militarist, who labelled Shameen one of 'China's [monuments of] national humiliation', effusively praised its 'tidy planning and cleanliness, [and its] tranquil scenery [which] does not differ much from the fairy-land of P'eng Hu' (Li Tsung-huang 1922: 8, *t'u-hua*).

Nora Waln (1933: 183–6) recalled a casual conversation in early 1925 with her four sedan-chair carriers who praised Shameen as an artefact of Western creativity and transforming power.

> 'When the island was woven', Number Two continued, 'the Westerners brought all sorts of materials. With these they built offices and homes of such pattern as had not been seen in China before. They planted flowering shrubs. Seeded green lawns. And used some magic force by which they make un-boiled water safe to drink and freeze ice here in tropic Canton even on the hottest days. . . . It was not intended that the Westerners should be comfortable or above water here. But they insolently made this tiny sand-bar nicer than any park in the proud ancient city of Canton. . . . My mother-in-law has a pleasure-boat. . . . The trip around Shameen is the trip most often ordered by her customers. . . .'
>
> 'It would take more courage than the Chinese soldiers possess to charge into this island, protected as it is by Western battleships. . . . The Westerners are doing no harm living here. All this wasted grumbling energy ought to be used to make another place as good as this. There are plenty of better sites.'

Shameen was seen as a place that inspired not hatred, but rather public envy and appreciation.

Although Shameen was closed to Chinese for permanent dwelling, an alternative site providing its Chinese residents with a similar socially symbolic function was readily available in the eastern suburb of the city called Tung-shan. In the hypercritical eyes of some Communist historians, Tung-shan was unmistakably an enclave of 'foreign imperialists and their warlord collaborators'. The 'religious wing of foreign imperialism' had allegedly taken the initiative in developing Tung-shan into a 'base of cultural encroachment'. Hence, a number of missionary enterprises such as schools, orphanages, churches, old people's homes, and a hospital were built there. Substantial investment in real estate by overseas Chinese contributed to the mushrooming of modern residential buildings and Western-style villas in Tung-shan from the late 1910s. It soon became an exclusive residential area for wealthy Cantonese, because of its reasonable distance from the hubbub of Canton proper, and, more especially, because of the concentration of foreign residents there. These latter indeed imparted the blessing of protection by the Powers. Hence, Tung-shan was never ravaged during the various military confrontations throughout the course of

Republican history (Ch'i Tzu 1965: 86–114). By the mid-1930s, it was proudly presented in an official guide to Canton as a 'popular residential section among officials of Modern Canton' because its Western-style residences were 'more comfortable and contain more conveniences than the old-style houses' in the old section of the city (Lee 1936: 29–30). The marked presence of Westerners and their culture in that district was seen more as an attraction, an advantage, and even a blessing, than as engendering humiliation or disgust.

Thus, the highly appreciative public perception and the fine image of Shameen and Tung-shan casts serious doubt on the sincerity and unfaltering commitment of at least a sizeable number of Cantonese to the rhetorical cause of anti-foreignism in Canton in this period.

Hong Kong

British Hong Kong, like Shameen, was also favourably perceived by many Cantonese as a successful model of modernization on Chinese soil, rather than just a shameful reminder of China's humiliating past. Admiration of this foreign enclave was sometimes aired publicly, and was done with the intention of ridiculing the socio-cultural inferiority of Canton and its people, in the hope of arousing their sense of urgency in catching up with the 'modern world'. In 1936, for instance, Generalissimo Chiang Kai-shek lectured a crowd in Canton on the importance of the New Life Movement for China. In his speech, he deplored Canton and the Cantonese for their general disrespect of civic order, which dragged the city into a state of great chaos and disorderliness. He lamented that whenever a Chinese national lived in Hong Kong, he would turn himself into a law-abiding citizen; but when he returned to China, he would instantly regress into an uncultured person. Chiang's critical view was further elaborated by a journalist who wrote in the leader of a Hong Kong daily. In his opinion, Hong Kong over-shadowed Canton in terms of cultural sophistication and the quality of its people mainly because of the fact that there were many more Europeans and North Americans residing in this British colony. These Western residents were all properly brought up, educated, and cultured in accordance with such a high standard that people of the weaker races could hardly attain. In addition, he added, prosperity in Hong Kong brought not only affluence to the society, but also a higher cost of living, which effectively drove away many undesired indigent and uncultured louts from the city (*HTJP* 1936: 2, 27 August). This, however, was not entirely true because Hong Kong, even as late as the end of the 1930s, was still regarded as a haven for jobs and opportunities for the many who came from Kwangtung. Political turmoil in Canton during the mid-1920s had driven many poor families from the vicinity of Canton to search for work in the colony.[8] In an interview of 24 coolies found on the colony's street by a Hong Kong labour officer, quite a few of them reported that they felt content with life there. One young woman was happy with her factory work and said she was better off than when she had been a worker in Canton. An elderly woman even commented that life was wonderful in Hong Kong compared to the country in Kwangtung (Gillingham 1983: 79–81).

By the late 1920s, the outward appearance of Hong Kong had been greatly transformed into one of the most spectacular cities in China. The cityscape was considered even more lovely than Shanghai's. Skyscrapers were majestically lined up in orderly fashion at the sea front, stretching all the way up to Victoria Peak. The 13-storey pyramid-shaped Hong Kong and Shanghai Banking Corporation building dominated the scene on the island. The prosperous side of Hong Kong had left even some of the most critical and nationalistic writers of the time with a rather positive impression.[9] If the cityscape of Hong Kong could win the 'conditional' admiration of an anti-imperialist writer, it is quite likely that it could have easily fascinated ordinary Cantonese too. For instance, in Chang Tzu-p'ing's semi-autobiographical novel *T'o-liao kuei-tao ti hsing-ch'iu* (The Planet which Strayed from its Orbit), the young hero and his friend travel from eastern Kwangtung to Canton via Hong Kong to take part in an open competition for a government scholarship. During their short stay in Hong Kong, they visit a number of spectacular places that highly impress these young men with their magnificence; and the emporiums they visit impress them most (Chang Tzu-p'ing 1928: 39). In another of Chang's novels 'Ch'ang t'u, Hsing Kuo wooes the heroine, Pi Yün, by inviting her for a weekend trip to Hong Kong, which is then commonly regarded by many people in Canton as a good way to enjoy life (1930: 330–5). It is the materialistic prosperity, the world-famous night-scene of the harbour, and the spectacular cityscape, that captures their minds and replaces the colonial, exploitative, and imperialistic image of Hong Kong with a rather uncritically favourable one.

Hong Kong had always been a safe haven for those war-sick Kwangtungese. For instance, the 1911 Revolution and the subsequent years of fighting between political and military factions in many parts of the Province drew at least 50,000 people across the border into the colony. The even more turbulent mid-1920s further aggravated this 'problem'. Although the Canton-Hong Kong strike and boycott in 1925–6 caused an exodus of Kwangtungese workers from the colony, who were in many instances unwillingly, even forced (Ho 1985: 16–20; T'sai Yung-fan 2001: 148–9), an even larger number of them ran in the opposite direction to Hong Kong as soon as the border was reopened after a settlement had been reached. From January until December 1927, 70,000 Kwangtungese had migrated to Hong Kong. The Canton Uprising in December 1927 and its subsequent turmoil brought another 30,000 Cantonese to the Colony. By January 1928, it was reported that about 80,000 Kwangtungese were still staying in Hong Kong waiting for the passing of the political storms in Canton (*NYSP* 1928: 2, 10 Jan.).[10] In 1927 and 1928, the proclamations of the extortionate financial policies of the KMT authorities in Canton caused another immediate exodus of rich Cantonese to Hong Kong, and many of them brought with them cases full of Hong Kong or foreign bank notes (*NCH* 1927, 17 Sept., 5 Oct.; *HTJP* 1927, 11–20 Sept.). To a number of Cantonese, especially the rich, the political stability and public safety of Hong Kong offered a perfect refuge in times of political turmoil. Many social notables and high-ranking officials from Canton, both Leftists and Rightists, bought properties in Hong Kong as a safeguard against any sudden change in their political fortunes.[11]

The popularity of Hong Kong currency in the Canton money market was an index of the public confidence, and of the lack of such confidence, in the socio-political positions of Hong Kong and Canton respectively. By the 1930s, the Hong Kong dollar had already established itself as a legitimate currency for Kwangtung foreign trade. This was a rather extraordinary phenomenon because Hong Kong was not a country exporting to Kwangtung although the colony's economic function as an entrepôt to Kwangtung involved the lion's share, namely some 54 per cent of the total volume, of imports into Kwangtung in 1935 (Ts'ai Ch'ien 1939: 2–4; Lee Tai-cho 1936: 4). Trading in Hong Kong dollars gave a range of advantages, which were not accorded to Kwangtung currency, such as over-drafts, lower interest rates and so on (Tsai Ch'ien, ibid. 15–16).

The growing public awareness of the more successful and 'healthy' economic structure of Hong Kong relative to Canton provided another boost to the strong position of Hong Kong currency in Canton (Lee Tai-cho 193: 3–4). Moreover, the frequent depreciation of the Chinese bank notes and coinages had further damaged the reputation of local currency in the eyes of the Cantonese.[12] On a number of occasions, political crises had brought about a temporary cessation of encashment of bank notes in Kwangtung because of the great shortage of liquidated assets of the Central Bank.[13] Therefore, it is not surprising to find that the rich in Canton always 'stored' or deposited a large amount of Hong Kong dollars as a reliable form of investment, which also facilitated their exodus to Hong Kong when necessary.[14] In times of political trouble, Hong Kong was usually flooded with wealthy Cantonese carrying with them sacks of Hong Kong banknotes. For instance, the news of the resignation of Chiang Kai-shek caused a panic amongst the wealthy class in Canton and ultimately led to a mass exodus of wealthy Cantonese to the Colony, bringing with them 'large bundles of Hong Kong bank-notes'. Hotels were said to be crowded with rich officials and opulent merchants (*NCH* 1927: 398, 3 Sept.). Such faith in Hong Kong, or Western, banknotes was seemingly also commonly shared by many ordinary Cantonese. For example, an elderly woman worker was vexed literally to death after she found out that her 300 dollars savings, which she had exchanged for Hong Kong notes and concealed 'safely' inside a wooden chest, were completely consumed by a colony of termite (*YHP* 1934: 1, 3 July).

Rhoads Murphey (1974: 101) is right to point out the failure of Canton to industrialize itself as a result of the geographical proximity to Hong Kong, where the more stable political environment and security provided a more nearly ideal ground for industrialists' investment. When the Canton's Yünnan hui-kuan looked for a secure place to have its public funds deposited, the manager chose a bank in Hong Kong (*HTJP* 1927: 2.2, 11 July). Similarly, at the 1928 annual meeting of the Chamber of Commerce of Kwangtung, it was unanimously agreed that the Headquarters of the proposed Shang-yeh yin-hang (Bank of Commerce) should be set up in Hong Kong, instead of Canton where the Chamber itself was based (*NYSP* 1928: 11, 19 Sept.). Even the river bandits and professional kidnappers always demanded that their protection fees and ransoms be paid in Hong Kong banknotes.[15]

In spite of its anti-imperialist rhetoric and propaganda, the regime in Canton, especially after 1927 with the ebbing of the tides of political radicalism, regarded Hong Kong, though still an 'imperialist enclave', as more a partner than an enemy. Hong Kong, for example, was welcomed as a source of financial aid to the stricken regime. During the Central Bank notes crisis in the summer of 1928, the much 'exhausted' Cantonese merchant communities could think of no better way to meet the government's extortionate policy of 'compulsory borrowing' than to appeal to Hong Kong merchant communities for a loan of 25 million yüan (*NYSP* 1928: 11, 16, 27–8 June). Although no concrete result was achieved after almost a month of intensive negotiation, this action showed the importance of Hong Kong in the economic minds of the merchants in Canton.

Colonial Hong Kong, being British and hence supposedly advanced, was also regarded as superior in the area of modern applied technology. Therefore, it is interesting and significant that the Canton administration, even at a time when the local regime was still professedly anti-imperialistic and steering on the course of revolutionary nationalism, placed orders for eight gunboats to be built by the Kowloon and Whampoa Dockyard, which was a British-owned company, in Hong Kong (*NCH* 1927: 100, 16 July; *HTJP* 1927: 3.2, 6 July). In a newspaper report about the construction of the largest cinema-plus-shopping complex in Canton, the huge six-storey structure was hailed by the reporter as both 'majestic' and 'extraordinarily strong' for the important reason that its piles were driven by a civil engineering company from Hong Kong.[16] The reputation of Hong Kong for being technologically advanced, relative to Canton, was also seen in an interesting libel case in Canton. The parents of a newly married bride sued the bridegroom for libel since the latter accused the former of not being a virgin. The significant aspect of this case was that the defendants invited a medical doctor from Hong Kong to give medical evidence on the virginity of the bride concerned. It is of course dubious that one can prove a former virgin was a virgin at a particular time in the past. But this implied the fact that the professionals from Hong Kong were regarded as having more authority in both their knowledge and judgement than their Cantonese counterparts (Chiu-chung fêng-fu 1934: 34).

Even in labour politics, Hong Kong had 'suddenly' become a source of learning after the cleansing of the 'Reds' from Canton. The system of free employment of workers of different unions, which was hailed as being very successfully carried out in Hong Kong, was adopted as a means to stop the years-long violent conflict between two militant unions that tried to monopolize all the menial jobs in Canton's dockyards for their own members.[17]

The relative freedom of the press in Hong Kong helped establish the popularity of Hong Kong newspapers in Canton. Especially since the establishment of the Republic, newspapers in Canton had been subjected to censorship, and it was not uncommon for defiant journalists to be arrested or even executed by both the 'warlord' and the 'revolutionary' regimes. As a result, the quality of news reportage in most newspapers in Canton was said to be affected and, hence, poor (T'an Yü-chien 1934: 3–9). This in return, might also help further strengthen the favourable image of Hong Kong among the Cantonese. Hong Kong daily papers were transported by train to Canton for sale. It was said that Cantonese always rushed to get a copy when they arrived each afternoon (Huang Ming-hui 1936: 10).

Hong Kong was sometimes favourably perceived as a city governed by a just system of law. For instance, in a letter of complaint by the Hong Kong Branch of the All-China Seamen Union against the attempt of its Main Office in Canton to take it over in reorganization, the complainant wrote in anguish that Hong Kong was a place of law unlike Canton where 'they could ... simply do what they want' (*HTJP* 1927: 2.2, 16 May). The merchant community expressed a similar high regard for the credibility of Hong Kong's legal system. A group of Canton merchants, who were the victims of the 'Big Fire' that swept over many parts of Canton during the last days of the Canton Commune, lost their confidence and faith in Canton's legal credibility after their claims for insurance on their destroyed properties were repeatedly turned down by the insurance companies, and an official inquiry into the matter was repeatedly postponed. In frustration, the claimants cited a legal case that they thought demonstrated the difference between the just English law and the arbitrary, unjust Canton legal code. In late 1927, a 'rice-hall' run by and for unemployed workers since the outbreak of the Great Strike caught fire. A number of private properties in the vicinity were also damaged. The Canton-based insurance companies denied any compensation to its claimants on the ground that the outbreak of the fire was due to military activities, a cause that could exempt the company from compensating its claimants. But, at the same time, the result of an official inquiry by the Hong Kong Government established the cause of the fire as a deliberate act of arson by the Communists and, therefore, those who had insured with any Hong Kong-based insurance companies were entitled to receive full compensation. The desperate Canton merchants used this case to support their criticism that in Canton, only 'arbitrary power exists, objective truth dies' (*yu chiang-chuan wu kung-li*). The Hong Kong Government was hailed for its just act (*NYSP* 1928: 11, 14 Aug.). In another example, when, in 1922, the editor-in-chief of the respectable publishing house, The Commercial Press, chose between Hong Kong and Canton for establishing a large-scale printing factory in the southernmost part of China, he eventually opted for the former mainly because, among other reasons such as infrastructure and availability of sites, the copyright of publications was well protected under British law (*Chang Yüan-tsi jih-chi* 1981: ii. 820–3). In a speech to the Students' Union of Hong Kong University in February 1923, Sun Yat-sen declared that it was the corruption of China and the peace, order, and good government of Hong Kong that had first turned him into a revolutionary

(Gillingham 1981: 30); Hong Kong as a living model of superior Western-style governance was, ironically, a source of inspiration to the champion of Chinese nationalism.

In the entertainment scene, Canton was sometimes implicated as inferior to Hong Kong in terms of the quality of its popular amusements. For example, the tea-houses in Canton where female singers from Hong Kong regularly performed were seemingly more popular. This could be deduced from the fact that the charge for tea per person in those tea-houses was always double that for those that had only local singers (*Kuang-chou nien-chien* 1935: 169). Moreover, it was known that whenever a Cantonese female singer wanted to enhance her reputation in the entertainment world in Canton, it was almost a matter of course that she had to be famous in Hong Kong as well. In other words, the value and prestige of a Cantonese sing-song girl increased in proportion to her popularity in Hong Kong. Many owners of this kind of tea-house preferred sing-song girls from Hong Kong because they were believed to be much better singers and entertainers than their Canton counterparts: after all, the best three divas in this form of art were all originally from Hong Kong (Chen Ping-han 1996: ii. 177–82).[18] Similarly, to form a 'Canton-Hong Kong troupe' (*Shêng-Kang pan*) and to be able to do well in both Canton and Hong Kong had become the ambitious goal for most Cantonese opera companies in Canton since the 1920s, and opera singers took great pride in being successful in both cities.[19] In terms of courtesans and the high-class brothel business, Hong Kong was hailed as *the* place where 'beauties of South China' congregated (Ting Yu Kung 1928: 8). Popular dailies in Canton were keen to publish news about visiting courtesans (as much as sing-song girls) from Hong Kong, despite the trivial nature of these stories. Their Hong Kong 'tag' helped, instead of jeopardized, their popularity in Canton.[20] Hong Kong was no longer looked down upon as a cultural backwater. It had become so highly prosperous a market that no Cantonese entertainers could afford to ignore it if they wanted to be successful and famous in South China. Hong Kong had become a place to be reckoned with.

These advantages enjoyed by Hong Kong helped the territory to win the admiration of many, but also generated jealousy and hatred in others. There were indeed jealous nationalists in Canton who had tried to retake Hong Kong from the British, or to sabotage it at least. Sun Yat-sen's dream of developing Whampoa, a deep-water port about ten miles east of Canton, was a means to the end of replacing Hong Kong as the largest port in South China (Ch'êng Hao 1985: 216–17). The heavy economic dependence of Canton and even Kwangtung on the entrêpot function of Hong Kong was always a nightmare to fanatical patriots in China. The year-long Canton-Hong Kong strike and boycott was believed to be a plan that, if it had materialized as intended, would have freed Canton from its economic dependence upon Hong Kong (ibid. 195–7).[21] Nonetheless, all these hostile attitudes towards the place of Hong Kong in Canton's existence do at least emphasize one common psychological feature—a deep-seated awareness of the inferiority of Canton in various aspects of life as compared with Hong Kong.

In the minds of these people in this period, the symbolic meanings of Shameen and Hong Kong were varied, but hardly hostile nor denunciatory alone. These 'imperialist enclaves' were also neither perceived nor hated as beachheads of one of China's enemies, but were viewed favourably, as symbols of stability, security, prosperity and, above all, respectable models of modern culture to learn from.[22]

3. ASPECTS OF PRO-FOREIGNISM IN CANTON: A CULTURAL PERSPECTIVE

Beauty and Dreams Redefined

The urban culture of Republican Canton, indeed, showed a strong Western influence. The process of acculturation from which this resulted is well illustrated by the changing concept of beauty at that time.

According to Wolfram Eberhard (1971: 271–304), the criteria for 'being beautiful' postulated by two Chinese writers, one in the seventeenth century and the other in the 1930s, share sufficient similarities for a continuity to be discerned. Most significant in this is the fact that the erogenous zones of the body receive no mention at all—a taboo not completely broken, he suggests, until as late as the 1960s.

Eberhard, however, is wrong as far as the timing is concerned. By the 1920s, the inclusion of the erogenous zones in the concept of beauty was already widely upheld in Canton. In an article 'On Woman's Beauty and Ugliness' published in a vernacular magazine, the author teaches his readers how to appreciate a beauty. The long list of the 'basic' parts of the female body to be appreciated includes the breasts, buttocks, thighs, and shins (T'ang Kê 1934: 6).[23] The spiritual quality of charm, which used to be cherished as an essential hallmark, has almost completely given way to sheer physical attraction. The new concept of beauty has taken a more sensual and erotic orientation, which is almost certainly a cultural expression of the influence of the West on Cantonese values.

The growing awareness of the breasts as an element of feminine beauty was indicative not only of the changing attitude towards sex, but also of the acceptance of Western standards of beauty; traditionally, breasts were considered as unimportant in the overall attractiveness of a woman, and thus could with justification be bound flat by a band. But at least from the 1920s onwards, natural 'big breasts' became the latest symbol of sensual attraction and feminine health, and buxom courtesans (especially those with large breasts) became popular, almost to the extent of being worshipped by brothel-goers (Sung Yü 1989: 298). In one official publication, the 'natural and big breasts of those blue-eyed blonde-haired Western women' were not only openly praised, but made out, by implication, to be the ideal towards which all Chinese women should strive. Physically, 'natural breasts' (*t'ien-ju*) symbolized better hygiene and health. Culturally, they became a symbol of women's liberation from 'feudalistic' bondage. Politically, they were seen as an efficacious 'Western means' of creating the kind of healthy and strong Chinese race urgently needed to strengthen the nation (Liu Yu-lun 1930: 207–9). A candid cartoon entitled 'Ideal Women of Today' simply shows a sculpture of a woman with permed blonde hair and exaggeratedly large breasts and hips (*KCTC* 1934: 4). This echoed what the famous, or infamous in the eyes of contemporary moralists, Chang Ching-shêng, alias Dr Sex, has said about the breasts of Chinese women. In his view, the most unsightly part of a Chinese woman, comparing to her Western counterpart, was her breasts, which were in 'a state of under-development' as a result of the Chinese custom of having them tightly bound. Flattened breasts, in addition to a general suppression of sex, helped contribute to an abnormal development of sexual desire and affected the normal physiology of Chinese women. As a result of that, Chinese women all looked ugly, with their tiny, flat noses, prominent cheekbones, thick lips, pale complexion, narrow hips, and so on (Chang ching-shêng 1927: 1–8). The possession of a pair of 'Westernized breasts' was seemingly seen as a crucial element in the breeding of a good-looking and both psychologically and physiologically healthy Chinese race. This growing obsession with natural, large breasts by local women was soon taken advantage of by shrewd surgeons who advertised in local newspapers their impeccable skills in 'restoring healthy natural beauty to flattened or degenerated' breasts, or their speciality in bringing 'beautiful shape to [women's] breasts'.[24]

In some advertisement illustrations, and magazine pin-ups, there was a clear aesthetic tendency to 'Westernize', or idealize, the facial features of Chinese women. The components of beauty in these drawings were usually permed hair, or fashionable short hair (the most popular hairstyle for young women after 1926),[25] large, deep-set eyes, and high-bridged noses.

Some of the pin-up drawings in a series of Cantonese comic books construct the ideal Chinese beauty with unmistakably Caucasian facial features. In those pin-ups featuring naked beauties, breasts and buttocks are always exaggeratedly drawn. In a drawing entitled 'The Frustration of Youth', a downcast young man is depicted day-dreaming about attractive, unclothed young girls in various seductive poses. Interestingly, all these 'dream girls' have short permed hair and look more like Western than Chinese ladies.[26] The popular obsession with the 'curves of beauty' (*ch'u-hsien-mei*), which was a Western 'import', was believed to have contributed to the popularity of the latest tight-fitting fashion in Western dress, which, in contrast to its Chinese counterpart, was so designed that the breasts and hips of the female body were invitingly outlined (Hsü Hsu 1946: 7).

It is worth mentioning in passing that similar popular accolades given to, and an obsession with, Western feminine physical appearance is seemingly re-emerging in present-day China. A journalist recently reported from Shanghai that 'after developing a taste for Coca Cola, rock music, blue jeans, break dancing, and eyebrow liner', some Chinese took one step further and had themselves Westernized by undergoing surgery to achieve rounder eyes and higher-bridged noses, and some women bigger breasts. It is claimed that in Shanghai alone, as many as one hundred women each day undergo surgery to enlarge their eyes.[27] Even forty years of ferociously authoritarian and xenophobic Communist rule have therefore failed to root out this kind of extrovert, pro-Western mentality from among its relatively well-indoctrinated subjects.

The once-appreciated older standards of inner beauty such as physical fragility, emotional delicacy, and melancholic sensitivity, were criticized as being socially regressive. In an article on the social position of Chinese women, the failure of the women's liberation movement was attributed to the widespread acceptance of these traditional 'destructive' standards of beauty by both men and women. Implicitly, the persevering, outgoing, and uncompliant character of Western women was believed to be one of the main reasons for the rise in their social position in Western society. Chinese women were urged to take up sports and such cultural hobbies as horticulture, painting, walking, and so on, as the means to build up their bodies. Physical fitness, a cultivated character, and education became the official standards of beauty (Li Hsüeh-ying 1935: 20–1). The substance of feminine charm had thus taken on an alien touch. But not everyone in Canton appreciated this form of 'modernization'. In a satirical overtone, a reader wrote to a newspaper about what a trendy modern woman looked like in Canton in the mid-1930s. According to his observation, these female 'modernites' were characterized by their heavy make-up, expensive Parisian perfume, low-cut blouses (intentionally to 'display their breasts'), sleeveless shirts (to expose their arms), short skirts (to reveal their thighs), and eagerness to show off in public their Western outfits and costly cosmetics; moreover, they showered flirtatious glances at bewitched male onlookers (Chü Ch'i 1934: 1). Criticisms aside, this was a vivid portrayal of how, in the popular view, a modern woman looked.

If a Western outlook could confer symbolic advantages to a Chinese body, the possession of a Westerner as one's mate was then an even more powerful symbolic asset. In a short newspaper article entitled 'The Bewitching Power of a Western Wife', the author noticed the latest trend of marrying Western women by 'bureaucrats and politicians' in Canton. He wrote that during the Ch'ing time, senior officials all kept concubines as a symbol of status. This old practice was denounced and had ceased after the establishment of the Republic. It was, however, replaced by the fashion of keeping mistresses. By the late 1920s, this was yet again replaced by a newly emerging trend among senior officials or politicians of marrying a Western wife. A Western wife did carry symbolic and practical advantages: first, her foreign nationality provided the husband with extra-territorial protection—a political privilege that was analogous to a talisman. Secondly, it revealed the power of the husband's charm and skill at courtship that impressed even the 'alien race' from afar. Thirdly, he could show off with pride that he possessed the right of 'communicating' (i.e. having intercourse) with 'the alien race' in 'creating a special specie[s] of national' (Hui You 1928: 8). Beauty and politics were intriguingly fused, with strong overtones of Occidentalism.

The male body also seems to have undergone a similar process of idealization along Western lines, though one that was less visible and less written about. Once again, illustrations in contemporary advertisements are revealing. In an advertisement for a tailoring company, a Chinese man is depicted in a well-cut Western-style suit, with tie, leather shoes, and well-combed Western-style short hair, adopting a somewhat foreign posture with one of his hands half inside a jacket pocket and his legs slightly crossed. But more symbolic is his round, robust, and tall body, fitting uncomfortably with the orthodox Chinese tradition of the ideal gentlemen.[28] In a number of advertisements for a Cantonese herbal tonic, half-naked men with a strong physique are featured. They are muscular, with broad shoulders, wide chests, and well-muscled necks and arms, and have fashionable, well-combed, short hair. One of these ideal men is drawn in a posture resembling that of a classical Greek discus-thrower. All these tend to suggest the desirability of a visibly robust male body, perhaps a new, alien, yet 'modern' and ideal symbol for the urban male.[29]

Even the ideal boyfriend or husband dreamed of by the modern city-girls in Canton was coloured with Western elements. In their view, he should be a university graduate, fashionable, and above all with a Westernized outlook (Cho Yu 1928: 20). In a collection of students' essays about their school lives, the editor has inserted a few 'satirical' (or realistic?) drawings by cartoonists showing the typical perception of contemporary male high-school and university students. They are invariably wearing foreign suits, with Western-style leather shoes and hats, ties, walking sticks, and sometimes with a cigarette (Shih-jih t'an hsün-k'an shê 1934). Two concerned readers wrote to a local newspaper about their contempt for what many young men were doing to become a 'modern man' (*mo-têng nan*)—to have themselves clad and decorated from head to feet in expensive Western-style apparels and accessories imported from Europe and North America. Fashionable hats, collared shirts, neck-ties, trousers, woollen overcoats, and leather shoes, all Western imports, were faithfully acquired by men whose anxiety to become 'modern' was irrepressible. Chinese imitations of these desirable items were dismissed as being inferior in all respects from style to quality. These 'modern men', like their female counterparts, were satirically compared to a 'flower vase'—an object that, however beautiful, was devoid of spiritual substance or soul (Li Hou and Ch'u shih 1934: 1). Like the pin-ups in the comics, the popular image of young gentlemen, the pillars of 'New China', reveals a strong Western savour. The propensity to idealize Western feminine beauty was getting close to the advocacy by Chang Ching-shêng (alias Dr Sex), whose pro-Western cultural values are self-evident,[30] of the total Westernization of the Chinese body (Leo Ou-fan Lee 1973: 270).

The idea of freedom in love (*lien-ai tzu-yu*), a symbol of Western individualism, was widely accepted by the young. Criticisms of the inhumanity of 'blind marriage' had intensified in Canton since the early 1920s, a legacy of the nationwide post-May-Fourth feminist movement. In a feminist magazine published in 1922, a female contributor strongly criticized traditional arranged marriage as 'a system of looting and barter' which had 'raped' the freedom of Chinese women for centuries. In its place, Western-style courtship resting on long acquaintance, and 'modern' marriage based on love and affection, were advocated (Chêng Ch'ên 1922: 27–8).

Westernizing Pleasures

Western-style entertainment, too, rose in popularity. To some, a feast of Western cuisine at a Western-style restaurant was regarded as an enviable experience. The food itself was not especially important; indeed, some Cantonese found it not particularly appealing. *Ch'ih hsi-ts'ai* (dining on Western cuisine), however, became an increasingly accepted symbol of social status and consumption capacity (Chiu-chung fêng-fu 1934: 13). Consuming imported wines and Western cuisine at Western-style restaurants became so popular as ostentatious social events among the militarists, politicians, and the rich, that a contemporary author labelled it a new social custom in Canton (Hu Po-an et al. 1922: ii. 8, sect. Kuang-tung). In the words of an alarmed traditionalist, the young had become so obsessed with *ch'ih hsi-ts'ai* that they 'wasted' most of their pocket-money on it (Ch'en Chi-t'ang 1972: 27). It is difficult to substantiate such an accusation. An official report tells us that the main attractions of Western-style restaurants and cafés in Canton were that they were fashionable and economical in cost compared with Chinese restaurants, and were hence doing very good business, even during the depression of the early 1930s (*Kuang-chou nien-chien* 1935: i. 110). Western-style restaurants and cuisine were also liked for being more hygienic and better cultured in table manners. As early as 1911, an advertisement for one such restaurant emphasized not only the quality of its cookery, but also its eagerness in 'studying [the ways of ensuring] hygiene [of its dishes]', and the cleanliness of its premises, which was also equipped with modern gadgets such as electric fans and lighting (*HTJP* 1911, 1 Sept.). From the advertisement of another restaurant in 1927, one can perhaps obtain a better picture of what a customer was generally looking for in dining at one of these fashionable places. This place, called *Kuo-min hua-yüan* (Citizens' Garden) and located just by the Municipal Government building, professed to provide the following attractions to its patrons: famous chefs who excelled at Western delicacies, an elegant and clean venue, and good service. The restaurant was furnished with a fountain, which was lit by electricity with 'magical light bulbs in different colours', a teak-made dance-floor whose style was copied from one in Western Europe, and a band of Filipino musicians who 'add exhilaration' to the venue with their Western popular music. Patrons were welcomed to dance every evening from eight o'clock to midnight (*KHP* 1927: 3, 9 Dec.). In a vernacular Cantonese language textbook written for Chinese learners of this dialect in Burma, one chapter was devoted to a situation in which the mistress of a household instructs her maids on how to serve at an upcoming Western-style dinner at home. According to her instructions, on the morning of the event, all the eating utensils must be thoroughly washed and the floor, table, and the chairs cleaned. The table has to be set in good order with all the cutlery and plates in their proper places. The correct way to serve each course of dishes was also described vividly and in detail. The chapter helps us to understand the symbolism of Western-style dining in the popular mind with its clear identification with orderliness and hygiene; and the very fact that it was essential enough to be included as a chapter in a practical book like this one is clearly an indication of the increasing popularity of Western cuisine and the awareness of Western table manners in urban Canton (Hsü Hsüeh-hang *c.*1920s: ii. 150–1).

A Cantonese novel reveals that to invite someone to dinner at a Western-style restaurant was regarded as something special, fashionable, and sometimes romantic. In Chang Tzu-p'ing's 'Ch'ang t'u' (The Long Journey; 1930: 109–10), when the heroine Pi Yün has just arrived in Canton, she is invited by Hsiao Szu, a native she has met en route, to a Western-style café on the top floor of a hotel. Pi Yün realizes that it is a popular place for dating. Western-style music and movies are played and shown there, and most of the customers are fabulously and lavishly dressed. This is their first date. A similar romantic value seems never to have been attached to the traditional Cantonese tea-house.

Western-style sports were imported into Canton alongside Western education, and were encouraged in schools by the education authorities, though limited budgets prevented all that encouragement from being put into action. Sports of this type were believed to be essential for building up physical vitality, nurturing and cultivating spiritual character, and fostering obedience and self-discipline among the young. At an education conference held in 1930, a panel proposed, on the issue of improving physical education in Kwangtung, that there should be at least one exercise ground, one volleyball court, one basketball court, one tennis court and one football pitch in every middle school. Western gymnastic equipment should also be installed if the financial situation allowed (Kuang-tung ts'ai-chêng-ting 1930: 109–10). Not one single form of Chinese traditional exercise was recommended.

Physical education, an imported concept, was believed to be a key to breed, so to speak, a strong and healthy stock for a nation, as it was interestingly brought out in a chapter of a Cantonese language book. The chapter is set in a situation in which two local primary-school students run into a group of Western schoolboys one day on their way to school. The passages include the conversation between these two Cantonese schoolboys who are amazed by how energetic, spirited, confident, and courageous those young Westerners can be. They believe that the fine qualities of these Western boys are by and large absent in their Chinese counterparts, including themselves; and the reason for that big difference, they believe, lies in their divergent attitudes toward physical education—Western school students are both enthusiastic and serious about physical exercises, but not the Chinese. The moral of this chapter, predictably, is that should the Chinese want to build a strong nation, they have to hold the right attitude towards physical education, just as Westerners were doing (Hsü Hsüeh-hang *c.*1920s: ii: 92–3).

The sensual pleasure of bodily touch seems to have contributed to the popularity of Western-style dancing in Canton.[31] We learn from a serialized short story that dancing had apparently become an integral part of 'modern marriage' celebrations (Hsi Hua 1933: 7). According to Nora Waln (1933: 196–7), even those professed patriots who often criticized the evils of Western imperialism in China were among the most enthusiastic dance-hall-goers in Canton during the 1920s. A Cantonese film director reminisced that he was approached by such senior officials as Sun K'o, Wu Chao-shu, and Wu Tieh-ch'êng to recommend a dancing teacher, since a dance party was sometimes held to greet visiting foreign officials (Kuan Wên-ch'ing 1976: 118). One of the main events for the 1926 official Double-Tenth celebration was a large-scale ballroom dance held in a Western-style hotel in Canton. The event was organized by the China Music Association, which was said to have contributed substantially to the promotion of Western dancing in Canton by running dancing courses taught by 'qualified instructors graduated from Europe and the United States'. Senior government officials and a number of foreigners took part in the event (*KCMKJP* 1926: 10, 8 Oct.). One month later, another dance-party was organized by the same body to commemorate the birthday of Sun Yat-sen. More than two hundred guests took part, all dressed up in 'lavish and seductively colourful clothes' (ibid. 4, 16 Nov.). Local politics thus found their expression in an explicitly Western cultural idiom. Public dance parties had been prohibited, for public security reasons, for some months during 1928. When the ban was lifted in early 1929, Cantonese reportedly once again indulged in a craze for Western dancing. The newly completed Nationals' Sports Hall was immediately 'converted' into a dance hall where enthusiasts danced round the clock for five consecutive days to celebrate the lifting of the ban as much as the Chinese New Year. Dance parties were also held in other locations in Canton, including one of the largest Western restaurants in the city, a few respectable hotels, and uncountable private venues (Hang 1929: 1). During the early and mid-1930s, Western dancing in public was banned. The popular enthusiasm for it, however, was unabated. Canton's police had received petition letters from citizens asking for the lifting of the ban on mixed-sex dancing performances held in public places such as theatres; these requests were turned down (*YHP* 1934: 1, 1 Oct.). In private circles, however, dancing apparently went on unchecked. In a suburban community in Canton in the same period, one household—an overseas Chinese family—was regularly hosting dancing parties in its mansion. To ensure that this pastime could be more widely enjoyed by the youngsters in the neighbourhood, its organizer (the 'thoroughly Westernized' daughter of the family) even held regular practice sessions for her interested, but inexperienced, neighbours (*YHP* 1934: 1, 15 Oct.).

Movies served as an important medium for the dissemination of Western cultural values and taste. They became one of the most popular pastimes in modern Canton. A student complained that his contemporaries were obsessed with the '3 M-isms: money-ism, mistress-ism, movie-going-ism' (Tsê An and Wei chih 1933: 30–1, 'Prose'). Another student wryly observed that, judging by the constantly large number of spectators flooding the cinemas 'like a run on the Central Bank', China was not likely to run out of cash for military defence (Wu Ju-chou 1933: 35). Provincial Governor Ch'en Chi-t'ang denounced *ch'ih hsi-ts'ai* and movie-going as the two prime examples of the spiritual pollution of the younger generation by materialistic and hedonistic Western culture (Ch'en Chi-t'ang 1972: 26).

The popularity of cinema-going and the domination by Western movies of Canton's film market was indicative of Cantonese receptivity to Western culture.[32] Apparently, Cantonese audiences preferred Hollywood movies to Chinese feature-films. The absence of Chinese subtitles in both silent and talking movies did not deter people from watching Western movies; nor did the quality of the screenplay appear to matter. Even a bad Western film, despite its inferior acting and ordinary theme, could become a blockbuster in Canton (Chung Ching-wên 1927: 109–13). In the opinion of some Cantonese, Chinese film companies for four major reasons rarely produced good movies. First, producers were too mean to invest in making good films; hence, most Chinese films were so badly produced that their images were blurred and their subtitles full of incorrectly written Chinese characters.[33] Secondly, directors were inexperienced and, hence, talented actors tended to be overlooked. Thirdly, the wages of actors were too low to attract or keep promising actors.[34] Fourthly, the poor performance of most Chinese actors could not match the ability of even an ordinary supporting actor in the West.[35] In the view of another critic, Cantonese were not truly uninterested in Chinese films; there was simply a serious shortage of Chinese productions of commendable quality, and one of the manifestations of this problem was the general absence of outstanding Chinese movie stars. In terms of the quality of the acting, movie stars from the West were said to be far superior to those of China because of the heavy investment committed by Western film companies in the long process of cultivating such silver-screen talent (Pai Tan 1923). As far as talking movies were concerned, it was even officially admitted that Western productions were far superior to the Chinese, both technically and artistically. As a result, it was not surprising that most Cantonese cinemas preferred to show Western talkies, although three out of twenty screened exclusively Chinese productions (*Kuang-chou nien-chien* 1935: 88, 161). But to the discomfort of the authorities, the film market in Canton was dominated by Western products. In the two years 1934–5, a total of 352 foreign-produced movies were shown in Canton's various cinemas. By great contrast, only 120 Chinese-made movies were shown (ibid. 159–61). Aggravated by the unsettled political situation, the film industry in 1920s Canton was stagnant, with merely four short-lived film companies producing fewer than ten films in total between 1923 and 1928 (Kuan wên-ching 1976: 127–8). Such a serious imbalance had aroused the concern of the local authorities who responded to this challenge of 'cultural invasion' with some resolute measures. In 1936, the Provincial government announced a set of regulations targeted at redressing this problem. They included: setting up a special task force of 'specialists' who would be responsible for previewing all imported films so that those that propagated obscenity, impropriety, imperialism, frivolity, or anything that would weaken Chinese nationalistic feelings, would be censored; another team of experts would be appointed for the purpose of selecting scripts for, and supervising the production of, Cantonese films to assure that they would promote nationalism and traditional ethics; to reserve at least 60 per cent of the broadcasting time in all cinemas in the province for exclusively showing Chinese movies.[36] It is not known how effective these measures were in stamping out this 'cultural invasion'. It was clear, however, that the popular predilection for Western cinema had reached an 'alarming' proportion.

In the first issue of *Hsi-chü* (*The Theatre*), the mouthpiece of the short-lived Research Institute of Performing Arts of Kwangtung (Kuang-tung hsi-chü yen-chiu-so), the editor trenchantly criticized traditional Chinese theatre as 'backward' due to its perniciously un-aesthetic nature, and as impractical because of its 'inability to speak for the masses' (*Hsi-chü* 1929: Preface). Ou-yang Yü-ch'ien, the Director of the Institute, argued that traditionally, Chinese despised the theatre and looked down on actors as 'mean people'. Hence, traditional theatre was wrongly adjudged as leaving few socially constructive and artistically refining legacies to Chinese society. In his view, since traditional Chinese theatre was devoid of a healthy tradition in the Western sense, the most effective antidote with which to 'progressivize' it was to borrow extensively from the Western theatrical tradition. To support his view, he quoted freely from Western theories of drama, especially on its utilitarian and social functions in modern society (Ou-yang yü ch'ien 1929: 1–64).[37] Thus, it is not surprising to find almost one-third of the 350-page first issue of the Institute's journal devoted to translations of Western works on the history, philosophy, theory, and scripts of the modern Western theatre.

In another article, the scripts of contemporary Cantonese opera were denounced in the most defamatory terms as being flooded with obscenity and violence, and having supernatural and over-commercialized stereotyped plots, operas themselves being irresponsibly performed by uneducated actors at the expense of the public good. In the view of its author, since the arts of a nation reflected the national character of its people, their refined and sophisticated theatrical tradition contributed to the refined quality of European *kuo-min* (citizens), providing a model that Cantonese would do well to emulate (Ch'u Chien 1929: 107–19).[38]

In the area of music, Western (especially classical) music was believed to possess transcendental and social functions that Chinese music lacked. An article published in an official daily in 1926 expounded the view that Chinese music had long lost its 'power to touch' (*kan-tung li*), while Western music alone still possessed the capacity 'to transform [a country's] customs, to purify the world, to nourish character, [and] regulate emotion'. The rhythm and harmony of Western music generated symphonic vibrations that stimulated the listeners' emotions and psyche. And classical music, with its element of 'beauty', was the best tool for unleashing this transcendental power (*KCMKJP* 1926, Supplement: 2, 4 Nov.).[39]

The obsession with the utilitarian value of Western music was probably attributable to the fact that most of the recommended texts and references for middle-school music teachers and students were non-Chinese publications.[40] An educationalist criticized the inadequacy of the teaching hours (three hours per week) spent on music education in Canton's primary schools, since the subject was believed to be very useful for the spiritual nourishment and intellectual development of children. He argued that if music education in the Western sense continued to be ignored as such, it was likely that before long Cantonese children would be found to have become 'rude, stupid and slothful' (Huang Hsin 1935: 4–5). A concerned writer advocated the establishment of a municipal symphony orchestra in Canton because he believed Western classical music to be a cultural weapon with 'magical' efficacy for rejuvenating the declining Chinese nation. In his view, a symphony orchestra was the only means to 'music-ize' (*yin-yüeh-hua*) the lower-class citizens so as to dispel the dull, unmusical, and suffocating atmosphere of life in the city (Ch'en Hung 1937: 23). Perhaps influenced by such views, the Municipal Radio of Canton spent on average 20 per cent of its broadcasting time playing Western music (Kuang-chou-shih chêng-fu 1934*a*: 28–32).

Such popular obsession with Western music was criticized by some musicians in Canton for contributing to the dwindling popularity of traditional Chinese music there. This situation was described in a newspaper article written by one of these concerned local musicians. Its author began with an appraisal of the government's efforts in promoting music education in schools and in the community, which was regarded as a means to modernize the school curriculum and to help strengthen spiritual health among the students and the general public. Music concerts were being held very frequently, and were popularly well received as a form of highly cultured amusement. The author, however, disliked the fact that such popular predilection for music was limited to Western music, which was mainly the result of a pro-West attitude commonly shared by the youngsters in the city. The increasing popularity of such musical instruments as violin, banjo, mandolin, and guitar in Canton was parallel to an opposite trend of diminishing favour towards traditional Chinese instruments. In his opinion, the people and the government in Canton should make a greater effort to popularize Chinese music in order to redress the aggravating situation of 'cultural invasion' (*YHP* 1934: 1, 11 July). It seems that the acceptance of Western music, or the extent of cultural invasion in this respect, had reached a level of serious concern.

Even in the field of Chinese painting, the urge to syncretize Japanese and Western techniques approximated to a fashion among the younger generation of Cantonese painters. The biographies of some of the more outstanding of these, from the late nineteenth century to 1940, reveal that the ideal image of a successful Chinese painter had gradually been modified to include as essential the possession of a relatively cosmopolitan outlook and taste.[41] P'an Chih-chung, a well-regarded Cantonese painter of the 1930s, grumbled about his student painters being so obsessed with Western painting techniques that the traditional Chinese skills and approach to art were very much despised (Li Chien-êrh 1941: 25–6). Contemporary pictorial magazines were fond of publishing Western-style oil and watercolour paintings by both Cantonese and Western artists, their motive being reflected perhaps in a slogan published in one pictorial amid reproductions of Western-style paintings, which reads: 'Friends! Let's strive for the breakdown of boredom in the art circles of South China!' By implication, Cantonese Chinese painting was believed to be dull (*P'iao-p'iao hua-pao* 1929: 3).

'Breeze from the West' in Cityscape

Further physical evidence of a Western-oriented life-style and consciousness was provided by the proliferation of Western-style buildings across Canton's cityscape. Most of the key government buildings, such as the headquarters of the Canton Branch of the KMT, the head office of the Bank of Kwangtung, the Provincial Finance Department, the Provincial Assembly building, and so on, were Western neoclassical-style structures. Interestingly, nobody tried to interpret, as some nationalistic Indians had, the symbolism of these Western-style buildings as 'colonial architecture visibly represent[ing] [the European] sense of mastery' (Metcalf 1989: 8–9, 250). On the contrary, the authorities were proud to show off their Western outlook by including in the 1934 official guidebook to Canton photographs of most of these modern government edifices. Unlike the government offices of the imperial era, which were usually hidden from the eyes of the public by walls and trees (Geil 1911: 80), these modern *yamen* were intended to command respect from the public by their huge size and overt presence. Western architecture was judiciously used for creating a new and 'modern' image of the Cantonese government.

A landmark in Canton in this period was the line of skyscrapers along the Pearl River waterfront. These high-rise commercial buildings were not a colonial legacy. It was the Cantonese who had planned and financed this modern skyline for their own city. The eight-storey New Asia Hotel, the twelve-storey Sun Company Building, and the fifteen-storey Ai-Ch'ün Building, the tallest in South China in the 1930s, were all built with overseas Cantonese capital. Most of the high-ranking officials of the Canton government attended the inauguration ceremony the Ai Ch'ün Building, giving official recognition to its symbolic meaning, and from the time it opened for business Ai Ch'ün became a popular place of rendezvous in the high-society life of the city (Hsien Tzu-lung 1986: 177–84; En Jên and T'an Shao-p'eng 1989: 28–36; Ou An-nien et al. 1987: 299–301, 304–6).

Due to the heavy investment by returned overseas Cantonese in the real estate market, a substantial number of new Western-style multi-storey residences had been built since the early 1920s, and this trend reached its peak in the decade after 1927 (Lin Chin-Chih and Ts'ang Wei-chi 1989: 688–708).[42] Western architecture was apparently chosen by the *nouveaux riches* as an ostentatious means to express their wealth and newly acquired social prestige. Photographs in Kuo Wên-fang's pictorial album on Canton show that the most common Western features on the façades of these new multi-storey residential buildings were curved and sometimes ornate lintels, the wooden window-shutters, the vase-shaped concrete parapets, and the triangular or round concrete plaques announcing the year the building was opened. Many social notables resided in the two-storey Western-style villas in the exclusive residential area of Tung-shan. Some of these villas are now, symbolically, being used as residences for high-ranking Party cadres.[43]

Western-style furniture was preferred for decorating these 'modern homes', as may be seen from contemporary commercial advertisements and comics. Most contemporary pin-up girls were photographed against the setting of a room furnished in modern Western-style furniture. On the cover of a Cantonese opera romantic comedy script, a newly wed couple, dressed in Western-style wedding suits, are depicted in the bedroom of their new flat, which is decorated and furnished in a Western manner. The happy ending of this opera, with the marriage of the protagonists, parallels the subject-matter of the drawing. It seems to suggest that a happy modern marriage will include a home furnished in modern style (T'ang Ti-shêng *c.*1930s). In an advertisement for a record company, a 'modern' family of five are shown enjoying music in front of an imported gramophone, with the parents comfortably seated on Western-style brocade sofas (*Hsiang-hua hua-pao* 1929: 25). All these drawings seem to idealize the essential symbolic function of Western-style interior decoration in a 'modern' and happy urban family. Similar cultural idealization was even more vividly revealed in another advertisement for a Chinese fabrics company in Canton. Captioned 'A Standard Bedroom' (*Piao-chun wo-shih*), the advertisement draws a scene of a corner of a bedroom, which is furnished with modern furniture and other accessories, and presumably is the way a *standard* bedroom should look in the modern world. The bed and the table, all Western-style of course, are covered with Western-style sheets and linens, while the floor is covered by a large Western-style carpet. One of the descriptions reads: 'When one enters into this room, [one will] feel everywhere simplicity, elegance, orderliness, and cleanliness; an aesthetic sense of beauty will be invoked in him' (*YHP* 1934: 8, 28 March).[44] The standard had been set, with a strong pro-West overtone, and apparently with a strong following as well. In the words of a satirical writer: 'Nowadays, all Chinese furniture shops are making Western-style furniture, [as if] preparing for those Westernised men and women living in this Westernised society [to get married and] form their small, Westernised families' (Hsü Hsu 194 : 33).

It is interesting to add that as early as the 1880s, the wealthy and the official families in Canton had already taken a strong interest in lavish Western furniture such as sofas, armchairs, sprung mattresses, and other expensive items that they eagerly acquired as collectibles or antiques. These had become essential objects of ostentatious exhibition in the home of a respectable or wealthy family (*YHKPK* 1996: 858).

In terms of municipal development, the Canton authorities consciously looked to Japan and the West for models. The Municipal Government, staffed mainly by returned students from the West and Japan,[45] tried to transplant a number of Western metropolitan symbols in the hope thereby of enhancing the reputation and image of Canton, and making it equal in status to its Western counterparts (*HCLCCN* 1934*c*: 10). The city wall, which had been 'one of the most imposing walls in China', one that 'any city of pride' should have kept, was torn down and its old symbolism thus destroyed (Franck 1925: 231; Lee Bing-shuey 1936: 13–14). Between 1922 and 1934, more than ten public parks were built to provide visitors with 'varieties of Western-style amusements', believed to be essential for the nourishment of physical and mental health. Miles of wide carriageways were opened, though some of these were too wide for the as yet not 'motorized' city (Franck 1925: 231).[46] A symbolic city flower was chosen, and a museum and two public libraries established. Even a racecourse was built, justified by the official line that this was something most big European and North American cities had (Kuang-chou-shih-chêng-fu 1933: 14, 16; LeeBing-shuey 1936: 138–9, 141–2).[47]

Modern Outlook, Western Outfits

At a time when the traditional gown and the Chinese-style jacket and trousers (*shan-k'u*) and 'Sun Yat-sen suit' (*Chung-shan chuang*) were still fashionable, an individual's preference for Western fashion might be more a symbolic expression of personal attitude and values than just a desire for a change in apparel. It might be interpreted as the physical expression of a person's preferences and propensity to imitate the mind-set of the Westerner. To those who could afford to choose, clothes were a mirror of character and value-orientation. If we assume that men usually dressed in a way that they felt appropriately represented their outlook, then the increasing popularity of Western-style costume in Canton may serve as visual evidence of the cultural acceptance of the West by a substantial portion of its inhabitants. By the mid-1930s, Western dress in Canton had become identified with social status, cultural level, and above all, modernity.

In government and unofficial publications, formal photographic portraits of officials and citizens alike tend to confirm the proposition that contemporary Cantonese preferred to present themselves in Western clothing at formal and socially important occasions. Government publications commemorating special official occasions always included group or individual photographs of senior staff dressed in full Western suits.[48] Chu Hui-jih, the newly appointed Commissioner of the Public Safety Department, wore a Western suit instead of police or army uniform, even though he was a senior military officer, for the official inauguration ceremony in October 1927 (*HTJP* 1936: 2.2, 3 Oct.). Similarly, when Ch'en Ming-shu was sworn in as the Chairman of the Kwangtung Provincial Government in 1928, he wore a Western full-dress suit with a topper (Kuang-chou-shih chêng-hsieh 1987: illus.). At the official welcoming party for the triumphant return of Huang Shao-hsiung and Ch'en Chi-t'ang from their military campaigns in eastern Kwangtung, the eighty-seven senior officials and social notables who attended were mostly in formal Western suits, and the banquet, which served foreign cuisine, was held at New Asia Hotel, then probably one of Canton's most exclusive dining places (*NYSP* 1928: 11, 13 Mar.). In another welcoming party for Liu Wei-chi, who was assuming office as Minister of Construction in the Provincial Government of Kwangtung, Liu himself and all the senior officials who greeted him at the quayside were all wearing light-coloured Western-style suits, with bow-ties or neck-ties, and, because of the hot weather, boaters, nicely in place (*HTJP* 1936: 2.3, 8 Aug.). In a photograph taken after a Congress of the Kwangtung KMT government, nearly all the cabinet ministers appeared dressed in Western suits (Kuang-chou-shih chêng-hsieh 1987: illus.).

This fashion was by no means confined to official circles, however. Respectable citizens did the same. In a magazine published by the alumni association of a prestigious high school, photographs taken during various social functions organized for its members show that all the participants, both men and women, wore formal Western suits or dresses (*Fang hai yüeh k'an* 2/2, 1936: 1). A photograph of a student group from Lingnan University shows that all fifty members wore Western suits, with neck- or bow-ties and Western-style hats as accessories (*Chung shê* 1930).

Advertisements for tailoring and drapery companies providing Western clothing predictably show the same trend. One of them reads: 'How can one be good-looking? How can one adapt to the [changing] needs of society? Love fashion! Western clothing!' (*KCTC* 1/1 1924: 14, *chi-tsa*). The intrinsic value of Western fashion was given so to speak a 'Darwinistic appraisal', as being 'progressive'. Another advertisement reads: 'Beautiful people mainly wear beautiful Western suits. This is because Western suits have the advantage of being light and convenient' (*Chien yen piao* 1, 1931: 9).

In the popular mind, Western clothing seemingly conveyed more symbolic power than mere good-looks, for it also symbolized intellect and perceptiveness. This was best reflected from cartoons drawn for the purpose of explicating, or visualizing, the meaning of the phrase *tu chü chih yen* (lit. the only one who has the eye), which was a pun to a well-known Chinese idiom *tu chü hui yen* (the only one who is insightful). In this cartoon, which was published in a popular local newspaper, three men are depicted against the backdrop of a modern city. Standing between two unappealing Chinese men who are clothed in traditional Chinese outfits is a nice-looking man (presumably an Englishman) with a trimmed moustache dressed in formal Western attire: top hat, a dark bow-tie, a winged collar, a dark tailcoat, and grey-striped trousers. This formally dressed gentleman is also wearing a monocle, which was described in the complementary text as one of the symbols of being a gentleman or bourgeoisie in the West. It was said to be a natural quality unique to Caucasians but denied to the Chinese because 'God does not give the Chinese people a deep or large enough eye socket' for wearing a monocle; a denial that was greatly regretted by the most Westernized Chinese in China (to the knowledge of that author, there was only one Westernized Chinese in Canton who was able to wear a monocle). What is interesting and symbolically important was that the monocle was here made analogous to the insightfulness to which the Chinese idiom *tu chü hui yen* refers. The underlying message was clear: gentlemen of the West were the only people who could see things perceptibly and intelligently (*YHP* 1936: 1, 5 Nov.). In another satirical cartoon entitled 'Respect the clothes, not their owner', two attractive young ladies are holding the sleeves of a Western suit, matched with Western trousers, hat, and neck-tie, worn by a limbless and headless wooden dummy. The embracing of Western fashion with its symbolic meaning and status of Western fashion would thus appear to have reached an 'alarming' stage (*Pan-chiao man-hua* 6/1 (1932: 5). An utterly infuriated reader wrote to a local newspaper complaining about the 'preferential' treatment that a specific category of men was commonly given at shops in Canton. His bitter experiences told him that shopkeepers would serve graciously only female customers, and any others who dressed in Western fashion; local men who dressed in Chinese outfits were generally ignored, and sometimes in a most humiliating manner (Liu P'ing 1934). Western attire was indeed taken very seriously by many locals.

Medicine advertisements unveil the cultural meaning of the Western outlook from another perspective. In a newspaper advertisement for a drug company promoting a brand of tonic pills for women, a listless and sad-looking Chinese lady, clad in an ordinary skirt and jacket, sits motionless on a sofa—representing one who has not tried these pills and thus remains unattractive with a pale complexion and a 'weak spirit' (*shên shu*). By way of contrast, after taking the pills, she is shown with fashionable Western clothes and accessories, standing upright and smiling cheerfully (*HTJP* 1927: 4.4, 17 Aug.). A substantial number of advertisements for Cantonese tonic pills, aphrodisiacs, and medicinal oils use drawings of young ladies, made up and dressed in Western style, as their subjects. Beneath the obvious visual appeal of these beautiful, and sometimes indeed scantily clothed and alluring, girls, lies the implication that the 'power' of these drugs can bring health and charm to their users, or, in the case of aphrodisiacs, can lead to a successful encounter with a beautiful partner. In an advertisement for Williams's shaving cream set in a Western-style restaurant, a supposedly handsome and robust Chinese gentleman, who is wearing a dinner suit with a bow-tie and a wing-collared shirt, is given an admiring glance by a young lady who is sitting at a table next to him. Symbolically significant is the caricature detail that she is in the company of another gentleman who is dressed in a traditional Chinese long gown—the inferiority of the Chinese attire was vividly constructed and demonstrated (*HTJP* 1929: 4.3, 27 Aug.). To be healthy, charming, and sexually attractive, a Western outlook is thus posited as essential. Even children do not escape. In two advertisements for children's medicine, the use of beautiful little blonde girls as a motif reinforces the cultural symbolism of the Western body representing the ideal of physical and spiritual health and loveliness. It seems to convey the message that by feeding Chinese children the advertised medicines, they can be made to grow as lovely and healthy as their ideal Western counterparts.[49] Imported packed beverages and foods manufacturers, such as Horlicks and Quaker Oats, also employed similar marketing tactics to persuade their Cantonese customers. In an advertisement for the imported malt drink Horlicks, a weak and sad-looking little boy, clad in a traditional long gown, is isolated by two friends of his who are cheerful, healthy, energetic, and, above all, dressed in Western-style clothes. These healthy boys are refusing to play with their weak friend, until he has turned stronger and looks happier after drinking Horlicks. Similarly, in a set of four advertisements for Quaker Oats, an apparently knowledgeable and perceptive doctor, who is clad in a suit and tie, gives advice to his patients, all dressed in traditional Chinese gowns or *ch'i-p'ao*, who are suffering from all sorts of trouble such as mental illness, intestinal ailments, and so on. These patients, after taking his medical and efficacious advice, 'naturally' are all cured (*HTJP* 1927: 2.4, 18 May; 1936 *passim*). Such advertisements tend to identify Western fashion and appearance with health, beauty, vitality, and all manner of other good points that both the younger and older generations should aspire to possess.

In real life, the obsession with Western fashion was widespread. One student complained that his contemporaries rejected Chinese clothing as backward and embraced Western garb as a symbol of modernity. Such a social phenomenon was seen in some quarters as an omen of the nation's collapse (T'sê An and Wei chih 1933: 23, 'Prose'). A concerned writer grieved at what she had overheard from the conversations between two middle-school students in the Central Park. They admitted that their main purpose of coming to study in Canton was to fulfil their dreams of 'wearing Western clothes and leather shoes every day, watching movies, [and] chasing after girls'. Having spent most of their time on these indulgences, and in view of the imminence of the school examination, they were planning to purchase a forged college certificate to keep their parents 'happy' (Ch'en Ching 1934: 1). Students were described to be so addicted to Western fashion that some Cantonese schools even proposed to the education authority that they should have their heads shaved (*KCTC* 33 1934: 5). At the peak of the New Life Movement in 1935–6, the provincial government adopted tough measures to battle against this problem of 'cultural invasion' of schools. Rigid codes of dress, including hairstyles, were stipulated by the authorities and imposed on every student. Under these rules, all uniforms have to be of Chinese-made fabrics only, and all kinds of luxurious and especially imported accessories were banned. Female students were not allowed to put on any make-up, have their hair dyed or nails painted, wear high-heeled shoes or skirts that were not long enough to cover the knees, and so on. Violation would be punishable in accordance with a range of penalties from writing a statement of repentance to expulsion (Kuang-tung shêng-chêng-fu 309, Oct. 1935; 332, May 1936). The severity of the policy reflected the seriousness of the problem, and there was no evidence to indicate that the austere government had won this battle outside the campus.

Women of the underworld were no less influenced by this trend of indulgence. Upper-class prostitutes began 'titillating with modernity' by wearing daring Western fashions, hairstyles, and make-up, and consuming imported liquor and cigarettes, in order to suit the taste of their more Westernized customers (Gronewold 1985: 59; Champly 1932: 80–6). A manual for brothel-goers recommended that its readers dress in Western suits to attract the attention of high-class courtesans (Hai-shang-chüeh-wu-shêng 1939: 82). By the middle of the 1920s, to follow Western-style fashion closely had become such a common subculture of the prostitute world in Canton that some concerned citizens contributed critical essays to a local official newspaper warning against the unhealthy impact of this phenomenon on the local women.[50]

It has been suggested that the extent of use of a foreign language in any given country may provide an inverse index of its attitude towards that foreign country. Since the German invasion of Czechoslovakia, for example, German lost its attraction to the Czechs, creating a void that was filled by Russian. But with the end of the War, interest in the Russian language declined as Soviet influence in the country increased (Krejci 1991: 15). By contrast, educated Cantonese seem to have had a different kind of sensitivity to foreign languages. Apparently unmoved by the incessant official rhetoric against 'foreign imperialism', educated youngsters in Canton enjoyed interlarding their speech with foreign words, phrases, and terms, which were usually unnecessary in that they could have easily been expressed in their native language. High-school students enjoyed uttering a few phrases of incorrect English in their conversations in public to show off their superior social status (T'sê An and Wei Chi 1933: 28, 'Prose'; Liang Yen-hsien 1934).[51] Young Cantonese regarded it as modern to address men as 'Mister' (*mi-ssu-t'o*), lady as 'Miss' (*mi-ssu*), and married women as 'Mrs' (*mi-ssu-shih*) (Tang Kê 1934: 10–11). This habit of introducing foreign words into speech was a means of showing off knowledge of a foreign language, which was (and indeed still is) popularly perceived as a yardstick of educational level, social status, and intellectual capacity. It is a consciously explicit pro-Western cultural gesture, resembling the penchant for English among the Bengali intelligentsia in the colonial era (Raychaudhuri 1988: 62–3). English was said to be 'recklessly used' (*lan-yung*) by some of the government departments as the fashionable medium for official correspondence. It had apparently reached such an 'alarming stage' that one of these departments felt obliged to issue an order exhorting its colleagues to give up the 'inveterate habit' (*KCHJP* 1933: 4, 18 Feb.).

Wearing Western outfits and having a 'mastery' of English were generally perceived as, so to speak, armour against social prejudice—i.e. it helped command respect from others. Sometimes, however, this Westernized appearance could not conceal a lack of substance underneath, as was vividly retold in a newspaper article contributed by a reader. One day, she recalled, a stylish young man boarded a bus in which she was also a passenger. He was wearing a beautiful Western suit and had a cigar in his mouth and a copy of an English newspaper under his arm. His up-to-the-minute appearance had attracted admiring glances from passengers, until a Western lady boarded the same bus. This lady, who sat right next to the 'Westernized' young man, politely asked him a simple question about the location of the YMCA. To the big surprise of everyone on board, the man apparently did not understand the question and, to save face, pretended not to hear. When the lady asked a second time, he still chose not to respond. Eventually, the lady surprised the passengers again by posing the question, in fluent Cantonese, to the bus driver. Deeply embarrassed, the young man dashed off at the next stop (Liang Yen-hsien 1934: 10). The author of this article wanted her readers to ridicule the irrationality of the fashion among the Cantonese youngsters of putting on a Western appearance as a means, though a deceitful one, of impressing their countrymen. Conversely, it revealed the blindly favourable attitude of the general populace towards those somewhat bourgeois cultural idioms imported from the West.

Even the afterlife was not spared this adoration of the West. A contemporary traveller was amazed to find, among items being burnt at a funeral in Canton, a life-size paper automobile with a paper Italian flag flying from its bonnet. A foreign flag was apparently considered useful in the next world, perhaps '[to guard] against property-confiscating generals and Tuchuns' (Franck 1925: 235–6). This trend certainly survived the waves of political campaigns against foreign imperialism, 'excessive' Westernization, and superstitious beliefs throughout this period in Canton. In 1934, a reader wrote to a local newspaper ridiculing the wide popularity of paper replicas of 'things Western' used for funerals in the city. Shops specializing in this trade displayed large boards outside their premises advertising their specialty in making 'beautiful modern paper work' which, in the critical eyes of this author, represented clearly the despicable and shameful pro-West mentality of the common people; even a Westerner's wind was said to be taken as a fragrance (*YHP* 1934: 1, 3 Oct.).

Glory to the West

Nobody in Republican Canton was more openly explicit and enthusiastic in advocating and publicizing their faith and confidence in the validity of Western culture to China's struggle for modernity than was a group of lecturers at Lingnan University. In the opinion of Ch'en Hsü-ching, the ring-leader, so to speak, of this group of advocates, Western culture far outstripped its Chinese counterpart in the areas of art, science, politics, education, philosophy, literature, religion, dress, cuisine, and so on. All the good points in Chinese culture, he believed, could also be found in Western culture, but not vice versa (Ch'en Hsü-ching 1934*a* 2–3).

Westernization was seen as the only hope for China's future. In the view of another advocate, all the qualities for being a strong nation could be found only in a thoroughly Westernized country:

> [Better] hygienic conditions; longer life-expectancy ... better and equal opportunity [for its people] to enjoy the material progress so that even its poorest [citizens] are never as poor as our country's; equal opportunity for education; better public order ... [and] more

> reasonable [measures of] social control... money-worship and utilitarian thinking relatively weaker; human affection more encouraged; the desire for scientific knowledge (*k'o-hsüeh yü*) stronger... knowledge [in general] more appreciated; civic consciousness stronger... altruistic and humanitarian ideas [more commonly] practised... (Lo Kuen-wei 1934: 151–2)

In terms of religion, Protestant Christianity and Catholicism, being more sacred and less superstitious (Ch'en Hsü-ching 1935*a*: 80),[52] were superior to Buddhism and Taoism (a misconception that is still held by the Communist government).[53] Western culture was highly regarded for being creative and progressive, in marked contrast to China's cultural inertia, which had impeded the country for centuries from making any 'healthy' cultural developments (Ch'en Hsü-ching 1935*b*: 142).

Fascism and imperialism were played down as temporary and uncharacteristic ulcers in Western society that would be eventually replaced by democracy—the mainstream of Western political culture (Ch'en Hsü-ching 1934*b*: 111). Even a dictatorial government in the West was believed to be more righteous than its Chinese counterpart: 'A modern Western form of dictatorship is good for a country and its people since it is designed for withstanding [aggression from] other countries. [But] the Chinese form of dictatorship is created only for the furtherance of the dictator's personal advantage, and is employed as a means of [absolute] control over the country' (Lü Hsüeh-hai 1935: 58). Beneath the idea of total Westernization lay a strong awareness of China's inferiority to the West—for Chinese intellectuals, the root of frustration at the country's failure in modern history (Ch'en 1979: 88–9).

The attitude of this group of scholars towards Japan was an unstable blend of admiration and hatred. On the one hand, Japan was still being regarded as China's enemy. On the other, Japan was also regarded as a successful Asian example of Westernization that China, and other Asian countries, should seek to emulate (Lo kuan-wei 1934: 151).[54] Sino-Japanese relations were interpreted and evaluated in terms of Westernization rather than imperialism.

The symbolic meanings and functions of the West to local Cantonese had become imperative. But it must be emphasized in passing that not all Cantonese had adopted a blindly pro-Western outlook. Total Westernization, no matter how appealing it seemed, was far from being achieved in Republican Canton. The persistence of some old 'bad customs' was an indication of this resilience. For instance, the official attempt to impose the use of the Gregorian calendar, which was accompanied by having the Chinese calendar abolished, was only poorly received by the multitudes and apparently accomplished little in the end.[55] The rising socio-cultural influence of the West had reached such an alarming level that some conservatives in the city felt the urgent need to rejuvenate the endangered indigenous culture and national pride. The official attempt to recompile the *Kuang-tung t'ung-chih* (Gazetteer of the Kwangung Province) was one of those efforts to remind the learned locals of their ethnico-cultural roots and the long and proud history of their native province.[56] In the early 1930s, the

Municipal Government also helped found semi-official organizations with a pro-tradition outlook, such as the Women's Association for Frugality and Morality (*Fu-nü chien-tê hui*), and the National Products Association (*Kuo-huo hui*) (Kuang-chou shih-cheng-fu 1934*b*: 18). The decision of Ch'en Chi-t'ang to reintroduce Confucian classics as a compulsory subject at school in 1934 represented the anxiety and the eagerness of the authorities to rejuvenate the traditional elements of Cantonese society in order to withstand the 'invasion' of Western cultures (Ch'en Shih et al.; Chin Chun; Hsü Chung-ch'ing, all in Kuang-chou-shih chêng hsieh 1987: 334–44). But what remains unclear is the far-reaching impact and effectiveness of these sporadic attempts as to revitalizing old traditions and eradicating Western cultural influences. The popular response towards the West in Canton followed its own logic and tempo, which had little to do with intellectual discourses or official rhetoric.

Anti-foreignism was only one side of the many expressions of Cantonese popular attitudes towards alien countries and their people. As we have seen from the examples above, Cantonese in this period were sophisticated enough to differentiate 'foreign' from 'imperialist'; though, ironically, not sophisticated enough to free themselves from generalized, and apparently imbalanced, perceptions of the West. Nevertheless, foreigners were no longer lumped into one simple category of outsiders inferior in all respects. A Cantonese might perceive and accept someone from the United States or Western Europe quite otherwise than if they were from Africa or South East Asia. Pro-foreignism, like anti-foreignism, was only one of many headings within this complex of popular attitudes towards foreigners (especially those from the successful Western nations), their countries, and their cultures. Political background and belief, social experience, cultural orientation and preferences, plus many other factors, combined to influence, and to some extent govern, the attitude of an individual towards a country and its nationals at a particular point of time in history. The complexity of the subject defies simple generalization.

4. POLITICAL ANTI-FOREIGNISM FROM A DIFFERENT ANGLE

Half-heartedness at the Top

Throughout the Republican era, jingoist fanatics in Canton kept anti-foreign, in particular anti-imperialist, propaganda alive. On the rhetorical level, the Canton government was impressively anti-imperialist and anti-foreign.[57] Politicians and officials, however, were not always sincere about anti-foreign or anti-Western rhetoric. Nor did ordinary citizens necessarily take these propaganda seriously. Behind the smokescreen of propaganda lies the reality of a general apathy towards these anti-foreign and anti-Western messages—a situation that no patriot or politician succeeded in changing.

Even during the 'high tide of anti-foreignism' in the mid-1920s, the sincerity of the Canton authorities in adopting a truly anti-foreign policy was dubious. When the Canton-Hong Kong strike and boycott of 1925–6 was at its peak, a number of senior officials of the Canton government, who usually stopped at Hong Kong en route to Canton or Shanghai, tried to convince the then increasingly belligerent Hong Kong governor, Cecil Clementi, that the whole idea of sustaining a boycott against Hong Kong was upheld by only a few Communist radicals and trade-unionists, and that their plan was by no means supported by the Canton government or the people. Sung Tzu-min and Sun K'o, two major figures in the group, told Clementi that if the labour activists had not been so obstinate, their government would have reached a settlement with the Hong Kong government much sooner.[58]

Political inertia became an openly serious problem for the Party bureaucracy. In 1926, still at the 'high tide of the national revolution', an official daily admitted that the Nationalist Party was running seriously short of 'healthy' members. The Party's admittance policy was too loosely coordinated and controlled; and quantity was stressed at the expense of quality with the new recruits. Some of them never attended any party meetings; and many had no knowledge about the Party's doctrine, or its organization (*KCMKJP* supplement 1926, 15 Oct.).[59]

The population at large was apparently no more anti-foreign than these inert officials. In spite of the somewhat histrionic accolades by many Chinese Marxist historians, in the various anti-foreign movements since the mid-nineteenth century deeds and commitments from the Cantonese were not that remarkable. Before the outbreak of the Opium War, for instance, foreign businessmen were apparently not hated by the local people, as described in some nationalistic history textbooks.[60] William Hunter's travelogues contain many instances of goodwill on the part of local officials and of friendly behaviour from the common people towards the 'foreign devils' at their Thirteen Factories.[61] The San-yüan-li type of anti-foreign collective violence was seemingly more officially plotted than truly spontaneous and died down as soon as the imminent threat had departed from the area (Polachek 1992: ch. 4; Mao Hai-chien 1995: 293–325; Wakeman 1966: 11–41). Throughout the Opium War, it was reported, especially in Chinese sources, that there was an abundant supply of Chinese traitors who were eager to serve the British invaders and their mischievous acts were held accountable for the humiliating defeats suffered by the Ch'ing forces (Waley 1960: pt. 5, esp. 222–3). In Canton, much like elsewhere in China where fighting broke out, the war with the British bothered few common people who lived outside the battlefields; there was not a reliable record of heroic acts in which the people took up arms to engage the invaders. On the contrary, many were anxious to make a humble fortune out of the war by peddling provisions (which no doubt were sold at a much inflated price) to the British, or by carrying heavy loads of supplies for them (Wakeman 1966: 48–9; Mao Hai-chien 1995: 311–13). During the British occupation of Canton in the mid-1850s, these 'imperialist soldiers' were surprisingly accepted by the local people who welcomed them as an efficient and honest peace-keeping force against the marauding secret societies associated with the T'aip'ings (Wakeman 1966: 174–6).

Having said all this, it must be noted that Cantonese were not necessarily blinded by this general acceptance of Westerners. There were occasional disputes that fit the profile of xenophobia. For example, in 1883, a fight broke out between a 19-year-old Chinese pedlar and an English officer of a British commercial vessel, resulting in the instant death of the pedlar at a pier close to Shameen. Although Chinese officials had come to the scene to investigate, they left without making any arrest after a lengthy discussion with the captain of the vessel, on the grounds that the case would be referred to the British Consul for further action. Utterly disappointed, the Cantonese spectators, about a hundred of them, then took the law into their own hands. They showered the vessel with rubble and rocks, set fire to the pier and the premises of the foreign company that was the agent of that ship. A number of vessels were burned as a result, and the British soldiers stationed nearby shot dead and wounded about a dozen Chinese. This incident, however anti-foreign it seemed to be, did not evolve into a popular movement against the British; it just died out quietly the next morning (*Shen pao* 1883, 19 Sept.). Even the well-organized and popularly supported boycott movement in 1905 was largely anti-American, rather than anti-foreign or anti-Western in nature, and not necessarily faithfully carried out. From local newspaper reports, it is known that the boycott of American goods in Canton persisted despite an official order against it and was due to the heavy presence of the city's elite gentry in the leadership of the movement and to the professedly wide supportive response of the people (ibid. 1905, 8 and 17 June, 10 and 20 July; Rhoads 1975: 85–91. Thanks to the participation of over a hundred local and non-Kwangtungese merchants in Canton, American trade with this port city, especially regarding oil, was significantly affected.[62] The annual reports of the Canton Customs, however, provide us with interesting information that the patriotic journalists and the American consuls seemingly chose to ignore in their reports. The British bystanders reported that despite the boycott, the total volume of American products imported via Canton did not show any sign of a drastic fall. American flour, contrary to what was stated by the American Consul in Canton, was imported into the port of Canton 'as usual'. Other foreign imports, such as a variety of Western-style hats, sweaters, knitwear, shoes and boots, and so on, continued to be freely imported into Canton in substantial volumes, and were preferred by local customers (*YHKPK* 1996: 436). For the year 1906, the Customs' annual report mentioned that although the boycott had not yet been called off completely, its intensity had already subsided considerably. It further elaborated that two American commodities, namely oil and flour, 'were not affected': for oil, there was an increase of more than 800,000 gallons, and for flour, a total of 274,932 *tan*, or 20,000 *tan* more than 1905, were imported into Canton (ibid. 445). The Customs' report also stressed that there was no convincing evidence to substantiate the rumour that the Lien-chou Incident of October 1905, in which five American missionaries were killed in northern Kwangtung, had anything to do with the boycott (ibid. 435).

Indifference at the Grass-Roots

In spite of successive waves of anti-foreign and anti-imperialist political campaigns launched by the local authorities throughout the period under study, there was apparently no short supply of Cantonese who displayed little interest in, and were unmoved by, calls for action. Some of them even behaved in a way that disheartened their fellow nationalistic citizens. Examples are abundant. For instance, in spring 1924, when Canton was packed with soldiers from various provinces who professed to support the cause of the nationalist revolution, ordinary citizens were affected more by a deep sense of worry than joy. Local merchants and businessmen, especially those who opened their businesses in the most prosperous parts of Canton, responded to the threatening presence of large numbers of the military in the city in a most unpatriotic, but practical, manner: by buying themselves a naturalized status and becoming a foreign, in particular Western, citizens. It was reported that more than half the total number of businessmen or merchants operating in these busy streets in the commercial areas had paid the Western consulates in Shameen a sum of 900 yüan in exchange for a stamped certificate, and, most importantly, a national flag of the country concerned, which would be hoisted in front of their premises if the political situation deteriorated and their lives and properties were under threat (*HTJP* 1924: 12, 1 Mar.).

During the turbulent mid-1920s, when the cries of anti-imperialism and anti-Westernism echoed loudly in the officially controlled mass media, and mass rallies were organized by the Revolutionary authorities, Canton was still remarkably safe for Westerners. Travelling in 1925, just before the outbreak of the Canton-Hong Kong strike, Harry Franck (1925: 250–1, 253–4, 258) was surprised by the safety of foreigners in Canton:

> [The] dangers to foreigners were really not great. For the Chinese it was another story... Kidnapping being a favourite Chinese sport, it was surprising to find no apparent tendency to steal the children of foreigners, surely a rich possibility... [The] foreigner really had less reason to worry about his wife and children anywhere in the streets of Canton than in any... American cities.

On his own, he wandered around and visited villages on the island of Ho-nan, which was a haven for outlaws in Canton. Even on the second day of the Canton Uprising in late 1927, Earl Swisher, a lecturer at Lingnan University, and his American colleagues could walk safely around the troubled parts of the city without encountering any molestation by either the government or the rebel troops (Rea 1977: 89–99). A possible implication of this was that the radical regime's ideological persuasion had simply failed to 'convert' the masses. One reason for this failure was the prevalent pragmatic attitude held by many towards the West and official campaigns against imperialism. At the peak of the strike and boycott against Hong Kong in July 1925, although many Cantonese workers willingly or unwillingly returned from the colony to Canton, it was also noted that quite a number chose to stay behind in Hong Kong. After a British-owned dockyard had posted an advertisement for recruiting coolies, to replace those who had deserted, hundreds of Cantonese workers instantly showed up for the jobs. In a shameless manner, according to one supporter of the boycott in Canton, many Cantonese teachers in Hong Kong anxiously sold their services as part-time censors to the colonial administration at a few dollars a day (Liang Ping-ao 1925). Another angry reader wrote in a local official daily about the 'capitulating mentality' held by many people around her. Very often she heard her friends disapprove this patriotic movement of strike and boycott by saying: 'Why is China still daring to launch such an anti-foreign movement when her weakness is already at its peak?' A senior official had once told her that there was no rush for launching a boycott against British and Japanese products; any serious boycott should start only after the stocks of those goods were cleared. A self-professedly 'civilized' old gentleman had lectured her: 'Why on earth must we boycott British and Japanese products which are both good in quality, and inexpensive?' (Lü P'ing 1925). Not surprisingly, then, the anti-British boycott and strike, though inaugurating a short period of recession in Canton, did not lessen the local appetite for Western imported goods. The 1926 Canton Customs reported a 'record high' for the total value (80 million *Haikuan tael*) of foreign goods imported into Canton; about 15 per cent of the total import were textile products, some of which were used in making uniforms for the Northern Expeditionary Army (*YHKPK* 1064–5).

Popular response to the strike and boycott was not always as enthusiastic as we are led to believe. At the peak of the strike, local attitudes in Canton towards the campaign were mixed and ambiguous. British Intelligence sources reveal the existence of a 'secret' trading link between the foreign communities in Shameen and Hong Kong, using local Cantonese peasants and traders.[63] Nora Waln's autobiography describes how a pedlar sold foodstuffs regularly to foreigners in Shameen, for which he was later arrested and executed. The author also recalls how intimidation by militant unionists forced a large number of passive Cantonese workers out of Shameen, and away from their foreign employers. Her Cantonese maid and chef hid to avoid the evacuation order imposed on Chinese employees by the pickets (Waln 1933: 215, 224–5).

Not all the strikers enjoyed the strike. Although they were given a small amount of strike funds and two free meals a day, life in the makeshift dormitories was miserable (ibid. 138). According to an official daily in Canton, severe hardships suffered by many undernourished and penniless strikers eventually took the lives of over 800 of them in less than two months after the strike began (*KCMKJP* 1926, 31 July). Many were seemingly intimidated into joining this 'patriotic movement'. In a Cantonese 'wooden-fish' song entitled 'Kung-jên tan wu-kêng' (The Grieving of a Worker Until the Fifth Watch of the Night), the songwriter, in the first-person, laments one such worker who was coerced to give up his well-paid job and take part involuntarily in the strike. This song also tells its audience that venality among the high-ranking officers on the strike committee is common, and ordinary strikers are brutally abused by the authoritarian and corrupt pickets and are forced to live in appalling and overcrowded conditions.[64]

No wonder, then, when a Kwangtung Central Committee for the Severence of Economic Relations with Great Britain called for another boycott against the British in June 1927, public response to the call for a meeting of all the interested parties was so poor that the announcement had to be reissued three times before enough delegates from labour and student organizations were gathered (*NCH* 1927, 18 June). In August, radical unionists in Canton declared another anti-British boycott in all the ports in Kwangtung. But it turned out to be

> a very half-hearted affair. Nevertheless, all shops with the exception of those in the vicinity of Shameen were forced by the police, acting on the orders of the KMT Committee, to exhibit white banners bearing the legend 'Oppose the British gunboat violence at Dosing, overthrow British Imperialism'... Owing to the threats of strong retaliatory measures that would be taken by the British Government should an anti-British boycott take place, no pickets were posted, and British trade was allowed to continue on its normal course... [The boycott] was engineered purely by the Labour Unions in order to keep the Hong Kong-Shameen strikers in funds.[65]

The tempo and the fervour were burning out fast.

The Shakee Incident on 23 June, 1925, or the Shakee Massacre (*Sha-chi ts'an an*) as it was officially called, was regarded by contemporary politicians and nationalists alike as an event of national humiliation and one of the major pivotal events in the modern history of the nation. Its anniversary date had become a commemoration day at school, which was presumably enacted on campuses, and by all men and women of letters in the city. Not every one in Canton, however, shared the official ideology underlying this official design. Just two weeks after this tragic event, which claimed, allegedly, over one hundred lives, readers of local newspapers had already shown signs of losing interest in it. In the observation of a patriotic reader who wrote of his concerns and disgust to an official daily in Canton, most newspapers in the city had already stopped publishing news related to the incident. Many of these newspaper offices rationalized their political apathy with the ludicrous excuse that their editorial decision was made to save papers. On the eve of each monthly commemorative day of the incident, he grieved, all sorts of excuses were given by the press to justify their temporary suspension of business, and to those which did continue to operate, none had published any extra or supplement or special feature that would have reflected the magnitude of this most glorious incident of martyrdom in the city's modern history. To his further annoyance, an ordinary issue of most newspapers in Canton had about eight pages, of which a substantial part was, allegedly, reserved for serialized 'obscene novels'. He emphasized that the press in the Western nations would surely have reported, and then followed up, very differently on a news story of this importance (T'ao wei 1925).

Slightly over a year after the Shakee Incident, the Governor of Hong Kong was officially invited by the Canton government to visit the city, to reciprocate an earlier official visitation to this British colony by the Chairman of the Canton branch of KMT, Li Chi-shên. The welcoming ceremony and receptions bore no sign of any 'old hatred' at all: the Chinese flagship in Canton fired seventeen guns as a personal salute; and 'whenever the Governor passed through the city, the streets were decorated with British flags . . . [and] absolutely cleared of the native population and lined with troops'.[66] Clementi was so 'warmly welcomed' by the Canton authorities that some nationalistic intellectuals were disgusted by this 'appeasing' gesture of their government.[67] But there were also many others who were pleased by such an improvement in bilateral relations between the two cities. One reader wrote to a local newspaper hailing the visit of Clementi as one of the 'happy occasions' that occurred for Canton in recent years. He interpreted the past few years when Canton was under the rule of radical leftist politicians as an era of hardship for the people, which was unmistakably a cosmographic sign of bad luck. And with this visitation of Clementi, which was interpreted as an auspicious sign and force of regeneration, he was confident that the spell of misfortune for Canton had already been dispelled and that the city had once again embarked on a path of prosperity and happiness.[68] In popular perception, this event was seen not as an act of shameful appeasement, but rather as a source of blessing, even to the extent of being a supernatural one.

In the face of general political apathy and, most importantly, official commitment to deradicalize local politics, the symbolism of the Shakee Incident lost much of its relevance. The second anniversary of the Incident passed quietly; 'nothing like a parade or demonstration was attempted, a memorial service only being held'. The authorities took 'the most elaborate precautions to prevent any incident in the [*sic*] Shameen and to prohibit any demonstration'.[69] The third anniversary also passed without trouble. On that day, an indoor commemoration gathering was organized. The Canton government, however, ordered that only one representative from each official department should take part and that provocative rhetoric was strictly forbidden (*HTJP* 1928: 3.3, 25 June). On the same occasion in 1929, 'radicals' had distributed anti-foreign pamphlets before the police arrived to disperse them; but such agitation hardly constituted a real threat to foreigners in Canton, nor did it spark off any anti-British or anti-foreign popular response.[70] Even commemorating the 'epic' May Thirtieth Movement had lost its patriotic and emotional appeal. Its second anniversary was marked in Canton with little enthusiasm from the general public. Only ten thousand people were mobilized by the local authorities for the occasion; the marchers devised no form of propaganda to interest bystanders, and there was no shouting of slogans at all (*NCH* 1927, 18 June).

Students and the Anti-Japanese Movement from a Different Angle

Although this chapter deals basically with Cantonese attitudes towards the West, a brief diversion to see how the Japanese were perceived will only further our knowledge of pro- and anti-foreignism in the same city, and from a somewhat wider socio-cultural perspective.

It is, therefore, interesting to note that even in the various anti-Japanese boycott campaigns in this period, which were supposedly more imminent and hence widely publicized, policy insincerity and official corruption were prevalent. On one of these boycotts protesting against the sending of Japanese troops to Shantung, a British diplomat in Canton observed that '[it] had never been rigidly carried out' and certain essential imports from Japan such as coal and chemicals were 'from the beginning excluded from its scope'.[71] Most ironic was that the Canton government, at the time of the boycott, openly solicited Japanese investment in the plan of reopening the official mint in Canton as a means to tackle the banknote crisis. Wen Chi-fêng, an overseas Chinese from Japan, was appointed as the chief manager of the mint only because of his close acquaintance with some Japanese financiers who eventually invested 3 million yüan in the plant (*NYSP* 1928: 11, 2 Mar.). Strongly worded anti-imperialist propaganda, though abundant, often served only to put a veneer of patriotism onto government's views.[72]

The 1928 anti-Japanese boycott revealed the intrinsic difficulties of organizing an anti-foreign boycott, especially when facing a half-hearted bureaucracy on top and indifference at the grass-roots. At the outset, a radical Kwangtung All-Occupations' Anti-Japanese Association was formed. To the alarm of Canton's merchants, this association proposed the formation of searching and picketing teams and a surcharge of 30 per cent imposed on the value of the remaining stocks of Japanese goods held by merchants. In response, the various merchant organizations in Canton formed their own independent Merchants' Anti-Japanese Organization;[73] and they refused to have their stocks of Japanese goods registered. Out of desperation, the radical Association retaliated by imposing a fine on individuals caught in possession of Japanese goods, and brought about the forcible closing down of a number of electrical supply shops and the confiscation of their contents. Goods seized were no longer redeemable, but were auctioned to the highest bidder.[74] The whole 'patriotic venture' became a melodrama of human covetousness and corruption. The governor of Hong Kong noted that the Canton government 'while clearly disapproving is helpless to interfere with the operations of the Japanese Boycott Committee whose members are busy enriching themselves in the old familiar manner'.[75] In another anti-Japanese boycott movement in 1933, open defiance by the general public was common. In one case, a high-ranking officer of the Boycott Committee was caught red-handed trading the 'enemy product' (*KCHJP* 1933: 14, 26 Feb.).[76]

The social impact of the Mukden Incident on Canton was also short-lived. A contemporary wrote that the subsequent anti-Japanese campaign was run only perfunctorily and then immediately called off when unconfirmed hearsay news of the evacuation of Japanese troops reached Canton (Li Han-ch'iao 1930: 135). In his 'Tsai shen ching li' (In the Deep Well), Ou-yang Shan (1948: 12–14) dramatizes this piece of social reality. The protagonists, a worn-out prostitute and a young worker, first meet on a crowded bus in 1931 when two students are appealing for donations to support the anti-Japanese resistance movement in the North. The prostitute attracts the young man's attention because she is the only one on that bus who gives money to support the cause.

For contemporary students, whose predecessors had once played so important a role in the May Thirtieth Movement and the Canton-Hong Kong strike, anti-foreign political radicalism had already lost its attraction. There were, no doubt, student-led anti-foreign nationalist movements in Canton throughout the 1920s and the 1930s, as many patriotic historians remind us.[77] This was, however, far from the full picture. In the view of one concerned student, the demoralization and depoliticization of contemporary students were mainly due to their obsession with Western materialistic culture, which had eventually 'polluted' their spirit. Politics no longer found any place in a student's ambitions. Instead, a flat in a skyscraper, Western cuisine, Western-style fashion and entertainment, and possession of an imported car became the 'standard objects of desire' for most of them (Ch'en Pei-ying 1934: 29). And if a student was lucky enough to read for an academic degree at a university abroad, his future would be guaranteed as bringing happiness, prestige, and success (Li Han-ch'iao 1930: 148–9). It is thus no surprise that although 1933 was officially proclaimed to be the 'Students' Year of National Products' (*hsüeh-shêng kuo-huo nien*), students' responses to this campaign in Canton were noticeably poor. One committed observer saw this in dismay as clear evidence of the triumph of selfishness and the failure of patriotism among his peers. Most students, he groaned, believed that imported goods stood for superiority and modernity. Thus, hairstyles, suits, and leather shoes came for preference from the United States, perfume from Europe, and hair-cream from Japan (Chang Lo-chih 1934: 30).

Under this cloud of apathy, even school military drilling, which aimed at cultivating patriotic feelings among students, was scarcely even nodded at by the bored staff, and was poorly received by the students, at least in some schools (*Shih-jih t'an hsün k'an shê* 1934: 56–8). A contemporary middle-school student wrote in his diary that as there were so many commemorative events related to nationalism, most students had already become numb to them, at the expense of their true meanings. Students, however, were still enthusiastic about these events not because of any commitment to patriotism, but merely because they were always celebrated off campus, sometimes in the form of a mass parade, which entailed the suspension of classes. When they helped put up political posters in the streets, they felt as though they were putting up New Year placards; all these political rituals, in his experience, had become void of their originally intended meanings and the nationalistic slogans were clichés (Huang Ch'ao-yu 1934: 87–8). In view of such political apathy and 'capitulation', the absence of a strong and radical student movement in Canton after 1927 seems not entirely due to the 'tactical fault', or active repression, of the KMT as John Israel suggests;[78] the students themselves are also to be blamed.

In fact, imperialism was not always hated by the general public as most Chinese history textbooks want us to believe. A 1929 opinion poll on KMT performance conducted by its Canton branch office, which had sent out 30,000 questionnaires in Canton, revealed some interesting findings. When being asked to identify and to rank in order of importance China's most serious and imminent threat, gambling and opium came out at the top of the scale, followed by the CCP, banditry, imperialism, warlords, local bullies, bad aristocracy, bureaucracy, unequal treaties, local ne'er-do-wells, and dishonest tax collectors. However, the director of the poll, who was a radical 'young Turk' in the Canton KMT, wrote: '[The respondents] do not hate bitterly [foreign] imperialism. They, however, feel that [their country] is being poisoned (*t'u tu*) by [the bad influence of] Communism.' Imperialism was undoubtedly identified as a threat to China's security; but it was not necessarily something to be bitterly hated, nor was it even seen as a source of 'poison' that could kill, as Communism allegedly could and would, their nation (P'u Liang-chu 1929: 214).[79]

A new facetious label, 'five-minute enthusiasm' (*wu fen-chung jê-tu*), was popularly used to describe the half-heartedness and transience of Cantonese anti-foreign sentiment in this period. It was also adopted as the title of a short story. 'Five-Minute Enthusiasm' ridicules the lack of patriotic commitment of Canton middle-school students as shown in the anti-Japanese boycott after the outbreak of the Shanghai Incident in 1932. Messrs S, H, and W are disappointed by the feeble non-resistance policy of the Nanking government against the invading Japanese. They all agree that the only way to save China is a boycott of Japanese goods, and they therefore swear to stop buying any 'enemy product'. But in less than one month, H and W have dishonoured their oath. When they meet again later, H and W defend themselves from the criticism of S:

> You moron! . . . In the crazy world of today, nothing must be treated too seriously. Do you think that your stern insistence on a thorough boycott would be commended by our government? . . . Moreover, there are four hundred million Chinese in this country. If only you is insisting on boycotting, do you think you will be powerful enough to kill all the 'dwarf-slaves' [Japanese]?

S's persistence, however, does not last long, either. When his uncle returns from a trip to Tokyo and brings him delicious tinned food as a gift, he accepts it gratefully (Kao Yu-yün 1933: 35–41). A Cantonese ballad compared allegorically the 'five-minute enthusiasm' to a flame-driven revolving lantern (*tsou-ma têng*):

> When the fire is [burning] strong, [you spin] as fast as if you could fly. [When your] fire-steam is beginning to die down, you stop intermittently. When the lamp-oil is completely exhausted, I am afraid that you can hardly move one inch further . . . All the figures [painted on the lantern are] depending on you to be animated. [However], no matter how hard you spin, it is just a [short-lived] posture; [since] in less than five minutes' time, [you] will become colder than a frozen corpse.[80]

This story and folk-song depict in miniature the larger reality of the fickleness and shallowness that marked anti-foreign sentiment in Canton in this period.

Some contemporary writers were dismayed by the general apathy towards the politics of anti-foreignism and anti-imperialism in Canton. Ou-yang Shan was one of them. Most of his pre-1937 novels are intended to unveil this 'ugly' unpatriotic side of the Cantonese people. In *Ch'i-nien chi* (The Seventh Anniversary of Death), he complains that only seven years after the Shakee Incident, the former political consciousness and active patriotism of the masses is all gone. The story begins with the hero moving into a shared flat owned by Wei San-tai and her second son, Ch'ang-lo. Ch'ang is not a filial son; all he wants his old mother for is to get more money for himself by pressuring her to sell their flat. On the seventh anniversary of the death of her eldest son, Ta-tê, who was shot dead in the Shakee Incident in 1925, Wei San-tai prepares a feast for Chu Chien, a good friend of Ta-tê who has visited her and paid his homage to Ta-tê's spirit tablet unfailingly over the last six years. Meanwhile, she tells her new tenant how her son's union has praised and commended his self-sacrifice. This time, however, Chu Chien does not show up. Teasing about his mother's rationalization for Chu's absence, Ch'ang-lo shouts: 'Unusual? You must be joking! People have already long forgotten the meaning of June 23 (the day of the Shakee Incident). They have let the [Shakee Incident] slip their memory these five or six years at least' (Ou-yang Shan 1935: 280). Refusing to believe this, Wei asks her new tenant to accompany her to look for Chu at the union. When they arrive, they realize that the union has been closed down for some time, and the premises are partitioned into three parts; two of them are being used as brothels, and the other an opium-den.

The story mourns for the death of an era—an era of political consciousness and conscience, political activism and revolutionary idealism. Ou-yang Shan complains that these young lives were wasted and betrayed by both their government and their people who chose to forget the meaning of their self-sacrifice. Wei Ch'ang-lo has replaced Ta-tê to symbolize the typical younger generation in Canton in the 1930s—mercenary, selfish, hedonistic, and politically apathetic. The importance of nationalist sentiment was rarely questioned, but the manifestations of which, in terms of its hostility towards the 'foreign' and in particular 'the West', were quite often not as sincere nor as glorious as they appeared to be. Pragmatism reigned over idealism.

The ideal and practice of anti-foreignism in Canton was rife with evidence of inconsistency. Such inconsistency was attributed to the government's awareness of the diplomatic difficulties involved, as well as to a lack of general interest in, and support for, any militant plan or hostile action against foreigners in Canton. The local populace appeared to be taking pride in its ability to borrow culturally from successful foreign, and especially Western, countries, rather than to be contemplating a violent end to centuries of arguably beneficial Sino-foreign interchange. In the cultural context of Republican Canton, popular attitudes towards the West were not necessarily always one-sided and belligerent.

Different and conflicting views on this issue could coexist in time and place, even in the same person, although on balance during this period modern Cantonese culture showed a strong leaning towards the West.

REFERENCES

Atwell, Pamela (1985), *British Mandarins and Chinese Reformers: The British Administration of Weihaiwei (1898–1930) and the Territory's Return to Chinese Rule* (Hong Kong: Oxford University Press).

Bergère, Marie-Claire (1989), *The Golden Age of Chinese Bourgeoisie, 1911–1937* (Cambridge: Cambridge University Press).

Cavendish, P. (1970), 'Anti-imperialism in the KMT, 1923–1928', in Jerome Ch'en (ed.), *Studies in the History of China and Southeast Asia* (Cambridge: Cambridge University Press).

Champly, Henry (1934), *The Road to Shanghai: White Slave Traffic in Asia*, trans. Warre B. Wells (London: John Long).

Chan, Ming K. (1975), 'Labour and Empire: The Chinese Labour Movement in the Canton Delta, 1895–1927', unpublished Ph.D. dissertation, Stanford University.

Chang Ching-shêng (1927), 'Hsing mei', in *Hsin wên-hua* 1/6 (Shanghai).

Chang Lo-chih (1934), in Kuang-tung chung-hsüeh hsüeh-shêng tzu-chih-hui (ed.), *Kuang-tung hsüeh-shêng* (*KTHS*), iv.

Chang Tzu-p'ing (1930), 'Ch'ang-t'u', *Tzu-p'ing hsiao-shuo hsüan* (Shanghai: Hsien-tai shu-chü), ii.

——(1933), *T'o-liao kuei-tao ti hsing-ch'iu* (Shanghai: Hsien-tai shu-chü).

Chang Yüan-tsi jih-chi (1981), 2 vols. (Peking: Shang-wu yin-shu-kuan).

Ch'en, Jerome (1979), *China and the West: Society and Culture 1815–1937* (London: Hutchison).

Ch'en Ching (1934), 'Lien-ko hsüeh-tzu t'i t'an-hua', *YHP*, 12 September.

Ch'en Chi-t'ang (1972), 'Hsin-li kai-tso', in Ssu-li Tê Ming hsing-chêng kuan-li chuan-k'o hsüeh-hsiao (ed.), *Ch'en Po-nan hsien-shêng nien-p'u* (Taipei).

Ch'en Hsü-ching (1934*a*), 'Chung-kuo wên-hua ti ch'u-lu', in Lü Hsüeh-hai (ed.), *Ch'üan-pên hsi-hua yen-lun chi* (*CPHH*) (Canton: Ling-nan ta-hsüeh hsüeh-shêng tzu-chih hui), i.

——(1934*b*) 'Tiu-yü i-pan huai-i ch'üan-pen hsi-hua chê ti i kê chien-shuo', in Lü Hsüeh-hai (ed.), *Ch'üan-pên hsi-hua yen-lun chi* (*CPHH*) (Canton: Ling-nan ta-hsüeh hsüeh-shêng tzu-chih hui), i.

——(1935*a*), 'Kuan yü ch'üan-pen hsi-hua ta Wu Ching-chao hsien-shêng', in Fêng En-yung (ed.), *Ch'üan-pên hsi-hua yen-lun su-chi* (*CPHH*) (Canton: Ling-nan ta-hsüeh hsüeh-shêng tzu-chih hui ch'u-pan-shê), ii.

——(1935*b*), 'Tsai t'an ch'üan-pen hsi-hua', in Fêng En-yung (ed.), *Ch'üan-pên hsi-hua yen-lun su-chi* (*CPHH*) (Canton: Ling-nan ta-hsüeh hsüeh-shêng tzu-chih hui ch'u-pan-shê), ii.

Ch'en Hung (1937), 'Chung-kuo hsin-ko-chü ti chuan-tso', *Hsi-chü i-shu* 1: 23.

Ch'en Pei-ying (1934), 'Hsiang-kang lü-hsing chih', *KTHS* 4.

Ch'en Ping-han (1996), 'Kuang-chou nü-ling i tang nien', in Kuang-chou shih jên-min chêng-fu ts'an-i shi (ed.), *Sui ts'an wên shih tzu-liao* (Canton), ii.

Ch'en Shih et al. (1987), 'Ming-tê shê h'u Hüseh-hai shu-yüan', in Kuang-chou-shih chêng-hsieh (ed.), *Nan tien sui yueh: Ch'en Chi-t'ang chu Yüeh shih-chi chien-wên lu* (Canton: Kuang-tung jên-min ch'u-pan-shê).

Chêng Ch'ên (1922), 'Fu-nü chieh-fang ti wo chien', *Ch'ün shêng* 1/1, November.

Ch'êng Hao (1985) (ed.), *Kuang-chou kang shih (chin-tai pu-fen)*, 2 vols. (Peking: Hai-yang ch'u-pan-shê).

Cheng K'ai-t'ang (1987), 'Ts'ung mou-ti Chi-tu-chiao ti fa-chan k'an tsung-chiao shêng-ch'ang ti t'u-jang', in Lo Chu-fêng (ed.), *Chung-kuo shê-hui-chu-i shih-ch'i ti tsung-chiao wen-t'i* (Shanghai: Shang-hai shê-hui k'o-hsüeh yüan).

Chesneaux, Jean (1968), *A History of Chinese Labour Movement* (Stanford: Stanford University Press).

Ch'i Tzu (1965), 'Kuang-chou-shih Tung-shan liu-shih nien nai fa-chan kai shu', *KCWSTL* 14/1.

Chien yen piao tsa chih (1931), 1/1 (Canton).

Chin Chun (1987), 'Ti-ch'ang tu ching', in Kuang-chou-shih chêng-hsieh (ed.), *Nan tien sui yueh: Ch'en Chi-t'ang chu Yüeh shih-chi chien-wên lu* (Canton: Kuang-tung jên-min ch'u-pan-shê).

Chin-tai Kuang-chou k'ou-an ching-chi shê-hui kai-k'uang: Yüeh hai-kuan pao-kao hui tsi (*YHKPK*) (1996), ed. Kuang-chou-shih ti-fang-chih pien-hsüan wei-yüan-hui pan-kung-shih and Kuang-chou hai-kuan-chih pien-hsüan wei-yüan-hui (Canton: Chi-nan ta-hsüeh ch'u-pan-shê).

Chin Wei, 'Sha-mien i pieh', in Mao Tun et al. (ed.), *Chung-kuo ti i jih* (Shanghai: Shêng-huo shu-tien, 1936).

Chiu-chung fêng-fu (1934), 'Ch'ih fan-ts'ai chih', *KCTC* 25.

——(1934), 'Kung-kai yen yin', *KCTC* 33.

Cho Yu (1928), 'Shang-hai ti lai hsin', *Ying shih* (Canton).

Chü Ch'i (1934), 'Hsien-hua shuo mo-têng', *YHP*, 17 September.

Ch'u Chien (1929), 'Yüeh-chü lun', *Hsi-chü* 1.

Ch'ün shêng pao hsing-ch'i tsêng k'an 1/1 (1935).

Chung Ching-wên (1927), *Li-chih hsiao p'in* (Shanghai: Pei hsin shu-chü).

Chung-kuo jên-min chêng-chih-hsieh-shang-hui-i Kuang-tung-shêng (1983) (ed.), *Kuang-chou chin pai nien chiao-yü shih liao* (Canton: Kuang-tung jên-min ch'u-pan-shê).

Chung shê (1930), 1/1, June (Canton: Kuang-chou ssu-li Ling-nan ta hsüeh Chung Shê).

Coble, P. M., Jr. (1980), *The Shanghai Capitalists and the Nationalist Government* (Cambridge, Mass.: Harvard University Press).

Croizier, Ralph (1988), *Art and Revolution in Modern China: The Lingnan (Cantonese) School of Painting, 1906–1961* (Berkeley: University of California Press).

Eberhard, Wolfram (1971), 'What is Beautiful in a Chinese Woman?', in *Moral and Social Values of the Chinese: Collected Essays* (Taipei: Ch'eng Wen).

Elvin, Mark (1989), 'Tales of Shen and Xin: Body-Person and Heart-Mind in China During the Last 150 Years', in Michel Feher (ed.), *Zone: Fragments for a History of the Human Body*, pt. 2 (New York: Urzone).

En Jên and T'an Shao-p'êng (1989) (eds.), *Kuang-chou chu-ming lao-tzu-hao* (Canton: Kuang-chou wên-hua ch'u-pan-shê).

Fang hai yüeh k'an (1928–1936) (Canton: Kuang-chou P'ei Ying chung hsüeh i-chiu-san-liu nien chi Fang Shê).

Fêng-su kai-kê wei-yüan-hui (1930) (ed.), *Fêng-su kai-ke ts'ung-kan* (FSKKTK) (Canton).

Fitzgerald, John (1996), *Awakening China: Politics, Culture, and Class in the Nationalist Revolution* (Stanford: Stanford University Press).

Franck, Harry A. (1925), *Roving Through Southern China* (New York: Century).

Geil, William Edgar (1911), *Eighteen Capitals of China* (London: Constable).

Gillingham, Paul (1983), *At the Peak: Hong Kong Between the Wars* (Hong Kong: Macmillan).

Gronewold, Sue (1985), *Beautiful Merchandise: Prostitution in China, 1860–1836* (New York: Harrington Park).

Hang (1929), 'Ch'ün hui yang shih chih tiao-wu k'uang', *KHP*, 12 February.

HCLCCN, see *Kuang-chou shih-chêng-fu (1934c)*.

Ho, Kit-yiu Virgil (1985), 'Hong Kong Government's Attitude to the Canton-Hong Kong Strike and Boycott of 1925–1926', Unpublished M.St. dissertation, Oxford University.

Ho Kuo-hua et al. (1946) (ed.), *Kuang-chou shih san-shi-wu nien-tu shang-yêh nien-chien* (Canton: Kuang-chou Shih Shang Hui shang-yêh nien-chien ch'u-pan hui-yüan hui).

Hsi Hua (1933), 'Ai yü yüan', *KCHJP*, 16 February.

Hsiang hua hua-pao (1928–9), 1–4 (Canton: Hsiang hua hua-pao shê).

Hsiao-tzu (1934), 'Fu-nü tou-fa chih t'i-pien', *YHP* 1, 1 July.

Hsi-chü (1929), vol. 1 (Canton: Kuang-tung hsi-chü yen-chiu-so).

Hsi Hua (1933), 'Ai yü yüan', *KCHJP*, 16 February.

Hsieh Fu-ya (1929), 'Jih-pen tsui-chin chih chin-pu', *KCMKJP* Supplement, 24–6 October.

Hsien Tzu-lung (1986), 'Kuang-chou Hsin-ya chiu tien', *Kuang-chou kung shang ching-chi shih liao*, ed. Chung-kuo min-chu chien kuo hui Kuang-chou-shih wei-yüan-hui (Canton: Kuang-tung jên-min ch'u-pan-shê).

Hsü Chung-ch'ing (1987), 'Wo shen-cha hsiao-ching hsin-ku ching kuo', in Kuang-chou-shih chêng-hsieh (ed.), *Nan tien sui yueh: Ch'en Chi-t'ang chu Yüeh shih-chi chien-wên lu* (Canton: Kuang-tung jên-min ch'u-pan-shê).

Hsü Hsu (1946), *Hsi liu chi*, 7th edn. (Shanghai: Yeh ch'uang shu-wu).

Hsü Hsüeh-hang (*c.*1920s) (ed.), *Hsin-pien Kuang-tung shêng-ch'êng pai-hua*, 3 vols. (Rangoon: Wên-hua chu-tzu kung-ssu).

HTJP, see Hua-tzu jih-pao.

Hu P'o-an et al. (1923) (eds.), *Chung-hua ch'üan kuo fêng-su chih*, 2 vols. (Shanghai: Kuang chi shu-chü). Reprinted by Shih-chia-chuan: Ho-nan jên-min ch'u-pan-shê, 1986.

Hua-tzu jih-pao (*HTJP*) (Hong Kong) (1911), 1 September; (1927) 11–20 September; (1936), 27 August.

Huang Ch'ao-yu (1934), 'Kuang-fu chi-nien', in Kuang-tung shêng-li ti-i chung-hsüeh-hsiao (ed.), *Shêng-i chung-hsüeh-shêng jih-chi hsüan* (3 vols., Canton), iii.

Huang Ching-hua (1972), *Chung-kuo chin-tai shih chang-shih* (Hong Kong: Chao yang chu-pan-shê).

Huang Hsin (1935), 'Lun hsiao-hsüeh ti yin-yüeh chiao-yü', *Kuang-chou yin-yüeh* 3/67.

Huang Ming-hui (1936), *Kuang-chou chi Hsiang-kang* (Shanghai: Hsin shêng-ming shu-chü).

Huang Yen-pei (1922) (ed.), *I-sui chih Kuang-chou shih* (Shanghai: Shang-wu yin-shu-kuan).

Hughes, E. R. (1968), *The Invasion of China by the Western World*, 2nd edn. (London: Adam & Charles Black).

Hui You (1928), 'Yang fu-jên ti mo-li', *KPP*, 15 March.

Hunter, William C. (1976), *Bits of Old China* (Taipei: Ch'eng Wen; first published London: Kegan Paul, Trench & Co., 1855).

'I chien jih to', *KCLPL* 12 (1934).

Israel, John (1966), *Student Nationalism in Republican China, 1927–1937* (Stanford: Stanford University Press).

Jên Po (1925), 'Ssu-chang ch'ung-ch'ih chih yüan-yin', *KCMKJP*, 8 October.

Johnson, Elizabeth (1984), 'Hakka Women', in Mary Sheridan and Janet Salaff (eds.), *Lives: Chinese Working Women* (Bloomington: Indiana University Press).

Kao Yu-yün (1933), 'Wu fen-chung jê-tu', in Kuang-tung chung-hsüeh hsüeh-shêng tzu-chih-hui (1933) (ed.), *Kuang-tung hsüeh-shêng (KTHS)* (Canton), ii.

KCMKJP, see Kuang-chou min-kuo jih-pao.

KHP, see Kuo hua pao.

Krejci, Jaroslav (1991), 'From the Margins to Centre Stage', *The Times Higher Education Supplement*, 15 February.

Kuan Wên-ch'ing (1976), *Chung-kuo yin tan wai shih* (Hong Kong: Kuang-chüeh-ching ch'u-pan-shê).

Kuang-chou hsin jih-pao (1933) (Canton: Kuang-chou hsin jih-pao shê).

Kuang-chou min-kuo jih-pao chiao-yü lan (1934–5) (Canton: Kuang-chou min-kuo jih-pao shê).

Kuang-chou nien-chien pien tsuan wei-yüan-hui (1935) (ed.), *Kuang-chou nien-chien*, 2 vols. (Canton: Kuang-chou nien-chien pien tsuan wei-yüan-hui).

Kuang-chou shih-chêng-fu (1933), *Kuang-chou shih chêng-fu liang-nien lai shih-chêng pao kao shu* (Canton).

Kuang-chou-shih-chêng-fu (1934*a*) (ed.), *Kuang-chou-shih chih po-yin-t'ai* (Canton, 1921–36).

——(1934*b*), *Kuang-chou shih-cheng-fu erh nien nai chi kung-tso pao-kao* (Canton).

——(1934*c*) (ed.), *Kuang-chou shih-chêng-fu hsin chu lo-ch'êng chi-nien tê-k'an (HCLCCN)* (Canton).

Kuang-chou-shih chêng-hsieh wên shih tzu-liao yen-chiu wei-yüan-hui (1987) (ed.), *Nan t'ien sui yüeh: Ch'en Chi-t'ang chu Yüeh shih-ch'i chien wên shih lu* (Canton: Kuang-tung jên-min ch'u-pan-shê).

Kuang-chou tsa chih (KCTC) (1924–1930s) (Canton: Kuang-chou tsa chih shê).

Kuang-tung chung-hsüeh hsüeh-shêng tzu-chih-hui (1933) (ed.), *Kuang-tung hsüeh-shêng (KTHS)* (Canton), ii.

——(1934), *Kuang-tung hsüeh-shêng (KTHS)* (Canton), iv.

Kuang-tung shêng-chêng-fu (ed.), *Kuang-tung shêng-chêng-fu kung pao* (Canton: 1920s–1930s).

Kuang-tung ts'ai-chêng-t'ing (1930) (ed.), *Kai-chin ch'üan shêng chung-têng hsüeh-hsiao chiao-yü fang-an* (Canton).

Kung-p'ing pao (KPP) (1924–1949) (Canton: Kuang-chou Kung-p'ing pao shê).

Kuo hua pao (KHP) (1927), 9 December.

Lee, Bing-shuey Edward (1936), *Modern Canton* (Shanghai: Kelly & Walsh).

Lee, Leo Ou-fan (1973), *The Romantic Generation of Modern Chinese Writers* (Cambridge, Mass.: Harvard University Press).

Lee Tai-cho (1936). *Hsiang-kang chih-pi yu Kuang-chou wu-chia chih ch'u-pu yen-chiu* (Canton: Kuang-tung shêng-li Hsiang-chin ta-hsüeh Shang-hsüeh yüan).

Li Chien-êrh (1941), *Kuang-tung hsien-tai hua-jên ch'uan* (n.p.).

Li Han-ch'iao (1930), *T'ui ch'uang chi* (Canton: Tai-shan shu-tien).

Li Hou and Ch'u Shih (1934), 'Mo-têng nan yü mo-têng nü chih pi-chiao', *YHP*, 19 September.

Li Hsüeh-ying (1935), 'Chung-kuo fu-nü tsen yang tsai nêng t'i kao ti-wei', *Hsin hsin* 1/1, January.

Li Tsung-huang (1922), *Hsin Kuang-tung kuan-ch'a chi* (Shanghai: Shang-wu yin-shu-kuan).

Liang Ping-ao (1925), 'T'a-mên p'u-shih Chung-kuo jên ma?', *KCMKJP*, 13 July.

Liang Yen-hsien (1934), 'Lung-k'ao fan-chüeh ti mo-têng ch'ing-nien', *YHP*, 17 October.

Liao Kuang-sheng (1986), *Antiforeignism and Modernization in China, 1860–1980* (Hong Kong: Chinese University Press).

Liao Shu-lun (1948) (ed.), *Kuang-chou ta kuan* (Canton: T'ien nan ch'u-pan-shê).

Lin Chin-chih and Ts'ang Wei-chi 1989) (eds.), *Chin-tai hua-ch'iao t'ou-tzu kuo nei chieh-yeh shih tzu-liao hsüan chi* (Hsia-mên: Fu-chien jên-min ch'u-pan-shê).

Liu Ching-chih (1988) (ed.), *Chung-kuo hsin yin-yüeh shih lun chi* (Hong Kong: Centre of Asian Studies, Hong Kong University).

Liu P'ing (1934), 'Tien-pan chao-tai ku-k'ê t'i yen-kuang', *YHP*, 23 September.

Liu Tsai-su (1926), *Kuang-chou kuai-lan* (Shanghai: Shih-chieh shu-chü).

Liu Yu-lun (1930), 'Wei ti-chang t'ien-ju yün-tung kao kê-ming fu-nü', in Fêng-su kai-kê wei-yüan-hui (ed.), *Fêng-su kai-kê ts'ung k'an* (*FSKKTK*) (Canton: Kuang-chou-tê-pieh-shih tang-pu hsüan-ch'uan-pu).

Lo Hai-sha (1937), 'Min-tsu fu-hsing yün-tung chung hsin-hsi-chü ti chien-li', *Hsi-chü i-shu* 1.

Lo Kuan-wei (1934), in Lü Hsüeh-hai (ed.), *Ch'üan-pên hsi-hua yen-lun chi* (*CPHH*) (Canton: Ling-nan ta-hsüeh hsüeh-shêng tzu-chih hui), i.

Lü Hsüeh-hai (1935), 'Wei ch'üan-pen hsi-hua-lun ta K'o Nan', in Fêng En-yung (ed.), *Ch'üan-pên hsi-hua yen-lun su-chi* (*CPHH*) (Canton: Ling-nan ta-hsüeh hsüeh-shêng tzu-chih hui ch'u-pan-shê), ii.

Lü P'ing (1925), 'Chê-shih shih-mo hua', *KCMKJP*, 9 July.

Mao Tun et al. (1936) (ed.), *Chung-kuo ti i jih* (Shanghai: Shêng-huo shu-tien).

Metcalf, Thomas R. (1989), *An Imperial Vision: Indian Architecture and Britain's Raj* (Berkeley: University of California Press).

Murphey, Rhoads (1974), 'The Treaty Ports in China's Modernization', in Mark Elvin and G. William Skinner (eds.), *The Chinese City Between Two Worlds* (Stanford: Stanford University Press).

Nan-yang shang-pao (*NYSP*) (1928) (Singapore:Nan-yang shang-pao shê), 10 January.

Ng Yong-sang (Wu Yang-shêng) (1936), *Canton: City of the Rams (Canton: M. S. Cheung).*

Ou An-nien et al. (1987), *Ling-nan chang ku* (Canton: Kuang-tung lü-yu ch'u-pan-shê).

Ou-yang Shan (1935), *Ch'i-nien chi* (Shanghai: Shêng-huo shu-tien).

——(1948), 'Tsai shen ching li', in *Shih-pai ti shih-pai-chê* (Shanghai: Ch'iao-fêng ch'u-pan-shê).

Ou-yang Yü-ch'ien (1929), 'Hsi-chü kai-kê chih li-lun yü shih-chi', *Hsi-chü* 1.

Pai Tan (1923), 'Ying-hsi tsa t'an', *KCMKJP*, 17 November.

Pan-chiao man-hua 6/1 (1932).

P'iao p'iao hua pao 1 (1929) (Canton: P'ing shê).

Raychaudhuri, Tapan (1988), *Europe Reconsidered: Perceptions of the West in Nineteenth-Century Bengal* (Delhi: Oxford University Press).

Rea, Kenneth (1977) (ed.), *Canton in Revolution: The Collected Papers of Earl Swisher, 1925–1928* (San Francisco: Westview).

Redfield, Robert, and Singer, Milton (1969), 'The Cultural Role of Cities', in Richard Sennett (ed.), *Classic Essays on the Culture of Cities* (New York: Prentice-Hall).

Rhoads, Edward J. M. (1975), *China's Republican Revolution: The Case of Kwangtung, 1895–1913* (Cambridge, Mass.: Harvard University Press).

Shih-jih t'an hsün-k'an shê (1934) (ed.), *Shih-jih t'an hao wai tsêng k'an hsüeh-shêng shêng-huo tê chi* (Shanghai: T'i-i ch'u-pan-shê).

Smith, H. S. (1939), *Diary of Events and the Progress on Shameen, 1859–1938* (Hong Kong: Ye Olde Printerie).

T'an Yü-chien (1934), 'Sze-shih-ch'i nien lai Kuang-tung pao-yeh shih k'ai lü', in Hua-tzu jih pao pien-chi pu (ed.), *Hua-tzu jih pao ch'i-shih-i chou-nien chi-nien k'an* (Hong Kong: Hua-jih jih-pao yin-yeh pu).

T'ang Kê (1934), 'Lun nü-jên ti mei yü ch'ou' and 'Wo ti chêng-hu nü-jên fa', *KCTC* 33, December.

T'ang Ti-shêng (*c.*1930s), *Yen Shui-shêng* (Canton: I-wên-t'ang shu-chü).

T'ao Wei (1925), 'Kuang-chou chih pao-chih', *KCMKJP*, 9 July.

Têng Chung-hsia (1980*a*), 'I nien lai Shêng-Kang pa-kung ti ching-kuo', *Ti-i-tz'u kuo-nei kê-ming chan-chên shih-ch'i ti kung-jên yün-tung* (Peking: Jên-min ch'u-pan-shê).

——(1980*b*), 'Sheng-Chiang pa-kung ti sheng-li', *Ti-i-tzu kuo-nei kê-ming chan-chêng shih-ch'i ti kung-jên yün-tung* (Peking: Jên-min ch'u-pan-shê).

Ting Yu Kung (pseud.) (1928), 'Kang-hua Pien Pien', in *KPP*, 15 March.

Ts'ai Ch'ien (1939), *Yüeh-shêng tui wai mou-i tiao-ch'a pao kao* (Shanghai: Shang-wu yin-shu-kuan).

Ts'ai Yung-fan (2001), *Hsiang-kang jên chih Hsiang-kang shih* (Hong Kong: Oxford University Press).

Tsê An and Wei Chih (1933), 'T'ien-hai sui-pi', *KTHS* ii.

Tsin, Michael Tsang-woon (1999), *Nation, Governance and Modernity in China: Canton, 1900–1927* (Berkeley: University of California Press).

Tzu-hang-shih (1919) (ed.), *Kuang-chou chih-nan* (Canton: Hsin hua shu-tien).

Waley, Arthur (1960), *The Opium War Through Chinese Eyes* (London: George Allen & Unwin).

Waln, Nora (1933), *The House of Exile* (London: Cresset).

Wood, Frances (1985), *Chinese Illustration* (London: The British Library).

Wu Ju-chou (1933), 'Hsin-nien sui pi', *KTHS* ii.

YHKPK, see Chin-tai Kuang-chou k'ou-an ching-chi shê-hui kai-k'uang.

'Yin-yüeh kan-tung li chih fên-hsi' (1926), *KCMKJP* supplement, 4 November.

Yüan (1924), 'Fan-tui Chi-tu-chiao ho fan ti-kuo-chu-i', *KCTC* 1/1.

Yüeh-hua pao (*YHP*) (1927–50) (Canton: Yüeh-hua pao shê).

Yung Shêng (1924), 'Ssu-chang chi tang yen-chin', *KCMKJP*, 15 April.

3

The 'Problem' of Opium Smoking in Canton

With official and moralistic views predominating on the subject of opium smoking, public statements about opium in China have always been characterized by emotionalism and outright denunciation. The main aim of this chapter is to get behind the arguments expounded in anti-opium literature of our period, in order to construct a more balanced view of certain political, social, and cultural issues related to opium smoking in Canton.

1. THE EXTENT OF THE PROBLEM—AN ENIGMA

It is never easy to know for certain the true extent of the problem of opium consumption in Canton throughout the period under study for the simple reason that neither the Ch'ing administrators nor their Republican successors displayed much urgency or concern about the necessity of keeping records of the number of opium divans or shops and opium smokers in this city. They were, however, concerned about the opium revenue. But since the collection of this revenue was farmed out to tax brokers most of the time, it came as no surprise that no relatively detailed official record of this prominent social phenomenon is available. All existing statistical figures on this trade, therefore, are largely sketchy and never continuous.

Writing in the early 1890s about the situation of opium smoking in Canton, a missionary states that 'in every Chinese town there are opium dens'; and that 'six out of ten adult men smoke opium'. Although 'no reliable statistics of the extent of the vice are attainable', he is convinced that opium smoking 'is an evil of great magnitude and continually increasing' (Turner 1982: 45–7). An anti-opiumist writes: 'Since Kwangtung is the old base of opium [importation], its high number of opium addicts is understandable' (Yü En-tê 1934: 181). The situation was certainly a worrying one. It is, however, uncertain whether the scale of the 'plague' was as bad as it was claimed. In 1884, when the cash-hungry local government announced its plan to tax the sale of prepared opium by farming out the endeavour to a merchant-run bureau, opium retailers in Canton and the island of Ho-nan, over a thousand people representing more than 1,600 opium retail shops excluding opium dens, gathered to form a guild and looked into the possibility of collective action, not against the idea of taxing sales of opium, but of introducing tax farming on the commodity.[1] This was not a small number, but did not reach the extent the Revd John Turner described.

Archival materials from the Canton branch of the Imperial Maritime Customs provided clues to the situation, despite the fact that this office always reminded its readers of the unavailability of any comprehensive and accurate statistics on both the situation of smuggled foreign opium and the traffic of Chinese opium. In the 1877 annual report of the Canton Customs house, it was estimated that a total of 15,000 *piculs* of opium was imported into Kwangtung during the year, of which 1,500 to 2,000 *piculs* was consumed in Canton and its adjacent rural districts. Meanwhile, no more than 160 *piculs* of Chinese opium was supposedly consumed by smokers in the city of Canton (*YHKPK* 1996: 181–5). Assuming that an 'ordinary' addict took on average 0.5 *tael* of opium per day, this amount of imported and native opium, if all was sold, could sustain the opium habit of approximately 18,500 people in Canton. By the end of the nineteenth century, the Canton Customs recorded a rise in the amount of both foreign and Chinese opium imported into Kwangtung: in 1895 and 1896, for instance, 5,900 *piculs* of foreign opium and 6,000 *piculs* of native opium were known to have been shipped into the province (ibid. 358, 365). On the surface, these figures represented a big leap from that of the 1870s. Attention, however, must be drawn to the fact that the statistics were for the whole of Kwangtung rather than Canton alone. Moreover, towards the end of the nineteenth century, as it was reported in these Customs reports, popular consumption of foreign opium was already increasingly being replaced by that of Chinese opium. Indian opium had by then become a commonly used ingredient, mixed with the native Chinese produce as a flavour enhancer. In the last year of the Ch'ing's rule, the Kwangtung Opium Suppression Bureau had submitted to Peking, in response to a nation-wide operation of data collection for the Chinese delegates at a International Conference on Opium Suppression held in the Hague, a 'detailed report' on the situation of opium smoking in the province. The report stated that in Kwangtung province the number of shops selling raw opium had decreased from 'originally' 2,051 down to 1,346, while shops selling prepared opium were down from 7,291 to 5,481. The report also proudly claimed that its 177 Opium Termination Institutions had succeeded in detoxicating 111,608 addicts, leaving in Kwangtung a total of 317,811 opium users (*Shen pao* 1910, 7 Sept.). The popularity of opium was indubitable, but apparently not to an apocalyptic extent.

Had the situation during the Republican and the Nationalist periods worsened? Despite Chinese Communist history books doing their best to demonstrate that the opium problem was aggravated in China throughout the Republican era for such familiar reasons as corruption of KMT, the rise of warlordism, and so on, not much substantial evidence has been produced when it comes to the case of Canton and Kwangtung. In fact, concrete and reliable information in this area is hard to come by. Extant and sketchy archival and unofficial materials, which are available for analysis during the time of this research, indicated that the problem, though still vividly there, might not have deteriorated as irreversibly as supposed. For example, a 1927 unpublished report of a social survey conducted by a small team of officers from the municipal government's Social Bureau stated that the authorities had succeeded in closing down a great number of unlicensed opium divans that had been operating 'freely' under the aegis of the 'guest soldiers' stationed in Canton between 1923 and 1925. The report provides some simple statistics on the number of licensed opium divans (for both smoking and retailing purposes) which are rarely mentioned elsewhere: 72 shops in Canton city proper including one floating establishment, and 255 in the whole area of Ho-nan island.[2] A Japanese source in the early 1930s notes that the number of male opium addicts in Kwangtung has decreased from 'the alleged past 33% to [the present] 10%' of the male adult population.[3] This general trend of decline may apply to Canton as well. During the early and mid-1930s, it was reported in newspapers that the number of low-class opium dens was mushrooming in Canton because more and more smokers, especially those from such low-income occupational groups as rickshaw-pullers and coolies, turned to a kind of adulterated opium sold mainly at these places. In 1936, there was believed to be about 400 of these establishments in Canton. It must be noted that many of these low-class divans were small or operated as a sideline by rickshaw companies whose clients were mostly rickshawmen (*YHP* 1933: 1, 25 June; 1934: 1, 4 Oct.; 1936: 9, 3 Nov.). Hence, the increase in the number of divans might not necessarily reflect a similar rise in the population of addicts. In 1937, a Canton Opium Suppression Committee was formed with the task of controlling the sale of opium, and implementing the scheme of compulsory registration of 'opium users' (*yen min*) in Canton. Under the combined efforts of extensive publicity, persuasion, and coercion, lasting for a period of over six months, a total of 21,721 opium addicts were reportedly registered, though the Canton Opium Suppression Committee believed, but without further explication, that these represented only half of the total number of drug addicts in Canton.[4] Even if the Committee's hunch might not be too far from the real picture, the number of opium users in Canton still only accounted for, at most, roughly 4 per cent of the city's population during the late 1930s.

Although slightly out of the time-frame of this study, it is still worthwhile to mention that on the eve of the 'liberation' of Canton in October 1949, a leftist newspaper printed an article under a somewhat sensational heading: 'The City of Rams has turned into a world of opium smoking and gambling.' To 'substantiate' its argument, the article wrote about the seriousness of the problem by citing police figures on arrest for the first quarter of 1949: a total of 199 people were arrested for 69 cases of opium violations and 493 people for gambling violations.[5] Such statistics, however, do not appear to be any more alarming than the situation during the 1920s, nor to indicate a serious deterioration. In 1928, for instance, the police force in Canton arrested a total of 2,547 people in connection with gambling and opium violations.[6] Without further substantive evidence, it is quite hard to believe that the problem of opium in Canton was truly as aggravated as professed. In June 1951, the new Communist authorities launched its first mass campaign against opium and narcotic drugs in Canton. A press release for this campaign provides us with some statistics pertinent to our discussion. It stated that since Liberation up to the date of the report, the city's police force had successfully uncovered and dealt with 214 cases of opium and [other narcotic] drugs production and sale, with 3,349 opium divans (probably including places where other narcotic drugs were sold) closed down, and 7,077 people arrested for drugs offences. Total seizures included: about 5.8 *piculs* of raw and prepared opium, 194 *taels* of morphine, 155 *taels* of heroin, 80 *taels* and 30 bags of 'red pills', 199 *taels* of dross opium, 13,000 lamps for smoking purposes, 12,555 smoking pipes, and 1,224 opium weights. In the first quarter of 1951, the authorities intensified its campaign of compulsory registration of drug users in Canton. Under the combined efforts of intensive publicity (blackboards and large banners painted with slogans and hung up all over the city), and intensive persuasion undertaken by the street associations and relatives of the drug addicts, the Opium Suppression Committee of Canton was quite happy with the result: a total of 4,762 addicts were eventually registered, of whom 1,069 had been smoking for less than ten years, 1,393 for 10 to 20 years, 705 for 20 to 40 years, and 89 for over 40 years. All these 'addicts' and 2,000 of their relatives were 'invited' to take part in a public event in which all the confiscated smoking apparatus and a heap of narcotic drugs were burnt in a public sports ground, in commemoration of a similar 'heroic act' by Lin Tsê-hsü in 1839 (*NFJP* 1951, 3 June). At a time when public surveillance of the urban populace had become increasingly effective, these figures could be fairly accurate in reflecting the extent of the problem, which was not as alarming as we are taught to believe.[7]

The true extent of the problem of opium smoking in Canton is an enigma. Politically it was a dangerous subject to write about, though no official censorship of it was ever formally legislated. In non-official contemporary guidebooks to Canton, even general information on opium divans did not appear. Considering the fact that these guides gave descriptions of prostitution and gambling, and indeed specific names and addresses for some brothels in Canton, the absence of similar information on opium might indicate an official blackout of information.[8] In comparison with the late-Ch'ing administration, successive Nationalist regimes in Canton appear to be more cautious in releasing data about opium within their jurisdiction. For instance, one could find in a late-Ch'ing official work a relatively lengthy description of the history and current situation of opium taxation in Kwangtung. A lengthy 1934 book of a similar nature, published by the provincial government, contains disappointingly little useful or detailed information on opium.[9] Since the KMT authorities in Canton officially publicized this southern city as 'the cradle of the Chinese Revolution', and the Nationalists as legitimate heirs of this Revolution whose origin was traced back to the Opium War, any report on the widespread persistence of an 'opium problem' would have spoilt that painstakingly constructed revolutionary image. At least one reporter was arrested for reporting the spread of illegal gambling and unlicensed opium smoking in the suburbs of Canton (*NYSP* 1928: 11, 27 Dec.).

Except for a brief period in July 1925, when a group of relatively radical journalists, who had seemingly a strong control over a pro-Nationalist local newspaper, *Kuang-chou min-kuo jih-pao*, released their deep frustration at the insincerity of the government and the military authorities in suppressing gambling and opium by printing, on consecutive days for over a month, a long list of locations in different parts of Kwangtung where illicit gambling and opium divans were (reported by readers) openly operated under the aegis of bribed officials or military officers (*KCMKJP* 1925, July and Aug. *passim*). Resolute efforts like this were, however, short-lived and rare.

Nevertheless, these statistics, fragmentary though they are, serve to reveal the KMT's predicament on the opium question. On the one hand, its authorities were eagerly promoting the image of a victimized China plagued by opium via a conspiracy of the foreign powers. On the other hand, it was also trying hard to conceal its failure in suppressing opium use. This led, therefore, to an ironic situation. While the government was making sensational allegations about the steady deterioration of the situation with opium, it withheld (or perhaps failed to produce) reliable figures that could have demonstrated how bad the situation was. When official statistics on the subject were occasionally released, they suggested only the mildness of the problem, relative to the well-nigh apocalyptic picture in official propaganda.

Although popular attitudes to opium smoking were apparently more ambiguous than inimical, it does not follow that the number of opium users had then to be constantly on the rise. Opium was seemingly losing its attraction for modern literati, whose Imperial-era counterparts had been regular users of the drug.[10] Modern education, the intensity of anti-opium publicity in schools, and the proliferation of anti-opium literary works,[11] all apparently helped to discourage young students from consuming opium (and most student magazines of this period do not even hint at the spread of opium or other drugs among student circles).[12] This was reflected by an opinion poll conducted by the KMT Canton Office in 1929. In this exercise, thirty thousand questionnaires were sent out to 'the public', which, in all likelihood, was referring to school students and the well-educated as judged by the kinds of questions asked, such as 'Do you believe in the Three Principles of the People?' According to this poll, 'many citizens of Canton' believed that opium and gambling were pernicious to China (P'u Liang-chu 1929: 214).

Moreover, although prolonged working hours and hard routine seemingly drove many to seek relief in opium, it does not follow that the drug must therefore be 'endemic' among the working class in Canton. In a 1934 survey of some three hundred Cantonese workers' families, only five workers were noted for spending a 'certain amount' of their income on smoking opium as a pastime (Yü Ch'i-chung 1934: 65–7).[13] Of the 609 inhabitants in the boat-people community of Sha-nan in Canton, only 15 men were opium addicts. In Chiu-fêng-hụang village, which had about 750 inhabitants, two opium divans were said to entertain about 70 clients (details of their addiction not known) per day

(Wu Jui-lin and Huang En-lin 1935: 153; Wu Jui-lin 1934*a*: 103). Even Canton's rickshawmen, supposedly the occupational group with the highest concentration of opium addicts, were not all drug users. According to a social survey of 600 rickshawmen in Canton, 70 admitted that they smoked opium in their leisure time (Wu Jui-lin 1940: 25). The figure was by no means low, but not as detrimentally high as implied in anti-opium propaganda.

Although the amount of revenue generated by auctioning the opium-sale franchise in Canton rose steadily throughout the Republican period,[14] this may not necessarily have been due to an increase in the number of addicts in the city, but perhaps was a result of competition among tax farmers bidding for the franchise, or due to the sheer insatiable greed of the government for more revenue. The increase in the volume of native opium imported into Canton during this period[15] may be explained by a corresponding increase in the volume of opium trade via Canton into the hinterland, or out to Hong Kong, Canton having always been an 'important entrepôt' for the region's opium trade (*HTJP* 1936: 2.4, 29 Aug.; *NFJP* 1952, leader, 3 June).[16] Although the opium habit was still prevalent, it was noted to be 'less common than it used to be'.[17]

In anti-opium literature, the abusive use of other narcotic drugs such as morphine, cocaine, and heroin was said to be spreading in Kwangtung due to an 'Imperialist conspiracy' to 'poison' (*tu-hua*) China.[18] The use of morphine and heroin, however, was apparently more common among the poorer classes in North China than in the South.[19] Although it is evident that the traffic in and consumption of drugs had at least the connivance of local Japanese authorities in Formosa (and in other occupied areas of China after 1937), active official support is harder to prove.[20] After all, the number of opium divans and retail shops in Canton did not increase sharply during the Japanese occupation: 199 opium divans and 120 prepared-opium retail shops.[21] Moreover, there is a lack of evidence that the Japanese involvement as such was a conspiracy operated in connivance with the other Powers; in fact, the Western Powers were seemingly sincere in enforcing the League of Nations' decision to restrict the manufacture of dangerous drugs internationally, and the British authorities, for example, also actively enforced the prohibition in British concessions.[22] Furthermore, the major motive behind the unrestrained Japanese policy on opium and narcotic drugs was seemingly not that conspiratorial. In the observation of a British diplomat: 'It can be said with reasonable certainty that revenue, rather than any ulterior motive, such as the systematic demoralisation of the Chinese people, has represented the ruling factor in the encouragement of the opium and drug traffic in North China.'[23] In this sense, the Japanese authorities, the Republican and the Nationalist governments, and the warlord administrations shared a common motive for generating revenue as the basis of their narcotic drugs policy. One of the most publicized substitutes for opium were the professedly Japanese-made 'red pills' (*hung wan*), which were heroin, morphine, or other narcotic drugs adulterated with caffeine, quinine, arsenic, and edible sweetened flour or rice-balls (Lo Yün-yen 1938: 9,10).

Similar substitutes, however, had been sold in China in the late 1900s, well before the arrival of these 'red pills' in the 1910s (Ball 1903: 496). Some Chinese preferred red pills to opium for two reasons. First, the red pill were inexpensive and much less time-consuming to smoke, compared with opium. Secondly, its cigarette-like flavour was, especially for beginners in drug abuse, a lot less strong and repugnant than opium. Its additional attraction was that it was said to be able to keep its smoker's body cool in summer and warm in winter (Ch'en Nien-ti 1935: 12–13). Furthermore, by the 1930s, the Chinese themselves had become major manufacturers of these pills (Lo Yün-yen 1938: 9).[24] One report from the Canton Delta revealed that a powerful clan in one village had manufactured the drug for three years until they were stopped by the army. To protect this lucrative source of income, this family had employed a formidable private army and had armed guards deployed at strategic locations around the village (*HTJP* 1936: 3.4, 11 Aug.). Thus, by attributing the narcotics problem solely to a conspiracy of the Powers, or to the demoralization of addicts, the government again tried to cover up its failure to solve this problem,[25] and to capitalize on it by linking it sensationally to current anti-Japanese politics and sentiment.

On the situation of other narcotic drugs use, the British Consulate-General in Canton reported in 1930:

> there appears to be little illicit consumption of or traffic in drugs in Canton . . . The seizures of smuggled narcotics other than opium by the Canton Customs during the nine months . . . were small quantities apparently for legitimate medical use and only smuggled to evade duty . . . Local medical opinion is that drug addicts are rare in Canton and there is no evidence of the sale of cheap injections or drugs such as is to be found in certain parts of North China . . . It is probable that there is some illicit traffic but that it is small owing to the wide-spread use of opium.[26]

The situation was far less serious in Canton, and also seemingly in South China.[27] And yet, by magnifying the scale of this problem, the Canton authorities were apparently quite successful in inculcating its people with fear and hatred of the 'conspiring' Japanese, and diverted public attention, as well as all the blame, to the foreign powers. The propaganda value of narcotic drugs was immense.

It is interesting to note in passing that the problem of red pills was escalating at an alarming speed in Hong Kong by the end of 1936, as opium shops were all reportedly also selling red pills and vice versa (*HTJP* 1936: 7, 19 Aug.; 1936: 2.4, 29 Aug.). The situation in Canton, however, was unknown. Narcotic drugs such as morphine injection, notwithstanding their advantage of being cheaper than opium, were apparently unsuccessful in out-competing the latter among the low-class drug addicts in Canton as they did in North China. Since further empirical evidence is not available, the explanation of this phenomenon can only be reduced to conjecture. It might be that the poorer opium addicts in Canton were, by comparison, still better off than the lower-class Chinese in North China; or that in the eyes of these low-class opium users in Canton, the recreational pleasure obtained from the ritual-like process of opium or red pills smoking, which always involved the gathering of friends or colleagues, was too great to be easily replaced by the relatively lonely act of hypodermic injection; or possibly that the cost of low-grade adulterated opium in this part of China remained low enough for the poor to consume throughout this period; or that the Cantonese were more aware of the greater danger of heroin and morphine addiction, and hence, as long as choice was available, they remained faithful to opium.

2. THE LANGUAGES OF ANTI-OPIUM POLITICS: OFFICIAL RHETORIC, UNOFFICIAL REALITY

Since the persistence of opium smoking in Canton throughout a large part of the Republican period was an embarrassment to its professedly revolutionary government, the Cantonese authorities were anxious to publicize a totally denunciatory view on opium consumption. Sun Yat-sen's will, which expounded his notion of opium suppression, was widely quoted in nearly all anti-opium writings of this period.[28] In official propaganda, opium smoking was denounced as a social evil that condemned China and her people to a long history of acute national problems and crises:

> Everybody knows that smoking opium is harmful and without one single benefit. It causes physical emaciation [and] moral degradation to its users. Today, China is [so] being tormented by [the problem of] national weakness, and an impoverished population, that her people can barely survive. All these are [evidences of the] spreading injury done by opium!... Our race has become so puny that we should no longer refrain from denouncing that... race-corrupting poison [called] opium!... The cause of the unequal treaties... is the Opium War!... If we want to abolish the unequal treaties, we must [first] suppress opium! (*FSKKTK* 1930: 8, 26)

In this emotional speech delivered by the chairman of the Opium Suppression Committee, opium was pinpointed as the culprit of the humiliating chapter of modern Chinese history: encroachment by the imperialist powers, national weaknesses, military defeat, socio-economic bankruptcy, and partitioning by warlords, all contributed eventually to her debasement into a 'semi-colonial country'.

> Our country is huge and full of natural resources... Unfortunately, since the massive growing of opium poppy [in China] began, all the good fields are used for growing this poisonous crop. With [the subsequent] decrease in food production, food shortages often occur... [Hence] production has become backward, [and our] economy is in a panicking state... Side by side with the increase in opium production is the number of smokers. Families are being ruined, and [their] fortune dispersed. There is nothing that [an addict] will not do. Many [become] bandits and scoundrels... Peace no longer exists... The reputation of the country is declining, [and] our race is being corrupted day by day.[29]

By the late 1920s, 4 June, the date Commissioner Lin Tse-hsü ordered the destruction of the confiscated Indian opium at Bogue, had already been officially designated as National Anti-Opium Day, which was celebrated in the form of a mass meeting attended by government officials and local schools representatives in Canton. Like most officially held political meetings, slogan shouting by participants was one of the many salient features of this occasion. To disseminate and highlight the official perceptions of opium smoking, the Propaganda Bureau of the Nationalist Party in Canton, for instance, publicized eye-catching slogans with concise and straightforward messages: '(1) Opium is a poisonous thing that kills people without a trace of blood. (2) Opium is a virus that destroys humankind. (3) Opium is a chemical weapon (*lü-ch'i pao*, lit. green-gas cannon) that [foreign] imperialists [in China] used in exterminating another race . . .'(*YHP* 1930:5, 3 June).

Such sensational views were also widely shared by anti-opiumists among the general public. A Cantonese writer stated that China's commitment to opium suppression was the sole key to her revival as an internationally respectable nation. It would help her to defeat the warlords, to rebuild her international image, to create prosperity, and, most importantly, to become a strong race.

> Imported opium is already enough to suck our marrow dry. Moreover, since farmers in our country stop growing anything but poppy, it causes a shortage of grains worse than any year of famine . . . After being sold [and consumed] in society, opium damages and weakens our race. Years of military carnage have brought our country's vital energy to the brink of extinction; [and] opium [alone] is already enough to undermine all . . . the attempts to have our country cleansed and revitalized.
>
> (Hsü Ching-yüan 1924: 1–2, 'Essays')

On another official occasion of opium suppression campaign, opium damages on the Chinese race was further elaborated and ascertained, even professedly supported by scientific evidence.

> According to scientific analyses, opium contains a large number of poisonous substances; so far, at least 20 kinds [of such substances] are identified. . . . Our countrymen have already developed a habit of inhaling opium. Although not so many of them display signs of [acute] intoxication as severe as it has been stated in the above, it is [not as good] when coming to [symptomatic signs of] chronic intoxication. [Opium users with these signs of chronic intoxication] are rendered into sick persons whose power of thinking and appetite for food is weakened and shrinks day after day; they are wan and sallow in complexions, incapable of working long hours, continuously haunted by evil of diseases, [to the extent that life is becoming] low, sordid, and a waste of time. Their bodies though still alive, their spirits, however, have already long withered. (Ou-yang Hui-tsung 1937: 10–11)

But how accurate were these allegations about opium smoking as the prime cause of all China's national problems? Undoubtedly, opium consumption in China must have caused her many social and political problems, though not necessarily to that degree or in that manner. Behind these sensational allegations are misconceptions and exaggerations about the adverse effects of opium smoking on at least the Cantonese society in this period. Some of these allegations, such as the indelible link between warlordism and opium revenue, were by and large substantiated (we will discuss these later). The rest, however, were mainly rhetoric serving the political purposes of those who made them.

Opium was being used by the Republican and the Nationalist governments as a convenient excuse for their notable lack of success in building the ideal society that they had aspired to. Hence, opium smoking was denounced as a problem only when it was linked, though arbitrarily, to bigger and more acute national, diplomatic, and racial issues. In other words, opium smoking might not have constituted a problem by itself, if the more sensitive factors of imperialism, nationalism, and warlordism had not been somehow forcibly related to it. In the official view, opium smoking could no longer be seen as a personal problem, but as an individual problem in a collective environment and thus a social, political, and national problem too.

Modern Western Imperialists as the Culprits?

Opium was introduced into China during the T'ang Dynasty. Since poppies were already grown in Szechwan, a poet at that time revealed in one of his poems that the sight of these exotic plants reminded him that his journey home (Szechwan) would be over shortly (Yung Tao, 'Hsi kuei ch'u hsieh ku', cited in I Wu 1969: 194–5). The extent of poppy plantation in China at that time, however, is not known. Nevertheless, it suffices to show that poppies had been grown locally in western China long before the nineteenth century; it was not a totally new commodity or plant that covetous foreign traders smuggled into China only since the eighteenth century, an argument that most anti-opiumists in China had eagerly put forward in order to highlight the guilt of the West by underplaying the role of Chinese opium in the political discourse of opium 'catastrophe'. Moreover, by the middle of the 1830s, opium was already known to be produced in substantial quantities in the provinces of Yünnan, Chekiang, Kwangtung, Kwangsi, Fukien, Kweichow, and Szechwan; by 1860, only a handful of China's provinces were reportedly free of opium production (Lin Man-hung *c.*1980s: 189–94).[30]

As early as Northern Sung times, the medicinal value of opium poppy had been widely recognized. The famous Su Tung-p'o recorded the medicinal benefits of opium in one of his poems:

> Grind them (the seeds of poppy) into white powder, [and] use them for preparing watery rice called 'Buddha porridge'. Elders [who suffer from] weak vital energy, loss of appetite, indigestion for meat, deficiency in the taste, [can be treated with opium] boiled with honey in an earthenware basin. It is also good for mouth and throat, [since it] regulates the lungs and nourishes the stomach. With them, one can shut the door and not go out for three years without a slight thought of regret. With them, recluses and joyful monks would become speechless. A cupful [of it will be enough] to make one burst into delighted laughter. Although I am in Huan Tsun, [I feel] as if [I were] touring Lo Shan.[31]

'Buddha porridge' was apparently not a euphemism, but a truly honorific name that signified the contemporary experts' high regard for the medical effectiveness of this drug. In a medical manual compiled by a group of elitist herbal doctors published in *circa* AD 973, the effectiveness of poppy in treating poor appetite and in suppressing some symptomatic side-effects of practising alchemy was well recognized, and the seeds of the poppy were also favourably called 'imperial rice' (*yü mi*), implying that this drug had been presented to, and used by, the imperial court (*K'ai-pao pên-tsao*, cited in I Wu 1969: 195). A Sung imperial-court doctor has also written that 'to take [opium] frequently is beneficial to [a man's] metabolic activity, since it activates the vital energy in his bladder'. Other Sung herbal doctors, however, pointed out that despite poppy seeds and plants being known for their efficacy in treating dysentery, patients did not always resort to them in the first place because they believed that poppy was so strong in costive properties that it could stop them from discharging all unwanted and pernicious substances from their infected bodies. These Sung medical specialists, however, still spoke highly of the medicinal functions of the poppy—'how could this (i.e. dysentery) be cured without this drug?' To make good and proper use of this plant, they advised users to mix it with few other herbs so that unwanted side-effects could be suppressed and its 'miraculous function' obtained.[32]

The medicinal value of the poppy continued to be noted by doctors and scholars in the Yüan Dynasty, and its list of advantages also grew as compared with that of the earlier period. In addition to treating dysentery, poppy seeds were said to be a powerful agent of fatigue relief and cough suppressant, an effective stimulant that could strengthen a person's vital energy (*chi*) in an instant, and generally good for bone-related illness because of its ability to penetrate one's kidneys.[33] It is interesting to note that some 'old China hands' gathered from popular folk stories in Kwangtung and Soochow that opium smoking had been prevalent in China under the Mongols until the last day of their rule. In these stories, opium was said to have entered China after the return of Kublai Khan from his Indian campaign; the habit was so extensive that the country was said to have been impoverished by it. The first emperor of the Ming Dynasty, even before he assumed the title of Emperor, had consulted the legendary maestro of geomancy Liu Po-wên on how to exterminate it. To follow Liu's counsel, he sought aid from heaven. 'On the third day of his oblation, it rained blood or red rain, which destroyed the entire poppy crop, no more was allowed to grow, and the desire for it ceased.' In the eyes of a concerned scholar, 'it is in this way only that one can satisfactorily account for the eagerness which was exhibited by Chinamen to obtain the article when it first reached their shores by sea'.[34] Perhaps not a point that can be easily substantiated by textual evidence, it still indicated the long history of opium consumption well before 'the coming of the West' in the late eighteenth century.

By the times of the Ming Dynasty, opium was said to have become a popular medicine, and its poppy a favourite ornamental flower for Chinese poets and literati (Ball 1903: 488; Yü En-tê 1934: 2–3, Wang Hsiang-chin, *Ch'ün-fang-p'u* and Wang Shih, *Lien hua shuo*, in I Wu 1969: 196). The renowned Ming herbalist Li Shih-chên wrote that:

> Opium poppy looks like [a] capsule in shape; its seeds look like corns which are edible, and [it] is an item of food presented to the imperial throne. . . . Poppy is planted in autumn and grows in winter. Its young stems are extremely good as vegetarian food. . . . Poppy flowers blossom for 3 to 4 days before withering. The 'pod' (ying), which is about 1 to 2 inches in length, grows at the top of the stem . . . and contains tiny white-colour seeds that can be used for preparing porridge and rice. Mix[ed] with water . . . they turn into thick creamy paste, which is ideal for preparing a soured bean-curd dish if added [to] green-bean powder. They can also be [processed] for oil. Despite their [seedcases being] commonly used for preparing medicines, they were not recorded in [old] herbal encyclopaedia[s], which indicates that they were not used often by the ancients. . . . [Opium] smells bitter and sour, and is slightly poisonous. It cures diarrhoea and proctocele. [Since it also] invigorates the vitality of a man's sperm, it is used by many men as an aphrodisiac. [Some people are] selling it by the name of 'Golden Pills' in the Capital city, [and claim that] it can cure all common types of diseases. This is just a trick played by scoundrels [on ignorant folk]. (Yü En-tê 1934: 5–6)

The late-Ch'ing geographer Wei Yüan wrote that the use of opium as one of the active ingredients in many 'effective prescriptions' had already been mentioned in a number of herbal medical books published in the Ming times. Opium, then, had not yet been smoked (Wei Yüan, 'Hai-kuo t'u chih', in I Wu 1969: 198).[35]

These quotations indicate, first, that opium had been widely used for centuries as an active component of home-made as well as prescribed medicine without causing much concern to its users and the herbalists. As early as 1589 a custom duty was levied on opium which was being imported under the name 'foreign medicine' (*yang yao*) by Portuguese merchants via Macao (Lo Yün-yen 1938: 39; 'Ying-shu yüan-liu k'o', I Wu 1969: 198). By the late seventeenth century, opium was being legally imported from South East Asia under the category of medicine; and the Cantonese had already been using it so much that they had developed an indigenous and 'improved method' of inhaling opium from a bamboo-made pipe (Kōsaka Junichi 1943: 40).[36] The fact that throughout the seventeenth and eighteenth centuries imported opium was levied a rather light tariff might be an indication of the official recognition of the medicinal value of the drug to the people.[37]

Secondly, the poem by Su Tung-p'o shows that even a layman such as Su knew quite well the medical value and euphoric function of opium. It is also an important indication that already in Southern Sung times opium was being used as a 'pleasurable drug'. This contradicts the allegation put forward by many late-Ch'ing and Republican anti-opiumists that opium had been used *only* as a medicinal drug since its introduction into China until the mid-Ch'ing period; and that since then, it was abused as a pleasure drug, and hence degraded from being a medicine into a vicious and demoralizing 'poison' (*tu p'in*).[38] Moreover, a prose piece written in the late Ming period about the romantic experiences of two brothel-goers in Canton shows opium already served at such places, and for purposes other than medicinal, in the city (Chou Yu-liang, 'Chu-kiang Mei Liu chi', in Chang Meng-chêng 1938: 88). This is not surprising given the fact that its aphrodisiac properties had already been known since at least the Mongol period. Therefore, the motives of opium consumption were apparently so individualized and hence complicated that any simple generalization and periodization are bound to be naive and futile.[39]

To substantiate the argument that the rise of 'massive addiction' throughout the late Ch'ing and the Republican periods corresponded to the decline in performance of contemporary Chinese national politics is no easy task. One historian alleges that the devastating impact of decades of political turmoil and socio-economic flux throughout the Republican era so frustrated the Chinese people that many of them consequently turned to opium and other drugs for psychological escape.[40] Some people might use opium for this reason. But it is highly doubtful that this was a major cause of opium consumption. Pessimistic thoughts and frustration fill Cantonese literary writings during this era. Youthful depression, boredom with life, dissatisfaction with political or social realities tormented many young Cantonese intellectuals.[41] Surprisingly, however, none of them ever mentions or recommends the use of opium or other drugs as a route for psychological escape from this anomie. Moreover, it is doubtful whether frustration alone could be enough to turn a person into an abusive opium user.

Was opium a Poison? Were Opium Users Criminals?

In spite of the slowly growing popularity of opium since Sung Dynasty times, opium consumption had apparently never been denounced as a problem by the establishment, and this 'poisonous' drug was never officially prohibited. One plausible reason for this is that because opium consumption was not then linked to any major moral, political, or social issues, and because the scale of opium trade and the extent of foreign involvement in it were not yet alarming enough to form the apparent threat to China's national security that it did in the early nineteenth century, it escaped condemnation as a pernicious drug.[42]

This also pointed to the fact that opium was not then viewed as a definitively harmful and poisonous drug in the way late-Ch'ing, and especially 'modern', anti-opiumists have seen it. The fact that most of the pre-Ch'ing medical records about poppy and opium use did not mention any possible pernicious side-effects of this drug urges us to rethink the plausibility of anti-opium literature of the late-Ch'ing and the Republican periods, which portrayed opium as nothing but a poison for its users. It was clear that the anti-drugs literature had chosen to ignore the medicinal value of opium in order to highlight one-sidedly the intoxicating and addictive qualities of the drug. A number of recent clinical and scholarly studies on the subject of opiate addiction, however, reveal a very different picture than that put forward in Chinese anti-opium literature. One of these studies points out the medical fact that 'opiates themselves produce no directly damaging or life-shortening effects on the body and that addiction itself is not a physically damaging condition' (Berridge and Edwards 1981: 75–86, 278–81). Another clinical report, authored by a team of physicians at the Narcotic Wards of the Philadelphia General Hospital and published by the prestigious American Medical Association in Chicago, arrived at a similar conclusion:

> The study shows that morphine addiction is not characterized by physical deterioration or impairment of physical fitness aside from the addiction per se. There is no evidence of change in the circulatory, hepatic, renal and endocrine functions. When it is considered that these subjects had been addicted for at least five years, some of them for as long as twenty years, these negative observations are highly significant. The study offers substantial grounds for the belief that were it possible to relieve the addict of his addiction complete rehabilitation could be expected. (Light et al. 1929–30: 115–16)

Drawing on their clinical knowledge, two American physicians wrote that symptoms of opiates intoxication 'are evidence of the use of excessive doses rather than of the condition when smaller doses are employed, and are observable, for the most part, only in advanced cases where great abuse, associated with insufficient food, the use of other drugs, or general unhygienic conditions, has been practiced' (Terry and Pellens 1970: 429).[43] Moreover, opium was commonly used as a medicine for its effective pain relieving quality.[44] Even an anti-opium writer acknowledged the medicinal value of opium, despite its alleged 'socially devastating' impact: 'Originally, poppy is an excellent disease-curing medicine. It can cure coughing, dysentery, "stomach-turning", vomiting; and can overhaul and strengthen [one's] energy-vitality, and so on... Opium occupies an remarkable position in pharmacology. It mitigates pain, promotes sleep, allays troubles such as diabetes, diarrhoea, excessive urination, and others' (Lo Tzu-ch'in 1933: 2).[45] Similar high regard on opium as a medicine that 'cures diseases' (*ch'ih ping chih hsiao tien*) was also noted, ironically, in a book of an anti-opium theme. In three full pages, all the favourable medicinal qualities of opium are listed and elaborated: to suppress acute and chronic pains arising from all kinds of diseases and complaints without causing the side-effect of loss of strength; to soothe blood circulation in patients with heart diseases; to relieve severe panting arising from neurotic or bronchitis problems; to quieten the symptom of vomiting arising from all kinds of gastric trouble, including ulcer; to suppress the diarrhoea symptom of dysentery, cholera, and tuberculosis; to help reduce the level of urinal dextrose in patients of diabetes; to treat chronic insomnia, and so on (Kao Hsiang-li: n.d.: 13–16).[46]

Opium was, if not a panacea, then at least a highly effective analgesic, rather than just a 'poison' as constructed in anti-opium rhetoric. Its importance as popular medicine was seemingly buttressed by the self-medication tradition of the Chinese, to whom hospitals and clinics were only a 'modern innovation' beyond the financial reach of the general public.[47] In fact, it was commonly believed that the growing popularity of opium consumption in Kwangtung since the Ch'ien-lung period was due to a somewhat accidental discovery of the medicinal efficacy of this drug by a chronically ill nun. According to this story, there was once a young widow from a wealthy household who was so heart-broken by the premature death of her husband that she decided to become a nun. A life of solitude and grief in the following decades cost her dearly in respect of health: her legs had become nearly paralysed and she could hardly sit or stand. Her parents had tried almost everything to redress her muscular complaint, but to no avail. To keep their daughter amused, the parents had once presented to her a set of playthings that they had received earlier from Canton 'factory' merchants; they included a crane made of bamboo, a lamp, a bottle of perfume, and some opium. One day, when she played with these curios, she discovered that they could be used to smoke opium. She also realized that her leg disease could be treated by inhaling the fumes, and the effect was miraculous: she felt comfortable and relaxed, she was able to stretch her legs at will and to walk as if the illness had completely gone. The next morning, however, her old complaint returned, and was subsequently relieved only after puffs of opium had been inhaled. From that time she was habituated to opium, which she smoked every day. Her leg problem, as a result, was gone as if, in the eyes of her relatives, a miracle had occurred. After the news of her 'miraculous' recovery had reached the neighbourhood and other villages in the area, patients who had been suffering from chronic or acute diseases such as malaria, dysentery, asthma, pain in the air passages, and stomach and liver troubles, began to imitate this nun by treating their complaints with opium; and all their diseases, we are told, were consequently cured. The medical reputation of opium was then spreading far and wide.[48]

An old resident of Canton reminisces vividly that his father was from time to time requested by their neighbours and good friends to give them a tiny portion of the opium ashes accumulated in the bowl of his expensive smoking pipe; these hardened ashes, which were commonly regarded as a powerful analgesic for the sick, and a longevity-boosting tonic for the healthy, would be drunk with water or tea. Being a modestly well-off gambling-house partner, his father could afford to consume high-grade opium whose ashes were generally believed to be in particular more efficacious for its medicinal functions; and that explains his father's popularity in the neighbourhood.[49] Moreover, as long as the self-medication tradition was alive, and opium easily available, the drug might be commonly prescribed by traditional Chinese doctors or herbalists. An anti-opiumist attributed the rise in opium addiction in China in the 1930s to the 'irresponsible actions of quack doctors' who readily recommended opium to their patients (Lo Yün-yen 1938: 18).[50] But it is unreasonable to denounce those doctors who prescribed opium to their patients as 'quacks', especially when the drug was actually effective for a number of minor complaints. Moreover, there is clinical evidence to show that patients who use opiates to the point of physical dependence do not necessarily become addicted, that is, taking it when there is no need, nor do they necessarily have to resort to it except when the disease recurs (Lindesmith 1968: 54–5).[51] Those Chinese 'quacks' who prescribed opium to their patients may also have learnt the pharmacological facts of opium from clinical experience.

An ironic case helps reveal the medicinal value of the drug. Lo-lo Chu-shih, a late-Ch'ing scholar who had composed a play with a strong anti-opium stance, wrote that the story was inspired by the real-life experience of another scholar-literati, Li Chien-lou. Li, who was praised by Lo-lo as a prolific composer of many beautifully written anti-opium popular songs, had fallen quite ill in his middle age, which consequently and ironically led him to resort to opium for treatment. Li indulged in opium smoking until, very likely, his death.[52] The medicinal power of opium was seemingly irreplaceable.

From the first-year admission record of the Canton Opium Addiction Termination Hospital, we learn that nearly half its inmates alleged that they consumed opium only for medical reasons such as treating stomach trouble, coughing, syphilis, and other chronic diseases.[53] 'Coughing' in this case might mean tuberculosis, pneumonia, or bronchitis. According to a newspaper advertisement in 1931, tuberculosis was ranked first among the causes of mortality in Canton.[54] Opium helped to 'alleviate symptoms, subduing coughing, expectoration and pain even if it could not touch the root cause' (Berridge and Edwards 1981: 67).[55] It was seemingly an important palliative especially for poor patients, since there was then no sanatorium for tuberculosis sufferers in Canton, and 'poverty is the factor in causing and intensifying' the disease (Lamson 1935: 341) In a social survey of 600 rickshawmen in Canton, 73 of them were noted as pursuing the opium habit in their spare time. Although the survey did not hint at the reasons for their consumption, it did show that more than 60 of these rickshawmen were suffering from diseases such as tuberculosis, coughing, chest pain, cardiac pain, stomach trouble, asthma, rheumatism, orthopaedic complaints, beri beri, and so on; for most of these complaints, opium was popularly known and clinically verified as an effective agent in treating some of the symptoms. Given the fact that these victims were too poor to afford any clinical treatment, as they all came from an indigent background, they were in all likelihood forced by circumstances to resort to opium for self-medication purposes, and these two sets of figures, therefore, seemingly help explain the cause of addiction for this group of users (Wu Jui-lin 1940: 24–6).

It must be mentioned that Taiwanese data from the Japanese colonial period provide even stronger and clearer evidence on similarly causative relations between opium consumption and medical treatment. In a contemporary detailed study on opium addiction conducted by a renowned Japan-educated Chinese physician in Taipei's Government Central Hospital, it was noted that the motive for using opium for the majority of habitual addicts, most of them workers employed in manual and low-paid jobs, was for therapeutic treatment for their illnesses (Tu Tsung-ming 1953: ii. 589–90, 594–5). Although the situation in Taiwan did not necessarily mirror other parts of China, it still showed that opium was rather popularly consumed by the city poor for its positive medical properties, just as evidence from Canton and Peking also indicated.[56]

In spite of this, these likely medical users of opium were still indiscriminately stigmatized as addicts, instead of as patients, in the admission record of the Canton Opium Addiction Termination Hospital.[57] Moreover, on the same admission record, the cause of addiction for the rest of the non-medical-users of opium was collectively classified as 'playing with it' (*wan nung*)—an intention to play down the complex social causes of opium consumption (especially among the working class) by playing up the individual and moral factors, which marginalized the public image of opium users as morally irresponsible, and thus less pitiable, pariahs.

By deliberately understating the medicinal cause and value of the opium issue in China, these anti-opium 'modern' physicians tried to redefine the functions of the drug from what it had been popularly construed and experienced into a highly ideological and much-filtered pharmaceutical interpretation. Opium users who resorted to the drug for its medicinal properties were described in the new discourse as 'ignorant people' who mistook (or were deceived by other equally ignorant people) opium as medicine.[58] This, however, did not do justice to many contemporary users of opium who had made a rational choice of a form of medication that they learned from their own or others' experiences was both affordable and therapeutically effective, as long as they were careful not to overdose. What had once been a rational choice was eventually rearticulated as irrational, ignorant, and even anti-social and anti-state.

Opium users were criminalized as well. Although inmates of this hospital were admitted for various reasons—being mainly referred there by the police for possessing unlicensed opiates, where some were admitted on a voluntary basis—they were just treated like criminals. Hence, all the inmates, before being formally admitted, were required to sign a pledge and confession in which the signatory

> has confessed without counter-pleading that [he has been] consuming opium or other toxic poisonous drugs. [But] now, [the signatory] realizes that opium or toxic drugs are goods which threaten our country and corrupt our race, and hence has decided to . . . stay in this Hospital where he will be treated for terminating the addiction . . . Under no circumstances will [he] withdraw from his treatment or leave this Hospital without the approval of the Head of this Hospital.

Before his official discharge, each patient was required to sign another pledge, with a complete set of his fingerprints inked on it, that he would not violate the Opium Suppression Ordinance in future (Kuang-chou-shih chieh-yen i-yüan 1937: 6–7, Tables).

Behind this official 'disease and criminal theory' of opium users was a strong class bias. Judged by the occupational backgrounds of its inmates—pedlars, workers, coolies, rickshawmen, and the unemployed—this was a hospital for mainly lower-class opium users (ibid. 2, Statistics). Their mediocre social backgrounds particularly made their dependence on opium into a 'disease', an 'act of crime'. Thus, during their two to three weeks of 'captivity' in this hospital, the inmates were required to attend a vocational training course which would allegedly 'reform them into healthy and productive citizens', despite the fact that most of them were already employed in decent jobs. In the eyes of the establishment, they were not only unproductive slouches who needed to be taught decent means of livelihood, but also spiritually deficient beings. Thus, an intensive 'spiritual training' programme was included as an important part of the treatment. The inmates were bombarded with compulsory lectures on a variety of anti-opium topics ranging from the origins of the Opium War to a meticulous reading of Sun Yat-sen's *Three People's Principles* and the 'Opium Suppression Ordinances'. They were also taught to take up such 'righteous' pastimes as reading, music, and sports (ibid. 18–23, Tables).

Moreover, despite the fact that a substantial proportion of the inmates consumed opium for a medical reason, the hospital administration in its annual report still preferred to believe that it was 'the weakness in their will power, [and] their poverty in knowledge' that had led them to abuse opium as a 'plaything'. 'Moral weakness' of the inmates was 'established' officially as the cause of their addiction, as well as of their failure to discontinue this 'pernicious' habit (ibid. 18).[59] Thus, these lower-class opium users were victimized and held responsible for China's opium problem; and it was this particular section of 'criminalized' opium users, rather than the upper-class addicts, that had aroused 'public' concern and apprehension. This might also help explain why opium smoking had not been condemned as a problem before the early Ch'ing period: opium then, though already quite popular, was used as a luxurious stimulant mainly by people in high society (Lo Tzu-ch'in 1933: 3).[60] The substantial increase since the late eighteenth century in both opium imports and the number of addicts among commoners had certainly alarmed many conscientious officials and the emperors, and contributed eventually to the court's determination in suppressing the drug, especially before 1842 (Chang Hsin-pao 1964: esp. chs. 2, 4). Moreover, the official policy of 'suppression by taxation' (*yu-chin yü chêng*), which had been implemented since the Opium War, was another expression of this class-biased anti-opium logic. To suppress opium consumption by means of taxing the drug would only affect the poor users, not the rich smokers (P'eng Yong-ou 1982: 109).[61]

A 'Playful' Drug for the Layabouts?

Opium users apparently took the drug for reasons of their own that defy simple generalizations. Although it might be true that some addicts started smoking opium for no better reason than simply 'playing with it', that all addicts must then have smoked for the same 'immoral' and 'playful' purpose does not follow.

Opium was sometimes consumed as a 'playful thing' (i.e. for recreational use) as much as for practical physiological aid.[62] Perhaps aware of the 'common knowledge' that those who ate regularly and well would not show physical deterioration from their addiction to opium, many better-off businessmen were among avid users of the drug. To them, 'opium sharpened their wits and helped them to drive shrewder business deals with their competitors'.[63] Business talks were commonly held in opium divans, floating brothels, or restaurants where a puff of opium had almost become a course on the menu. To those who preferred a more private atmosphere, offices or shops were an alternative.[64]

Consumption of superior quality but unlicensed imported opium at business premises had become so common that it provided a fertile ground for official extortion and corruption.[65] On one occasion, the Canton government was shrewd enough to make use of this piece of common knowledge for its political ends. In the summer of 1928, when the government was desperately seeking for a huge loan of 10 million yüan from the mercantile community in Canton to stabilize the rapidly depreciating Central Bank notes, most officials of the two Chambers of Commerce procrastinated as an act of defiance against this high-handed policy of compulsory borrowing (*NYSP* 1928: 11, 12 July). Then one evening a team of Opium Suppression inspectors raided the premises of these chambers of commerce. As a result, eleven businessmen were caught red-handed smoking unlicensed opium; among them was the chairman of the General Chamber of Commerce, who had been very outspoken against this policy. The raid succeeded in quietening the disgruntled chambers, and the required loan was subsequently collected with no further delay (ibid.).

A substantial number of opium smokers apparently came from the city poor.[66] In contemporary social novels, opium smoking was sometimes particularly associated with urban poverty, ignorance, and demoralization among the 'exploited' toiling masses.[67] Reports prepared by the Opium Suppression Bureau of Kwangtung Province in the late 1930s and the early 1940s indicated that the majority of opium users in Kwangtung, as in other parts of China, were the 'poor and miserable' (*ping ku*) or the 'outright poor' (*ch'ih ping*). To alleviate the financial burden for these indigent opium smokers, this bureau had introduced, probably in the late 1920s, a measure of issuing a special category of opium-smoking permits for 'the poor', which cost substantially less than the ordinary ones.[68] At one time, when the bureau sold 7,200 copies of such ordinary permits province-wide, a total of 67,100 copies of special permits for the poor were issued.[69] In the case of Canton, according to the number of registered smokers as recorded by the city's Anti-Opium Committee during the first quarter of 1937, there were about 5,000 'ordinary smokers' as compared to nearly 13,000 'poor smokers'.[70] Among these urban poor, opium was consumed for a number of practical or therapeutic reasons.

In the early 1930s, there were about 15,000 rickshawmen in Canton. Life for them was by no means easy. They were required to work long shifts, from six o'clock in the morning until three in the afternoon; or from 3 p.m. to 6 a.m. the following day. Their income was so meagre that the majority were said to be unable to afford to get married (Huang Wên-to 1933: 2–3). A survey conducted in 1934 by the Canton municipal government of some five thousand rickshawmen in Canton showed that opium smoking was the second most favourite pastime among them, next to alcohol.[71] In another relatively detailed survey of 600 rickshawmen in Canton conducted during the late 1930s, its author, a professor of sociology in Lingnan University, wrote that since pulling a rickshaw was physically a highly strenuous job, very few rickshawmen in Canton could stay in this profession for over ten years. Of the 600 rickshawmen studied, about 80 had indicated their regular consumption of the drug in their spare time, for, in all likelihood, a therapeutic or stimulant purpose to help them to overcome those unwelcoming physical signs of poverty such as tuberculosis and malnutrition (Wu Jui-lin 1940: 24–8). This was shown in a casual conversation between a concerned journalist and a rickshawman who was also an opium addict in Canton. One evening, this journalist had hailed a rickshaw. On board the rickshaw, he noticed that the puller looked exceedingly weak and fragile with his skeletal physique, as if he had just undergone a serious illness. To the surprise of this journalist, however, this apparently undernourished rickshawman was pulling his loaded rickshaw at such a high speed that he described the ride as extraordinary. When asked where he got his energy, the rickshawman told his curious customer that he just had a fix at a low-class opium den and that was how he could be as strong as a tiger. He then went to elaborate that he usually visited an establishment that sold cheap, adulterated opium twice a day, where he spent about fifteen minutes in one instance and 10 cents per visit, which was described by him as both economical and effective, especially for a low-income addict like he was (Hung Lang 1933: 1). The practical importance of opium for this group of smokers should not be underestimated.

In the reminiscences of a Cantonese opera actor, the pains of prolonged and routine labour drove many of his colleagues to 'heavy addiction'. Musicians in a Cantonese opera troupe in this period were usually required to work continuously from about eleven o'clock in the morning until eight in the evening. After a one-hour break, they would be required to work again until one o'clock in the morning. Then they would get another hour of rest before returning to play for the morning session (*t'ien-kuang hsi*) which lasted until dawn (Ch'en Cho-ying 1983: 313).[72]

To these underfed and overworked labourers, opium was not only one of the few affordable types of recreation, but also an important aid to hard work. It did not seem to destroy their stamina, or ruin their working life.[73] The persistence of opium smoking among the urban poor might be due to a general awareness of the stimulant power of opium in increasing endurance, lessening the pains of prolonged toil, keeping the body warm (Spence 1975: 146 n. 19; Wu Yü et al. 1988: 351–2; Berridge and Edwards 1981: 36), quenching thirst and allaying pangs of hunger,[74] and, in the words of an American physician, providing temporary relief to visceral neuralgias and rheumatism so common among the poorer classes of working people (Terry and Pellens 1970: 100). Opium helped them to 'forget their miserable life . . . mingle with a better world . . . [and] turn the horrible reality into a happy, slow-moving dream' (Kazantzakis 1982: 239–40). The physiological and psychological power of opium was noted in the observation that a man of low morale always came out from an opium den as a 'totally different person'; and thus opium smoking was commonly called 'beating the tiger' (*ta lao-hu*), a metaphor of the vitalizing power given by the drug to its users who, after a few puffs, were jocularly described as being strong enough to kill a dozen more tigers than the legendary Wu Sung (Kōsaka 1943: 41).[75]

This corroborated the general situation of opium consumption found in other parts of China. A recent historical study brought to our attention the fact that Western travellers in late-imperial China (such as Isabella Bird, Colbourne Baber, and Elizabeth Kendall) were generally impressed by the much-neglected fact that opium smoking among Chinese workers, particularly sedan-chair coolies and junk crews, did not produce any remarkable damage, and their work performance, honesty, and good-nature displayed no sign of inferiority to an non-user. Among these smokers, opium played a highly meaningful role in their working lives:

> Smoking by workers such as these was clearly a normal form of relaxation, a sign of camaraderie that grew up on long journeys and a sociable way of spending the evenings.... It had also a therapeutic value, since workers like these must have suffered more than their fair share of chills, aches, sprains and hunger-pangs, brought on by arduous work through irregular hours in all kinds of weathers. (Newman 1995: 782–3)

Opium smoking by prison inmates, though officially prohibited, was common.[76] At least since late Ch'ing, prisons in Canton had been so badly managed that gambling and opium smoking were openly conducted round the clock under the effective protection of prison caretakers who received as rewards handsome amounts of illegitimate income (*Shen pao* 1911, 24 Jan.). This 'tradition' apparently survived into the Republican era, at least well up to the early 1930s.[77] In one institution, officers and inmates collaborated and ran an opium-cum-gambling den. Some non-addict inmates became addicts by the time of their discharge.[78] However, it was perhaps the narcotic function of opium that induced some prisoners, both addicts and non-addicts, to become habituated to the drug which, with its euphoric function, was seemingly important for them as a means of overriding the boredom of prison life, and which with its medicinal properties perhaps made bearable the appalling conditions in the cells. In 1926, four merchant associations in Canton requested the government to rebuild its dilapidated detention centre where ventilation and lighting were bad, the floor was damp, and crawling worms and insects abounded. This small place was tightly crowded with 800 inmates; and those too weak to occupy a bunk were forced to sleep sitting on the floor (*KCMKJP* 1926: 10, 30 Sept.).[79] Thus, when a cholera epidemic broke out in Canton in 1927, it claimed the lives of 'a number of' inmates (*HTJP* 1927: 2.2, 22 Aug.). Opium therefore might be crucial for their very survival in a harsh environment.

Not all opium smokers were poor, or smoked for the sake of survival or medication. Some opium users were scholar-literati who smoked for pleasure. A few of them even immortalized their euphoric experiences in poems or prose pieces;[80] Hsia Kuan-pu, who was said to be well known for his paintings and poems, seemingly enjoyed to display his intellectual talent by giving to friends as gifts his compositions of amusing but somewhat moralistic couplets that were then engraved on the smoking pipes of the recipients (*Yen hua*, Ah Ying 1957: 765–6). Some consumed it as a status symbol. By the early Ch'ing period, opium was said to be a luxury item of consumption for pleasure for wealthy families (Lo Tzu-ch'in 1933: 3). By early Republican times, it was said that the homes of most middle- and upper-classes families in Kwangtung usually had a room reserved for smoking superior-quality opium, in which guests were received and entertained (Umeda Ikuzō 1913: 17).[81] The recreational use of opium was an agreeable subculture within Cantonese high society. On the long dowry-list of a bride from a wealthy family in Canton were found quantities of expensive imported and local opium,[82] and smoking pipes of different sizes, one of which was made from rhinoceros horn. An old maid, whose duty was to serve opium to the bride, was also included in the list (T'un Huang 1927*a*: 4.4).

As discussed earlier, upper-class consumption of opium was not viewed as a social vice or a moral problem, probably because of the common knowledge that the drug would be harmless to well-to-do smokers who could afford good food and comfortable living conditions (Ball 1903: 494). An anti-opiumist noted that since its consumption by upper-class users was regarded by the common people as a rich man's pleasure, these folk then gradually came to imitate and indulge in this respectable form of upper-class pastime themselves. In the writer's view, opium consumption had to be publicly denounced in order to make addicts ashamed of their habit. To this end, a stigmatized image of opium smoking was said to be necessary (Yü En-tê 1934: 248).

Some smoked opium for practical ethical reasons. A late-Ch'ing gazetteer recorded that 'many rich Chinese encourage their sons to stay at home and smoke opium rather than indulging in debauchery or gambling' (Spence 1975: 145). This was not fictitious. Old Cantonese informants reminisce that even by the late 1930s 'a number of' wealthy Cantonese families still tried to keep their wastrel sons at home, instead of letting them squander the family fortune in gambling-houses and brothels, by encouraging them to become habituated to opium—a drug generally known to be efficacious in soothing excessive sexual impulses and creating a state of idleness and lack of ambition, but without causing any physical harm to these well-to-do users.[83] For a similar reason, a famous Cantonese opera actress had reportedly succeeded in preventing her good-looking husband from being unfaithful to her by encouraging him to indulge in opium smoking (*YHP* 1936: 2, 3 Nov.).

From the late Ming onwards, opium smoking seems to be closely linked with prostitution. By the late Ch'ing, most brothels in Canton and Shanghai served opium to their customers who used it as an aphrodisiac, or as a euphoric 'stimulant' for refreshing their spirits (Umeda Ikuzō 1913: 17; Wang Shu-nu 1933: 307–8; Spence 1975: 144 n. 4; Yü Chiao-ch'ing 1909: 19). Opium sometimes figured as a motif in late-Ch'ing erotic woodblock printing, and on smoking paraphernalia.[84] By the 1930s, opium continued to be served in brothels. But in order to compete, many opium shop owners hired up to five 'opium beauties' (*yen hua*), or 'opium prostitutes' (*yen chi*), as hostesses to attract customers. It was said that the seductive act of preparing a smoking pipe by one of these beauties was alone enough to get some men sexually excited; and if both parties agreed, sex might be traded on the premises (Kōsaka 1943: 41; Wu Yü et al. 1988: 336).[85] A contemporary writer noted that many young addicts started smoking opium simply out of desire for these attractive women (Ch'üan Shêng 1924: 6. *Wên-i*).

It is interesting to note that patriotism might boost, rather than discourage, the sale of licensed opium. Such national loyalty was artfully used by a professedly patriotic sing-song girl as justification for her addiction to opium. Pai Yü-mei, a popular sing-song girl in Hong Kong and Canton in the 1920s, was interviewed by a newspaper columnist after she was found out to be an opium addict. On being asked how she started to smoke opium, she replied assertively that following her election as Chairwoman of the Canton Sing-song Girls Union a few years ago, she could cope with her much-increased workload only with its help. When being further asked why she preferred opium to other stimulants, she said that since the existence of the revolutionary government and the success of its great nationalistic enterprise depended heavily on the revenue brought in by the franchised sale of licensed opium, she herself, being an 'office-bearer of the Union [and] an outstanding national [citizen] under the flag of the Revolution', must hasten to express her love for her country, and her allegiance to the Party, by consuming opium. She criticized the columnist's view of the immorality of opium smoking as regressive and hypocritical. She added that she had persuaded, and would continue to persuade, her friends to start smoking licensed opium too. She opined that the younger generation should also promote the sale of licensed opium, as a means to show their support to the great cause of the Revolution and the Nationalist Government (Leng Yen 1927: 4.1). Judged by the perplexed response of the columnist, Pai's motive for smoking opium was an unusual and bizarre one.

Do Users Have to Be Addicted and Therefore Poor?

Some anti-opium literature tries to foster a somewhat problematic image of opium smoking that the drug, because it was imported and expensive, inevitably helped devastate the economic lives of its users whose dependence on it could rarely be sustained economically for a long period of time. The poorer section of the smoking population was especially hard-hit by such economic depredation. Such argument, however, is built on two assumptions, which are not unproblematic.

First, the holders of this view seem to have ignored the fact that there was no shortage of smokers in China who could easily afford to indulge themselves in expensive Indian opium. Moreover, before the Anglo-Chinese Ten-year

Agreement was enforced in 1908 and the price of Indian opium began to soar, 'foreign mud' in Canton was not always unattainably expensive for the smokers. By the end of the 1870s, for example, a *tael* of foreign opium in Canton cost 0.45 *tael* of silver, compared to 0.36 *tael* of silver for Chinese opium; the price difference was not huge (*YHKPK* 1996: 184). In the words of a British officer working for the Imperial Maritime Customs in Canton, any smoker with the financial means would opt for Indian opium, mainly for its distinctive rich flavour (ibid. 154). This also helped explain, at least partly, why the importation of Indian opium into Canton enjoyed a steady growth throughout the second half of the nineteenth century up to the end of the 1900s.[86] When the supply of Indian opium to Kwangtung was gradually restricted as a result of successive opium suppression campaigns in China during the late 1900s and the early 1910s, its price reached a record high. The sale of this drug, however, was not affected (e.g. see *YHKPK* 1996: 415, 423, 468). Since Indian opium was generally recognized as the best product in existence, wealthy and finicky smokers in Canton were not deterred by its cost. Opium merchants in Canton also continued to purchase Indian opium, which was used mainly for blending with Chinese opium to enhance the flavour of the inferior local product (ibid. 399; Miners 1987: 236–7).

Secondly, proponents of the 'impoverishment theory' on the socio-economic impact of opium seem to have ignored the important fact that by the end of the nineteenth century imported opium had already been out-competed by Chinese opium in terms of quantity, apparently an outcome of the latter's competitive lower price.[87] Moreover, as the cost of imported opium began to soar after the export of Indian opium had been progressively regulated in the face of the mounting pressure from Whitehall since the early 1910s and the success of an effective suppression of opium by the Chinese government, the price gap between Chinese and Indian opium was further widened. By 1918, although smuggled 'foreign mud' could still be purchased at a very high price, inexpensive Chinese opium dominated the local opium market (*YHKPK* 1996: 365, 481, 617–18, 1007–8; Miners 1987: 244–5).[88] The truly indigent smokers who could not afford native opium of superior quality opted for a variety of cheaper alternatives, which were either low-grade native opium or dross opium, or an adulteration of foreign opium with a cheap Chinese product, lard, and pig's blood (Miners 1987: 236–7), or other even lower-cost opiate derivatives such as the infamous but increasingly popular red pills (*hung wan*) (Ch'en Nien-t'i 1935: 12–13). There was apparently a range of opiate products from which a smoker in Canton could choose that met their personal tastes and budgets (*YHKPK* 1996: 921).

Annual figures on the prices of opium in Canton are not available at the time of this research. Sketchy information, however, may help us to grasp the situation. Between 1909 and 1910, a tael of foreign opium was priced at two silver dollars and fifty cents, while a tael of Chinese opium at less than two (Kuang-tung ch'ing-li-ts'ai-chêng-chü 1910: bk. 7, 12). In 1912, when the anti-opium campaign was still actively enforced by the early Republican administration, a *tael* of imported opium cost 5 yüan, which was considered by the Canton Customs as very high. This ushered in a wave of opium smuggling from Yünnan, which was considerably cheaper in retail price (*YHKPK* 1996: 1000–7). In 1919, the official price for a *tael* of foreign imported opium was 15 yüan; the same amount of Yünnan opium cost 4 yüan, and opium from Ch'ang-chou 2 yüan (Yü En-tê 1934: 179). In Hong Kong during the same period, cheap Chinese opium (retailing at HK$2 a *tael*) was much welcomed by local addicts and caused a drop by half in the sale of Indian opium, which retailed at HK$14.5 a *tael* (Miners 1987: 236–7). By 1920, China's effort at eradicating native opium in the past decade had come to a halt, as provincial militarism helped effectively defy any attempt to eliminate this lucrative source of local revenue.[89] Widespread cultivation of the native opium poppy was reported. Supplies of native opium were so abundant that in Fukien province the price of raw opium had dropped from HK$16 to 90 cents a *tael* in the space of two years (Miners 1987: 244). The situation in Canton might have been similar to that of Fukien. In 1927, a British official source stated that the price for a *tael* of opium sold by the Hong Kong Government monopoly was HK$14.50, while a respectable brand of Chinese-prepared opium could be purchased at 2 dollars a *tael*.[90] In 1928, the official retail price of a *tael* of prepared opium in Canton was 5–6 yüan, which in all likelihood was for the superior grade of the drug; most of the opium consumed then was of Chinese origin (*YHP* 1928: 2, 10 Feb.). In 1930, when political instability was seriously affecting the opium supply from the south-western provinces, the retail price of prepared opium (probably superior grade) in Canton was 6 dollars a *tael* as compared to 5 dollars in 1927. The prices of raw opium from Yünnan and Kweichow in 1927 were 2.4 and 2.3 yüan respectively.[91] The cost of opium in Kweichow, Yünnan, and Szechwan during the 1920s was much lower—mainly between 40 cents and 1 yüan for a *tael*, depending on quality (P'eng Kuo-liang 1981). Smuggling opium from these provinces into Canton, therefore, was widespread. This smuggled opium provided the poor consumers with a cheap alternative. In the reminiscences of an old resident of Canton, Mr Cheng, who lived in this city until 1950, the official price for a *tael* of medium-grade opium in Canton in the 1930s was about 3.5 yüan. All these figures on the opium retail price in Canton and its adjacent areas, however fragmentary, indicated that the cost of this commodity, especially native produce, though suffering from fluctuation at times, remained largely stable at less than five 5 yüan a *tael*. The question remains to be answered, was opium an economically devastating indulgence for its smokers?

This is not an easy question and no answer will satisfy all critics without running the risk of overgeneralizing a complex situation. Whether a habit of opium consumption was detrimental to the economic capability of a smoker depended on a range of variables: family size and financial situation, the amount of daily intake of opium, the kind of opium smoked (the price gap between Indian and Chinese opium could be substantial), where the opium was smoked (smoking in a brothel or a high-class divan cost more than at home), and so on.

No generalized assumption on all these variables is possible for naturally variation among individuals could be very high. What one can safely point out at the time of this research is that the economic devastation of opium on its users was not an indisputable fact as it was commonly portrayed in contemporary anti-opium literature. In addition to what has already been pointed out above—abundant supplies of low-price opium and other cheap opiate derivatives—the general consumption level by smokers also has to be considered. According to Mr Cheng, who had lived in Canton until 1950, an 'ordinary' addict was said to have consumed about 0.1 *tael* a day, while the heavily addicted needed more; he does not believe that smoking opium alone could ruin one's family fortune for he did not know any case personally. In 1922, the British Consul-General in Canton mentioned in a dispatch an estimate of the amount of opium required annually for legitimate local consumption in Macao: 'One of my informants states that the number of opium-smokers in Macao is 6,000 or between 6 and 7 per cent of the population; that these may be said to consume an average of 20 taels weight per annum each.'[92] That suggested a daily intake of an average of 0.05 *tael* of opium for a smoker, which was hardly an alarming figure in terms either of the amount consumed or the economic cost incurred. A detailed statistical study on opium addiction in Japanese Formosa was concluded thus:

> As for the consumption of prepared opium quantity for the licensed opium smokers—the products sold in 1900. This year [1900], it can be counted as the most using year, from which, the maximum quantity reached 200,927 kg. The index number was at 100. The quantity of opium issued to individual licensed opium smokers used to be about average consumption for each person 3.3 g. per day, but decreased to 15,945 kg. in 1938. The smoking quantity index was at 8. Each person per day consumed 4.0 g. in average. In 1940, each person per day consumed 3.3 g. only, decreased again in average.
>
> (Tu Tsung-ming 1953: 602–3)

Although there is no possible way to know the actual amount of opium consumed by each individual smoker, these figures still indicated a general situation that was, at least, not as catastrophic as it was commonly depicted in anti-opium writings. There was no convincing reason to presume that smokers in Canton consumed more opium than their counterparts in Macao or Japanese-controlled Taiwan. Most opium addicts in the boat-people community in Canton's Sha-nan in the mid-1930s spent 20 to 60 cents a day on this indulgence. Richer addicts were said to have spent more on the drug (Wu Jui-lin 1934*a*: 103; 1934*b*: 53–4). In the two opium dens in Chiu-Fêng-huang Village not far from Canton, a patron spent an average of 20 cents on one visit; the stimulation brought about by one trip seemed to be enough for to last a 'normal' user the day (Wu and Huang 1935: 153).[93] A 1934 research study on workers' families in Canton shows that the addict interviewees spent 'a minimum of ten cents per day' on opium (Yü Ch'i-chung 1934: 67). This was seemingly not a big sum of money for the ordinary people; to place a small bet on a local lottery then cost about the same amount of money (see Ch. 4). Poor addicts there might also cut the cost of their habit in the ways that boat-people in San-shui County commonly employed. First, they would not patronize opium dens; they smoked only at home. Secondly, instead of using proper smoking paraphernalia, they would improvise with whatever home utensils were at hand. Thirdly, smoked opium might be reused until its stimulative potential was exhausted (Wu Jui-lin 1971: 53–4). In connection to the last point, it is important to note that dross opium was also valuable and enjoyed a degree of popularity among the poorer customers because of its cheapness.[94] In Canton during the 1930s, a number of low-class opium divans sold this kind of mixture of dross and raw opium, at a price (16 copper coins in 1935) that could be afforded by smokers even from some of the lowest-income groups (Chu Yang 1935: 20). Rickshawmen in Canton were among the major patrons of these low-class dens. During the first half of the 1930s, when most rickshaw pullers in Canton earned in average 30 yüan a month, a relatively better-off addict rickshawman 'usually' spent 20 to 30 cents on opium for a respectable brand every day. But to many who smoked on a tight budget, dross opium or some other adulterated form, a 'kick' of which cost as little as 5 cents, was a welcome alternative (Hung Lang 1933: 1; Hai Lung 1934: 1).[95] In a report prepared by the Canton Opium Addiction Termination Hospital, opium smokers in the city, in view of the pressing needs of making ends meet, had decreased the amount of the drug taken at the times when the market price of opium soared.[96] Sometimes, an addict might even take the 'drastic' action of giving up the habit for good. Chu Ting-ho, who was once a popular Cantonese opera actor, was a case in point. This not-so-lucky actor, who had been turned down by opera companies for casting, had faced serious financial problem. To maintain a balanced budget, he was determined to abstain from his costly indulgence in opium, and subsequently managed to make ends meet (*KPP* 1934: 3.3, 31 Jan.). These consumers of opium were seemingly much more rational than they were portrayed in anti-opium literature. The extent of the economic devastation of opium on the city poor was, therefore, disputable.

In most anti-opium writings, opium users were classified indiscriminately as 'addicts', without taking into consideration the fact that opium could be used occasionally without the consumer being habituated to it. The effect of opium on these occasional small-doses users, unlike heavy addicts, might be more positive than deleterious. Moreover, there are wide differences in individual susceptibility and resistance to opium, and in the amounts consumed daily (Terry and Pellens 1970: 429).[97] In Japanese Taiwan, individual variations of opium consumption per day could be very wide indeed: in one case the amount of intake was 0.4 g, while it was 45 g in another (Tu Tsung-ming 1953: 575–8). Furthermore, clinical studies on opium addiction conducted in the United States during the 1920s had already revealed that conventional wisdom on addiction at the time was highly problematic. In many anti-opium writings in China, for instance, addiction was generally described as the inevitable fate for all smokers. In such anti-opium rhetoric, no differentiation was made between smokers and addicts; and addicts, because of physiological dependence on the drug, would be portrayed as continually having to increase their daily dose of opium to satisfy their insatiable demand for stimulation and to suppress withdrawal symptoms until their physical constitution would be completely devastated, their moral fibre and individual integrity totally shattered, to the point of descending to theft or banditry, and would ultimately die as a result of violence or intoxication.[98] Addiction, however, was not as straightforward as that. There were cases of opium smokers who were able to abandon their smoking habit without suffering from any withdrawal symptoms after a period of using the drug.[99] Evidence also indicated that although a user's needs will almost invariably climb at first, eventually a standard dose will establish itself; for opium is self-regulating and a person will get sick if he smokes too much of it (Hogshire 1994: 23). Most opium smokers were able to maintain a certain level of opium consumption rather than continually increasing their dosage.[100] Revd Terada, Pastor of the Protestant Episcopal Church of Taipei, Taiwan, pointed out that the Chinese of the better class are seldom addicted to it; addicts were found almost entirely from the lower class. He added that since these addicts were generally poor, the amount of opium they were able to buy was very limited, the daily consumption of one person varying from 6 to 12 *sen* (cents) worth of the drug (Philippine Commission 1905: 62–3). This was also true for smokers in Canton. When opium prices soared as a result of grave political uncertainty, as in the late 1930s. opium smokers in Canton would and could decrease the amount of opium consumed by half (downward from a few *chien* to a few *fen*) in order to make ends meet, instead of doggedly holding onto their usual dose.[101] Such rational flexibility on the part of opium smokers should have urged the anti-opium medical profession in Canton to rethink the true nature and extent of opiate addiction. The same report also mentioned the need of a modern laboratory for undertaking accurate scientific tests on determining whether or not an opium smoker was addicted to the drug. This seems to imply that, first, addiction to opium was not so easily detected or established, and, secondly, that not every opium user was also an addict.[102] Sometimes, even withdrawal symptoms can be emotional rather than physiological, which brought serious doubt to whether addiction was truly as enslaving and damaging as had been conventionally assumed.[103] All these facts, however, were played down in anti-opium literature, so that all opium users were unquestioningly reduced to suicidal psychotics who rush down the cul-de-sac of self-destruction (Lo Yün-yen 1938: 2, 13–17).

The number of occasional users in Republican Canton is not known. A social survey of a boat-people community in Canton notes fifteen opium addicts in this village, and twenty users not yet habituated to the drug (Wu Jui-lin 1934*a*). The first-year admission record of Canton's Opium Addiction Termination Hospital also reveals the interesting fact that there were sixty-nine inmates who asserted that they were 'non-addicts' (*wu yin chê*), and who claimed that they were arrested and forced to undergo treatment 'out of misunderstanding'.[104] These 'non-addicts' might be occasional users with none of the craving for opium of true addicts. The presence of 'occasional users' added more ambiguity to the term 'addiction'. Western medical research on opiate addiction in the 1920s and 1930s had already confirmed that 'morphine or some other opiate may be given to a patient over a long period of time without creating an independent craving'. Moreover, there are marked physiological, and especially psychic, differences between true opiate 'addicts' and those who habituate to it (Lindesmith 1968: ch. 3). However, neither the establishment nor the contemporary medical profession seems interested in these ambiguities, preferring to present the 'problem' in a way they assume to be socially and morally convincing.

Formidable Threat to the Race, the National Defence, and the Economy?

The physical and social effects of opium smoking on the Chinese and their society were also inevitably generalized. In anti-opium literature, opium smoking was commonly held accountable for causing 'marked deterioration' in the physical health of its users, and was denounced as a major primary threat to the physiological and genetic well-being of the Chinese race. The image of opium 'addicts' was negatively stereotyped:

> [All] addicts of dangerous drugs can be easily recognized by their appearance. Their complexions are grey and pale; their appearance derelict and weak. [They] grow old precociously: [their] hair turns grey easily, their pupils are contracted, teeth loosened, skin dried, [and] their voices quiver. Thus, disparaging people always call them 'opium ghosts', which is a very accurate description [of their dereliction]. Moreover, they also [suffer from] poor digestion, constipation, insomnia, irregular heart-beat, impotency, cessation of menstrual cycle, and so on. (Lo Yün yen 1938: 19)[105]

Since all opium-eaters were invariably constituted as such, 'Their strength is weakened and spirit withered. [As a result,] they spend all day lying on bed smoking opium, without doing anything for their career; their meanings of life is completely shattered by poppies.'[106] An official anti-opium publication pointed out that an opium user could never hide his 'true identity' as a drug addict simply because his appearance was so emaciated that it could be distinguished fairly easily: blackened teeth, shrunk nose, burnt and dark-colour lips, coarse voice, contracted pupils and yellowish eyegrounds.[107] In a contemporary anti-opium *Yüeh-ou*-style folk song, the opium addict is derogatorily caricatured:

> [His] lips [are always half-open] like blowing air to a burning fire, [and] his face as dark as [a smoked] altar. He is [so weak and hunched that] either his shoulders are always higher than his ears, or his . . . ears are on his shoulders. He becomes as thin as a wooden stick. [So thin and weak] that he dares not stand facing the wind, lest he will be blown away. You, opium ghost, wake up when evening is approaching, and retreat in [to] a corner [of your home] during daytime . . . [108]

More seriously, the leftist writer Ou-yang Shan (1948) depicts the prostitute protagonist in one of his 1930s works as a sallow addict whose ailing and emaciated body eventually robs her of life.[109]

It is, however, wrong to assume that all opium dependants must develop symptoms of physiological emaciation and psychological depression similar to those of heavy addicts. The effect of opium on smokers was, in fact, a lot more complex and diverse. Western medical and scientific reports show that 'the effects of opiates on the body and bodily functions have uncovered either only minor injurious effects or none at all that can be traced directly to the drug.' Clinical records also reveal persons who have used the drug in small doses for long periods of time but without being tormented by any physical degeneration, depression of sex activity, bodily malfunction, or even weight loss. An addict could live and work like any normal human being when receiving a satisfying quantity of the drug (Lindesmith 1968: 39–40; Berridge and Edwards 1981: 84–6, 280; Lewin 1931: 2–26; Terry and Pellens 1970: 501). In the words of two physicians who compiled a medical anthology on opium for the United States Social Hygiene Bureau in 1928:

> There is a popular belief extant that practically anyone can detect the so-called 'dope fiend', that he is a miserable, emaciated, furtive individual with pinpoint pupils, trembling hands, sallow complexion and characterized by a varied group of moral attributes ... As a matter of fact, not even one of these characteristics need be present and it is safe to say that in many cases only one or another of them exists and by no means would suffice to give the ordinary observer an idea of the true situation ... and that quite possibly the average physician, unaccustomed to dealing with the condition, might have difficulty in determining its existence. (Terry and Pellens 1970: 2)

Another clinical study on opiate addiction in the United States in 1929–30 contains detailed and interesting findings on the physical characteristics and physical fitness of addicts during administration of morphine:

> A careful examination in ninety-six cases together with information gained from the supervision of the physical examination in 450 additional cases by the interns on service gave the following results: The large majority of the patients were between 20 and 40 and their physical status conformed closely to that of normal persons of that age and group. Some showed emaciation which sometimes reached an extreme degree, but many were muscular and well developed and a number were obese. The skin was sallow in many cases, but this change in colour was practically always present in patients who lived a rather unhygienic sedentary life. On the other hand, the skin of those who followed healthy outdoor occupations had the colour of excellent health.... Sixty per cent of these ninety-six patients showed scars of previous abscesses ... [they were] caused by improperly disinfected hypodermic needles by the irritating diluents used with either morphine or heroin.... The pupils were practically always contracted when the patient had had his usual quantity of the drug. They reacted to light and in accommodation, though somewhat more sluggishly than normally.... The extra-ocular movements were normal. The eye-grounds did not show any abnormality of either retina or the vessels.... Sixty per cent of the ninety-six patients examined exhibited a particularly high degree of pyorrhea and dental caries. Before attributing these changes to the continued use of drugs, one must bear in mind that these people are notorious in their lack of care of the teeth and failure to consult a dentist.... Otherwise, the oral cavity showed nothing abnormal. The throat (40 per cent) showed a chronic inflammatory condition, but these persons are excessive smokers, a factor to be borne in mind. The thyroid was not palpable in one single case.

> The chest, as a rule, of normal shape with good expansion.... Heart sounds were of good quality.... We have been unable to detect any marked physical deterioration or impairment of physical fitness aside from the addiction per se.... We believe that the existence of considerable emaciation in certain cases is caused by the unhygienic and impoverished life of the addict rather than by the direct effects of the drug.
>
> (Light et al. 1929–30: 13–20)

This was, however, just an old wisdom now scientifically proven. Writing on the subject of opium in Canton, a nineteenth-century missionary noted that 'the effects of the practice are certainly not such as to strike the eye of the uninitiated, nor are emaciated cases so frequently seen as some would lead us to suppose' (Turner 1982: 43) In early 1900s, a group of leading Chinese merchants with an anti-opium stance had told an official delegation from the United States Government that there was a difference between the well-to-do and the poor people in the extent to which the use of opium injured them: 'The well-to-do are better fed and clothed and as a result have more resistance, enabling them to smoke opium with less injury and suffering' (Philippine Commission 1905: 79). The diverse variations of opium effect had been noticeable for a long time.

In the context of Canton, such observations, probably due to the moral and political sensitivity of the issue, were not often made known. It is thus preposterous to assume that the physiological and psychological effects of opium on its Cantonese (and Chinese) users were totally different from their Western counterparts, or more predictably and noticeably devastating. For example, social surveys conducted by Lingnan University on two rural communities in Canton in the early 1930s note the 'problem' of opium smoking there, but report nothing about a 'physical degeneration' suffered by the habitués—a phenomenon which, if it existed, could hardly have escaped the critical eyes of the researchers, who were unreserved in their bigoted remarks about village life (Wu Jui-lin 1934*a*; Wu Jui Lin and Huang En-lin 1935). A similar absence of negative descriptions is noticeable also in a social survey of 600 rickshawmen in Canton during the second half of the 1930s (Wu Jui-lin 1940). In the same survey, nearly 20 per cent of the rickshawmen interviewed were said to be in a dissatisfactory state of health.; fatigue, skin troubles, tuberculosis, muscle pains, stomach ache, venereal diseases, and irritation in eyes and ears were among the most common complaints diagnosed. All these ailments and diseases, however, were pointed out as a direct outcome of malnutrition and an unhygienic lifestyle (such as refusal to take baths regularly, and appalling living conditions) on the part of these workers rather than the effect of opium addiction (ibid. 25–6). An impressed journalist in Canton was amazed by how opium helped enhance the efficiency of a skeletal rickshawman who looked desperately ill to this client (Hai Lung 1934: 1). In this case, the emaciated appearance might be due to undernourishment and impoverishment. On the contrary, treatment could do more harm to an addict, and sometimes even be fatal. According to the records of the Addiction Termination Hospital in Canton, 33 per cent of patients lost weight during the course of treatment. Moreover, a substantial number of them reportedly suffered from a variety of physiological complaints when they were abruptly withdrawn from the drug;[110] it was then that they became truly 'sick persons'.[111] No wonder the budgetary items of an opium treatment rehabilitation institution in Canton included a moderate sum of expenditure for funerary purpose for its inmates; an estimated 2 per cent of inmates would die during treatment,[112] but data from Taiwan between 1929 and 1934 reveals an alarming rate of 10 per cent fatalities (Tu Tsung-ming 1953: 597). It might be true that some poor addicts might look emaciated due to their hard life and poor diet.[113] The cause, however, was thus a social one rather than opium alone.

An interesting article describes in detail how a 70-year-old Cantonese man maintained a healthy body and happy life with the aid of opium (this article will be discussed later) (Ch'üan Shêng 1924, *Wên-i*) Opium smoking was not necessarily detrimental to a smoker's longevity, even if a strong dosage were being taken regularly for a long period of time. Levels of tolerance apparently varied with individuals (Lewin 1964; 2–25).[114] Scanty data from Canton indicated that about 20 per cent of officially registered opium smokers in early 1937 were in the age group 50–60 or over; there was no shortage of long-living addicts.[115] It is for Taiwan that relatively more detailed data on the age distribution of opium smokers are available for analysis. In 1940, there were 7,058 males registered as opium users. Of these smokers, the largest age group was of those between 58 and 74. One male smoker was 105, while two female users were 90 (Tu Tsung-ming 1953: 600). However, all contemporary anti-opium literature accused opium of causing a rise in the mortality rate in China, even though none of these works substantiated their allegations with evidence. For instance, a Cantonese writer argued that since most opium users, as a result of intoxication, suffered from vascular problems or brain or lung damage, 'a high mortality rate has inevitably resulted'. Moreover, 'the physique of the opium addicts is so weakened that their reproductive power can no longer be strong. Hence, most of their offspring [suffer from] mental retardation or poor health. The infant mortality rate is, as a consequence, also certainly above normal' (Lo Tzu-ch'in 1933: 17–18).

Sensational allegations such as these were only partly true. First of all, the size of the population of Canton was apparently undisturbed by the alleged problems of opium consumption. (By 1934 it had topped one million (*HCLCCN* 1934: 37)) Secondly, extant records of the mortality rate in Canton reveal no sign of any 'marked increase' in this period. Nor did opium overdosage (which must be differentiated from using opium purposely to commit suicide), though bound to happen accidentally from time to time, constitute a major cause of death in this city (ibid. 214–16).[116] The fact that the best-selling book in late-imperial Kwangtung, the almanac, contained a section on teaching its readers how to apply emergency first-aid to a victim suffering from opium poisoning suggests the commonness of this knowledge among the literate population; such knowledge might well be helpful in bringing down the number of casualties incurred from opium overdosage.[117] The few extant records of the various public hospitals in Canton provided some clues into the situation. For the whole year of 1918, for example, the Canton Hospital (Po-ch'i i-yüan) had admitted four in-patients for 'opium addiction' and a further four for 'opium poisoning'. All were successfully cured and eventually discharged (Kuang-chou Po-ch'i i-yüan 1919: 58). Between December 1936 and June 1937, for another instance, the Municipal Hospital of Canton had reportedly treated eight patients for 'opium poisoning' and 119 others had undergone to break the addiction treatment (Kuang-chou-shih shih-li i-yüan 1937: 42–3). None of these figures are not that worrying. Thirdly, although opium was seemingly a popular means of suicide (either by swallowing or smoking an overdose) from at least the late Ch'ing period, the number of deaths related to it was still insignificant in the overall mortality map of Republican Canton.[118] Moreover, the availability of opium would not have been a factor in the decision of a determined person to commit suicide as there were plenty of other methods open to them.

On the point of congenital addiction the allegations were true only in part. Western medical evidence from the same period shows that if a mother was suffering from chronic opium intoxication during pregnancy, congenital addiction was possible for her child, though by no means inevitable or universally predictable. According to a report prepared by the United States Committee on Drug Addictions in 1921, 90 per cent of the physicians who responded to a questionnaire about congenital addiction expressed serious doubt about the allegation (Terry and Pellens 1970). The situation in Republican Canton was no clearer. First of all, congenital addiction was mainly applicable to heavily addicted mothers, whose number in Republican Canton is virtually unknown. Certainly there were women who used opium in Canton, but there were seemingly few of them. The 1937 admission record of the Opium Addiction Termination Hospital shows that only eleven out of a total 1,139 inmates were women (Kuang-chou-shih chieh-yin i-yüan 1937: 3, Statistics). The 1941 admission record of another treatment institution reveals a similarly heavy imbalance between the sexes—171 adult males to four adult females.[119] Moreover, not all female opium users were necessarily heavy addicts, and likely to transmit their opium habituation to their offspring. Since congenital addiction was far less likely to be transmitted by the father of a baby, the male-dominated scene of opium consumption in contemporary Canton should not have been a serious threat to the genetic prospects of the Chinese race.[120] Therefore, although the fathers of both Ch'ü Ch'iu-pai and Lu Hsün are said to have been opium addicts (Spence 1975: 146), neither man appears to have inherited that 'fatal habit' from his father.[121] The famous 'Christian General' Feng Yü-hsiang, despite the fact that both his parents were opium addicts, was a physically well-constituted man with apparently no record of drug abuse (Lary 1985: 40).

China's military defeat by both her domestic rebels and the foreign powers during the nineteenth century was attributed to the wide spread of opium addiction in the army, which had allegedly ruined its physique and corrupted its morale. This allegation is hard to prove. First, the proponents of this view all cited as evidence an 1832 imperial edict that reprimanded two senior officials for their failure to suppress the rebellion of a Yao tribe on the Kwangtung–Hunan border; one of the major reasons for this military fiasco was that the troops were so loosely disciplined that many of them were addicted to opium and therefore unfit for battle.[122] However, they did not provide further substantial evidence to prove an undisputable link between military failure and opium smoking.[123] The T'aip'ing, Nien, and Yao rebels were not victorious;[124] and the humiliating defeat inflicted by the foreign powers on Ch'ing forces was more attributable to the former's superior weaponry and logistics than to what seems the over-simplistic reason of opium addiction among the Chinese soldiers.[125] After all, the Ch'ing forces did fight bravely in a few battles against the invading British, despite the latter's superiority in firearms and military tactics (Waley 1960: 205–10; Mao Hai-chien 1995: 440–5). Throughout the second half of the nineteenth century and the mid-twentieth century, there were apparently very few reports that suggested a relationship, however vague, between opium addiction and China's military weakness. Instead, contemporary newspapers enjoyed publishing reports of the country's achievements in military modernization; many also recorded the reporters' favourable impressions of the soldiers' excellence in their regular drills. Although opium continued to be consumed privately and illegally by officers and the rank-and-file, there was no clear evidence that the problem was both prevalent and critical.[126]

Opium addicts were also criticized as being a main source of recruits for bandits. A Cantonese scholar writes that of the 'thirteen million' bandits in Kwangtung, many 'must be recruited from those who have lost their families and properties as a result of opium [addiction]' (Lo Tzu-ch'in 1933: 14–15). A penniless, desperate addict, suffering from withdrawal, might resort to pilfering to obtain the money for a relieving puff. But that he joined the bandits and plundered the countryside because of the drug is a serious allegation that requires convincing proof. It is also difficult to know how many of these addict-bandits had already habituated to opium before they joined their 'brothers'. Moreover, if opium could devastate the Ch'ing soldiers, how could it at the same time bestow prowess on the addict-bandits?[127] Such extreme opposite effects produced by opium make sense only when all the factors of dosage amounts and the particular physiological and psychological reactions of the individual user are taken into account. Opium thus could produce a state of mental and physical lethargy and a loss of ambition in some, but inflate the personality of others to the extent that they became aggressive heroes (Terry and Pellens 1970: 506–7). Anti-opium rhetoric ignored these important complicating factors, and opium was used by the establishment as a convenient scapegoat for China's failure, as much as its own, to bring peace and stability to the country.

Nor it is fair to assume that addicts always wasted their entire family fortune on opium and ended up destitute. The inmates record of Canton's Addiction Termination Hospital shows that opium addicts or users were mostly normal citizens with stable occupations (Kuang-chou-shih chieh-yen i-yüan 1937: 2,

'Statistics').[128] The inmates record of its counterpart in Taiwan further supported this impression: opium addicts who had undergone compulsory treatment to break their addiction worked in a variety of trades such as rickshawman, tailor, prostitute, actor/actress, businessman, coalminer, maidservant, barber, and so on (Tu Tsu-ming 1953: table 18). During the 1930s, the city's two hundred or so low-class opium dens were not serving customers who were truly destitute, but mainly rickshaw pullers who stayed in Canton for the purpose of bettering their own and their relatives' lives in the native village (Han Ping 1933; Wu Jui-lin 1940: 4–7, 20–1). Sketchy official data on this city's crime rate for the late 1920s do not indicate any deterioration in law and order. Although Canton was not a safe city—there were over 8,000 suspects arrested on criminal charges in 1928 for instance—there was an absence of any clear evidence that attributed the cause of all crime largely to opium addiction (Kuang-chou-shih shih-chêng-fu t'ung-chi ku 1929: 87–93). Although the number of theft cases in Canton substantially increased during the years 1931–3, this may have been due more to an increase in urban unemployment—a repercussion of the worldwide economic depression—than to opium addiction (*Kuang-chou nien-chien* 1935: ii. 109, ch. 16).[129] Also, as discussed earlier, many well-to-do Cantonese merchants and businessmen, despite being opium users, were not ruined by their indulgence in the drug.

Contemporary anti-opiumists condemned opium addiction for producing layabouts whose productivity was so low that the economy of the country was seriously damaged. A Cantonese scholar even wrote an article to elaborate how the opium problem was destroying China's agricultural economy. In his view, since the majority of Chinese peasants already lived in poverty, additional substantial expenses incurred by opium consumption only 'chained them' further to perpetual indigence. Moreover, since opium addiction was detrimental to efficiency and productivity, the income of addicts' families was then badly affected, and the country's agricultural output also steadily fell. The culminative, as well as cumulative, effect of all these factors was the widespread abandonment of arable land. Opium was charged as the cause of the 'bankruptcy' of the Chinese countryside (Lo Tzu-ch'in 1933: 12–19).[130]

But how accurate were these allegations? A study of the agricultural economy in Republican Kwangtung tells us that the much-publicized 'bankruptcy of rural economy' in Central and South China was, to a certain extent, illusory. Instead, the rural economy of Kwangtung in this period grew steadily, enjoying a long period of prosperity until the impact of the worldwide Great Depression hit China in the early 1930s (Faure 1989). Extant Canton Customs reports from the mid-nineteenth century to the early 1930s also revealed a general trend of development and progress in the province's agricultural economy, albeit with occasional setbacks and problems such as technological backwardness. In areas where occasional drops in production or export of commodities such as silk and sugar cane occurred, the problems always lay with the inferior quality of the commodity (in the case of silk) as a result of general uninterest in quality control or technological improvement, or in plagues of parasites or diseases that destroyed the crops, but were never due to opium or its alleged socio-economic impact. In spite of occasional fluctuations, tea, rice and fruit growing, and other agricultural sidelines such as pickles and dried mandarin orange skins, enjoyed a stable growth (*YHKPK* 1996: *passim*). The Customs report did mention that the province's agricultural economy suffered from a recession after 1927 when a whirlwind of radical peasant movements swept through the Kwangtung countryside, which resulted in serious disruption to the lives of the peasants and left large stretches of land fallow (ibid. 1081–2). Contemporary scholars also pointed out that unequal distribution of land, heavy taxation, and high rent, rather than physical degeneration of the peasants or the abandonment of fields, were the major causes of the 'agrarian problems' in Kwangtung (Ch'en Han-seng 1936: ch. 1; Ch'en Ch'i-hui 1977: i. ch. 4).[131] The social surveys of three rural communities in Canton conducted by a local sociologist during the mid- and late 1930s did not indicate that opium smoking had disrupted productive work among the addicted villagers. In the report on Sha-nan, it was even stated that everyone in the settlement was diligent and productive. Meanwhile, in Hsia-tu Village, everyone, besides those who were either too young or too old, worked in a variety of jobs, mainly agricultural, and contributed to the household budgets. Although Hsia-tu was by no means a well-off community, the easy availability of jobs and the enthusiasm of its villagers in utilizing this 'natural' advantage enabled most of its households to make ends meet and even make monthly savings of a few dollars. Moreover, addicts in these communities were not identified as a factor of concern to public security, or as a source of family problems (Wu Jui-lin 1934*a*: 43–7; 1940: 248, 265–9). The conventional agricultural activities in these villages on the outskirts of Canton, in fact also in a large part of the Kwangtung province, had never been threatened in any serious manner by the growing of poppies. It was true that poppies had been grown in some poorer counties of Kwangtung, such as Swatow, Wêng-yüan, Lo-ting, Hsin-fêng, and Tung-kuan, but the scale of this was not big, and the authorities did succeed in eliminating most of it during the early years of the Republic.[132] According to a historical study on the percentage of crop area devoted to poppies in China in the 1910s, the situation in Kwangtung, like that of most other provinces with the exception of Kweichow, Szechwan, and Yünnan, was apparently mild, with 16,000 *mou* affected, or 0.04 per cent of the province's total arable land.[133] In 1924, The International Anti-opium Association reported that very little poppy was grown in Kwangtung for two reasons. First, the local people had never given any serious attention to cultivation, and consequently the quality of Kwangtung opium was poor. Secondly, the neighbouring provinces produced such enormous quantities that it was easier to buy than cultivate. The problem of poppy growing, however, re-emerged in some districts in Swatow, 'which with the neighbouring districts around Amoy produce a high quality opium grown from India opium seeds' (International Anti-opium Association 1924: 3). The reason given was the need of money, ironically, by the troops of

Ch'en Chiung-ming, who had been an ardent crusaders against opium and other vices in Canton during the early 1920s, but now compelled the farmers to cultivate poppies against their will. The farmers were said to be very much discouraged as they did not want to plant poppies, and 'as usual they have gone to the foreign missionaries for help and advice... [but] there is little that they can do for themselves'.[134] Official Chinese and British sources, however, told a different story: that the farmers in this area preferred to grow poppy, a highly lucrative crop grown during the slack season (*Chü-tu yüeh-k'an* 1928: 48). In some remoter parts of the counties of Chieh-yang, Ch'ao-yang', and Fêng-shun, it was reported in 1930 that poppies were still grown extensively, well after the departure of Ch'en from this region in 1926. An informant told the British consul there that the value of raw opium from the year's harvest was estimated at around 700,000 dollars; some of the prepared opium was sold to the government Opium Prohibition Bureau, but considerable quantities were distributed by illicit dealers. The Consul, however, added that 'details regarding the growth and the sale of opium are difficult to obtain... [and] actual statistics are not available'.[135] Even though the problem might be a serious one, it was still confined to these 'remoter parts' of the north-east region in the province. After all, the quality of soil and the climate in Kwangtung was not ideal for growing poppies; a good harvest in this province, the Imperial Maritime Customs at Canton observed, was not possible (*YHKPK* 1996: 373).

Although there were more addicts in the city than in the countryside,[136] the problems of productivity and work efficiency were apparently no more noticeable there. Better-off users of opium such as merchants and businessmen continued to work with normal efficiency.[137] Opium consumption was not even an issue of concern in a social study of workers' families in Canton.[138] Poor users such as the city rickshawmen also appear not to be ruined by the drug, and kept up their shifts of long hours (Huang Wên-to 1933: 3–4; Wu Jui-lin 1940: 13–14). After all, the annual and decennial reports of the Customs office in Canton revealed a promising trend of steady growth in trade and business and economic prosperity to this city from the late-Ch'ing period to the eve of the Japanese invasion in 1938.[139] Even the beggars in Canton did not display much evidence that they were all victims of this 'poisonous drug'. Most of them were said to be seasonal visitors from China's north-eastern provinces to Canton. During the winter months in the early 1930s, these roving beggars, as a rule, marched all the way from the north in isolated groups along the Hankow–Canton railroad. Once in Canton, they divided themselves into smaller groups and begged in different areas; they pooled and shared their takings together (*KPP* 1933: 3.2, 29 Nov.). They were seemingly impoverished or dispossessed peasants, not opium druggies.

All these half-truths, or fallacious, often sensational, allegations of the devastating effects of opium smoking on Chinese society at large and Canton in particular, were intended more to arouse patriotic sentiment among the general public than to provide accurate information about the true extent of the problem. Truth had no place in the political reality.

3. THE LESSER-KNOWN VIEW: FAVOURABLE PERCEPTIONS OF OPIUM SMOKING

Opium had become such a politicized and emotional issue that writings that gave a somewhat different view of the subject were a rarity. This does not, however, mean that the popular idea of opium consumption must be a universally condemning one. Favourable perceptions did exist, even if only implicit and seldom publicized.

A favourable attitude towards opium came out in a number of idioms heard in popular speech. For example, public premises for opium smoking in Canton were commonly called 'chatting rooms' or 'chatting places' (*t'an-hua shih* or *ch'u*), instead of 'opium dens', as they were derogatorily referred to by the Western missionaries. It is not known when this terminology was first adopted. But by our period, 'chatting room (or place)' had established itself. This morally neutral, and even somewhat intimate, term was not necessarily intended to camouflage from the public the real purpose of such places,[140] since no citizen would have been so easily deceived, and the places were in fact operating legally and openly under licence.[141] Instead, it may represent a conscious attempt, by opium users and traders, to dissociate the drug from the politicized values and stigmatized image put out in anti-opium propaganda. It also hinted that opium smoking might be an agreeable form of leisure; and that this 'chatting place' was no pernicious den where sick addicts indulged in their vicious practices. It might be just an agreeable public room where any ordinary habitué might entertain himself and his guests, or meet friends regularly, as non-addicts did in teahouses. A contemporary writer noted in his own investigation in the city's opium dens that in them 'addicts', though strangers to each other, apparently enjoyed such ad hoc companionship and chatted incessantly on a wide range of topics, but with the latest social and crime news of Canton being their favourite (Chu Yang 1935: 21). An anti-opium article stated the attraction of these chatting rooms in the eyes of their users: the strong but delightful aroma of opium, and the chance to forget about time by becoming immersed into conversation over a wide range of topics including, of course, gambling and prostitution.[142] In fact, not every chatting place fitted into the stereotype image of an opium den as a tiny, dark, and sordid room, poorly ventilated, and hidden in a back alley where addicts crouched side by side on greasy wooden beds to indulge in their drug trips.[143] Smaller establishments were, however, not all the same: some could be tidy and clean, others unhygienic and smelly (*YHP* 1933: 1, 25 June; 1934: 3.2, 10 Apr.).[144] There was, moreover, no shortage of large and ostentatious establishments. In late-Ch'ing, many of these high-class smoking houses were clustered in the western district (Hsi-kuan) outside the city wall, which was also known for its concentration of commercial shops and mansions of wealthy local merchants. These shops were described as luxuriously furnished, and their patrons, who chatted, dined, and smoked there, squandered money like 'droppings and soil'.[145] A Cantonese writer had written a rare description of one of these high-class, or 'big' in his word, opium-smoking shops in the mid-1930s:

> Most of these big opium shops . . . are located in western-style buildings with good ventilation [near broad] carriageways! The signboards they hung up at the front doors are very artistic [in design]. In addition, the characters of their shop names are also printed in red ink on [long and large] scrolls of white cloth, which are [all] hung up high in eye-catching locations. A great sum of money is spent on the interior decoration of these places. All the smoking beds, tables and chairs are made of red wood. [The shop is] divided into two wings: one accommodating seats in an open hall, the other private rooms. A private room costs one small silver dollar, while it costs 40 cents for using the open hall. [The premises are] equipped with electric fans during summer, and heaters in winter. When one enters [one of these shops, one will be impressed with its] coolness in summer and warmth in winter, and its fabulous furniture. Its attendants are called 'zither attendants', who always display a smile on their faces and serve well. All the smoking utensils are clean and elegant. [Most of these shops have] ten to twenty smoking beds, while some even have 30 to 40 beds. . . . Each bed is numbered in Arabic numerals . . . engraved on a whitish iron plate; they all look very good to me. . . . (Chu Yang 1935: 20)

Many of these high-class opium dens seem to have displayed at the entrance couplets in classical Chinese composed specially for their shops, which might help maintain a respectable image in the eyes of both their patrons and the passers-by.[146] In 1937, as an integral part of a 'serious' official campaign to eliminate opium smoking in Kwangtung, the government issued an order to all opium shops in the province to stop using 'chatting room' in their names. As replacement, all shops had to use the official designated name 'Kung-ying hsien-ch'i chieh-yen shou-hsi suo' (literally translated as 'Government-managed Outlet that Sells Opium for Smoking and that Terminates Opium Addiction within a Fixed Period of Time) (Kuang-chou-shih chin-yen wei-yüan-hui 1937*a*: 26). This uninvited change in nomenclature represented the authorities' assault on opium smoking by de-neutralizing and reformatting the old ambiguous image of opium in the popular mind. But the old ambiguity refused to depart. The city's telephone directory printed the names of at least thirteen opium-smoking shops that subscribed to the use of this municipal telephone service; the same 'privilege' was seemingly denied to gaming houses and brothels, which also existed in plenty in Canton (Kuang-chou shih tzu-tung tien-hua kuan-li wei-yüan-hui 1936).

At a time when all narcotic drugs were labelled by the establishment 'poisonous drugs' (*tu p'in*), and their consumption 'inhaling poison' (*hsi tu*), opium was instead popularly known as 'black rice' (*heh mi*), due to its dark colour; and its consumption 'eating black rice' (*shih heh mi*), by analogy with the staple 'white rice' (*pai mi*) of the Cantonese (Kōsaka Junichi 1943: 31). Such an analogy was not without any significant meaning; opium was favourably compared to rice for its popularly perceived nourishing and stimulant power.[147] In recognition of its strong stimulant effect, opium was also widely known in

Canton as 'the tiger rubber' (*lao-hu chiao*)—the physical strength of its users, under the effect of opium, was analogous to that of a tiger. The phrasing seemingly indicated the physiological importance of opium to its users, no less than its acceptable cultural position in Cantonese society. In this period, smoking licensed opium might be considered as a 'bad habit', but not necessarily as any kind of shameful crime.

There seems to be a close link between opium smoking and the theatrical world. Many Cantonese opera actors and musicians, due to their stressful and tedious work, sought both relief and stimulation from opium (Ch'en Cho-ying 1983: 313).[148] It was perhaps because of their familiarity with opium that the drug had occasionally become a theme in some scenes. In a passage from 'the best script' (*shou-pên hsi*, i.e. most popular piece) of a famous Cantonese opera actor called Shêng Kuei-yung, opium smoking is seen as a pleasurable and agreeable pastime. In this excerpt, a wastrel is scolding his wife who blames him for selling her jewellery in order to pay his debts incurred by opium smoking and other vicious habits. In defence of his opium habit, he hits back against his nagging wife:

> Lying down straight [on the bed to] smoke opium is the most enjoyable [pastime I have ever had]. Everyone says that longevity can be brought about by smoking opium; [and its efficacy] far exceeds that of ginseng and *pei-chih*. I should prefer to die if you force me to give up prostitution, gambling, opium smoking and drinking . . . Tell me, will there be an end to this kind of happy life?[149]

Grading such material as an actor's 'best script', the editor of this compilation, and to some extent his readers, display a nonchalance about the moral implication of the passage. Perhaps he is saying that opium smoking is just a culturally sanctioned way of relaxing? The social survey on Sha-nan likewise tells us that 'a large number of the inhabitants in this community regard opium smoking as the most pleasurable, the most comfortable way of alleviating sadness and boredom' (Wu Jui-lin 1934*a*: 103).

To some Cantonese writers, opium smoking was just a subject for humour, another indication of a relaxed attitude to this 'vice'.[150] One such humorist's concern was not for the pernicious effects of opium, but rather for the absurd and hypocritical nature of official 'opium suppression' measures. In the early 1930s, the Canton government taxed not only opium, but also smoking paraphernalia such as pipes and oil lamps. If a user smoked in places other than a public chatting room, he was required to purchase a one-day permit for smoking opium and using the tools (Kōain Seimubu 1939: 4). In the euphemisms of officialdom, opium was laudably and approvingly called an 'opium addiction termination drug', the monopoly of opium sale 'opium suppression', and opium retail shops 'anti-opium institutes' (Kōsaka Junichi 1943: 31). Our Cantonese author noted that on a one-day permit opium smoking tools were preposterously termed 'anti-opium apparatus'. Thinking this must be some latest scientific invention that could wean thousands of Chinese addicts, including himself, from their 'vicious habit', he consulted famous Western-trained doctors in Canton about the discovery. An addict friend of his even flew all the way down from Nanking, hoping to be cured by this new apparatus. But to his disappointment, all these experts, who charged enormous consultation fees, told him that they had heard nothing about it. He ended his piece on a note of sarcasm: 'As modern people say: "Exercise can drive away illness; [and] exposure can enhance knowledge." After finding out that [this anti-opium apparatus does exist as least on paper], I believe more and more in [the wisdom of] that [aphorism]' (Lu Wên-lung 1933: 7). In a serialized novel, one scene is set in a opium divan in Canton. Its author, however, treats the venue more as a topic of humour than of vice: 'They walk into some business premises which are a so-called "opium-temperance shop". As the name "opium-temperance shop" implies, this place is filled with guests who come, apparently, to have their opium smoking habits terminated. They all lie down on the beds, [and] conduct their opium-addiction-termination work with great concentration ...' (Ssu-ma I 1933: 14). This rather light-hearted perception of opium could be dated back to at least the late-Ch'ing period. One of the greatest humourists of Kwangtung at that time was Ho T'an-yü, an intellectual as well as an opium addict. At least on two occasions he had impressed his friends and clients with amusing couplets on the theme of opium that he composed. In one of them he used the names of five different kinds of opium and tobacco to contrast with five types of moon-cakes, which was praised as witty and technically skilful (Chien Yu-wên 1973: 43–5).

Criticisms of official opium policy, and defence of the interest of opium users in Canton, were sometimes explicit. For instance, the Canton authorities once proposed to intensify its search for unlicensed opium in order to protect the opium revenue. A journalist at once expressed his doubt about the proposal, because an increase in house-search by the already abusive inspectors might cause even greater disturbance to the citizens. In his opinion, the major concern of the government should be not its coffers, but the convenience of opium users; and the authorities should return to its old policy of limited interference (*HTJP* 1928: 2.2, 9 June).

Pro-opium-smoking views in writing, though rarely published, did occur. It is interesting to find that one of them, entitled 'Quick Notes from a Chatting Place' (*T'an-hua-ch'u su chi*), appeared in a seemingly pro-government magazine in Canton. The article begins with a general discussion, and denunciation, of the practice of opium smoking especially among the young. However, the ambiguous stance of its author emerges when he drops his official line and instead details the usefulness of opium. In terms of its recognized value in traditional Chinese pharmacology, he opines, the 'soothing' (*yu*) and 'temperance-inducing' (*chien*) properties of opium were excellent as an antidote for correcting, and hence restraining, the excessive element of fire in the body. On this account, opium was believed to be the only medicine that could tame an uncontrollably prodigal wastrel whose insatiable lust and unruly behaviour could be attributed to his body's excess of fire.

This author also records a conversation with a 70-year-old gentleman opium addict who is described as having the look of a middle-aged man. When asked how he was able to stay so young, the old man answers proudly:

> Opium and sex are the two things that I rely on to stay young... Everything which is [normally] good for human beings can become harmful if [we] fail [to understand] its nature. [And] everything which is [normally] harmful to human beings can be turned advantageous to man if [we can] master its way (*tao*). Most people spend days and nights on smoking opium... But I smoke [opium] unfailingly only after meals, and in an amount that I have never exceeded. This is how I nurture my bodily vitality (*ch'i*).

This revelation wins over our author, who concludes that if all opium users could master the 'way' of opium smoking as this wise old man has done, the drug could be of immense medicinal value:

> I am greatly convinced [by the teaching of this old gentleman]. Opium is a [precious] thing which must not be allowed to disappear from all societies of the human race. [It has the power] to enhance attentiveness, elevate the spirit, vitalize [a man's] sperms, [and] cure diarrhoea. All these extraordinary and powerful functions are absent from many herbal medicines. Why then do people criticize it as an evil thing? [It is] because its users over-dose themselves. Even if a man takes too much highly tonic drugs and food [that are good for him], it is rare that he will not be killed by [overdosage]... [Some] Chinese smoke opium like [consuming] food [and hence smoke] more than a few times every day. By doing so, [we must] know that it is not opium which damages [their health]: it is rather the users who injure themselves.[151]

Opium is not seen as a truly harmful drug so long as the user does not overdose. Nor is it simply for escapists. Instead, opium is hailed as a tonic enhancer that could be highly beneficial to the health of its users, provided that they consume it in the proper way.

To further support his argument, the author cites the example of his two friends: one a regular customer of an opium divan, the other always ordered to stay at home by strict parents who tried to keep him from opium. After a few years, however, the friend who frequented opium divans remained unaddicted, while the other friend had become heavily dependent on the drug. This example reaffirms his opinion: that there is no way to stop a person from smoking opium, and hence the important thing is to teach users how to enjoy the pleasure of it without ruining their physical health and moral integrity.

As though to justify the practice, he describes in detail the great euphoric pleasure invoked by opium:

> When the desire to smoke [opium] emerges, a user can see nothing in his eyes but sorrowful clouds, pitiful mist, bitter rain and melancholy wind. But after smoking [a few puffs, he will transcend] to a state of ultimate happiness—the sky becomes all clear, and a sense of cosmic unity begins... At this stage, everything [that he sees] is picturesque stars and happy clouds, clear sky and a bright sun. Such anomalous transcendence (*pien tai*) of the grand earth, mountains and rivers, goes beyond the control of the Creator; [and] his feelings of happiness and sorrow can no longer be regulated by the Gentleman in

Heaven . . . In my view, from ancient antiquity to the present time, this (opium) is the only genuine plaything [of mankind].

In his view is also that, since men commonly indulge in prostitution and inebriation, opium has been unfairly singled out as 'the only vice' which 'wastes [a man's] time, ruins [his] business, devastates [his] morals, [and] harms [his] health'. Moreover, with the carnal desires of men forever changing, only opium smoking can assure its users a steady lifetime's recreation because of its addictive quality. The euphoric properties of opium offer users a pleasurable, as well as a lifelong means of relieving sorrow (Ch'üan Shêng 1924: 6–9, *Wên-i*).

A similar highly ambiguous view on opium smoking is also found in a late-Ch'ing publication entitled *Yen hua* (Conversations on Opium), authored by Chang Ch'ang-chia, a scholar from Kiangsu province who himself was also an addict. The aim of this book is straightforward: to dissuade people from indulging in opium. Its content and arguments, however, are far more ambiguous than it seems. First, its ambiguity is manifested by the fact that all four prefaces written for the book by scholar-literati companions of the author did not display much critical disdain towards opium indulgence, but words of amazement at the euphoric pleasure the drug bestowed on its users. For instances, in the preface written by Ch'en Han-hua, opium was favourably compared to the drug of immortality prepared by Taoist alchemists; its aroma, colour, and fumes when heated were described as 'wonderful' (*ta hao*). His readers were told: 'Is there a need to set [oneself] free from it? One may gain [something] by indulging in it. On the stalk [of a poppy plant an addict sees] the personification of a Buddha's body.' Indulgence in this pleasurable drug was depicted as 'to make life happier' (*hsing lê jên-shêng*). In another preface, Sun Fan-wên wrote that 'poppies come from a plant that was brought and nurtured here (i.e. China) by a Buddha from the West' (Chang Ch'ang-chia 1957: ii. 765–7, Prefaces). Secondly, throughout the main text of the book, the author puzzled his readers with comments that qualified the anti-opium stance of the book. The book does, as a matter of fact, contain passages of strong-worded advice to readers to avoid the drug for its addictive narcotic property and its destructive effects on the addicts. On the property and functions of opium, the author's attitude was clearly ambiguous. Some parts of these lengthy passages are worth quoting in full:

> The nature of opium is temperance-inducing (*chien*). For being temperance-inducing, it helps reduce [the tempo] in a hundred kinds of [human] affairs. Opium is soft in texture. For being soft, it helps lower the element of fire in various [kinds of entities]. As a result [of these qualities, opium] is the only antidote for curing [metaphorically] wastrels and those who are ferocious, temperamental, and fearless perpetrators of the most evil acts. Mr. Lien Ch'êng has stated in his *The Purposes of Daffodil* [that this flower] can move the feelings [of man]. I say this is also true [of] opium. When one is craving [for it], in his eyes he can see nothing but sad clouds and bitter fog, bitter rain and sorrowful wind. When the craving stops after a feast [of the drug], the sky becomes clear and fine, and in between his eyebrows he see only fresh breeze. By then [he sees only] twinkling stars and magnificent clouds, bright sky and shiny sun. Alas! . . . The sadness and happiness of these men can no

longer be controlled by God in the Heaven... From the point of view of the present-date [people], this [opium] is unique among all the rare and beautiful things since antiquity. Every man has a hobby that helps him to pass the time. [Some] may obsess with flowers, [some] with wine, [some] with bamboo, [some] with games of chance. If these obsessions become excessive, they could cause a senseless loss of time, jeopardize one's enterprise, harm one's physique and damage morality. However, [these hobbies] are not criticised; it is opium alone which is being blamed. Is this not due to the short-sightedness [on the part of the critics]?... Opium is in fact an invaluable matter in this world. Its magical and efficient qualities of boosting spirit, strengthening sperms and stopping diarrhoea, can never be found in all other herbal medicines. Why is it, therefore, always denounced by people as something bad? It is only because those who take [this drug] do not show any restraint [in using it]... It is clear that opium does not harm man; it is man who harms himself with opium.... Is opium then a beneficial matter? [If yes,] then how come its long-time users all look skinny and thin? Is opium then harmful? [If yes,] then how come [its users are all] swift in action and high in spirit?... Not another wonderful drug as such has ever been invented since antiquity.... Now [let me] present you with a... motto: 'There is no need to stop smoking [opium], and one must not smoke too often either'.

(Ibid. 769–71, 778)

The fact that Chang Ch'ang-chia was an opium addict and a proponent against opium added significance to these passages in the sense that his ambiguous position and views on the functions and worthiness of opium might well be an honest revelation based on his years of first-hand experiences with the drug whose effects on its users defy any simple generalization.

Socially, opium was not a totally destructive economic force.[152] In Canton's rural communities Chiu-fêng-huang and Sha-nan, both the opium and gambling divans were required to pay a daily surcharge to the village organizations, which would be mainly utilized for funding major religious festivals in these villages (Wu Jui-lin and Huang En-lin 1935: 122, 153; Wu Jui-lin 1934*a*: 103–10). During temple fairs, itinerant opium sellers always congregated in host villages to make money; the fees that they paid to the fair organizers helped contribute to the funding of the events. In Chung-shan county, when its chamber of commerce planned for a fund-raising Cantonese opera performance, booths for opium smoking and gambling were permitted as a means of attracting audiences (*HTJP* 1927: 3.2, 10 June). Treated on a level with any other shop, opium divans and their contributions were not deemed sacrilegious where the funding of temple fairs was concerned. In the eyes of many ordinary Cantonese, opium smoking was not a major moral issue, nor a monstrously pernicious habit to be condemned out of hand.[153]

It is interesting to note that by the early 1930s, most opium-using rickshawmen in Canton patronized low-class opium-smoking shops that ran under the same roof as a rickshaw company. These shops sold cheap adulterated opium, which was a mixture of prepared Chinese opium, opium dross, and flavours (sometimes condensed coffee solids were used). Low-income rickshawmen and coolies preferred to patronize these shops not only because of the inferior-grade opium sold there, but, more importantly, these places allowed smokers to sleep over for no extra charge, to smoke in the morning, and settle the bills in the evening. The latter was described by some of these truly indigent rickshawmen as crucial for their working lives as they had to smoke in the morning to gain the needed strength for a day of hard work, but they did not have the money in the morning to do so. This system of payment gave them the flexibility an ordinary opium den did not. Without this morning fix, they might not be strong enough to strive for another day (Han Ping 1933: 1). Such social and economic importance of opium was also revealed in another example outside Kwangtung. Eighty per cent of the porters who carried heavy loads of salt from Szechwan to Kweichow were said to be opium addicts. When the price of opium was normally low (40 to 50 cents per *tael*), they spent less than 10 per cent of their wages on opium. On the infrequent occasions when the cost of the drug was high, they had to spend half their daily wages of 60 cents on it. When a conscientious writer tried to persuade them to give up opium, they rebuked him: 'We can only afford to smoke opium, but not to quit.' And their reason was a convincing one. That they could live on the remaining 20 or 30 cents from their daily wages after paying the opium bill; but if they had stopped smoking opium, they would not have the strength to carry salt for at least a month or two, and they would have certainly starved to death because of a lack of income. The importance of opium to the poor was significant (Chang Hsiao-mei 1987: 250–1).[154]

Two more examples of popular perceptions of opium might help build up a favourable image of the drug. First, Chinese opium had been believed to be far less poisonous than its Western, or more appropriately Indian and Central Asian, counterparts since at least the early nineteenth century. Hsü Nai-ch'i and Têng T'ing-chêng, two proponents of opium regulation (in contrast to prohibition advocated by Lin Tse-hsü and Huang Chüeh-tzu), had expounded in their memorials that since the 'nature of soil in China is moderate and mild' (*Chung-yüan tu-hsing ho-p'ing*), the opium on which it grew was 'cheap in price and weak in [stimulating] power'. Moreover, the way opium was prepared in China was said to be markedly different from that of the West—poppy in China was processed by means of boiling, and this resulted in reducing the level of poison in the drug by a considerable degree. As a result, in the opinion of these officials, locally produced opium inflicted substantially less harm on its users and even if a user was addicted to it, his habit could be terminated fairly easily. That explained, they argued, why among the population of opium smokers in China one found not only beggars and ne'er-do-wells, but also gentlemen with an admirable record of longevity (Ma Mo-ching et al. 1988: 52–4). The same picture of Chinese opium was further painted by two prominent late-Ch'ing statesmen, Li Hung-chang and Tseng Kuo-fan, in their memorials (petitions or reports) to the throne advocating lifting the ban on growing poppies in China as one of the weapons for the Chinese in the 'commercial war' against the economic threat of the Powers. Both of them held the view that locally grown opium, and the poppy from which it was made, was much less pernicious and addictive than its 'Western' counterparts. Moreover, since locally produced opium was sold much cheaper than imported opium, the economic burden to be shouldered by addicts in China would be substantially reduced, which advantaged the Chinese economy by depriving the Western Powers of a lucrative source of income. Once the Western import of opium was stopped, they argued, restrictions on Chinese opium would then be tightened until the problem of opium consumption was uprooted in China (I Wu 1970: 448). People outside the official circle apparently shared this somewhat favourable view of Chinese opium (it is not clear if this opinion was first originated by officials or civilians). A Cantonese newspaper in the mid-1880s published a leader that argued for lifting the ban on poppy planting in Kwangtung and other provinces; one of its main arguments being that Chinese opium was far less 'poisonous' than the Indian 'mud'.[155] Another late-Ch'ing source elaborated that Chinese grown poppies contain a level of 'narcotic quality' (*mi hsing*) measured between 7 and 15 per cent, depending on the species of the poppy, as compared to a highly pernicious level of 25 per cent for opium grown in India, Britain, and France. Chinese opium, it concluded, was less damaging to its users than foreign opium (ibid. 199–200). A relatively scientific laboratory report also confirmed that the pernicious impact of opium smoking on an addict was a lot less than morphine injection because a certain amount of morphine intake into a human body through smoking was lost on its way from the smoking pipe to the addict (Tu Tsung-ming 1953: 593).

Secondly, as the various sources above have pointed out, since Chinese opium was believed to be less addictive than foreign opium, addiction to it was also believed to be easily cured. An 1881 newspaper article described opium as 'a wonderful product in the world of medicine' for its effectiveness in treating many different kinds of particularly stubborn and nasty diseases. If properly administered, opium could be very beneficial to its users, whether or not they were ill. A tiny dose of opium, served with wine, could bring the following benefits to anyone: gain in weight, healthy muscles and complexion, stronger bones and joints, refreshment in spirit, heart, and mind, and even longevity. The article then went on defending opium by saying that it did not inflict any harm upon smokers, but the fire a smoker used did. The reason, it claimed, was obvious: fire released an element of poison that, once inhaled, would certainly cause harm to humans. Since opium smokers were regularly exposed to fire during the act of smoking, their constitutions were also consequently damaged. He even stated that addiction to opium was almost natural, just like one could be addicted to rice if it had been consumed regularly for a long period of time. It added, however, that opium addiction could be easily cured. Its author suggested an effective prescription, which was composed of a simple mixture of wine and prepared opium. If consumed regularly, one's addiction could be terminated without any side-effects in about one hundred days (*Shen pao* 1881, 28 Feb.) Similar herbal-medicine prescriptions to break opium addiction were abundant and readily available to anyone. These prescriptions were occasionally printed in newspapers, books, anti-opium tracts, and self-medication manuals;[156]

anti-opium herbal medicine was also distributed free of charge to addicts by the various charity halls and, especially, the Anti-opium Society of Kwangtung, from the late 1900s.[157] Interestingly, even Lin Tse-hsü, the anti-opium 'hero', had stated in a memorial to the throne that opium smokers of strong physical constitution would be only lightly addicted to the drug and their habit could be so easily terminated that even medication was not needed. In contrast, all heavy addicts were unmistakably men of weak constitution. Taking prescribed herbal medicines, however, was the only way to have their habit terminated. He then listed different 'effective prescriptions', which he had collected from experts, for the inspection of His Majesty (Ma Mo-ching et al. 1988: 67–71). By the early 1940s, the authorities in Canton, to lure addicts to enrol in its anti-addiction programme, also propagated this image of opium addiction as a 'sickness', curable in this case, under the close supervision of the 'modern' medical profession.[158] This perception of opium smoking as an easily rectifiable habit-cum-disease seemingly provided opium smokers with much-needed psychological reinforcement.

These ambiguous perceptions reflected, to an extent, the popular wisdom on opium consumption that contradicted the one-sidedly abhorrent image of opium portrayed in official anti-opium propaganda: smoking opium, though by no means harmless, was not as devastating as officially described. This popular wisdom, as has been discussed above, was not wholly fallacious, but was at least partly vindicated by clinical evidence from outside China.

During the short-lived late-Ch'ing reforms and the early years of the Republic, Canton witnessed a relatively successful campaign against opium smoking. Students staged street parades preaching anti-opium messages. In 1907, the newly founded Anti-Opium Society succeeded in lobbying for the closing down of numerous opium divans in Canton. The first Republican Provincial Assembly also ordered the arrest of several well-to-do smokers (Rhoads 1975: 94–6, 124–5, 253, 264). On the eve of the 1911 Revolution, progressive Cantonese opera troupes performed anti-opium scripts as a means to reform the 'demoralized Cantonese society'.[159] However, whether these efforts had far-reaching effects is doubtful. For example, although opium divans were strictly ordered to close, private consumption was still tolerated in 1913 (Umeda Ikuzō 1913: 17). As vehicles for popular Cantonese opera, scripts with an anti-opium theme were hardly common.[160] Popular attitudes towards the notion of opium smoking were in no way consistent, nor unvaryingly hostile. The existence of such alternative views on the moral issue of opium rendered a true suppression of the 'vice' a distant reality for the already half-hearted administration in this period.

4. *OPIUM AND THE REVOLUTIONARY GOVERNMENT*

Except for a brief period during the late 1900s and the early 1910s, and again in the early 1920s, the Cantonese authorities were never sincere about their much-publicized plans for opium suppression.

The value of the opium revenue was so important to the Canton government that any whole-hearted attempt to wipe out the drug was considered unfeasible. Ironically, opium revenue was used by successive regimes in Canton for the nationalistic purposes of first, strengthening the local government during the late-Ch'ing period, and later financing the Republican experiment: the National Revolution, and, above all, its expensive war machine.

Since the mid-nineteenth century, the opium tax, though despised by some Governor-Generals of Kwangtung, had been greatly valued as an important source of income for the local government. By the eve of the 1911 Revolution, opium tax and licence fees had brought in more than half a million *taels* of silver to the coffer of Kwangtung; this revenue was largely spent on the huge costs of military training, salaries for the army, subsidies on education, and repaying foreign loans (Kuang-tung ch'ing-li-ts'ai-chêng-chü 1910: bk. 6, 1–3; bk. 7, 11–15).

Contrary to what KMT and CCP history books say, Canton and Kwangtung in the early years of the Republic (1912–16), under the control of a pro-Yüan Shih-k'ai military administration, was proved to be one of the most sincere and determined republican regimes in enforcing the anti-opium cause: the authorities were tough on eradicating poppy farms in Kwangtung, tightened surveillance against opium smuggling, and penalized a number of corrupt officials who were protecting illicit sales of opium.[161] All this, however, was still insufficient to uproot the problem completely. During the seven years of rule by the Yünnanese and the Kwangsi clique, smuggling opium from China's south-western provinces into Kwangtung was termed a routine 'military exercise' in which government gunboats were openly involved (Li P'ei-shêng 1921: 136–7). This system rarely failed, because under normal conditions, the foreign-run Canton Customs was not allowed to search a Chinese warship.[162]

Ch'en Chiung-ming, after capturing Canton from the Kwangsi clique in 1920, proclaimed the suppression of opium and gambling in Kwangtung. At one point during this time, 'opium devils' (*yen kuei*) were said to be 'out of sight' in Canton (Li Tsung-huang 1922: 205); some 130,000 *taels* of the drug, seemingly unlicensed opium, were confiscated and burnt for three consecutive days at the Parade Ground in the eastern suburb, and the elimination of this cheap but illicit source of opium had been so successful that many junkies were reportedly forced to resort to morphine injection. To address this unexpected problem with morphia, the opinion emerged that opium should be legalized and that Canton should enter into agreement with the international anti-opium community to monitor the situation. Ch'en was also said to be very interested in making arrangements for Canton to become a member of the International Anti-opium Association (*YHPK* 1996: 1008; *KCPN* 1980: i. 229, 233). However, the stamina and the sincerity of the government in enforcing its strict rule against official and upper-class involvement in trading opium is dubious, since it was noted that 'nobody has been executed' on those grounds, though violations were common (Li Tsung-huang 1922: 205). Moreover, despite all these measures against opium smoking,

Ch'en's government, in face of financial stringency especially during the last months of his regime, had apparently lost much of its early zeal in suppressing opium; he even used the opium revenue as one of its securities for borrowing a huge loan from a Japanese bank (*KCPN* 1980: i. 228). And with the expulsion of Ch'en by Sun Yat-sen's forces, these short-lived and limited efforts at restricting opium smoking in Canton came to an end anyway.

Sun Yat-sen is always officially portrayed as an ardent anti-opium patriot. One of his denunciatory writings against opium smoking was even officially promulgated as a moral tenet that should be learnt by every good citizen. In it, Sun pronounced his deep hatred and his call for an uncompromising war against opium: 'Any one who advocates... for the legalization of opium selling, or indicates any inclination of surrendering to, or making compromise with, the evil force of opium, is the public enemy against the people's wishes.' In some official publications, Sun's portrait and this anti-opium tenet were printed side by side with that of Lin Tse-hsü; he was then officially promoted to an anti-drug hero and the successor to China's most famous, beloved, and staunch anti-opium crusader whose great but unfinished anti-opium enterprise was then passed onto the 'father of the nation'.[163] In reality, however, the government of Sun Yat-sen also relied heavily on the opium and gambling revenues for survival. Some of his undisciplined soldiers not only used opium, gambling, and prostitution as financial sources, but also patronized them (Franck 1925: 268, 275). Soon after his return to Canton in February 1923, after Ch'en Chiung-ming had fled the city, Sun's revolutionary government established a Opium Suppression Bureau, which monopolized the wholesale of prepared opium in Canton and that year brought to his administration an income of 6 million yüan.[164] In summer 1924, opium-divan owners in Canton went on strike to protest against the heavy surcharges levied on their business. The combined monthly income brought by opium and gambling revenues in 1925 totalled 5 million yüan.[165] The decision by the government of Sun Yat-sen to monopolize opium caused considerable concern to the British government, which reported the matter to the League of Nations. The report stated that

> an anti-opium bureau was established at Canton... [which] is in reality a bureau for the Government sale of opium, although nominally an anti-opium drug is supposed to be sold. Licences were at the same time issued to opium dens, who are required to buy amounts varying from 1 to 5 oz. a day according to the class of house. But the sales have been few, as the military have also been dealing in the drug themselves, despite orders to the contrary from the generalissimo, and on one occasion they held the secretary-general of the bureau to ransom for 10,000 oz. of opium.... The bureau is based on the system which Yuan Shih-kai attempted to institute in 1914–15, with the difference that the opium dens to be regulated were at that time already in existence, whereas it now appears that the bureau is to establish fresh ones. Its twenty-two regulations... are taken by the public to mean only that they may not smoke unlicensed opium, and their insincerity is regarded as proved by the clause dealing with the purchase and 'chopping' of stocks in the hands of the dealers at the time the regulations enter into force, for, if they were genuine, there

would be no necessity for 'chopping' opium which was to be destroyed or converted into anti-opium medicine. It is stated in the local press that the bureau has announced that any person may obtain opium for retailing, 92 dollars being payable for 100 dollars' worth of opium.... In the month of February 152 opium divan licences had been issued for the city of Canton alone, not including the establishments run by the Yunanese soldiery... Indeed, it has been asserted in the Chinese press that there are some 500 licensed dens in Canton city, and that branches, to be farmed out to the highest bidder, are to be established in all the towns in the province. A fee of 20 cents is said to be levied on each lamp in the Canton dens. Large quantities of opium are being landed in Canton almost daily, some for the anti-opium bureau, but a considerable amount for individual generals and their troops, who find its sale a profitable source of income.[166]

Although Sun might dislike opium at heart, the attractiveness of the substantial opium revenue proved to be too great for him to push harder for whole-hearted action to outlaw it. To the contrary, extant official documents issued by his office indicate clearly that his concern with the issue of opium came mainly, if not only, from financial considerations: how to ensure the opium tax could be properly and efficiently collected and transferred to the coffers of the Nationalist government rather than to that of individual military commanders. In one of these orders, which he sent to military commanders stationed in the province, he begged for their cooperation with local inspectors, who were dispatched by the Opium Suppression Bureau to various counties to take over the management of this lucrative source of revenue on behalf of Sun's regime based in Canton. Throughout this edict, Sun tried to persuade his military commanders of the importance of this source of 'military revenue', not the evil of opium smoking (*Kuo-fu ch'üan-chi* 1961: vii. 133, 223–4, 412–13). Most ironically, Sun had at least once presented a board of commendation with his own calligraphy to a Wan-yi Company, which was in all likelihood an opium tax-farming agent, for its generosity in giving to the government a voluntary contribution of a 'certain' amount of money for the purpose of meeting its 'military expense' (ibid. 443). Up to the eve of Sun's death, his government still propagated, intensively and extensively, the outright suppression of opium and gambling in Kwangtung. The authorities, however, were only relatively tough on crushing unlicensed gambling houses, but remained largely half-hearted towards opium smoking. As a result, Canton, not to mention the other 'remoter parts' of the province, was still full of opium divans although the number of patrons had dropped since they were not certain about the will of the authorities (*KCMKJP* 1925: 7, 17 June). Soon after Ch'en Tsê, a former admiral, had been inaugurated as the new director of the Opium Suppression Bureau in December 1925, he lost no time in putting forward a plan to raise 300,000 dollars from the opium taxes with which the dilapidated gunboats once under his command would be overhauled and prepared for action again. To ensure his plan could be implemented, he not only decided to abandon any plan of banning opium divans, but also ordered that no less than 300 such shops should be open in Canton; to save face, these opium divans would be ordered to operate under the name 'institute for treating opium addicts' (*HTJP* 1925: 1.3, 12 and 18 Dec.). To many politicians in the 'revolutionary' camp, opium and its handsome revenue were beyond doubt convenient means to an end.

In 1926, when the National Kuomintang government almost exclusively drew its income from Kwangtung, 7 per cent of the total revenue, or 4.5 million yüan, came from the lucrative opium tax (Chia Shih-i 1932: i. 111; Fitzgerald 1990: 755–7). Two years later the government monopoly on opium wholesale was sold to tax-farmers at 700,000 yüan per annum. Each month, in addition, these tax-farming companies were required to pay to the Kwangtung armies a sum of 160,000 yüan as protection fee.[167] The year 1928, therefore, was described by a British diplomat in China as a year that 'Canton took a further step in the downward path' of opium 'suppression' work. The abolition of the Opium Suppression Bureau and the farming out of the monopoly of sale of the 'anti-opium medicine' marked the end of whatever residual official sincerity in the eradication of opium consumption in Kwangtung.[168] In 1932, the charge for this wholesale monopoly was increased to more than 12 million yüan, allegedly as a result of the tightening of border vigilance which ushered in a substantial decrease in opium smuggling but also a boom in legitimate opium business (*Kuang-tung sheng-chêng-fu kung-pao* 1932: 5, no. 183, April). The opium and gambling revenues were crucial for financing first the Northern Expedition,[169] and later Ch'en Chi-t'ang's separatist movement.[170] Fully aware of its lucrativeness, the successive Canton regimes in this period were predictably reluctant to enforce any genuine opium suppression policy.[171]

Many senior and middle-ranking officials, moreover, had vested interests in the lucrative opium business. For instance, the brothers of General Huang Shao-hsiung, Chairman of the Kwangsi Government, were main partners of the Liang Kwang Company, which bid for the first monopoly of wholesale opium in Canton.[172] But with the fall of Huang and the rise of Ch'en Ming-shu in Kwangtung politics by 1930, Ch'en's uncle, Ch'en Yü-hsing, who himself was a leading farmer of raw opium, was appointed as director of the new Kwangtung Opium Suppression Bureau—an official body that oversaw the collection of opium revenue rather than its enforced suppression.[173] When he submitted his resignation in 1930, the brother of Canton's chief of police, Ou-yang Hsi, had already indicated his interest in taking over the position.[174]

Not surprisingly, the official anti-opium agency was a hotbed of corruption. In 1927, for example, the new Head of the Opium Suppression Bureau ordered the arrest of his predecessor Li Ch'êng-i on the charge of misappropriation of public funds (*HTJP* 1927: 2.2, 6 May). However, since Li was a good friend of Chiang Kai-shek who was said to be impressed by his remarkable work of raising opium revenue during the critical years of the Northern Expedition, the latter interfered by ordering the Cantonese authorities to extradite Li to Nanking for trial (ibid. 1.3, 24 May). Li was so extradited, but the trial never took place, and he was eventually released because of 'insufficient evidence' (ibid. 1.3, 22 June; 1.3, 14 July). Apparently, Li was not the only one here who may have misappropriated public funds. After his arrest, the Opium Suppression Bureau was paralysed because all senior staff appointed by Li promptly fled. His hapless successor later begged Li to write to these absentees and ask them to resume duty (ibid. 1.3, 2 June).

Almost every year throughout this period, the Canton administration launched a 'new' project of opium suppression in order to maintain a self-deceiving 'moral stance' on the issue. All these schemes, however, existed only as empty words. For instance, in 1927 Chu Chia-hua, a member of the provincial government, proposed a comprehensive plan for suppressing opium consumption in Kwangtung.[175] Ironically, just as Chu was advocating his blueprint, the Opium Suppression Bureau announced new measures, including privatization of the wholesale monopoly of opium, to increase opium revenue in the province (ibid. 1.3, 2 June; 3.2, 30 June). The privatization plan was swiftly approved (ibid. 1.3, 29 June; 3.2, 25 July), while Chu's suppression scheme was never implemented; and the 'vice' persisted untouched.

In March 1930, the Canton government issued a circular to local KMT branches defending its lack of success in suppressing opium by blaming unscrupulous officials and criminals (ibid. 1930: 1.3, 3 Mar.). One month later, however, the government announced the founding of a Kwangtung Opium Suppression Bureau, whose publicized function was to oversee the opium suppression work in the province (ibid. 3.3, 4 Apr.). In fact, this bureau was 'directly engaged in selling opium under the guise of anti-opium medicine'; and 'in one place... [was] used as an opium den'.[176]

A new Finance Minister in 1933 announced his plan to ban gambling and opium smoking in the province. But shortly afterwards he changed his mind after realizing the huge amount of revenue that these 'vices' had been supplying to the establishment (*KCHJP* 1933: 4, 2 Feb.). In another case, when a virtuous and daring junior official launched a one-man crusade against opium and gambling in his county, mainly by posters denouncing these 'vices', both the county and provincial authorities were so alarmed that this officer was ordered to stop his campaign immediately, in case it jeopardized the financial strength of the county (*HTJP* 1930: 4.3, 25 Apr.)

After the wholesaling of opium had been monopolized in 1913, the term 'opium suppression' was also redefined. 'Suppression' refered only to opium that was not imported, taxed, and sold through the official body of the Opium Suppression Bureau. 'Opium suppression' was nothing more than a means to protect official sales. The Bureau's team of inspectors were quite efficient in 'suppressing opium',[177] since they were entitled to a commission that amounted to 20 per cent of the fine paid by a convicted suspect arrested by them.[178] Probably due to this commission system, the number of arrests relating to unlicensed opium in Canton dramatically increased, from 688 cases in 1922 to 2,600 in 1928.[179] But the system backfired. Inspectors were sometimes too eager in searching out violators, and became a source of social nuisance. They conducted relentless home searches without warrants and shamelessly extorted money from the suspects. At one time, the Opium Suppression Bureau was compelled to replace all its inspectors with new recruits; the police authorities also notified these inspectors that they should not search a civilian home unaccompanied by police; but all to no avail (*HTJP* 1928: 2.2, 12 June).[180]

Senior Opium Suppression officers also violated the ban on unlicensed opium.[181] In late 1928, in the midst of an official anti-opium campaign, a department head and two of his senior colleagues in the Opium Suppression Bureau were caught red-handed smoking untaxed opium at an opium divan. They were fined a mere 200 yüan, and released without dismissal from office; though the department head later resigned after realizing that 'circumstances were turning unfavourable to him' (ibid. 1.3, 11 June).

Embarrassing case like this prompted the authorities to make yet another face-saving public gesture by proclaiming in 1929 the 'Ordinance on the Scanning of Opium Addicted Civil Servants' (*Kung-wu-yüan chin-yen k'ao-chêng t'iao-li*) to improve the efficiency, integrity, and honesty of civil servants.[182] Whether or not this ordinance was effective is not known. But it certainly did not end the official role in the perpetuation of the licensed opium business in Kwangtung.

In late 1933, Ch'en Chi-t'ang imposed a short-lived prohibition against opium and gambling in Canton. As a result, many public opium divans were forced to move away from the heart of the city to the southern suburb in Honan, and some moved to the resort town of Shen-chen at the border with Hong Kong. This campaign, which probably lasted until the fall of Ch'en in July 1936, did not aim at any proper eradication of these 'vices', but a relocation of these forms of public amusement to the outskirts of Canton where opium and gaming businesses were allowed to continue as usual; and the substantial revenues from these businesses continued to flow uninterrupted into the government treasury. Problems of access caused to the customers were soon overcome by the free shuttle-bus services linking this part of Honan with Canton city provided by the owners of the relocated premises. Moreover, many 'private' opium divans or gambling houses, which entertained regular customers only, continued to operate secretly inside the city. In June 1934, the municipal government of Canton announced the plan that the newly developed area of Ta-sha-tou in the western suburb would be designated as a 'commercial quarter' to which all the licensed opium divans, gambling houses, and brothels in the city would be ordered to move.[183]

When the Nanking government implemented the New Life Movement in Canton from August 1936 until the next spring, opium smoking was attacked in official publications for being one of the many harmful habits that caused great damage to its users, to society, and to the country. In reality, however, the official organizing committee did not invest much effort in suppressing opium seriously throughout this half-year-long campaign. The committee, however, had sent delegates to help organize an Anti-Poisonous Drugs Convention in Canton, and they assisted in its publicity work. School students, civil servants, and members of official worker unions were also mobilized to take part in a mass demonstration against opium and narcotic drugs. It also publicized extensively that all 'poisonous drugs' (*tu-p'ing*) such as cocaine, heroin, and other narcotic opiate derivatives were banned with immediate effect, but the ban on opium smoking would be enforced only four years from then, hopefully in 1940 (*HTJP* 1936: 2.2, 1 Sept.). Meanwhile, the authorities announced the immediate enforcement of two measures: all opium users were to be registered, and all opium dens had to close down; opium could be purchased only at officially approved shops from September 1936. However, the plan to have all addicts registered turned out to be less smooth than expected; and the deadline had to be postponed time and again (*YHP* 1936: 9, 3 Nov.; Kuang-chou-shih chin-yen wei-yüan-hui 1937*a*: 16). In respect of closing down all opium dens, many licensed opium divans continued to operate smoothly in Honan, especially in areas outside the police jurisdiction, so much so that a local newspaper speculated that the authorities had already had the plan postponed (*YHP* 1936: 9, 26 Oct.). Moreover, this professedly anti-opium government continued to express concern over a drop in opium revenue for Kwangtung. In the hope of addressing this issue, a new director was appointed to the Opium Suppression Bureau, whose major task was to reverse the situation so that the income from opium sales and taxes would be resuscitated. Money, rather than suppression, was still a key concern to this new Nationalist administration in Canton (*HTJP* 1936: 2.1, 24 Aug.). The anti-opium mission of the movement was apparently confined to propaganda rather than active suppression.[184]

The founding of the Canton Opium Addiction Termination Hospital in 1937, shortly after the Nanking government had overthrown the Ch'en Chi-t'ang regime and assumed control over the province, was less an act of goodwill than a publicity showpiece intended to dramatize the 'benevolent image' of the new administration. The hospital was claimed to be able to terminate opium addiction in an average of two weeks. There was also an optimistic forecast that, with the aid of this hospital, in about four years all opium addicts in Canton would be cured.[185] In this manner the new government appeared as the saviour that would deal with China's centuries-long opium problem.

But what did 'cure' mean? According to the hospital's first annual report, inmates would not be given opiate substitute during the final three days of treatment; if they did not show any withdrawal symptoms, they would be considered as 'cured'.[186] Western medical evidence, however, shows that opium addicts could relapse even after more than five years of abstention (Lindesmith 1968: 50–4). The addicts' relapse rate in Canton, though not recorded, may have been high, due to the easy availability of opium in this period. This particular institution was more interested in boasting about the number of inmates 'cured', seemingly without concern for the real problem of relapse, than in the medical control of addiction, and, least of all, in the long-term treatment of the addicts. It is the height of irony that, while this hospital was founded to impress the public with the new government's commitment to anti-opium measures, the authorities had no plan to close their 300 opium retail and smoking outlets (*ch'ou hsi so*) (*KCPN* 1980: ii. 485). The continuous existence of opium in Canton and

Kwangtung was a result of the clearly ambiguous and arguably half-hearted attitude of successive governments towards the drug. Opium was, therefore, a denigrated but nevertheless welcome accomplice of both the Republican and the Nationalist revolutions.

Canton's 'problem' of opium smoking during this period, was, in many respects, a far more complicated social phenomenon than it was portrayed in contemporary anti-opium literature. The true extent of the problem, and its alleged devastating impact, were distorted in order to meet the socio-political purposes of anti-opiumists, and of the hypocritical authorities. To some, opium was certainly a source of social evil. But to many more, it was a desirable and 'necessary' drug. The social and political functions of opium smoking in Canton in this period were far more meaningful and extensive than the stigmatized image of 'vice' suggested.

REFERENCES

Ah Nan (1997), 'Pei-p'ing ti pai-mien fang-tzu', in K'o Ling (ed.), *Erh-shih shih-chi Chung-kuo chi-shih wên-hsüeh wên-k'u, 1900–1949: Tien-t'ang yü ti-yü* (Shanghai: Wên-hui ch'u-pan-shê).

Ah Ying (1957), *Ya-pien chan-chêng wên-hsüeh chi*, 2 vols. (Peking: Ku-chi ch'u-pan-shê).

Ball, J. Dyer (1903), *Things Chinese*, 4th edn. (Hong Kong: Kelly & Walsh).

Becker, Gary S., and Murphy, Kevin M. (1988), 'A Theory of Rational Addiction', *Journal of Political Economy* 96/4.

Berridge, Virginia (1999), *Opium and the People: Opiate Use and Drug Control Policy in Nineteenth and Early Twentieth Century England* (London: Free Association Books).

—— and Edwards, Griffith (1981), *Opium and the People: Opiate Use in Nineteenth-Century England* (London: Allen Lane).

Byron, John (1987), *Portrait of A Chinese Paradise: Erotica and Sexual Customs of the Late Ch'ing Period* (London: Quartet Books).

Canton: Its Port, Industries & Trade (1932), (Canton: Canton Advertising & Commission Agency).

Champly, Henry (1934), *The Road to Shanghai: White Slave Traffic in Asia*, trans. Warre B. Wells (London: John Long).

Chang Ch'ang-chia (1957), *Yen hua*, in Ah Ying (ed.), *Ya-pien chan-chêng wên-hsüeh chi* (Peking: Ku-chi ch'u-pan-shê).

Chang Chên-chih (1929), *Mu-chien Chung-kuo shê-hui ti ping-tai* (Shanghai: Min-chih shu-chü).

Chang Hsiao-mei (1987), *Kuei-chou ching-chi*, cited in Kuei-chou shê-hui k'o-hsüeh pien-chi pu et al. (eds.), *Kuei-chou chin-tai ching-chi shih tzu-liao hsüan chi* (Ch'êng-tu: Sze-chuan-shêng shê-hui k'o-hsüeh yüan), i.

Chang Hsin-pao (1964), *Commissioner Lin and the Opium War* (New York: W. W. Norton & Co.).

Chang Kung-p'ing (1993), *Têng-yü yü-shêng shu*, 3 vols. (Taipei: Lung-wên chu-pan-shê ku-fên yu-hsien kung-ssu).

Chang Tzu-p'ing (1928–30), *Tzu-p'ing hsiao-shuo hsüan*, 3 vols. (Shanghai: Hsien-tai shu-chü and Lo ch'ün shu-tien).

Ch'en Ch'ien (1989), *Hsiang-kang chiu-shih chien-wên lu* (Kuang-tung jên-min ch'u-pan-shê).

Ch'en Ch'i-hui (1977), 'Kuang-tung t'u-ti li-yung yü liang-shih chan hsiao', in Hsiao Ch'êng (ed.), *Ming-kuo erh-shih nien-tai Chung-kuo ta-lu t'u-ti wen-t'i tzu-liao*, 2 vols. (Taipei: Chêng wên ch'u-pan-shê, and Chinese Research Materials Centre).

Ch'en Cho-ying (1983), 'Hung ch'uan shih-tai ti Yüeh pan kai-ku'ang', *YCYCTLH*.

Ch'en Han-seng (1936), *Agrarian Problems in Southernmost China* (Shanghai: Kelly & Walsh).

Ch'en Hua-hsin (1983), 'Yüeh-chü yü Hsin-hai kê-ming', *YCYCTLH*.

Ch'en Nien-ti (1935), 'Hung wan', *Jên-chien shih* 20.

Ch'êng Hao (1985) (ed.), *Kuang-chou kang shih*, 2 vols. (Peking: Hai-yang ch'u-pan-shê).

Ch'i wan hua shê (1910) (ed.), *Chung-kuo shih ta hai* (Canton: Shêng ch'ün shu-chü).

Chia Shih-i (1932), *Min-kuo hsü ts'ai-chêng shih* 1 (Shanghai: Shang-wu yin-shu-kuan).

Chia-yin nien hsin t'ung-shu (1914) (Canton: n.p.).

Chien Ch'êng-jun et al. (1995), *Fei Hsiao-t'ung Lu Tsun nung-t'ien wu-shih-nien* (Ku-ming: Yünnan jên-min ch'u-pan shê).

Chien Yu-wên (1973), 'Ho Tan-yü ti yu-mo', *Kuang-tung wên-hsien chi k'an* 3/3.

The China Year Book (1912–1930s), ed. H. G. W. Woodhead and H. T. Montague Bell (London: Routledge & Sons).

Chin-tai Kuang-chou k'ou-an ching-chi shê-hui kai-k'uang: Yüeh hai-kuan pao-kao hui tsi (YHKPK) (1996), ed. Kuang-chou-shih ti-fang-chih pien-hsüan wei-yüan-hui pan-kung-shih and Kuang-chou hai-kuan-chih pien-hsüan wei-yüan-hui (Canton: Chi-nan ta-hsüeh ch'u-pan-shê).

Ch'iu Ho-chin (1924) (ed.), *Yüeh tung ming yu ch'ü pên* (Canton: Ta hsin shu-chü).

Chu Hsiu-hsia (1930), *Pa-yüeh chien* (Shanghai: Hsien-tai shu-chü).

Chu Yang (1935), 'Kuang-tung ti ya-pien', *Jên-chien shih* 30 (October).

Ch'üan Shêng (1924), 'T'an-hua-ch'u su chi', *KCTC* 1/1, December.

Ch'üan Yüeh shê-hui shih-lu (1911), (Canton: Tiao-cha ch'üan Yüeh shê-hui chü).

Chung-kuo jên-min chêng-chih-hsieh-shang-hui-i Kuang-tung-shêng Kuang-chou-shih wei-yüan-hui wên-shih tzú-liao wei-yüan-hui (1980) (ed.), *Kuang-chou pai-nien ta-shih chi (KCPN)*, 2 vols. (Canton: Kuang-tung jên-min ch'u-pan-shê).

Chü-tu yüeh-k'an 22, 23 (1928), (Shanghai: Chung-hua kuo-min chü-tu hui).

Courtwright, David T. (2001), *Dark Paradise: A History of Opiate Addiction in America* (Cambridge, Mass.: Harvard University Press).

Faure, David (1989), *The Rural Economy of Pre-Liberation China: Trade Expansion and Peasant Livelihood in Jiangsu and Guangdong* (Hong Kong: Oxford University Press).

Fêng-su kai-kê wei-yüan-hui (1930), (ed.), *Fêng-su kai-kê ts'ung k'an (FSKKTK)* (Canton: Kuang-chou-tê-pieh-shih tang-pu hsüan-ch'uan-pu).

Fitzgerald, John (1990), 'Increased Disunity: The Politics and Finance of Guangdong Separation, 1926–1936', *Modern Asian Studies* 24/4.

Franck, Harry A. (1925), *Roving Through Southern China* (New York: Century).

FSKKTK, see Fêng-su kai-kê wei-yüan-hui.

Gillingham, Paul (1983), *At the Peak: Hong Kong Between the Wars* (Hong Kong: Macmillan).

Hai Lung (1934), 'Yü hou ch'ün-hsüan ti hsia-chi yen-shih', *YHP*, 10 April.

Han Ping (1933), 'Hsia-chi yen-shih fang-wên chi', *YHP*, 25 June.

HCLCCN, see Kuang-chou shih-chêng-fu (1934).

Hogshire, Jim (1994), *Opium for the Masses* (Washington: Loompanics Unlimited).

Hsiang-yen ts'ung-shu (*HYTS*) (1909–1911), (Shanghai: Kuo-hsüeh fu-lun-shê).

Hsü Ching-yüan (1924), 'Kuang-chou tsui chin chih chü tu yün-tung lun', *Kuang-chou tsa chih* 1/1.

Hu P'o-an et al. (1986) (ed.), *Chung-hua ch'üan kuo fêng-su chih*, 2 vols. (Shih-chia-chuan: Ho-nan jên-min ch'u-pan-shê). First published 1923 (Shanghai: Kuang chi shu-chü).

Hua-tzu jih-pao (*HTJP*) (Hong Kong: Hua-tzu jih-pao shê).

Huang Wên-to (1933), 'Kuang-chou-shih jên-li-chê shih-yeh ti tiao-ch'a'. *Nan-ta ching-chi* 2/1, January.

Hung Ching-kiang (1989), 'Ya-pien liu-ju Chung-kuo ho Shang-hai shou-hai ching-ku'ang', in Shang-hai wên-shih yen-chiu kuan (ed.), *Chiu-Shang-hai ti yen tu ch'ang* (Hong Kong: Chung yüan ch'u-pan-shê).

Hung Lang (1933), 'Chê-fu k'ou-chung chi chieh-yen-tiao', *YHP*. 5 May.

I Chien-ch'uan (1937), 'Kuang-chou-shih ch'ing-tu ta hui ch'ou-pei ching-kuo', in Kuang-chou-shih chin-yen wei-yüan-hui (1937*b*).

I Wu (1969) repr., 'Ying-shu', *Chung-ho yüeh-k'an shih-liao hsüan-chi* (Taipei: Wên hai chu-pan-shê).

——(1970) repr., 'Yen ku', *Chung ho yüeh k'an shih-liao hsüan-chi: ti-erh chi* (Taipei: Wên hai ch'u-pan-shê).

International Anti-Opium Association, Peking (1922), *The War Against Opium* (Tientsin: Tientsin Press).

——(1924), *Opium Cultivation and Traffic in China: An Investigation in 1923–1924* (Peking: The International Anti-opium Association).

Kao Hsiang-li (n.d.), *Ya-pien liu-tu shih* (n.p.).

Kazantzakis, Nikos (1982), *Japan, China: A Journal of Two Voyages to the Far East*, trans. George C. Pappageotes (Berkeley, Calif.: Creative Arts Book Co.).

KCPN, see Chung-kuo jên-min chêng-chih-hsieh-shang-hui-i Kuang-tung-shêng Kuang-chou-shih wei- yüan-hui wên-shih tzu-liao wei-yüan-hui (1980).

Kōain Seimubu (1939), *Kanton no sembai jigyō* (Tokyo: n.p.).

Kolb, Lawrence (1928), 'Drug Addiction', *Archives of Neurology and Psychiatry* 20.

Kōsaka, Junichi (1943), 'Ingo yori mitaru Kanton sha kai so', *Minzoku Taiwan* 3/4–5.

KPP, see Kung-p'ing pao (1924–1949).

Kuang-chou min-kuo jih-pao (*KCMKJP*) (Canton: Kuang-chou min-kuo jih-pao shê).

Kuang-chou nien-chien (1935), ed. Kuang-chou nien-chien pien tsuan wei-yüan-hui, 2 vols. (Canton: Kuang-chou nien-chien pien tsuan wei-yüan-hui).

Kuang-chou Po-ch'i i-yüan (1919) (ed.), *Po-ch'i nien pao 1918* (Canton: n.p.).

Kuang-chou shê-hui tsa chih 1 (*c*.1910s) (Canton: Kuang-chou shê-hui tsa chih shê).

Kuang-chou shih-chêng-fu (1934) (ed.), *Kuang-chou shih-chêng-fu hsin chu lo-ch'êng chi-nien tê-k'an (HCLCCN)* (Canton).

Kuang-chou-shih-chêng-fu t'ung-chi hui k'an (1929).

Kuang-chou-shih chêng-hsieh wên shih tzu-liao yen-chiu wei-yüan-hui (1987) (ed.), *Nan t'ien sui yüeh: Ch'en Chi-t'ang chu Yüeh shih-ch'i chien wên shih lu* (Canton: Kuang-tung jên-min ch'u-pan-shê).

Kuang-chou-shih chieh-yen i-yüan (1937) (ed.), *Kuang-chou-shih chieh-yen i-yüan nien pao* (Canton).

Kuang-chou-shih chin-yen wei-yüan-hui (1937*a*) (ed.), *Kuang-chou shih chin-yen wei-yüan-hui kung-tso chi-yao* (Canton: n.p.).

——(1937*b*) (ed.), *Kuang-chou shih ch'ing tu yün-tung tê k'an* (Canton: n.p.).

Kuang-chou-shih ch'ing-tu yün-tung tê k'an (1937).

Kuang-chou-shih hsin-shêng-huo yün-tung wei-yüan-hui (1937) (ed.), *Kuang-chou-shih hsin-shêng- huo yün-tung chi-yao ti i chi* (Canton: n.p.).

Kuang-chou shih shê-hui chü (1941) (ed.), *Shê-hui tê k'an* (Canton: Kuang-chou shih shê-hui chü).

Kuang-chou-shih shih-chêng-fu t'ung-chi ku (1929) (ed.), *Kuang-chou-shih shih-chêng-fu t'ung-chi nien-chien. Ti i wei* (Canton: Kuang-chou-shih shih-chêng-fu).

Kuang-chou-shih shih-chêng-t'ing (1924), *Kuang-chou-shih shih-chêng pao kao hui k'an*.

Kuang-chou-shih shih-chêng-t'ing shê-hui-tiao-cha-ku (1927) (ed.), *Ti sze lei: shê-hui pu-liang shih-yeh* (Canton).

Kuang-chou-shih shih-li i-yüan (1937) (ed.), *Kuang-chou shih shih-li i-yüan nien pao (1936)* (Canton: n.p.).

Kuang-chou tsa chih (KCTC) (1924–1930s), (Canton:Kuang-chou tsa chih shê).

Kuang-tung ch'ing-li-ts'ai-chêng-chü (1910) (ed.), *Kuang-tung ch'üan shêng ts'ai-chêng shuo-ming shu*, 2 vols. (Tientsin: Ching-chi hsüeh hui).

Kuang-tung shêng-chêng-fu (1920–30s) (ed.), *Kuang-tung shêng-chêng-fu kung-pao* (Canton).

Kuang-tung shêng-chêng-fu min-chêng-ting chin-yen kung-tso pao-kao shu (1940), (Canton: n.p.).

Kuang-tung shêng chin-yen chü chieh-yen liu-i-so ch'êng-li i-chou-nien chi-lien tê-k'an (1942), (Canton: n.p.).

Kuang-tung shêng-chêng-fu ts'ai-chêng-t'ing and Kuang-tung ts'ai-chêng tê-pai-yüan kung-chü (1934) (eds.), *Kuang-tung shêng ts'ai-chêng chi shih*, 3 vols. (Canton: Kuang-tung-shêng chêng-fu ts'ai-chêng-t'ing).

Kuang-tung-shêng hsi-chü yen-chiu-shih (1983) (ed.), *Yüeh-chü yen-chiu tzu-liao hsüan (YCYCTLH)* (Canton).

Kuang-tung shêng hsüan-an-shih kung-ch'u (1912–20s) (ed.), *Kuang-tung kung pao* (Canton).

Kung-p'ing pao (KPP) (1924–1949) (Canton: Kuang-chou Kung-ping pao shê).

Kuo-fu ch'üan-chi (1961), 6 vols. (Taipei: Chung-yang wên-hua kung-ying shê).

Lamson, Herbert Day (1935), *Social Pathology in China*, 2nd edn. (Shanghai: Commercial Press).

Lary, Diana (1985), *Warlord Soldiers: Chinese Common Soldiers, 1911–1937* (Cambridge: Cambridge University Press).

Lattimore, Owen (1975), *Manchuria: Cradle of Conflict*, rev. edn. (New York: AMS Press). First published 1935.

Leng Yen (1927), 'Ch'u ku yü hua', *HTJP*, 7 May.

Lewin, Louis (1964), *Phantasia: Narcotic and Stimulating Drugs* (London: Routledge & Kegan Paul).

Li P'ei-shêng (1921), *Kuei-hsi chü Yüeh chih yu-lai chi ch'i ching-kuo* (Canton: n.p.).

Li Tsung-huang (1922), *Hsin Kuang-tung kuan-ch'a chi* (Shanghai: Shang-wu yin-shu-kuan).

Light, Arthur B., and Torrance, Edward G. (n.d. [1929–30]), *Opium Addiction* (Chicago: American Medical Association).

Lin Man-hung (*c.*1980s), *Ch'ing-mo shê-hui liu-hsing hsi-shih ya-pien yen-chiu* (Taipei: n.p.).

Lindesmith, Alfred R. (1968), *Addiction and Opiates*, 2nd edn. (Chicago: Aldine).

Liu Shih-hsin (1937), 'Ch'ing-tu yün-tung yü min-tsu fu-hsing', in Kuang-chou-shih chin-yen wei-yüan-hui (ed.), *Kuang-chou-shih ch'ing-tu yün-tung tê k'an* (Canton).

Liu Tsai-su (1926), *Kuang-chou kuai lan* (Shanghai: Shih-chieh shu-chü).

Lo Tzu-yin (1933), 'Chung-kuo ya-pien wen-t'i ho tui yu nung-ts'un ti yin-hsiang', *Nan-ta ching-chi* 2/2, May.

Lo Yün-yen (1938), *Tu-p'in wen-t'i*, 2nd edn. (Changsha: Shang-wu yin-shu-kuan).

Lu Wên-lung (1933), 'Chieh-yen chih-liao ch'i-chu', *KCTC* 23.

Ma Mo-ching et al. (1998) (eds.), *1729 nien–1949 nien Chung-kuo chin-tu shih tzu-liao* (Tientsin: Tientsin jên-min ch'u-pan-shê).

Maddux, James F., and Desmond, David P. (1981), *Careers of Opioid Users* (New York: Praeger).

Mao Hai-chien (1995), *Tien-chou ti pêng-k'uei* (Peking: San-lien shu-tien).

Miners, Norman (1987), *Hong Kong under Imperial Rule, 1912–1941* (Hong Kong: Oxford University Press).

Nan-fang jih-pao (*NFJP*) (1950–present), (Canton: Nan-fang jih-pao shê).

Nan t'ien sui yüeh.

Newman, R. K. (1995), 'Opium Smoking in Late Imperial China: A Reconsideration', *Modern Asian Studies* 29/4.

NFJP, see Nan-fang jih-pao.

Nan-yang shang-pao (*NYSP*) (Singapore: Nan-yang shang-pao shê).

The Opium Trade (1974), 6 vols. (Wilmington, Del.: Scholarly Resources Inc.).

Ou-yang Hui-tsung (1937), 'Chin-yen li-shih yü chin-yen chien-tu', in Kuang-chou-shih chin-yen wei-yüan-hui (ed.), *Kuang-chou shih ch'ing-tu yün-tung tê k'an* (Canton).

Ou-yang Shan (1948), *Shih-pai ti shih-pai-chê* (Shanghai: Ch'iao-fêng ch'u-pan-shê).

'Pên yüan ch'ou-pei ching-kuo', in Kuang-chou-shih chieh-yen i-yüan (ed.), *Kuang-chou-shih chieh-yen i-yüan nien pao* (1937).

P'eng Kuo-liang (1981), 'Hsi-nan san shêng Ch'uan Tien Ch'ien chin-tu yü chin-yen chih yen-chiu 1911–1940', Kuo-li Chêng-chih ta-hsüeh li-shih hsi shuo-shih lun-wên (Master's thesis, University of Kuo-li Chêng-chih ta-hsüeh).

P'eng Yang-ou (1982), *Hêh-chieh yüan-yün*, in Ah Ying (ed.), *Wan-Ch'ing wên-hsüeh ts'ung-ch'ao. Hsiao-shuo*, iii (Peking: Hsin-hua shu-chü). First published 1909.

Philippine Commission, Opium Investigation Committee (1905), *Report of the Committee appointed by the Philippine Commission to investigate the use of opium and the traffic therein and the rules, ordinances and laws regulating such use and traffic in Japan, Formosa, Shanghai, Hong Kong, Saigon, Singapore, Burma, Java and the Philippine Islands/ Bureau of Insular Affairs, War Department* (Washington: Government Print Office).

Pruitt, Ida (1967), *A Daughter of Han: The Autobiography of a Chinese Working Woman* (Stanford: Stanford University Press).

P'u Liang-chu (1929), 'I-nien lai chi Kuang-chou tang-chêng', in *Kuang-tung Kuang-chou tang-chêng kung-tso kai-ku'ang pao-kao* (Canton: n.p.).

Rhoads, Edward J. M. (1975), *China's Republican Revolution: The Case of Kwangtung, 1895–1913* (Cambridge, Mass.: Harvard University Press).

Rowntree, Joshua (1895), *The Opium Habit in the East: A Study of the Evidence and Report of the Royal Commission on Opium, 1893–5* (Westminster: P. S. King & Son, and E. T. W. Dennis).

Sheridan, James E. (1966), *Chinese Warlord: The Career of Feng Yü-hsiang* (Stanford: Stanford University Press).

'Shina chikaiji no ahen mondai', *Shina* 22/4 (1931).

Shu pao (1965), (Taipei: Tai-wan hsüeh-shêng shu-tien). First published 18 April 1884 to 4 April 1885 (Canton: Kuang-chou Shu-pao shê).

Skog, Ole-Jørgen (2000), 'Addicts' Choice', *Addiction* 95/9.

Spence, Jonathan (1975), 'Opium Smoking in Ch'ing China', in Frederic Wakeman Jr. and Carolyn Grant (eds.), *Conflict and Control in Late Imperial China* (Berkeley: University of California Press).

Ssu-ma I (1933), 'Chou-tai jên-shêng', *KCTC* 20.

Sultzberger, Hartman (1884) (ed.), *All About Opium* (London: Wertheimer, Lea).

Sung Yü (1989), *T'ang-hsi chin-fên* (Hong Kong: I yüan ch'u-pan-shê).

Szasz, Thomas (1975), *Ceremonial Chemistry: The Ritual Persecution of Drugs, Addicts, and Pushers* (New York: Anchor Press and Doubleday).

Sze yin ch'i (*c.*1920s), (Hong Kong: Kuang-mou hao).

Têng Yü-shêng (1911) (ed.), *Ch'üan Yüeh shê-hui shih-lu ch'ü-pien* (Canton: T'i-cha ch'üan Yüeh shê-hui-chü).

Terry, Charles E., and Pellens, Mildred (1970), *The Opium Problem* (Glen Ridge, NJ: Patterson Smith). First published 1928.

Tieh Ma (1931), 'Jui-yüeh-fen chi Kuang-chou shê-hui', *Chien yen piao* 1/1.

Tsui-mien-shan-jên (*c.*1920s), *Kuang-tung heh-mo ta kuan* (Canton: n.p.).

Tu Tsung-ming (1953), 'Statistical Studies on Opium Addiction in Formosa, Eighth Report', in *Tu Tsung-ming yen-lun chi* (Taipei: Tu Tsung-ming p'o-shih huan-li chi-nien chiang-hsüeh chih-chin kuan-li wei-yüan-hui), ii.

T'un Huang (1927*a*), 'Yü yu t'an chia-chuang', *HTJP*, 9 June.

——(1927*b*), 'Yen lin', *HTJP*, 27 June.

Turner, J. A. (1982), *Kwangtung or Five Years in South China* (Hong Kong: Oxford University Press). First published in 1894.

Tzu-hang-shih (1919), *Kuang-chou chih-nan* (Canton: Hsin hua shu-tien).

Umeda Ikuzō (1913), 'Kanton no iji oyobi eisei', *Shina* 4/9, May.

Waley, Arthur (1960), *The Opium War Through Chinese Eyes* (London: George Allen & Unwin).

Wang Tsung-hsien (1974), *Kuang-tung wên-wu ts'ung-t'an* (Hong Kong: Chung-hua shu-chü).

Wu Jui-lin (1934*a*), 'Sha-nan tan-min tiao-ch'a pao kao', *Ling-nan hsüeh pao* 3/1.

——(1934*b*), *San-shui tan-min tiao-ch'a* (Canton: Ling-nan ta-hsüeh shê-hui yen-chiu-so).

——(1940), *Kuang-chou-shih liu-pai jên-li-chê fu shêng-huo ts'ang-ku'ang chih tiao-ch'a* (Canton: Ling-nan ta-hsüeh shê-hui-hsüeh hsi shê-hui tiao-ch'a-so).

——(1971), 'San-shui tan-min tiao-ch'a' (Canton: Ling-nan ta-hsüeh shê-hui yen-chiu-so, 1934), reprinted in Lou Tsu-k'uang (ed.), *Folklore and Folk Literature* (Taipei: The Orient Cultural Service).

——and Huang En-lin (1935), 'Chiu Fêng-huang ts'un tiao-ch'a pao kao', *Ling-nan hsüeh pao* 4/3.

Wu Yü, Liang Li-ch'êng, and Wang Tao-chi (1988), *Min-kuo heh-shê-hui* (Nanking: Kiang-su ku-chi ch'u-pan-shê).

YCYCTLH, see Kuang-tung-shêng hsi-chü yen-chiu-shih.

Yen Ching-yueh (1934), 'Crime in Relation to Social Change in China'. Unpublished Ph.D. dissertation, University of Chicago.

'Yen-kuan fu' (1910), in *Piao tu ch'ui hsin chi* (Canton: Shêng-ch'êng Liu yüeh chin kuan).

YHKPK, see Chin-tai Kuang-chou k'ou-an ching-chi shê-hui kai-k'uang (1996).

Yü Chiao-ch'ing (1909), 'Ch'ao Chia fêng yüeh chi', *HYTS* 1.

Yü Ch'i-chung (1934), *Kuang-chou kung-jên chia-t'ing chih yen-chiu* (Canton: Kuo-li Chung-shan ta-hsüeh ching-chi tiao-ch'a-ch'u).

Yü En-tê (1934), *Chung-kuo chin yen fa-ling pien ch'ien shih* (Shanghai: Chung-hua shu-chü).

Yüeh-hua pao (YHP) (1927–50) (Canton: Yüeh-hua pao shê).

4

Gambling in Canton: Myth and Reality of a Calamity

This chapter examines the official perceptions of gambling that were held during our period, getting behind their rhetorical language, and critically assessing them and their shortcomings in order to understand the motives that underpinned such views. Popular perceptions of gambling are also studied, revealing what gambling meant to the Cantonese, and how widespread this pastime was.

1. *THE OFFICIAL AND THE ORTHODOX PERCEPTIONS OF GAMBLING*

Condemnation

Although Confucius seems to have held a somewhat ambiguous attitude towards gambling,[1] orthodox Confucianism has no place for it.[2] An anti-gambling treatise of the late eighteenth century condemns it as 'the three wastes', a quite usual view commonly found in nearly all anti-gambling literature:

> [Gamblers] shuffle [*ma tiao* dominoes] for days and nights, without adequate sleep, without any spare moment for meals... They have [even] forgotten about their friends, [and] abandoned books and music. This is [what I] call a 'waste of time'... [When gambling with these dominoes], three people join hands to crush the fourth one... [Their minds are] filled with deceptive tricks... [and they intrigue so much that their] spirits are disturbed, [and] their faces turn pale yellow. This is [what I] call a 'waste of mind-and-heart'. All these must cause illness and insanity [to them]... [When gamblers] win, all that happens is that more counters are exchanged [for more betting]. When [they] lose, deeds of debt are signed. Family houses, land, [and all the] precious antiques that they inherited from their ancestors, are sold [as a result]... This is [what I] call a 'waste of wealth'.

Its author also believes that a heavily indebted gambler would not hesitate to violate the divine moral principles by selling his wife and children. Gambling was seen as a genuine threat to the Confucian moral codes of conduct, and its ideal social and family order. Since gambling was a selfish and aggressive act of self-aggrandisement and profit-seeking, it was denounced as 'lack of sensitive concern for others' (*pu-jên*), 'lack of public-spiritedness' (*pu-i*), and 'unwise' (*fei chih*). In the family context, it was allegedly a major source of domestic contention between father and sons, and among brothers. Thus, gambling was also detested as 'improper' (*wu li*) (Yao T'ung 1849).

In anti-gambling poems collected in the *Ch'ing Bell of Poesy*, gambling was condemned as morally and socially devastating, and all gamblers as doomed to the fate of total bankruptcy, either from their inevitable losses in games, or from swindling. They would eventually degenerate into beggars, bandits, burglars, or prostitutes (Chang Ying-ch'ang 1960: 426, 772, 828–9).[3] Gambling, which provides 'improper'—unpredictable and unworked-for—access to wealth, runs contrary to the Confucian concept of wealth as something to be earned through the proper legitimate course. It also denies the tenet of 'repose in poverty'. Gambling, by condoning the somewhat anarchic rule of chance, luck, disorder, and irrationality, potentially threatens the ethical system of Confucianism, which built heavily on harmony and order.[4]

Interestingly, these late-Imperial Chinese anti-gambling writings differed markedly from their Western counterparts in one major respect: that the main worry of its authors was about the breakdown of the established ethical values and the socio-political order, rather than any concern about the incompatibility of gaming with any system of religious belief as they most often appeared in the English anti-gambling texts (Newman 1972: 1–3). Traditional Chinese anti-gambling discourse, in sharp contrast to similar thinking in Western countries such as Britain, where Christian values and faith had made their impact, displayed much less, if any at all, influence of religious thought. This, however, did not mean that religion, especially popular religion, played absolutely no role in the culture of gambling in this part of China. On the contrary, popular religion was a significant factor in facilitating popular participation in gambling and in helping to perpetuate this form of illegal amusement. This point will be discussed in detail later in the chapter.

It is also worth noting in passing that most anti-gambling treatises targeted only certain forms of gambling. For instance, the first treatise cited above singled out the popular *ma tiao* dominoes; while most anti-gambling poems collected in the *Ch'ing Bell of Poesy* criticized mass indulgence in the 'flower lottery' and *fan tan*, rather than all kinds of gambling indiscriminately. Officials and upper classes in late-Ch'ing Kwangtung were particularly concerned with *fan tan*, 'flower lottery', 'pigeon lottery', and 'surnames guessing' games.[5] But there was seemingly no moral treatise denouncing other popular forms of gambling such as the 'pigeon race', 'cricket fight', 'sugar cane guessing', or 'official promotion game'. This might imply that not all games of chance were indiscriminately denounced as gambling; and that where the line was drawn might depend only on circumstances.[6]

Nevertheless, gambling, legal or not, was consistently criticized by officials and concerned intellectuals. In the words of a party rhetorician:

> Gambling does no good [but] causes hundreds of [kinds] of calamities [to society]... There are many men and women, adults and teenagers, who do nothing but gamble

at *mahjong* every day from morning until night . . . Are not [the rising number of] burglaries in Canton, and banditry in the countryside, all attributable to the gambling dens on the island of Ho-nan? Since [these people] waste all their energy on gambling, they are naturally unfit for any decent jobs. Thus, the productivity of society is suffering from great losses. (Tê 1930: 27–8)

Gambling was also said to be so pernicious that it could reduce a wealthy man to a helpless mendicant, who 'will inevitably fall into the fate of committing suicide, or becoming a bandit' (Chin Tsê-ching 1930: 8).

The Expansive Rhetoric: Late Ch'ing

A close study of the official anti-gambling discourses between 1860s and 1936 reveals that the issue of gambling was progressively used by successive political regimes not only for the innocent aim of wiping out this form of 'social evil' in its controlled territories, but also for the calculated motive of defaming their political opponents in order to exaggerate their own achievements and hence justify their mandate.

In 1863, for the first time in the history of Kwangtung, a popular form of gambling, the 'surnames guessing' game, was officially allowed to be operated in the open, which brought to the provincial treasury a handsome income that was subsequently used for building a new examination hall complex to replace the one destroyed by a fire during the siege of the T'ai-p'ing rebels. Since then and until the eve of the collapse of the Manchu regime in 1911, various forms of gaming had been intermittently permitted by the authorities to operate legally, paying to the cash-hungry administration a huge sum of money. During this long period of time, we are told that 'public opinion' against legalized gambling, formed and organized mainly by morally conscientious local upper classes and officials, was strong and widespread. A lack of extant documentary materials in this area, however, prevents us from knowing these opinions in detail. Existing materials, however scanty, indicated that the major concern of these anti-gambling voices was the government's irresponsible role in legalizing this supposedly socially pernicious pastime, and its ethical consequences on individuals and their families (Tsou Lu 1936: 243–4; Kuo Shuang-lin and Hsiao Mei-hua 1995: 254–9).

The late-Ch'ing reform brought to the reformers a good opportunity to materialize their plan of suppressing legalized gambling in the province. On 30 March 1911, under the auspices of Viceroy Chang Ming-ch'i, as much as under the pressure of some 'progressive' politicians from the Provincial Assembly, gambling in the province was formally prohibited. The occasion was celebrated with a huge procession through the streets of Canton. The two-and-a-half-hour-long parade included a number of school students and voluntary associations, and it was well attended by thousands of curious onlookers who packed the main streets. The procession was in all senses a pageant, and its atmosphere carnival-like. There were fourteen lion-dance teams, one of which consisted of women, a few dozen decorated floats on which costumed performers showed off their acrobatic skills (*piao shih*), an 'uncountable number' of military and civilian musical bands, teams of amateur dramatists who performed short plays with an easy-to-understand anti-gambling theme, and many other exhibits and programmes to disseminate the theme of this parade—gambling was bad for individuals and society—to the audience (*Shen pao* 1911: 8, 9, 10 Apr.). Sensationalism prevailed: 'a man was covered from head to foot with pawn tickets, or clad in most beggarly garments; a man selling his child for cash to sustain his gambling habit; criminals in cangue (a portable pillory), chains, and handcuffs followed by an executioner with sword in hand.'[7] The theme was clear: that gambling was detrimental to morality and social and domestic harmony.

The Expansive Rhetoric: The Early Republic

During the early years of the Republic, the new military-governor of the province Ch'en Chiung-ming, who had been an outspoken assemblyman against legalized gambling before the Manchu dynasty crumbled, continued to follow up the late-Ch'ing campaigns against gambling. Extant orders issued by the governor's office on the subject of anti-gambling show that gambling was attacked for its devastating effects on domestic harmony, and was held as a major cause of theft, banditry, and official corruption (*Kuang-tung kung-pao*, 1912 no. 11, 13 Aug.; no. 54, 2 Oct.). His effort, however, came to an end when political rivals supported by Yüan Shih-kai in Peking forced him out of office.

Ch'en Chiung-ming returned to power and retook Canton in the autumn of 1920. There immediately followed another large-scale campaign against gambling in the province. The campaign, engineered by some voluntary associations in Canton including a local Christian organization and a middle-school student group, was intended mainly to wipe out legalized gambling that had been allegedly 'protected' and 'actively promoted' by the Kwangsi militarists who had Kwangtung under their control since 1917 (*CTKL* 1936: 233–8; *KCPN* 1980: i. 207, 214). The 1920 campaign was kicked off with a highly publicized parade that resembled in many ways the one of 1911. It reportedly had 12,000 participants of different voluntary or official associations and schools in Canton. Participants carried large boards inscribed with slogans and cartoons; many others dressed up in sensational costumes, for enacting drama of an anti-gambling theme. Some dressed up like crippled beggars, crying out in most pitiful tone that they were victims of gambling; some put on the costume of a hanged man, shouting that that was the fate for all gamblers; some acted as thieves, while others as desperate gamblers selling their wives and concubines. There was one theme in these lampoons that had not appeared in earlier anti-gambling campaigns: a group of participants dressed up as prominent late-Ch'ing and early-Republican officials who were held responsible for lifting the ban on gambling in Kwangtung. These ridiculed personalities, including

Li Hung-chang, Lung Chi-kuang, and those 'hypocritical gentry and merchants' who had persuaded the government to lift the ban, were accused of having committed a crime that was analogous to 'a devastating flood and a ferocious beast', which seriously disrupted the normalcy of the Cantonese society: 'gentlemen and ladies have transgressed the bounds of decency', bankruptcy, selling ones' wives and children, suicides, banditry, theft, and so on, had become so common that one even lost count of them (Ch'en Ting-yen 1992: i. 273–4). For that, they were given a dehumanised representation: the actors who represented them all wore 'masks that hardly looked like a human being at all' (*Shen pao* 1920, 8 Dec.; *CTKL* 1936: 236–8)

The Expansive Rhetoric: 1920s–1930s

In 1925, when Canton was under the control of the reorganized KMT, the Canton authorities, under the order of its military commander Chiang Kai-shek, launched a short-lived campaign against gambling in the province. In an edict issued by the provincial governor, the political and military enemies of the KMT Canton government since 1913 were identified as the ringleaders of the unforgivable crime of 'poisoning' the people of Kwangtung with legalized gambling. In this proclamation, interestingly, the late-Ch'ing officials who helped lift the ban on gaming were not mentioned at all. Another prominent figure of the anti-gambling cause, Ch'en Chiung-ming, was also left out. A large part of this announcement was devoted to accusing a list of militarists, all from Kwangsi, Yünnan, Kweichow, and Hunan, who had been former allies but later became enemies of Sun's 'revolutionary' forces, of their selfish and wicked roles in promoting gambling for its revenue. These enemies of the Nationalist regime were attacked on three charges. First, they lifted the ban on gambling and subsequently pocketed all the proceeds themselves. Secondly, they encouraged gambling by collecting protection fees from gaming houses in their garrisoned areas. They reportedly urged their rank and file to loot so that the latter would get the money to gamble in local dens, which were obliged to pay protection fees to these commanders. Thirdly, as a result of all these misdeeds, soldiery misconduct was rampant, people's moral standards had plunged, public order had crumbled, all trades had regressed, and labourers and merchants suffered from grave economic despair (*KCMKJP* 1925: 3, 20 June; *CTKL* 1936: 236–8).

The year 1925 was one of great turbulence not only for Canton but also for most parts of China. It was a year when the Northern Expedition was intensely under way, when the death of Sun Yat-sen helped tear apart the superficial unity within the Nationalist camp, when a radical mass movement was in its heyday in Canton and the province, and when the year-long Canton-Hong Kong boycott and strike began. This brief campaign against gambling (and opium smoking) was seemingly more a political act of pampering especially the radical wing of the Party, the moralistic local merchants, and the Christian communities that had been attacking legalized gambling, and to sustain the 'revolutionary fervour' of the labour unionists who were the most active supporters of the campaign.[8] Moreover, it was also apparently utilized as a propaganda stunt that aimed to deceive the people into supporting the 'virtuous' Nationalist government by holding Sun's political enemies responsible for bringing about massive suffering, such as high taxation and socio-political chaos, to the people during the first two decades of the Republic in Kwangtung.

The Expansive Rhetoric: Late 1930s

In 1936, shortly after the overthrow of the separatist rule of Ch'en Chi-t'ang, the succeeding pro-Nanking government in Canton launched a large-scale anti-gambling campaign in the province to demonstrate its determination to 'liberate' the people of Kwangtung from the calamity that had been incurred by the tolerant policy of the former regime.[9]

One thing that distinguished the 1936 campaign from the previous ones was, relatively, the substantial amount of publicity texts and journalist reports that survive. This might be ascribed to: the eagerness of the administration to push forward this campaign; the Party's anxiety to mobilize the general public in supporting the crusade through an effective use of the mass media, a political technique that the KMT in the mid-1920s had been only an apprentice but was by now a maestro; and the local journalists' great interest in following the campaign. Large, eye-catching anti-gambling banners, drawings, and pennants were mounted on bamboo scaffoldings erected strategically on major streets in the city. In addition to the parade already mentioned, writing competitions were held and school students were strongly 'encouraged' by the municipal educational authorities to take part. Senior government officials were invited to deliver anti-gambling speeches on numerous public occasions at places such as public parks, schools, the recently completed and highly publicized Sun Yat-sen Memorial Hall, and on the airwaves through the Municipal Radio Broadcasting Station. To keep the campaign alive and the public mobilized, the Party and the government held publicity meetings regularly, which civil servants, military officers, school students, and others were 'invited' to attend.[10] As a result of all these, the campaign was indeed a carnival of propaganda.

Hundreds of anti-gambling writings were gathered into five or more volumes published for the occasion. These official and semi-official documents are a rich body of texts that enables us to analyse the ideological and rhetorical structures of the representations of gambling in depth. In most of these treatises, the 'old' theme of the moral and social downfall allegedly caused by gambling was reiterated. Gambling was held to be a major cause of banditry, family tragedies, suicides, bankruptcies, moral ruin, and physical emaciation.[11]

However, in the 1936 oratory, many of these 'old' themes were further expanded in terms of deliberation, and coated in more sophisticated political language. First, Kwangtung people were now singled out, and stigmatized, as *the* gamblers of China. Although this was not the first time the Kwangtung people were criticized for that reason, the tone of accusation, and the length of deliberations that the discourse encompassed were unprecedented. As a senior official elaborated in a radio broadcast programme on the theme of gamble suppression:

> The people of Kwangtung were, among all other provinces of China, the most fond of gambling.... It is, therefore, nowhere in China other than Kwangtung that [an official] organisation like [the] Anti-Gambling Committee can be found.... This time, the aim of the government to enforce its ban on gambling is not so simple. Its most important aim is to salvage our decadent race and to help revitalise it; to save our country from threat and stringency.... Gambl[ing] suppression is about saving [our country] from extinction.... We need to understand the reasons why the Chinese race (*Chung-hua min-tsu*) could be so degenerating and weak for over a thousand years. Why [China] could be so dispirited to such a worrying degree?.... The major reasons for this degeneracy, in my opinion, are obvious: the life-style of our people [is] too decadent. The bad habits shared by our countrymen are just too many, in particular their obsession with opium smoking and gambling (*CTKL* 1936: 82–6).

An accusation was even 'explained', by another senior official, in structuralist terms: 'Geographically speaking, since Kwangtung is at the frontier and close to the sea, [the characters of] its inhabitants are rich in adventurous and opportunistic qualities. This has been so since antiquity... Regrettably, [these natural gift of theirs] are mostly misused, and deformed into a ludicrous mentality of thoughtless spending [on gambling]' (ibid. 8). Another source stated: 'Before the [1936] Prohibition of Gambling, officials competed among themselves in lavish spending; people indulged in an indecent and frivolous life-style. [Hence] the entire Kwangtung seemingly strove to survive inside a ring of gambling' (ibid. 30).

Although it might be true that many Kwangtung folk were fond of gambling from time to time, this was hardly a phenomenon unique to the province. In the same period, organized gambling in Shanghai was apparently not only more varied in its forms, but also on a much bigger scale (P'ing Chin-ya 1989: 111–25).[12]

Secondly, one of the most frequently quoted slogans of the campaign was 'The prohibition of gambling is [the way that] the Central Government relieves the people of Kwangtung from bitterness and pain.'[13] Another frequently reiterated message was that the 'bitterness and pain' suffered by the people of Kwangtung was attributed largely to the greed of those corrupt officials, militarists, and politicians of the Manchu, and then the warlord regimes. With its former Kwangtung enemy being criminalized, the Nanking government was able to present itself as saviour of the Kwangtung people, and hence rationalize and glorify its takeover of the province as an act of 'liberation', just as Ch'en Chiung-ming, Sun Yat-sen, and Chiang Kai-shek did to the 'corrupt regimes' that they had toppled during the early 1920s.[14] Furthermore, the campaign also heavily publicized the righteous image of the new administration by emphasizing that it had no misgivings about 'sacrificing' the huge amount of gambling revenue for the benefit of the Kwangtung people. In fact, however, the new government had sacrificed virtually nothing simply because the gambling tax, which had been always retained by the separatist regime as a provincial tax, had never been in the coffer of the Central Government.[15] Moreover, according to a financial administrator who was sent by the Central Government in Nanking to Canton to reform the fiscal structure of the separatist regime, since the income of Kwangtung had been significantly larger than that of most other provinces, the sudden abolition of the huge gambling revenue 'would not be too difficult' to be offset by stricter measures of expenditure control (*HTJP* 1936: 2.4, 5 Sept.). In other words, the 'sacrificing' of this 'immoral source of revenue' served the new administration well: it promoted its public image and helped legitimize its rule over the province, without any true financial loss.

Thirdly, these anti-gambling writings, in a manner strikingly similar to the contemporary debate on opium smoking, deliberately exaggerated the socio-economic disruption allegedly caused by gambling in Kwangtung. In order to debase the image of Ch'en Chi-t'ang's separatist regime, gambling was arbitrarily tied to issues of national survival, and its moral and social repercussions overstated. Thus, it was denounced not only as a threat to the gamblers themselves, but also to their families, friends, neighbours, the society, and even the country. It caused socio-ethical degeneracy to the country, and threatened the construction of the national economy because of its pernicious effect on the productivity of the people. Gamblers were blamed for wasting both precious time and resources (their money and energy) that could have been funnelled into the purpose of 'building the nation' (Fitzgerald 1990: 18–19, 24). To add a 'scientific' social Darwinist touch to the discourse, the problem of gambling in Kwangtung was criticized for hindering the social progress of China and, most importantly, pushing the nation backwards down the path to extinction.[16]

In connection with this issue of nation-building, gambling was further criticized for its incompatibility with the official model of an ideal citizen advocated by the New Life Movement, which was widely propagated as the key to revitalizing the nation. Gambling was blamed for fostering among the people an 'inhuman, irrational, shameless, dishonest, unrighteous, and discourteous' lifestyle (*YHP* 1936: 9, 7 Oct.). In one anti-gambling essay, gambling was 'diagnosed' as a 'psychological disease' that allegedly contributed to 'the fall in people's morality, [and brought] chaos and impoverishment to the people'. Gamblers were said to be poisoned by six different kinds of mentality (*hsin li*), all contradictory to the Confucian ideal of a gentleman. In the first of these, gamblers were believed to be consumed by the ambition to win; and this would just mould them eventually into violent scoundrels who would kill unhesitatingly for money. In the second, gamblers were all obsessed with luck and chance. They dreamed so much about winning an instant fortune that they never observed the proprieties of earning one's money by being honest, hard working, frugal, and prudent.[17] Thirdly, since all forms of gambling involved cheating, gamblers took it for granted that cheating was a way of life. Fourthly, since all gamblers were selfishly and obsessively pursuing their own dream of instant wealth, they never contributed anything good to society. Fifthly, since money came easy to gamblers, they all spent lavishly on alcohol, prostitution, and opium smoking, and hence stirred up the 'wind of lavish consumption'. Sixthly, since gamblers exhausted themselves by their long hours of gambling in dim and poorly ventilated dens, they were all spiritually degraded and physically emaciated. Their laziness would not only ruin their own life, but also the future of their country (*CTKL* 1936: 43–6, 51–4).

Two more new themes were surfacing in the 1936 campaign rhetoric. First, the countryside and its rural culture were increasingly implicated as a major culprit of the persistent problem of gambling in Kwangtung. It is true that, in previous campaigns against gambling, county cities, market towns, and administrative villages were also criticized for having not tried hard enough to wipe out this form of 'vice'; at times, local 'mischievous gentry' (*ê shen, lüeh shen*) or local bullies were blamed for protecting the operation of illicit gaming. These pre-1936 reports and official statements, however, were more concerned with describing the situation of, and the problems facing, gambling suppression campaigns than passing prejudiced judgements on the spatial aspect of the problem. For instance, although the city of Canton was described in these narratives as the place where the ban was most effectively enforced, which was factually true, the city was not explicitly idealized at the expense of the countryside.[18] Although it might be true that instances of violation of the ban on unlicensed betting were more easily found in areas far away from Canton or other county cities (for the limited reach of the state in the countryside had always been a problem for this region), villagers were rarely believed to be more prone to this 'evil hobby' than city folks, not until, at least, 1936.[19] In the 1936 anti-gambling discourse, however, the role of the city was explicitly acclaimed, though not unreservedly, while the countryside was increasingly stigmatized. As already discussed in an earlier chapter, popular attitudes towards the city among the urbanites were becoming increasingly favourable at the expense of the countryside by the 1930s. It was, therefore, no surprise to detect in this social campaign a similar anti-rural attitude in some of the publicity materials. In a long newspaper article on the topic of anti-gambling, its author, when expounding the difficulty of suppressing gambling in Kwangtung, attributed the problem to the unavailability of amusement to the people living in the countryside: gambling, as a result, was the only form of amusement they knew. The city, in this author's view, did not have such a problem because there were public parks, cinemas, amusement parks, and even well-paved broad avenues that its residents could stroll along to spend their leisure time 'healthily'. Participation in normal and decent amusements for all village people, he implied, was the only way to ensure a successful campaign against gambling.[20] In another piece of writing, its author held that although gambling was popular among city dwellers, its popularity among villagers, and therefore its pernicious impact on the rural culture, was 'perhaps even greater'. He then expounded on the reasons for the popularity of gambling in the countryside. First, it was the serious shortage of amusement facilities in villages that deprived a peasant, after a day of hard labour, of any amusement other than gambling. Secondly, since most peasants were uneducated and therefore incapable of discerning the right or wrong of a particular form of entertainment, their weakness was easily exploited by bookmakers who turned these country folks into gamblers. The fate of all these 'ignorant peasants' was a predictable one: they would become slack in work, which would bring them poor harvests; to survive and ensure a supply of stake money they would sell their children, pawn their farm land, and, when all possible sources of income were exhausted, eventually join the ranks of bandits or thieves (*YHP* 1936: 9, 7 Oct.). The imagined representation of the peasantry in rural China as backward and poor, just as they were constructed in the discourse of China's 'rural bankruptcy' shared by many academics inside and outside China in this period,[21] was further reinforced, and in return, offered these anti-gambling publicists a convenient and unambiguous answer to complicated questions about the popularity and the socio-cultural implications of gambling for the nation.[22]

Another emerging theme in the 1936 anti-gambling discourse was the invocation of the 'Father of the Nation' to rally public support to the campaign. The rising cult of Sun Yat-sen helped add colour to both the anti-gambling and anti-opium campaigns in 1936 and thereafter. The idea was not entirely new. As early as 1925, in an official statement issued together with a set of publicity guidelines released by the Propaganda Bureau of KMT in Canton, Sun's contribution to the crusade against gambling had already been exaggerated.

> In 1912, the military forces of Yünnan and Kweichow invaded Kwangtung, which caused great disorder and chaos [to the region]. All kinds of gambling, [as a result], were easily available everywhere; a serious calamity that brought suffering [to the people of Kwangtung]. Fortunately, [our honourable and] great Commander-in-Chief Sun had [subsequently] prohibited and annihilated [gambling]. It was not until the launching of the Northern Expedition that this ban on gambling was lifted. . . . [T]he present campaign aims entirely at bringing happiness to the people. It is also intended to put into practice the ideals of our Party of saving the nation and its citizens, as well as fulfilling the will of [the late] Premier Sun in strict enforcement of the ban on gambling (*CTKL* 1936: 219–23)

Fifteen years later in 1936, Sun's role in suppressing gambling was again glorified; but this time, it was done more elaborately. In one anti-gambling essay written by a KMT partisan for the campaign, the determined action by Sun to uproot gambling was described in vivid detail:

> After suppressing the rebellion of the Kweichow and Yünnan armies [in Kwangtung], [our honourable] Premier Sun, who felt pain [to know about] how the calamity of gambling is bringing disaster to the nation and injuring its people, had ordered without delay the Governor and the Military Commander of the Kwangtung Province to prohibit and eradicate all kinds of gambling [under their jurisdiction]. Capital punishment was swiftly imposed on the violators of this ban. With the great determination in enforcing [this rule], the dark cloud that hovered over the Province, was all swept away at the stroke of a broom. It was only [some time] later when [our honourable] Premier Sun had passed away, and the Northern Expedition was launched, that enforcement [of the ban] became

slack; this was, however, inevitable as a result of the circumstances, which was beyond our control.[23] (ibid. 32–3)

In these passages Sun was portrayed as a great, compassionate, and morally upright man of principle, as much as a committed fighter against social evils, in this case gambling. The campaign was shrewdly, and conveniently, utilized as a means of boosting the personality cult of Sun, which, like other methods the KMT Propaganda Bureau employed, was intended to boost the image of the Party as the legitimate ruler and the saviour of a stricken nation.

2. FALLACIES, AMBIGUITIES, AND REALITY: THE PROBLEMS OF THE OFFICIAL VIEWS ON GAMBLING

The Statesmen, Militarists, and Officials

Many official Chinese writings on gambling sought to give the impression that only corrupt or errant officials enjoyed taking part, and that it bred corruption in officialdom (ibid. 69–71).[24] But this was not always true. For instance, Chang Yin-heng, a Kwangtung man and a highly regarded court official specializing in foreign affairs, who keenly supported the Hundred Days Reform, was an addicted *fan tan* gambler. Every evening after dinner, he had to play *fan tan* with his entourage, relatives, and friends. He enjoyed it so much that he always insisted on having the role of croupier.[25] Wu Tieh-ch'êng, a prominent KMT official from Canton, was a skilful *mahjong* player. In 1932, he represented the Nanking government on a negotiating mission to Manchuria, in the hope of winning Chang Hsüeh-liang's allegiance to the central government. Wu cultivated Chang's friendship for some time, and entertained him by playing *mahjong* with him. Wu's mastery of the skill impressed Chang so much that he eventually agreed to support the Nanking administration (Chu Hsiu-hsia 1977: i. 104–5).[26] It is interesting to note that although the recorder of these two anecdotes was himself a prominent KMT official (Yeh Yün-shêng and Yeh Pai-heng 1946: 50–1), he did not criticize, even slightly, such 'despicable' pastimes indulged in by these eminent statesmen. Gambling was not seen as necessarily harmful to the meritorious performance of a respectable official. Sometimes, as in the story just recounted, it even contributed to the making of history.

There are serious problems in the array of images and representations constructed by zealous supporters of these socio-political movements and incorporated into the contemporary anti-gambling rhetoric. In the following sections, these images will be deconstructed and the reality re-examined.

The Ch'ing Officials

One major area of fallacy is found in the stigmatized image of the Manchu regime and its officials; they were accused of bringing about the 'calamity of gambling' in Kwangtung, which was a highly problematic representation intended to mislead the public. In the compendium of essays devoted to the anti-gambling campaign of 1936, numerous contributors chose to hold a simple view of history by blaming the deposed Ch'ing regime for China's ultimate failure in both domestic and international affairs, with the failure to crush gambling as a manifestation of both its incompetence and its wickedness. One such official orator, Huang Kang-pu, for example, wrote that

> Our country was a state of propriety and righteousness, its people, therefore, rarely picked up the bad hobby of gaming. During the last years of the Ch'ing regime, [the combined forces of] corruption in the administration and invasion by the foreign Powers had led to the wide circulation of heterodox and evil thought, and the popularity of dissident [acts]. In consequence, our people were no longer able to follow the path of order and normalcy. Our old standard of morality had gradually collapsed and disappeared. Such circumstances facilitated the rise of corrupted officials and mischievous men [who helped sustain the calamity of gambling].[27] (*CTKL* 1936: 41)

It is beyond doubt that the period of late Ch'ing marked an intensification of the problem of legalized gambling in Kwangtung. It is, however, quite a different matter to blame solely the Ch'ing administration and its officials for *causing* this problem.

To start with, the Ch'ing government, like its Ming predecessor, did try to enforce its elaborate anti-gambling ordinances.[28] Moreover, many Manchu monarchs had shown sincere concern about the problem of gambling and, in response, passed edicts aimed at suppressing it in the society and, in particular, among the bannermen and officialdom (Kuo Shuang-lin and Hsiao Mei-hua 1995: 217–40). But the fact that the Court had to reiterate its order against gambling time after time indicated not only the weakness of the state over this matter, but also, more importantly, the wide popularity of gambling in, at least, Kwangtung. Gambling in general, and various forms of lottery and *fan-tan* in particular, enjoyed such a high degree of popularity among the populace that the local authorities were rendered almost powerless in suppressing them effectively.[29] Corruption and bribery also played a crucial role in frustrating the efforts of the Ch'ing court.[30] In the observation of the British Consul in Canton, the prevalence of *fan-tan* before 1900, despite the official prohibition against it, was due to the fact that the operators of this line of business had substantially bribed local officials, street-level administrators, and residents in the neighbourhood to ensure that their businesses could be run freely (*YHKPK 1892–1901* 1996: 945). Thus, when *fan tan* was legalized in 1900, the vested interests of the local *yamen* runners in Fo-shan were so seriously affected that they resolved to operate their own illegal dens (*Fo-shan chung-i hsiang chih* 1923: ch. 15 p. 27). In fact, one of Li Hung-chang's main arguments in lifting the ban on *fan tan* was that a considerable number of unruly officials were deeply involved in either protecting gambling or operating bookmaking businesses in Canton, which made it virtually impossible to have any official control of them (ibid. ch. 11 p. 20).

This problem with the state persisted throughout the 1900s until the early 1910s when the government launched a strong campaign against gambling in Kwangtung. On the eve of the 1911 Revolution, a Hong Kong daily published a lengthy leader that cast serious doubt on the workability of the Ch'ing authorities' plan to eradicate gambling in the province. The journalist pointed out that any strictly enforced official ban would only drive the bookmaking business underground. Given the limited capability of the state to control effectively this vast stretch of territory, and the countless number of people engaged in the lucrative bookmaking business, if all these professional bookmakers were forced to operate underground, the local government would, as the writer foresaw rightly, be overwhelmed and the gambling situation only exacerbated (*HTJP* 1911, 19–21 Apr.).

Secondly, not all senior officials who had served in Kwangtung between 1857 and 1912 were in support of legalized gambling. There was no shortage of 'virtuous' governors and viceroys who committed zealously to the cause of gambling suppression. For example, An Tuan in the early 1860s, Chang Shu-shêng in the mid 1870s, Ma P'i-yao in the early 1880s, and the last Viceroy of Ch'ing Kwangtung Chang Ming-ch'i, were a few of those senior mandarins who were notorious for their determination and strict measures against gambling in Canton and other major towns in the province (*CTKL* 1936: 243–4, 252–3; *CSL* 1995: v. 227, 454–6, 463).[31] Chang Ming-ch'i even won high regard from the American Consulate General for his 'strenuous efforts' and remarkable success in 'the crusade' for the suppression of licensed and private gambling in Canton and throughout the province.[32]

Thirdly, not all the allegedly corrupt senior officials who had served in late-Ch'ing Kwangtung and played a role in lifting the ban on gambling were downright 'corrupt' or unconcerned about the possible social impact of legalization. For instance, Liang-Kuang Viceroy Li Han-chang (served 1889–94), who was nicknamed by his contemporaries as 'big pocket' for his allegedly infamous role in 'protecting legalized gaming' and receiving huge sums as bribes from local bookmakers, played an apparently much more complicated role than conventionally assumed. To start with, his decision to make use of a lottery to generate revenue for the province had obtained the full support of the imperial court too. Moreover, in spite of his role in lifting the ban on the 'surnames guessing' lottery, he never intended to milk, indiscriminately, all forms of gambling for the sake of raising revenue. In a memorial to the Grand Council in Peking, Li presented an investigation report, prepared at the request of the Councillors, on whether a form of lottery, called the 'lesser surnames guessing' lottery, or more commonly 'white pigeon lottery', should be legalized to help fund the imperial navy. In this report, Li argued rather sternly against the idea of lifting the ban on this particular form of lottery on three major grounds, one of which was that the simple method and the low stakes required for betting would easily entice a great number of 'ignorant men and women' to indulge in it. His conclusion was a firm negative: the damaging impact of this specific form of lottery would, in his estimation, certainly exceed that of the other lottery of which he had earlier approved (Li Han-chang, 1969: ii. 853–7). Furthermore, the tarnished image of Li Han-chang as 'the viceroy who was most corrupted by local bookmakers' handsome bribery', an image questionably promoted by historians, is apparently not supported by much evidence. Their prejudice against Li is probably influenced by an anti-gambling essay that won second prize in a literary competition organized by a local Christian group in the early 1920s. *Ch'ing Shih-lu* (*The Veritable Records of the Ch'ing Dynasty*) did contain an imperial edict that instructed the Governor of Kwangtung, Ma P'i-yao, to look into the accusations raised by two censors about Li's misconduct by embezzlement (*CSL* 1995: vi. 292–5). In Ma's report of his investigation, a handful of Li's aides and assistants were implicated and subsequently expurgated. The viceroy, however, was not only cleared, but also praised by Ma for his good record of performance (ibid. vi. 313, 323). Other extant sources such as *Shen pao* and *Nan-hai hsien-chih* (*Gazetteer of Nan-hai County*) do not contain much evidence to substantiate this accusation against Li.[33]

Fourthly, both contemporary anti-gambling writers and present-day historians overlooked the great complicity of the situation of gambling when appraising the 'far-reaching' good work of some committed Ch'ing officials in their campaigns against this form of social evil. For instance, the 'good record' professedly accomplished by Viceroy Chang Shu-shêng (served during 1879–82 and 1883–4) should not be taken for granted.[34] Although Chang was undoubtedly trying hard to tackle gambling, and his determination was most vividly reflected in a public proclamation in which he listed out the harsh punishments to be imposed on any offenders against the ban (ibid. v. 454–5, 463; vi. 17; *Shen pao* 1880, 29 Aug. and 3 Oct.; 1881, 2 Jan.), unofficial evidence such as newspaper reports indicated the persistence of the common problem of illicit gambling within the provincial capital and in many other parts of Kwangtung during his governorship. Similar irony can be observed in Canton and the province under the rule of another ardent anti-gambling governor Tan Chung-lin, Li Han-chang's successor (*CSL* 1995: vi. 313, 323).[35] The determination and achievements of the strict and upright Governor Ma P'i-yao were also inflated. Although he is described as a tough fighter against gambling, which was conventionally believed to have led to his 'sudden mysterious death', extant documentary evidence from the imperial court or his memorials does not support this view. At least during his brief governorship in Kwangtung, the operation of legalized gambling in the form of the 'surnames guessing' lottery remained intact and continued to supply the cash-hungry provincial government with an important source of revenue; Ma, at least in official records, had not done much to 'rectify' the situation (ibid. 290–310). Rampant and uncontrollable corruption on the part of local petty officials and soldiers along with common protection of and involvement in illicit gaming on the part of local bullies and elite nullified the already half-hearted and inconsistent efforts against gambling in the province throughout the half century preceding the fall of the Ch'ing Dynasty.[36] In spite of their good faith and great determination in wiping out gambling, just like Commissioner Lin Tse-hsü had tried to do with opium, the eventual failure of these 'virtuous' officials in this great enterprise revealed the true extent and the nature of the problem, which was beyond the reach of not only a handful of zealous bureaucrats but also the Ch'ing state.

When attacking these late-Ch'ing officials' roles in legalizing gambling, many anti-gambling orators used the words 'to commence gambling' (*k'ai tu*) to underline the guilt of the fallen Manchu regime for opening the floodgates of this social calamity. Rhetoric as such was intended to mislead the public in believing that Canton and Kwangtung had been free of this social evil before these 'corrupt' officials lifted the ban on it. This, as all the evidence shows. was at most only partially true. Legalized gambling in Kwangtung was doubtless a new phenomenon since the 1860s. This, however, does not mean that gambling had never existed in this part of China before then. Gambling, like many other things in China, has a long history predating the 1860s. Some early-Ch'ing scholars mentioned in their works the popularity of gambling in Kwangtung.[37] Therefore, when those late-Ch'ing officials endorsed specific forms of gambling in Canton or other parts of the province, they did not 'commence gambling' or open the floodgates in the true sense of the words, but only granted official permission, and hence assumed the authority of taxing it, for the operation of gambling that had already been in open existence anyhow. In the reminiscences of an old resident of Canton, the major difference between the pre- and post-legalization period was that gambling, in the latter phase, could operate openly without fear of official intervention (Chung Chiao 1925, 2 June).

Lastly, anti-gambling orators and historians alike wanted their readers to believe that these 'mischievous' high-ranking officials, who had lifted the ban on gambling in late-Ch'ing, pocketed a large part of the revenue generated, since this revenue was supposedly never spent in any meaningful way. These criticisms on corruption, however, are apparently based on impression and not substantiated by much evidence.[38] Moreover, legalized gambling began in 1860, after a group of elite academics had successfully petitioned the authorities, and had purchased the monopoly of running the 'surnames guessing' lottery as a means to raise funds for rebuilding the Provincial Examination Hall, which had been burnt down by the T'aip'ing rebels (Tsou Lu 1936: 243). The revenue was spent meaningfully, rather than senselessly, at the instigation of the local elite rather than the criminal element. Reading through the memorials on the subject of legalizing gambling in Kwangtung submitted by such senior officials as Li Hung-ping, Kuo Sung-t'ao, Chang Chih-tung, and so on, one would not fail to be impressed with their genuine concerns about the state of affairs in the province(s) they governed.

Kuo Sung-t'ao, for instance, lifted the ban on the 'surnames guessing' lottery at the time when Kwangtung and Kwangsi were still being pressed by rebels associated with the crumbling T'ai-p'ing rebellion and by roving bandits who had been hitting the countryside hard well before he assumed governorship there. To finance military campaigns against these enemies of the state was by no means easy, as Kuo revealed in his diary. Thus, a large part of this lottery revenue was utilized for maintaining the army for the good of the state and society, a decision that was also supported by his senior colleague in the province (Wang Hsien-ch'ien 1969: ii. 925–6).

In April 1885, when Chang Chih-tung made a similar decision on the same form of lottery, his main concerns were twofold. First, to utilize this handsome source of revenue in meeting the urgent need of reinforcing the coastal defence in Kwangtung and Kwangsi; the war with the French was not yet over and a French naval fleet was still blockading the South China coast. Chang, who was in support of war against the French, found the acute shortage of military funds distressing. Secondly, the Portuguese in Macao, in Chang's view, were a potential threat to the security of Kwangtung. One of Macao's major sources of income, running the 'surnames guessing' lottery, which was banned in Kwangtung although most wagers came from this province, had to be stopped and funnelled back to the Chinese territory where the sum could be spent meaningfully. Chang realized the impotency of the local government in preventing its people from betting on this lottery, which was being run by an extensive network of bet collectors working for bookmakers based in Hong Kong and Macao (Yüan Shu-i et al. 1998: i. 296–301).

The reason behind Li Hung-chang's decision to legalize *fan tan* in 1900 differed somewhat from that of his predecessors. Circumstantial evidence indicates that his decision to lift the ban on this form of much-ostracized gambling might not have been his own idea, but that of the Court, whose urgent need of funds to deal with the national crises caused by the Boxer debacle was apparent.[39] Even a harsh critic of Li, Liang Ch'i-ch'ao, stated that the decision to lift the ban on this controversial form of gambling was an expedient measure adopted by the Viceroy to alleviate the imminent problem of funding the normal operation of the provincial government during the turbulent Boxer Uprising of 1900; after all, Li realized the impossibility of suppressing this form of gambling in Kwangtung (Liang Ch'i-ch'ao 2001: 90). By 1910, gambling revenue brought his provincial treasury a handsome 4.4 million *taels* of additional annual income; all this income was supposedly spent on maintaining a modern police force and funding education in both Canton and many other counties (Kuang-tung ch'ing-li-ts'ai-chêng-chü 1910: bk. 7 pp. 27–38; Rhoads 1975: 165). Meanwhile, however, all other forms of gambling, including the 'surnames guessing' lottery, were prohibited, though the ban was short-lived. The legalization of *fan tan* was also intended to check the growing problem of soldiers' corrupt involvement in protecting unlicensed divans for this form of gambling.[40] The decisions made by these administrators might have aggravated the 'calamity' of gambling in the province, but their motives were clearly more complicated, and more well intended, than generally assumed. Historical complexity, however, was given no place in moralistic writings against gambling.

It is quite clear that legalized gambling in the late-Ch'ing period was well thought out. Not all kinds of gambling were legalized. Moreover, gambling was not necessarily without its worthy social and even patriotic side, despite the possibility that some vested interests might also take advantage of the situation.

The 'Warlords'

Political reasons required all official KMT anti-gambling publications to foster the distorted impression that the 'warlords' of early-Republican Kwangtung legalized all kinds of gambling simply either to finance their military dictatorship or for personal embezzlement. Hence, it is not surprising to find the lifting of the ban on gambling by Lung Chi-kuang, a Kwangsi clique general who put a forceful end to the two-year rule of the T'ung Meng Hui revolutionaries in Canton in 1913,[41] condemned as a selfish move to consolidate his regime in Kwangtung (Tsou Lu 1936: 245; Hu Pu-chin 1936: 254). This accusation, however, is only partially true. When Lung lifted the ban on gambling in 1914, he did not mean all kinds of gambling, but only two forms of lottery. Furthermore, the lottery was considered, even by a contemporary ardent anti-gambling politician, as socially less devastating than such 'pernicious' forms of gambling as *fan tan*, which could be played anytime anywhere (Tsou Lu 1936: 242). Given the fact that the financial situation had reached a crisis-point three months earlier when the value of the Canton bank notes plummeted by 30 per cent, Lung's decision to legalize only two forms of lottery was already a sign of restraint (*Kuang-chou nien-chien* 1935: ch. 21 p. 2). Anti-gambling literature, moreover, underrated the fact that Lung Chi-kuang's decision partially to lift the ban was prompted by the outbreak of a devastating flood in the West River region three months earlier. Thus, the tax levied subsequently under this entry was called 'Rewards-giving Lotteries for Flood Relief' (*shui-tsai shan-hou yu-chiang i hui*). In 1915, another devastating flood destroyed the embankment in Canton and left a large part of the city inundated. The lottery revenue, which amounted to 800,000 yüan annually, was essential for relief and reconstruction work: by mid-April 1915, the provincial Relief Bureau had already distributed to victims of the flood a total sum of 437,578 yüan for helping them to rebuild their destroyed houses (Tsou Lu 1936: 245; Hu Pu-Chin 1936: 254; *Kuang-chou nien-chien* 1935: ch. 21 p. 2; *KCPN* 1980: i 140).[42] Moreover, the Canton administration continued to make arrests of gamblers and bookmakers who violated the official ban on other forms of gambling. These offenders were seemingly released only after a fine had been paid, and all the stake money was confiscated and funnelled into the local police coffers for use for a more meaningful social purpose.[43] Gambling revenue therefore did sometimes serve respectable and constructive social purposes, rather than all being embezzled by the mischievous warlords.

Between 1917 and 1920, under the auspices of the ruling Kwangsi militarists, the ban on most forms of gambling was lifted. Those 1936 anti-gambling orators pinpointed these Kwangsi warlords for being responsible for 'poisoning' the Cantonese people with legalized gambling. By saying this, however, they apparently hid the important fact that when the decision on lifting the ban on *fan tan* was made, Sun Yat-sen, their much-revered hero, was the leader, though a short-lived one, of a 'united government' of the south-western provinces in which Kwangsi was also represented. Instead of 'poisoning' the people of Kwangtung, the gamble revenue was utilized in meeting the huge financial cost of feeding the 'revolutionary' armies and preparing for the Northern Expedition. In the eyes of a local British Customs officer, this source of revenue was in a way beneficial to the populace because they were spared from the negative impact that could have been incurred by an increase in local tariffs (*YHKPK 1912–21* 1996: 995–6).

A total ban was once again enforced in late 1920, after the forces of Ch'en Chiung-ming had driven away those Kwangsi militarists from Canton.[44] Prohibition was so successfully enforced that 'the gambling dens were all closed... and there was a feeling of hopefulness all round'.[45] However, the prohibition was only 'effectively' implemented in the city of Canton; illicit gambling continued to be found in suburban areas and most parts of the countryside in Kwangtung.[46] Even in Canton, a contemporary army officer noted that some bold, errant army officers continued to offer protection to illegal gambling establishments.[47] Ch'en's *coup d'ètat* against Sun in June 1922 unleashed political instability in Canton and the region. As a result, by September 1922, illicit gambling dens, either under the armed protection of soldiers or the 'prominent elite', had been reported to be mushrooming throughout the city (*Shen pao* 1922; 12 Aug.). Before long, Ch'en yielded to the difficult circumstances by expanding sources of revenue for his hard-pressed regime in anticipation of a military showdown with his adversaries. Liu Hsüeh-hsün, the infamous but wealthy bookmaker, who had been running a successful bookmaking business in Kwangtung since the 1880s, was said to have reached a deal with the cash-hungry Ch'en, who was given a 'donation' of 140,000 yüan in cash in return for his revocation of a charge against Liu for failing to pay the Treasury a huge sum of rent earned from a government-owned estate under Liu's management (*KCMKJP* 1923:6, 11 and 13 Aug.). Ch'en was ousted in January 1923 by a joint force from Yünnan, Kwangsi, and Kwangtung who were 'loyal' to Sun Yat-sen. After he was forced out of Canton by the pro-Sun allied forces and had established a regime in eastern Kwangtung, this once champion of the anti-opium and anti-gambling causes, in the face of increasingly imminent military and financial pressures, had eventually to revert to his earlier uncompromising attitude towards these 'vices' by taxing them. These gambling and opium revenues helped not only sustain the strength of Ch'en Chiung-ming's army, but also his rule over the eastern part of the province for two more years in this final phase of his military career (ibid. 1923: 6, 29 Dec.).

The expedition to oust Ch'en Chiung-ming from Canton resulted in the gathering of a huge military force in Canton. The regional forces, marched in and set up their respective headquarters in different parts of the city and the suburbs, running them as their own spheres of influence which were, by and large, beyond the control of Canton's municipal police or Sun's Commander-in-Chief's office. Gambling of different kinds resurfaced swiftly, mainly in areas adjacent to the garrisons where thousands of 'guest army' soldiers were stationed (Chung 1922: 39–40). A contemporary traveller noted that in some parts of the city where gambling dens proliferated, 'gambling went on noisily, often all night'. These mat-covered structures were 'filled with long tables, where hundreds of coolie-clad men came several times a month' to gamble (Franck 1925: 238). At its peak between 1923 and 1925, many of these gambling places, whether licensed or not, operated very openly, with many of them located in the most bustling parts of Canton. Both men and women gambled in these places, which were often packed with spectators of all ages.[48] By 1926, when the Nationalist government in Canton was determined to cleanse the city proper of all the various types of gambling except the lottery, and many unlicensed gaming houses that had once flourished throughout Canton were either forcibly closed down or scared away, this illicit business, however, was surviving in the city suburbs and its neighbouring counties.[49] As a result, newspapers in this period were filled with reports of the arrest of unlicensed bookmakers. In one case, the police chief of a district was arrested for accepting bribes and protecting illegal gambling. (*KCMKJP* 1926: 10, 29 Oct.) Two women were apprehended, one for operating a *fan tan* booth, and the other for running a 'flower lottery': an indication of the popularity of gambling among women[50] and their involvement in this trade.[51]

The 'Father of the Nation' and his Nationalist Followers

The portrayal of Sun Yat-sen as an ardent anti-gambling hero was no more than a reflection of the Party's intense interest in mythologizing 'the founding father of the nation', for obvious political reasons. The historical, or the real, Premier Sun, however, was, as all extant evidence suggests, neither a faithful nor a committed fighter against this form of 'social evil'. Searching through *Kuo-fu ch'üan-chi* (*The Complete Works of the Father of the Nation*) for his writings or speeches on the theme of anti-gambling is a disappointing endeavour: there is only one piece of a document—a public speech delivered to an audience of 'military men, politicians, and the people' in Canton in 1923, that touched on the issue of gambling suppression. This speech did not, in fact, address the problem of gambling alone, but also other important issues, namely, how to reform the quality of China's civil servants, and how to reduce the size of the army as the first step to demilitarize, and thus stabilize, the country. Gambling suppression in Kwangtung took up only an insignificant proportion of this speech. Moreover, the brief statements that touched on the issue did not show that Sun had spent much thought on how to resolve the problem of legal and illicit gambling operated and protected by the allied soldiers whom he himself had invited to Kwangtung to help him oust his enemies. Furthermore, and also ironically, Sun admitted in this speech that the Canton administration, of which he was supposedly the head, had allowed these allied forces to legalize gambling as a contingency measure to meet the 'guest army's' repeated requests to their host to provide pecuniary support to pay their troops. Sun rationalized his, and his administration's, role in the 'calamity of gambling' by saying that: 'Those who allowed the legalisation [of gambling] in the first place are not guilty. We are guilty of not being able to exterminate gambling swiftly enough' (*Kuo-fu ch'üan chi* 1961: iii. 245–7). In his own words, Sun Yat-sen, the professedly gambling-fighting hero, admitted his role in bringing about this unfortunate 'calamity' to Kwangtung. Moreover, though he sounded repentant of his failure to prevent the cancer from spreading, he, in this speech and seemingly in other places or writings, did not work out any substantive plan to bring an end to the problem of army misconduct and legalized and illicit gambling in territories under his control. Furthermore, the Party orator's story about Sun's heroic role in suppressing gambling in the last years of his life was, undoubtedly, a fallacy. All evidence indicates that the short-lived anti-gambling campaign of 1925 was launched officially on 20 June 1925, nearly three months after Sun's death; it was Chiang Kai-shek, the Commander-in-Chief of the Nationalist Revolutionary Army, who ordered the enforcement of the ban on gambling (*KCMKJP* 1925: 3, 20 June; *CTKL* 1936: 227).

Chinese Marxist and Nationalist historians invariably try to protect the 'revolutionary' image of Sun Yat-sen by dissociating him from the sin of legalized gambling in Canton. The KMT's version of events was that the lifting of the ban on gambling was dictated by the unruly army officers from Kwangsi and Yünnan against the wishes of Sun. Thus, as soon as Sun had ousted these 'guest' troops from Canton, he proclaimed a ban on all kinds of gambling in the province. Any person who was caught running a gambling business could be executed on the spot.[52] This narrative, however, apparently intended to cover up, on at least two counts, Sun Yat-sen's long record of seeking Cantonese bookmakers' help in generating gambling revenues to finance his revolutionary enterprise. First, Sun's relations with the bookmaking syndicate in Canton certainly predated the late 1910s. While he was still a young apprentice of revolution plotting an uprising in Canton in 1895, Sun had solicited 'support' from a rich and ambitious local man, Liu Hsüeh-hsün, whose fame and wealth was derived from his monopoly of managing the 'surnames guessing' lottery in the province. Although there was not much evidence to show that Sun had received any substantial and direct aid from Liu,[53] the strong pragmatic tendency of Sun's personality did not prevent him from wooing and currying favour with local bookmakers throughout his political career. In the course of plotting the ill-fated Waichow Uprising in 1900, Sun made another approach to the same bookmaker, whose ambition stretched far beyond local fame and wealth. Through the mediation of his Japanese 'friends', Sun tried to win over Liu and his lottery revenues. Harold Schiffin recounts the events, by utilizing Feng Tzu-yü's *Kê-ming i-shih* (*Anecdotes of the Revolution*), most vividly:

> Before asking for money, Sun offered Liu a fabulous inducement. For the time being, he wrote, a five-man government would be sufficient. Whether its chief would be called 'Emperor' or 'President' would be left up to Liu, since Sun had declared that Liu should have the post.... Not a moment could be lost if China was to remain intact, and he hoped that Liu... would quickly send him one million dollars.... In closing he (Sun)

> repeated his offer: Liu would definitely be head of the new government, since his original candidate, Li Hung-chang, had decided to accept the post of peace negotiator. Liu's appointment had already been announced to the revolutionary army, he declared, and would later be made public. (Schiffrin 1968: 238–9)

Sun was not concerned about the justification or moral implications of using gambling revenue in financing the revolution.

Secondly, Sun supported the act of lifting the ban on a wide assortment of gaming by the 'guest' troops in Canton and Kwangtung. In 1917 and 1922, when Sun Yat-sen returned to Canton to lead an united military regime of the south-western provinces, he, as already pointed out in the above, was more than a willing accomplice in utilizing gambling as a contingent source of revenue, which brought almost 20,000 yüan daily into the coffers of the Canton treasury and the regional forces (Hu Pu-chin 1936: 255–6). Despite Sun's occasionally retrospective moralistic criticism against gaming (*Kuo-fu ch'üan chi* 1961: iii 246), gambling revenue was, however, gratefully made use of to sustain the revolutionary government under his leadership and to finance the various military expeditions by KMT against its enemies. In late 1922, a special bureau for raising revenue was established. In early 1923, this bureau released a public statement announcing its decision, and the justifications, to farm out the operation of *fan tan* and the 'pigeon lottery' to the highest bidders. This was believed to be the only feasible and the quickest means to generate substantial revenue without the need to increase the tax burden of the majority (*Shen pao* 1923, 10 Feb.). Throughout the latter half of his political career, he neither said nor accomplished much in addressing the problems of legalized and illicit gambling in territories under his control. In the critical commentary of a traveller to Canton in 1924, Sun was responsible for the proliferation of several vices in the city:

> Early in the century . . . of such nefarious memory in Sun's eyes, *fan-tan* had been prohibited . . . and there was a mighty bonfire of opium and gambling paraphernalia . . . Now under the great idealist reformer [Dr Sun] who, by his own administration, overthrew them, there were gambling, opium, and prostitution 'joints' without number, wide open everywhere, for the enriching of the government rascals and the realizing of large sums for mercenary troops overrunning the district. One had only to push aside a dirty once-white canvas curtain almost anywhere, even along the Bund, to find a *fan-tan* game in full swing. (Franck 1925: 268–9)

Although Sun did proclaim a ban on gambling in May 1924, his sincerity, and the effectiveness of the ban, were dubious. A few months after its proclamation, Sun instructed one of his senior aides to assume the directorship of the Revenue Raising Bureau, which handled revenues from gambling and opium. This bureau lasted until the formal inauguration of the Nationalist Government in Canton in July 1925 (Lo I-ch'ün 1983: 220–1). Afterwards it was incorporated into the Treasury of the Provincial Government (Kuang-tung-shêng chêng-fu ts'ai-chêng-ting 1934: iii. 973). Sun's half-heartedness, or perhaps even unwillingness, in suppressing gambling had upset those partisans who were in favour of a tougher course of action in this matter. Not long after the death of Sun, one group of these prohibitionists, who apparently controlled the local KMT newspaper *Canton Republican News*, caused a lot of embarrassment to the Party and the municipal government by printing in this daily, on consecutive days, an announcement to the readers to request their active participation in providing the newspaper with the locations and other related details of illegally operated gambling and opium dens in and outside Canton. This information was subsequently serialized in this Party newspaper for weeks, which, as the original announcement stated, was intended to pressure the authorities into addressing the problems more staunchly.[54]

In June 1925, the Provincial Governor of Kwangtung proclaimed another ban on gambling (Kuang-chou-shih chêng-hsieh 1987: 357). In the same year, however, 10.5 million yüan of gambling revenue, the third largest item of income for the administration, was collected under the deceptive title of 'rations for army' (*ch'ou hsiang*) (Chia Shih-i 1932: i. 111).[55] In 1926, when the Nationalist administration survived almost exclusively on taxes from Kwangtung, gambling revenue supplied 20 per cent, or 11.5 million yüan, of its total income (Fitzgerld 1990: 757).[56] Therefore it is clear that gambling revenue helped sustain the rule of both the warlords and the Nationalists in Kwangtung, and it also contributed to the eventual success of the Northern Expedition.

This source of revenue brought to the city's coffers a handsome monthly sum of 1.5 million yüan by late 1928. These revenues were crucial to the running of Canton and Kwangtung at a time of political instability and, subsequently, of social rehabilitation. Canton, it must be noted, suffered heavy financial losses when a substantial portion of its reserves was looted by the 'rebel' forces during the Canton Uprising in December 1927; this event also brought to this city a great deal of destruction, especially in its commercial districts.[57] After the purgation of the communists and radical unionists following the suppression of this uprising, the political situation in Canton and the province remained unstable because local military leaders disagreed with Chiang Kai-shek over his belligerent attitude towards the KMT Left government in Wuhan; this had eventually led to a rift between Chiang's Nanking regime and the military government in Canton. To exacerbate the situation, a serious famine swept across a substantial part of Kwangtung in 1928. To relieve the suffering of the affected peasants, the provincial government allocated millions of yüan of contingency funds to those counties that were most hard hit (*YHP* 1928: 4–5, 15 Nov.). Furthermore, even by 1930, the financial situation of the provincial government, as well as Canton, was still suffering from a combination of unfavourable factors: huge budgetary deficits, unfulfilled quotas of land tax, heavy borrowing and debts, debasement of local currency as a result of a lack of public confidence in it; all these problems had been perennial since the early 1920s after Canton was rendered a 'cradle of Chinese Nationalist revolution' (Kuang-tung shêng-chêng-fu ts'ai-chêng-t'ing 1934: i. 46–68).

It is wrong to assume that the Nationalist regime in Canton never heeded public opinion opposed to a full-scale legalization of gambling, or that they never tried to contain its spread. Throughout the late 1920s, the military administration based in the city of Canton did try to keep the city proper (commonly referred to as 'Ho-pei', meaning literally 'north of the [Pearl] River') free of legalized and illicit gambling, to avoid embarrassment since in official propaganda and rhetoric the city was proudly presented as 'the cradle of Chinese revolution'. Legalised assorted gambling, as a result, was confined geographically to Ho-nan, or the part of the city south of the Pearl River, which was under the rule of a minor 'warlord' Li Fu-lin who maintained amicable relations with the Nationalist government based in Canton.

In mid-1928, a rumour went round that the government was going to lift the ban on an assortment of forms of gambling in Canton proper (*NYSP* 1928: 3, 22 Aug.; 1928: 2, 14 Sept.). Before long, bookmakers gathered in Canton contemplating the prospect of business expansion. One of them, a former chief of the local police force, was reported to have expressed great interest in bidding for the franchise of managing the gamble revenue for one year at a sum of 1.2 million yüan. He planned to divide the city proper into four quarters, in each of which 30 'clubs' for an assortment of gambling would be open for business (ibid. 11, 21 Sept.). Two other bookmakers presented the government with a proposal for operating dog-racing in Canton (ibid. 11, 20 Sept.) But public opinion was strongly against lifting the ban. The Twenty-one Guilds of Swatow telegraphed a strongly worded condemnation of the government and the plan (ibid. 11, 21 Sept.). However, it was strong reaction from overseas Cantonese communities that eventually nipped the proposal in the bud.[58] In an official reply to the criticism mailed in by overseas Chinese in Singapore, a spokesman of the Finance Department wrote that a total suppression of gambling was not feasible given the serious shortage of funds to meet the heavy military expenses. The government, however, could at best contain legalized gambling to 'districts that have never imposed a prohibition against gambling' (*NYSP* 1928: 2, 8 Oct.) It was not sure for how long the Canton city administration was able to resist this tempting source of income. It was clear, however, that the Finance Department started taxing the playing of *mahjong* in Canton city from August 1928. The job was farmed out, as was the usual practice, to a private company which, to ensure a smooth operation of the scheme, dispatched teams of inspectors to different quarters of Canton to impose a three-tiered system of charges on *mahjong* players in especially commercial establishments such as leisure clubs, brothels, restaurants, and guest houses (ibid. 11, 2 Oct.).[59] At almost the same time, Ch'en Ming-shu, a member of the Canton Division of the Central Political Council, had publicly stated his intention to outlaw all forms of gambling in Canton and Kwangtung; he proposed that the Canton Division of the Central Political Council, the Party's highest authority in the province, should examine the matter (*YHP* 1928: 4, 24 Aug.). There seemed to be, however, no record that this issue had ever been discussed in subsequent meetings of this political organ; the plan of maintaining a gamble-free city remained unfulfilled. Gambling revenue continued to pump into the Provincial Treasury: a handsome and much-needed amount of 14.6 million yüan for that year (*CTKL* 1936: 239). The situation throughout the final years of the 1920s and the beginning of the 1930s seemed to have remained the same as both the provincial government of Kwangtung and the municipal government of Canton continued to enjoy a yearly income from gambling revenue of 14 million yüan, despite the fact that Ch'en Ming-shu had declared a full-scale prohibition of gambling with effect from 1930; Ch'en's good intention apparently existed only on paper (ibid.; Kuang-tung shêng-chêng-fu ts'ai-chêng-t'ing 1934: i. 6)

In the official anti-gambling rhetoric of 1936, every yüan of the immense revenue from gambling was said to be embezzled by senior officials of, first, Li Chi-shen's, and then Ch'en Chi-t'ang's, separatist government (1929–36). Gambling was thus conveniently made a scapegoat for the prime cause of the widespread corruption that existed in Canton's officialdom (*CTKL* 1936: 30 and esp. 69–71). Here again we seem to find exaggeration. In the first place, corruption in Chinese officialdom existed long before the legalization of gambling (Balazs 1964: 9–10, 42, 212, 223). Browsing through *Hua-tzu jih-pao*, a contemporary Hong Kong newspaper, one finds not much evidence indicating the exacerbation of the problem of corruption in connection with gambling. Secondly, although there might be cases of corruption and embezzlement involving the gambling revenue, Kwangtung's history of legalized gambling shows that this revenue also contributed substantially to local society rather than just being a source of bribery for officials. In an official report on the fiscal situation of Kwangtung published in the early years of Ch'en's rule, it stated, rather candidly, that successive revolutionary governments in Canton had almost exhausted every possible source of income and, as a result, its people, as compared with nationals in other provinces such as Kiangsu, had to shoulder a heavy burden of taxation. Even that, however, was not quite enough to alleviate the fiscal pressure on the government, which was further handicapped by the fact that the amount of taxation raised from farmlands constituted less than 20 per cent of the government's total income. In spite of all these shortcomings, the report pointed out cursorily (probably to avoid causing embarrassment to the self-professed 'revolutionary' administration) that the provincial treasury had no shortage of reserves, and this was ascribed to the huge income levied on legalized gambling and opium; the gambling revenue supplied over 30 per cent of the total income to the government (Kuang-tung shêng-chêng-fu ts'ai-chêng-t'ing 1934: i. 67). These revenues that allegedly 'caused pains and bitterness to the people of Kwangtung' served a more meaningful purpose for the community as a whole; it was a viable alternative to increasing further the rates for regular and additional items of taxation that would have brought even greater misery to a wider section of the populace.

Throughout the separatist reign of Ch'en Chi-t'ang, gambling taxation accounted for between 12 and 17 million yüan per year (Fitzgerald 1990: 761). Apparently the gambling revenue was crucial for maintaining the military forces of this separatist regime, as much as for building 'Modern Canton'. By the mid-1930s, the budget of Canton municipal government was being nourished by a six-digit income under the dubious entry of Special Entertainment Taxation (*tê-chung yü-lo-shui*), which was in all likelihood income draw from taxes imposed on *mahjong* playing in public establishments, and on a form of lottery called 'mountain shop' lottery (*Kuang-chou nien-chien* 1935: ch. 9 pp. 12–14; Kuang-tung shêng-chêng-fu ts'ai-chêng-t'ing 1934: iii. 974) During Ch'en's rule, Canton, and to some extent Kwangtung, experienced its 'golden age' in modern history—infrastructure tasks were carried out, the manufacturing industry grew, higher education was promoted, and large-scale agricultural projects came to fruition (Kuang-chou-shih chêng-hsieh 1987: 358; Sha Tung-hsun 1989: 193–209; Ch'êng Hao 1985: ch. 7).

After 1933, Ch'en Chi-t'ang tried instead to tighten up the regulation of legalized gambling in Canton, probably as a result of his ambitious 'Three-year Plan' to build a socially and morally upright city.[60] The ban on gambling in Canton proper was once again proclaimed. Most gaming businesses, as a consequence, were forced to move either to the gambling resort of Shen-chen at the border with Hong Kong, or to the southern part of Ho-nan island, just a few kilometres away from their original lairs.[61] But this moral campaign of Ch'en Chi-t'ang turned out to be a short-lived and insincere one. Ch'en Chi-t'ang's close relations with the wealthy bookmaker Huo Chi-ting, however, proved on occasion to benefit the public interest as well. Since Huo owed Ch'en a favour for the latter's decision to maintain a tolerant policy on gambling, he felt obliged to help him out from a provincial financial crisis in early 1934, when the value of the Cantonese banknote plummeted. Huo 'kindly lent' 3.5 million yüan to the government for stabilizing the currency (*KCPN* 1980: ii. 457). It was perhaps because of such fiscal, and arguably social, significances of the gambling revenues that, in 1936, when a Canton Industry Association petitioned the newly instated pro-Nanking administration to relieve the people of 'severe maltreatment and pain' (*k'o-nüeh t'ung-ku*) by abolishing 'severe miscellaneous exactions by officials' (*k'o chüan tsai shui*), gambling-related taxes, though denounced for their pernicious effect on the society, were not considered as one of those exactions (*YHP* 1936: 6, 25 Aug.). Meanwhile, the local police seemingly did the least by occasionally closing one or two of those back-lane divans at 'public request'.[62] 'Private' gambling also persisted. Western-style gambling clubs (*chü lo pu*), which admitted selected members only, were said to be highly popular among senior officials and military officers. Hence, these exclusive establishments, which were usually located in the busy part of the city, were able to prosper without interference; and the biggest one of them was allegedly run by a close relative of the military strongman Ch'en Chi-t'ang (Kuang-chou-shih chêng-hsieh 1987: 358–9).

The 1936 anti-gambling campaign was a relatively sincere one. For the first time in Republican Canton, a seven-man Anti-Gambling Committee was formed to oversee the campaign. Severe anti-gambling ordinances were proclaimed (*CTKL* 1936: 33–6, 221–2); and they were seemingly so effectively enforced that playing was said to be 'entirely suppressed', which left tens of thousands of former gambling-house employees jobless (ibid. 57: *YHP* 1936: 3, 5, 9; 7 Oct.).[63] However, this campaign was not faultless and the local people's propensity to gamble, though under greater restriction, persisted. Even at the peak of this moral crusade, the local authorities still noticed that gambling activities continued to exist, legally, under the guise of recreation such as billiards and 'many other forms of play' that were offered at the city's many amusement parks and markets, which were reportedly patronized by 'countless number of ignorant women' in the city (*YHP* 1936: 9, 26 Oct.). Moreover, despite the authorities' strict enforcement of the ban, eye-catching advertisements of at least two kinds of state lottery, one of which was marketed as both a 'shortcut to affluence' and a way to help one's nation in building her aviation structure and highways, could still be read every day consecutively for months in a local newspaper.[64] The state lottery was apparently not viewed as just any lottery, but, as a young writer elaborated in his prize-winning essay, as a 'beneficial lottery operated by the government with a morally upright attitude' (*CTKL* 1936: 92). Nonetheless, the 1936 campaign did not last long. By 1938, most forms of gambling had reappeared, shortly after being legalized by the Japanese occupation authorities. Once again the Cantonese were able to enjoy gambling as much, and as openly, as before (Wu Yü et al. 1988: 159–60; *YHP* 1938: 7, 3 and 4 May).

The vicissitudes of official inquisition against gambling in Canton seem to have affected very little the prosperous bookmaking businesses on the island of Ho-nan, which was under the firm rule of General Li Fu-lin, a locally powerful gangster-turned-militaryman nicknamed 'the King of Ho-nan', who was also a self-professed ardent supporter of Sun Yat-sen and Chiang Kai-shek (Franck 1925: 256–7; Li Fu-lin 1995).[65] Before the completion of the Pearl River Bridge in 1929, the many gamblers who visited these establishments across the river also helped boost the business of the ferry-boats. In order to attract customers, the big gambling houses in Ho-nan erected large and conspicuous neon-lit signboards that could be seen clearly from the Bund on the Canton side (Kuang-chou-shih chêng-hsieh 1987: 359). Although the ban on 'flower lottery', *fan tan*, and other 'miscellaneous' forms of gambling had been upheld by the pro-Nationalist Canton administration throughout the late 1920s, these games were operated without a break by bookmaking companies in Ho-nan.[66] Since officers in Li Fu-lin's forces were more or less tolerated for taking bribes from the island's bookmakers, the ban existed as no more than a vague suggestion.[67] Gambling in Ho-nan, both legalized and unlicensed, prospered virtually uninterruptedly throughout the Republican era (*CTKL* 1936: 79; Hsü Chu-ch'êng 1982: 146).

3. *THE GAMBLERS AND THEIR GAMBLING: INDIVIDUAL AND SOCIAL CALAMITY?*

Anti-gambling literature and rhetoric from the late Ch'ing to 1936, as we have noted earlier, warned the populace, with good intent, about the devastating social, economic, and political impacts of gambling on the society and the nation. The stereotyped images that were projected of gambling and gamblers were, however, to a large extent exaggerated for the purpose of publicity. Although there may be cases to support such charges, it is doubtful whether all gamblers trod the same path of self-destruction. As a modern researcher on gambling points out:

> Most of the [anti-gambling] writers' formulations [to the effect that gambling has disastrous consequences] are based on unsystematic observations of individuals addicted to gambling... By scrutinizing the life histories of gamblers who did ruin themselves... these writers hypothesized in an *ex post facto* manner that gambling in general leads to such social destruction. There are many drawbacks and dangers in such a method of reasoning.[68] (Tec 1964, cited in Dunkley 1985: 18)

Official Canton records from this period reveal that the socially 'disastrous consequences' of gambling might be far less serious than was depicted in the official publicity. Although gambling seems to have been a favourite pastime of many desperadoes and malcontents,[69] there is little evidence that their misconduct was attributable to their liking of gambling.

Calamity on the City's Outskirts?

During the late 1930s, the Department of Sociology of Lingnan University in Canton had conducted a series of social surveys covering a range of issues such as the living conditions of workers and ethnological studies on villages in the vicinity of the city. The social surveys conducted by Lingnan University on three rural communities in the vicinity of Canton provide us with rare first-hand information on the social impact of gambling. In Chiu Fêng-huang, a settlement with 750 residents, there was only one *fan tan* divan. This gambling-house was first opened only in 1932, though the village was founded in the seventeenth century. Every day, the divan was patronized by about twenty villagers, all of them coming in late afternoon after they had finished their work (Wu and Huang 1935: 153).[70] Although this survey provides no detail of the impact of gambling on this village, it does not hint that gambling constituted any problem to this community. Gambling was not seen as a financial threat to the villagers' lives, though their average income was said to be meagre. Nor did it damage the familial and social orders of the village.

In the village of Sha-nan there was no gambling-house. *Mahjong*, a fashionable form of gambling, was much liked in Sha-nan. Women and children were particularly fond of one kind of game called the 'shop lottery' (*p'u p'iao*). Its popularity was fostered by the convenience in betting—a courier was sent to the village every day by the bookmaking company to collect stake-money or deliver prizes. Each day, this company received some two thousand bets from villages in this area. Other popular forms of gambling included dominoes, card games, dice-throwing, 'official promotion game' (a board game), the rustic 'win-a-roasted duck' game (*shao-ya pao*, a game in which the winners were paid in roasted ducks), and a children's board game called 'cock' (Wu Jui-lin 1934: 110–11). When the villagers wanted to play *fan tan*, they had to travel by a free shuttle ferry provided by the den to another village on the other side of the river. Although most adult males in Sha-nan were said to be fond of gambling, the problem caused by gambling was apparently mild. In the first place, most of the gamblers played only when they were free from work. They did not abandon their work for gambling; nor did they gamble so much that their physical and mental health was destroyed. Indeed, the physical health of the majority of adult villagers was said to be 'apparently very good' (ibid. 109, 112–13). They were, through and through, recreational, rather than pathological, gamblers.

Secondly, although most gamblers in this village were said to like gambling so much that they flocked to the *fan tan* den as soon as they received their wages, excessive gambling, to the extent of devastating personal and family lives, was seemingly rare. In the social survey on this community, not one single case of such misbehaviour was mentioned.[71] Although the report does mention that the two big 'pigeon lottery' fans of the village lost about six yüan every month, the lack of information on their financial backgrounds rules out any attempt to assess the impact upon them and their families. But to those in this village who were keen players of *mahjong*, and those who bet regularly on lotteries, their stakes were so small that it could hardly bring any catastrophic consequence to normal life (ibid. 110).

Thirdly, although most villagers enjoyed gambling, it does not therefore follow that they were addicted to it, and did nothing else in their leisure time. Gambling was certainly not the only form of leisure available to the villagers. The research team identifies twelve other forms of popular leisure activities, chatting with friends in the local tea-house being the most popular of all (ibid. 102–4). This contradicts the common anti-gambling assumption that the expansion of the gambling problem was to be attributed to the severe shortage of proper pastimes available to the masses.[72]

Fourthly, in contrast to the much-cited assumption in nearly all the anti-gambling literature of whatever period, public security in this village, which was hailed as 'very peaceful and safe', was unaffected by the popular interest in gambling. The researchers were told that 'in the past three years, [only] one case of pilfering was reported... [and] more serious crime was totally unheard of' (ibid. 101).

The third surveyed rural community, Hsia-tu Village, was located south of Canton. When this survey was being conducted in 1937, all forms of gambling had already been outlawed by the newly formed pro-Nanking government, which also reportedly had the rule strictly enforced. As a result of such enforcement, which was also applied to opium prohibition, the village office had been deprived of a major source of income. In the observation of the investigators, however, opium and gambling continued to be openly available, though illicitly. They also held that further enquiry into the operation of these surreptitious enterprises was 'highly difficult' (Wu Jui-lin 1941: 239, 288). However, this survey, given its coverage on various aspects of life of the villagers, still allowed us to assess, though indirectly, the impact of gambling on this community. Although the report mentioned the villagers' persistence in practising their 'bad habits', namely gambling and opium, an examination of their patterns of spending did not indicate that any family in this community was suffering from that; the largest item of expense for the average family was food, not betting. Moreover, throughout the report, there was no mention of any demoralization on the part of the villagers, or deterioration of the public order, that were attributable to these 'bad habits'. After all, as the survey concluded, the economic condition of most families in this community was, by comparison, substantially better than that of many of their counterparts in Central and North China (ibid. 301).

Calamity in the City?

In Canton proper, the situation might have been relatively more worrying, which seemed to tally with sociological observations made on gambling behaviours in Europe and North America.[73] Gambling was often condemned for breaking up happy families or causing domestic disharmony, and local newspapers occasionally published reports to proselytize their moralistic concern about such harmful effects of gambling on good citizens of Canton. One such report stated that Mr Ma, an addictive gambler, had stabbed his wife to death and fled the city, after having failed to obtain money from his wife for further betting (*HTJP* 1931: 1.4, 25 Mar.). In another case, a small businessman, who earned his living by collecting bets on the 'flower lottery' for a lottery company, was reportedly killed by a close relative of his in a fight arising after the latter's attempt to cheat in a game had been discovered (*KCMKJP* 1923: 7, 22 Aug.). There was also a case in which a woman was tied up by her husband and badly beaten for having lost all her few hundred yüan of savings in the 'flower lottery'. When she was screaming for help, her neighbours reportedly responded only by nodding their heads (ibid. 1925: 9, 25 May). An anti-gambling essay illustrated the pernicious effects of gambling on domestic harmony with a few 'true' stories. A woman was said to have tried to use her 5-year-old daughter as a wager. When she was dissuaded by her neighbours, she grew so infuriated that a fist-fight broke out. In another case, a young lady from a wealthy family lost all her possessions in gambling. She then borrowed heavily from a loan shark and failed to repay her debt. She was threatened at knifepoint to compel her to return home for money. When her parents realized what had happened, they fainted away and later died of sorrow (Ku Yü 1936: 267). In September 1930, a local newspaper reported that two cases of suicide were caused by losses in gambling.[74] At about the same time, a woman committed suicide by swallowing opium after she had lost on *mahjong* games all the 300 yüan savings that her husband gave her (*KHP* 1931: 2.4, 28 Jan.). In another event, a Manchu man was found hanging himself in a public toilet; he was saved by a cleaner. He told his rescuer that he tried to take his own life because he dared not return home to see his wife, as he lost all the money that he got, by pawning his wife's clothes and his own at the gaming table (ibid. 2.4, 16 May).

However, 'classic cases' such as these are not easily found in local newspapers, and therefore should not be taken as typical instances. Mishaps of this kind did undoubtedly occur, but were not seemingly out of control nor had become so common that countless reports about them could be easily located in local newspapers. Perhaps one may argue that the 'calamitous impact' of gambling on individuals and their families was not necessarily reflected by the quantity of reports found in local newspapers, for these tragic incidents might be hidden from the public and therefore escape the notice of local journalists. The same problem of lack of quantitative evidence, however, also precludes us from obtaining an indisputable picture of the 'calamitous effect' of gambling on individual gamblers and their families.

In comparison, there were relatively more reports in local newspapers about the devastating effects of gambling on public order in Canton, especially during the turbulent early and mid-1920s, when legalized and illicit gambling in Canton and its suburbs was commonplace as a result of unrestrained interference by unruly troops stationed in the city.[75] The following examples are randomly chosen to illustrate the extent of the problem; some of them also show the problematic representations of gambling as a calamity.

Our first example concerns a shooting incident in front of two bookmaking companies that operated legalized lotteries within the city of Canton. On a winter evening in 1923, a small group of armed gunmen marched to the scene of the crime where they demanded extortion money from those *t'ai tzu-hua*, or 'flower-lottery carriers' (a kind of middleman who lived on commissions to be paid by lottery companies for helping them to collect stake money from betters in different parts of Canton), who were about to submit their collected wagers to the companies. When some of them refused to comply, an exchange of verbal abuse between the two parties ensued. Enraged, this group of bullies shot at one of the daring carriers. The shooting caused great panic to ordinary betters and passer-bys, and a stampede followed. Shops on that street were all closed instantly. The victim died on his way to the municipal hospital (*KCMKJP* 1923: 6, 21 Sept.).

A police constable claimed that he was attacked by a group of six suspicious-looking men before dawn. The officer reported that when he tried to stop these men for interrogation he was first verbally abused and then nearly stabbed. In defence, he pulled out his pistol and, at the same time, blew his whistle for assistance. This group of bullies, we are told, fled in fear. However, no sooner had the constable filed his report, than a man arrived at the same police station to launch a complaint against the same constable. In his declaration, this man said that he was a 'flower-lottery' carrier by profession. On the evening of the incident, he was on his way home after collecting six yüan in wagers from a better. He was stopped by the constable who, as this man alleged, took him to a dark corner and seized half the money. The constable, however, retorted that this gambler fabricated the story to evade serious charges. The officer-in-charge dismissed this man's allegation as doubtful. One of the reasons he gave, most interestingly, was that this man, because of his profession, did not have any credibility; his work was also said to have provided him with ample opportunities to mingle with criminals and, therefore, 'there was no guarantee that his demeanour could be any different [from those inferior characters]'. This man was subsequently arrested and sternly interrogated. The reporter of this piece of news, like the police officer, held a biased attitude towards the profession of gambling. In spite of the controvertible nature of the case, this reportage was given a prejudiced title: 'Gambler trumps up charges against policeman' (ibid. 1923: 7, 27 Aug.).

A newspaper used the sensational headline 'A ferocious gambler ran after his brother and tried to kill him' for a piece of news, that, according to the text, was far from a straightforward case. The story was that: One day a fishmonger named Li Lin turned down a request for a loan by his half-brother, Li T'i, who was an addictive gambler and opium smoker. The report stated that the latter had a record of stealing money from the shop to sustain his bad habit of gambling. But on that day, when he was refused sternly by Li Lin, he grabbed a chopping knife from the kitchen and chased after him, until he was stopped and overpowered by a group of neighbours and a policeman. This seemed to be an indisputable case until Li T'i's statement was made. In his statement, Li T'i claimed that Li Lin had recently tried to force him to collude with him in a fraud on an insurance company; a demand that he had strongly resisted. Since then, Lin's family disliked him utterly. On the date of the incident, Li Lin and his father beat Li T'i for no obvious reason. To protect himself, Li T'i stated that he rushed into the kitchen and grabbed a chopper to stop the perpetrators. We do not have further details on the outcome of this case, but the way the case was reported apparently displayed a strong bias against Li T'i, not because the evidence was substantial enough to point to his guilt, but mainly because of his 'record' of being a gambler and opium smoker (*KHP* 1929: 2.4, 17 June).

In a story with the headline 'A gambling maid stole in collusion [with someone else]', a maid was reportedly apprehended after her master had informed the Public Security Bureau of her theft of a considerable amount of his jewellery. From the beginning of the investigation, the police had already identified the maid as the suspect because of her 'cunning character and her fondness in betting on the "flower lottery" '. She finally admitted her role in the crime after 'she was threatened' by the investigating officers. The report then went on to describe how she had colluded with another maid in the same neighbourhood and had the valuable jewellery stolen and sold; the money they got had already been 'squandered' (*KCMKJP* 1923: 7, 13 Oct.). It is interesting to note that, throughout this report, there was no evidence that might have indicated a possible link between the maid's 'fondness in betting on the "flower lottery"' and her misdeed, despite the headline clearly pointing to that link. Biased narrative of this kind, when being coated by the supposedly impartiality of news reportage, might not only reinforce the stigmatized image of gambling and gamblers, but also strengthen the imaginary fear of this form of 'bad habit' and its practitioners.

News like this might well help readers to form an exaggerated image of gambling as a ruinous activity.

The Extent of the 'Calamity' in Numerical Terms

In all these cited cases, the pernicious effect of gambling could be vividly felt. But whether the devastation was widespread enough to become an 'epidemic' or if every gambler or better was under the gambling spell, is arguable indeed.

In a report to his superiors in Washington, DC on the suppression of gambling in Canton and Kwangtung in the last months before the fall of the Ch'ing Dynasty, the American Consul in Canton wrote that '[a]n authoritative statement places the number of gambling houses in Canton in recent years at 10,000, employing at least 50,000 men and frequented by not less than the same number of habitual gamblers'.[76] The reliability of these figures is hard to confirm, for the Consul's report did not provide us with any further details. These numbers, though they should not be taken uncritically, still reflected the wide popularity of gambling among the local population. In the newspaper advertisement and prizes announcement of a lottery company in Canton in 1919, it was noted that draws were done four times a month, and for the specific week of this announcement, a total of 617,294 tickets had been sold in and outside Canton. This figure represented only one form of lottery; the popularity of the lottery was apparent, but not necessarily its devastating effects.[77]

Contemporary police records were one of the many ways to measure the social impact of gambling on Canton. During the early years of the Republic, the Canton District Attorney Office (*Kuang-chou ti-fang chien-ch'a tien*) published a monthly table of fines imposed on convicts of crimes such as illegal possession of opium, violation of the ban on various forms of gambling, theft, fraud, bribery, and so on. Extant records show that a significant portion of these cases involved 'gambling' violations. For instance, the table for February 1915 showed that of the total 21 cases listed, 12 were related to 'gambling', while the figure for May of the same year was 9 out of a total of 30, and for July was 36 out of 59.[78] These statistics, though indicating the existence of a social problem in Canton, were far from revealing an alarming picture of illicit gambling in this largest city of South China.

Canton police records of 1922 and 1923 show that a total of about 350 cases of violation of the ban on gambling were dealt with. But only 18 people were apprehended, and it is not known if they were subsequently charged.[79] This was hardly an alarming figure, though it is not known if gambling was also related to other crimes in this city. In 1928 and the first half of 1929, some 4,000 people were arrested for 'violating the rules on opium or gambling'. However, between 1926 and that first half of 1929, only 45 culprits went on trial for opium or gambling offences. In 1929, as few as 28 inmates in the two prisons in Canton were serving sentences related to gambling or opium charges.[80] Police records reveal that between 1931 and 1934 a yearly average of about 110 people were tried for gambling-related charges (*Kuang-chou nien-chien* 1935: ch. 16 p. 108 table).[81] These figures again do not tell how gambling might have been related to other criminal activities in Canton; moreover, they show no alarming increase when compared with statistics for 1922–3. Although gambling might lead some gamblers to commit such unlawful acts as usury, pilfering, and so on, there is no evidence to prove that the number who did so was great. On the contrary, a Western study on gambling published in the late 1940s suggested that the presumption that gamblers were more prone to commit crime was largely unsubstantiated.[82] After all, in the annual reports of the Canton municipal government in the period between the early 1920s and the mid-1930s, gambling was never hinted at as a threat to public security.

An official report prepared by the Social Investigation Unit of Canton Municipal Government provides us with some rare data on the number of legal gambling houses in Canton and Ho-nan, in the period between November 1926 and January 1927. This was a time after the uncontrollable situation of unapproved gambling run by the 'guest armies' had been largely rectified, and the Canton authorities had begun to restrict legalized gambling to the suburbs. Therefore, the figures in this report might not reflect the extent of the gambling problem in Canton during the worst time, but they could well be showing the general situation of legalized gambling in this city and its vicinity at a relatively 'normal' time up to 1936. According to this report, Ho-pei (lit. 'north of the river'), which referred to the city proper of Canton on the north bank of the Pearl River, was basically free of *fan-tan* and other miscellaneous types of gambling. These forms of gambling, however, were available in Ho-nan and Fa-ti (on the south bank, the latter famous for its flower farms); both places were only a short distance from the city and could be easily reached by the hundreds of sampans that plied between the shores. There were thirty-seven *fan-tan* houses altogether in Ho-nan and Fa-ti. Three bookmaking companies, which operated the legalized 'mountain shop' lottery in this area, and another three companies running the 'white pigeon' lottery, were all based in Ho-nan. In addition, there were in Fang-ts'un (also in Ho-nan) four gaming houses where 'ox dominoes' (*niu-pai*) was played. In the same district was also one house for 'miscellaneous gambling'. In Canton proper on the north bank, the five branches of the bookmaking companies that were operating the 'mountain shop' lottery in Ho-nan helped facilitate the bets for people living in this part of the city. The report ended with an observation: the commonest forms of gambling for people in Canton were, in order of popularity, *mahjong, p'ai-ju* (another form of dominoes), and poker. These games were commonly played nearly everywhere, especially in restaurants, hotels, clubs, shops, and even homes. The main reason for their huge popularity, according to this report, was the fact that they were not commonly seen as either gambling or problematic, and this was especially so in the case of *mahjong*, which was widely regarded as a form of amusement.[83] The above numbers did not indicate that Canton, including its suburbs, was being seriously plagued by a social problem of gambling to an extent that was comparable to a disaster. The thirty-seven *fan-tan* houses, for example, though certainly an eyesore to local anti-gambling lobbyists, would lead one to wonder how it was possible for this rather small number of gaming houses to cause a truly extensive pernicious impact on an urban society with a population of over one million. The six lottery companies there appeared to indicate the popularity of this form of gambling rather than the extent of damage it inflicted on the community.

Other official data also help gauge the extent of social devastation allegedly caused by the 'epidemic' of gambling. In official statistics on suicide in Canton, for example, financial loss from gambling does not even get entered as a cause.[84] In fact, a contemporary survey on working-class families in Canton shows that gambling was not even rated by the interviewed workers as among their five most favourite pastimes.[85] The survey also reveals that although many families occasionally borrowed money or pawned belongings to survive financial crises, none of them did it for any reason related to gambling (Yü Chi-chung 1934: 67–71). By September 1936, just before the ban on all forms of gambling was strictly enforced, a journalist estimated that in Ho-nan, where gambling in the forms of lottery and *fan-tan* were most tolerated, a total of forty-eight gaming houses were to be affected by the upcoming prohibition; all of them were small businesses operated by four to five persons (*HTJP* 1936: 2.4, 2 Sept.). Their popularity, as reflected in this figure, was seemingly not as widespread as the term 'epidemic' suggests.

In an interview with more than 5,000 rickshawmen in Canton, only some 200 of them identified gambling as their major form of pastime (*Kuang-chou nien-chien* 1935: ch. 7 p. 53). Another relatively detailed study of 600 rickshawmen in Canton, which was the result of a research project by a professor in the Department of Sociology of Lingnan University, provided us with further details on the 'problem' of gambling during the period 1936 and 1937 when the survey was conducted. Out of the 600 rickshawmen interviewed in this study, a total of forty indicated that they considered gambling as one of their hobbies (*shih-hao*), while nineteen admitted that gambling was the only pastime they knew. In the moralistic view of the author of this report, rickshawmen were inhibited both by their poor educational background and difficult living conditions from having any awareness of 'superior hobbies' (*kao-hsiang shih-hao*); prostitution, alcohol consumption, cigarettes, opium, and gambling were the only forms of leisure they enjoyed (Wu Jui-lin 1940: 24–5). In this report, however, gambling appeared neither as popular nor as common as described in contemporary anti-gambling literature.

Black Hole of Impulsive and Compulsive Gambling?

It is impossible to know how many Cantonese were gamblers in this period, and it is very hard to define what a gambler, or 'habitual gambler', is. A gambler is not necessarily an addictive, or habitual, player. Likewise, it goes against the grain to say that a petty gambler, who plays only once in a while with an insignificant sum as his stake, is, strictly speaking, not a gambler. It is also hard to differentiate clearly a 'frequent gambler', who bets from time to time, from a 'habitual gambler', who is supposed to be addicted, in pathological sense, to gambling. It is after all quite likely, as discussed above, that the majority of Cantonese were petty gamblers, while there may have been a minority of people who could be categorized as addictive gamblers, and an even smaller minority on the other hand who took a strong moral stance against gambling.[86]

An interesting point was mentioned in the research on rickshawmen, above: the number of respondents who indicated that gambling was one of their favourite pastimes was significantly fewer than those who did actually gamble. Such discrepancy in numbers arose, as the researcher described, from the probable reason that although many of these rickshawmen were fond of gambling, many did not have the money to do so. Moreover, since the timing of the interviews coincided with that of a whole-hearted anti-gambling campaign in Kwangtung under the aegis of the Nanking government, it was said that a number of rickshawmen were deprived of the chance of pursuing this 'hobby' (Wu Jui-lin 1940: 24). This raises an important point about gamblers that all contemporary anti-gambling literature seems to have ignored: these gamblers apparently did not bet blindly in disregard of, or without any concern with, their actual financial situations or capabilities. Not everyone who was fond of gambling had to be a compulsive player, as many of them could well be recreational gamblers who wagered only when they had the spare money to do so, and their wagers were small, not necessarily the other way round; this seems to have tallied with the findings of detailed anthropological and psychological research on gambling done in other parts of the world.[87]

It is interesting to note that in the reminiscences of an old resident of Canton, most of the victims of gambling who had ruined their families by losing their entire fortunes were wastrels from rich families or well-to-do merchants themselves. Poor gamblers, our informant tells us, rarely played to the extent of having their family ruined mainly because they lacked the financial stakes; and if they tried to borrow stake-money from their relatives or neighbours, their reputation for indigence caused them to be turned down.[88] Contemporary anti-gambling essays apparently did not bother to differentiate compulsive or pathological from recreational gambling; the problems engendered by the latter pattern of betting could be far less severe than that of the former. Many betters seemed to be rational gamblers, meaning that they bet according to their financial capabilities, and rarely squandered all their fortunes. Therefore, when South China was still suffering the effects of the worldwide Great Depression during the early 1930s, the bookmaking business also suffered and experienced a plunge in income.[89] The experience of a market town in Nan-hai County not far from Canton showed that the culture of gambling of its people could be altered remarkably by a significant change in the economic situation. Before the recession, the economy of this town was said to have been greatly benefited by the business of its gambling houses and lottery companies. In 1934, when the area was under the curse of the Depression, its numerous local bookmaking businesses suffered severely as a consequence. Business was so poor that, in the description of an observer, even those once addictive gamblers had become rare visitors to these houses (*YHP* 1934: 1, 6 July). In the observation of the young Ch'en Chiung-ming, many villages did not have any gambling houses because their residents were just too poor to have any spare money for that (Ch'en Chiung-ming 1987: ii. 109).

An anti-gambling essay, ironically, provides us with rare information on the limited extent of damage done by gambling to the community. This essay set out to warn its readers of the danger of being obsessed with lottery gambling. The essayist argued that the threat of the lottery on the populace was much worse than the threat of *fan-tan* (a much-criticized form of gaming). He justified his view by saying that lottery bets could be easily placed at numerous collection points scattered throughout the city, but *fan-tan* could be played only in a limited number of gaming houses. Moreover, he pointed out that in most people's eyes, using a gambling house was considered a disgraceful act that only a subhuman was capable of (*shih wei-jên chih tzu-ko*); those who cared about their own reputation and moral integrity, therefore, were reluctant to play in a gambling house. Furthermore, since students and soldiers were prohibited from, and women and children dared not visit these places, the actual number of people who fell prey to the pernicious impact of *fan-tan* was, as a result, small.[90] It was quite obvious that the common folk were capable of knowing which games involved a higher risk, and higher turnover, and hence were to be avoided. The financial and social 'destructiveness' of the *fan-tan* game, as pointed out by many anti-gambling writers, could be much higher than other games of chance. But knowledge of that could help ward off a good many from it. Although the essay continued to elaborate on the damage of lottery on obsessive betters and the society, it contained hardly any substantiated and only clichéd evidence.

It is also important to note that most betters were seemingly incapable of placing substantial stakes on the 'pigeon lottery', which was allegedly a highly pernicious form of gambling in the eyes of its late-Ch'ing and Republican opponents. According to a contemporary writer, when the 'pigeon lottery' was first legalized in Canton during the late nineteenth century, its popularity was low because of its small amount of prize money. In spite of that, this form of lottery gradually enjoyed wide popularity because its small prize money was justified by the low limit it set on a bet. As a result, most people, especially women, who normally did not have as much spare pocket money as men, could afford to place a bet on it (Chung Chiao 1925, 3 June). Another news report stated that the lottery was much less harmful to individuals for one major reason: in a lottery, a better was required to place his or her bet in cash, while for *fan-tan* and other forms of dominoes or card games a gambler was allowed to bet in chips. Betting in cash effectively helped restrain a better from raising stakes too easily; in contrast, betting with chips facilitated progressive gambling and escalation of wagers (*KPP* 1934: 3.3, 31 Jan.). Moreover, between 1926 and 1930, the revenue generated by 'shop and pigeon lotteries' combined amounted to approximately three million yüan a year for the entire Kwangtung province (Kuang-tung-shêng chêng-fu ts'ai-chêng-ting 1934: iii. 979–85). This was not truly a huge sum in terms of per capita distribution, though its importance to the stringent government was beyond doubt. In other words, given the allegedly wide popularity of lotteries in Canton and the province, and the actual income that the government collected, the amount of stake money that betters placed on average could be neither substantial nor truly devastating as alleged.

Other evidence also reminds us that when we fathom the 'social devastation' of gambling, we should not ignore the possibility that many betters were not necessarily the compulsive type and that they did not necessarily stop only after they had lost total their fortune at the gaming table. Extant records of the Canton District Attorney Office published during the mid-1910s showed the amount of money, in all likelihood the stake money, which this office confiscated from convicted violators of the anti-gambling ordinances. In many cases, the sum seized from individual offenders amounted to one or two dollars, and in some cases no more than a few dozen copper coins.[91] Although these data were not detailed enough to provide us with a definite picture of, for instance, the frequency of gambling, the exact sum of the stakes regularly wagered, or the social background of these betters, they still indicated the possible existence of moderate gamblers who would not, and could not, spend their entire fortunes, and their family's, on betting. Moreover, this set of data did not support the allegation that all gamblers had to be of the compulsive type and that they would not stop until they lost their last coins in gaming and had squandered their entire family fortune. Both types of gambler apparently existed and hence the betting behaviour and fate of gamblers should not be loosely stereotyped, and the assumption about the disastrous consequences of gambling requires further proof.

The surveys on Sha-nan and Chiu Fêng-huang show that gamblers were not necessarily always addicted to gambling, as many of them bet for recreational purposes. Nor did they inevitably lose their self-restraint and engage in impulsive, irrational, and heavy betting that would ruin their lives.[92] The ability of gamblers to exercise self-control is shown vividly in modern research on gambling in the United States, which finds that most racetrack betters are cautious and moderate, and in Europe, where gamblers' betting behaviours are so diverse that any simple generalization is impossible (Herman 1967: 97–9; Newman 1972: ch. 5; Wen-lang Li and Smith 1976: 190–1). In late-Ch'ing Kwangtung, a Cantonese writer recalled that his father had been an addictive gambler before the death of his grandfather. After the latter's death, his father shouldered the responsibility of keeping his own family, whose fortune had plummeted. Consequently, his father from then on ceased gambling (Chang Tzu-p'ing 1989: 8). In the reminiscences of a former army officer who was once a compulsive gambler playing regularly with very substantial stakes, he was able to stop his 'bad habit' literally overnight, after he lost in one evening every dollar that he had won earlier in the same night in a domino game. This experience was too shocking for him—he claimed that 10 million dollars had changed hands, and he felt so humiliated that he subsequently withdrew from all forms of gambling for well over three years (Chang Kung-p'ing 1993: 627–36). From the same autobiography of this retired army officer we learn that a gambler such as he always played with great caution; in his case, he observed very closely the advice of three elderly, experienced gamblers that one has to exercise great restraint when gambling. By 'restraint', he referred to his ability to leave a gaming table without hesitation as soon as he lost all the money in his pocket and never borrowed a penny for further betting. He held that if gamblers, he himself being an example, could hold fast to this wise advice, they would never lose to the point of depleting their entire family fortune. A gambler's wisdom as such should not be totally disregarded; there might well be a substantial portion of gamblers who could think and act according to the wise advice of these veteran gamblers (ibid. 625–6).[93] The capability of exercising self-control among gamblers helped contain the pernicious impact of gambling significantly.

Gamblers' self-control seems to have been fostered through familiarity with various forms of anti-gambling writings, and oral literature that they may well have been taught since childhood. One of such writings was the *Chu Yung-ch'un's Maxims for Family Management* (*Chu-tzu chih-chia ko-yen*) which first appeared in the early Ch'ing. An illustrated and annotated popular version of the book was produced, seemingly at a later date, and widely read by the Cantonese throughout the late-Ch'ing and Republican periods, and even up to the 1960s (*Dai Kan-Wajiten* 1989: vi. 44; Hayes 1985: 80, 83).[94] One of the maxims on family management advises: 'Do not covet wealth that one should not think of' (*mo tan i-wai chih ts'ai*). Four young men are drawn playing *mahjong*, and the inscription reads: 'Acquaintance with wicked young men must lead to trouble' (Chu Yung-ch'un n.d.: 6, 16). In another characters-learning text for women and children, the readers are warned against the bad effects of opium smoking and gambling. Gamblers, according to the text, would only end up financially bankrupted, deserted by friends and relatives, and causing great unhappiness to their parents (*Kung-ho shih-yun fu* etc. 1911: pt. 4 pp. 6–8). Similar warnings of the dangers of gambling were also given in a popular collection of moral teachings on righteous behaviour (*Ming-hsin pao chien* 1919: 17).

Moralistic folk songs also helped spread the anti-gambling message, and could be effective warnings against excesses at the gaming tables. In one item of 'wooden fish'-style Cantonese folk song, the pernicious social effects of *fan tan* are warned against in its lively vernacular lyrics.[95] The highly amusing and popular 'dragon-boat' (*lung chou*) songs, with equally lively, vernacular lyrics, also helped publicize the conventional wisdom to refrain from gambling, especially compulsive gambling. 'A Virtuous Wife Dissuades her Husband from Indulging [in Vices]' (*Hsien ch'i chien fu*), with its long moral treatise on the destructive effect of gambling on a happy family, might convince many of its listeners. Another *lung-chou* song called 'A Gambler Cries at a *Fan-tan* Table' (*Tu-tsai ku tan*) captures the melancholic and remorseful repentance of a tearful man who loses all his money at a *fan-tan* table. The song 'A Virtuous Wife Scolds Bitterly at [Her] Gambler [Husband]' (*Ching-chieh-fu ta ma tu-tsai*) retells the story of an addictive gambler who, after losing all his money at *fan-tan*, persuades his wife to work as a prostitute in order to obtain the money for sustaining his 'bad habit'. His unreasonable request is turned down by his virtuous wife who is also joined by a neighbour in cursing her husband for his shameless act. In the end, he is so ashamed of himself that he becomes 'wordless' in face of this barrage of scolding.[96] In the boat-people community of Shanan, one of the folk songs locally most often sung is about the bad effects of gambling on the harmony of domestic life. Since these folk songs were mainly sung by women, especially mothers, to their children, their moral impact on the youngsters may have been far-reaching (Wu Jui-lin 1934: 145).[97] All these anti-gambling songs emphasize the idea that having a decent job and abstaining from gambling is the only way to 'win money'. In early Republican years, some progressive Cantonese opera troupes also performed scripts that condemned gambling.[98] In *Yen Jui-shêng*, an opera hit since the 1910s, the protagonist's indulgence in gambling is attributed to his insatiable greed for money, which becomes his motive for killing his courtesan girlfriend. He also eventually takes his own life (T'ang Ti-shêng *c.*1930s). The moral lesson against excessive gambling manifested in this commercially successful opera, a dramatized true story, must have spoken clearly to its audiences.

Kinship organizations could also help contain, if not eliminate, the spread of gambling. Most lineages' genealogy carried a section of 'family instructions' (*chia hsun*) with advice on how to attain some of the Neo-Confucian ideals of family conduct. Often, instructions against gambling were given (Furth 1990: 197). The genealogy of a Liang lineage in the county of Nan-hai stipulates that if a male clansman is caught gambling at a 'flower lottery', 'pigeon lottery', or *fan tan*, he is to be punished with loss of his claim to a share of the ceremonial pork,[99] a punishment that symbolizes loss of the offender's socio-political rights, and lineage membership, in his village (Baker 1968: 52).

In the late Ch'ing, various local gentry tried to contain the spread of legalized gambling in their communities. In 1861, for example, a missionary in Canton recorded that all the shopkeepers living in a street called Shu-ssu chieh (Book of Poetry Street) closed their shops 'and refused to open them until the governor-general of the province, whom they had petitioned on the subject, promised to issue an order directing the district ruler to close a gaming-house that he had permitted to be opened in the street'. Such concern of the local gentry-merchant community explained why gaming houses in Canton were in general in back- or side-streets during the late-Ch'ing period (Gray 1972: 385). In one village in the county of Shun-tê, they banned gambling permanently. A stone stele with a full inscription of the text of the prohibition was erected in the village (*Shun-tê hsien chih* 1929: ch. 6 p. 27).[100] In the market-town of Chiu-kiang in Shun-tê, the Chü lineage organization petitioned the Republican government, and was subsequently granted permission to maintain a ban against all forms of gambling in their section of the town (Tsu Lou 1936: 247).[101] Village elders of Sha-nan, the rural community in Canton, were also able to stop villagers from gambling at poker, which was outlawed at the request of the *fan tan* monopoly company in Canton (Wu Jui-lin 1934: 111). Towards the 1920s, when gambling in Canton was legalized by the ruling Kwangsi militarists, one street's business association voted to prohibit *fan tan* houses from operating there (Tsu Lou 1936: 247).[102] In the early 1920s, mid-1925, and 1936, the Kwangtung Christian Church organized large-scale anti-gambling campaigns targeting the student community. In its 1920s campaigns, essay and drawing competitions were held, and the prize-winners published.[103]

Whether such forms of collective control and publicity aimed at 'reforming' Cantonese gamblers were effective in the long term remains doubtful. But the effects of school education, add to persuasions and warnings given by close relatives and friends, must have been powerful in controlling the otherwise impulsive and irrational behaviour of gamblers. Although all these moral lessons, warnings, publicity campaigns, and attempts at social control might not keep every gambler away from gambling, they may have helped bring to mind the danger of indulging in it.

Were Bookmakers Bullying Swindlers?

Another conventional assumption about gambling was expressed in the common saying that 'nine out of ten forms of gambling are swindles' (*shih tu chiu p'ien*). In anti-gambling writings of every stripe, gamblers were always assumed to be cheated, and were all seen as prey to the ingenious and devious tricks played upon them. Thus, in dice games, specially made dice filled with mercury were believed to enable a skilful croupier to throw the outcome of a game. In *fan tan*, he was also said to be able to cheat by adding in pieces of button while counting. And even in lotteries, which were generally believed to be a relatively honest form of gambling, cheating was said to be commonplace. With some forms of lottery, although it was a rule that all the numbers or characters to be drawn had to be placed in a sealed box and hung from a beam outside the lottery company for some time before being opened, tricks could still be played at the moment of disclosure of the drawn characters, enabling the company to minimize its loss and maximize its gain.[104]

Although swindles in gambling undoubtedly existed, it is questionable that they were necessarily widespread, undetected, or easily accomplished. Moreover, the assumption that gamblers were too unsophisticated to be aware of being cheated, or that (though aware) they submitted quietly, further reinforced the stereotypical image of gamblers as the helpless prey of swindlers. From the recollection of a once-compulsive gambler, we learn that aficionados of poker or dice games were always on high alert to trickery. Moreover, the motto to 'Play only with someone you know, not strangers' (*tu shu p'u tu shêng*), which was extremely familiar to betters, could well help maintain a player's vigilance (Chang Kung-p'ing 1993: 626).

With some forms of gambling, cheating, while possible, was very difficult. For instance, in the 'flower lottery', the lucky character was chosen the night before its announcement. It had then to be sealed in a red envelope. The next day, the sealed envelope would be folded into a cone, tied to a red string, and hung up outside the lottery premises, in the presence of many betters. Only after that would gamblers put their stake-money on their favourite characters. We get the impression that gamblers knew how to protect themselves from being cheated. Some of the more cautious took pains to have their wagers and their choice of characters sealed in a red paper envelope so that the details would remain unknown to the lottery company and the chance of being cheated thereby minimized. Moreover, since a good reputation was absolutely essential for a lottery company's survival, few of them were said to be willing to risk cheating on the outcome of a game. At the opening of the sealed envelope with its lucky character, the presence of a large crowd of vigilant spectators would anyway render cheating very difficult (Li Han-ch'ung 1988: 114–16).[105]

One case of alleged cheating is vividly recorded in a contemporary magazine. A lottery company in Canton was said to be always cheating its customers by hiding the original character-paper, and announcing to the public a different one prepared at the last moment. On this occasion, however, the original character-paper accidentally slipped from the announcer's hands. The gambler spectators became so infuriated that a riot almost broke out and troops were called. However, the soldiers refused to disperse the crowd, in case they were thought to be lending support to swindlers. Instead, they demanded that the company compensate all betters by paying them thirty times the total of their stake-money.[106] This incident reminds us that the presence of the state and its readiness to support legitimate but deceived betters could help minimize malpractices by dishonest bookmakers. It also brings out an important point that cheated betters did not easily yield to the circumstances, and were usually determined to pursue the suspects until justice was done.

This was by no means an isolated incident. Other occurrences revealed similar aggressive reactions by indignant victims of bookmakers' swindles. For instance, a Mr Huang was said to be notorious for deceiving women betters in the 'flower lottery': on a number of occasions he had allegedly turned down a winner's request for collecting her windfall with the excuse that the betting characters written on the ticket were illegible, or the stamp on the ticket did not match the one on the receipt, and so on. One day, he turned down a demand from another winner, but this time the woman was a feisty character. Under her leadership, a group of men and women had the crook surrounded, and threatened to have him beaten up if the award was not paid to her instantly. In the end, the trembling Huang yielded to the demand and paid the woman the full amount she had won

(*KCMKJP* 1923: 7, 11 Sept.). In another context, an angry winner, accompanied by a group of women, headed towards the bookmaking company and demanded the immediate payment for her winning lottery ticket, which the latter announced invalid because of late submission. The news report stated that these women were prepared for physical violence if their demand was turned down (ibid. 7, 25 Sept.). On the same day, another lottery bookmaker was threatened with his life by a group of indignant winners who failed to get anything from him because the paper that was inscribed with the winning characters had been taken away forcibly by a group of soldiers who had allegedly received bribes from this company. They chased him from his office to his residence until they dispersed at the sight of an approaching team of armed policemen (ibid.). Although these reports do not tell us the outcome of the two incidents, the responses of these disillusioned betters demonstrate that they did not submit to trickery quietly. Gamblers were apparently sophisticated enough to deter deceits, and the bookmakers were not at all free to do whatever they wanted.

This last point was vividly shown in another dispute involving a well-to-do better and a seemingly trustworthy agency of a local lottery company based in Ho-nan. This agency was originally a money exchange shop that took up a sideline business of selling lottery tickets. Since it was an old shop with a good reputation, local punters were happy to place their bets through it. A few months before the dispute occurred, the original owner of this shop died, and it changed hands. A local resident, Mr Huang, had patronized this shop for a long time. The shopkeeper trusted him so well that sometimes he could place a bet without paying at once; the payment would be settled a few days after the draw. One day Mr Huang placed another bet on a lottery without paying. It then came to his notice that the characters that he had bet on were drawn and he had won first prize. Exhilarated, he immediately sent his maid to the shop and asked for the official receipt of his bet, which would entitle him to collect the prize money. The shopkeeper, however, regretted that since Mr Huang had not left the betting money, his bet was not valid. Having found out that the shopkeeper had placed the bet but kept it for himself, Mr Huang first bitterly cursed the shopkeeper in front of the premises, and then filed a complaint to the local police, who, however, could not help because of a lack of substantiated evidence. Eventually, Mr Huang turned to a local personage from the prominent Kiang household. Under the mediation of the highly respectable Kiang, the two parties agreed to have the dispute settled: the shopkeeper split the windfall with the disgruntled Huang (*YHP* 1932: 1, 14 Nov.). Although his action was both legally and technically legitimate, the fact that this agent had to yield to pressure revealed that a bookmaker was not untouchable.

Bookmaking companies themselves were not invulnerable to swindling either. One magazine reports how a Cantonese businessman named Li once won 600,000 yüan in a 'flower lottery' by playing a simple trick on a lottery company in Canton. It was a rule that the 'flower lottery' was drawn twice a day. In the reported case, shortly after the announcement of the day's first draw, Mr Li got into a sedan-chair and rushed to a local lottery company. He knew very well that he would not be able to make a last-minute bet for that game, and he also knew the result of the draw. By the time his sedan-chair arrived, the drawn characters, as expected, had just been announced. After he was told that the last drawn characters were 'yung shêng', he smiled and informed the lingering crowd that he was lucky to be late since the drawn characters were not what he would have betted on. Pretending that he felt relieved, he handed over to the lottery company his sealed wager of 20,000 yüan in cash for the second draw of the day. As the company saw it, Mr Li would obviously not bet on the characters 'yung shêng'. In order to minimize possible loss, they cheated by changing the result of the next draw to 'yung shêng' again. However, they fell into his trap, these being precisely the characters Mr Li betted on. He won the top prize—thirty times his original stake-money (Han Pi *c.*1920s: 2–3).

Another gambler's trick took even more amazing form. A Mr Chü was an experienced *fan tan* gambler, so skilful that as soon as the bowl was lifted, and even before the croupier started to extract the porcelain buttons, he could count ahead of the croupier and 'foretell' the outcome of the game. He always played with a big cigar in his hands, acting, literally, as a smokescreen to hide his trick of 'spitting buttons'. After the bowl had been lifted, and if he knew he would lose that game, he puffed cigar-smoke to the centre of the gaming table. At that moment, he would spit out one or more buttons onto the table, and hence manipulate the outcome to his advantage. His trick was so faultless that in three months, he won so much money from the *fan tan* dens in Canton that he was eventually refused admittance (*Kuang-chou shê-hui tsa chih c.*1920s: 3). These stories, though somehow sensationalized, show that cheating was not the monopoly of the companies. Both gamblers and bookmakers could be swindlers as well as victims. These reports cannot be verified, but at least show that the bookmaking companies that operated this popular, and allegedly highly pernicious form of gambling in Canton were sometimes perceived as more trustworthy and honourable than the betters.

Gambling Houses, Race Courses, and Prosperity

The assumption that gambling-houses were the seed beds of crime might be true only to a certain extent. Pickpockets, for instance, may have found the crowded environment of gambling divans an ideal ground for practising their misdeeds. Some of these dens might be poorly lit and ventilated, noisy, chaotic, filthy, and packed with men of loose reputation and 'complex backgrounds'.[107] By contrast, a former resident of Canton also recalls that well-lit and 'wonderfully and lavishly' decorated gambling establishments were plentiful on the island of Ho-nan (Hsü Chu-ch'êng 1982: 146).[108]

It is interesting to note that sometimes a local gambling house could be as big as a present-date resort. Shen-chên, a market-town bordering the New Territories of British Hong Kong, was reported to have three of these massive well-organized 'gambling places' (*tu ch'ang*). According to the report of a journalist who had visited one of them, they were a great deal more than just a venue for betting. In addition to a wide choice of gambling games, this place also supplied its customers with Chinese and Western cuisine, quality opium, and wines that were served by attractive waitresses. If a customer wanted to stay overnight, he could choose between a well-decorated room and floating pleasure boats of various sizes. For entertainment, this establishment erected a theatre in which Cantonese opera was performed nightly. Other forms of amusement included Chinese chess competitions, scriptures chanted by Buddhist nuns, and a 'floating pageant' (*ch'iu-shih*), which was originally a religious festival parade of people dressed up in colourful and historical costumes. The scale and management of this establishment, and the wide variety of non-gambling entertainment available, had left a highly positive impression with this journalist, who concluded that even those well-established gambling houses in Macao were completely outshone. Visitors to this place were said to have found it so enjoyable that they forgot about going home (*YHP* 1934: 1. 13 Sept.).

In Canton, establishments like this one seemingly did not exist. During the heyday of legal and illegal gambling in the city in the early and mid-1920s, however, there were a few houses that resembled, though on a much smaller scale, the one described in Shen-chên. In the heart of Canton, for example, there was an illicit gaming house where sing-song girls were hired to perform to attract customers. The place was said to be particularly popular among gamblers and unlicensed prostitutes. Also in the bustling part of Canton was another illicit establishment that reportedly arranged film shows and traditional opera to entertain its clients. All these places were under the open protection of the army or the local police, who, of course, received a handsome sum from bribes in return (*KCMKJP* 1923: 6, 7 and 10 Aug.).

Given the opportunity of making easy money, it is no surprise that loan-sharks and crooks should hang around gambling houses looking for likely targets.[109] Moreover, during the chaotic years of 1923–5, there were reports of sporadic cases of violent clashes between rival groups of soldiers or local bullies who tried to extend their control over both licensed and illicit gambling in Canton. In one of these cases, for example, after a private was gunned down when he demanded a protection fee from a gambling house that was located outside his territory, a feud ensued between two groups of unruly soldiers in a busy quarter of the city (ibid. 1923: 7, 1 Nov.). In another incident, three soldiers lost their bets at a gaming house. Before leaving, they demanded that the croupiers give some of their stake-money back, which, of course, was refused. When they tried to vandalize the place, they were beaten up and then chased away by the 'guardians' of the house, who were also soldiers. In revenge, these three soldiers returned shortly afterward with some thirty soldiers, and a street battle then followed (ibid. 7, 22 Nov.).

There is, however, little evidence to show that gambling-houses were particularly unsafe to visit, or that they were necessarily a breeding-ground for violent crime. For security reasons, these houses usually employed many security guards (*ta shou*) whose conspicuous presence ensured that their customers had a safe place to gamble.[110] For many illicit houses during the early and mid-1920s, bribing the police, the army, and local bullies, trebly ensured the safety of their businesses. Such links between bribed officials and unlicensed bookmaking activities could be traced to at least the mid-nineteenth century, when many illegal gambling houses were under the effective protection of, and sometimes even the management of, *yamen* constables;[111] in an 'extreme' case, an illicit 'pigeon lottery' ring was operated, probably by junior officials, inside the *yamen* of the Provincial Viceroy (Ching Hsiao 1935: 146–7). The missionary John Henry Gray, who was also a long-time resident, noticed that 'the Namhoi and Pan-Yu magistrates at Canton have actually converted some spare rooms near the outer gates of their respective *yamens* into gaming houses'; 'similar devices' were also noted by him in other district cities in Kwangtung (Gray 1972: i. 385). At the start of this century, many legal *fan tan* houses in Canton were even guarded by soldiers.[112] An American traveller in 1924 noted that 'troop-protected gambling in Canton included lotteries of every description... Some troop-stations went so far as to put up advertising-signs of colored boards and paper lanterns declaring that all patrons would be well guarded while "conversing" inside' (Franck 1925: 269). Another Westerner made a similar comment on the gambling district in 1920s Macao: 'Many of the gamblers have no other home than these dens. Many are employed by the syndicate as guards against pickpockets. The streets are full of police, both uniformed and plain-clothes men, but it is seldom that a whistle is heard within the gambling district in Macao' (Lilius 1930: 88). Hence, with this official blessing, robbery, kidnapping, and other forms of violent crime, which were not uncommon to Republican Canton,[113] seldom involved gambling-houses. Visiting a gambling-house was seemingly safer than taking a walk in the countryside of Canton, where violent crimes were commonplace.[114] It was perhaps because of this reason that in extant contemporary drawings of *fan-tan* houses, children, under the auspices and accompaniment of adults, were vividly present as spectators inside these establishments.[115] Moreover, in the late 1920s and mid-1930s, when gambling was under relatively strict surveillance and regulation by the state, newspaper reports of incidents of various kinds that had taken place in licensed gambling houses (mostly located in Ho-nan) seemed to follow at least two patterns. First, most cases concerning the disruption of public order in the vicinity of gambling houses were about fist fights among gamblers themselves, brawls between croupiers and gamblers, or aggressive behaviour of betters who thought they had been deceived, and so on; very few of these reported cases were what could be understood as 'violent crimes' that targeted operators or customers of these places indiscriminately.[116] Secondly, when mishaps as such occurred, the local police were able, in most cases, to react swiftly and assume control over the situation.[117] This indicates that the state had agents close to these establishments, and this was probably because almost all the licensed gambling houses, especially those specializing in card and domino games, were concentrated in two areas of Ho-nan that were also within the jurisdiction of the Canton Public Security Bureau.[118] The fact that gaming houses were one of the popular hang-outs for many off-duty policemen might also have helped to keep undesirable elements away from these places (*KHP* 1927: 11, 6 Dec.).

It is interesting to note that the anti-gambling writings of the Republican period also revealed some typical contemporary assumptions of the superiority of things Western. In a radio broadcast speech by a senior provincial official, the 'absence of gambling' in modern Western countries was believed to be one of the reasons for their national success:

> When we are in our country, we always think about playing *mahjong* for leisure. However, once we were in a foreign [Western] country, all such desires [for gambling] would disappear completely. [We would] forget about *mahjong*, and our life would become more upright. Why is it so? It is because in foreign [Western] societies, the custom of gambling just does not exist. Since they [the Westerners] already complain about the lack of physical and mental energy to deal with all their righteous businesses, how can they have any spare time [to waste on] playing *mahjong*? When [Western] foreigners need entertainment to drive away boredom, their societies naturally provide them with many graceful pastimes for their enjoyment. They do not need to gamble at *mahjong*.

Moreover, since all Westerners were assumed to abstain from gambling, their life-span in consequence was believed to be longer and their physique healthier than those of the Chinese (Li Hsun-huan 1936: 66, 18).

This pro-Western attitude fostered a double standard in the official policy towards gambling. Although gambling was condemned in official rhetoric and in moralistic 'public opinion', the government endorsed the proposal by a bookmaker to build a racecourse in the eastern suburb of Canton. The plan was said to be welcomed by most Cantonese (*NYSP* 1928: 2, 17 Aug.; 1928: 3, 25 Oct.). Ironically, none of these anti-gambling treatises even mentioned horse racing in Canton, though it was conspicuously alive. In Ch'en Chi-t'ang's ambitious 'Three-year Plan' for the building of a modern Kwangtung, one of many public-works projects was the construction of concrete spectator-stands for the racecourse (*HCLCCN* 1934: 24–5). Officially, horse racing was not conceived of as gambling, but as 'an important facility of game and sport that can be found in most big cities' (Kuang-chou-shih chêng-fu 1929: 453). It was glorified as an effective Western means of modernization:

> Inquiries show that horse racing has a very noble origin. All countries in Europe and America hold races in Spring and Autumn. In . . . [big] cities like Peking, Tientsin, Hankow, Shanghai and so on, [horse racing] is also organized. [Horse racing] helps promote sports among the citizens, and stimulates [their] martial spirits . . . arouses their interest . . . in country sports, and in philanthropic activities. (Kuang-chou-shih chêng-fu 1933: 16)

In the view of a contemporary journalist, horse racing, together with dancing, opera music, movie-going, and visiting public parks, was among the finest forms of entertainment available to citizens of civilized countries. In an official publication on the financial situation of Kwangtung, the budgetary data concerned with the construction of the racecourse was printed under the category of 'Education and Culture'.[119] Probably for this reason, horse racing was the only game of chance that was not suppressed by the authorities in the 1936 anti-gambling campaign.[120]

Information on the history and the organization of horse racing in Canton is very sketchy. But it is apparent that the sport/spectacle was widely enjoyed as a high-class pastime by the elite. From a rare piece of reportage on one of these races, it is known that nearly all the major figures in the Kwangtung government, and the compradores of some of the big foreign firms in Canton, joined the other five thousand people as spectators at a one-day event (*HTJP* 1931: 1.3, 6 Apr.).[121] Stake-money was involved, and lottery tickets issued. In 1933, a one-day event brought more than 10,000 yüan of income to the coffers of the municipal government, which was said to be used for the construction of a hospital for 'ordinary citizens' (Kuang-chou-shih-chêng-fu 1933: 16).

On the local level, gambling did sometimes contribute to the welfare of a community. In the village of Chiu Fêng-huang, the *fan tan* gambling-house paid about three yüan per day to the government as tax, and of this one-third was funnelled into the public coffers of the village. In the village of Sha-pei, also on the outskirts of Canton, the more prosperous *fan tan* den there contributed to the chest of the village temple a daily sum of 2.5 yüan, plus another 15 yüan of tax per day to the government. All these offerings would be used mainly for funding the annual local temple fairs, which were among the few joyful events in these communities (Wu and Huang 1935: 153; Wu Jui-lin 1934: 109–10). In some villages in this area, such financial contributions were crucial to the success of the event.[122] During temple fairs, therefore, temporary gambling-dens or booths would always be set up in the vicinity of the host temple. Bookmakers were required to pay a fee to the temple, and a bribe to the local police. Their presence also contributed by attracting sought-after crowds to the venue, a 'bustling crowd' being commonly held to bestow a highly auspicious blessing on a locality (Ho 1994; Ward 1979: 29). Outside Canton, this economic importance to some market towns was crucial. For example, in 1934 a market town called Kang Tou was reportedly suffering from a deep recession. Commerce declined, and opium and gambling businesses, which had once brought great prosperity, also dwindled sharply. To rejuvenate their businesses and to lure old customers back to their establishments, bookmakers there tried out a number of gimmicks including organizing large-scale dragon-boat races on religious festivals and staging free Cantonese opera shows performed by the sensational all-female opera companies from Canton. These free entertainments, especially the latter, helped draw huge crowds to this town and partly resuscitated its dying *fan tan* business (*YHP* 1934: 1, 6 July). An anti-gambling critic pointed out, albeit rhetorically, that where gambling dens prospered, so also did brothels, restaurants, opium dens, and other luxury consumer businesses (Huang Lin-shêng, *CTKL* 1936: 46).

It was, therefore, no surprise that after the pro-Nanking Kwangtung government had imposed a strict ban on gambling and opium in the province, it was soon faced with a serious challenge from many county administrations who refused to remit to the Provincial Treasury a substantial portion of local revenue on the grounds that their financial condition was aggravated by the prohibition; the normal operation of the local government was acutely affected by the loss of these two sources of income (*Kuang-tung shêng-chêng-fu kung pao* 356, 1937: 49, 30 Jan.). In other words, gambling also helped boost the local economy, and was also, inversely, an indicator of a place's prosperity (*CTKL* 1936: 29).

The lottery, the most popular form of gambling in Canton, served noble causes too. The first legal lottery in Canton, namely 'surnames guessing' game, was introduced as a means to raise funding for repairing the Examination Hall partly burnt down in a military conflict. Since then and up until the early Republic, most forms of licensed lottery were intended for the purpose of raising funding by the local government to meet the cost of political contingency or public projects. In the case of 'shop lottery' (*p'u piao*), for instance, its original 'missions' were to finance emergency relief for victims of a devastating flood and to fund the government in its formidable task of reforming the chaotic currency structure.[123] By the mid-1920s, the major source of income for Canton's only orphanage came from a 2 per cent tax levied on the prize money of the infamous 'pigeon lottery' (*KCMKJP* 1925: 6, 25 Apr.). Throughout the 1920s and the early 1930s, different forms of lottery existed legally and illicitly under various names in Canton and the province. The extensive popularity of the lottery had attracted the attention of many local respectable organizations, both official and unofficial, which turned to it as a legitimate means of fund-raising. In 1926, for example, the director of a government-funded charity, which was a school for indigent citizens called the Institute for Educating the Poor (*P'ing-min chiao-yang yüan*), requested an official licence to operate a lottery based on the model of 'shop lottery' for, in all likelihood, the purpose of fund-raising. In 1928, a seemingly semi-official body called the Association of Canton Women Consoling the Anti-Communist Armed Comrades (*Kuang-chou nü-chieh ju-chih wei-lao tu-chieh wu-chüan tung-chi hui*) submitted a similar application for a licence to run a lottery game in Canton. Although both applications were turned down by the Provincial government on the grounds that this would have infringed on the bookmaking company's franchise of running the 'shop lottery' in the city, it was not known if other similar applications existed and how many of them were endorsed (Kuang-chou-shih shih-chêng-fu, no. 341, 1929: 81–2, Dec.). The fact that these notable organizations chose to employ a lottery as a tool for raising funds indicated at least two significant characteristics of this particular form of gambling: it was both hugely popular and considerably much less pernicious for individuals and society than other games such as *fan tan* and shooting dice.[124]

The wide popularity of the lottery was probably also due to the way that it was played. First, in nearly all forms of lottery operated in Canton, betters were required to pick a set of numbers or Chinese characters on their wagered tickets. This, perhaps, as pointed out by sociologists and anthropologists, was particularly appealing to a better because it bestowed a sense of self-determination, of being able to exercise control over one's destiny, of self-reliance and autonomy, feelings usually denied in daily life (Wen-lang Li and Smith 1976: 192–3; Newman 1972: 13–19). Secondly, anyone could place a bet on various forms of lottery conveniently through extensive networks of collectors that penetrated far and deep into the local society, and the minimum stake required was usually very low. It therefore enabled people from all walks of life—from rich officials to poor bondservants, from troublesome children to beggars—to wager on it.[125]

To sum up: the publicized official views on gambling in Canton were apparently so conditioned by rhetoric and so generalized that they produced only a distorted, and politicized picture of the 'problem'. Ironically, however, this strongly worded anti-gambling propaganda carried no weight with the administration, which continued to display reluctance in enforcing any far-reaching plan against the 'vice' it condemned.

4. *POPULAR PERCEPTIONS OF GAMBLING*

Some Favourable Views

In spite of the fact that gambling was always publicly condemned in official propaganda, Cantonese popular attitudes towards it seem to have been little affected. That also explains why gambling remained popular among local residents throughout the period under study.

Gambling in the general view was an enjoyable and socially meaningful pastime, as long as its players did not overindulge in it. The popular saying 'Ah Po's Father's Dead' (*Ah Po ssu lao-t'ou*), meaning 'indifference', originated in the commercial heart of Canton, Hsi-kuan, in the mid-1920s. The proverb was said to have evolved from a true story. Ah Po, a rich young wastrel, was an addictive gambler, and a regular visitor to the gambling-houses in Hsi-kuan. Once, when he was playing in a gambling den, one of his servants rushed in to break the news of his father's death, and requested him to return home immediately. Ah Po, however, was so absorbed by the game that he sent his servant away with a message that 'he is too busy to care about it' (*lan li*). From that day on, the story of Ah Po spread all over town. But instead of criticizing him, people made a joke of his 'laughable' reply. It seemed there was nothing morally wrong about gambling, unless one indulged in it as excessively as Ah Po did (*HTJP* 1927: 4.4, 19 May).

In a piece of humorous writing called 'The Divination for *Fan Tan*' (Po tan), an obsessive *fan tan* gambler patronizes a fortune-teller in order to obtain divine betting tips. In the end, the gambler gets this reply from the fortune-teller: 'If one obsessively bets for a long time, one will only lose. If one is greedy, one will only lose . . . [Hence, my advice is] to make your mind-and-heart austere, [and] to restrain your hands [at the gaming table]. Your request [, therefore,] can never be answered by means of divination' (K'ung pa-an 1934: 12). Except in such cases of overindulgence, gambling was not commonly seen as a problem.

This view was shared by many contemporary betters. For instance, in a newspaper article entitled 'The Philosophy of Gambling' (Tu t'i chieh-hsüeh), its author held a rather ambiguous attitude towards gambling. He began by saying that it was hard to determine if gamblers were good or evil because one could find them in both categories. He then went on to give his clichéd and unsubstantiated analysis on the psychology of the gambler, which he casually characterized in two words: covetous and indolent. But before he ended his essay, he advised his readers that 'to be content is the most important attitude towards life' because 'the failure of a man's life is without exception a result of his covetousness, just like the failure of gambling [for a gambler] lies in his greed'. The essay, though sounding moralistic, did not ask its readers to stay away from gambling, but to refrain from being covetous when playing (*YHP* 1934: 1, 19 Oct.).

To some, gambling was not considered morally wrong at all. For instance, a report about a famous sing-song girl called Ta Yin-lien stated that she had just announced a list of seven expectations she had of a man she would consider marrying. Of the seven criteria, it is interesting to find that opium smoking was out of the question. Brothel-going and gambling, however, were not problems as long as the man had no other 'bad' habits (*KPP* 1928: 8, 29 Mar.).

In a short article published in a KMT newspaper's supplement, its author wrote sarcastically of what he envied most in Canton. In addition to leading the life of a wealthy man in a luxurious mansion with all the modern facilities, bodyguards, maidservants, beautiful women, and so on, a lucky night out in a gaming house with handsome winnings was also something that he highly envied ('Hsien sha', *KCMKJP* 1925, 14 July '*Hsiao Kuang-chou*' column).

Although there was no shortage of moralistic songs with an anti-gambling theme, there were also folk songs that sounded out the unpretentious and positive views of the people towards gambling. In an extract of a vernacular song, 'A *Fan tan* Croupier is Tired of Gambling' (Tu lieh chih tan-kuan), which was compiled in a song-book entitled *A Big Collection of Famous Songs* (Ming-ch'ü ta-ch'üan) published probably in the 1920s, such a favourable attitude was most vividly, and amusingly, displayed towards both bookmaking and its industry:

> In retrospect, my serious trouble began after the death of my parents. Since I have not read any books [in my childhood], I was thoroughly uneducated. Not only was I not equipped with any skill for making a living, but also full of [bad] habits. Idling away the time, I went astray before long. . . . I specialized in running unlicensed [*fan tan*] houses, never bothered if that was right or wrong because I saw in it only as a means of livelihood. I took the opportunity of the government's quest for defence funds to operate [licensed] gambling. If I had not done that, many others, no doubt, would have had done so. . . . My business is booming ever since its first day of inauguration. By now I have already

amassed a few coins, and am contemplating to [spend them on] buying a few shops, though my wealth is still a long way from that of the four richest families [in Canton]. Some people never say one good word on prostitution, gambling, alcohol consumption, and opium smoking. If you ask for my opinion, I shall tell you about my high regard of gambling [among those four forms of habit]. It is by all means fair to charge ten per cent on the rewards of a winning better [as my income]. [Moreover,] although [gambling] can kill, it can also save a person's life; numerous people have been transformed into men of great wealth because of [winning in] gambling. . . . If I had not had been involved in the bookmaking business, I would not have been able to become as rich as I am now. Come, my shop assistants, let's lose no time in opening for business! If we are lucky [today], we may run into a young wastrel.[126]

Gambling here was perceived as serving some important and meaningful economic and social functions to its players and the larger community. It brought hope to betters, and would harm mainly those who had the financial means to squander. The huge popularity of gambling in this part of China could well be attributed to such a practical view on gambling seemingly shared widely by the local populace.

Such a favourable attitude towards gambling was not new to Canton. In 1882, when a Governor-General strictly enforced a ban on gambling in Canton and the province, a lengthy leader published in a Shanghai newspaper *Shen pao* challenged the wisdom behind this official policy. It began with an attack on the official prejudice against gambling as a legitimate means for both bookmakers and betters to acquire wealth. Its author saw no major difference, but a lot of similarities, between the nature of gambling or bookmaking businesses and that of any other profit-making mercantile or commercial enterprise: both were consciously profit-seeking, at times ruthless, and able to inflict harm on customers and the community. Many merchants were criticized by this author for being involved in economic crimes such as hoarding, swindling, and profiteering without the least interference by the authorities. The traps that these immoral merchants laid were even more dangerous than gambling because, whereas the latter was operated in broad daylight, these traps were largely set up surreptitiously 'in the dark'. 'These covetous beings,' said the author, 'their shrewdness exceeds that of the gamblers, but their malicious mind-and-heart also surpasses that of the gamblers.' He also disliked the fact that when local officials were trying to suppress gambling among the common people, they themselves indulged in it in the sanctuary of *yamen* and official residences (*Shen pao* 1882, 8 Mar.). Gambling, despite still being regarded as a vice in this leader, was not perceived as particularly malicious or more so than many legitimate businesses run by scheming merchants. The harm that gambling was supposedly inflicting on individuals and the community was read from an alternative, perhaps even more realistic, perspective. It is very likely that this view was shared by many residents of Canton, as the legalization of the 'surnames guessing' lottery in 1897 was reported by the British Consul as a great success that won public acceptance and support from all levels of the society (*YHKPK* 1996: 944).

In spite of the fact that anti-gambling writings stressed heavily the danger of swindling in all forms of gambling, the common people did not always share this opinion. A 1910 dragon-boat folk song that ridiculed the insincerity of the official campaign against gambling in Canton gave the advice that some forms of gambling have to be either avoided, as with *mahjong*, which was too time-consuming, or suppressed, as with 'pigeon and flower lotteries', which could be easily used to defraud. The folk song, however, continues:

> Only *fan tan* is played with great fairness. You can bet on the odds [of one to four] as you wish. If you lose, it is entirely up to you to decide if you would like to continue to stake. With only ten per cent of a stake taken away [by the bookmaker] as the charge, a winning bet is paid 90 percent of the total stake money [placed on winning number]. 'Shop lottery' and 'mountain lottery' [are also fairly played] as there are two hundred characters from which a better can choose at his will, without being misled or cheated. The drawing of the odds is conducted in the open [to ensure no room for swindling]. A lottery winner is by no means unfairly treated for receiving as prize money 80 per cent of the total money staked in a draw. The national treasure, as a result, has become heavily dependent on this source of revenue. The government, in consequence, is doing whatever it can to perpetuate the existence [of these forms of gambling]. ('Chin-tu chih kung-tan' 1910: 89–91)

Given that *fan tan* was strongly criticized by the anti-gambling politicians as being the most pernicious form of all gambling, the presence of such a popular appreciative view of it forces us to reconsider the truthfulness of these criticisms.

In some late-Ch'ing literature, gambling was not seen as something worthless, immoral, and pernicious. In the epilogue to an essay about the history of various forms of gambling, its author gave his sincere advice on when one should, and should not, play. He opined that one might gamble

> on leisure days, rainy days, [and] extremely cold or hot days; after drinks; after illness; [in] private chambers where windows are shiny and tables clean; with lavish guests, [or] gentle and refined guests . . . when celebrating success in the Civil Examinations, [or] when one has failed in them . . . when staying with people who know little about literature or poetry; when one is disappointed by a minor setback . . . [and] when beautiful women are sitting nearby.

He also listed the occasions on which gambling should be avoided: on wedding days; when strangers and unfamiliar guests are present; when one's playing partners are the greedy, temperamental, or arrogant type; and so on. Moreover, one should not gamble continuously for days and nights (Chin Hsüeh-shih 1849: 19–20). Thus as long as one knew how and when to gamble, it could be a highly enjoyable entertainment.

In late-Ch'ing and Republican Canton, the wide popularity of various forms of gambling was largely attributed to the prevalence of such a favourable image of, and attitude towards, gambling as an amusement rather than a vice. Some forms of gambling, judging by the rules by which they were played, looked more like amusement than straight gambling: these included cricket fighting, quail fighting, wild pigeon fighting, guessing the weight of a joint of meat or a fish, orange or sugar-cane cutting, and guessing the length of rods.[127] In an investigative report prepared by the Social Bureau of Canton Municipal Government in 1927, the popularity and consistent survival of many forms of domino and dice games in this city, which the local authorities had great difficulty in suppressing, was largely because, among other factors, they were commonly taken as legitimate entertainment, and 'no longer as a problem of gambling'.[128] In many villages and towns, although organized public gambling was forbidden or regulated, private playing with dominoes or dice at home was still favourably accepted as a way to relax (*hsiao-hsien*).[129] In some rural settlements near Canton, organized public gambling, though illicit, prospered during the slack seasons for farming when farmers there played *fan tan* and 'pigeon lottery' for leisure (*YHP* 1934: 1, 6 July). In their analyses on how to eradicate gambling, two prize-winning anti-gambling essays reminded their readers of the importance of correcting the long-held positive view of gambling by those from all walks of life in Canton and the province. Both rich and poor were said to be indulging in various forms of gambling activities which were traditionally acceptable and unquestioned leisure pursuits. In the view of these writers, such fossilized ideas have to be uprooted and swiftly replaced with a consistent programme of thought reform that would help educate the people on what real entertainment—such as cookery, flower arranging, toy making, exercise, etc.—should be (*CTKL* 1936: 99–114). The value of the amusement unleashed by gambling was seemingly appreciated by a great many people.[130]

Contemporary guidebooks on Canton display a similarly favourable attitude towards gambling. Two of them, one published in 1919 and the other in 1926, both contain a section on gambling in their chapters on entertainment, in which concise explanatory notes on the rules of each of the most popular forms of gambling in Canton are given. But in order not to be suspected of promoting this form of 'morally damaging' pastime, the editors claim that they have shortened the descriptions, for which they apologize to readers in a postscript (Lui Tsai-su 1926: 116–18; Tzu-hang-shih 1919: ch. 4 pp. 6–7).

Long Live Mahjong

In the mid-1920s, three Chinese tobacco companies promoted their products by inserting in every packet of cigarettes a picture of either a *mahjong* domino, a playing card, or one of the ancients as depicted in the 'flower lottery'. An official daily criticized these companies for 'flattering [the bad taste of] the society, [and] following the [vulgar] trend'. Gambling, by implication, was very much in popular demand (*KCMKJP* 1926: 4, 14 Oct.).

Mahjong had been commonly played in Kwangtung and Fukien since the mid-nineteenth century, but it was only in the 1920s that its apparently increasing popularity had started to arouse the concern of the authorities.[131] In a 1927 government report on vices in Canton, *mahjong* was specifically singled out as one of the many forms of 'gambling', which, as time went by, was increasingly taken by the general public as a form of entertainment. The changing popular perception of *mahjong* was said to have become so worrying from the authorities' perspective that the game, though still being played with stakes, had ceased to be seen as gambling at all.[132] In 1928, Ch'en Ming-shu, the chairman of Kwangtung provincial government, was worried by his observation that *mahjong* was increasingly accepted by the general public as an agreeable means of social gathering. Anyone who refused to play *mahjong* was usually laughed at for being doltish or anti-social (*NYSP* 1928: 11, 13 Sept.). In this period, *mahjong* was generally regarded as a 'noble form of pastime', which was 'even popular among officials' (*KCMKJP* 1926: 4, 14 Oct.). Thus, villagers in Sha-nan also picked up this 'fashionable form of leisure' which they regarded as the 'most pleasurable form of gambling'. Whenever they played, small crowds of spectators were always attracted to the scene (Wu Jui-lin 1934: 110). Gambling became just another reason for social gathering.

A reader had written about his concern over the wide popularity of *mahjong* and its pernicious impact on society. In his analysis, *mahjong* posed an even more serious threat to an individual and the community than other forms of gambling. The attraction of *fan tan* and other games that were commonly played in a gambling house was mainly confined to those 'lower-class' denizens who did not mind being seen in such lowly places; 'middle- and upper-classes gamblers always avoid these places to keep up their appearances'. The time a better spent on the lottery was short, and since the game itself was straightforward and boring, its attractiveness was not as strong. *Mahjong*, however, was not only played but enjoyed by many people ranging from senior officials and important people to pedlars, schoolchildren, and the most ordinary people of all ages. These people took the game as 'normal entertainment' and a family routine, so much so that it would 'exhaust their energies and strip them of all their possessions' (*YHP* 1934: 1, 27 Mar.).

The appeal and the public acceptance of *mahjong* was vividly revealed in popular culture. In a serialized story entitled 'The Lady from the West Gate' (Hsi-kuan hsiao-chê), nearly all the female protagonists, some of them well educated and from respectable families, are *mahjong* addicts who play at a club for hours every day. Whenever they meet, they talk much about their previous games, and gossip. In this story, the author also stated that in Li-chi Bay, a popular resort in the eastern suburb of Canton, huge bamboo structures were built to accommodate local Cantonese who went there to play *mahjong* during holidays (Kuang Lao-chiu 19: 47–52) In another social novel about a group of courtesans and their wealthy businessmen clients, it is noted that playing *mahjong* at brothels or private club, in the company of beautiful courtesans, was almost a daily routine to most businessmen. At the *mahjong* tables, business relations were cultivated, business partners introduced and established, and market news exchanged (Sung Yü 1989).[133] All these, however, were not fictitious. *Mahjong* was popularly played both in private and in public. By the mid-1930s, *mahjong* had already gained such popularity that there existed a Cantonese idiom that reflected the psychological importance of this game in the hearts and minds of many local people: '[I] would rather not have meat in [my] diet, than give up the sight of bamboo (a synonym of *mahjong*)' (*ling k'o ch'ih wu ju, pu k'o k'an wu chu*) (*YHP* 1936: 9, 1 Sept.). *Mahjong* was especially popular among well-off housewives who understandably had the luxury of time to spend on it. In one particular case, which was said to be widely talked about by 'faithful followers' of this game, a wealthy widow, who had spent most of her leisure time on playing *mahjong* with friends at home, died of a heart attack at a *mahjong* table after she was overjoyed by winning a game.[134] Overstressing oneself was indeed a problem to be avoided. *Mahjong*, however, did bring joy to that poor widow and to many of her contemporaries.

The joy of playing *mahjong* was visualized in at least one contemporary calendar poster entitled 'Amusement for Famous Stars' (*Ming-hsing shou-hsien*). The poster is set in the living room of a luxurious mansion, which is designed, decorated, and furnished in an impressively 'modern' manner, with Western-style lamps, chairs, curtains, carpets, and so on. The people, six ladies and three children, are also clad in 'modern' clothes with Western-style accessories. The atmosphere is an unmistakably light-hearted and joyous one: all the people were drawn with hearty smiles, they were painted in bright colours, the infants and children are healthy and well clad (Chang Yen-fêng 1994: i. 58). A poster like this helped transmit only the positive values and image of *mahjong* to its audience. It is not clear how many calendar posters on this motif existed. Since this kind of commercial calendar targeted the mass audience, with themes that always applied to the taste and preferences of such people, they are visual evidence of the popular perception of this social phenomenon. In this case, *mahjong* was undoubtedly highly perceived as a respectable form of amusement for classy people, especially women; it brought great joy to their families and posed no threat to their decency and that of their households, but rather helped them nurture domestic happiness and harmony.

After the proclamation of a short-lived ban on the game in 1932, a cartoonist vividly captured the people's wishes for the 'return' of official sanction of the game in a drawing entitled 'Hope Your Soul will Return'. A funeral flag, which was used for guiding the soul of a deceased person back to his terrestrial abode, was pictured, and on it were written the characters of some representative *mahjong* dominoes (*Pan-chiao man-hua* 1932: 2). This public sentiment about the game was not fictitious, however. In late August, 1936, just shortly before a new administration enforced a strict ban on gambling, local newspapers were filled with reports of an interesting phenomenon in Canton: numerous people, aware of the imminent ban, spent the last few days and nights gambling, especially playing *mahjong*. Many 'enthusiasts' were reported to have played consecutively for three days and nights. On these 'last' few evenings, this game was extensively and intensively played in local restaurants and hotels, where the sounds of *mahjong* and players' exhilaration were said to have filled the air in those neighbourhoods. This sudden upsurge in popular interest in this game also helped bring along a brief boom to local restaurant and hotel businesses in Canton (*YHP* 1936: 9, 1 Sept.). In 1936, shortly after a new administration had reimposed the ban on gambling, the Restaurants and Tea-Houses Guild petitioned the government to lift the ban on *mahjong*. The petitioners claimed that the game was a noble form of entertainment that won the admiration even of Westerners who, consequently, had introduced it into their countries. The fact that playing was also enjoyed by such historical figures as Wu Tsao and Liu I (a twelfth-century general) vindicated, allegedly, its harmlessness *vis-à-vis* the moral integrity of its players. Moreover, *mahjong* was said to be commonly played at restaurants as nothing but a social game that cheered the spirits of its players and enriched their friendships. Hence, *mahjong* was claimed to possess the social function of 'nurturing the vitality of a society' (*pei-yang shê-hui ti shêng-ch'i*). In addition, *mahjong* was said to have played an indispensable economic function too. The revenue it helped generate was a source of blessing to the local administration, and the prosperity of local restaurant business also benefited a long list of other trades related to catering and services.[135]

One of the plausible reasons for its high popularity was that people played *mahjong* as a game of skill, rather than just for money. A late-Ch'ing local gazetteer points out that it was very popular among scholar-officials, who played in order to train their innovative skill. Although the author criticizes *mahjong* as a vice, he ironically describes in detail the 'deeper meanings' of the game.[136] A contemporary journalist states that since *mahjong* gambling involved a mastery of skill instead of sheer luck, it gave its players a unique sense of achievement and satisfaction not found in most other forms of gambling. For this reason, he wrote, some *mahjong* fans were too proud to stoop to play *fan tan*, or lottery (despite its handsome prize)—games that required no more than sheer luck.[137] When attacking *mahjong* in an anti-gambling essay, its author grieved that all the resources, time, and talent that had been 'wasted' by players on this game should have been channelled to the more meaningful purpose of building China into a strong nation. In his view, *mahjong* players were mostly capable and intelligent, just the kind of 'talented persons' that China needed to manage her reforms. Although this may be an overstatement of the intelligence of *mahjong* betters, it still reflected the trend that *mahjong* was then popularly perceived as a game of intellect for, and by, intelligent people.[138] Extensive anthropological, sociological, and psychological research on gambling behaviours make the interesting observation that gambling that requires skill to play has a special attraction for it gives people a sense of control over their lives, the opportunity to participate in the decision-making process that affects their fate, and the chance to establish prestige and status by demonstrating to others their excellence in that skill (Campbell 1976: 220–7; Wer-lang Li and Smith 1976: 190–3; Newman 1972: 144–53; Scheibe 2000: 148–53). Hence, the game won many 'faithful supporters', and its unsurpassed popularity was established.

Some Cantonese were so bewitched by the magic of *mahjong* that they even used it as a standard of measurement to gauge their conditions of existence.

During the late 1970s, the gradual re-emergence of the game in Communist Canton was commonly interpreted as a good omen of the 'return' of long-lost individual autonomy. Occasional and light-wager gambling continues to be seen as a symbol of personal and, to some extent, social freedom.[139]

EARTHLY AMUSEMENT, DIVINE BLESSING

The high popularity of *mahjong* indicated that many Cantonese conceived of gambling in a flexible way. The thin line between 'acceptable games' and 'vicious gambling' was not drawn simply along the money divide, but also considered the attitudes of the players, the way they played, and the size of betting. Likewise, many other forms of 'gambling' that were indiscriminately denounced by anti-gambling writers in this period had seemingly been played and enjoyed as 'games' of great entertainment-value by the Cantonese for centuries.

For instance, Cantonese children were commonly said to like 'gambling [with] sugar canes, and mandarin oranges' (*tu chieh tou kan*). The rules were simple: to bisect sugar cane shoots at one stroke with a chopper, and the player who could cut it from end to end won; to peel open mandarin oranges, and the one whose orange had most pips won (Ch'u Ta-chün 1974: 302; Pao 1936: 12; Baker 1981: 33–4).[140] The research on Sha-nan village in Canton also shows that children there were especially fond of 'gambling' with a particular kind of board game (Wu Jui-lin 1934: 111). All these gambles, or games in the eyes of most Cantonese, were apparently an important source, and innocent form, of recreation for the local children.[141]

In pre-Communist Canton, cricket fighting was a highly popular form of gambling, as much as an entertainment, for gamblers and non-gamblers alike.[142] In addition to 'fights' conducted on a private basis, large-scale and well-organized contests were held every autumn on the outskirts of Canton. By the time a main fight was staged, terraces of temporary bamboo buildings—shops, restaurants, tea-houses, opium shops, dormitories, theatres, gambling-booths, etc.—were erected near the venue. Free opera performances were also provided by the organizing committee. The atmosphere was gay and festive. Some people no doubt came just to gamble; but a lot more came to enjoy the festivities, maybe gamble a little, watch the fights and the people as curious spectators, and perhaps just to show off.[143] The cricket owners themselves invested much time and effort in taking care of their pets. To them, the game itself was a source of prestige, and a test, as much as a proof, of their expertise. The pecuniary part of it just added more excitement to the game (Wu Yü et al. 1988: 103–4).[144] Like temple fairs, cricket fights might be enjoyed by most visitors as a festival and an occasion of free entertainment rather than merely an event for gambling.[145]

Sometimes gambling was employed as a means to test, and prove, one's foresight on mundane affairs. For example, a lawsuit in which a rickshawman sued the chief doctor of a hospital for stealing his baby boy and substituting a girl, attracted great public attention in the early 1930s. Although the defendant had behind him the support of his hospital, the plaintiff won the sympathy and backing of public opinion. Some people then bet on the outcome of the case; and most wagers were on the side of the rickshawman (Ta Fu *c.*1920s: 2). This might be a gesture of popular support for the plaintiff, who from the beginning was assumed to be innocent because of his humble class background. Hence, gambling here implied something more than the sheer greed for pecuniary reward. It might be a symbolic act of moral commitment and support, and an expression of the desire to see justice done. It was also not a way to escape from life, as many anti-gambling writers assumed the act of gambling to be; but, instead, was a bizarre, and pleasurable, means of keeping in touch with reality.

To most people, gambling was not only an agreeable form of relaxation after a hard day's slog, but also an essential source of hope. Perhaps with the exception of some true Confucianist, Buddhist, and Taoist priests, most Chinese were, indeed still are, outright and fervent believers in the cult of wealth.[146] To the majority of the less well-to-do Canton residents, and to those who did not want to spend the rest of their lives as poor working men, gambling was the only available short-cut to affluence, provided one were lucky enough to win. No matter how remote the chance might be, gambling was commonly regarded as a hope to those who did not possess a better alternative means of getting rich;[147] and it was, and is, certainly a way—neither moral nor immoral—to fulfil that irrepressible human desire for wealth.[148] In the words of an anti-gambling writer, since Chinese people were generally poor, their strong desire to gain a windfall by means of a game of chance was also prevalent (*CTKL* 1936: 234–5). It is therefore not surprising to find in a widely read text for the young (used to teach the written characters as much as to provide moral instruction), the popular saying: 'An [ordinary] man can never get rich without a windfall; as a horse can never grow healthy without [feeding on] wild grown vegetation' (*jên wu hêng-ts'ai pu-fu, ma wu yeh ts'ao pu fei*). This popular saying is not generally perceived as promoting heavy or hectic gambling, but occasional light gaming with self-control in order to gain some unexpected profits.[149] According to the lyrics of another folk song, 'Tu lieh chih tan-kuan', 'gambling [helps] many people become tycoons' (*Ming-ch'ü ta-ch'üan c.*1920s: 16).

The importance of this source of hope to the multitudes is seen in the popularity of the lotteries in Canton during this period. By the 1920s, at least five different kinds of lottery were thriving there.[150] The 'pigeon lottery' and the 'flower lottery' (their rules have been discussed earlier) had been very popular among the Cantonese since at least the mid-nineteenth century. In our period, the 'pigeon lottery' was so popular that it was drawn thrice daily. The 'flower lottery', despite its much-publicized 'pernicious moral effects', was still drawn twice a day. In addition there were the equally popular 'shop lottery' (*p'u p'iao*), and 'mountain lottery' (*shan p'iao*). In the former, lots were chosen from a group of shops' names. It was drawn once every five days. In the latter, as with 'pigeon lottery', lots were chosen from the first 120 characters from the character-learning text *Ch'ien tzu wên*. In each draw, which took place once every ten days, thirty characters were drawn, and matching fifteen of them would be enough to win the first prize. 'Mountain lottery' was so popular in the mid-1920s that as many as 120,000 betting tickets could be sold for each draw (*KCMKJP* 1925: 7, 2 June).

The main attraction of lotteries was probably their convenience and easiness to play and, more importantly, their low stakes, and hence low risk, alongside an enormous amount of prize-money. For 'pigeon lottery', the minimum stake was as little as 5 cents. A good bet would be awarded ten times the amount of the stake. For 'mountain lottery', the minimum wager was only 10 cents, and the first prize was fixed at about 20,000 yüan (Liu Tsai-su 1926: 117). Most people, therefore, could afford to purchase a hope, a dream, at a very low cost. It was, therefore, no surprise that lotteries were very popular among women, who seemingly had less spare money to spend on entertainment than their male counterparts. For them, inexpensive chances as such were doubly tempting (Chung Chiao 1925, 3 June; *YHP* 1933: 1, 30 Apr.).

Lotteries were also easy to play. Betters just needed to choose certain characters, or names of ancients, from pools of lots that they had been familiar with since childhood. Even the trouble of making a trip to the bookmakers to place their bets was spared them, because well-organized networks of collectors were deployed by most lottery companies for collecting bets from, or delivering prizes to, the doorsteps of their clients.[151] This 'courier' service provided a great deal of convenience especially to the rural betters, as we have seen in the case of Sha-nan. Within the city, numerous corner-shops collected lottery bets for bookmaking companies (Wu Jui-lin 1934: 110; Hsü Chu-ch'êng 1982: 147). To facilitate the bets of women, some bookmaking companies employed a ring of stake-collectors consisting of 'nosy women' whose duties were to collect wagers from women clients and to encourage more females to play (*KCMKJP* 1925: 7, 2 June).

A Cantonese writer reminisces how his poor but shrewd teacher father won a small amount of money from the lottery, which eventually enabled him to save enough to open some private schools. With this change of fortune, his family was pulled out of dire poverty. In his view, to get rich by gambling, as in his father's case, was morally more justifiable than by abusing one's social position as many bad heads of clans did (Ch'ang Tzu-p'ing 1987: 8–9).

To its players, the lottery embodied an attainable hope,[152] the pursuit of which was seemingly further stimulated by the popular belief that 'An [ordinary] man can never get rich without a windfall' (as mentioned above). To most Cantonese, 'to enrich oneself by means of a windfall' (*fa hêng-ts'ai*) was not necessarily a fantasy, and by no means a sin. Instead, it was commonly conceived as a divine reward for one's good deeds, as something predestined, though it was not easy to know who had that good fortune and when it would be materialized. Gambling was believed to be one of the commonest ways to realize that destiny. Since winning a windfall was predetermined, one need not gamble hectically to obtain it because that would not help to bring an early outcome; the divine scheme of reward is fixed. Thus, the idea occasioned no conflict with the orthodox teaching against excessive indulgence in gambling. In the mental universe of countless people, gambling had a noble, and perhaps even divine, role to play.[153] Fortune-tellers therefore benefited from this fatalistic attitude towards betting. One of the commonest gimmicks in their advertisements in local newspapers was their ability to advise their clients on the optimal time to bet, or their expertise in face-reading, or selecting good *feng-shui* sites for burying ancestors.[154]

The Cantonese obsession with the idea of *fa hêng-ts'ai* came out in many facets of life in Canton. For instance, the Chinese New Year was believed to be the best time of year to test one's luck in the matter of a windfall for the rest of that year, which could be most efficaciously accomplished by means of gambling (Baker 1979: 138). Hence, in Sha-nan, Western card games, normally forbidden because of an injunction by the *fan tan* bookmaking companies, were allowed to be played for three days during the Lunar New Year (Wu Jui-lin 1934: 111).[155] In Canton, gambling was commonly accepted, and widely played, as an essential part of New Year customs and celebration programmes.[156] Even in the Chinese New Year of 1937, shortly after the large-scale anti-gambling campaign, local police were said to turn a blind eye for a few days on the common violation of the ban on gambling (Ch'ing Shui 1937: 6). One of the most popular good-luck New Year greetings was 'hêng-ts'ai shun-li' (wish you good luck in [wining] unexpected profits) (Liu Wan-chang 1972: 20).

We find a number of Cantonese lottery players who seem eager to seek supernatural assistance to better their chance of winning. A contemporary poet humorously records that he and his friends always offered a substantial quantity of food to a deity at a local temple, in order to seek lottery tips from it through divination. This provided them with an excuse for regular meetings and the chance to enjoy culinary feasts, but above all to bask in a 'delusion of discarding poverty' (*fa chiung mi*) (Shih-yu shih-jên 1934: 11). Fortune-telling was also a highly popular resort. Some well-known fortune-tellers in their advertisements emphasized their 'good record' of giving accurate predictions on the *hêng-ts'ai* fate of their clients.[157] It was not uncommon that such means as divination, spirit-mediums, and shamans were employed to solicit tips for lottery betting.[158] Ever since the lottery gained wide popularity in Canton and the province since the late Ch'ing, worshippers at temples were noted for praying frantically for blessings in games. During the 1930s, betters were still seen flocking to local temple festivals, with lottery tickets in hand, and praying and begging for the deities' blessings on their stakes. Their enthusiasm to seek heavenly benison drove many of them even to such state-sponsored and supposedly secular occasions as memorial services for revolutionary martyrs. One of the most spectacular commemoration events was held for the Nineteenth Route Army in the autumn of 1932. In this week-long event, numerous men and women flocked to the main altar of one particular site to make offerings, mumble prayers, and perform divinations over dice or lottery characters written on pieces of paper hoping to ensure that their numbers or characters would win (*YHP* 1932: 1, 14 and 20 Nov.). Gambling was not seen as something immoral or sinful, but as a legitimate way to receive heavenly reward that was predestined in one's life.[159] Hence, it was not uncommon in local temples to find religious paraphernalia donated by lottery winners as thanksgiving offerings to the deities whose blessing was believed to have brought them the windfalls.[160] The lure of winning big prizes, as vividly described by a late-Ch'ing scholar, plunged the 'bewitched countrymen into [a state of] madness [in which they] constantly day-dreamed [about winning lotteries]' (Chu Hsiu-hsia 1977: 40).

Gambling was also something for jocularity as well. A contemporary poem, entitled 'The Hum of a Lottery Buyer' (Mai p'iao yin), revealingly captures the feelings of the ordinary lottery betters. It is about a man who dreams day and night of getting rich. He tries all he can, but still fails. Every day, he mentally works out his great plan of how to spend his money when he gets rich. Besides purchasing land, he will also marry many concubines, and buy a team of maidens to serve him. He will raise his social prestige, and enhance his physical attraction by buying and wearing Western-style suits and accessories. Patronizing beautiful courtesans and prostitutes will also be an essential part of his fantasized lifestyle. But how can he get rich? He finds himself too old to be a pimp, too poor to be a speculator in the real estate market, and too unattractive to seduce a wealthy widow. In deep frustration and on the brink of losing all hope, he passes by a booth where lottery tickets are sold. After reading the advertisement about the high prizes of the lottery, he immediately regains courage for the pursuit of his dream:

> If I win the first prize, I would immediately burn fire-crackers as an act of thanksgiving [to the god]. After that, [I would go to] collect my bounty of [perhaps] 30,000 or 50,000 yüan. [With this amount of money], I would almost certainly have a happy and easy life. [By then], I would be instantly transformed from being a 'poor ghost' into a rich man. My clothes, my cuisines, my residence, and my means of transport would be classy... [I would] reside in a Western-style mansion, with girls accompanying me wherever I go. What a romantic life it would be! How happy life would then be!... I must buy two or three of these lottery tickets even though I have to pawn my [remaining] worn-out trousers [in order to get enough money for that]. (Shih Ch'ih 1934: 1)

The dream was seemingly not an impossible one. It was nearly as true as reality, and possessed an almost magical property as a fountain of hope.

All anti-gambling literature dwelt more or less exclusively upon losers in games of chance.[161] This might serve the political purpose of highlighting all the negative aspects of gambling. However, gamblers were not necessarily constant losers, especially in lotteries, a truth that was acknowledged even by writers in the anti-gambling camp.[162] In fact, one of the biggest attractions was that many ordinary men and women did win. And their very existence helped other gamblers to believe in the possibility of *fa hêng-ts'ai*, and reassured them that their dream was not unachievable.

A journalist reminisces about the early 1930s, when there was an old lady who earned her living by mending torn clothes at a makeshift booth in Canton. She was abandoned by her first husband, and subsequently cohabited with a poor man. One day she won the first prize of a lottery, which turned her into a rich woman overnight. But the good time did not last long. After learning about her windfall, her first husband, whose status was still legitimate, suddenly showed up and insisted on receiving her back to his family. The old lady refused, and took the case to court. As a result, she spent all her wealth on the lawsuit, which secured her a divorce from her first husband (Hsü Chu-ch'eng 1982: 147).

Not all lottery winners were as unlucky as this elderly seamstress. A T'ai-shan village history records the story of a lucky better-turned-businessman. Poor Mr Su worked as a watchman in Macao in the early Republican period. His concubine chanced to pick up a lottery ticket that had been thrown away by a rich woman who thought she had lost the game. It turned out, however, to be a first-prize ticket which eventually entitled them to a bounty of 20,000 yüan. With that sum of capital, they started a rickshaw company in Macao, and operated a ferry plying between his native village and the Portuguese colony (Li I-chi 1960: 366–7).

Another successful and happy story concerned a group of sixteen blind men and women who were residents of a local charitable house for the blind. One day, the report stated, one of them told his housemates that he had a strange dream, which was interpreted by them as unmistakably an omen from Heaven. Each of them contributed an insignificant sum of 2 cents for purchasing a lottery ticket, which, in their minds, was what the dream was about. To their delight, their ticket won the first prize and they were rewarded with a bounty of about 1,000 yüan. Each of the winners was given a fair share of the reward and a celebration feast was held in front of the institution. This joyous incident provided residents in this neighbourhood with a hot topic for gossip (*KPP* 1928: 6, 25 Apr.).

The recorders of these two anecdotes do not say a word about gambling being a vice. To enrich oneself by means of the lottery was nothing to be ashamed of. It was seen as legitimate and morally justified, and probably the only available quick way, especially for an ordinary man or woman, to get rich. These 'true stories' provided the poor and the ordinary people with concrete enough evidence on the plausibility of their dreams of winning and the presumptions about *fa hêng-ts'ai*, and Heaven's intervention in earthly affairs.

Thus it is no wonder that lottery players became frantic when lots were drawn. In the Macao of the 1920s, a traveller records the scene before the announcement of the winning ticket outside a large building owned by a 'pigeon lottery' syndicate:

> The street is blocked by a crowd of coolies, messengers from the vendors, or ticket-holders who mumble prayers to their special deities to send them luck: the dope fiend, for a few moments' escape from his misery; the dainty prostitute, for regained freedom from a life into which she had been sold by her fan-tan crazed parents; the coolie, for money to buy an extra bowl of rice. (Lilius 1930: 79, 83–5)

In Canton, the conspicuous celebration by lottery winners had become a common sight. Before the draw or the announcement, excited crowds usually gathered in front of the lottery companies. The winners always fired long strings of fire-crackers to celebrate, which was in fact a religious means of communicating with the divinities, and announced 'their promotion from just-another-ordinary-man to the rank of the rich' (Wang Sun-chia 1934: 2; Li Han-ch'ung 1988: 115). Gambling provided hope to all walks of life. This source of hope appears as a particularly important stabilizing force to a society in which social security for the urban poor barely existed. With it, the tension generated by the problem of urban poverty might be, to some extent, relieved.[163]

To the general public, gambling was an agreeable part of life. There was a place that adopted the word 'tu', gambling, in its name.[164] Another linguistic point is that vernacular Cantonese was full of 'taboo words' thought to be detrimental to the luck of gamblers, which most Cantonese therefore took pains to avoid at all times.[165] In the common mind, the importance of gambling was immense.

Gambling was a much more intricate and complex social and political issue than it was portrayed in official propaganda. It served significant social and cultural functions, and met a social need. Its persistence in this period not only showed up the failure of the élitist plan to superimpose on the general public a moralistic orthodox ideology, which the government believed to be conducive to the modernization process, but also demonstrated the ability of the people to keep their preferred, though denounced, form of pastime. This crusade against the vice of gambling required a much greater ideological commitment, mastery of collective resources, and ruthlessness of application. It was a task that the totalitarian Communist regime would prove to be more capable of undertaking than its predecessors were. Although professedly a 'people's government', the present Communist regime continues to view the 'problem' of gambling as narrowly and puritanically as their predecessors did.[166] The people's wishes are still denied with respect to this popular pastime, though the state is apparently fighting a losing battle in its attempt to enforce strictly its ban on all forms of gambling. In Canton and many other parts of China, *mahjong* is returning rapidly and is widely played in private without interference. With the inauguration of the highly popular state-run lotteries such as the 'horse-racing lottery' (*ma p'iao*), the 'sports lottery' (*t'i-yu ts'ai-p'iao*), and the 'soccer lottery' (*tsu-ch'iu ts'ai-p'iao*, which is in fact either legalized betting on international and domestic soccer matches, or just simply a lottery) in Canton, the old popular wisdom of turning gambling into a meaningful socio-economic agent, rather than suppressing it uncompromisingly, has once again been enacted by a cash-hungry and de-radicalized government.[167]

REFERENCES

Alexéiev, Basil M. (1928), *The Chinese Gods of Wealth* (London: School of Oriental Studies and the China Society).

Amaro, Ana Maria (1988), 'Fai-vut-lau', in *Review of Culture (Macau: Instituto Cultural de Macau)* 2/6.

Baker, Hugh D. R. (1968), *A Chinese Lineage Village: Sheung Shui* (London: Frank Cass).

——(1979), *Ancestral Images: A Hong Kong Album* (Hong Kong: South China Morning Post).

——(1981), *Ancestral Images Again: A Third Hong Kong Album* (Hong Kong: South China Morning Post).

Balazs, Etienne (1964), *Chinese Civilization and Bureaucracy*, trans. H. M. Wright (New Haven: Yale University Press).

Bergler, Edmund (1957), *The Psychology of Gambling* (New York: Hill & Wang).

Campbell, Felicia (1976), 'Gambling: A Positive View', in William R. Eadington, and Charles C. Thomas (eds.), *Gambling and Society: Interdisciplinary Studies on the Subject of Gambling* (Springfield, Ill.: Charles C. Thomas).

Chang Chên-chih (1929), *Mu-chien Chung-kuo shê-hui ti ping-tai* (Shanghai: Min-chih shu-chü).

Chang Hsin-tai (1898), 'Yüeh yu hsiao chih', Wang Hsi-pu (ed.) *Hsiao-fang-hu-chai yü-ti ts'ung ch'ao* (Shanghai: Chu i t'ang). ix.

Chang Kung-p'ing (1993), *Têng-yü yü-shêng shu*, 3 vols. (Taipei: Lung-wên chu-pan-shê ku-fên yu-hsien kung-ssu).

Chang Tzu-p'ing (1989), *Tzu-p'ing tzu-ch'uan* (Taipei: Lung wên ch'u-pan-shê ku-fên yu-hsien kung-ssu). First published 1932.

Chang Yen-fêng (1994), *Lao yüeh-fêng-pai kuang-kao hua*, 2 vols. (Taipei: Han-shêng chu-pan-shê).

Ch'en Chiung-ming (1987), 'Hsiang Tzu-yi-chü shen-ching chin-tu ti-an', in Hsü Yen-tung et al. (1986–8) (eds.), *Kuang-tung wên-chêng shu pien* (Hong Kong: Kuang-tung wên-chêng pien-yin wei-yüan-hui).

Ch'en Hua-hsin (1983), 'Yüeh-chü yü Hsin-hai kê-ming', Kuang-tung-shêng hsi-chü yen-chiu-shê (ed.), *Yüeh-chü yen-chiu tzu-liao hsüan* (*YCYCTLH*) (Canton: n.p.).

Ch'en Li-fu (1986), *The Confucian Way: A New and Systematic Study of 'The Four Books'*, trans. Shih-shun Liu (London: Routledge & Kegan Paul).

Ch'en Ting-yen (1995) (ed.), *Ch'en Ching-chuan hsien-shêng nien-pu*, 2 vols. (Taipei: Li Ao ch'u- pan-shê).

Ch'êng Hao (1985) (ed.), *Kuang-chou kang shih (chin-tai pu-fen)* (Peking: Hai-yang ch'u-pan-shê).

'Chê-pan chê-pan' (*c.*1920s), *Kuang-chou shê-hui tsa-chih* (Canton: Kuang-chou shê-hui tsa-chih shê).

Chia Shih-i (1932), *Min-kuo hsü ts'ai-chêng shih* (Shanghai: Shang-wu yin-shu-kuan).

Ch'iao Kang I Yüan T'ang (1989), *Liang-shih chia-pu* (Hong Kong: Ch'iao Kang I Yüan T'ang).

Chin Hsüeh-shih (1849), 'Mu-chu hsien hua', in Chang Ch'ao, Yang Fu-chi, and Shen Mou-tê (eds.), *Chao-tai ts'ung-shu pieh-chi* (n.p.: Shih k'ai t'ang).

Chin Tsêng-ching (1930), 'Kai-kê fêng-su shih jên-lui tsui-ta ti nu-li', in Fêng-su kai-kê wei-yüan-hui (ed.), *Fêng-su kai-kê ts'ung k'an (FSKKTK)* (Canton: Kuang-chou-tê-pieh-shih tang-pu hsüan-ch'uan-pu).

Chin-tai Kuang-chou k'ou-an ching-chi shê-hui kai-k'uang: Yüeh hai-kuan pao-kao hui chi (YHKPK) (1996), ed. Kuang-chou-shih ti-fang-chih pien-hsüan wei-yüan-hui pan-kung-shih and Kuang-chou hai-kuan-chih pien-hsüan wei-yüan-hui (Canton: Chi-nan ta-hsüeh ch'u-pan-shê).

'Chin-tu chih kung-tan' (1910), in Ch'i wan hua-shê (ed.), *Chung-kuo shih ta hai* (Canton: Shêng ch'ün shu-chü).

Ching-chieh-fu ta ma tu-tsai (n.d.) (Canton: Tsui ching t'ang).

Ching Hsiao (1935), 'Ch'ing-tai Yüeh-tung hsieh-tou shih shih', *Ling-nan hsüeh pao* 4/2 (June).

Ch'ing Shui (1937), 'Kuang-chou-jên ti chiu-li hsin-nien fêng-su', *Ko yao* 2/37.

Ching-hai tsung-pao (2000), July 1893 to Dec. 1895 (Shanghai: Shanghai shê-hui ko-hsüeh yüan and Ao-men chi-chin hui).

Chou Ku-ch'êng (1930), *Chung-kuo shê-hui ti chieh-kou* (Shanghai: Hsin shêng-min shu-chü).

Chu Hsi-nung (1965), 'Shih-nien lai ti Chung-kuo nung-yeh', in Chung-kuo wên-hua chien-shê, *K'ang-chan chien shih-nien chih Chung-kuo* (Hong Kong: Lung-mên shu-tien).

Chu Hsiu-hsia (1977), *Yüeh hai chiu wên lu*, 2 vols. (Taipei: Chung wai wên k'u).

Ch'ü Ta-chün (1974), *Kuang-tung hsin yü*, 2 vols. (Hong Kong: Chung-hua shu-chü). First published 1700.

Chu Yung-ch'un (n.d.), *Chu-tzu chih-chia ko yen* (n.p.: n. pub.).

Chung (1922), 'Liang ke yen-ti ti shêng', *Ch'ün shêng* 1/1.

Chung Chiao (1925), 'Kuang-chou tu-po hsüan-kê lü-shuo', *KCMKJP*, '*Hsiao Kuang-chou*' column.

Chung-kuo jên-min chêng-chih-hsieh-shang-hui-i Kuang-tung-shêng Kuang-chou-shih wei-yüan-hui wên-shih tzu-liao wei-yüan-hui (1980) (ed.), *Kuang-chou pai-nien ta-shih chi (KCPN)*, 2 vols. (Canton: Kuang-tung jên-min ch'u-pan-shê).

——(1986), *Sun Chung-shan san-tzu tsai Kuang-tung chien-li chêng-ch'üan* (Peking: Chung-kuo wên-shih ch'u-pan-shê).

Clotfelter, Charles T., and Cook, Philip J. (1991), *Selling Hope: State Lotteries in America* (Cambridge, Mass.: Harvard University Press).

CSL, see Kuang-tung-shêng t'i-fang shih-chih pien-wei-hui pang-kung-shih and Kuang-chou-shih t'i-fang-chih pien-wei-hui pang-kung-shih (1995).

CTKL, see Kuang-tung-shêng chin-tu wei-yüan-hui (1936).

Dai Kan-Wa jiten (1989), Morohashi Taksuke, 14 vols. (Tokyo: Taishukan Shoten).

Dunkley, John (1985), *Gambling: A Social and Moral Problem in France, 1685–1792* (Oxford: The Voltaire Foundation).

Eadington, William R. and Thomas, Charles C. (1976) (ed.), *Gambling and Society: Interdisciplinary Studies on the Subject of Gambling* (Springfield, Ill.: Charles C. Thomas).

Fêng-su kai-kê wei-yüan-hui (ed.), *Fêng-su kai-kê ts'ung k'an (FSKKTK)* (Canton: Kuang-chou-tê-pieh-shih tang-pu hsüan-ch'uan-pu).

Fitzgerald, John (1990), 'Increased Disunity: The Politics and Finance of Guangdong Separation, 1926–1936', *Modern Asian Studies* 24/4.

Fo-shan chung-i hsiang chih (1923).

Franck, Harry A. (1925), *Roving Through Southern China* (New York: Century).

Furth, Charlotte (1990), 'The Patriarch's Legacy: Household Instructions and the Transmission of Orthodox Values', in Kwang-ching Liu (ed.), *Orthodoxy in Late Imperial China* (Berkeley: University of California Press).

Gamble, Sidney D. (1921), *Peking: A Social Survey* (New York: George H. Doran).

Gorer, Geoffrey (1967), 'British Life—It's a Gamble', in Robert D. Herman (ed.), *Gambling* (New York: Harper & Row).

Gray, John Henry (1972), *China. A History of the Laws, Manners and Customs of the People*, 2 vols. (Shannon: Irish University Press). First published 1878.

Han Pi (*c.*1930s), 'Chuan tu', *Kuang-chou shê-hui tsa-chih* 1.

Hayes, James (1985), 'Specialists and Written Materials in Late Imperial China', in David Johnson, Andrew J. Nathan, and Evelyn S. Rawski (eds.), *Popular Culture in Late Imperial China* (Berkeley: University of California Press).

HCLCCN, see Kuang-chou shih-chêng-fu.

Herman, Robert D. (1967), 'Gambling as Work: A Sociological Study of the Race Track', in id. (ed.), *Gambling* (New York: Harper & Row).

Ho, Kit-yiu Virgil (1994), 'Cantonese Opera in a Rural Setting', in Göran Aijmer and Åsa Boholm (eds.), *Images and Enactments: Possible Worlds in Dramatic Performance* (Gothenburg: Institute for Advanced Studies of Social Anthropology).

Hsien ch'i chien fu (n.d.) (Canton: I wên t'ang).

Hsü Chu-ch'êng (1982), *Chiu wên tsa i* (Hong Kong: San lien shu-tien).

Hsü Yen-tung et al. (1986–8) (eds.), *Kuang-tung wên-chêng shu pien*, 4 vols. (Hong Kong: Kuang-tung wên-chêng pien-yin wei-yüan-hui).

Hu Pu-chin (1936), in Kuang-tung-shêng chin-tu wei-yüan-hui (ed.), *Chin-tu kai lan (CTKL)* (Canton: n.p.).

Hua-tzu jih-pao (*HTJP*) (Hong Kong: Hua-tzu jih-pao shê).

Huang Lin-shêng (1936), Kuang-tung-shêng chin-tu wei-yüan-hui (ed.), *Chin-tu kai lan (CTKL)* (Canton: n.p.).

Huang Tsun-shêng (1941), *Ling-nan min-hsin yu Ling-nan wên-hua* (Canton: Min-tsu wên-hua ch'u-pan-shê).

Hui-t'u tseng-kuang yen-wên (n.d.) (Hong Kong: Ch'en-hsiang-chi shu-chü).

Kai-liang Ling-nan chi-shih (n.d.), ed. Ling-nan shih-shih shê (n.p.: n. pub.).

Kavanagh, Thomas M. (1993), *Enlightenment and the Shadows of Chance: The Novel and the Culture of Gambling in Eighteenth-Century France* (Baltimore: Johns Hopkins University Press).

KCPN, see *Chung-kuo jên-min chêng-chih-hsieh-shang-hui-i Kuang-tung-shêng Kuang-chou-shih wei-yüan-hui wên-shih tzu-liao wei-yüan-hui* (1980).

KCTC, see *Kuang-chou tsa-chih* (1924–30s).

KTFCL, see *Kuang-tung fêng-ching lu.*

Ku Yü (1936), 'Kuang-tung tu-huo li-shih', Kuang-tung-shêng chin-tu wei-yüan-hui (ed.), *Chin-tu kai lan (CTKL)* (Canton: n.p.).

Kuan Wên-ch'ing (1976), *Chung-kuo yin tan wai shih* (Hong Kong: Kuang-chüeh-ching ch'u-pan-shê).

Kuang-chou li-pai liu (*KCLPL*) (*c.*1933–5) (Canton:Kuang-chou li-pai-liu shê).

Kuang-chou min-kuo jih-pao (KCMKJP) (Canton: Kuang-chou min-kuo jih-pao shê).

Kuang-chou nien-chien (1935), ed. Kuang-chou nien-chien pien tsuan wei-yüan-hui, 2 vols. (Canton: Kuang-chou nien-chien pien tsuan wei-yüan-hui).

Kuang-chou shê-hui tsa-chih 1 (*c.*1920s) (Canton: Kuang-chou shê-hui tsa-chih shê).

Kuang-chou shih-chêng-fu (1933), *Kuang-chou shih chêng-fu liang-nien lai shih-chêng pao kao chu* (Canton: n.p.).

Kuang-chou shih-chêng-fu (1934) (ed.), *Kuang-chou shih-chêng-fu hsin shu lo-ch'êng chi-nien tê-k'an (HCLCCN)* (Canton).

Kuang-chou-shih chêng-hsieh wên shih tzu-liao yen-chiu wei-yüan-hui (1987) (ed.), *Nan t'ien sui yüeh: Ch'en Chi-t'ang chu Yüeh shih-ch'i chien wên shih lu* (Canton: Kuang-tung jên-min ch'u-pan-shê).

Kuang-chou-shih shih-chêng-fu (1921–36) (ed.), *Kuang-chou-shih shih-chêng kung pao* (Canton).

Kuang-chou-shih shih-chêng-fu t'ung-chi ku (1929), *Kuang-chou-shih shih-chêng-fu t'ung-chi nien- chien. Ti i wei* (Canton: Kuang-chou-shih shih-chêng-fu).

Kuang-chou-shih shih-chêng-t'ing shê-hui-tiao-cha-ku (1927) (ed.), *Ti sze lei: shê-hui pu-liang shih-yeh* (Canton).

Kuang-chou tsa-chih (1924–30s) (*KCTC*) (Canton: Kuang-chou tsa-chih shê).

Ku'ang Lao-chiu, 'Hsi-kuan hsiao-chê', *KCLPL* 4.

Kuang-tung Ch'i-tu-chiao chu-tu hui (1925), *Chu-tu hui chêng wên hua chieh-hsiao* (Canton).

Kuang-tung ch'ing-li-ts'ai-chêng-chü (1910) (ed.), *Kuang-tung ch'üan shêng ts'ai-chêng shuo-ming shu*, 2 vols. (Tientsin: Ching-chi hsüeh hui).

Kuang-tung fêng-ching lu (*KTFCL*) (1988) (Canton: Kuang-tung jên-min ch'u-pan-shê).

Kuang-tung kung pao (1912–1920s), ed. Kuang-tung-shêng hsüan-an-shih kung-ch'u (Canton: n.p.).

Kuang-tung shêng-chêng-fu kung pao (1920s–30s), ed. Kuang-tung shêng-chêng-fu (Canton).

Kuang-tung shêng-chêng-fu ts'ai-chêng-t'ing and Kuang-tung ts'ai-chêng tê-pai-yüan kung-chü (1934) (eds.), *Kuang-tung shêng ts'ai-chêng chi shih*, 3 vols. (Canton: Kuang-tung-shêng chêng-fu ts'ai-chêng-t'ing).

Kuang-tung-shêng chin-tu wei-yüan-hui (1936), (ed.), *Chin-tu kai lan (CTKL)* (Canton).

Kuang-tung-shêng t'i-fang shih-chih pien-wei-hui pang-kung-shih and Kuang-chou-shih t'i-fang-chih pien-wei-hui pang-kung-shih (1995) (ed.), *Ch'ing shih-lu Kuang-tung shih-liao (CSL)*, 6 vols. (Canton: Kuang-tung-shêng t'i-tu ch'u-pan-shê).

Kung-ho shih-yung fu ju san szu wu tzu shu (1911) (Canton: Lin Shu Ko).

Kung Pa-an (1934), 'Po tan', *Kuang-chou tsa-chih (KCTC)* 29.

Kung-p'ing pao (KPP) (1924–49) (Canton: Kung-p'ing pao shê).

Kuo-fu ch'üan chi (1961), 6 vols. (Taipei: Chung-yang wên-hua kung-ying shê).

Kuo Shuang-lin and Hsiao Mei-hua (1995), *Chung-hua tu-po shih* (Peking: Chung-hua shu-ch'ü).

Legge, James (1899) (trans.), *Confucian Analects*, Bk. XVII, 'Yang Ho', in Chu Wên-hua (ed.), *Chu-shih hsiao-chêng hua-ying Szu Shu* (Shanghai: Shang-hai shu-chü).

Li Fu-lin (1995), *Li Fu-lin kê-ming shih-liao: Li Fu-lin chiang-ch'ün ts'an-chia kê-ming ching-kuo tzu-shu* (Hong Kong: Wên-hua chiao-yu).

Li Han-chang (1969), *Ho-fei Li Ching-lo kung (Han-chang) chêng-shu*, ed. Li Ching-yü, 2 vols. (repr. Taipei: Wên hai ch'u-pan-shê).

Li Han-ch'ung (1988), 'Hua-hui tu-po chung chung', in Kuang-tung shêng chêng-hsieh wên shih tzù-liao yen-chiu wei-yüan-hui (ed.), *Kuang-tung fêng-ching lu* (*KTFCL*) (Canton: Kuang-tung jên-min ch'u-pan-shê).

Li Hsun-huan (1936), 'Chin-tu yü fan-yung kuo-min ching-chi', in Kuang-tung-shêng chin-tu wei-yüan-hui (ed.), *Chin-tu kai lan (CTKL)* (Canton: n.p.).

Li I-chi (1960), *Yen-hai hsiang tu shih* (Hong Kong: published privately by Yü Chung-hüan).

Li T'iao-yüan (1937), 'Nan Yüeh pi chi', in Wang Yün-wu (ed.), *Ts'ung-shu chi-ch'êng* (Shanghai: Shang-wu yin-shu-kuan). First published in 1778.

Li Tsung-huang (1922), *Hsin Kuang-tung kuan-ch'a chi* (Shanghai: Shang-wu-yin-shu-kuan).

Liang Ch'i-ch'ao (2001), *Li Hung-chang chüan* (Tientsin: P'ai-hua wên-i ch'u-pan-shê).

Lilius, Aleko E. (1930), *I Sailed With Chinese Pirates* (London: J. W. Arrowsmith).

Liu Tsai-su (1926), *Kuang-chou kuai lan* (Shanghai: Shih-chieh shu-chü).

Liu Wan-chang (1972), 'Pa-kung ti Kuang-chou kuo nien jih-chi', in Chou K'ang-yen (ed.), *Kuang-tung fêng-su chui lu* (Hong Kong: Ch'ung wên shu-tien).

Lo I-ch'ün (1983), 'Sun Chung-shan hui Yüeh chung-chien chêng-ch'üan huo ti Kuang-tung chêng-chü', in Chung-kuo jên-min chêng-chih-hsieh-shang-hui-i (ed.), *Sun Chung-shan san-tzu tsai Kuang-tung* (Canton: Kuang-tung jên-min ch'u-pan-shê).

London Missionary Society (1920s–1930s), Reports from South China District Committee, London, The School of Oriental and African Studies Library.

Lu Yen (1981), *Hsiang-kang chang-ku* (Hong Kong: Kuang-chüeh-ching ch'u-pan-shê).

Ma Chia-hui (2001), 'Hu Shih ta ma-chiang', *Ming pao*, 5 July.

Ma P'i-yao (1969), *Ma Chung-chêng (p'i-yao) i-chi*, ed. Ma Ch'i-shen and Ma Ch'i-chang (repr. Taipei: Wen hai ch'u-pan-shê).

McMillen, Jan (1996), 'Understanding Gambling: History, Concepts and Theories', in id. (ed.), *Gambling Cultures: Studies in History and Interpretation* (London: Routledge).

Mêng Yüan-lao (1987), *Tung-ching mêng hua lu*; vernacularized and abridged by Sun Ming-sun (Taipei: Shih pao wên-hua ch'u-pan ch'i-yeh yu-hsien-kung-ssu).

Ming-ch'ü ta-ch'üan (*c.* 1920s) (Shanghai: Pai-tai kung-ssu).

Ming-hsin pao chien (1919) (Canton: Tsui Ching t'ang).

Murray, Dian H. (1987), *Pirates of the South China Coast, 1790–1810* (Stanford: Stanford University Press).

Nan-fang jih-pao (NFJP) (1950–) (Canton:Nan-fang jih-pao shê).

Nan-hai hsien chih (1910).

Nan-yang shang-pao (*NYSP*) (Singapore: Nan-yang shang-pao shê).

Newman, Otto (1972), *Gambling: Hazard and Reward* (London: Athlone).

Pan-chiao man-hua 7/7 (1932) (Canton: Pan-chiao man-hua shê, 1929–32).

P'an-yü hsien hsü chih (1968) (Taipei: Hsüeh-shêng shu-tien). First published 1931.

Pao (1936), 'Kuang-tung fêng-su pien pien t'an', *Yüeh fêng* 2/3.

Piao tu ch'ui hsin chi (1910) (Canton: Shêng-ch'êng Liu yüeh chin kuan).

P'ing Chin-ya (1989), 'Chiu Shang-hai ti tu-po', in Shang-hai wên-shih yen-chiu kuan (ed.), *Chiu Shang-hai ti yen tu ch'ang* (Hong Kong: Chung yüan ch'u-pan-shê).

Rea, Kenneth (1977) (ed.), *Canton in Revolution: The Collected Papers of Earl Swisher, 1925–1928* (San Francisco: Westview).

Rhoads, Edward J. M. (1975), *China's Republican Revolution: The Case of Kwangtung, 1895–1913* (Cambridge, Mass.: Harvard University Press).

Rowe, William T. (1989), *Hankow: Conflict and Community in a Chinese City, 1796–1895* (Stanford: Stanford University Press).

Scheibe, Karl E. (2000), *The Drama of Everyday Life* (Cambridge, Mass.: Harvard University Press).

Schiffrin, Harold (1968), *Sun Yat-sen and the Origins of the Chinese Revolution* (Berkeley: University of California Press).

Sha Tung-hsun (1989), *Yüeh hai chin-tai-shih t'an* (Canton: Hua-nan li-kung ta-hsüeh ch'u-pan-shê).

Shen pao (1842–1949).

Shih Ch'ih (1934), 'Mai p'iao yin', *KCLPL* 20, August.

Shih-yu shih-jên (1934), 'Mai pai-ko-p'iao', *Kuang-chou tsa-chih* (*KCTC*) 30.

Shu pao (1965) (Taipei: Tai-wan hsüeh-shêng shu-tien). First published in Canton by Kuang-chou Shu-pao shê between 18 April 1884 and 4 April 1885.

Shun-tê hsien chih (1929); repr. (Taipei: Chêng wên ch'u-pan-shê, 1965).

Spanier, David (1987), *Easy Money: Inside the Gambler's Mind* (London: Sphere).

Sung Wên (1990), 'Chung-kuo ku-tai ti chin-tu', *Nan-fang jih-pao* (*NFJP*) Weekend Suppl. (Canton: Nan-fang jih-pao shê).

Sung Yü (1989), *T'ang-hsi chin-fên* (Hong Kong: I yüan ch'u-pan-shê).

Sze yin ch'i (*c.*1920s) (Hong Kong: Kuang-mou hao).

Ta Fu (*c.*1930s), 'Tou lung chuan fêng yü tu-tu kuan-hsi', *Tien-têng-tan* 12.

Tan-tsao hsiang tzu-chih-hui pao kao shu (1925)

T'ang Ti-shêng (*c.*1930s), *Yen Shui-shêng* (Canton: I wên t'ang shu-chü).

Tawney, R. H. (1932), *Land and Labour in China* (London: George Allen & Unwin).

Tê (1930), 'Kai-kê fêng-su chung ti shih-chung chung-yao kung-tso', in Fêng-su kai-kê wei-yüan-hui (ed.), *Fêng-su kai-kê ts'ung k'an* (*FSKKTK*) (Canton: Kuang-chou-tê-pieh-shih tang-pu hsüan-ch'uan-pu).

Tec, Nechama (1964), *Gambling in Sweden* (Totowa, NJ: Rowman & Littlefield).

Tsou Lu (1936), 'Tu huo', in Kuang-tung-shêng chin-tu wei-yüan-hui (ed.), *Chin-tu kai lan* (*CTKL*) (Canton: n.p.).

Tu-tsai ku tan (n.d.) (Canton: I wên t'ang).

Tzu-hang-shih (1919), *Kuang-chou chih-nan* (Canton: Hsin hua shu-tien).

Wang Hsien-ch'ien (1969) (ed.), *Kuo (Shih-lang) Sung-t'ao tsou-kao*, 3 vols. (Taipei: Wên-hai ch'u-pan-shê).

Wang Sun-chia (1934), 'Mai lien-pang', *Kuang-chou tsa-chih* (*KCTC*) 26.

Ward, Barbara (1979), 'Not Merely Players: Drama, Art, and Ritual in Traditional China', *Man* NS 14.

Warner, John (1981) (comp.), *Hong Kong Illustrated: Views and News 1840–1890* (Hong Kong: John Warner).

Weinstein, David, and Deitch, Lillian (1974), *The Impact of Legalized Gambling: The Socioeconomic Consequences of Lotteries and Off-Track Betting* (New York: Praeger).

Li Wen-lang and Smith, Martin (1976), 'The Propensity to Gamble: Some Structural Determinants', in William Eadington and Charles Thomas (eds.), *Gambling and Society: Interdisciplinary Studies on the Subject of Gambling* (Springfield, Ill.: Charles C. Thomas).

Wu Yü, Liang Li-ch'êng, and Wang Tao-chi (1988), *Min-kuo heh-shê-hui* (Nanking: Kiang-su ku-chi ch'u-pan-shê).

Wu Jui-lin (1934), 'Sha-nan tan-min tiao-ch'a pao kao', *Ling-nan hsüeh pao* 3/1.

——(1940), *Kuang-chou shih liu-pai jên-li-chê fu shêng-huo ts'ang-ku'ang chih tiao-ch'a* (Canton: Ling-nan ta-hsüeh shê-hui-hsüeh hsi shê-hui tiao-ch'a so).

——(1941), 'Kuang-chou shih Ho-nan tao Hsia Tu ts'un ch'i-shih-liu chia tiao-ch'a', *Ling-nan hsüeh pao* 6/4 (June).

——and Huang En-lin (1935), 'Chiu Fêng-huang ts'un tiao-ch'a pao kao', *Ling-nan hsüeh pao* 4/3.

Wu Yü, Liang Li-ch'êng, and Wang Tao-chi (1988), *Min-kuo heh-shê-hui* (Nanking: Kiang-su ku-chi ch'u-pan-shê).

Yang Yin-shen (1935), *Chung-kuo yu-i yen-chiu* (Shanghai: Shih-chieh shu-chü).

Yang Yü-shu (1936), 'Kuang-tung tu huo shih', in Kuang-tung-shêng chin-tu wei-yüan-hui (ed.), *Chin-tu kai lan* (*CTKL*) (Canton: n.p.).

Yao T'ung (1849), 'Chieh tu wên', *Chao-tai ts'ung-shu pieh chi*.

YCYCTLH, see *Kuang-tung-shêng hsi-chü yen-chiu-shih*.

YHKPK, see *Chin-tai Kuang-chou k'ou-an ching-chi shê-hui kai-k'uang* (1996).

Yu Ch'i-chung (1934), *Kuang-chou kung-jên chia-t'ing chih yen-chiu* (Canton: Kuo-li Chung-shan ta-hsüeh ching-chi tiao-ch'a ch'u).

'Yü k'o tan tu' (1907), *Sze yin ch'i* (Hong Kong: Kuang-mou hao).

Yüan Shu-i (1998) et al (ed.), *Chang Chih-t'ung ch'üan chi*. 6 vols. (Shih-chia-chuang: Ho-pei jên-min ch'u-pan-shê).

Yüeh-hua pao (*YHP*) (1927–50) (Canton: Yüeh-hua pao shê).

Yün Shêng (1936), 'Chin tu tsai chin-jih Chung-kuo chih i-i', in Kuang-tung-shêng chin-tu wei-yüan- hui (ed.), *Chin-tu kai lan* (*CTKL*) (Canton: n.p.).

5

The Worlds of Prostitution in the Early Republic

This chapter does not claim to be a comprehensive history of prostitution in Canton. It is concerned, rather, with the differing social perceptions of prostitution and prostitutes, and presents an alternative, though possibly no less realistic, view of the job and life of those of that profession in Canton in this period.

1. AN ENIGMATIC 'PROBLEM'

The Problems with Assumptions

In order to discredit their predecessor regime, official Chinese Communist historians hold that the problem of prostitution in Canton during the Republican period, as in the rest of China, indisputably grew worse.[1] Most social historians of this subject also generally believed that due to the lowering of the moral standards in relation to sex, the persistence of the system of concubinage, the inferior social and family position of Chinese women, and the growing pauperization of rural and urban dwellers, the 'problem' of prostitution became further aggravated during this period (Gronewold 1985: ch. 4; Hershatter 1991: 265–6).

It is arguable, however, that the lowering of moral standards and the growth of permissive attitude towards sex and love necessarily led more and more young women to prostitute themselves. Prostitution as a profession was still socially and morally despised—a deep-seated perception that was not easily altered by any change in attitudes towards sex. Nor was the concubinage system, women's low social position, or poverty new to Chinese society. Prostitution, moreover, exists in every human society, both affluent and poor, past and present.

Poverty has always been assumed to be a major culprit among the causes of prostitution in modern China (Warren 1994; Ping Chin-ya 1989). This seemingly straightforward cause, however, was not without ambiguity. To start with, poverty, like richness, has never been an concept easily grasped, or something so concrete and unambiguous that it could be discerned by everyone in the community; there is always someone who is poorer, or richer, than somebody else. There are, of course, extremes of materialist conditions that can be easily and indisputably recognized by most people as 'poor' or 'rich'. Prostitutes in this part of China, however, did not all come from a social or family background that was obvious enough to be convincingly categorized as 'poor'. As a matter of fact, many of the presumptions on the causes of prostitution—extreme poverty, abduction, orphan girls who had nowhere to turn, and so on—hardly match the many known biographical profiles, though sketchy, of prostitutes in this period. Records show that many of them, by the time they entered into this business, were not as poor or helpless as they were always depicted in official anti-prostitution treatises; and many of them did become prostitutes of their own free will, though unhappily. Economic need, instead of poverty, was apparently an important factor that facilitated the decision by a woman (or her family's decision to sell her to a brothel) to work as a prostitute. This factor of 'economic need', however, always worked with an integral set of other reasons, ranging from personal to familial or circumstantial, in the process.[2] Women prostituted themselves for a variety of reasons; poverty and abduction were only two among a wide range of possibilities.[3] A journalist in Canton, who professed to have a good knowledge of this profane business, mapped out the general backgrounds of prostitutes (both clandestine and licensed) in this city after consulting a hotelier and an official of a local tax brokerage company specializing in collecting brothel taxes. It was noted in this finding that nearly two-thirds of all the prostitutes in Canton entered the business by choice and for reasons that had little to do with 'the pressure of circumstances' (*huan-ching ya-po*), and only a tiny fraction (less than sixty out of a total of 5,800 in the authors' estimate) were believed to be victims of abduction or force (*KPP* 1928: 8, 8 June).[4]

The fundamental question is, therefore, whether, compared with the past, the problem of prostitution really grew worse during the Republic or not.

The Problem with Numbers

It is impossible to know exactly how many brothels and prostitutes existed in Canton at any given period. Surviving sources tend to indicate, however, that their number in Republican Canton was falling rather than rising, especially as compared to the situation in late-Imperial times.[5] A late seventeenth-century Cantonese scholar wrote that 'before his times', the extent of both the lavishness and the prosperity of the floating-brothel business in Canton had surpassed even that of Ming-dynasty Nanking. The author of an early nineteenth-century travelogue was told by local Cantonese that the number of these brothels, though then by no means few, was only about one-tenth of what it had been 'thirty years ago' (Chang Hsin-tai 1898: ix. 306). Hence, it seems that their number had been steadily decreasing since early-Ch'ing times.

Official statistics for Republican Canton show that the number of licensed brothels actually remained quite stable. In 1911 and 1913, there were respectively 166 and 169 such brothels in Canton (*HTJP* 1911, 14 Sept.; Umeda Ikuzo 1913: 16); in 1926, an official survey indicated that there were 131 (Wang Shu-nu 1988: 333; Chen Li-chu et al. 1991: iv. 533). Of these, 70 were high-class establishments. This was, nevertheless, a significant drop—assuming constant size—compared with the some 400 in the mid-nineteenth century (Wang Shu-nu 1988: 266, 333). An English work on the commerce of Canton published in 1932 stated that there were 61 prostitute houses in the city (Canton Advertising 1932: 88). They were classified, among a list of others, as shops related to 'Daily Life Necessities'—evidence of the favourable popular perception of this business (a subject that is discussed in detail later in this chapter). There is no way to know how these data were collected and where they came from. The total figure, however, was apparently too small to represent the overall picture. An internal document entitled 'A Survey Chart on the Lives of Prostitutes in the City [of Canton]', which was prepared by two senior official from the Social Bureau of Canton Municipal Government in 1930, gave a relatively detailed description of the situation of prostitution (rather than the conditions of prostitutes as its title suggests), in the city. There were, according to this document, a total of 110 brothels in Canton: 25 high-class, 38 middle-class, and 47 low-class establishments (Kuang-chou-shih shê-hui chü 1930: 14–15). An allegedly systematic survey of 1934 shows that there were about 300 brothels of all classes in Canton, though the number of high-class establishments had fallen to 17 (*Kuang-chou nien chien* 1935: ch. 7 pp. 60–2). But the greatest sign of 'improvement' was in the reduced number of floating brothels. A senior mid-Ch'ing official was perplexed by the proliferation of all classes and sizes of these floating brothels operating on Canton's waterfront. According to his rough estimate, some 8,000 women earned their living by this kind of prostitution (Chao I 1975: 32), though the possibility should not be ruled out that this rather alarming estimate was based on the popular misconception that most Tanka women (women from the boat-people community) worked as prostitutes.[6] Nevertheless, an official record of 1924 shows that there were fewer than 100 licensed floating brothels in Canton (Kuang-chou-shih shih-chêng-fu 1924: 16), while another official report of 1927 indicates that this number had dropped further down to 69 (Ch'en Li-chu et al. 1991: iv. 533). The data given in a Social Bureau's internal document indicated that slightly over 400 prostitutes worked in a total of 52 floating brothels of all classes in 1929 to 1930 (Kuang-chou-shih shê-hui chü 1930: 14–15). According to the allegedly 'first systematic' census in Canton in 1932, of the 100,000 boat people only about 1,000 (700 women, probably including maids, and 300 men) were said to be working on the 300 or so floating brothels.[7] The discrepancy in the total number of floating brothels between the last two sets of data is remarkable and could be attributed to the different ways the information was gathered. The source of the 1930 figures came from the 'flower taxes' brokerage companies, while the census was carried out mainly by teams of student volunteers from the city's middle schools. There is no way to know for sure which set of figures is more accurate. Statistically, however, it remains that the actual number of brothels did not increase in any dramatic manner in real terms, a fact supported by the actual number of prostitutes employed by the floating brothels on the Pearl River.

The number of prostitutes in this period also shows no sign of rapid increase, especially compared with the mid- and late-Ch'ing periods. A Republican writer estimated that high-class courtesans alone in Canton in mid- and late-Ch'ing times had numbered in the region of 5,000. On top of this were countless numbers of lower-class 'mobile prostitutes' (*liu ch'ang*) mainly from other provinces. A mid-Ch'ing official put his estimate of prostitutes working on the floating brothels in Canton at 8,000 (Chao I 1975). An official census released in the autumn of 1911 indicated that 2,758 women were working as licensed prostitutes in the city of Canton (*HTJP* 1911, 11 Sept.). According to a 1928 estimate prepared casually by a concerned journalist with his friends from a prostitution-tax brokerage company, there were altogether about 5,800 licensed and sly prostitutes in Canton (*KPP* 1928: 8, 8 July).[8] According to the Social Bureau's internal document, which was cited earlier, however, there were 972 licensed prostitutes working in Canton between 1929 and 1930, consisting of 188 high-class, 272 middle-class, and 512 low-class harlots (Kuang-chou-shih shê-hui chü 1930: 14–15).[9] Published records of Canton municipal government, however, if they can be relied on, indicate that the number of licensed prostitutes in the mid-Republican period remained between 1,000 and 1,500 (Kuang-chou-shih shih-chêng pao-kao hui k'an 1924: 224; *Kuang-chou nien chien* 1935 ch. 7; Ch'en Li-chu et al. 1991: ix. 533).[10] Even taking into account the presence of an estimated 2,600 unlicensed prostitutes in the city,[11] the total number was still quite insignificant compared with the Ch'ing period, when the 'flowery business' (*hua shih*) was remorsefully claimed by some Republican writers to have been at its peak and its best.[12] Fires that broke out in the brothel quarter during the late-Ch'ing and the early-Republican periods, coupled with the intermittent military carnage of the 1910s and 1920s, were seen as detrimental to the brothel business in Canton (Wang Shu-nu 1988: 302–3). That these misfortunes were only occasional and apparently did not last very long as contemporary newspaper reports show that the 'flowery business' recovered shortly after such incidents had subsided (*HTJP* 1914: 3.4, 5 Jan.; 1924: 1.2, 29 Feb.).

Not all misfortunes, however, were as short-lived. During 1933 and 1934, when the adverse effects of the worldwide Great Depression hit this part of China, the 'flowery business' was also reported to experience a serious recession as a result of the weak economy. In Hong Kong, for example, we learn from contemporary newspaper reports that the brothel business was badly hit, though it was the high-class bordellos that the recession most affected. In the city of Shao-hsing, the recession led to a drop in the number of prostitutes to about sixty. The brothel business there became so slim that even the once lucrative tax-brokerage rights of levying prostitution-related taxes had failed to attract any bidders (*YHP* 1934: 1, 23 and 24 Mar.). Similarly in Yung-ch'i, a market-town in the heartland of the sericulture industry in the Pearl River delta, the number of brothels had dropped from nearly thirty at its peak to a mere two. The businesses of local restaurants and musicians were also badly hit as a consequence (*YHP* 1933: 1, 27 Apr.). Although the situation in Canton was not as bad, business in general was still hardly satisfactory. These examples of vicissitudes remind us that the simplified and gloomy picture of prostitution as a persistently exacerbating problem in Republican society was more a rhetorical myth than historical reality. The economic recession cost jobs in the services industry and had certainly made life difficult for many employers and employees in this business. But general impoverishment did not cause a surge in the prostitution business, which, on the contrary, was trimmed. As discussed earlier, poverty alone did not suffice to explain the causes of prostitution.

Although this study stops at the mid-1930s, it is still important to note in passing that in spring 1951 the early Communist authorities in Canton recorded a total of 277 prostitutes in the city (Kuang-chou-shih jên-min chêng-fu pan-kung tien 1951: 13). This figure might be a realistic number because, first, it was drawn from statistics on prostitutes provided by the city's Public Security Bureau. Secondly, this set of data, published in March 1951, might well be referring to the situation of Canton during the early months of the Communist takeover, when the new regime was trying hard to stabilize the country by adopting a tolerant attitude towards many forms of 'feudalistic customs', including prostitution (Vogel 1969: 31–2, 65). It was only from autumn 1951 that the local authorities in Canton began to intensify its social and political campaigns to clean up the city through puritanical measures. Even in the official campaign to 'reform' prostitutes, in which these women were rounded up by the People's Liberation Army and shipped off to a training camp where they were 're-educated' through hard labour and ideological indoctrination, only 221 prostitutes were reported to have been 'benefited'.[13] In other words, the small number of prostitutes recorded was not necessarily a result of any official anti-prostitution action that might have scared away these women; the scale of this 'problem' might simply not be as wide as many Communist party historians have imagined.

Clandestine Prostitution: An Ever-Worsening Problem?

The allegedly large numbers of unlicensed prostitutes in Canton increased the difficulty of obtaining reliable information on the overall situation. If the official statistics for licensed prostitutes were marked by obvious flaws, so much more difficult was it to make a realistic estimate of the number of unlicensed prostitutes. Both writers of that time and present-day historians, however, prefer to believe that the problem of clandestine prostitution was serious, and was getting steadily worse.[14] But their arguments were not, and are not, supported by any convincing evidence.

To start with, the phenomenon of undercover prostitution was seemingly first problematized in the anti-prostitution discourse during the mid-1920s, when Canton politics had entered a phase of revolutionary radicalism under the control of the newly reorganized KMT. In most of these official or intellectual anti-prostitution opinions, as seen from the numerous articles that appeared in a local official daily, clandestine prostitution was presented as a recent but speedily worsening social problem and as a reaction to the soaring of Canton's prostitution-related taxes that drove brothel-goers away from licensed establishments to the illicit but cheaper alternative. In this kind of literature, a clandestine prostitute was also commonly depicted as woman of weak moral fibre: covetous, greedy, and addicted to sensual pleasure (Ch'en Li-chu et al. 1991: iv. 470–1). The weakness of this pejorative generalization is obvious. In another article from the same daily, generalization went to the other extreme: that all undercover prostitutes were, in fact, pitiable for they were all thought to have come from poor families and had been forced to sell their bodies by their merciless and violent procurers (ibid. 477–9). Either way, these criticisms and stories were seemingly constructed in such a manner as to cause such a sense of outrage among their readers that they would condone the revolutionary causes of the expansive party-state. Covert prostitution, unlike the licensed type, implied a failure of the state's mechanism of social control over an individual's body and desires, and therefore had to be addressed immediately to restore order to the society. The politicized anti-prostitution discourse conjured up the powerful image of a devastated China, which was being plagued by poverty, socio-economic inequality, and exploitation; and national salvation could be attained only through the recipe of reform dictated by the Nationalist regime. It is clear, however, that this kind of political rhetoric does not improve our understanding of the real situation or condition of undercover prostitutes in the city. First, unlicensed prostitution was not a new problem in the mid-1920s. In 1895, we learn from a local newspaper that a case of theft took place in an unlicensed brothel in the walled city of Canton. It was also mentioned that this particular locality was notorious for its concentration of such bordellos (*HTJP* 1895, 5 Feb.).[15] This 'social problem' could be antedated by at least thirty years, and possibly even much longer.

Secondly, the scale of the problem might not be as truly alarming as it was depicted in the anti-prostitution propaganda. Police records that have survived also provide hints of the state of unlicensed prostitution in Canton. During the first two weeks of April 1921, for instance, the Public Security Bureau launched a series of campaigns targeting covert prostitutes, which was probably a means to publicize the reforming spirit of Canton's first and nascent municipal government. Teams from a special task force were sent out to inspect all classes of hotels and restaurants, and to arrest such women when found. A contemporary newspaper reported that the campaign was a genuine one—sudden raids had been conducted day and night, closely monitored by enthusiastic senior police officers. The result, however, is somewhat interesting. In spite of all these high-handed efforts, the police made less than one hundred arrests during the campaign; a number that had, however, impressed the reporter, who aired his concern about the lack of space in local prisons to house these women (*HTJP* 1921: 2.3, 4 April and 1.3, 14 April). Drastic measure against unlicensed prostitutes as such might be unprecedented, but the actual number of arrests, given the scale and sincerity of the effort, only indicated the fact that the extent of the problem might be a lot smaller than it was officially portrayed. Then in 1923, some twenty unlicensed prostitutes were arrested and fined by the police (*Kuang-chou-shih*

shih-chêng pao-kao hui k'an 1923: 314); in 1928, this number rose to about 1,200, and constituted the second largest category of apprehension (*Kuang-chou-shih shih-chêng t'ung-chi hui k'an* 1929: 90). This remarkable increase might have been due simply to the growth in the number of unlicensed prostitutes in Canton; no doubt, too, the police force was more efficient in making arrests (with a reward system that helped to boost the enthusiasm of the rank and file), and the municipal administration was keeping better records.

It is interesting to note in passing that during 1924, when Canton was packed with infantrymen who were friendly to the Nationalist government under the leadership of Sun Yat-sen, the situation of covert prostitution was reported to have worsened as a result. In order to work in peace, many unlicensed prostitutes bribed those cash-hungry military officers in return for their protection. Bribes were paid on either a daily or weekly basis. With military blessing, these ladies were said to be able to operate freely at local hotels, unwillingly tolerated by policemen who dared not antagonize those hard-bitten soldiers (*HTJP* 1924: 1.3, 1 May). One tends to infer from this that the situation of unlicensed prostitution can only have worsened as a consequence. This, however, is not a substantiated conclusion. Extant newspapers point out that unlicensed prostitutes had become more visible in public places, but not much was said about any steep rise in their numbers. Available documents from the municipal administration did not record any note of serious concern about a deterioration in the situation either. Moreover, there seemed to be a strong reason for both the military authorities and the municipal government to control, if not to uproot, this link of clandestine prostitution and soldiery misconduct: revenue. Since licensed prostitution was one of the major sources of revenue for both the city and the military administrations (to be discussed in detail later in this chapter), covert prostitution would only produce a negative impact on their incomes. It was unlikely that the higher authorities would have tolerated the spread of such abuse and done nothing to avert this allegedly deteriorating problem, which was pointing directly at the vested interests of the 'revolutionary regime'; prostitution-generated revenue was simply too important for sustaining and financing the nationalist revolution.

There would seem to be no way to obtain a truly accurate picture of prostitution in Republican Canton. Official and unofficial statistics, though not without their weaknesses, suggest a different situation from the emotionally charged accounts of Republican writers and modern historians. Whether prostitution in Republican Canton was a 'permanent sore' or not is a question that remains unanswered.

2. *CONFLICTING PERCEPTIONS OF PROSTITUTES*

Victims of Exploitation, Agents of Destruction

For reasons of political and ideological necessity, Chinese Communist historians have commonly described prostitutes as victims of the 'semi-feudal', 'semi-colonial', and exploitative capitalist Republican society under the 'reactionary' rule of the Nationalist Party (*NFJP* 1951, 17 Oct.; *KTFCL* 1988: 238–43). Poverty and abduction are given as the two main reasons girls entered the profession (Wu Yü et al. 1988: 400–15; K'ang Shu-chên 1990).[16]

Conscientious writers in Republican Canton, however, also fostered this pitiable image of prostitute. Prostitution was no longer seen as a delightful pastime, but as 'a symbol of a nation's impoverishment, corruption, and decadence' (Gronewold 1985: 2). In Ou-yang Shan's short story 'Tsai shen ching li' (In the Deep Well), the torments suffered by the prostitute were perhaps representative of the perception held by many post-May Fourth 'conscientious' writers. Village-girl Liu Fei-yün lives with her alcoholic and abusive uncle. One day, when her uncle threatens to sell her as a whore destined for Singapore, she escapes to Canton where she finds herself alone and helpless. Consequently, she becomes a prostitute in order to support herself and, later, her pseudo-mother and a syphilitic 'sister'. Her life as an unlicensed prostitute is depicted as being hard. She is usually rewarded for a day without business by a severe beating from the madam of the brothel (her pseudo-mother).

Helpless submission to customers' physical abuses was dramatized in vivid language. One day, a hairy and robust vegetable hawker, who is well known for his harshness in abusing girls, comes to patronize Liu again. As soon as he sees her, he grasps her skinny body so tightly that it is 'like a crab squeezing its prey'. With all his weight he presses down on her breasts. He rubs his dirty feet over her face, tugs at her tongue with his blackened fingers, and twists her into a ball. When Chao Szu, a worker who tries to persuade Liu to leave this 'deep well', sees this, his pity for her turns into rage, and he throws the vegetable hawker out. Liu, however, is not pleased because a regular client has been lost. She cries out in despair:

> She closes the wooden door hurriedly, tears open her shirt, and takes off her trousers. Then she comes close to me and shouts: 'Look! Take a good look at the scars on my body! Do you think you have done me a good turn by booting him out? Right! He's gone now. But for me it means another round of whipping, another torture-session of burning [by my madam]...' After a while she is exhausted... She lays her head on my thigh, and bursts into tears. (Ou-yang Shan 1948: 21)[17]

Physical emaciation and ravaged health was held to be another 'necessary consequence' of working as a prostitute. Although Liu is just 20, she is already so worn out that she looks old far beyond her years. At the end of the story, she is described as 'having a pale and aged face', while 'no part of her body is not worn out and weak'.[18] She also suffers from tuberculosis. But even in this very bad state of health, she goes on working. Her physical debilitation aggravates the inevitable process of spiritual corruption. She loses any sense of purpose and forgets any dream for her future. She becomes a neurotic, staring at her reflection in the mirror, then smashing it, and biting her wooden comb until it breaks (ibid. 17).

Liu's 'last assignment' is to be hired out to four Shanghai workers for a month. She is obliged to sleep with them day and night. In the end, she disappears from her filthy 'workplace', and probably dies of tuberculosis.

Life as a derelict prostitute is already pitiable enough. But in order to highlight the plight of these women, Ou-yang Shan describes the appalling working environment of Liu in great detail:

> Whenever I walk into that room [where Liu sleeps with her clients], it smells pungent and stinks . . . of herbal medicine, and medical sulphuric cream. The floor is strewn with drops of thick phlegm, empty tin-cans, charcoal ash, and blood-stained paper. Table and chairs are covered with dust, dirty clothes, hair, pieces of broken glass, and a wooden comb with teeth missing. On the wall hangs a calendar with pictures of girls in out-of-date fashion, most of whom are [disfigured] with . . . [sketched-in] moustaches, breasts, and genital organs of both sexes. (ibid. 27)

Ou-yang Shan's intention, in short, was to educate his readers that to be a prostitute in this period was the most miserable fate that could befall a woman.

In a short play written by a high-school student in Canton, the torment of its heroine was similar to Liu Fei-yün's. The setting of the play is a cold midwinter evening in the countryside in the North. The prostitute Lien Lien is dragged by her hair from a brothel by a vindictive fat madam who is punishing her for being infected by venereal disease, which drives many regulars away. She has been mistreated on this account for some months already before being thrown out now. Her too-thin clothes and short skirt hardly suffice to keep her warm in the bitter cold. For three days, she has no food. Shivering in the icy weather, she feels she has lost everything, even her sense of existence.

Suddenly, she spots a man walking towards her. Overcome by desperation as much as joy she tries everything she can, from flirting to begging, to get him to stop. The young man ignores her until she offers to sit naked on the snow-covered pavement for five minutes in return for twenty cents. In addition, this man will whip her for half a cent per stroke. When the abuse is over, blood oozes from the new wounds on Lien's already scarred back. With over one yüan in her hand, however, she feels the world is once again good to her. Her mind is now so full of images of hot food that she pays no attention to the pain that wracks her back. She hurries to a restaurant which is twinkling with neon lights (Lei Li-pin 1934: 126–30).[19]

Expectedly, anti-prostitution reformers and intellectuals in Canton had been eagerly promoting this miserable image of prostitute. In a commemorative volume of collected essays published for an official campaign against 'bad customs' in Kwangtung, such an image of prostitution was invoked to solicit public support to the cause:

> In brothels run by these procuresses, these girls are even much more pitiable and inhumanely treated, though this is rarely known to people not in this trade. For instance, if a prostitute is poor in business and fails to earn any money [for a few days], she will be punished with whipping and abusive reproaching by her procuress. Since these prostitutes are [as] afraid of their madams as if they are tigresses, they dare not [be] insubordinate [to these abuses but] reveal their bitterness only quietly in private. Therefore, prostitutes are all eager to entertain their clients without daring to be slack, lest pain will once again shower upon them. (*FSKKTK* 1930: 216)

Behind this tragic image of prostitutes lay a familiar political message: that these unwilling and abused victims of the 'flesh trade' could be rescued only with the people's active support of the kind of radical and intrusive social reforms overseen by the Nationalist Party.

In the concerns of these anti-prostitution commentators, the imminent plague of syphilis was another problem that required immediate rectification. In the discourse of venereal diseases, the prostitute was identified as the carrier and the unwilling victim. On the grounds of saving these poor girls from this form of incurable disease, as much as preventing its spread to the community, the authorities were asked for stronger regulatory action to avert the exacerbation of the problem (*HTJP* 1924: 3, 28 Mar. and 1.3, 7 Apr.). Venereal diseases were also said to be something new to China's metropolises, and the number of people inflicted grew each year. This, it was believed, would only disrupt the otherwise 'healthy' social order and corrupt the genetic quality of the Chinese race (Ch'en Li-chu et al. 1991: iv. 530–1; *YHP* 1933: 1, 12 Feb.). Syphilis, however, was not new to China: it had been there since at least the late Ming (Dikötter 1995: 127). What was new was the heavy emphasis that it received in anti-prostitution discourse from the early 1920s. Browsing through extant late-Ch'ing and early-Republican Cantonese anti-prostitution writings, it appears that very rarely were venereal diseases highlighted, or represented, as a problem. In these early documents, the danger of prostitution lay chiefly in its immoral social and familial repercussions, the trickery with which most brothel-goers were said to be preyed upon, and the 'predictable' insincerity of prostitutes to their patrons (Hsiao-tian-shih 1907; Ch'i wan hua she 1910). The fear of venereal disease, and the discourse against it, seemed to have arisen from a larger context of rabid nationalism against foreign imperialism, the critique of 'modernity' and an unfamiliar urban culture, and the growing concerns over public hygiene and the regulation of sexuality and individual lifestyle especially in the city.[20] In this discourse, the role of prostitutes had been subtly expanded from being a threat to the moral integrity of the local society to becoming an accomplice in corrupting China's modern civilization.

Reputable Women with a Bad Name

Some people, however, saw prostitutes simply as victims of an unjust social system, who were to be portrayed as pitiable, rather than wicked or despicable, characters. Biographies of courtesans in random notes of the late Ch'ing, in contemporary local newspapers and magazines, in a 1931 courtesan's guide, in the published reminiscences of a brothel-goer, and prostitute-characters as depicted in *Yüeh-ou* folk songs, show that morally these women often surpassed ordinary men in happier circumstances. Such literature is full of praise for their extraordinary sensitivity, strong commitment to love, cultural refinement, and spirit of filial pious self-sacrifice that prompted them to work as courtesans in order to save their families from destitution (Chou Yu-liang 1914: 87–90;

Chih-chi-shêng 1974: 5267–80; Chiu-chung-fêng-fu *c.*1930s; Yu Chiao-ch'ing 1909: 18–33; Clementi 1904).[21] This favourable portrayal of prostitutes was probably intended to depict the hardship they suffered in their profession as even more unbearable and pitiful—and thus render more convincing and justifiable an attack on the society that tolerated this. Liu Fei-yün, the derelict street-walker in Ou-yang Shan's 'Tsai shen ching li', is also portrayed as a compassionate and patriotic woman. She is the only passenger on a public bus who gives money to students asking for donations to support the anti-Japanese resistance campaign in 1932 (Ou-yang Shan 1948: 12–14). And, as already mentioned, she continues to prostitute herself, despite her serious ill-health, in order to maintain her syphilitic 'sister' and elderly 'mother' (ibid. 25).[22]

In reality, it must be added, such 'kind-hearted prostitutes' did exist. From time to time in local newspapers one comes across reports about the good deeds of some of these women. During the early months of the 1911 Revolution, four prostitutes from different high-class brothels in Canton came forward to donate a handsome amount of cash and a collection of expensive jewellery to the revolutionary militias in support of their cause. Knocking on the doors from household to household, they asked their fellow citizens to show their support of the new government in kind. This group of zealous women even planned for a similar campaign in Macao (*HTJP* 1911, 28 Dec.). The following story is an instance. One day, in 1924, in Hong Kong, a woman hawker was selling vegetables on a busy street. She was caught by an Indian policeman for unlicensed hawking. This woman, we are told, looked very sad and hapless because she did not have the money (3 dollars) to pay her fine. Moreover, when she was apprehended, she was carrying a baby on her back and a small child stood close behind her. Such a pathetic scene attracted a big crowd. Among the crowd was a well-dressed young prostitute who came forward, paid the fine for this poor mother of two, and withdrew from the scene quietly. Onlookers were impressed (*HTJP* 1924: 1.3, 7 Apr.). At times, commitment to philanthropy was done collectively. Prostitutes in Canton and Hong Kong had seemingly formed a 'tradition' of taking part in public charities. In response to a call for donations for plague relief in 1893, for instance, a blind sing-song girl (an occupation that was popularly perceived as unlicensed prostitution) in Canton had bequeathed a tiny, but symbolically meaningful, sum of one copper coin that won her heart-felt applause from the public. She was probably not the only prostitute who took part in this event. Two years later, a group of prostitutes, under the leadership of a 'sister' from a low-class brothel in the old city of Canton, presented a collective donation of 20 *taels* of silver to a recently founded charity hall (*shan t'ang*) located in the vicinity of her workplace. This act of good faith, we are told, represented the wishes of these women who tried to redeem sins committed in previous lives (*huan hua-chai*), which caused them to work as prostitutes (*HTJP* 1895, 5 Mar.).[23] Occasionally, similar collective efforts at charity were more organized and bigger in scale. In winter, 1911, for example, an eye-catching advertisement appeared in a respectable Hong Kong newspaper consecutively for nearly a fortnight. This public notice, entitled 'Learned Women in the Flowery Business Participating Enthusiastically in Public Charity', tells us that in response to a call for charity donations (the benefited institution is not mentioned in the ad but was probably a charitable hospital in Canton), the two guilds relating to the 'flowery business' in Hong Kong had initially decided to show their support by asking their members to make a contribution of 30 cents out of each 'flowery feast' transaction. Later on, the notice reads, the guilds realized that this had increased the cost of running this business, which was already in a state of financial difficulty. The guilds, therefore, decided to stop imposing this tax on their members. Instead, businessmen and 'sisters' in this trade were encouraged to donate as much, or as little, as they pleased. In response, a group of high-class prostitutes actively promoted this act of charity among their 'sisters', whose benevolence was recorded in a newspaper announcement that contained a long list of names including those of the organizers and donors from this occupation. Quite a few of these women even donated a sum equivalent to one month of their income (e.g. *HTJP* 1911, 16 Dec.).

Similar acts of benevolence were recorded in Canton throughout the Republican period until the eve of the Japanese invasion. In a 1921 funfair organized by the Nationalist military authority in Canton for the dual purposes of fund-raising and showing gratitude to the army, high-class prostitutes joined hands with many other professional entertainers as well as social notables, including the wives of some prominent KMT officials and military commanders, to make this event a big success. They contributed to the cause by singing, at a charge, on the requests of donors; some of them also donated a modest sum to the chest. These women were able to think nationalistically and act accordingly in their own ways (*KHP* 1921: 8, 30 July).[24] In November 1936, to celebrate the 50th birthday of Generalissimo Chiang Kai-shek, a group of high-class prostitutes in Canton Ch'en-t'ang initiated a donation campaign in the hope of 'catching up with the pace of the rest of the country, which is zealously launching a fund-raising campaign to purchase warplanes that shall be sent to the Generalissimo as birthday gifts'. They obtained from the local government copies of donation record books and had them distributed to a number of their 'sisters' working in high-class brothels. On the collection day, prostitutes from the various high-class establishments formed small groups and spent long hours visiting the city's restaurants, tea houses, and, of course, brothels, to solicit donations. To motivate these women, tax-farming companies for the local prostitution tax arranged a competition for this event; the top three women who collected most donations were awarded large silver-plated shields and other trophies that many courtesans were said to like. Although the total amount of donations raised was not really substantial, the fact that this event was favourably reported in at least one respectable local newspaper is indicative of the public recognition of some of the commendable qualities of these women (*YHP* 1936: 9, 1 Nov.).[25]

The generosity of these prostitutes indicated their relative economic well-being, a fact that most anti-prostitution writers seemed to ignore. In this period, despite the efforts of writers and reformers to promote the image of prostitutes as pitiable, the perception of many people that these women lived lives of comfort was not altered. A reader wrote to a popular Canton pictorial to express his simple view of prostitutes: they would 'love' their clients only if being treated 'properly' by them. That included frequent visits, substantial tips, gifts of jewellery and expensive fashions, being driven in limousines, dining at Western-style restaurants, and spending hours of leisure at cinemas and department stores' entertainment complexes, all, needless to say, at the expense of their clients. Prostitutes, however, were not singled out for taking such a practical attitude towards love. This author continued to make similar sarcastic remarks about Cantonese actors, young girls of the new generation, and housewives in general (*Chu-kiang hsing-ch'i hua-pao* 1927: vol. 4, 18). The analogy itself was a meaningful one: that prostitutes, in this reader's mind, and probably also in many others', were not more disingenuous or materialistic than other contemporary women; they were not stigmatized blindly in that sense. On the other hand, putting such views in writing helped reaffirm the common perception that these pragmatic girls led a life of luxury, and this positive image could have assisted a desperate woman to decide to enter this ill-famed business.[26]

A compilation of *Yüeh-ou*-style vernacular love-songs written in the 1920s provides us with further clues to the expression of this favourable view of prostitutes.[27] As their nineteenth-century prototypes had done, many of these songs praised the devotion and sincerity of courtesans towards their lover-clients, who, by comparison, were far less honest.[28] More interestingly, the turbulent political situation of the first decade of the Republican era seemed to help to elevate the image of prostitutes, who were sometimes considered as morally superior to, and socially more useful than, warlords bent on destruction. This is illustrated by the following words from a song entitled 'Working As a Whore Like Us':

> [A]fter they (the warlords) have gained power, they rage about waging war [against other warlords] . . . They always slip away as soon as their stomachs have been satisfied with [our] food . . . Although we are considered decayed flowers and rotten willows, we can still speak out loudly. We may be doomed to be whores, [but our sense of] sisterhood still allows us to resolve disputes by discussion.[29]

This might be an indication of public disapproval of the warlords' misconduct. The image of prostitutes that was so favourably portrayed in this song, however, should not be dismissed as unimportant; it is a vindication of the existence of a supportive popular attitude towards this profession. Prostitutes were seen to be more 'constructive' than military men because at least they provided the public with entertainment, and supported the virtue of freedom of speech. In another song on a similar theme, prostitutes are said to be more dignified than obsequious officials, and their way of earning an income more conducive to moral pride.[30]

Even a swindling prostitute's misdeeds were more justifiable than a warlord's. One of these prostitutes, when asked whether she had ever felt remorse over her misbehaviour, answered confidently:

> I have been involved in this business for years. Swindling is my way of doing business and that is how I can earn the money that keeps me alive. [But] all the men whom I have

squeezed enjoyed [my services and do not mind having been squeezed]. I have never heard a word of complaint... Swindlers abound in this world. Am I the only one?... At present, are those men who are armed with swords, go about in motor-cars [and] wear the fearsome visage of a warlord, really gifted with the military talent of Sun Tzu or Wu Ch'i? They do not know how to defend their country against foreign aggression, how to stop civilians from being massacred, how to deal with the issue of unequal treaties, and yet they never feel ashamed of living in spacious Western-style residences... Aren't these men also profiting by harming others? (Ching Fo 1934: 3–4)

These words stunned the moralist writer so much that he could hardly make any further comment. Prostitutes might be seen as sufferers of abuse and exploitation, but they were not necessarily perceived as socially and morally inferior to other people.

In the course of building his 'revolutionary base' in the South during the early 1920s, Sun Yat-sen had invited the military interventions of various regional forces to drive off his old enemies from Canton and its vicinity. There was, however, a heavy price to pay: Canton was flooded with soldiers from different regions who quarrelled and even at times fought between themselves for all sorts of reasons, and their loose discipline posted a serious threat to law and order in the city. This proliferation of soldierly misconduct aroused the concern of some men of letters who expressed their incriminations against it through humorous prose, some of them being published in a respectable Hong Kong newspaper. One of these prose pieces, whose long title may be shortened to 'Soldier-like prostitutes, prostitute-like soldiers', tries to make an analogy between prostitutes and soldiers in order to ridicule the latter. It states that soldiers not only shared many prostitutes' behavioural traits, such as insincerity about love and avarice, but also excelled at them and surpassed those soldier-like hard-hearted harlots. The distinction between these two groups of people, therefore, was said to have become invisible. The fusion, however, was never a complete one. For a 'true prostitute', we are told, would never feel ashamed to be a harlot, but would if asked to join the army. Moreover, although the common people could not be harmed by prostitutes, they were always subjected to molestation by soldiers. In the end, our humorist called for measures to be taken immediately to rectify this worrying phenomenon of 'prostitute-ization' of military conduct (*HTJP* 1924: 3.4, 21 Apr.). Like many satirical essays on the same theme, this one appears to criticize both the military and prostitutes. A closer look, however, reveals that the disparagement of prostitutes in this essay is only a stylistic technique to highlight the humorist's denunciation of the misconduct of soldiers; the low status of prostitute did not necessarily render these men of letters unable to appreciate the good side of these women, and to represent them in a favourable light.

With the increase in the number of clandestine prostitutes in this period who were believed to be engaged in the trade for reasons of debauchery or greed, many Cantonese intellectuals and reformers began to see prostitutes in a somewhat different light: they were perceived to be the cause of their own downfall rather than victims of society. A contemporary writer, K'ung Fu-an, noted that most pre-Republican prostitutes were to be pitied because they were generally forced into the profession by economic hardship or other reasons beyond their control. In Republican Canton, however, many women prostituted themselves simply to earn more money, or to chase their illusory dream of modern 'moral freedom'. This was far less deserving of sympathy.[31]

K'ung's opinion accorded with that of a writer on the subject in Shanghai, in whose view all prostitutes in Shanghai, with the exception of the most servile low-class harlots, were vicious and should be treated with caution instead of sympathy. He repeatedly warned his readers that most prostitutes were money-grubbing, and they should guard against being deceived because, behind their flirtation, these women were insincere and dishonest about affairs of the heart (Hai-shang-chüeh-wu-shêng 1939: 3–4).

It is perhaps due to this jaundiced view of contemporary prostitutes that Canton saw an upsurge of interest in the romantic life stories of virtuous high-class courtesans and the refined tradition of superior brothels in Imperial Kwangtung. This was reflected by a proliferation of articles, poems, and books on the subject. K'ung Fu-an was one of these writers of nostalgia. In the preface to his book on prostitution in Ch'ing-period Kwangtung, he stated that in view of the disappearance from 'present-day' brothels of the kind of beauty who was well versed in the arts of singing, composing poems, painting, calligraphy, and conversation, his book was intended to record the life histories and accomplishments of famous Cantonese courtesans and anecdotes about them, before they faded from the popular memory (*LNFY c.*1930s: 1–7).[32]

It must be added, however, that the 'emergence' of unlicensed prostitution did not replace its registered counterpart which apparently continued to do well until banned in 1936. Moreover, the negative perception of contemporary prostitutes was not a dominant attitude because the sympathetic image of these women persisted. Although many viewed this 'modern' form of prostitution with fear because of its unregulated nature and its presumed link with syphilis, many also perceived clandestine prostitutes with great sympathy for they saw in the lives of these girls a bitter history of being forced by unfortunate circumstances to sell their bodies (Ch'en Li-chu et al. 1991: iv. 468, 528–9, 547, 584; *KPP* 1927: 8, 8 July). Furthermore, writings praising the good virtues and character of contemporary high-class prostitutes—qualities that were supposed to have been long gone in the eyes of nostalgic writers on brothel high culture—continued to be seen as late as the early 1930s: their acts of filial piety towards their parents or siblings, their loyalty and generosity to friends or patrons, their persistence in refusing sexual demands from customers they did not like, and so on (*Chu-kiang hsing-ch'i hua-pao* 1927: vols. 4, 6, 7, 8; Lo Li-ming 1962).[33] The good side of these ill-reputed women had not been totally forgotten in the modern era, and these conflicting perceptions persisted, neither one ever outdoing the other.

An experienced brothel-goer reminisces that in Hong Kong and Canton in the 1930s, to work as a prostitute at a high-class brothel was generally seen as one of the very few opportunities available to a girl of lower-class background to climb up the social ladder. This was because it was only at these venues that a young prostitute was given the opportunity to meet rich patrons from high society; and not infrequently their courtship would eventually lead to marriage. It might not be her major concern whether she would be married into a rich family as first wife or concubine; what mattered more was the opportunity for her to become a member of a respectable and wealthy family because that would guarantee a prosperous and comfortable life not only for herself, but also her natal family. There was a common saying that 'If a daughter is married into a wealthy family, her natal family will [as a result] be able to afford to have pork at every meal' (*i nü chia hao-mên, ch'üan chia chi chu-ju*). These popular high-class prostitutes, who were courted by the rich and famous, were a source of pride for their parents and relatives; they were thus regarded as daughters with great expectations (Lo Li-ming 1962: ii. 4.).

In the period under review, the public image of prostitutes became more complicated, varied, and unpredictable, yet at the same time more realistic. Prostitutes were simultaneously despised, respected, and pitied. These conflicting images indicated that in their long crusade against prostitution, reforming politicians, officials, and intellectuals had apparently failed to transform or alter the ways the phenomenon was popularly perceived. Their 'civilizing' efforts could at best arouse the concern of some well-informed citizens, lead to the issue of regulatory measures governing the 'proper' ways the brothel business should be conducted, but were not able to erase the persistent views of the general population or replaced them with a new set of ideas actively promoted by the modern elite. To change the mindset of the people was a mission beyond the reach of successive Republican and Nationalist governments in Canton, who lacked the true qualities and the powers of an absolute modern state.

3. *ALTERNATIVE PERCEPTIONS OF THE 'SUFFERING' OF PROSTITUTES*

'Ruthless Exploitation' under the Heel of the Madam?

As already pointed out, one of the most often used images of prostitutes in anti-prostitution writings was that they led a life of regular abuses and severe exploitation by their procuresses or madams. Such images might not be publicity stunts in the sense that real-life examples of this sort could be read occasionally in contemporary documents. A newspaper article featured the case of a pitiable prostitute whose story, we are told, should be studied by everyone to arouse public concern about the sad conditions that many such women were suffering. The contributor of the article wrote that he met this prostitute, Chin Lan, in a brothel in the northern Kwangtung city of Shao-kuan. Chin Lan was not the kind of courtesan most customers preferred: she was reticent and sad-looking. Learning that our writer-client was a sincere, compassionate man, Chin Lan began to tell him her bitter life story. She was from Hunan and married to an army officer who disappeared in action. Deceived by a villain, who convinced her that he knew the whereabouts of her husband, she followed him to Kwangtung where she was eventually abducted and sold into the brothel. Since she refused to entertain her guests with a smiling face, her madam had been whipping her for four months, but even that was not enough to make her yield. She pleaded to the writer to help her out as she said her madam was arranging a deal to sell her to a low-class brothel where she would be forced to provide sex for any men 'thirsty of carnal desire' (*KPP* 1928: 8, 3 Apr.).

Exploitation and misery were not seen as the exclusive preserve of low-class prostitutes, or as a phenomenon new to the 'modern age'. Ch'ing-period random notes on high-class prostitutes tended to reinforce the miserable image of all classes of these ladies in Canton. For instance, in the biographies of twelve high-class courtesans of the late-Ch'ing period, most were described as suffering from serious emotional trouble as a result of their quasi-captivity,[34] interference by the madams in their love affairs,[35] or being forced to have sexual intercourse with clients they disliked.

However, a madam's intervention in the love affairs of her girls was not always attributable to covetousness. In the 1920s, and probably in the Ch'ing period too, there were parasitical, often good-looking and suave, crooks who preyed on well-off prostitutes.[36] It might have been out of concern to prevent their girls from being cheated that madams interfered in the affairs of their 'daughters', for whom they had often developed an affection based on years of mutual dependence.

Contemporary moralists' writings on the subject of prostitution tended to perceive brothel madams as a species of subhuman blood-sucker who resorted to all forms of abuse to maintain absolute control over their girls, exploiting them ruthlessly[37]—a picture that was neither fantasy nor universally true. A physically abused prostitute was no good to a money-hungry madam if her attractiveness—her economic value—was reduced by a scarred body. The image of 'the wicked brothel madam' (*ngo pao*), however, was often casually exploited by journalists to give a sensationalized touch to news of unfortunate incidents occurring in the 'flowery world'. For instance, in a report about a prostitute who died of a skin eruption which bears the emotional heading 'The Pitiless Inhumane Malevolent Brothel Madam', one would feel disappointed at failing to find convincing evidence illustrating the madam's wickedness. The story, in fact, was a simple one. One day, a young prostitute had a severe rash. Before long, her madam turned to supernatural healing by paying for elaborate rituals and praying at various temples, but to no avail. She then resorted to modern medical advice, which, however, was eventually dismissed for being untrustworthy. In desperation, the madam resorted once again to a traditional supernatural recipe—pasting all over the patient's body strips of paper soaked with rice wine and then covering her with layers of thick blankets for days. This was too much for the poor sick girl who died one day later (*HTJP* 1921: 2.4, 13 May). In this sad story, the madam could at most be blamed for her distrust of modern medicine, but even this was not unique to her or the business that she happened to represent. Her caring attitude toward the poor girl was indicated by her acts of faith at the local temples and her resorting to the divine realm for rescue. These acts were ignored in this narrative, however.

In another example, a newspaper report on the attempted suicide of a young prostitute was entitled 'The Blame is on the Evil Madam'. In this case, a young courtesan, Miss Mai, tried to drown herself by jumping into the Pearl River. She was fortunately rescued by some nearby marines. In her narrative of the event, we learn that she was a Fukienese who was sold to a brothel in Canton when she was a child. She met a young military officer about a year earlier in her brothel. They fell instantly in love with each other and the officer even proposed to 'buy her out' from the bordello. However the 'evil madam', we are told, succeeded in fending off the request by setting the price unrealistically high. Then, one evening, another client of this prostitute was so inebriated that he had to stay overnight with her in the brothel. The next morning, the officer chanced to visit his girlfriend and saw the stranger in her bed. Outraged, he scolded the girl and declared an end to their intimate relationship. This paved the way for the abortive attempt to take her own life (*HTJP* 1921: 1.3, 20 May). Miss Mai's tragic story, however, was only partly attributed to the 'wickedness' of her madam and specifically to her demand for an unaffordable amount of ransom. The madam was not as evil as the headline boasted because at least she did not stop the couple from seeing each other, nor did she threaten the girl with violence. The tragedy was apparently triggered off by a misunderstanding on the part of Miss Mai's lover that she had been unfaithful to him. This also revealed the interesting fact that not all prostitutes were expected to sell sex to anyone who could pay, a subject that will be discussed in greater detail later.

Courtesan–madam relations was not always perceived as exploitation by the parties involved, for the long period of acquaintance between the two had the potential to foster mutual concern and intimacy,[38] and hence to minimize mistreatment (Hershatter 1991: 269). An example of exploitation being minimized by emotional attachment may be seen in *T'ang-hsi chin-fen* (The Romance of Courtesans in West Point), a social novel set in Hong Kong in the 1920s. Yü Shan and Yin Shan, the novel's two prostitute heroines, are sold to a modest but high-class brothel by their foster-mother. Both of them are treated well by their madam. They are given fine clothes and expensive jewellery to wear and enjoy the best of foods. The madam never forces Yü Shan to receive clients whom she dislikes. When the business of her brothel is seriously affected by the Canton-Hong Kong strike, Yü Shan's lover proposes to buy her out from the brothel. But Yü Shan is so emotionally attached to her madam, and sympathetic to her in the current crisis, that she refuses to leave her (Sung Yü 1989: 16, 115–19). Later in the story, after Yü Shan becomes disillusioned with her lover, she releases her anguish and frustration by sleeping with all the clients. Her 'promiscuity' arouses the concern of her madam who tries hard, though without success, to dissuade her from ruining herself in that way (ibid. 193–4). Hence, a madam did not always let profit blind her conscience and, to some extent, her moral responsibility to her girls.

In the case of another high-class prostitute, Tsai Hung, the moral responsibility went in the opposite direction. Tsai Hung was very popular among 'drinkers' (i.e. patrons of high-class brothels) in Canton. Although she was eager to end her career by finding the right man to marry, her captiousness inhibited her from resolving the matter promptly. When a Mr Fung, the owner of a theatre in Canton, proposed to her, she knew that he was the right candidate. To respect the customs of local brothels, Tsai Hung, despite her status as a 'free body' (meaning she was not pawned or sold to the house and in theory could come and leave at will), requested that Mr Fung negotiate with her madam on a price for her release. Since her madam did not want to see the departure of one of her most popular girls, an 'unreasonably' high price-tag of 3,000 yüan was put on Tsai Hung's release, which was double what the businessman wanted to spend. This infuriated Mr Fung so much that he proposed that Tsai Hung elope with him. Tsai Hung, however, refused, and, it was reported, lectured him about the consequences, such as the condemnation of the other girls if she ran away from her madam as proposed. In the end, she came up an alternative plan that was eventually followed: having placed a sum of 1,500 Hong Kong dollars in the drawer of her dressing table, she took with her a few of her favourite dresses and then left the house with almost everything intact. She believed that this would not harm her madam, who accepted the news of Tsai Hung's departure as fait accompli. After a short interval, Tsai Hung even returned to visit her madam and discussed the arrangement of a ritual, 'to hang up red [lanterns]' (*kua hung*), at the brothel, which would formally recognize her retirement from the business (*KPP* 1928: 8, 7 and 11 May). Tsai Hung's considerate sensibility towards her madam indicated perhaps a deeper emotional relationship between a prostitute and her madam.

The memoir of a contemporary 'drinker' contains many similar stories of the earnest relations between madams and their girls. The following is one of these examples, a reconstruction based upon the experience of a famous 'poet courtesan' in early-1930s Canton. Purple Orchid, our drinker friend reminisced, was brought up in a well-off family. She was educated at a respectable high school for girls. When she was 16, she lost her virginity to a young philanderer. The scandal was taken seriously by her strict father who was so upset that eventually he refused to let her stay in his house. By the arrangement of her mother, Purple Orchid lodged at a hotel in Hong Kong. During her lengthy stay there, she realized that the guests next door were a 'mother' with her two 'daughters' who were in the business of unlicensed prostitution. The procuress, named Pa Ku, was remembered as a considerate madam. She told Purple Orchid that her two 'daughters' entered out of desperation—one was ejected from home by her stepmother, the other worked to pay a debt for her ne'er-do-well boyfriend. Pa Ku added, however, that despite this business relationship, she cared about the welfare of her girls: they slept with only one client a day at most, she chose only gentlemanly clients for them, and she did not force them to serve men whom they disliked. After a period of fraternization, Pa Ku tried to help Purple Orchid out of her financial stringency by persuading her to work as an entertainer at a high-class brothel in Canton. She was then introduced to a Aunt Chiu, madam of a top-class brothel. Both Pa Ku and Aunt Chiu sympathized greatly with the unfortunate experience of Purple Orchid. They both agreed that Purple Orchid should entertain guests at dining tables only, unless there were clients for whom she was willing to provide further intimacy. For Purple Orchid, the brothel became a temporary refuge where she could wait for the chance to meet a suitable man to marry and where her pressing problem of subsistence could be solved. With the support of these considerate madams, Purple Orchid became a highly successful high-class courtesan in Canton and, later, Hong Kong (Lo Li-ming 1962: iv. 7–71).

It is interesting to note that Aunt Chiu's restraint was said to have stemmed from her religious belief in the existence of a supernatural realm of justice (ibid. 31–2). She, and probably many other madams in this business, believed that by treating her girls decently and considerately, she would earn herself merits in the eyes of divine beings. Accumulation of these merits would assure her a better life in the future, and in the after-world too. This fear of retributive punishments might act as an restraint to a madam maltreating a prostitute. It was by no means a magic bullet that ended all abuses against these girls, but was at least a strong psychological deterrent that might help reduce or minimize molestation.

The popular discourse of retributive punishments was revealed in the report of a real case. A woman nicknamed 'Fat Woman Number Four' had worked as a pimp and a madam. She had amassed so much money that she bought herself a mansion and lived on its rent. One evening, however, she had a bad nightmare. She dreamed of a robust man forcing his way into her bedroom and scolding her bitterly for enticing his wife to be unfaithful to him. In anger, he took out a knife and stabbed her in the abdomen. At this point, she awoke, in panic. She found on her abdomen that a huge sore was emerging. Convinced that she was being haunted by a malevolent spirit, the next morning she sought help from a Taoist priest. While the exorcist ritual was in progress, she was frightened by the reappearance of the apparition, which punched her in the back. She fell from the bed, wept copiously, and began to vomit blood. Her fate was sealed. The report claimed that to those who knew this woman, this was undoubtedly a retributive and deadly punishment for her sinful career in the 'flesh trade' (*KPP* 1928: 6, 5 Apr.). Reports such as this could convince the madams in this business that such retribution was indeed real.

Nor was the coercion exercised by a madam always effective in forcing girls to act against their will. Ta An, once the most 'eminent flower' in Canton, for instance, was only willing to entertain romantic and famous scholars. Once, her madam received 500 *taels* of gold from a rich man in return for Ta An's company. Ta An, however, refused. When her madam insisted, she went on a hunger strike; and that put her madam in a difficult position (*CKMH* 1974: 5268–9). Similarly, Yü Liang, another famous courtesan, refused to eat after her madam repeatedly intervened in her love affairs with poor scholars. Her hunger-strike was effective because the madam was eventually penitent (Yü Chiao-ch'ing 1909: 26).

In some cases, frustrated courtesans threatened to commit suicide, an effective measure of self-defence which served as a warning to mischief-making madams. For instance, when Fêng T'sai, a highly popular sing-song girl in late-Ch'ing Canton, fell in love with a scholar she refused to entertain anybody else, threatening suicide as a warning against intervention by her madam. Later, when the madam tried to force her to sleep with a rich patron, she refused by attempting to hang herself, though she was in fact saved. Eventually, Fêng was allowed to leave the brothel and, with her substantial savings, opened her own establishment, making a monthly payment to her former madam in return for her freedom (*LNFY c.*1930s: 54–8). The case of another prostitute, Chou Sui-ying, in mid-1920s Canton was even more dramatic. Sui-ying's parents passed away while she was very young. She had worked as a bondservant in a household until she was forced into prostitution by her mistress. It was said that for four years she was often whipped by her madam for failing to entertain her patrons willingly and nicely. Sick and tired of all this, Sui-ying, one evening, tried to drown herself. Fortunately, she was rescued by a boatman. When her madam learned about this, the report goes, she was overwhelmed by a deep sense of guilt so much so that she decided to let Sui-ying go. Instantly, Sui-ying became a free person, and she was also given a modest sum of 50 yüan, which was to be used, at her madam's request, for finding a suitable man to marry. We are also told that Sui-ying, despite her prostitute background, was very selective in choosing the right man. She listed seven criteria for her ideal man, among them that she should have the status of a principal wife and his recognition of this once-abusive madam as mother-in-law (*Chu-kiang hsing-ch'i hua-pao* 1927: iii. 20). The last clause raises doubt about the genuineness of Sui-ying's accusation of her madam's inhumane treatment against her and indicates instead the good terms she continued to enjoy with this 'wicked' woman even after their business relations had ended.

An over-abused prostitute could simply run away and seek help from the police (*KCHJP* 1933: 15, 22 Feb.). This also indicates that not all prostitutes were restricted in their movements, though virgin prostitutes (not yet receiving clients), because of their high market value, might be closely watched,[39] while control over 'wilful' prostitutes could be difficult. Examples of this abound. For instance, on one chilly morning in Macao a brothel madam found out that three of her girls had run away during the night. All three fugitives took away with them all the cash and the jewellery that she had lent them (*HTJP* 1914: 1.3, 7 Jan.). In another report we are told that a brothel madam had two foster daughters who were enticed by some riff-raff to run away from their 'mother'. They hid in the native village of these undesirables. The identities of the two young prostitutes, however, was later known to a local bully, Ah Lung, who also fancied these attractive girls and hence lost no time in reporting the case to the county office. Ah Lung had been an officer in the local militia, and this former official position had connected him to the power echelon in the locality. With the aid of his county official friends, the two girls were 'rescued' from the riff-raff and placed in the 'safe custody' of Ah Lung. The greatly disappointed rabble, however, were determined to take revenge. They went back to Canton to inform the brothel madam of the whereabouts of her 'daughters'. She eventually found the woman who was allegedly responsible for persuading the girls into hiding and took her to the local police (*HTJP* 1921: 2.3, 4 Apr.). This drama of Ah Lung revealed not only the ability of a disgruntled prostitute to run away from a brothel, but also the vulnerability of a madam though she was usually depicted in anti-prostitution literature as an incorrigible devil.

The exercise of power by a madam over her girls was not unlimited, especially when the girls were smart enough to take full advantage of the protection offered by the state. The dramatic case of Hsiang Chün, a high-class prostitute in Hong Kong, is an interesting example. Hsiang was a good-looking girl and her presence brought handsome income to the brothel where she worked. Her madam, as a result, treated her well, until one day she noticed that Hsiang had fallen in with a mediocre man of modest income. The madam became very suspicious of this handsome young man, who was believed to be a professional swindler trying to cheat Hsiang of all her (and the madam's) possessions and, perhaps, even make her leave the bordello. To prevent her from doing anything disloyal, she locked up all Hsiang's jewellery and expensive clothes. This, however, angered Hsiang so much that she decided to take revenge in a drastic way. On one carefully chosen afternoon, Hsiang went to the police station, reporting that she had been badly molested by her madam. She could even show to the duty officers bruises on different parts of her body as 'evidence'. Then she made two requests of the officers: first, she would like to leave the brothel and to marry the man in question, and, secondly, she wanted to have her confiscated possessions back. Impressed by this hard evidence of abuse, the policemen escorted Hsiang back to her brothel, went into her room, and forced open the locked wardrobe for her. This took place when the madam was out of town; when she returned, she was threatened by the police to bring charges against her for molestation, which sounded frightening enough to inhibit her from pursuing the happy Hsiang (*HTJP* 1929: 4.4, 17 Sept.).

Sometimes, a madam could be found surprisingly weak in the face of the 'free body' prostitutes. For example, once the madam of a brothel in Canton was distressed by a serious drop in business in her establishment. After close investigation, she was convinced that it was mainly due to the fact that all her girls had a reputation for keeping Cantonese opera singers as paramours, an act that was generally disliked by contemporary 'drinkers'. The madam, we are told, did not have the right or the power to interfere in the personal liberty of her girls. Nor had she the determination to dismiss all the girls from the brothel—'their roots in this establishment are too deep to be pulled out easily'. Eventually, the madam found a simple resolution: she closed down her brothel on the grounds of financial stringency and had it reopened some months afterward. All the newly recruited prostitutes were subjected to a 'thorough' examination on their previous histories of employment to ensure that they did not have a record of intimate association with Cantonese opera stars (*Chu-kiang hsing-ch'i hua-pao* 1927: vii. 5). A madam was not empowered to oppress her inmates at will, nor had the madam in this case chosen to resolve the problem in a way that could be considered as oppressive. Her reluctance to dismiss her girls forcibly also displayed a madam's willingness to deal with her prostitutes calmly and rationally.

Working in a Living Hell?

Exploitation and the maltreatment of prostitutes, while by no means eradicated during this period, were not necessarily becoming more common and widespread either. It seems that high-class prostitutes in Republican Canton, as in other Chinese coastal cities, could be so much better-off than most contemporary women that it casts serious doubt on whether they were financially exploited or physically maltreated in the true sense of the words.

First, with regard to their working environment, surviving sources show that high-class brothels in late-Ch'ing and Republican Canton were no filthy dens, but clean and lavishly decorated floating establishments. A late nineteenth-century European traveller recorded the glamour of these 'flower boats':

> These boats resemble enormous Venetian Gondolas. The greatest part of the hold is taken up by the saloon, furnished with the best style of furniture. In the middle is placed a large round marble topped table; the chairs are of Chinese ebony elaborately carved, whilst the saloon is lighted up by European swinging lamps... The front of the boat is equally carved and gilded, and the whole line of splendidly illuminated boats offers in the evening an enchanting view.[40] (Schlegel 1894: 5–7)

Cantonese brothel-goers also found them comfortable and luxurious. One recorded that most of the famous courtesans lived in their private compartments on these boats, and access to them was strictly limited to very close friends. Their rooms were clean, and decorated according to their personal tastes. In one case, all the window frames were elaborately carved; the curtains were made of pearls; ivory sculptures were displayed, and the table held a bowl of ink and other accessories for brush-writing. It was said of this particular woman that 'When one enters [her room], all that is vulgar is banished in an instant. No client who is not a literatus or scholar has ever been admitted' (*LNFY c.*1930s: 40).

In another case, the enormous income earned by a popular late-Ch'ing courtesan enabled her to lead an extravagant life. Her bedroom was particularly lavishly furnished:

> In her room, all the screens are embroidered, [and] windows elaborately [carved]. The tables and chairs of sandalwood are finely carved...On a shelf are displayed antique

bronze sacrificial tripods. [There is also] a screen of marble, a Yu-K'u-style cauldron [from the Sung Dynasty], a fine red vase, and other [precious items], each of them worth a few hundred taels of gold! Her flat wooden pillow is decorated with gold-plated rhinoceroses whose sparkle would startle anyone. Beneath the bed is . . . [a sculpture of] a gold lion and a seal carved from a piece of precious stone . . . On the wall are hung a number of music-box clocks.[41] (*CKMH* 1974: 23)

By the late 1920s, the working and living environments of popular courtesans were apparently no less extravagant. A contemporary brothel-goer reminisces that once he visited a prostitute whose room was luxuriously and elegantly decorated, the wall hung with scrolls and brush paintings presented to her by 'well-known men' (Ts'un shih 1988: 244). Another old-style scholar wrote that he was once invited to a feast at a high-class brothel in Hong Kong. When he entered the living room of this establishment, he was amazed by the large number of scrolls hanging on the wall, given to the courtesans of the house as gifts. These calligraphies were mainly verse and couplets composed by the social notables who frequented the place. Some of them, however, were not that good at all in the critical eyes of this scholar 'drinker' (*HTJP* 1921: 2.4, 13 May). A European traveller once again was very impressed by the tidiness, cleanliness, and luxury of the city's floating brothels: 'The floor of the principal room where "transaction" take [*sic*] place is covered with a precious carpet. The furniture is usually in excellent taste. Lamps of rare designs, with crystal ornaments, are suspended from the ceiling' (Leeuw 1934: 75–6). Inside a 'blue house' on land,

> It was cool and immaculate. A bright matting covered the floors. There were hangings, severe and straight, of green and white cloth threaded with gold . . . The upper part of the walls, including the doors, were of lattice work with beautiful wood carvings. Many scrolls were hung on the walls which shows, no doubt, the charming and virtuous sentiments [of their prostitute owner] . . . Against the walls were cabinets containing rare porcelains and there were rugs of silk and camel's hair everywhere . . . She opened a door in the corridor. It was a small room of sandalwood, a room that might belong to a palace. She turned and resumed the conversation in which she had been so well trained. (ibid. 106–8).

In a short article intended to reveal 'the misery' of low-class prostitutes in Canton, its author used emotive language in order to impress his readers. But surprisingly, the conditions of the low-class brothels he described in this article were not as bad as those portrayed in Ou-yang Shan's short story 'Tsai shen ching li'. There was nothing in these brothels that truly upset its author, except that the areas in which they were located were crowded with men who had flocked there to look around. Its author visited three of these brothels at random. The first was said to be 'plainly decorated [and] poorly lit', while the other two were both 'nicely appointed and clean' (Chou Hsia-min 1934: 8–9). Even the tiny floating brothels on which the 'water-chicken' (low-class Tanka prostitutes) worked were said to be beautifully decorated and impressively clean (Hu P'o-an et al. 1923 ii. 13, ch. 7).[42] A 1926 Canton guidebook also commented that some of these lower-class floating brothels were 'unusually clean and tidy, well decorated and furnished' (Liu Tsai-su 1926: 115). The reputedly decent and hygienic environment of most brothels in Canton, in great contrast to the filthy and degraded establishments in Victorian London (Harrison 1979: 221–4), may have been due to the supposedly frequent inspections conducted by the local health authority (once a week for low-class brothels, and bi-weekly for others) as stipulated by the Prostitution Control Regulations.[43]

Unlicensed brothels did not have to be filthy or oppressively tiny either. A reader wrote an article to a local newspaper describing his experience of visiting a top-of-the-range clandestine bordello located in a prime suburban area. The house was an impressive Western-style bungalow, built of concrete and stones, guarded by palisades and a huge iron gate of artistic design, and curtained with attractive, colourful fabrics. Once inside the building, he was led into a small living room where he was served with tea and cigarettes by an attractive middle-aged woman. This room, though small, was beautifully decorated with exquisite furniture and paintings of a kind one would expect to find in the homes of nobility. This was the perfectly decent workplace of three unlicensed prostitutes. To his disappointment, the madam told him smilingly that her girls had regular clients staying the night but that he would be welcome to visit again. While leaving he met a stunningly attractive girl who, together with this appealing establishment, had made such a great impression on this reader that he could hardly stop thinking about it (especially about her) for the rest of the night (Ai Ai 1928, 29 Mar.).

What captured the attention of many contemporary, 'ordinary' writers on prostitutes was their lavish clothing. Writing in the late-Ch'ing period, Yü Chiao-ch'ing was impressed by the gorgeous, and fashionable silk clothes of some high-class courtesans, which were in sharp contrast to the simple cotton garments worn by ordinary women (Yü Chiao-ch'ing 1909: 19). In an extreme case, a popular courtesan wore only silk, and all her hairpins were made of precious stones (*CKMH* 1974: 5276). By the 1930s, prostitutes in most treaty-ports were keen followers of Western fashion (Wang Shu-nu 1988: 308–9).[44] Even streetwalkers in Canton usually dressed lavishly (Lo-ti-jên 1930: 2; Chang-lao-yeh 1930: 2). And contemporary cartoonists' impressions of prostitutes were of stunningly fashionable women whose appearance hardly shows any sign of misery or traces of maltreatment (e.g. *Pan-chiao man-hua* 7/2 (1932: 6); 9/6 (1932: 5)). The fact that many prostitutes, especially those employed in the high-class establishments, dressed so well tempted many social critics to believe that these women entered the business to make money to fulfil their insatiable desire for expensive clothing (Ch'en Li-chu et al. 1991: 470–1).

The basic working environment of most prostitutes in Canton in this period, therefore, appears not to have been as grim as we are sometimes led to believe. Of course, a relatively comfortable workplace and fancy clothing did not necessarily mean that life as a prostitute was easy or enjoyable. When we examine other aspects of a prostitute's life, however, it seems unlikely that outright exploitation and maltreatment were the only things she experienced.

Rules of Respect

In late-Imperial times, maltreatment of prostitutes by their customers at high-class brothels, though existent, was apparently uncommon. A traveller recorded: '[I]t must be said to the honor of the Chinese that they behave, even in the flower-boats, with the utmost decency . . . I never saw a simple improper gesture, nor even a simple caress as would be tolerated in Western society.' (Schlegel 1894: 4). As a Cantonese 'brothel-song' tells us, brothel-goers were always prevented from taking advantage of a girl at will (ibid. 5).

Improperly behaved clients, even in exclusive brothels, however, were sometimes found and accounts of their misbehaviour towards the girls could be read occasionally in local newspapers. On one such occasion, a bully with certain political power forced a sing-song girl, who had repeatedly refused his sexual demands, into a 'transaction' with him. During intercourse, this revengeful man inserted, unnoticed, into this poor girl's vagina a sort of odorous material that made her private parts stink for days (*KPP* 1928: 8, 18 Apr.). This, however, was apparently an isolated case rather than a common occurrence. It was also clear that many powerful clients behaved 'properly' when visiting brothels, and in the memory of contemporary 'drinkers' molestation of prostitutes was certainly not the order of the day. In another much-publicized case, Ah Hung, a high-class prostitute, was slapped across the face by a client, who was a 'powerful man' in the local tax brokerage firm responsible for collecting duties on prostitution, for refusing to let him into her room (*KPP* 1928: 8, 20 Apr.). This incident, however, was slightly more complicated than it first appeared to be. Some anxious brothel-goers even investigated this affair and surmised that the unfortunate prostitute herself should also be blamed for her improper treatment. It was stated that on the night of the incident, Ah Hung returned to her brothel from a flowery feast, slightly drunk. She retired to her private chamber, undressed, and lay naked on her bed. At this point the powerful client arrived. He knocked on Hung's door and demanded her company. Feeling tired and irritated by this late visit, Hung, a Shanghaiese, ridiculed this unwelcome visitor with exceedingly obscene language in her dialect, presuming that he was a local Cantonese. The officer, however, understood the Shanghai dialect. He was furiously jealous that Hung had received other clients but not him. Our investigator wrote that this unfortunate incident, ironically, turned Hung into a famous character who consequently received a lot more invitations from 'drinkers' than before (*KPP* 1928: 8, 25 Apr.).[45] Another interesting point is that this rather minor affair drawing so much public attention is indicative of the rarity of similar cases of abuse in the high-class brothel world.

Maltreatment of prostitutes by customers in most brothels, perhaps with the exception of the very low-class establishments, might be effectively minimized in the first place by a number of unwritten customs and rules that a brothel-goer was expected to observe, and in the second by the long process of courting, especially between high-class courtesans and their clients. Shanghai's brothels in this period provide us with interesting examples of a kind of establishment that was also found in Canton. A manual for Shanghai's brothel-goers in the late 1930s warned readers not to violate any of the 'ten commandments' that governed the behaviour of clients in high-class bordello. These rules imposed restraints on a client's conduct, ranging from his use of language when conversing with a courtesan, to the minute details of table manners. For instance, readers were strongly advised not to hug their knee-caps with their hands, or to support their cheek on their hand while sitting. Inside a brothel, they should not step on a doorsill. While dining, they should avoid breaking dining utensils or cutlery; chopsticks should not be placed across the top of rice-bowls. Inside a courtesan's room, the visitor was advised not to move about freely, nor open any drawer without permission. Violation of these rules would attract a reprimand and the contempt of both the prostitutes and the brothel's staff (Hai-shang-chüeh-wu-sheng 1939: 69–71). At high-class brothels in Canton and Hong Kong in the 1930s, an improperly behaved brothel-goer—such as those who had tried to caress a girl's body notwithstanding her refusal—could be denied any services by the both the madam and the prostitutes. A high-class brothel was a respectable place in which the manners of both customers and prostitutes were expected to remain within the principles of decency and propriety at all times (Lo Li-ming 1962: ii. 41). It is not surprising to find, therefore, that Republican Peking's brothels were highly acclaimed for their orderliness and tranquillity compared with their counterparts in the United States (Gamble 1921: 249).

Was forced sex part of the exploitation of prostitutes? Some, especially high-class ones, were apparently less exploited than is generally believed. In order to win their bodies, a client was required to follow an established pattern of courting customs that were both expensive and demanding. A client would first be required to meet a high-class prostitute initially at an elaborate 'flower restaurant' where they would be entertained by conversation and singing for something under one hour—an expensive initiation that not all brothel-goers could afford (Lo Li-ming 1962: i. 1–8; Hai-shang-chüeh-wu-sheng 1939: 9). After more rounds of such meetings, a besotted client determined to go further would start visiting the 'lady's' brothel, in which he would hold expensive tea parties and banquets in order to get close to the courtesan.[46] After a few such occasions, if the courtesan agreed, the client would approach her madam and negotiate a price for spending a night with her. On the appointed evening, a small banquet would be held at the brothel attended by close friends of the client. According to the reminiscences of one brothel-goer, this party usually had the gay atmosphere of a family gathering, rather than a straightforward sexual transaction. And only some hours later, after it was over and his friends had left, could the client retire to bed with his long-sought-after lady (Ts'un Shih 1988: 243–5; Lo Li-ming 1962: i. 1–8).

An 'intimate patron' of a high-class courtesan was 'obliged' to 'give face' to her and her brothel by occasionally holding big banquets there, especially during civic or religious festivals (Liu Wan-chang 1928: 24).[47] Moreover, he needed to keep his lady happy by buying her gifts. In one case, a rich businessman in Canton spent three years patronizing a popular courtesan before he eventually won her body; and once she even refused to entertain him, though he eventually paid her 3,000 yüan just to attend his banquet (Wu Yü et al. 1988: 438–9). In 1930s Hong Kong, a former regular brothel-goer writes that it was not unusual for a client to spend over 10,000 Hong Kong dollars, and two to three months, courting a popular prostitute before she agreed to accept him as a more intimate client (Lo Li-ming 1962: iii. 6).[48] The long process of familiarization between courtesan and client probably helped reduce the psychological pressure suffered by a prostitute through having to have sex with an otherwise total stranger. This privilege of long courting was apparently denied to a large number of ordinary Chinese women. Hence, it is interesting to note that from the point of view of 'poor' brothel-goers, it was they who were 'exploited' by prostitutes in this long process of financially exhausting courtship. Prostitutes were believed to be adept at playing tricks on them that squeezed the last penny from their wallets (Ah Mên 1928: i. 3).

Patrons of high-class brothels did not expect to receive instant or casual sexual favours during their visits. For 'raw sex', most would opt to go to lower-class establishments where 'bodies' were more readily sold. It is, however, interesting to find that some Cantonese brothel-goers seemingly possessed an ambiguous, even hesitant, attitude towards purchasing sex from brothels. To them, it was morally wrong, and even sinful, to demand casual or frequent sexual favours from prostitutes, including the low-class ones. This attitude was reflected in an article that recorded the experience of a regular to low-class brothels. This man, we are told, was once seriously ill. One night on his sickbed he had a dream in which he was led to a dark, chilly alley, and entered a dimly lit house where he was struck by the sight of a woman's face, as pale as quicklime, and by a strong odour of foul air. On closer observation he was appalled at how ugly the woman was, with a big mouth, thick, dark eye-brows, round eyes resembling those of mouse, thin and untidy hair, and a chicken-like skin. This woman introduced him to other 'ladies' in the house. They all had bound feet, wore heavy make-up, dressed in colourful lingerie, and served their guests with wine that was as murky as muddy water. They insisted that he should stay the night there. He asked where he was, and was told that this was the purgatory for brothel-goers. Frightened at the answer, he wept and begged for mercy. When he asked the way home, he was led and then pushed into a big dark cave. At this point he woke up, terrified. Since having this dream, the man swore that he would never again visit a low-class brothel in his life (*HTJP* 1912, 18 Apr.). By patronizing these low-class establishments where one's sexual desire could be fulfilled instantly, one also took the risk of committing a sin that would lead to divine punishment. Inferring from this author's logic, one might at best visit a brothel for pleasure, not for 'raw sex', and therefore low-class whorehouses should be avoided. Carnal pleasure, of course, might be sought, but only occasionally and with respect to the rules of restraint generally observed in established brothels. This principle of avoiding casual sex on the part of brothel-goers might help explain their willingness to observe the rules of respect especially in high-class bordellos.

It must be mentioned in passing that the orderliness of most brothels, including the high-class ones, was not unchallenged, and at times could be seriously disrupted by undisciplined clients. This was revealed by occasional newspaper reports of disturbances or rows at brothels. Most of these cases involved unruly off-duty soldiers who paid little respect to brothel etiquette (e.g. *KPP* 1928: 6, 22 May and 8 June).[49] These, however, should be taken as isolated incidents rather than a general pattern; the news value of these cases is indicative of this point.

Most historians of Chinese prostitution believe that low-class whores were the most exploited and abused group of prostitutes in 'old China'. These girls are always described as helpless and silent victims of maltreatment. Their sufferings and exploitation were presumably best reflected by the frequent straightforward sexual services that they were forced to provide to a large number of men in a day's work. It seems logical to assume that in terms of both working conditions and treatment by clients, low-class harlots were inferior to their high-class 'sisters'. But this picture of inferiority was, and still is, constructed mainly upon insubstantial 'reports', general assumptions, or contemporary anti-prostitution literature (e.g. Ping chin-ya 1989: 247–8; Wang shu-nu 1988: 351–4). However, the world of low-class prostitution in Canton (Hong Kong too) received little attention from contemporary pretentious writers on this subject and, henceforth, remains largely hidden. Relatively bias-free and reliable information is difficult to come by and always sketchy when available. Judging by such data, however, the assumed link between low-class prostitution and maltreatment is not an unquestionable one. The following examples, drawn from news reports and archival records of a charity organization, may give us some food for thought.

One evening at around nine o'clock, a small group of off-duty infantrymen visited a low-class brothel in Canton. They asked for Yin Tsai, one of the inmates they fancied, to accompany them at a 'tea party' (*ta cha-wei*) in the brothel. (*Ta cha-wei*, in the parlance of the local brothel world, meant a client and his favourite prostitute would have tea and snacks inside her bedroom, but he would not spend the night there) (Lo Li-mung 1962: i. 7.) To the disappointment of this group of visitors, Yin Tsai already had a man to serve. She politely asked her disappointed customers to come early on another day. The soldiers, however, not only refused to leave, but also forced their way into her bedroom and demanded favours. Both Yin Tsai and her guest tried but failed to reason with them. Out of frustration and jealousy, these violent men broke furniture in the bedroom and even beat up the poor girl and her courageous client. In view of this, the madam of this brothel ran to call for police intervention. Seven men were eventually apprehended. During their interrogations at the local precinct, they repeatedly apologized for their misbehaviour. Apparently to avoid antagonizing the army too much, these men were discharged after signing a pledge against similar misconduct in the future (*KPP* 1928: 6, 24 Apr.). This piece of sketchy information provides us with a rare glimpse into this hidden world. First, this report showed that even a low-class prostitute did not have to receive as many clients as were available; she was not public property, so to speak. Secondly, if the work schedule of Yin Tsai represented that of most of her 'sisters', it is then clear that they were not expected to work round the clock to satisfy the sexual demands of needy clients. By nine in the evening, she had already entertained her last guest of the day and was apparently in no mood, or need, for more. Thirdly, her madam, as far as the report reveals, had neither forced Yin Tsai to entertain this eager group of clients, which could have brought more income, nor allowed her to be maltreated, even at the risk of herself being hurt by the soldiers. Protection of a prostitute against abuses, though it came late in this case of Yin Tsai, did exist. Last but not least, the availability of such non-sexual services as 'tea parties' at Yin Tsai's brothel, as well as the principle of serving a limited number of clients, indicates that some sort of rules of respect were applied even in low-class whorehouses, allowing them to be run with 'decency' and in reasonable order.

In the Po Leung Kuk archive is kept the brief biographical account of T'ai Tsai, a low-class prostitute in Hong Kong. This poor girl was born in Shanghai but sold to a brothel in Kwangtung when she was 5 years old. By 13, she had been resold three times. Since she was 14 she had been asked by her foster mother to entertain Western and Chinese customers on a small floating brothel. For the whole year as a prostitute, as she told the interviewer, she had served two Western and four Chinese clients (Po Leung Kuk 1911: pt. 1). This hardly fits the stereotyped picture of a low-class whore who was generally assumed to sell her body against her will to an unlimited number of men around the clock.

A Life of 'Selling Smiles'

Some prostitutes were so spoilt by their customers that the quality of their services, it was lamented, had plummeted compared with late-Ch'ing times. Their work-load seemed to have become much lighter than that of their predecessors. Sometimes the roles were reversed and it was the clients who served their beloved courtesans (for details, Hai-shang-chüeh-wu-shêng 1939: 9, 14). The proud manner of some of these high-class courtesans rendered abuse against them unlikely. As a contemporary recorded:

> Prostitutes of this class never ask your name [—a basic courtesy]. They do not know how to entertain their clients with singing. When I ask them questions, they reply in terse monosyllables. Very seldom do they [take the initiative to] talk to you. [Some of them even] do not utter a single word as long as the banquet lasts. Occasionally, [if you] venture to touch their hands, they immediately avoid you... When the banquet is over, they [immediately] and rudely ask their clients to pay. When given copper coins, they will throw them onto the floor to test their genuineness... Even towards a client who has patronized [a prostitute] ten times before, her attitude is just the same. Her icy manner makes you feel as if you are sitting in a snow-bound room. (Hu Po-an et al. 1986: ii. 4, ch. 7)

A brothel-goer wrote in 1928 that the most popular courtesan in Shao-chou (in northern Kwangtung), Hua Lin, earned herself the nickname 'thermos jug' among her 'fans'. She was called as such because of her outward indifferent disposition, but inward passionate character. Her passion for a client she liked, however, was said to be short-lived and rarely lasted more than 24 hours (*KPP* 1928: 8, 1 May). Another highly popular high-class prostitute in Canton, Leng Hung (Cold Red), whose cold manner and impudent attitude towards customers, combined with her suggestive expression, had 'captured' a great number of fans. She was so icy, dour, and haughty that to see her smile was regarded as a brothel-goer's once-in-a-life-time experience (Hao-chi-sheng 1928: 2). Another brothel-goer wrote that popular high-class prostitutes in Hong Kong shared a similar demeanour. He pointed out that most of them had a habitual haughty expression, the kind of look that seemed to signal to their clients that they were 'holy and inviolable', and their 'demands over all matters have to be fulfilled to their satisfaction' (*KPP* 1928: 8, 15 Mar.). Hence, the common description of the prostitute's lot as a 'life selling smiles' (*mai hsiao shêng-ya*) was not always true. Smiles, it seems, were only sold to those who could pay well. A Cantonese song tells how even low-class Tanka prostitutes could be snobbish, money-oriented, and very impolite to customers. Niggardly or improperly behaved clients were always refused and scolded as 'doomed prisoners' (*chien ting*) or 'sick cats' ('Shui-chi chien ch'a', in Chi-hsien-hsiao-yin *c.*1926: 52), and sometimes even punched (Hua-ts'ung-fên-tieh 1934: 21). A local writer recorded that Cantonese prostitutes were well-known for their aloof attitude and recalcitrant demeanour. At the slightest excuse, they could 'explode' in front of their customers. 'Flower feasts' were always impolitely and hurriedly served, and the prostitutes arrived and left at will without notifying their clients. Nor did they even bother to remember the names of their regular clients, which was considered an insult to a brothel-goer. The writer lamented that some prostitutes did not even provide their customers with the basic service, which was bartering smiles for money (K'ung Fu-an 1934: 16). Another Cantonese reiterated that most prostitutes in Canton had become so arrogant that when they attended 'flower feasts' they stayed only briefly, entertained their clients perfunctorily, and left earlier than they should. He proposed, somewhat sardonically, that these girls should be punished by the government accordingly (Ping Lan 1934: 14).

A social novel about the life of two courtesans in 1920s Hong Kong shows that some prostitutes could be very wilful. Once, one of them becomes angry with one of her regulars who she mistakenly thinks is chasing another girl. She takes revenge on him by deliberately losing heavily in a *mahjong* game in which he asks her to play a few rounds for him. Then, without a word to him or his friends, she simply leaves. That evening, the deeply embarrassed customer waits for hours at her brothel for her return, in the hope of begging her pardon. Anticipating this, the prostitute stays elsewhere that night (Sung Yü 1989: ch. 17). In another non-fictional case, a popular high-class prostitute in Canton named Hsüeh Ch'ün was reported to have castigated an intimate client of hers for being unfaithful to her. The man was a dentist and had established a 'close relationship' with Hsüeh Ch'ün for over a year. This intimacy, however, was disrupted by another prostitute, who was a former workmate of Hsüeh Ch'ün, with whom the dentist fell in love. One evening, Hsüeh Ch'ün received the news that the pair were having a secret liaison at a local hotel. She rushed to the place and caught them red-handed. The furious Hsüeh Ch'ün then berated the couple and cursed the unfaithful client in exceedingly foul language. In fear and trembling, the dentist expressed remorse and placated her by asking his 'paramour' to return to her brothel. Hsüeh Ch'ün then left the hotel in a victorious mood (*KPP* 1928: 8, 9 June). The prostitute had even more standing, in this case, than her client, despite his 'superior' social status as a surgeon and a customer.

Wilful behaviour as such, however, occasionally backfired. Sweet Peach, a high-class prostitute in a county capital not far from Canton, was well known for her haughty attitude towards clients, which, however, did not stop her from becoming popular in the local 'flowery world'. Although many of her regular patrons had tried to appease her by inviting her to drinking parties or banquets, she was not at all impressed. These disappointed men, reportedly, continued to be ignored by her. Then one night Sweet Peach ran into an equally proud, but also strong-willed, client who was a senior officer in the local police force. She was late to an appointment with this officer at a restaurant. Upon arrival, she did not apologize for that and, as a result, he scolded her. She, did not take that lightly and retorted by making sarcastic remarks about him. Infuriated, the officer ordered his body-guards to tie her up, and threatened to charge her for 'maltreating a client'. The report did not say anything about Sweet Peach's reaction to all the fuss: she seemingly did not beg for mercy in tears. But it did mention that 'someone' came to arbitrate the dispute. Eventually Sweet Peach was released unhurt on the condition that the officer would not be charged for the feast, nor owe any fees to her brothel (*KPP* 1928: 6, 26 Mar.).

In the 1920s and 1930s, popular courtesans and sing-song girls alike were always trailed by faithful fans who tried all means to win their favour. In dance halls, restaurants, and theatres frequented by their sex-idols, plenty of these 'chicken chasers' (*chui chi k'o*) or 'maternal uncle teams' (*chiu tuan*) could be seen (Mo-têng-nü 1934: 4).[50] One random note about a beautiful but choosy prostitute tells how, when a rich client was successful in winning her after a long and expensive courtship, the news dismayed many of those hopeful clients whom she had turned down (Hsin-tung-fang-shuo 1931: 29).

Many prostitutes not only took great pride in their popularity, but capitalized on it as well. Once, two of the most popular courtesans in Canton, namely Red Flower and Angel, competed with each other for fame. With the financial support of certain clients, Red Flower spent several thousand yüan on a grand banquet to which all the prostitutes in Canton were invited. In response, Angel organized a similar feast at the same restaurant. In order to show off her generosity, all the prostitutes in the city, both licensed and unlicensed, are said to have been invited. On the day of the feast, so many clients and other courtesans sent her baskets of flowers as a greeting that the whole neighbourhood was fragrant with their scent (Ts'un Shih 1988: 245–6). For prostitutes who flourished, their ill-famed job could apparently still be an enjoyable one that bestowed on them the kind of power, frivolity, and prestige about which most contemporary women, as well as men, dared not even dream.

Wealth and Power

Some prostitutes were able to enjoy a wide range of 'privileges' normally denied to ordinary people. With military officers being regular customers of brothels, these girls seemed to be protected from harassment by unscrupulous ordinary soldiers, abusive clients, or riff-raff generally (Wan Yung 1930: 97; Chu Hsia-min 1934: 8). In fact, prostitutes could be as much bullies as military men. Like common soldiers, they often refused to pay fares on public transport or to buy tickets to cinema shows (*NYSP* 1928: 24, 12 Sept.). They also got away with sabotaging the dignity of powerful men such as inflated army officers and government officials because these men 'enjoyed being hit' by their favourite courtesans, even in public ('Yang-ch'êng chao-yao-ching', *KCMKJP* 1926: 4, 1 July).

The common perception of the prostitute as a poor, exploited 'money-tree' (*yao-ch'ien shu*) whose income was always reaped by her madam was not universally true. Some high-class prostitutes were able to save enormous amounts of money with no interference from their madams. Late-Ch'ing random notes on prostitution were full of descriptions of the affluence of famous courtesans in Canton. The popular courtesan Pu Hsiao-ku, for instance, was so well-off that she was able to turn down almost all invitations from her clients, including the rich and powerful. To free herself from the vociferous protests of her madam she purchased a number of mansions by the river, in which she spent the rest of her life 'reciting Buddhist scriptures and burning incense' (Yü Chiao-ching 1909: 21). Another famous courtesan became betrothed with a dowry of her own savings of a few thousand *taels* of gold, though her lover in the end was too proud to marry her because her personal wealth was much greater than that of his family (ibid. 28). Although these cases may not necessarily help illustrate the experiences of prostitutes in later times in Republican Canton, they still provide us with evidence that we should hesitate to assume that all prostitutes were indigent and invariably subjected to ruthless financial exploitation by their madams.

Cantonese prostitutes in the Republican period were seemingly no worse off, and this was manifested in a number of ways. Some prostitutes were so wealthy, for instance, that they became the prey of good-looking scroungers.[51] One affluent clandestine prostitute was swindled out of a box of expensive jewellery (Tsui-mien-shan-jên *c.*1920s: 33–5). A journalist ridiculed the fact that a prostitute earned much more than a teacher (*KCMKJP* 1926: 4; 9 Nov.). Cantonese brothel-goers were also well known for their profligacy in placating prostitutes which allegedly dwarfed even that of the big spenders in Central China (Wang shu-nu 1988: 304–5).[52] In Hong Kong in the 1930s, many successful high-class prostitutes were able to save substantial amounts of money from their income. One of them, Hsiao Fêng, was very generous in providing financial assistance to the poor and needy. Her good deeds, as local legend goes, were eventually rewarded when she married a good husband, became a legitimate wife, and led a happy family life (Lo Li-ming 1962: ii. 39–40).

The riches of some prostitutes was evident in another case. During the mid-1920s, the 'flowery business' in Hong Kong and Canton suffered as a result of the political turmoil in South China. The year-long Canton-Hong Kong Strike struck a further blow to brothel business especially in the Colony. In this period of difficulty, three enterprising prostitutes from a high-class bordello there came up with a plan of rescue. Inspired by their counterparts in Shanghai, these three 'sisters' envisioned that business could be rejuvenated if costs could be cut and gimmicks employed to attract clients. They planned to rent a small flat, have it renovated luxuriously, and hire a team of attractive young maids and, most importantly, a reasonably good chef. This was intended to help a client save on costly 'flower banquets', which usually took place at exclusive restaurants. To fund this project, these three 'sisters' pooled a sum of 10,000 Hong Kong dollars, which was indeed not a small amount by contemporary standards.[53] The business of this new establishment was reportedly prosperous (*KPP* 1928: 8, 26 Mar.).

It is interesting to note from contemporary newspaper reports that the relative wealth of some prostitutes had rendered them the targets of petty crime. Examples of this abound, and the phenomenon seems to have long antedated the period of this study.[54] One evening in 1895, a group of five men visited a brothel in the Bund in Canton. While being served with tea and snacks, they pulled out revolvers and knives and demanded money. Although the report did not mention any loss on the part of the inmates, the madam was robbed of more than ten *taels* of platinum (*HTJP* 1895, 2 Feb.). For Shao Ya, a former prostitute in Canton, a burglary case at her flat cost her dearly. Shao Ya had worked in a high-class brothel until she was married to a government bureaucrat as a concubine. Marital life for her, however, was an utterly unhappy experience: it was characterized by ceaseless quarrels with the principal wife. Unwilling to submit herself to this fate, she moved out from this household into a flat at her own expense, thanks to her shrewdness in amassing substantial income from her lucrative job. One evening, when returning home from a film with her maid, she found that her flat had been ransacked by burglars who took away a handful of trophies worth more than 3,000 yüan. These included one precious jade bracelet, one pair of diamond earrings framed with platinum, a certain amount of cash, and some expensive apparel (*YHP* 1934: 1, 27 Mar.). In the case of a brothel robbery in Hong Kong in 1910, jewellery worth 130 dollars was taken away (*HTJP* 1910, 26 July). In 1911, a penniless brothel-goer was caught stealing clothes from a prostitute whom he had visited. He hoped to pawn these goods to pay the bill for the visit (*HTJP* 1911, 29 July).[55] In the same year, a prostitute in Hong Kong took two of her clients to court for stealing cash from inside her chamber (*HTJP* 1911, 21 Sept.). Another brothel visitor was sentenced to six months in prison, in addition to a flogging and being put into a cangue (pillory), for stealing personal items such as clothes and a golden ear-pick from three prostitutes in a high-class brothel (*HTJP* 1911, 10 Nov.). Two maids working for a high-class prostitute were sentenced to imprisonment for stealing from their mistress jewellery worth over HK$200 and some cash (*HTJP* 1912, 10 Jan.). A ruffian in Hong Kong was sentenced to six months of hard labour and cangued for four hours for robbing a prostitute of her golden necklace (*HTJP* 1921: 1.3, 19 Apr.). A less fortunate prostitute was robbed on her way back to the brothel of a golden necklace, a cultured pearl necklace, and a jade pendant, all costing over HK$100. No one was apprehended for this (*HTJP* 1915: 1.3, 28 May). In a burglary case, a prostitute lost one diamond ring worth HK$400 (*HTJP* 1915: 1.3, 30 Apr.). There were also brothel-goers who were caught for stealing trousers, petty cash, smoking pipes, and even an electrical fan from prostitutes (*HTJP* 1915: 1.3, 12 May; 3.4, 13 May; and 1.3, 16 May). A prostitute from a middle-range brothel in Kowloon reported to the police that she was hypnotized by a young client and then robbed of one pair of golden bracelets, two gold rings, one golden waist-watch, a pair of golden earrings, and one jade bracelet (*HTJP* 1921: 1.3, 12 May). A 23-year-old prostitute named Red Rose fell victim to fraud. She had paid one of her customers, who claimed to be a dealer of expensive furniture from Italy, a sum of HK$260 for several items of imported home furnishings. The goods, however, were never delivered (*HTJP* 1927: 2.3, 21 May). A prostitute in Canton reported to the police that a regular patron of hers had stolen: one jade ring which worth HK$300, one gramophone, and many of the latest gramophone records (*YHP* 1932: 3, 18 Nov.). Most of these examples refer to the experiences of prostitutes in Hong Kong not because it was unique in this respect, but because such occurrences were better documented. Similar occurrences could most probably be also observed in Canton. All these cases share one common point: that the prostitutes were victims rather than perpetrators of petty crimes, and this was so because of their relative affluence in the eyes of criminals.

The affluence of some prostitutes and their semi-luxurious lifestyle was reflected in the kinds of goods advertised in a magazine that published mainly photographs and profiles of popular courtesans in Hong Kong. Advertisements of jewellery shops, Western-style clothing shops, fashionable hair salons, and high-class Western restaurants, suggest that its readers, who were mainly prostitutes and brothel-goers, were potential, or regular, consumers of these luxury goods and expensive services (*Hua ying* 1, 1931).[56] These fashionably clad prostitutes, alongside women socialites from notable families, were said to help set the trends of high fashion for the local women who could afford to follow (*KPP* 1928: 8, 31 May). The act of pairing these two categories of women in the discussion was already in itself an interesting indication of the presence in this period of an ambivalently positive popular attitude towards seemingly prosperous prostitutes, a topic that is further discussed later.

Another indication of the affluence of some prostitutes in Republican Canton was that they patronized male entertainers. Along with other rich women, they delighted in chasing famous Cantonese opera stars—an expensive 'hobby' because these actors were already quite rich. We learn from contemporary reports that some prostitutes spent a fortune, or even their entire savings, on appeasing and enticing their favourite actors to maintain intimate relations with them. Such intimacy, which was built upon purely materialistic interests, was said to have been short-term, usually lasting as long as the girls were able to supply their idols with expensive gifts. The careers of many high-class prostitutes were ruined as a result.[57] This phenomenon had become so common that it was adopted as the theme of a Cantonese opera, a comedy about a well-off prostitute, Hua Ying, who tries to woo a famous opera actor Ch'iu Tsai. Hua is a fanatical fan of Ch'iu. Once, on finding out that Ch'iu is lodging at a local hotel, she bribes the hotel receptionist to give her a room next to his. In order to seduce him, she sings aloud a love-song. Noticing that Hua is dressed lavishly and bedecked with sparkling jewellery, the licentious and swindling Ch'iu gives in to temptation, and she offers him a diamond-ring for sleeping with her. Ch'iu takes the ring, but then slips away. Realizing she has been cheated, Hua sets off to search for her truant idol.[58]

Stories about rich courtesans as such were not uncommon. Whenever the superstar Ma Shih-ts'êng returned to Canton from overseas performances, for instance, it was said that the concubines of wealthy men and well-off courtesans, wearing lavish clothes and heavy make-up, would greet him at the pier. Some of them, it was said, even rolled bunches of bank notes into a ball, and threw them at him by way of ostentatious greeting (Wan Yung 1930: 93).[59]

It was held to be fashionable for famous Shanghai prostitutes, and their Cantonese counterparts too, to keep secret lovers for their own pleasure. They provided these 'little ghosts' (*hsiao-kuei*) with flats, expensive clothing, good food, and pocket-money. In return, the 'lover-slaves' were required to provide sexual services exclusively for their mistresses (Hai-shang-chüeh-wu-shêng 1939: 145–7). These well-off prostitutes were probably the first group of Chinese women to struggle and earn their way up the social ladder by hard work, albeit in an ill-famed profession. However, unlike daughters and wives in respectable families, they retained a high degree of control over their wealth, and were apparently quite free to spend it however they liked. By patronizing secret lovers, a certain amount of lost pride, dignity, and self-confidence might be regained, and a feeling of power in the ability to manipulate and to exert absolute control over at least some men could be enjoyed—a revengeful and self-reassuring act denied to most women in male-dominated China.

Means of Self-Protection

It is a simplistic view that all prostitutes have to work in horrendously abusive circumstances and be subjected to all kinds of maltreatment helplessly and silently. Contemporary materials, however, show that these women, even though some of them might work in a far-from-ideal environment, did not always take unfair treatments by their customers lightly. Prostitutes, like other citizens of this city, commanded certain knowledge of how to safeguard their own interests as much as their bodies. Self-protection was an instinctive drive.

Although abduction and the selling of women were propagated as the main causes of prostitution, it was also clear that many of these women did not submit quietly or passively to their ill fate. In a suburb of Canton, for example, there was a young wastrel who had squandered all his inherited fortune on gambling and opium smoking. As a last resort to obtain cash for sustaining his addictions, he tried to pawn his good-looking wife to an unlicensed brothel. To this end, he plotted to deceive his suspicious wife: he first asked her to accompany him on a visit to 'a friend', who was actually the madam of the brothel, and then tried to persuade her to stay once there. His normally obedient wife, however, found that too much to bear. She scolded her husband at the top of her voice for trying to force her into prostitution and compared his immoral act to that of a beast. She also recounted all his unseemly acts as a husband to the curious customers in the house. Before she left, she chided the madam for her part in this act of sin. Her husband then followed her home. Upon arrival, this infuriated wife first started another round of angry cursing against her husband to disgrace him in front of his neighbours, then she locked him out for the whole evening in revenge (*KPP* 1928: 6, 3 May). This unfortunate woman was saved by her instinctive reactions: fury and determination. In a less fortunate case, a woman from Kiangsu was allegedly deceived by some crooks and sold to a brothel in Canton. Dismayed by her disgraceful work and abusive procuress, she escaped, and sought help from a police station in the neighbourhood. Since she had no relatives in Kwangtung, she was referred to a charitable refuge for children and women, through which a marriage with a decent man was to be arranged at her request (*KPP* 1928: 6, 9 May). In another incident, it was reported that two girls from a lower-class brothel were able to run away with their clients on the same night; their lover-clients enlisted the service of an automobile, which greatly facilitated their escape plan (*YHP* 1934: 6, 15 Sept.). There was also the case of a concubine who disliked her husband's interference in her private life and gambling habit and sold herself into a brothel in Hong Kong. There, she found her madam too temperamental and abusive. One day she just sneaked out of the brothel and travelled back to Canton where she stayed safely with her adopted father (*YHP* 1934: 6, 11 Sept.). In the case of Hsiao Chi, a prostitute who had worked for high-class brothels in Canton and a county town in eastern Kwangtung, she was remembered for her shrewdness at running away from houses that she disliked. Twice she fled from the brothels to which she had pawned herself as a prostitute. On each occasion, she connived with her lover to work out an ingenious plan of escape that eventually helped her to regain freedom.[60] When Li Hsiao-cheng, a teenager brought up by a retired madam, was ordered to serve her first client, the encounter ended unhappily. On the night of her defloration, the poor girl found her client's repeated demands for sex so annoying that she refused to comply. Infuriated by her resistance, perhaps understandable for a man who had paid a substantial 100 yüan for the privilege, he resorted to violence to release his frustration on her, and allegedly beat Hsiao-cheng with a porcelain pillow. The poor girl, however, was not subdued quietly; she reacted by first crying aloud to draw the attention of the house's inmates and then dashing off to seek police protection. The man was arrested and awaited charges, while Hsiao-cheng was released at her madam's request (*YHP* 1934: 5, 2 July).

These cases reveal that the means of self-protection was not necessarily denied to the women who were forced to enter this business in this part of China. The fact that these prostitutes, both the experienced and fresh recruits, knew quite well where to seek effective protection against abuses, is an indication of the commonness of such knowledge, which was probably eagerly circulated and widely shared within their community. If they were determined to leave the business, their resourcefulness always enabled them to find a way out, which indicates also that those who remained were probably willing partners rather than passive victims.

Prostitutes were, in theory, protected by law against their madams' mistreatment. A police regulation stipulated that inspectors were to pay unexpected visits to brothels to ensure the proper treatment of prostitutes by madams and customers.[61] The effectiveness of such enforcement, however, is not known. But if this rule was indeed properly enforced, then general assumptions about the maltreatment of prostitutes must be reconsidered.

Even though police patrols might not be that reliable, many mistreated prostitutes did not hesitate actively to seek protection from the state. Police and unofficial records show that not all prostitutes would quietly endure abuse. For example, two prostitutes poured scorn on a policeman who had collected a bribe from their brothel. The humiliated officer then beat them up and ordered the closure of the whorehouse. Their madam, however, reported the incident to the police headquarters, and the culprit was duly reprimanded (*HTJP* 1928: 1.3, 3 Aug.). It is worth noting that in this case, as well as the next, the madam was on the side of her girls rather than the unreasonable clients, as was more normally described in anti-prostitution literature. Once when an off-duty officer felt disappointed at the services of a prostitute, he broke into a rage, started making false accusations against her for stealing his gold watch, and demanded compensation. The girl refused and invited the madam's arbitration. Noticing the determination of these women, the angry officer withdrew from the brothel, but returned with a group of colleagues from the barracks. They burst into the prostitute's chamber, destroyed the furniture, and tried to take away her expensive clothes. The madam reacted swiftly by blowing a whistle, catching the attention of the neighbourhood police. This eventually led to armed conflict between this group of unruly soldiers and the local police which lasted hours (*HTJP* 1924: 12, 30 Apr.). In another incident, once when an off-duty soldier visited a low-class brothel, he demanded to examine the whore's genitalia before having sex with her. When this was refused he lost his temper and threatened to whip the woman. She yelled for help, whereupon policemen were called in and the soldier arrested (*HTJP* 1928: 1.3, 9 June). In a similar case, a group of off-duty soldiers were ordered by the outraged madam and her girls to leave the brothel for this unjustified demand. This time, however, the frustrated customers took vengeance. They returned shortly with more than ten men, forced their way into the brothel, and beat up everyone in sight. All the inmates shouted for help, and the local police reacted promptly and made one arrest (*KPP* 1928: 6, 8 June). In another case, the brave madam of a low-class bordello had stopped a group of bullying off-duty soldiers from harassing an inmate of the house by shouting for police intervention. The soldiers were apprehended and later released after signing a pledge eschewing misconduct in the future (*KPP* 1928: 6, 8 June). In another context, a low-class prostitute, Yang Mei, was literally begged by a penniless customer to have sex with him, but she refused firmly on the ground that she served only those who could pay. The desperate man then began to break ornaments in her room. Yang Mei responded with shouts for help, which were promptly answered by the security men of the brothel who also instantly called for police assistance. The troublemaker was arrested by officers who arrived to the scene swiftly (*KPP* 1934: 3.4, 31 Jan.). Apparently, even a low-class prostitute knew quite well how to protect herself in the face of unreasonable demands. Another point of interest that is common to all the above incidents was that every madam sided with her girls; they were not accomplices to abusive brothel-goers.

It is interesting to note in passing that there was no trace of any secret society involvement in the operation or the protection of the local prostitution business. It is indeed surprising to find that contemporary newspapers, which published a great deal of news related to prostitution, extant municipal archival records in Canton, and those unofficial contemporary writings on the subject, contained no information at all that indicated any relation between the business of prostitution and the triads, whose influence on the local society was presumably immense in this part of South China. The absence of materials prevents us from making any definite or substantiated conclusion about the link between these two presumably natural partners. But it suffices to conjecture here that the seemingly insignificant interference by the local triads in the world of prostitution in Canton might be an indication of the effectiveness of the state's protection over these women, which was a welcome outcome of taxing prostitutes, and that might also help explain why prostitutes in this period were apparently willing to pay the rather heavy taxes levied on them.[62]

It should be also pointed out that in places where the rule of law was relatively better enforced than in Canton, prostitutes were prone to settle disputes with abusive madams or clients by legal actions. In Hong Kong, a number of litigation cases were initiated by wronged prostitutes against their customers and, occasionally, their madams. For instance, an inmate of a high-class brothel in the red-light district of West Point took one of her clients to court for beating her. He was charged with maltreating her by forcing her to drink wine mixed with vinegar and then punching her on the face, hands, and waist. This was because the jealous defendant was angry with the plaintiff who was accused of taking a

PLATE I The Waterfront of Canton in the Early 1930s. The Tallest Building in this Picture, which Housed The Sun Department Store, was the Locus of Urban Pride for Many Local Residents.

Source: *Kuang-chou chih-nan* (Canton: Kuang-chou shih-chêng-fu, 1934), p. 195.

PLATE 2 One of the Busy Streets in the Commercial Hsi-Kuan District in Canton in the Early 1930s. Western-Style High-Rise Buildings, by Then, had become a Symbol of Prosperity and Urban Pride for many Local Cantonese.
Source: *Kuang-chou chih-nan* (Canton: Kuang-chou shih-chêng-fu, 1934), p. 116.

PLATE 3 This Satirical Cartoon Entitled 'Respect the Clothes, not their Owner' (chih ching lo-i pu-ching jên), Revealed the 'Alarming' Stage of Popular Pro-Western Attitude, which was Symbolically Expressed in Unquestioned Embracing of Western Fashion by Ordinary People.
Source: *Pan-chiao man-hua*, vol. 6, no. 1 (1932), p. 5.

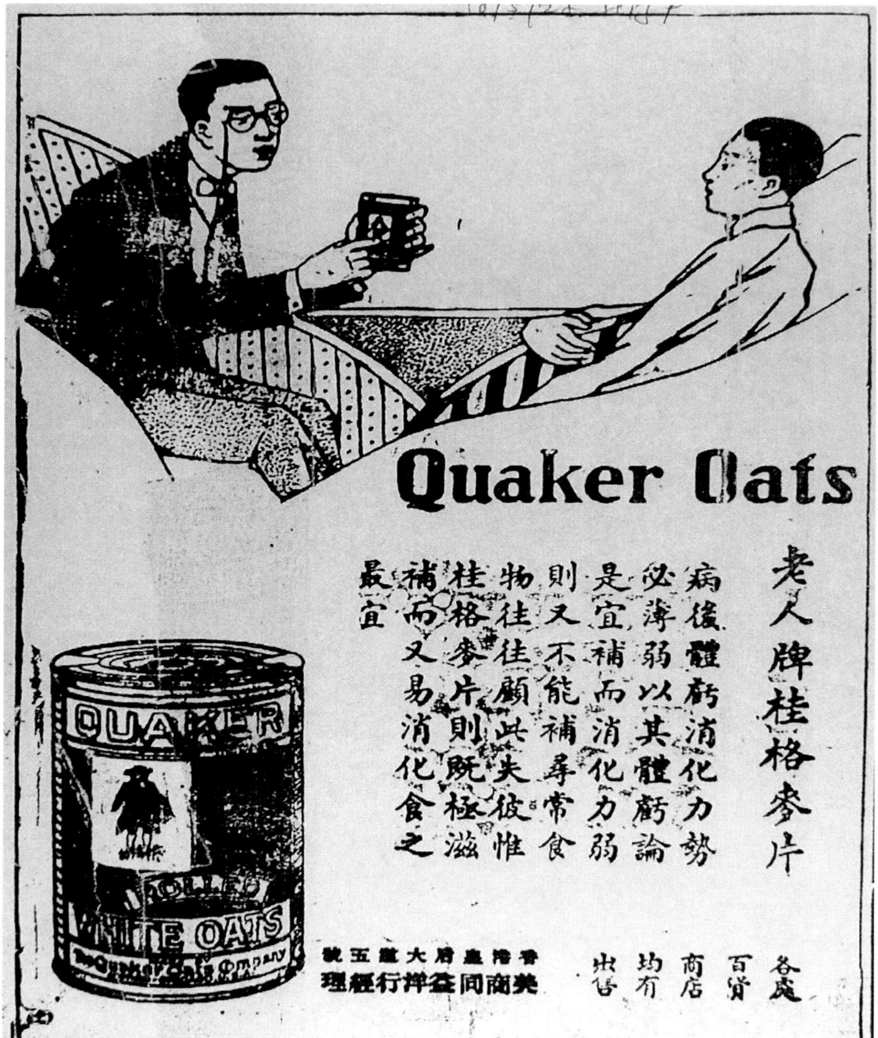

PLATE 4 The Quaker Oats Company Published a Series of Advertisements to Promote its Product Throughout the 1920s and the 1930s. Many of these Advertisements Shared One Interesting Theme—an Ill or Recuperating Man or Woman, Always Clad in Chinese Clothes, Receiving 'Smart' Advice from a Modern Doctor or Modern-Looking 'Wise Man' Whose Expertise Knowledge of Modern Medical Science is Symbolically Represented by his Formal Western Attire, to Take the Product for Strengthening his or her Body. Chineseness, in this Context, Stood for Weakness and Need of Care. The Superior Cultural Status of the West, and its Science, was Clearly Revealed.

Source: *Hua-tzu jih pao*, 1927: 18 May.

PLATE 5 Pro-West Mentality was also most Vividly Expressed in many Contemporary Medicine Advertisements. This One, Entitled 'A Different Person Before and After' (ch'ien hou liang jên), was for a Drug Company Promoting a Brand of Tonic Pills for Women. A Listless Chinese Lady, Clad in Chinese Skirt and Jacket, Sits Sadly on a Sofa—Representing One who has not Taken the Pills and Hence Remains Weak and Unattractive. By Way of Contrast, after Taking the Pills, She is Shown with Fashionable Western Clothes and Accessories, Standing Upright and Smiling Cheerfully.
Source: *Hua-tzu jih pao*, 1927: 17 August.

PLATE 6 The Title of this Cartoon is 'Tu chü chih yen' (lit. the Only One who has the Eye), which was a Pun to a Well-known Chinese Idiom 'tu chü hui yen' (the Only One who is Insightful). Standing between Two Unappealing Chinese Men who are Clothed in Traditional Chinese Outfits is a Nice-Looking Man (Presumably an Englishman) who is Wearing a Monocle, which was Described in the Complementary Text as One of the Symbols of being a Gentleman or a Bourgeoisie in the West. Monocle, According to the Text, was only for the Caucasians and Denied to the Chinese because 'God does not give the Chinese People any Deep or Large Enough Eye Socket' for Wearing it. Monocle was here made Analogous to Insightfulness. The Underlying Message was Clear: Gentlemen of the West were the only People who could see Things Perceptibly and Intelligently. *Source*: YHP, 1936: 1, 5 November.

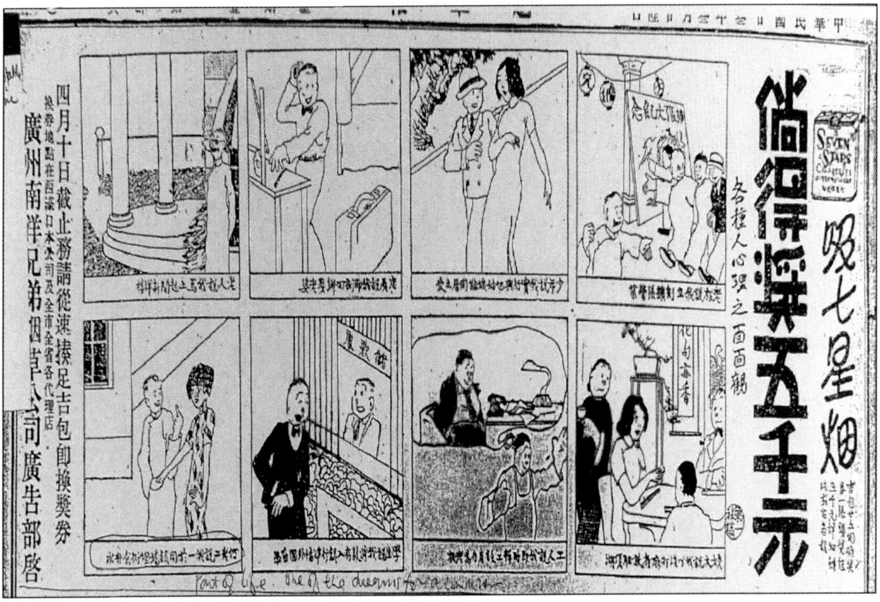

PLATE 7 In this Advertisement by a Chinese Tobacco Company, the Popular Favourable Attitude Towards Prostitution was Revealed. The Advertisement, which was about a Lucky Draw Organized by that Company, Depicts how Different Types of Winners would Spend the Handsome Prize Money of 5,000 Dollars. The Drawing on the Bottom Left Hand Corner Shows that a Mr. Ho would use the Bounty to 'Purchase' and to Marry a Prostitute, Ying-chiao, from her Brothel.
Source: YHP, 1934: 4, 26 March.

PLATE 8 Inmates of Canton's Addiction Termination Hospital Receiving Treatments of 'Spiritual Training'. In the Official Rhetoric, Opium Addiction, among other Causes, was Simplistically Ascribed to the Psychological 'Problems' Suffered by Opium users.
Source: Kuang-chou-shih chieh-yen i-yüan (ed.). *Kuang-chou-shih chieh-yen i-yüan, nien-pao* (Canton: 1937).

PLATE 9 A Rare Glimpse of the Interior of a Gambling-den in Canton. Similar Establishments were Described as Proliferating in the Back Lanes of the City During the Early 1920s.
Source: Harry A. Franck, *Roving Through Southern China* (New York: The Century Co., 1925), p. 264/5.

PLATE 10 The Exterior of One of the Twelve Gambling-Houses of Macao in the 1920s. Its Entrance was Guarded by a Uniformed Man Armed with, Seemingly, a Rifle.
Source: Aleko E. Lilius, *I Sailed With Chinese Pirates* (London: J. W. Arrowsmith, 1930), p. 32.

PLATE 11 A Row of 'Flower Boats', or Floating Brothels, Docked on the Pearl River in Canton.
Source: Aleko E. Lilius, *I Sailed With Chinese Pirates* (London: J. W. Arrowsmith, 1930), p. 151.

PLATE 12 A 'Flower Boat', or Floating Brothel, in Service in Canton in the late-Ch'ing Period.
Source: Kuang-tung shêng-li Chung-shan t'u-shu-kuan ed., *Kuang-tung pai-nien t'u-lu* (Canton: Kuang-tung chiao-yu ch'u-pan-shê, 2002), vol. 1, p. 101.

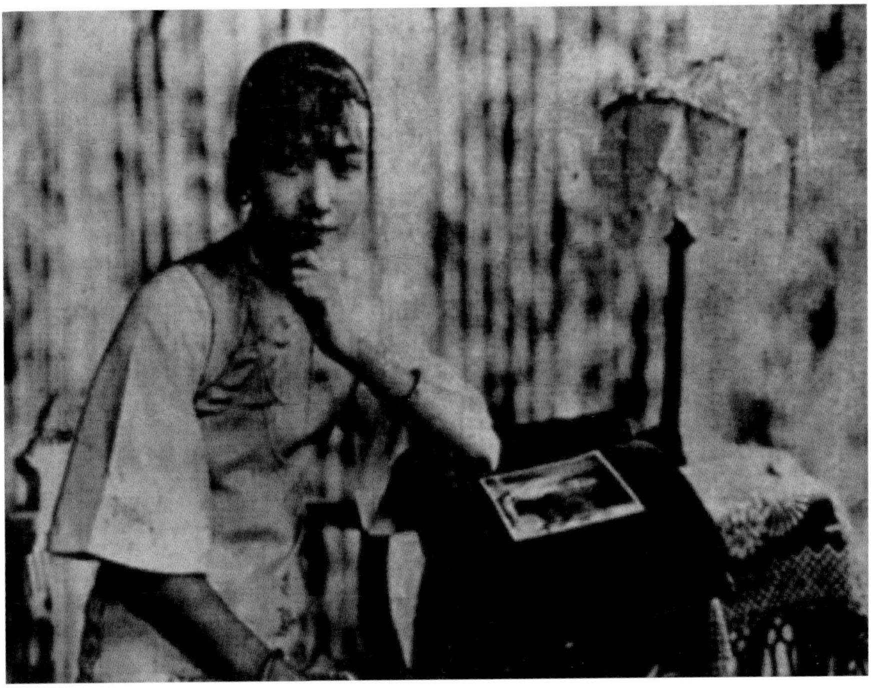

PLATE 13 Photographic Portrait of Hua Tsai, a Prostitute from a High-Class Establishment in Canton in the Late 1920s.

Source: Kuang-tung shêng-li Chung-shan t'u-shu-kuan (ed.). *Kuang-tung pai-nien t'u-lu* (Canton: Kuang-tung chiao-yu ch'u-pan-shê, 2002), vol. 1, p. 269.

PLATE 14 One of the Many Photographic Portraits of Courtesans that Appeared on Contemporary Vernacular Magazines. This one, Depicting 'Yellow Rose' who was Apparently a Popular 'Dance Girl' in Canton, Appeared in a Monthly Entitled *Wu-chia pao*, no. 2 (Nov. 1931).

PLATE 15 The Scene of an Anti-Prostitution Procession held in Canton in 1922.
Source: Kuang-tung shêng-li Chung-shan t'u-shu-kuan (ed.). *Kuang-tung pai-nien t'u-lu* (Canton: Kuang-tung chiao-yu ch'u-pan-shê, 2002), vol. 1, p. 136. The event was supported by Ch'en Ch'iung-ming's reformist government. The demonstration, however, was seemingly not so well participated, which was perhaps a sign of the popular perception of prostitution as an acceptable pastime.

PLATE 16 Li Hsüeh-fang, one of the Most Influential Cantonese Opera Singer and Actress of the 1910s and the 1920s, Helped 'Modernize' the Stage by Breaking the Male-Dominant Tradition of this Form of Opera, and Introduced Sensational Costumes and Plots Since the Early Republican Times.
Source: Ch'iu Sung-ho (ed.) *San-tung-wu po-wu-kuan Yüeh-chü tsang p'in* (Hong Kong: Hong Kong Regional Council, 1992), p. 10.

PLATE 17 Photographic Portrait of Ma Shih-ts'êng, was One of the Major Figures who Helped 'Modernize' and Commercialize Cantonese Opera During the 1920s and 1930s. The Western-Style Military Uniform he was Wearing was, in Fact, one of the Many 'Sensational' Costumes that he had Used on Stage.

Source: Ma Shih-ts'êng, *Chien-li chuang yu chi* (Canton: n.p., 1931).

PLATE 18 Hsüeh Chüeh-hsien, One of the Most Influential Actors in Modern Cantonese Opera, Cross-Dressed and Posed for a Studio Photograph in Seductive Western-Style Costume. Popular Demand for Sensation and Novelty was Clearly Reflected by the Adoption of this Kind of Costumes in Local Opera.

Source: Kuang-tung shêng-li Chung-shan t'u-shu-kuan (ed.). *Kuang-tung pai-nien t'u-lu* (Canton: Kuang-tung chiao-yu ch'u-pan-shê, 2002), vol. 1, p. 350.

strong liking to another brothel-goer (*HTJP* 1913, 29 Apr. and 7 May). In another case, a prostitute from the same area disliked her madam for mistreating her and, on the advice of one of her intimate clients, solicited help from a senior British official responsible for Chinese affairs. Under official intervention, she was allowed to walk free from this particular brothel with three other inmates to join another house in the same area (*HTJP* 1913, 29 Apr.). In the case of another prostitute, Chou Hsüeh-ying, her madam sued her for elopement. She was later arrested by a detective while leaving an expensive hotel in which she and her wealthy paramour stayed. Hsüeh-ying was eventually acquitted after a British legal consultant, enlisted by her lover, had successfully defended her case at the police station (*HTJP* 1921: 3.1, 13 Apr.). When former prostitute Wei Feng-chin was sued by her lover for stealing a diamond ring and a sum of cash from her, she did not just sit back and let fate take over. Instead, she hired a British lawyer to defend her innocence (*HTJP* 1915: 3.4, 13 May). Prostitutes, despite their presumably low social status and humble backgrounds, were well aware of their right to legal protection and sought it when needed.

The state was only one of the prostitutes' protectors; there were other unofficial means of protection too. When they were not ready or willing, many prostitutes were seemingly able to turn down the sexual demands of their clients, as a consequence of this madams might sometimes inflict punishment on their girls. This, however, was not always the case. A madam was keen to preserve the good atmosphere of her establishment, and scars on a prostitute's body might substantially lower her attraction and market value. If a prostitute was forced by her madam to sleep with a client whom she disliked, she could be very resourceful in getting out of it. One of the most common excuses was menstruation, because menstrual blood was generally considered as polluting, and the mere sight of it was said to bring bad luck to men (Eberhard 1967: 64; Gulik 1961: 151; Hai-shang-chüeh-wu- shêng 1939: 142).[63] Sometimes, an excuse was not even needed. A contemporary source tells that Cantonese prostitutes were well known for insisting on their right to refuse a client even though he had paid for her body. In bed, a prostitute might still refuse his demands and be vocal about her refusal. Sometimes, she might simply run away, leaving her disappointed client to spend the night alone (Ts'un Shih 1988: 243–5). Since this trick usually worked well, some experienced prostitutes used it as a means to solicit more tips (*pai shui*) from the client before consenting to his sexual demands (Wang Shu-nu 1988: 305).

A prostitute's 'right of refusal' was a common characteristic in Canton's brothels, at least the high-class ones, and was adopted as the theme of at least two vernacular songs. In one of them, the frustrations of a spurned customer are vividly described. The song also shows the extent of a prostitute's haughtiness (*chia tzu*), especially to clients she disliked:

> My reason for visiting a brothel is to seek happiness, not to watch your impudent behaviour. When a customer asks you to come [and entertain him], he surely has in his

> mind-and-heart a desire to enjoy 'the wind and moon' (i.e. the carnal pleasure of love-making)...I would rather you were aloof and taciturn during the banquet, than recalcitrant in bed...How could you be so happy when serving us wine, but becomes so aloof on going to bed?...What can a man do about it?...You neither pay me any attention nor howl [at me], but just lies there motionless...[When] I...try to touch your breasts, [you] suddenly scold me: 'What an annoying man you are!', and stand straight up [and leave]... So anxiously do I look forward to the dawn that my neck grows as if elongated as I look out for the sun. But cock-crow has not yet been heard. I have almost decided not to pay the bill—but that would mean a loss of face...I can hardly suppress my anger...I must be [cursed] for murdering you...in a previous life...Why must you keep torturing me by thwarting my desire?... ('Li chi-fu', in Chi-hsien-hsiao-yin *c.*1926: 51–2)

Interestingly, when such a thing happened, a customer could only put it down to bad luck; he was the one who suffered, not the prostitute.

It must be noted that not all prostitutes were, however, reluctant to sell their bodies. A contemporary writer complained that Canton's prostitutes had become even more hasty in asking their clients to 'buy' their bodies, sometimes only after one or two meetings (Ping Lan 1934: 13). The girls who joined the profession as 'free-body persons' (*tzu-yu shen*) could be very selective in choosing 'ideal' clients, and go to bed with them perhaps even with some pleasure (Ts'un Shih 1988: 237). At times, a haughty high-class prostitute might turn down the sexual demands of even her lavish clients, but would not hesitate to establish sexual liaisons with the young handsome clients she fancied (*YHP* 1934: 5, 9 July). Her right to choose was not denied, and she could discriminate between clients if she wished.

If most prostitutes were able to defend themselves against unfair treatment, then the feisty ones would probably react even more strongly. For instance, when a certain Miss Huang opened a snack shop in Canton that sold cold dairy drinks, which were in vogue then, she attracted customers by employing flirtatious young women as waitresses. The gimmick worked: many men from the neighbourhood became regulars as a result. One day, two off-duty prostitutes stopped by the shop. Two elderly customers mistook the good-looking pair for waitresses and impolitely caressed their hands and bodies. Outraged by this intolerable misconduct, the girls reacted first with verbal abuse, and soon followed that up by throwing soft-drink bottles at the old men. The fight, which scared away all the customers, resulted in the intervention of the police, and the prostitutes were asked to pay the shop compensation of a few yüan (*KPP* 1928: 6, 18 May).

At times, a mistreated prostitute could be saved by her chivalrous customers, as the following examples reveal. A sing-song girl named Shao Ying was once impolitely treated by an intimidating young wastrel after he was refused her company inside the private chamber of the restaurant. He ran onto the podium and pulled her down by force. A group in the audience in the same restaurant was furious at the unreasonable treatment that the female entertainer received. They first shouted at the bully to stop and then threatened to beat him up if the latter procrastinated. The frightened lout dashed off and never returned

(*KPP* 1928: 6, 21 May). The second instance involved two 'wild chickens', as unlicensed prostitutes were known in the local idiom. One evening at the pier, these two prostitutes, after serving a powerful client on board a pleasure boat, were harassed by a group of aggressive hoodlums. They shrieked for help, and answered promptly by the 'scouts' of their client. Outnumbered by the aggressors, the scouts reported to their master who, outraged by the discourteous treatment of his girls, rushed ashore and fired a few shots in the air with his pistol. The pier was cleared of all living souls in a matter of seconds (*KPP* 1928: 8, 11 May).

Given the social discrimination (though not without ambiguity) against this profession, prostitutes fostered a strong sense of vocational identity and solidarity among themselves, which was also an effective means of self-protection. The particular environment that they worked in, usually a small community under one roof, encouraged the cultivation of a bond among girls who probably also shared similar unhappy backgrounds and histories. Sometimes this bond provided an girl with practical help rather than just an emotional attachment. For example, a local merchant, Mr Yüan, fell in love with a prostitute called Shao Hsing. Since he was already married to an aggressive wife, Mr Yüan dared not propose to marry her as a concubine and could only meet his beloved paramour at the brothel behind his wife's back. His wife, however, was later informed of this secret affair. She wrote a letter of remonstrance to Shao Hsing, warning her to leave Mr Yüan alone, and berating her in abusive and obscene language. Shao Hsing read the letter in anguish. She was determined to fight back. Two notoriously bad-tempered prostitutes, who were said to be 'sisters' of Shao Hsing, were instantly mobilized to her camp. The furious three marched straight away to Mr Yüan's abode and demanded an audience with his wife. The two parties then started a brawl, which soon resulted in violence. The fierce Mrs Yüan mobilized her maids, who attacked the challengers with brooms and sticks, while the latter defended with umbrellas. In the end, Shao Hsing and her party were forced to retreat; she was also slightly hurt on the forehead. The very terrified Mr Yüan, as the report stated, visited his prostitute lover the same evening to give her his personal apology and compensation in the hope of mending the jeopardized relations (*KPP* 1928: 8, 7 May). In another example, a Tanka prostitute named Sze Mei was reportedly saved from the hands of a vengeful man who claimed to have been inflicted with venereal disease by her in their intimate encounters. This man, backed by his nephew, demanded pecuniary compensation from Sze Mei who insisted that she had not seen him before. When he threatened to throw her into the river, she screamed for help, and that drew the attention of other boat-people anchored nearby. They rushed to her help and notified the police. These two men were so frightened at this that they dashed off instantly (*KPP* 1928: 6, 15 Mar.). Similar 'collective' action was noted in another incident involving a prostitute and her misbehaving client. In this event, Chin Tsai, the prostitute, was slapped on the face by a client at a local club. Instead of taking the mistreatment quietly, she rushed back to her brothel where she easily mobilized a group of nearly twenty 'sisters' who came forward to seek justice on her behalf. They gathered in front of the club and loudly upbraided the delinquent man for hurting their 'sister'. The angry crowd finally dispersed only after the police intervened (*KPP* 1928: 6, 27 Apr.). These dramas reveal the sisterly solidarity that a mistreated prostitute could rely on when defending herself.

It is worth mentioning that prostitutes, as a group, did not necessarily lack organization, thereby being left to quiet exploitation by the authorities, as some historians allege (e.g. Wu Yü et al. 1988: 436; Lu Yen 1981: ii. 106). On the contrary, they could on occasions be well organized in defending themselves against unreasonable and excessive demands. In traditional China, brothel-owners set up their own trade association (Gulik 1961: 179). In the 1900s, for example, the 'flower boat' owners in Canton staged at least two industrial strikes against 'unreasonable' increases in the 'flower-feast surcharge' imposed by tax brokers (Kuang-tung ch'ing-li ts'ai-chêng chü 1910: 38–41, 'Shui-ju pu: Chêng tsa ke-chuan'). The madams of brothels in one district in Canton had also petitioned the authorities over replacing the old practice of levying random surcharges on their establishments, and the monthly and festival surcharges solicited by *yamen* clerks, with a fixed and regular tax (ibid. 40). In the County of Shao-hsing, when the news reached other brothels in the area that an unruly off-duty soldier had stabbed a madam during a row, the entire 'flowery business' in the city went on strike in protest. The incident caused such a heavy loss to the city's treasury that the tax brokerage company was busy in arbitrating the dispute (*HTJP* 1919: 1.3, 23 Apr.).

In July 1927, the arrest of a few blind sing-song girls on the charge of clandestine prostitution caused an uproar among their fellows in Canton. In less than twelve hours hundreds of them were mobilized and marched to the local police station where their 'sisters' were being detained. They demanded their immediate release, and an undertaking by the head of that police station that no similar incident would occur in future. They sat in protest in front of the police station until these demands were eventually met (*HTJP* 1927: 3.2, 11 July).

The effectiveness of collective action had convinced the sing-song girls in Canton to organize a guild for themselves. A public meeting was called, which was spontaneously and enthusiastically attended by a large number of girls in this business. Although a formal sing-song girls' guild was already established in 1924, when labour politics was at its zenith in Canton, many sing-song girls did not join it for it was dominated by a few male labour activists. Three years later they submitted a new application for setting up another body that would be more capable of representing their interests (*HTJP* 1924: 1.3, 18 Apr.; 1927: 1.3, 16 May).

In December 1928, low-class brothels at the eastern end of the city went on strike against the proposal by a tax brokerage company to impose an additional surcharge on brothels. Although the proposed rate of increase was quite small (an additional ten cents on each bill), the reaction was unexpectedly strong. All brothel-owners in that area gathered together, and decided to go on strike until their demands were acceded to. Plans for a public demonstration were also devised. Realizing the determination of the brothel-owners over the issue, the tax brokerage company was finally forced to yield (*NYSP* 1928: 11, 3 Dec.).[64] These incidents show that prostitutes and brothel-owners were able to mobilize themselves effectively whenever outside encroachment became unsustainable. The fact that they could act together as one united body for their common good also indicated that relations between madams and prostitutes were not necessarily frozen into an irreconcilable polarity. Moreover, it implies that prostitutes saw their profession, albeit one of ill-repute, as legitimate and acceptable as other occupations. The fact that an officially registered trade union existed for the 'flower business' (*Hua-chieh kung-hui*) also indicates the extent of the integration of this 'disreputable' profession into society. Their collective action against excessive encroachment was therefore seen as perfectly legitimate.

There were at least three possible factors that contributed to the growth of cohesion among prostitutes in Canton. First, the geographical distribution of brothels tended to foster group cohesion and facilitated collective action when needed.[65] Secondly, since prostitutes were often invited by clients to attend parties held in different brothels or restaurants, there was an opportunity for them to get to know other 'sisters' (Liu Tsai-su 1926: 113–15). Prostitutes could, moreover, organize parties for themselves. In the late-Ch'ing period, for instance, the courtesan Chün T'ien was well known for her enthusiasm in organizing singing and drinking parties for all 'ladies' on the evening of every full moon (Yü Chiao-ch'ing 1909: 28). By the late 1920s, it is not known if this kind of regular gathering was still held. Annual and religious festivals, however, continued to provide occasions for congregating at local shrines.[66] It is clear that prostitutes could and did gather when they wished to do so. Thirdly, available biographies of contemporary both low- and high-class prostitutes, revealed the interesting fact that many of these women worked for more than one brothel in their careers.[67] Such mobility allowed a prostitute to expand her networks of 'sisterhood' with inmates of different establishments, as much as of her clientele. Sometimes, this sentimental and practical bond, or comradeship, lasted well after they had left the business.[68]

Happy Hookers

Although contemporary Cantonese literature about prostitution always contained scenes of sobbing prostitutes recounting their miserable life stories, it would be a mistake to leap to the conclusion that all prostitutes were treated cruelly. As we have seen earlier, not all shared the same experiences. Some prostituted themselves of their own free will in the expectation of earning quick money or of climbing the social ladder. A prostitute's 'tear-jerking' account could, of course, be simply fictitious. This is best shown in a story about a late-Ch'ing's provincial official who had served in Canton. Once, this official boarded a ferry that he did not realize was a clandestine floating brothel. Nor did he know that Miss Pu, nicknamed 'Chuang-yuan fu-jên' (Wife of the First-Class Graduate from Civil Examination), one of the most famous and beautiful courtesans in eastern Kwangtung, was also on board. Realizing that this official was a high-ranking one, Pu seduced him without any difficulty. When they arrived in Canton, Pu would not release her client and tried to persuade him to marry her by telling him how miserable her life was:

> [When recounting her sad life story, her] tears poured down like never-ending rain. Although he had tried a hundred ways to have her sent away, she still refused to leave. In the end, she only [agreed to] return home after five-hundred taels of gold had been offered to her. He remained unaware, however, of her skill in soliciting money [from other rich clients] in just the same way. (Yü Chiao-ch'ing 1909: 32)

Some prostitutes were certainly well aware that exaggerating the 'misery' of their lives could help them win the sympathy of their customers.

In an article intended to reveal the conditions of the lowest class of prostitutes in Canton in the early 1930s, the author recalled that upon entering a low-class brothel they were immediately received by two seductive girls. When the girls learned of the 'academic' purpose of their visit, however, they looked unhappy, presumably realizing they were unlikely to extract any money from the visitors. After both of them were given one yüan as 'greeting money', however, they started to recount tales of their miserable life as low-class whores. At the end of the interview, one of them was so gratified that she could not stop smiling (Chou Hsia-min 1934: 8). It is, of course, possible that these prostitutes exaggerated their sorrows to satisfy the curiosity of the inquisitive client anxious to 'prove' his assumptions about the ill-fated life of these suffering girls.

There could have been other practical reasons for a prostitute to flaunt her tragic life story, such as securing return visits by innocent and compassionate clients anxious to monitor her treatment. Moreover, there was always the chance that a greatly affected client might proffer marriage.[69] In Shanghai, it was well known to experienced brothel-goers that certain madams cheated inexperienced clients by pretending to mistreat their favourite girls, in the hope that they would be driven by conscience to pay handsomely for their release (Hai-shang-chüeh-wu-shêng 1939).[70] Cantonese prostitutes were doubtless equally skilful at playing the same trick. A contemporary Cantonese wrote that four tricks were most frequently played by shrewd prostitutes on their simple-minded clients: to flirt, to scold, to cry, and to threaten to commit suicide. The latter two forms of ruse, according to the author, were usually employed effectively by the astute prostitutes to capture the affections of their wealthy clients; these hoaxes were not often used on less well-to-do patrons (*KPP* 1928: 8, 29 Mar.). Of course, not all the miserable life stories were necessarily fabricated. To believe them, however, also ran the risk of perpetuating an untruth.

Another case of such misconception was recorded in a local newspaper. On a hot summer day in Canton, a 14-year-old prostitute was heard screaming for help from a hotel room occupied by a Westerner. Policemen were, as a result, called to the scene. They forced their way into the room to find this young lady in tears because her private parts were bleeding heavily. After further investigation, the police arrived at an account of the incident: a hotel attendant arranged the services of an illicit young virgin-prostitute for a Western man who lodged at the hotel, and the defloration turned out to be so extremely painful and traumatic for this girl that she lost her self-control and screamed for help. The policemen had the attendant arrested and charged him for forcing the young girl to sell her body against her own will. To protect this poor girl from further exploitation, the police sent her to the custody of Chi-liang So, a refuge centre for female orphans and 'rescued' prostitutes (*KCMKJP* 1923: 6, 27 Aug.). This, however, was not the end of the story. A few days after this horrific incident, the same reporter found the 'poor' victim of illicit prostitution in the lobby of another local hotel. He found out that this girl was not sent to the refuge shelter as was initially proposed. Instead, she was released as a free woman after paying a fine of 30 yüan. But to his big surprise, this 'poor' girl was now transformed and exuberant, and not only continued to solicit customers at hotels and restaurants, but also recounted loudly, joyfully, and proudly to her friends and clients the story of her shrewdness in escaping the fate of being sent to the refuge shelter (*KCMKJP* 1923: 7, 29 Aug.). What had appeared to be tragic and miserable turned out to be illusory and deceptive.

Not every prostitute perceived herself as leading a miserable life in a living hell. In the same serialized Cantonese opera script discussed earlier, the female protagonist enjoys her life as a popular and well-off prostitute. Introducing herself to the audience, she sings:

> Some prostitutes are so anxious to keep alive in their minds-and-hearts integrity and shamefulness, which render them perpetually unhappy. However, I always think differently. [In my opinion], life is lamentable [and short]. [Thus, when one is] happy, one must not think about sad things [because] it is useless to be madly preoccupied with [apprehensive thoughts about one's future]. Of all kinds of women, prostitutes should be the most romantic and felicitous. [It is because she can afford] to buy expensive and beautiful clothes, and to match [them with accessories of] gold and jade... [Moreover, she] feeds herself with good food, and lives in spacious quarters. Furthermore, she is always accompanied by [numerous] 'temporary husbands' who provide her with happy diversion every night. She is free to come and go from her brothel without [any] family authoritarian restraints. As for money, she can earn and spend it [easily and freely]; and there are always clients who are anxious to offer such emoluments and worry that their presents might arrive late. (K'u Tieh 1927: 3.4, 2 July)

Surely, there is a sense of pride and achievement, rather than complacency, in this monologue.

Some prostitutes took pride in their relatively superior economic and living conditions. They also enjoyed showing off by parading themselves in public decked out in expensive clothing.[71] A scholar noted that a prostitute's 'rich apparel of brilliant silk makes her much better dressed than any class of women save the rich. On the streets she is the object of attention for those who wish to see the new style in feminine dress' (James Wiley, cited in Hershatter 1991: 274). The well-being and self-confidence of especially high-class prostitutes were also noted by two senior officials from Canton's municipal administration. In a report on the situation of prostitution that they submitted to the city's Social Bureau, lives in high-class brothels and low-class whorehouses were described as 'sharply different, like heaven and hell'. Although they did not elaborate on the 'hellish' working conditions of the low-class prostitutes (besides mentioning their low income), they did characterize some aspects of life for the high-class courtesans. They commented that although these women had first entered this ill-repute business out of ignorance or misguided intent, most of them, once they got used to their work, were happily willing to stay in the trade. In this report we also learn that almost one-third of all high-class prostitutes did not live in brothels; they lived in their own flats, or shared an apartment with some of their intimate 'sisters'. An average high-class courtesan spent each month a sum of 50 to 100 yüan on living expenses. It was reported that a prostitute of this class could comfortably earn enough money to cover her living expenses by entertaining clients at the drinking table alone, without the need to 'accompany' them overnight, not to mention the substantial amount of 'special income' (tips) that they usually received (Kuang-chou-shih shê-hui chü 1930: 14–15). One could detect a note of envy in the officers' report.

A contemporary *Yüeh-ou* song reveals that being a prostitute was sometimes perceived as even more fortunate than being a daughter of a rich family:

> Compared with a girl from a wealthy family, I am cheaper than mud. But such girls are not easily married off. If they marry a debauched husband, shame will be brought to their families—far worse than our degraded brothel life. It matters little if we choose not to marry [because] we can still pass our days by combing our hairs and being served bowls of rice and tea . . . Alas! these words are not intended to inflate my worthiness, but having realized that human relationships in this world are so fickle, I don't wish to be involved anymore.[72]

In another *Yüeh-ou* song, prostitutes were seen as fortunate women with ample chances to become familiar with different types of men from whom to chose a husband.[73] Unlike most ordinary women, they could avoid the emotional pain caused by 'blind marriage'. In the song 'Repaying the Flower-Debt' (*Huan hua-chai*), a prostitute is described as willing to sell her body while still young and attractive for at this golden age of her life, she will be admired, appeased, and wooed by a large number of her 'followers' who will bring her both companionship and money.[74]

Some prostitutes might dislike their job at first, but once they were used to brothel life, enjoy it. In the social novel *T'ang-hsi chin-fên* (mentioned earlier), for instance, Yin Shan is sold into a brothel by her foster-mother. She adapts quickly to the comfortable life there, gains weight, and looks more attractive than before because of the better diet and easier lifestyle. Her elder sister, also a prostitute, is soon spoilt by this comfortable life and becomes very choosy about her food. When Yin Shan has sex with her first customer, she enjoys the experience thoroughly. Throughout the story, she, like most other girls in the brothel do, enjoys her sexual encounters with most of her regular clients, an enjoyment that colours an otherwise monotonous life.[75] A former Shanghai prostitute reminisces that prostitutes used a number of arguments to justify their existence to themselves. One of the 'craziest idea was it wasn't men having fun with us, but us having fun with them and they still had to pay good money' (Zhang Xinxin 1987: 33). A perceptive traveller recorded that 'like the coolies, these women of the 'flower boats' face life with a cheerful demeanour, as if, true fatalists, they are not going to be any more miserable than necessary over the lot to which the gods have assigned them' (Franck 1925: 222). Although not a respectable profession, it was undoubtedly one of the most lucrative alternatives to starvation and poverty. To some, it brought an exciting and easy life in a dynamic city.[76] In a survey conducted in Shanghai in 1948, more than half the 500 prostitutes interviewed were satisfied with their job mainly because it provided them with a relatively secure livelihood in a period of economic uncertainty. Fewer than a quarter were unhappy with their current circumstances (Hershatter 1991: 274). This favourable self-perception seemingly helps to explain the difficulty that the 'new' socialist regime was facing in 're-educating' these women during the early 1950s. Many of them did not share the official perceptions of the meanings of their lives since they did not see anything wrong with their relatively easy work, comfortable living conditions in brothels, and, to some, the emotional satisfaction that sharing life with their 'sisters' provided. On the contrary, strictly regimented, and even brutal at times, 're-education' reforms imposed forcefully by the paternalistic state on prostitutes eventually deprived this group of women of their old privileges and lives of luxury. For many of them the harsh life at the labour camps was unbearable and tortuous; and, for some, their lives were destroyed and dreams shattered.[77]

This positive side of the prostitute's life is also ironically acknowledged by Ou-yang Shan in his anti-prostitution short story 'Tsai shen ching li'. To the chief protagonist, being a whore is better than living impoverished and abused in her village. At one point, she defends her preference to remain a whore:

> [Morally] we may be shallow and cheap. However . . . there are countless numbers of wives in respectable families who, after giving birth to children, have to endure being beaten by their husbands, and work laboriously all day long with too little food to eat. Are these women not more to be pitied than me! Their bodies also become infected by all kinds of diseases which will eventually kill them . . . Do these women deserve all this? . . . Although they are more passive, kind-hearted and virtuous than we [prostitutes] are, compared with them we are still free to eat [what and where we want], to wear [whatever we like], [and] to die [unencumbered]. (Ou-yang Shan 1948: 30)

This view may have been shared by many prostitutes in this period.[78]

Some prostitutes in Canton were perceived by the public as lewd characters whose strong desire for money and a luxurious lifestyle was their main motive for entering the profession. This group of prostitutes were said to be willing to sell their bodies without remorse; some of them were indiscriminate in picking up their customers, and spent their 'easy money' freely and happily on buying up the latest fashion, to the envy of many simple-minded women (*KCMKJP* 1924: 7, 15 Apr.; 1921, 18, 19, and 21 June; *KHP* 1929: 2.4, 1 Mar.). A research project conducted in 1934 on boat-people in the county of San-shui cited randomly chosen cases of three prostitutes who 'always wore a broad smile' and served their patrons well. All three had chosen to become prostitutes and seemed to enjoy their job. In one case, the young woman had been married to a fisherman. But she grew to despise him for earning too little and left him to work as a prostitute (Wu Jui-lin 1937*b*: 51–2). These cases from San-shui do not speak for the situation in Canton, but they may still usefully reflect some of the possible attitudes of this class of woman towards the profession in this part of Kwangtung, including Canton.

Positive self-perception as such was a reflection of the willingness of some of these women in Canton who prostituted themselves for the simple practical reason of earning easy and quick money. Money provided them with not only materialistic comfort, but also a degree of self-assertiveness that commanded respect, perhaps reluctantly, from the common folk. Such a pragmatic attitude in the popular mentality, which was epitomized in the common Cantonese saying 'Laugh at a penniless man, but not a prostitute' (*hsiao p'in pu-hsiao ch'ang*), apparently helped to bring this about (Lo Li-ming 1962: i. 40). An article published in a contemporary daily in Canton informs us of a similar observation. The article, which bears a social-scientific title, 'An analytical categorization of the reasons leading to the moral decline of prostitutes in Canton', was contributed by a reader (who occasionally contributed articles on famous prostitutes or sing-song girls from Canton and Hong Kong) who claimed to have a wide knowledge of prostitution in this city. This report was said to be prepared with the assistance of a group of close friends of its author, including an officer from a brothel-taxes brokerage company and attendants of a handful of local hotels frequented by prostitutes. In the estimates of this investigator, of the 5,800 or so prostitutes in Canton, less than 60 were either enticed or abducted into the business, while slightly over 2,000 entered under the 'pressure of [economic] circumstances'. For the rest, he wrote, they prostituted themselves willingly for the sake of money. He lamented that the prevalence of voluntary prostitution was attributed to the wide acceptance of that common attitude, 'Laugh at a penniless man, but not a prostitute' (*KPP* 1928: 8, 8 June). This might also explain why some former prostitutes seemingly did not mind re-entering the business after they had left it.[79]

It must be noted that not all prostitutes necessarily ended up as the derelict and pathetic streetwalkers they were commonly depicted to be in contemporary highbrow literature. To begin with, not all prostitutes spent their whole life in brothels. Many of them took their job at a brothel as a temporary measure of contingency, and left this 'transient refuge' as soon as they could.[80] Marriage to a rich man, either as a concubine or a wife, offered a prostitute an invaluable chance of climbing the social ladder. It was noted that 'the prestige of being associated with a wealthy and powerful family gives her a position far above anything she has probably known in the past', while the offspring she bears 'are all accepted as legitimate children and heirs of their father' (Gamble 1921: 260). Late-Ch'ing random notes on famous Cantonese courtesans show that many were redeemed by marriage to rich patrons and led a comfortable life thereafter. Even in Ou-yang Shan's 'Tsai shen ching li', an originally low-class prostitute manages to climb the social ladder from being the concubine of a warlord to eventually becoming an executive member of the official Women's Association (Ou Yang-shan 1948: 18). At the end of another social novel, the prostitute-heroine Yü Shan is married to a rich businessman as his first wife, and lives happily in a two-storey Western-style villa. The marriage is described as bringing good luck to her husband whose business begins to prosper after that (Sung Yü 1989: 410–11).

But this was no fiction. In the 1930s in Hong Kong and Canton, it was not uncommon that high-class prostitutes were married to wealthy men as their legitimate first wives (e.g. Lo Li-Ming 1962: ii. 40, 44). A visitor from Canton wrote what he observed about prostitutes in Ping-shi, a county capital in northern Kwangtung, after a stay of three months there. Most of the 200 or so brothels in this city served a prosperous mercantile community. To his amazement, nearly all the girls were virgins and entertained their clients with drinks or singing, rarely sex. Many of these prostitutes, once they had amassed substantial savings, left their jobs and returned to their place of origin for good. Those who had given their consent to a marriage proposal from a passionate client, usually after a lengthy period of expensive courtship, were married as principal wife and lived a decent life of material comfort (*KPP* 1928: 8, 17 Apr.). A contemporary journalist recorded the case of Hsing Tsai, a high-class prostitute in the Chiang-men County, south-east of Canton. For three years, she was eagerly wooed by a former Ch'ing senior official who eventually married her as principal wife. He paid a sum of 2,000 yüan to the brothel to release her from the establishment, and another 250 yüan for a ritualistic farewell banquet, with her 'sisters' taking part. Hsing Tsai was also given 750 yüan for purchasing furniture that she liked in Hong Kong for their new flat and a collection of fashionable items for her wardrobe. From then on, she led a life of relaxation and comfort and was said to have commanded great envy from many 'sisters' in the trade (*KPP* 1928: 8, 26 May). The happy married life of Ling Ling, another high-class prostitute in Canton, attracted the envy not only of her counterparts, but also of journalists. Ling Ling was married to an American diplomat widower and settled down comfortably in Berkeley, California. The news of her revisiting Hong Kong was followed closely by a handful of newspaper columnists who eagerly updated their readers on the latest information about this fortunate former prostitute. We learned from this gossip column news that Ling Ling was practising Chinese calligraphy as her pastime and that she had recently arranged for her aged mother to emigrate to California. During her brief stay in Hong Kong, she visited many of her old friends, including one at the 'prestigious' Hong Kong University. She also went to Macao where a small reunion party was organized with three of her former colleagues—all had once been famous in the world of high-class prostitution in Canton, but then left the profession and led a life of material comfort with their wealthy husbands or paramours (*KPP* 1928: 8, 17, and 20 Apr.).

There were many other occupations for a retiring prostitute to choose from once she had left the brothel for good. Some remained in the world of entertainment. From the Po Leung Kuk (1924–5, pt. 2) files, we learn about former prostitutes who, after amassing enough savings and thus deciding to leave the trade, became apprentices of the art of Cantonese opera in the hope of becoming opera singers in the future. The nascent but steadily expanding Chinese film industry was apparently an attractive option for retiring prostitutes. A journalist mentioned the names of three former Cantonese prostitutes who succeeded in establishing themselves in the movie world in Canton and Shanghai (*KPP* 1928: 8, 16 June). Working as a sing-song girl at local tea-house restaurants was another major alternative for those prostitutes who had mastered well the art of singing. Contemporary journals recorded numerous cases of such career shifts. Some sing-song girls were said to have taken the sideline of unlicensed prostitution, though mainly targeting men whom they fancied.[81] The emerging business of massage provided these women with another alternative means of livelihood. A local newspaper noted that in the past this business was dominated by masseurs. Such men, though good at the skill, were mostly 'filthy... opium addicts who perhaps are able to bring comfort to one's body, but their outlook is unacceptable and repulsive to their customers'. As a result, masseuses had become increasingly favourable among patrons of massage services, and this encouraged a number of young women from poor family backgrounds and 'roving prostitutes' to learn the skill and to join the trade (*YHP* 1934: 1, 3 Oct.). For the more enterprising few, their substantial savings helped materialize their ambitious ventures. From a newspaper report we learn that a small group of high-class prostitutes, in response to the official's call for 'abolishing prostitution', collectively resigned from their 'ill-reputed' job. To attain 'economic independence', they worked industriously at amassing capital for investing in the weaving industry (*HTJP* 1921: 4, 15 Apr.).

The fate of a prostitute-turned-concubine was beyond any simple prediction, and an oppressive life subjected to the abuses of her husband's principal wife was certainly only one pattern out of the many.[82] Some of them, due to their physical attractiveness and stronger intimacy with their husbands (fostered by their long premarital courtship), could be quite powerful, even, for example, accompanying their husbands to social functions, a role usually reserved for the principal wife (Sung Yü 1989: 410).[83] In an allegedly true story about power getting out of hand, an affluent businessman Mê takes the prostitute Pei as a concubine. After moving into his house, Pei becomes increasingly dominating to the point where Mê's principal wife, who is more submissive in character, is forced out of the house. Meanwhile, Pei conspires with her paramour to kill Mê, but fails, and in panic she bolts. Eventually, Mê is happily reunited with his wife (Chi'en 1934: 27–8).[84] In another incident, a man was accidentally poisoned by his concubine—who had been a prostitute in Macao before marrying him. The poisoned drink was prepared by this woman who intended it to be consumed by her husband's principal wife, who had a history of antagonism towards the perpetrator. The man was saved, and the wicked woman was expelled from the household (*Chu-kiang hsing-ch'i hua pao* 1927: iii. 19). A similar, but allegedly real, story was described by a concerned reader and printed in a local newspaper. In this narrative, we are told that a former *yamen* clerk in Tung-kuan County fell for a low-class prostitute in Canton whom he kept as a mistress. His principal wife in the village secretly followed her husband to Canton where the illicit couple were caught red-handed. The man, however, refused to leave his beloved mistress. Hoping to keep her husband, the principal wife asked to stay with them in Canton. The three then lived together under one roof. In the beginning, the mistress pretended to be submissive to the principal wife. Soon, when she could rely on the man's obsession with herself, her attitude towards the principal wife became disrespectful. Whenever the husband was out of town, her new paramour came to visit her and, at times, stayed overnight. The husband dismissed his principal wife's repeated admonitions, as the groundless suspicions of a jealous woman. At the end of the story, we learn that the principal wife fell seriously ill. Her husband, who was out of town at the time, wrote to ask his mistress to send the sick woman to hospital, but that was never done. The poor woman was left to die on her sickbed (*KPP* 1928: 8, 26 May).

It must be pointed out that although most prostitutes perceived marriage as the ideal way of quitting the profession, they were not all desperate to leave their jobs by grasping indiscriminately at any available client to marry. Some high-class prostitutes were well known for their fastidiousness in choosing matrimonial partners. Wu K'o, a high-class prostitute in Canton, is an example. An intimate client of Wu K'o contributed a short essay to a local newspaper about her ideal husband, which was based upon a long and sincere conversation between the prostitute and him. In this record, we learn that Wu K'o had been working as a high-class harlot for a few years. Until recently, she enjoyed her work so much that she 'rarely considered it anything bitter'. Lately, she was tired of her unsteady relations with her 'male friends'; she wanted to leave the brothel and to lead the 'normal' life of an ordinary married woman. She, however, sighed over the difficulty of finding the right man to marry. Among her numerous faithful clients, none was able to meet her five basic requirements: he must be good-natured and handsome; reasonably rich; have a pair of well-positioned and thick eyebrows; preferably married but without a concubine; without any liking for opium and gambling (*KPP* 1928: 8, 15 May). Wu K'o might have been bored by her job, but she was not desperate to start a new life until she found the right man to marry. After all, working as a high-class prostitute was by no means a horrifible or unbearable lifestyle for her.

The experiences of two other prostitutes, as reported in a respectable Hong Kong newspaper, illustrate this point from another perspective. In the first report, a high-class prostitute named Fêng Shan was said to have a long, intimate relationship with a client, Mr Huang, who had even paid her madam the first instalment for her release. At a 'flower banquet' organized by Mr Huang, Fêng Shan fell for his dentist friend Mr Ch'en, who was also bewitched by her. The couple then began an affair, leaving the distressed Mr Huang aside. Before long, Fêng Shan fell for a nephew of her dentist lover. This time, however, she was refused, as this young man's conscience did not allow him to pursue her, though he was obsessed with her coquettishness (*HTJP* 1915: 1.3 and 2.2, 28 Apr.). This anecdote revealed the fact that a prostitute was not always willing to marry anyone available. In this case, she had a selection of choices and, despite her status as a 'pawned prostitute', was in no desperate need to be hurriedly married off. The second report concerned a prostitute in Canton who was shot and seriously wounded by a policeman. The perpetrator was later found to be a keen patron of the prostitute Ch'i Mei. He was infuriated at first by her refusal to marry him, and later by her disdainful treatment of him. It was also reported that Ch'i Mei was tired of working in brothel and was looking for the right man to marry before she met this policeman client. Up to the time of the tragedy, Ch'i Mei had not yet found the right man, and had turned down the proposals of a number of her clients on the grounds that they were not good-looking enough (*HTJP* 1915: 1.3, 3 May). Ch'i Mei, seemingly liked many of her colleagues, preferred to be careful and selective in her choice.

4. *PROSTITUTION AS AN ACCEPTABLE AND PLEASANT PASTIME*

Undoubtedly, some Cantonese did denounce prostitution as a strongly corrosive influence on moral character and physical health, or capable of corrupting otherwise happy families and, above all, society. Brothel-going could certainly lead to financial bankruptcy, and to the transmission of venereal diseases to spouse and offspring ('Ch'ang-liao su-yu' n.d.: 53–5). Since the early 1920s, both the local government and concerned intellectuals in Canton helped build up a nationalistic discourse on prostitution. Citizens were taught to look at prostitution not only as a social or moral problem, but a menace to the survival of a healthy and strong nation, detrimental to the Chinese race (*KCMKJP* 1924: 3, 14 Apr.; 1929: 12, 18 June; Ch'en Li-chu et al. 1991: iv. 468–70).[85]

Not every Cantonese, however, shared this critical view of brothel-going. On the contrary, most seemed to hold an ambivalent, if not openly favourable, attitude towards patronizing prostitutes as an agreeable form of entertainment. Some also considered it a necessary social evil.

Agreeable Entertainment

With the exception of some moralistic treatises, contemporary Cantonese literature on prostitution rarely attacked brothel-going as an unworthy form of entertainment. Brothels were commonly regarded as a pleasurable playground for men if they knew how to refrain from overspending, how to avoid being cheated by greedy prostitutes, and how to keep away from disease-infected girls. Although sounding a warning against swindling whores, one writer still held that no young men should avoid visiting a brothel, though they should not indulge heavily in the practice. To visit a brothel occasionally with close friends, and chat and dine with attractive and hospitable prostitutes, was considered an enjoyable and memorable experience. It could even enrich one's knowledge about one's society to know about the brothels where most social functions took place (Hai-shang-chüeh-wu-shêng 1939: 4 (Preface), 110). A Cantonese writer who recorded his experience of patronizing prostitution aired a similar ambivalent attitude. After describing at length the great pleasure of being accompanied by two charming high-class prostitutes at the dining table of a 'flower feast', this author dramatically charged his stance by asking his readers not to be easily taken in by such sensual pleasure, because, in his view, obsession with prostitutes could lead a wealthy man to bankruptcy, moral and economic. He concluded, however, by saying that since it was unavoidable for men to patronize prostitutes occasionally, they should restrain themselves from being obsessed by it (Huai-ping-tzu 1911, 13 Sept.). Another Cantonese reminisces how at the age of 15 he was taken by his uncle on a trip to Canton. Anxious to show him the 'big-city life', the uncle went with him to a gambling house and then to a floating brothel whose beautiful and talkative courtesans, luxurious decor, and gay ambience deeply impressed the young country visitor. Brothels were apparently agreeable enough places for teenagers to visit in the company of an adult without giving cause for concern (Têng Fei-p'eng 1978: 22–3).[86]

The popular perception of the brothel is explicit in the lyrics of a *Yüeh-ou* song: 'Paying visits to these stunning beauties is not necessarily a bad thing. One will not be driven mad by these beauties if one's mind-and-heart is enlightened [after listening to this song and having appreciated its lesson].'[87] The message of this song is: Do not betray the love of a sincere prostitute, or overindulge in brothel-going.

A nineteenth-century French anthropologist, J. Jacobus, had stated that visiting a brothel in China, unlike in Europe, was not regarded as a furtive or secret affair, but a normal activity that was engaged in openly and publicly (cited in Henriques 1962: i. 258 n.). A similar view was expressed by a Chinese diplomat who defended the decent image of 'flower boats' in the same period:

> Certain travellers have taken it into their heads to describe . . . flower boats . . . as places of excess. That is incorrect. The flower boats serve this purpose just as little as the concert halls of Europe. This is a favourite amusement of Chinese young men. These water parties are arranged especially in the evening in the company of ladies who have accepted invitations to them. These ladies are unmarried (*sic*): they are musical and are invited for this reason . . . This is a pleasant way of beguiling slowly passing time. On the boats is to be found everything that an epicure can possibly wish for; and in the cool of the evening, with a cup of deliciously perfumed tea, the women's harmonious voices and the sound of musical instruments are not considered a nocturnal debauch.[88]

This apologia may be a little disingenuous, but it was appropriate enough to point out that a brothel-goer was looking for something more than just sex. Like hetaerai in ancient Greece (Evans 1979: 34–40), Chinese courtesans provided their customers with the kind of intellectual female companionship for which their wives were not normally trained. High-class brothels were the place where literati and officials relaxed, congregated, and made political or business deals (Larsen 1987: pp. xv–xvi; Gulik 1961: 178–9).[89]

By 1920, few brothel-goers visited brothels for the intellectual company they provided, though a great many were in search of more than sex alone. Some went there to entertain their guests with a banquet, to listen to the sweet singing of the courtesans,[90] to chat with the prostitutes, many of whom were articulate conversationalists, or to meet their colleagues or business partners there as at an informal club house (Lee Bing-shuey 1936: 96; Henriques 1962: i. 260; Kung Fu-an 1934: 13–14; Lo Li-ming 1962: *passim*).[91]

Food played a significant role in Cantonese brothel culture. Contemporary advertisements of local restaurants emphasized, as one of their main attractions, their proximity to the red-light district where most of the high-class brothels were located.[92] Most high-class brothels were also quasi-restaurants, with professional chefs catering for the clients. Most meetings between high-class prostitutes and their patrons took the form of small feasts or more sumptuous banquets (Liu Tsai-su 1926: 113–15).[93] Even the names of most of these establishments sounded more like restaurants than brothels.[94] It was said, moreover, that the cuisine served on 'flower boats' was often superior in quality and less expensive than many high-class restaurants. Most of these boats were scenically located by the banks of the Pearl River, providing an ideal retreat from the heat of the summer nights (Schlegel 1894: 4). Such attractions must have helped to reinforce the favourable perception of brothels as 'resorts' within the bounds of the crowded city of Canton.

Low-class brothels were not necessarily viewed less favourably. Vernacular poems sometimes captured the happy experiences of visitors to these establishments, in which no feeling of guilt at all is detected. The poem entitled 'Shui-chi t'ing' (Water-chicken Boats) is a good example:

> How happy one is before the ['water-chicken'] boat! To cruise on this boat of pleasure and enjoy the scenery all around [is a memorable experience]. The boat is beautifully decorated and polished to sheen... [which] heightens the romantic atmosphere... The singing clocks, the hanging scrolls of calligraphy and painting are [all] delightful... [A pair of brightly lit lanterns] helps dispel [any feelings of] human misery... In the hot season when you put on your silk clothes... your prettiness excites me [further]. From the corner of your eyes comes a message of romantic love... and I feel I have encountered Hsi Shih... (Chi-hsien-hsien-yin *c.*1926: 58)

The pleasure of cruising on the same kind of low-class floating brothel was vividly recorded in another poem, 'Fang t'ing yu ho':

> What beautiful scenery! It helps a man to rid of himself of his sorrow. On a fine evening when the full moon in the sky... [and] the weather is hot, people go out to look for a cool

place [in which to relax] ... I come to Shakee where ... a cluster of small boats [is] anchored along the pier ... I also notice the 'sisters' dressed in beautiful clothes and seated in the bow of these vessels ... Without any feeling of shame, they call out [to the passers-by] on land ... Sometimes, [bewitched customers] press their 'breads' (breasts) ... which are ... soft, smooth, and rich in oily cream. Then will one hear the cry: 'Don't touch!' ... My friends! Remember my words whenever you are free, and take a trip on one of these boats. [It costs] no more than places on land. [But by doing this, you might] even hook a few beauties. [You can], moreover, escape the heat [of the summer evening] ... which is better than spending your silver-money in a brothel on shore ... But most importantly, you must refrain from over-indulgence. (Ibid. 58–9)

The pleasure was indisputable, and the experience was certainly not seen as shameful or regrettable.

There were other indications of the predominantly favourable social perception of prostitution. It seems that very few writings on the subject in Republican Canton challenged the legitimacy of brothels as a venue for both serious social functions and open leisure activities. In the *Canton Yearbook* for 1935, the chapter on prostitution made no mention of the immorality of brothel-going, concentrating instead on the municipal government's concern for the deplorable physical conditions of certain low-class establishments, the alleged maltreatment of some prostitutes by their madams, and the illegal employment of young girls as maids in brothels (*Kuang-chou nien-chien* 1935: 62–3, ch. 7). In the early 1930s, when the government launched a series of publicity campaigns against the 'bad social customs' in Cantonese society, the problem of prostitution, though labelled as a major vice, was only lightly targeted in comparison with other vices.[95]

Local guidebooks also published information about brothels. In two of these, the addresses and telephone numbers of a selection of different classes of brothel, their prices and services, were listed. This information was clearly intended to facilitate visits to such establishments which, in the eyes of the editors, provided a less harmful and immoral form of entertainment than gambling.[96]

Latest news or gossip about famous high-class prostitutes had nearly become a regular feature for many local pictorial magazines, many of which were published weekly. Many of these magazines were by no means disreputable tabloid-like publications. On the contrary, their upright nature was indicated by the fact they featured articles and reports on such serious subjects as traditional-style Chinese painting and painters, personnel movement in local government, the impact of the Communist uprisings in Hai-fêng and Canton, tourist sites both local and overseas, the Cantonese opera world, Hollywood and Chinese movies and film stars, students' feedback on modern education, and so on. The fact that news about high-class prostitutes was given a not so insignificant space in these general-interest magazines was clearly a sign of public acceptance of this form of entertainment.[97]

Local newspapers also reflected this favourable reception of prostitution. Up until the mid-1930s, many local dailies, such as *Kuo hua pao, Kung-p'ing pao,*

Yüeh hua pao, and to a lesser degree the Hong Kong-based *Hua-tzu jih-pao*.[98] contain significant coverage on the world of high-class prostitution, despite their reputation for being serious journals. These newspapers did not show bias against local prostitutes in the sense that news, big or insignificant, as long as it had something to do with these women, would find its place in a column of local reports. Anecdotes of famous prostitutes and information on the brothel world, in addition to a wide range of subjects that were supposed to be entertaining to the readers, also appeared regularly in the supplements of the former three journals. In this sense, prostitution was considered favourably as a part of daily life in Canton. This last point was even more vividly reflected by an eye-catching advertisement published in a local newspaper. This commercial was intended to promote a special brand of Chinese cigarettes by announcing an upcoming lucky draw organized by a tobacco company. Under its large-print title 'If I win the 5,000 dollar prize' is a set of eight cartoons, each telling how a winner would make good use of the award. These include a factory worker who resigns from his job to start his own business, a young man who hurries to marry his sweetheart, a student who finances his overseas education, and so on. One of these eight cartoons, somewhat pertinent to our discussion here, depicts a happy man, holding a prostitute by her hand. He says that he can buy her off from the brothel so that she can lead the easy life of a married lady (*YHP* 1934: 4, 26 Mar.).

To some, as a *Yüeh-ou* song noted, patronizing a brothel helped one to forget the reality of growing old:

> In no time one grows old, and scarcely blink before the autumn wind comes blowing. Man's affairs of a full twenty years are as drifting weed on the surface of the water... Though like a fallen chrysanthemum shivering in icy weather, one can still withstand the seasonal cold like an aged pine... [One is] hardly a fool for knowing how to enjoy [life], losing oneself in the embrace of a bevy of beauties humming a few lines of a *Yüeh-ou*... [and] choosing a companion who can strum a tune on the *p'i-p'a*.[99]

Prostitution had a psychologically soothing function, and brothels provided a happy refuge for escapists. A contemporary journalist noted that the more successful tabloids and pictorials in Canton concentrated on news and anecdotes about the cinema world, sing-song girls, prostitutes and brothels to pander to the taste of the general reader. Though information of this kind was 'not useful for 'mending' the affairs of this world', it did provide readers weary of reading about massacres or robberies with an alternative source of diversion and a temporary escape from the harsh realities of social disorder and political instability. For some Cantonese, prostitution was a delightful means of escape (*Hsiang hua hua-pao* I, 1928: 1, Preface).[100]

Chin Man-ch'êng, a disciple of Chang Ching-shêng (alias Dr Sex), argued that prostitution would persist for as long as the younger generation ignored his advice regarding sexual liberation and free love. Prostitution provided men with those same kinds of pleasure that they were not free to enjoy elsewhere (Chin Man-ch'êng 1928: 50). Brothels, therefore, provided these young men with the venue for experimenting with romance and exercising their freedoms in this respect. It might be due to this favourable reception of prostitution among the urban youth that a local traditional medicine company capitalized on it. In one of the illustrated advertisements of the company's tonic pills which was hailed for its magical power in rejuvenating an exhausted male body and its sexual strength, a well-dressed young man clad in a Western suit is depicted receiving an intimate caress from a seductive prostitute. The drawing was captioned with a couplet: 'Young people are having great time in patronizing prostitutes; [but] excessive indulgence in sex and alcohol drains dry their renal power.' The commercial did not ask its male readers to stay away from prostitution, but to announce the 'good news' to these young men that having a pair of weak kidneys resulting from frequent patronage of prostitution was no longer something to worry about after the birth of that product (*HTJP* 1928: 4.4, 2 Aug.). For a modern urban young man, paying a visit to prostitutes was neither a sinister nor a shameful thing to do.

Surprisingly, prostitution was a favourite pastime for 'modern' students. This might have been an extension of the practice among traditional literati of patronizing courtesans.[101] Unlike their predecessors of imperial times, however, this new generation of literati-customers were looking for unambiguous sex rather than intellectual companionship. In Ou-yang Shan's 'Tsai shen ching li' (1948: 32–3), the protagonist has many regulars who are college students in Canton, and even entertains them at school dormitories. In another short story about the 'alternative' extra-curricular activities of a university student in Canton, philandering and visiting brothels are among his major pastimes. He is so experienced in brothel-going that he is nicknamed 'the great athlete of sleeping with beauties' (*mien-hua chien chiang*) (Hua-ts'ung-fên-tieh 1933: 19–21). A contemporary journalist recorded the conversation of his neighbours—four local students—while they were playing *mahjong* on three consecutive evenings. They were so excited by the game, as much as by the recollections of their last visit to a brothel, that they began to discuss the visit with raised voices in lurid detail (Wan Yung 1930: 88–9). A newspaper report ascribed the proliferation of clandestine prostitutes to their popularity among students, who could enjoy their services without having to visit a brothel. Every weekend, when a boarding school in Canton released its students for a break in the city, many of them would stay at local guesthouses where the receptionists, at their request, would arrange the company of a clandestine prostitute. The problem was reported to have become so serious that as many as sixty students were found to have venereal disease. In the hope of containing the situation, teachers were deployed to inspect the local guesthouses frequented by their students (*HTJP* 1927: 2.2, 17 Oct.).[102] Thus we are provided with an alternative picture of the subculture of contemporary students, not all of whom were as morally superior as was generally believed.

Nor were all modern educationalists necessarily better than students in this respect. The scandalous news of a Canton primary school principal patronizing an unlicensed prostitute triggered off strong reaction from the pupils. The angry students called for an urgent meeting with the school's Board of Directors to demand the immediate replacement of the schoolmaster. The latter eventually submitted his resignation in disgrace (*KPP* 1925: 6, 15 May). In another case, the headmaster of a public school in San-sui County was suspected of bringing a prostitute with him on a study trip organized by the school for his students; she pretended to be his wife. The school's student union, after the trip, demanded a public apology from the headmaster who seemingly did not comply (*YHP* 1932: 3, 20 Nov.).[103]

'Necessary Evil'

Some Cantonese were tempted to regard prostitution as a 'necessary evil'. One writer saw the social value of prostitution in the 'fact' that it helped minimize incidents of rape. In his view, the practice of the rich keeping concubines disadvantaged the poorer class of men because it substantially reduced the number of marriageable women available to the latter. They were fortunate if they could save enough money to pay for a prostitute and relieve their sexual impulses, but rape was the only way out, it was argued, for those too poor to afford anything else (Wan Yung 1930: 33–5).[104] Although exaggerated, this reveals an alternative view of the social function of prostitution in male-dominated Canton.[105]

Prostitution was also commonly perceived as an acceptable alternative to starvation or destitution for a woman in dire straits. Lo Li-ming, a contemporary writer and a regular to high-class brothels, reminisced that many women in this business were brought up in a decent family but were driven by unfortunate personal or familial circumstances into this ill-reputed profession. These women considered their jobs as a kind of temporary shelter, and would leave as soon as good fortune returned to them. He reminded his readers to read the pitiable experiences of these women with respect instead of contempt.[106] This perception of prostitution as a refuge could be easily found in newspaper and magazines articles of this period, which also reflected the popularity of such a view.[107] An abolitionist opined that whenever a woman was mistreated by her relatives, or whenever she wanted to free herself from a stifling life in an authoritarian family, opportunities for her to lead an independent life were so few that she would most likely end up in a brothel. In the eyes of this concerned intellectual, the core of the problem of prostitution in China lay in the family structure and domestic authoritarianism and the lack of economic independence of her women.[108] Another concerned writer questioned the feasibility of the government's advocacy to abolish legalized prostitution on the grounds that the authorities had not worked out any alternatives for the women involved. Given the weaknesses in the economy and educational resources, this author doubted the practicability of such a plan that would further limit the job opportunities for women on the breadline (Ching-chien 1924: 3). All these voices tended to reflect one common view on this profession—that it served some meaningful social purposes. This might provide a brothel-goer with a kind of psychological comfort that helped him rationalize his visits and lessen his feelings of guilt.

Interestingly, some viewed prostitution as a 'necessary evil' in a religious or moral sense. To them, brothels and prostitutes were ethically justified as part of the heavenly design of karma in which both the prostitutes and the brothel-goers were living out their predestined punishments. In a nineteenth-century Cantonese ballad, for example, a murderous stepmother and her accomplice are said to be reborn as whores who would suffer the ultimate humiliation of remaining uninterred after death.[109] In most nineteenth-century *Yüeh-ou* love-songs, prostitutes were seen as condemned sinners repaying their 'flower debts' incurred in previous lives, and therefore undergoing a form of retributive punishment. This karmic view of prostitution was still in currency during the Republican period. In the 1920s version of *Yüeh-ou* songs, both prostitutes and brothel-goers suffering from 'fornication-related' misfortunes such as bankruptcy or infection with venereal diseases were seen as sinners being punished for sins committed in previous lives. Sometimes, we are told, a prostitute, instead of being on the receiving end of retributive punishment, metes it out to the brothel-goers, especially rich but parsimonious patrons who earned their wealth by exploiting others:

> [You may] blame me for trying again to 'disembowel you with a sword' (i.e. solicit an unfairly large sum of money from a customer)... [But since there are] so many people whom you have castrated (i.e. squeezed), [now] is the time for me, your slave, to do the same to you... Need I remind you that the few yüan [that you have paid me] were hardly earned by you in honest ways. [Such money] can be only scattered into the 'flower forest' to buy suggestive smiles from us. But no money gained immorally can be kept for long... Though nobody can do anything now about [the way you earned it], Heaven will settle the account with you.[110]

The brothel had become an 'execution ground' of retributive punishment in the karmic order. And the existence of prostitutes was justified by their dual role as both sufferer and executant in this divine scheme of justice.

In short, Cantonese perceptions of prostitution was far from being one-sidedly negative. Some viewed it as an agreeable form of entertainment; others saw it serving positive social functions; while others justified it on ethico-religious grounds. Condemnation was never entirely absent, but such disapproval was inadequate to alter the generally favourable view, and the widespread patronage, of prostitution in Canton.

5. *OFFICIAL PERCEPTIONS AND CONTROL*

Ambivalence and its Pecuniary Causes

Ambivalent attitudes towards prostitution were shared no less by the city authorities. Although denounced as one of the 'bad customs' (*pu-liang fêng-su*) in an official campaign for social reform in 1930, the issue of prostitution was a low-profile one.[111] Throughout this period, the Cantonese authorities never attempted to eliminate prostitution altogether, or even to take drastic action to suppress the 'vice'. A few nominal measures were, however, implemented: a handful of reform shelters for ex-prostitutes were established; occasional calls for the registration of prostitutes in the naive hope of controlling the profession;[112] girls under 16 were prohibited from working in brothels; health inspectors were randomly sent to local brothels to check the hygiene conditions and whether the girls were being treated humanely (*Kuang-chou nien-chien* 1935: 62–3, ch. 7; Lee Bing-Shuey 1936: 96). These measures, however, were chiefly concerned with the maltreatment of prostitutes and the provision of a more hygienic service to brothel-goers, and hardly amounted to a sincere attempt to eradicate the practice.

The government had no long-term plans for the relief of prostitutes. The founding of the refuge shelter for girls and women (*Chi-liang So*) was proclaimed as a first step towards the suppression of prostitution, but this institution was hardly successful in fulfilling this aim. First, it was not devoted entirely to the care of prostitutes. Lost children, runaway domestics (*mui-tsai*), 'procured' girls who had been recovered, and homeless women were also received there. Secondly, in the early 1920s, there was only one such refuge in Canton. Its insignificant monthly budget of 400 yüan limited the number of inmates to fifty, and restricted the quality of rehabilitation work (Li Tsung-huang 1922: 28). The entire institution was run by only one supervisor, one accountant, one inspector, and one teacher.[113] By the end of the 1920s, the number of its inmates at any one time had grown to about 400, and the annual budget to about 7,500 yüan (*Kuang-chou-shih shih-chêng t'ung-chi hui k'an* 1929: 102–3, 231). However, its effectiveness as a true institution of relief remains dubious. Even the official view of this institution was critical and unfavourable. It was criticized for its inadequate funding and poor management, which rendered it a quasi-prison and discouraged prostitutes from seeking assistance there (Ma Huan-huan 1930: 216). Once admitted, an inmate was not allowed to leave the premises until discharged.[114] And instead of being given any real vocational training, inmates, in 'compulsion of their freedom' (Franck 1925: 272), were eagerly married off to men seeking mates (Li Tsung-huang 1922: 28).[115] A combination of poor management and corruption was responsible for at least one incident in which the inmate's marriage was arranged with an unauthorized man.[116]

One of the major reasons for the lack of determination to eliminate prostitution was the lucrative tax on the business. Since 1904, an excise tax had been levied on brothels in Canton, an operation in which tax-farmers were actively involved. Originally, the excise tax was intended to finance the organization of the River Police Department, but it was gradually channelled towards the funding of a variety of government projects, such as the building of schools and the repair of dykes.[117] On the eve of the 1911 Revolution, the local administration had become so dependent on this source of revenue that the rate imposed on the licensed brothels was increased by 20 per cent (*HTJP* 1911; 14 July).[118] When the local government, as a means to stabilize the socio-political situation, ordered the abolition of all surcharges on the 'flower business' shortly after the revolutionary movement in Central China began, all the brothels in Canton celebrated by letting off fireworks and making pilgrimages to local temples (*HTJP* 1911, 1 Nov.).

It is not clear how long this benevolent rule lasted. It is clear, however, that the 'flower tax' was once again imposed in late 1913 and was farmed out to a tax brokerage company for an annual sum of 200,000 yüan (*HTJP* 1914: 1.3, 6 Jan.).[119] By the early 1920s, prostitution-related revenue had become a major source of income for both provincial and municipal governments. In 1922, the 'flower-feast surtax' was the fourth largest source of revenue for the municipal government. It brought to the treasury coffers a handsome injection of 650,000 yüan, 8 per cent of the municipal income for that year. There was a surcharge on the number of rooms in a brothel (*hua-liu fang-chuan*), and an additional surcharge on top of the 'flower-feast surtax' for funding ditch-dredging projects.[120] The 'flower-feast surtax' was so lucrative that in 1922 and 1924 a substantial portion of it was usurped by the Yünnanese militarists, who occupied Canton at Sun Yat-sen's request, from the municipal government, and despite months of negotiation it was never fully reclaimed until these 'guest' soldiers were driven away from Canton by force in 1925.[121]

Throughout the 1920s, both the leftist and rightist regimes in Canton continued to enjoy the pecuniary benefits from this source of revenue, despite the occasional call for the elimination of prostitution. During the early 1920s, the 'flower-feast surtax' provided the municipal government with a much-needed yearly income of 510,000 yüan, the second largest item of revenue for the city administration. Most of these money went to finance the various municipal projects relating to, in particular, policing work and education (Li Tsung-huang 1922: 12, 40). In 1925, the 'flower-feast surtax' accounted for some 450,000 yüan, or 13 per cent of the municipal treasury's total surtax income. In 1926, the amount collected had increased to 680,000 yüan, or 18 per cent of the total surtax income. It was in that same year that the government proposed issuing licences to streetwalkers as a means of raising revenue. But in the face of 'ferocious criticism' by the various women's associations in Canton the plan was eventually abandoned (*KCMKP* 1926: 10, 28–Oct.). Nevertheless, from 1928 until the fall of Ch'en Chi-t'ang in 1935, the annual revenue from the 'flower-feast surtax' alone remained at about 450,000 yüan (*Kuang-chou-shih shih-chêng t'ung-chi hui k'an* 1929: 227, 229; *Kuang-chou nien-chien* 1935: 102, ch. 9). Prostitution-related revenues continued to be used for funding infrastructure projects and vocational education.[122] In late 1920s, for example, in the standard minimum charge of 3 yüan that a patron paid to a high-class brothel for his visit and non-sexual services included 50 cents of 'flower surtax', 30 cents of military expense surcharge, 20 cents of municipal charge, 15 cents of sewage dredging charge, 40 cents of educational charge, and 20 cents of art and craft charge. Both a madam and a prostitute would get an equal share of 60 cents each (Kuang-chou-shih shih-chêng-t'ing 1927).[123] In 1933, the standard minimum charge for the same service was increased to 4 yüan, of which 2.6 yüan went to the government coffer as taxes (*KPP* 1933: 3.2, 16 July). The range of public projects that it funded, and the substantial sum that it contributed, inevitably hindered the official determination to suppress prostitution (Lee Bing-shuey 1936: 95).[124] Even in fall 1936, when the newly inaugurated pro-Nanking KMT authorities in Canton announced its determination to suppress all kinds of vices in Kwangtung, with prostitution being one of them, there was little sign to indicate to the enforcement of such a plan in the area of prostitution. Instead, there were proclamations of revised measures on taxing 'flower feast' and of an order that prohibited public servants to visit 'places of improper entertainment' in uniforms (Kuang-chou shih-chêng-fu 551, 1936: 15, 15 Oct.; 552, 1936: 115, 31 Oct.).

Therefore, from the early twentieth century to the late 1930s, prostitution revenues in Canton and Kwangtung cherished a 'proud record' of playing the honourable role of funding the late-Ch'ing reform, the local police forces of the various regimes, the Republican and Nationalist municipal administrations, the Northern Expedition, and the modernity projects of the local KMT government.[125]

It is interesting to note that despite the importance of this source of revenue for local administrations, the registration fee levied on a prostitute remained quite stable between the mid-1910s and the late 1920s. The actual increase in this form of revenue seemingly came mainly from the actual amount of surcharges imposed on 'transactions', or, in other words, on the patrons.[126]

The lure of this source of revenue explains the survival of the 'beautiful courtesan contest' (*hua-pang hsüan-chü*) into this period. Such contests were particularly favoured by scholar-gentlemen (*ming shih*). From the meagre surviving sources, it is known that the first contest of this kind in which the participants were required to be both beautiful and accomplished in the arts was held in 1904, sponsored and organized by a newspaper company (Wang Shu-nu 1988: 302). The frequency of these contests is not known, but they were apparently held from time to time. In 1925, at the peak of the leftist rule in Canton, a scholar-gentleman organized a successful contest of this kind (*KCMKJP* 1926: 5, 29 Oct.). Three years later, a tax-farmer in Canton requested official approval to organize another contest, though, this time, it was to be conducted differently: votes in the form of tickets were to be distributed to the brothels with girls taking part in the contest. Participants would then implore their clients to purchase from them as many tickets as possible, because the one who sold most tickets would win the title. In spite of being 'heatedly criticized' by two local women's associations, the municipal authorities acceded to the proposal after the tax-farming company had agreed to pay the municipal government 2,000 yüan in return (*NYSP* 1928: 11, 10 Aug.). Sketchy information revealed that this kind of contest survived through the early 1930s, and perhaps even longer. In 1933, a similar gala was held in Canton although its timing was criticized by some patriotic citizens as being insensitive to the gloomy mood of the nationals as a result of the Shanghai Incident. Nonetheless, the contest was held as scheduled, which was favourably reported in local newspapers (*KPP* 1933: 3.2, 19 June). This practice won a certain amount of public support, and a magazine article defended such contests as morally acceptable, its author comparing them with international beauty contests, and argued that both were ethically justifiable.[127] Popular supportive views of this kind probably helped the government rationalize its tolerance of the 'vice'.

The late-Ch'ing administration had openly expounded its view of prostitutes as taxable 'goods'. An official publication concerning Kwangtung financial policy published in 1909, stated that:

> It is known that prostitutes are the most indecent and degraded [group] in the whole of society. [They can] eat and dress well without ever tilling [the soil] or weaving... Viewed superficially, prostitutes are those who cream off the 'profits' [from society]. Nonetheless, their existence in a city, which is full of local and expatriate merchants, can also bring prosperity... Thus, prostitution cannot at this stage be suppressed. Moreover, it is almost impossible to prohibit it because the already serious problem of clandestine prostitutes will only be aggravated, and further damage social morality. Hence, it is better to tax these women so that some control can be kept over them, and allocate the revenue for local use. (Kuang-tung ch'ing-li-tsai-chêng-chü 1910: 40–1)

Although such pragmatic views on prostitution are not found in official publications of a later period, the fundamental perception of sex-workers as an exploitable 'asset' and a necessary evil was deep-rooted. It was a rationalization that allowed the government free rein to use prostitutes as a source of revenue for the funding of local projects, and as a means to prosper a city. When the Canton Bund was completed in the late 1910s, for example, a local official devised and implemented a plan to boost land values in the newly reclaimed area, successfully persuading entrepreneurs to build a number of Western-style multi-storey buildings, a theatre for Cantonese opera, and an amusement park. In the advertisement for this stretch of newly developed land printed in a government daily, potential investors were reminded of the great commercial opportunity of this area because brothels and military barracks were said to be soon established there; the former, as it is claimed, would bring about commercial prosperity, and the latter public security (Kuang-tung shêng hsüan-an-shih kung-ch'u 1915: 21). Certain brothel-barons, before long, agreed to move most of their establishments, then located within the walled city, into this area (K'ung Fu-an 1934: 14–15);[128] this confirms the fact that throughout the period there was no plan to banish brothels to relatively remote parts of the city in order to suppress them,[129] as the government attempted to do with gambling houses and opium dens. Unlike the latter two, brothels in Canton, being considered acceptable business enterprises, were allowed to continue operating during the brief official campaign against social vices in the mid-1930s (Kuang-chou-shih chêng-hsieh 1987: 30).

In fact, such an official 'functional' view of prostitution has a much longer history in China. Prostitution was seen officially as a trade that not only helped prosper a community by stimulating brothel-related businesses, but also provide employment to such city 'poor' as sedan-chair carriers, servants and maids, actors and musicians. An early nineteenth-century Chinese scholar praised brothels, gambling-houses, and theatres as 'charity halls for the poor' (Wang Shu-nu 1988: 340–1).

The lack of organized public opinion could have been another factor contributing to the half-heartedness of official policies aimed at eliminating prostitution. The criticisms of intellectuals regarding its 'pernicious' social consequences never gained impetus, and it is doubtful whether they had any impact on the public at large. At most, these moral preachers may have caused short-lived embarrassment to the authorities. Although certain organizations were persistent in taking a lone stand for the elimination of the vice, their voice was so weak and their effect so small that they find no mention even in contemporary writings on the subject.[130] A concerned citizen groaned that despite increasing public concern over the problem of prostitution, nothing practically effective had been achieved leading to its abolition. He recalled a relatively large-scale anti-prostitution campaign organised by the Christian groups in Canton in 1922. Although this two-month-long crusade succeeded in arousing the public awareness of the issue, it was unable to sustain the people's interest nor to accomplish anything thorough. The campaign died down quietly (*HTJP* 1924: 13, 13 May).

More importantly, any criticism of prostitution on social grounds was swamped by the popular acceptance of it as an agreeable form of entertainment, as discussed earlier, and it was generally understood that prostitutes themselves were opposed to official plans for the abolition of their profession. In a *Yüeh-ou* song entitled 'Fei-ch'ang' (The Abolition of Prostitution), the narrator, as if a prostitute herself, summarizes the apprehensions of her co-workers on this issue:

> When there is nothing else to abolish, then it's 'eliminate the prostitutes'. But where can we sisters be settled, there are so many of us? They say if we learn skills at school our chances of getting a new job [and] travelling a different road for the rest of our lives will be easier, but I have spent the first half of my life in this 'smoky, flowery' place . . . and am good at nothing but finger-guessing games and singing. Suddenly there is this talk about making us reform, but where can we find enough customers to marry us, just like that? There may be one or two patrons who can understand us and show pity, but not all of them [are good enough for us to] take them home [as husband]. Perhaps we should shave our heads and become nuns . . . But our carnal thoughts are far from extinguished, so it would be hard to live out our days as vegetarians . . . We fear that employers will despise us and refuse us jobs, not to mention the miniscule monthly income which will scarcely buy flowers [for our hair]. . . We still have charm . . . and are young . . . how could we bear loneliness night after long night . . . ? While nobody can help plucking a beautiful flower when he sees it, how can we [beautiful] flowers be sure that those flower-obsessed butterflies will never come back? And by then we would be unlicensed . . . As for brothels, I dare not say they do no harm, but since men are merely looking for . . . happiness and distraction . . . they don't take them seriously. And when business in all trades is bleak, [brothels] can foster prosperity.[131]

The unwillingness of the prostitutes to abandon their lucrative jobs, the popular perception of the social usefulness of brothels and the technical difficulties in abolishing prostitution, and the uncontrollable growth in the number of unlicensed prostitutes (which merely indicated the depth of this entrenched social practice), all provided the government with excuses for not tackling the 'problem' with determination.

Ambivalence and its 'Official' Causes

The great popularity of brothel-going among military and government officials and politicians certainly undermined any serious attempt to abolish prostitution. There was a long tradition of military and civil officials patronizing brothels,[132] a tradition still very much alive in the 1920s and the 1930s. After Ch'en Chiung-ming's troops had taken Canton in 1911, for instance, the concentration in the city of army officers, infantrymen, and the rather unruly militiamen was said to have helped revitalize the declining brothel business in Ch'en-t'ang and the East Bund, where many brothels had been destroyed by a fire in 1910. High-class brothels in Ch'en-t'ang were usually crowded with inebriated senior army officers who delighted in firing their pistols into the air. Different groups of militiamen competing for the favour of their favourite prostitutes always ended up in fighting at brothels which caused serious disturbances to the citizens and tainted the image of the revolutionary cause. Ch'en-t'ang being in close proximity to Shameen, the Legation Quarter located there complained about this to the Canton government, and as a result Ch'en Chiung-ming ordered the closure of all brothels in the city (K'ung Fu-an 1934: 13–14; *HTJP* 1912, 10 and 12 Jan.). Needless to say, this injunction caused great inconvenience to local civilian brothel-goers, who had to travel to Fo-shan to meet their favourite prostitutes who had been forced to move there to ply their trade (K'ung Fu-an 1934: 17). The injunction, however, was not as effective when applied to those lustful soldiers and unruly militiamen who flooded into Canton by the hundreds after the collapse of the Manchu administration. There were reports of brothels that continued to operate unabated with the support of these revolutionary militiamen (*HTJP* 1912, 10, 26, and 31 Jan.). The seriousness of this open violation was reflected by the fact that the revolutionary headquarters had to dispatch a special force of 120 soldiers to ensure the successful implementation of this rule in the city's red-light districts (*HTJP* 1912, 12 Jan.). With the retreat of Ch'en Chiung-ming from Canton in mid-1912, brothels reopened (*KCPN* 1980: i. 135), and it is said that the new military bosses from then until the mid-1920s were once more dedicated patrons of brothels (K'ung Fu-an 1934: 15). In this period, military victory celebrations were often held in high-class floating brothels anchored along the scenic Pearl River.[133] Politicians, military officers, social notables, and powerful businessmen also mingled in these brothels where political deals were settled, and first-hand information on political plots, military movements, and monetary speculation was traded (Kuang-chou shih chêng-hsieh 1987: 360).[134]

Early generations of Chinese reformers or revolutionaries were not hostile to prostitution. On the contrary, all evidence suggested that there were keen patrons of prostitution among this group of idealists. Examples abound. In the reminiscences of Wu Chih-hui, a group of young reform-minded scholar-officials in Tientsin, including Sun Mo-han, who was later appointed as ambassador to France, often met and exchanged views on matters big and small in brothels where, in addition to buying favours, they also gambled and smoked opium (Lo Chia-lun et al. 1969: xvi. 249). In the reminiscences of Tsou Lu, a prominent KMT official, most of the provincial councillors in late-Ch'ing Canton enjoyed visiting brothels. Being a councillor himself and under peer pressure, he and Ch'en Chiung-ming (also a councillor and later a prominent military man) had once joined their colleagues for a 'flower feast' with, the author wrote, great reluctance (Tsou Lu 1984: 141). During the last days of the Manchu rule in Canton, public security was escalated after a series of assassinations of senior government officials. To intensify the hunt for revolutionaries, many plain-clothes detectives were dispatched to one of their favourite places—brothels, the others being guest houses and restaurants. In the testimony of an arrested assassin, the revolutionaries moved around from brothel to brothel to avoid having a permanent abode. Although it was not clear if they patronized the prostitutes during their time in these premises, their choice of these seedy places was rather unexpected (*HTJP* 1911, 5 and 23 Sept., 20 Oct.). It was Hu Han-min, a young revolutionary and loyal follower of Sun Yat-sen, who ordered the lifting of the ban on legal prostitution after the departure from Canton of his rival Ch'en Chiung-ming (*KCPN* 1980: i. 135). A journalist wrote half-jocularly that since 'millions of dollars of military expenses came from the ['flower'] taxes', people should visit brothels more often to help contribute to the Republican revolution, and to forget about the misery of life (*HTJP* 1912, 27 May). Another wrote jokingly that local prostitutes should consider raising their charges because their services, first, facilitated the work of those military officers who made deals and important decisions at the dining tables in brothels, and secondly helped boost the economy and hence taxation by squeezing the money from the wallets of those niggardly citizens who would otherwise never donate to the great cause (*HTJP* 1912, 5 Aug.). In Hong Kong, there were small teams of young men and women who called on restaurants, brothels and theatres to ask for donations for funding the Republican forces in Canton (*HTJP* 1912, 23 Jan.). In the eyes of these young Republicans, prostitution was no embarrassment to their revolutionary ideals. After all, the ban was originally a political contingency rather than a moral consideration.

This 'old link' between the revolutionaries and the world of prostitution did not diminish as the revolutionary enterprise in Canton grew. As soon as the news of Sun Yat-sen's success in winning the parliamentarians' nomination for president in spring 1921 spread, the overjoyed Nationalist politicians celebrated by driving seventeen vehicles slowly along the commercial boulevards of the city. The excited passengers drew public attention by beating gongs and empty cans, waving the Party and military flags, and shouting aloud slogans wishing Sun 'ten thousand years of age'. To the surprise of a reporter onlooker, present amid this group of prominent politicians was a popular high-class prostitute named Pien Ying. Her close acquaintance with a 'prominent politician' from this group endowed her with the privileges of mingling with these social notables and of taking part in political functions of such importance (*HTJP* 1921: 1.3 and 2.4, 11 Apr.). To create a festive ambience for the President's inauguration ceremony, the municipal administration commissioned a large number of pennants and small flags, on which were printed celebratory messages for the event. The city's brothels, together with all the rickshaw and bus companies, were supplied with these publicity materials, and they were ordered by the authorities to hang them up in conspicuous places in or outside their premises and vehicles on the date of the inauguration (*HTJP* 1921: 1.3, 29 Apr.). Meanwhile, visiting brothels continued to be a popular pastime for many military personnel. In spite of repeated warnings against brothel-going by military men ordered by Ch'en Chiung-ming, the military head of the Canton regime, it was never easy to stop senior officers from visiting brothels. There were cases of inspection teams sent out by the Army that were kicked out of brothels by senior military officers who disliked being disturbed. It was also widely reported in the newspapers that both military officers and infantrymen were involved in protecting the operation of unlicensed prostitution at many guest houses; and with this military backing, the local police force rarely dared to interfere into the business of these women (*HTJP* 1921: 1.3, 9 and 12 Apr., 18 May). In one case, the head of a government department was twice spotted patronizing unlicensed prostitutes and gambling in his exclusive abode. Military policemen had tried to investigate but were turned back. When his lawyer neighbour reported to the police that his concubine was seen being seduced by this 'prominent official' in his house, the police sent out a team of special forces to investigate. They were, however, taken aback when the man pointed a pistol at them. He eventually managed to drive away safely with two suspected unlicensed prostitutes and the concubine, leaving the powerless police officers behind (*HTJP* 1921: 1.3, 5 Apr.). Even the nephew of Liao Chung-kai (Minister of Finance in the Canton-based Nationalist government), a senior secretary at the Ministry of Finance, was described as a heavy addict of gaming and prostitution, so much so that his uncle had to issue a warning to all colleagues warning them to stop visiting brothels or face a reprimand (*HTJP* 1921: 1.3, 7 Apr.).

Not so surprisingly, even officials in the Revolutionary government of the mid-1920s (considered as the radical era in the city's modern history) were often regular patrons of high-class brothels, and seem to have found no ideological clash between brothel-going and their political activities (*KCMKJP* 1926: 11, 15 July; Franck 1925: 275).[135] Instead of suppressing this form of popular pastime,[136] the Revolutionary government chose to 'tolerate' and milk it. In 1926, for example, the government ordered all floating brothels in Canton to be parked at specific points so as to facilitate control and, above all, taxation (*KCMKJP*

1926: 10, 18 Aug.). In the same year, when the local administration announced a plan to raise the amount of surcharges on the 'flowery business' and to legalize unregistered prostitution, three women politicians serving in the Nationalist government telegraphed an angry letter of complaint to all major press in the region (*KCMKJP* 1926: 5, 30 Oct.; 1926: 10, 2 Nov.). Although the latter plan never materialized, the revenue generated from prostitution continued to fund the local government and its revolution.

After the outbreak of the Tsinan Incident in 1928, General Li Chi-shen, as an official gesture of mourning for those killed, placed a one-month prohibition on government employees attending banquets in 'public places', including brothels. But even for that short period the order was openly defied, and Li had to deploy plain-clothes detectives to patrol the red-light districts. In a number of raids on brothels more than twenty army officers and bureaucrats were arrested, among them the mayor of the city of Kiang-men. Those arrested were stripped of their honours and dismissed from office (*HTJP* 1928: 1.3, 4 June; *NYSP* 1928: 11, 14 June).

The author of a short article in a Cantonese magazine of late 1930 lamented the fact that certain officers of the respectable Nationalist Revolutionary Army—his neighbour being one—were enthusiastic frequenters of brothels. They saw themselves as folk heroes, loved and surrounded by beauties, while their frivolity and free spending, and the protection they afforded local brothels from harassment by local bullies, made them especially welcome (Wan Yung 1930: 90–2, 95–8).[137] It was in county cities distant from Canton that such liaison between government officials and prostitutes became unrestrained and open. From a report on a 'flower contest' held in the county city of T'ai-shan we are told that this grand event was treated with utmost respect by the local authorities. The contest was well attended by a long list of local officials and social dignitaries including representatives from the local Kuomintang office, the local official newspaper, the local police headquarters, the local magistracy, and so on. It was in all likelihood that the competition was inaugurated by one of the officials who attended (*KHP* 1933: 2.4, 25 June).

During the last years of the 1930s, before the 'golden decade' in modern Canton history was brought to an abrupt end by the Japanese invasion, prostitutes and local officials had apparently resumed their old cordial relations. As in the earlier period discussed above, prostitutes were keen to promote their public image and to have their self-confidence strengthened by shrewdly clinging, even symbolically, to the official establishment, and by taking advantage of the rising tide of nationalism. On the eve of Chiang Kai-shek's fiftieth birthday in late 1936, for example, a group of high-class prostitutes in Canton took the initiative in organizing a donation campaign within the 'flowery business' with the ambitious aim of raising enough money to purchase one warplane that would be sent to the generalissimo as a birthday present. To motivate their 'sisters' better, the organizing committee encouraged them to compete; those who succeeded in making the most contributions would be commended and awarded with huge silver-plated disks or vases. For a few consecutive evenings, these zealous prostitutes formed themselves into small teams and marched through the city to call at restaurants and tea-houses in the city's red-light quarters. The tax-farming company that handled the prostitution revenues agreed to surrender a portion of its income to the cause in order to help boost the morale of these participants. Meanwhile, 'sisters' in other counties apparently joined this campaign. In one county, any prostitute who succeeded in raising 50 yüan was allowed to work without wearing her 'flowery badge' (a kind of identification card) for six months. In the end, although the total amount of money raised was inadequate for buying the warplane, the event was jubilantly conducted and was apparently enjoyed by those who had taken part in it. The occasion was favourably reported in the local press; one story described the good deeds of these women as an act of unrestrained generosity (*hao-ch'ing*) (*YHP* 1936: 9, 1 Nov.).

In sum, the limited knowledge we have of prostitutes and prostitution during the period under review has been distorted by the presumptive views and misconceptions of those who have written on the subject from particular a priori political or moral standpoints. Generalized views and moralized observations do not help us to understand the complex subject of prostitution in Republican Canton. The diverse experiences of prostitutes in Canton show that many conventional assumptions about the severe hardship suffered by these unfortunate women were not always true. Moreover, popular perceptions towards prostitutes and brothel-going in Canton in this period were not necessarily as scathingly critical as the writings of social reformers or moralistic officials might lead us to believe. A well-off and popular high-class prostitute could well be perceived and regarded very differently by the general public from a poor and worn-out whore. And to many Cantonese men, visiting a respectable and well-kept brothel was by no means an immoral or ignominious act; it was an acceptable pastime.

REFERENCES

Abrams, Lynn (1988), 'Prostitutes in Imperial Germany, 1870–1918: Working Girls or Social Outcasts?', in Richard J. Evans (ed.), *The German Underworld: Deviants and Outcasts in German History* (London: Routledge).

Ah Mên (1928), 'Shih-t'ang yü fêng shên', *Hsiang hai hua-pao* 1.

Ai Ai (1928), 'Yeh yu meng chi-tou chi-shih', *Kung-p'ing pao* (*KPP*) (Canton: Kung-p'ing pao shê).

Aijmer, Göran (1984), 'Birth and Death in China: Musings on a Taiwan Groups', *Ethnos* 49/1–2.

Canton Advertising and Commission Agency, The (1932) (ed.), *Canton: Its Port, Industries & Trade* (Canton: The Canton Advertising and Commission Agency).

Chan-ch'i-ho-chu-jên (*c.*1926), *Hsin Yüeh-ou chieh hsin* (*HYOC*) (Canton: n.p.).

Chang Hsin-tai (1898), 'Yüeh yu hsiao chih', *Hsiao-fang-hu-chai yü-ti ts'ung ch'ao* ix, ed. Wang Hsi-pu (Shanghai: Chu i t'ang).

Chang-lao-yeh (1930), 'Liu k'o-shui shih', *Wu-hsien man-hua* 1/5.

'Ch'ang-liao su-yu' (n.d.), Chi-hsien-hsiao-yin, *Kai-liang Ling-nan chi shih* (Canton: Ta hsin shu-chü).

Chao (I) Ou-Pei (1975), 'Yen pao tsa chi', in *Pi-chi hsiao-shuo ta kuan*, 5th edn., vii (Taipei: Hsin Hsing shu-chü).

Ch'en Fei-nung and Yu Mu-yün (1982), *Yüeh-chü liu-shih nien* (Hong Kong: Wu hsing chi shu pao shê).

Ch'en Hsü-ching (1946), *Tan-min ti yen-chiu* (Shanghai: Shang-wu yin-shu-kuan).

Ch'en Li-chu, Huang Hsiu-hua, and Kuan Li-chen (1991) (eds.), *Kuang-tung fu-nü yun-tung li-shih tzu-liao*, 8 vols. (Canton: Kuang-tung-shêng fu-nü lien-ho-hui, Kuang-tung-shêng tang-an kuan).

Chi-hsien-hsiao-yin (*c.*1926), *Kai-liang Ling-nan chi shih* (Canton: Ta hsin shu-chü).

Ch'i wan hua shê (1910) (ed.), *Chung-kuo shih ta hai* (Canton: Shêng ch'ün shu-chü).

Ch'ien (1934), 'Pu kan hui shou', *Shê-hui heh-mu* 14.

Chien Ch'iu et al. (1975), 'Ch'ang-chi chih heh-mo', *Pi-chi hsiao-shuo ta kuan*, 7th edn. (Taipei: Hsin hsing shu-chü).

Chih-chi-shêng (1974), 'Chu-kiang ming hua hsiao ch'uan' (*CKMH*), in *Pi-chi hsiao-shuo ta kuan*, 5th edn., ix. 10 vols. (Taipei: Hsin Hsing shu-chü).

Chin Mang-ch'êng (1928), *Yung-hu kê-ming ti ching-jên chih* (Shanghai: Mei ti shu-tien).

Ching-chien (1924), 'Wei fei-ch'ang chien i-kê tsung-yao wên-t'i', *HTJP*, 28 Mar.

Ching Fo (1934), 'Mai shên chê yen', *Kuang-chou tsa-chih* (*KCTC*) 20 (Canton: Kuang-chou tsa-chih shê).

Chiu-chung-fêng-fu (*c.*1930s), *Ling-nan fêng-yüeh shih* (*LNFY*) (Canton: n.p.).

Chiu-chung-fêng-fu (*c.*1910s.), 'Ping szu chih k'u', *Kuang-chou shê-hui tsa-chih* 1.

Chou Hsia-min (1934), 'Kuang-chou hsia-chi chi-nü chih ta hsieh chên', *KCTC* 33 (Canton: Kuang-chou tsa-chih shê).

Chou Yu-liang (1935), 'Chu-kiang Mei Liu chi', in Chang Mêng-chêng and Chu Yüan-liang (eds.), *Ch'ing-lou yün yü* (Shanghai: Chung yang shu-tien).

Chu-kiang hsing-ch'i hua-pao (1927).

Ch'ü Ta-chün (1974), *Kuang-tung hsin yü*, 2 vols. (Hong Kong: Chung-hua shu-chü). First published 1700.

Chung-kuo jên-min chêng-chih-hsieh-shang-hui-i Kuang-tung-shêng Kuang-chou-shih wei-yüan-hui wên-shih tzu-liao wei-yüan-hui (1980) (eds.), *Kuang-chou pai-nien ta-shih chi* (*KCPN*), 2 vols. (Canton: Kuang-tung jên-min ch'u-pan-shê).

CKMH, *see* Chih-chi-shêng.

Dikötter, Frank (1995), *Sex, Culture and Modernity in China: Medical Science and the Construction of Sexual Identities in the Early Republican Period* (Hong Kong: Hong Kong University Press).

Eberhard, Wolfram (1967), *Guilt and Sin in Traditional China* (Berkeley: University of California Press).

——(1972), *Cantonese Ballads: München State Library Collection* (Taipei: Oriental Cultural Service).

Evans, Hilary (1979), *The Oldest Profession: An Illustrated History of Prostitution* (London: David & Charles).

Fêng-su kai-kê wei-yüan-hui (1930) (ed.), *Fêng-su kai-kê ts'ung k'an* (*FSKKTK*). (Canton: Kuang-chou-tê-pieh-shih tang-pu hsüan-ch'uan-pu).

Franck, Harry A. (1925), *Roving Through Southern China* (New York: Century).

FSKKTK, *see* Fêng-su kai-kê wei-yüan-hui.

Gamble, Sidney D. (1921), *Peking: A Social Survey* (New York: George H. Doran).

Gillingham, Paul (1983), *At the Peak: Hong Kong Between the Wars* (Hong Kong: Macmillan).

Gronewold, Sue (1985), *Beautiful Merchandise: Prostitution in China, 1860–1836* (New York: Harrington Park).

Gulik, Robert Hans van (1961), *Sexual Life in Ancient China: A Preliminary Survey of Chinese Sex and Society from ca. 1500 B.C. till 1644 A.D* (Leiden: E. J. Brill).

Hai-shang-chüeh-wu-shêng (1939), *Chi-nü ti shêng-huo* (Shanghai: Ch'un ming shu-tien).

Hao-chi-shêng (1928), 'Lêng Hung yü nan-hsin', *Hsiang hai hua-pao* 1.

Harrison, Fraser (1979), *The Dark Angel: Aspects of Victorian Sexuality* (Glasgow: Fontana/Collins).

Henriot, Christian (2001), *Prostitution and Sexuality in Shanghai: A Social History (1849–1940)* (Cambridge: Cambridge University Press).

Henriques, Fernando (1962–8), *Prostitution and Society: A Survey*, 3 vols. (London: Macgibbon & Kee).

Hershatter, Gail (1991), 'Prostitution and the Market in Women in Early Twentieth-Century Shanghai', in Rubie S. Watson, and Patricia Buckley Ebery (eds.), *Marriage and Inequality in Chinese Society* (Berkeley: University of California Press).

——(1997), *Dangerous Pleasures: Prostitution and Modernity in Twentieth-Century China* (Berkeley: University of California Press).

Ho, Kit-yiu Virgil (2001), ' "To Laugh at a Penniless Man Rather than a Prostitute": The Unofficial Worlds of Prostitution in Late-Qing and Early Republican South China', *European Journal of East Asian History* 1/1.

Hsiang hua hua-pao (1928–9), 1–4 (Canton: Hsiang hua hua-pao shê).

Hsiang-yen ts'ung-shu (*HYTS*) (1909–11) (Shanghai: Kuo-hsüeh fu-lun-shê).

Hsiao-tian-shih (1907) (ed.), *Sze yin ch'i* (Hong Kong: Kuang mou hao).

Hsin-tung-fang-shuo (1931), 'Su kan chi', *Wu-chia-pao* 2 (Canton).

Hsü Fu-chin (1948), *Kuang-tung min-chien wên-hsüeh ti yen-chiu* (Hong Kong: Hai ch'ao ch'u-pan-shê).

HTJP, see *Hua-tzu jih-pao* (Hong Kong: Hua-tzu jih-pao shê).

Hu P'o-an et al. (1986) (eds.), *Chung-hua ch'üan kuo fêng-su chih*, 2 vols. (Shih-chia-chuan: Ho-nan jên-min ch'u-pan-shê). First published 1923.

Hua-ts'ung-fên-tieh (1933), 'Ta-hsüeh shêng k'o-wai', *KCTC* 20.

Hua ying (1931), i (Hong Kong: Published privately by Ching-shao-êrh-lang).

Huai-ping-tzu (1911), 'Hua-chiu su', *HTJP*, 13 Sept.

HYOC, see *Chan-ch'i-ho-chu-jên.*

HYTS, see *Hsiang-yen ts'ung-shu.*

K'ang Su-chên (1990), *Ch'ing-lou hên hsü chi* (Ch'ang-ch'un: Chi-lin wên shih ch'u-pan-shê).

KCHJP, see *Kuang-chou hsin jih-pao.*

KCLPL see *Kuang-chou li-pai liu.*

KCMKJP, see *Kuang-chou min-kuo jih-pao.*

KCPN, see *Chung-kuo jên-min chêng-chih-hsieh-shang-hui-i and Kuang-tung-shêng Kuang-chou-shih wei-yüan-hui wên-shih tzu-liao wei-yüan-hui* (1980).

KCTC, see *Kuang-chou tsa-chih.*

KHP, see *Kuo hua pao.*

KPP, see *Kung-p'ing pao.*

KTHS, see *Kuang-tung chung-hsüeh hsüeh-shêng tzu-chih-hui.*

Kuang-chou hsin jih-pao (1933) (*KCHJP*) (Canton: Kuang-chou hsin jih-pao shê).
Kuang-chou li-pai liu (*KCLPL*) (*c.*1933–5) (Canton: Kuang-chou li-pai-liu shê).
Kuang-chou min-kuo jih-pao (*KCMKJP*) (Canton: Kuang-chou min-kuo jih-pao shê).
Kuang-chou nien-chien (1933), ed. Kuang-chou nien-chien pien tsuan wei-yüan-hui, 2 vols. (Canton: Kuang-chou nien-chien pien tsuan wei-yüan-hui).
Kuang-chou-shih chêng-hsieh wên shih tzu-liao yen-chiu wei-yüan-hui (1987) (ed.), *Nan t'ien sui yüeh: Ch'en Chi-t'ang chu Yüeh shih-ch'i chien wên shih lu* (Canton: Kuang-tung jên-min ch'u-pan-shê).
Kuang-chou-shih jên-min chêng-fu pan-kung tien (1951) (ed.), *Kuang-chou ching-ku'ang tiao-cha* (Canton: n.p.).
Kuang-chou-shih shê-hui chü (1930), 'Tiao-cha pên-shih-nei ch'ang-chi shêng-huo piao', Canton Municipal Archive, 10/4/1406.
Kuang-chou-shih shih-chêng-fu (1924), *Kuang-chou shih-chêng kung-pao* (Canton).
Kuang-chou-shih shih-chêng-t'ing (1924), *Kuang-chou-shih shih-chêng pao kao hui k'an* (Canton: Kuang-chou-shih shih-chêng-t'ing).
Kuang-chou-shih shih-chêng-t'ing shê-hui-tiao-cha-ku (1927) (ed.), *Ti sze lei: shê-hui pu-liang shih-yeh* (Canton).
Kuang-chou-shih shih-chêng-fu, *Kuang-chou-shih shih-chêng-Kung pao*
Kuang-chou-shih shih-chêng-fu t'ung-chi nien-chien (1929).
Kuang-chou-shih tiao-cha jên-k'ou wei-yüan-hui (1932), *Kuang-chou-shih êrh-shih-i-nien jên-k'ou tiao-ch'a pao kao.*
Kuang-chou tsa-chih (*KCTC*) (1924–30s) (Canton: Kuang-chou tsa-chih shê).
Kuang-tung ching-ch'a-t'ing chu-t'i chi-kuan chi-t'ing chi ch'ang-chi kuei tsê (*c.*1910s) (Canton).
Kuang-tung ch'ing-li-ts'ai-chêng-chü (1910), *Kuang-tung ch'üan shêng ts'ai-chêng shuo-ming shu*, 2 vols. (Tientsin: Ching-chi hsüeh hui).
Kuang-tung chung-hsüeh hsüeh-shêng tzu-chih-hui (ed.), *Kuang-tung hsüeh-shêng* (*KTHS*) (Canton).
Kuang-tung ch'üan shêng ts'ai-chêng shuo-ming-shu (1910).
Kuang-tung fêng-ching lu (*KTFCL*) (1988) (Canton: Kuang-tung jên-min ch'u-pan-shê).
Kuang-tung shêng hsüan-an-shih kung-chü (1915) (ed.), *Kuang-tung kung-pao* (Canton).
K'ung Fu-an (1934), 'Chu-kiang hua shih', *KCLPL* 20.
Kung-p'ing pao (*KPP*) (1924–49) (Canton: Kung-p'ing pao shê).
Kuo hua pao (*KHP*) (1911–50) (Canton: Kuo hua pao-shê).
Lamson, Herbert Day (1935), *Social Pathology in China*, 2nd edn. (Shanghai: Commercial Press).
Larsen, Jeanne (1987) (trans. and introd.), *Brocade River Poems: Selected Works of the T'ang Dynasty Courtesan Xue Tao* (Princeton, NJ: Princeton University Press).
Lee, Bing-shuey Edward (1936), *Modern Canton* (Shanghai: Kelly & Walsh).
Leeuw, Hendrik de (1953), *Cities of Sin* (London: Neville Spearman).
Lei Li-pin (1934), 'Hsin Fu', in Kuang-tung chung-hsüeh hsüeh-shêng tzu-chih-hui (ed.), *Kuang-tung hsüeh-shêng* (*KTHS*) (Canton), iv.
Lethbridge, Henry J. (1978), 'The Evolution of a Chinese Voluntary Association in Hong Kong: Po Leung Kuk', in id. (ed.), *Hong Kong: Stability and Change* (Hong Kong: Oxford University Press).
Leyda, Jay (1972), *Dianying: Electric Shadows: An Account of Films and Film Audience in China* (Cambridge, Mass.: MIT).

Li Ma-chu (*c.*1926), Preface, *Hsin Yüeh-ou chieh hsin* (*HYOC*) (Canton: n.p.).

Li Tsung-huang (1922), *Hsin Kuang-tung kuan-ch'a chi* (Shanghai: Shang-wu yin-shu-kuan).

Liu Fu-ching and Wang Ming-k'un (1992), *Chiu Kuang-tung yen tu ch'ang* (Hong Kong: Chung-hua shu-chü).

Liu Tsai-su (1926), *Kuang-chou kuai lan* (Shanghai: Shih-chieh shu-chü).

Liu Wan-chang (1928), 'Kuang-chou ti chiu sang su', *Su Yüeh ti hun sang* (Canton: Chung-kuo min-su hsüeh hui).

Liu Ying (1935), 'Chu-kiang ch'i yü chi', in Chang Mêng-chêng (ed.), *Ch'ing-lou yün yü* (Shanghai: Chung-yang shu-tien), ii.

LNFY, see Chiu-chung-fêng-fu.

Lo Chia-lun and Huang Chi-lu (1969) (eds.), *Wu Chih-hui hsien-shêng ch'üan chi*, 18 vols. (Taipei: Chung-kuo Kuo-min-tang chung-yang wei-yüan-hui tang-shih shih-liao pien-hsüan wei-yüan-hui).

Lo Li-ming (1962), *T'ang-hsi hua-yüeh hêng*, 4 vols. (Hong Kong: n.p.).

Lo-ti-jên (1930), 'Chung-yang kung-yüan', *Wu-hsien man-hua* 1/6.

Lu Yen (1981), *Hsiang-kang chang-ku* (Hong Kong: Kuang-chüeh-ching ch'u-pan-shê), ii.

Ma Huan-huan (1930), 'Fei-ch'u ch'ang-chi', *FSKKTK*.

'Mei-nü ti ching-sai yü hua-chieh hsüan-chü' (1930), *Wu-hsien man-hua* 1/7.

Mo-têng-nü (1934), 'Wen chi ch'i wu', *KCTC* 29.

Nan-fang jih-pao (*NFJP*) (1950–) (Canton: Nan-fang jih-pao shê).

Nan-yang shang pao (*NYSP*) Singapore: Nan-yang shang pao shê.

Ou-yang Shan (1948), 'Tsai shen ching li', *Shih-pai ti shih-pai-chê* (Shanghai, Ch'iao-fêng ch'u-pan-shê).

Pan-chiao man-hua (1929–32) (Canton: Pan-chiao man-hua shê).

P'ing Chin-ya (1989), 'Chiu Shang-hai ti tu-po', Shang-hai wên-shih yen-chiu kuan (ed.), *Chiu Shang-hai ti yen tu ch'ang* (Hong Kong: Chung yüan ch'u-pan-shê).

Ping Lan (1934), 'Lo sha hai shih shih-chêng-fu hui-i i-shih-lu', *KCTC* 26.

Po Leung Kuk (1978), *Centenary History of the Po Leung Kuk* (in Chinese) (Hong Kong: Board of Directors of Po Leung Kuk).

Remick, Elizabeth (2002), 'Taxing Prostitution in Republican Guangzhou', unpublished paper presented at Association for Asian Studies Annual Meeting, 4 April.

Schlegel, Gustav (1894), *A Canton Flower-Boat* (Leiden: E. J. Brill).

Shang-hai wên-shih yen-chiu kuan (1989) (ed.), *Chiu Shang-hai ti yen tu ch'ang* (Hong Kong: Chung yüan ch'u-pan-shê).

Sinn, Elizabeth (1994), 'The Protection of Women in 19th-Century Hong Kong', in Maria Jaschok and Suzanne Miers (eds.), *Women and Chinese Patriarchy: Submission, Servitude and Escape* (Hong Kong: Hong Kong University Press).

Sung Yü (1989), *T'ang-hsi chin-fên* (Hong Kong: I yüan ch'u-pan-shê).

Su T'ung (1992), *Hung fên* (Hong Kong: Tian-t'i tu-shu yu-hsien kung-ssu).

Têng Fei-p'eng (1978), 'Yang-ch'êng hua-hsü', *Kuang-tung wên-hsien chi k'an* 8/1.

Tien Chung-chi and Sun Chang-hsi (1984), *Chung-kuo hsien-tai hsiao-shuo shih* (Chi-nan: Shan-tung wên-i ch'u-pan-shê).

Tsou Lu (1984), *Tsou Lu hsien-shêng wên-chi*, ed. Chung-kuo Kuo-min-t'ang and Chung-yang hui-yüan-hui t'ang-shih wei-yüan-hui (Taipei: Chung-yang wên-chien kung-ying-shê).

Tsui-mien-shan-jên (*c.*1920s), *Kuang-tung heh-mo ta kuan* (Canton: n.p.).

Ts'un Shih (1988), 'Yen-hua hsüeh lei hua Ch'en-t'ang', in Kuang-tung shêng chêng-hsieh wên shih tzu-liao yen-chiu wei-yüan-hui (ed.), *Kuang-tung fêng-ching lu* (*KTFCL*) (Canton: Kuang-tung jên-min ch'u-pan-shê).

Tu Yün-chih (1972), *Chung-kuo tien-ying shih*, 2 vols. (Taipei: Shang-wu yin-shu-kuan).

Tung-kuo-hsien-shêng (1990), *Chi chia fêng yüeh* (Shih-chia-chuang: Peh-yüeh wên-i ch'u-pan-shê).

Tzu-hang-shih (1919), *Kuang-chou chih-nan* (Canton: Hsin hua shu-tien).

Umeda Ikuzo (1913), 'Kanton no iji oyobi eisei', *Shina* 4/9, May.

Vogel, Ezra (1969), *Canton Under Communism: Programs and Politics in a Provincial City, 1948–1968* (Cambridge, Mass.: Harvard University Press).

Wan Yung (1930), 'Ping hou luan t'u' and 'T'an tu chiang-chien', *Wan jên tsa-chih* 1/3.

Wang Shu-nu (1988), *Chung-kuo ch'ang-chi shih* (Shanghai: San lien shu-tien).

Warren, James Francis (1994), 'Chinese Prostitution in Singapore: Recruitment and Brothel Organization', in Maria Jaschok and Suzanne Miers (eds.), *Women and Chinese Patriarchy: Submission, Servitude and Escape* (Hong Kong: Hong Kong University Press).

Wolfe, Arthur (1975), 'The Women of Hai Shan', in Margery Wolfe and Roxane Witke (eds.), *Women in Chinese Society* (Stanford: Stanford University Press).

Wolfe, Barnard (1980), *The Daily Life of A Chinese Courtesan Climbing Up a Tricky Ladder* (Hong Kong: Learner's Bookstore).

Wu Hao (1989), *Fêng yüeh T'ang-hsi* (Hong Kong: Po i ch'u-pan-shê).

Wu-hsien man-hua (1929–1930s) (Canton: Na-fang fu lun shê).

Wu Jui-lin (1934*a*), 'Sha-nan tan-min tiao-ch'a pao kao', *Ling-nan hsüeh pao* 3/1.

——(1934*b*), *San-shui tan-min tiao-ch'a* (Canton: Ling-nan ta-hsüeh shê-hui yen-chiu so).

Wu Wu-yao (1986), *Fa ts'ai pi-chüeh*, in Chung Hsien-pei (ed.), *Wu Yen-jên hsiao-shuo hsüan* (Chêng-chou: Chung chou shu hua shê).

Wu Yü, Liang Li-ch'êng, and Wang Tao-chi (1988), *Min-kuo heh-shê-hui* (Nanking: Kiang-su ku-chi ch'u-pan-shê).

Yang Chieh-tseng and Ho Yüan-nan (1988), *Shang-hai ch'ang-chi kai-tso shih hua* (Shanghai: Shang-hai San-lian shu tien).

Yang Pu-wei (1967), *I-kê nü-jên ti tzu-chüan* (Taipei: Chüan-chi wên-hsüeh ch'u-pan-shê).

Yü Chiao-ch'ing (1909), 'Ch'ao Chia fêng yüeh chi', *Hsiang-yen ts'ung-shu* (*HYTS*) 1/4 (Shanghai: Kuo-hsüeh fu-lun-shê).

Yüeh-hua pao (*YHP*) (1927–50) (Canton: Yüeh-hua pao shê).

Zhang Xinxin and Sang Ye (1987), *Chinese Lives: An Oral History*, ed. and trans. W. J. F. Jenner and Delia Davin (New York: Pantheon), 33.

6

Cantonese Opera as a Mirror of Society

One sunny winter afternoon in 1990, the news of the death of one of the most popular stars in the world of Cantonese opera reached a village in the Canton Delta via a radio broadcast from Hong Kong, which was illicitly but commonly received by the thousands in this region. When the news broke, a European anthropologist and I were in that village, discussing local customs and kin relationships with a group of village men and women in the comfortable mansion of a local notable. All the villagers present, without exception, were shocked by the news and responded by much sighing at the unfortunate lost of a superstar and their old-time idol. Our inquiries had, by comparison, suddenly become unimportant, and were subsequently ignored, as conversations in the following hours were shifted to this Cantonese opera diva (which disappointed my European anthropologist friend a lot), and every elderly villager present contributed to this ad hoc form of collective memory by giving their appraisals of the excellence of her singing and acting and of which scripts and what roles that she had performed had impressed them most; some could even retell in vivid detail the scenes and the lyrics that they had enjoyed and called to mind most. The cultural power and the emotional importance of Cantonese opera to its audiences, as this anecdote shows, can be very strong indeed. Like any art form, Cantonese opera in this period was a socio-cultural product of its society. Therefore, to study Cantonese opera—its scripts and theatrical technique, its performers and audiences—will contribute to our knowledge of the mental worlds of its contemporaries, as well as of aspects of life in Canton.[1]

1. INTELLECTUALISTIC PERCEPTIONS AND MISCONCEPTIONS

A popular form of entertainment does not automatically enjoy universal critical acclaim and acceptance. On the contrary, there are always people who question the social relevance and cultural value of such entertainment (Frith 1987: 133; Gans 1974: 3; Docherty et al. 1987: 89).[2] Cantonese opera, being popular, was hardly exempt. Criticisms of it not only provide us with a different view of some aspects of this popular form of entertainment, but also, though ironically, with insights as to why Cantonese opera should have been so popular.

In *Ho lang pi-chi* (Notes of the Lotus Colonnade), one of the few extant late-Ch'ing sources that touch briefly on Cantonese opera, the author's contemptuous view was perhaps typical of the scholar-literati of his time:

> Those [troupes which] are taught by teachers from Kwangtung and perform mostly in cities and villages are called local troupes... They employ many actors. Their stage properties and customs are very splendid and beautiful... [They] perform complete scripts (*chêng pên*)... [which] are long enough for a whole-day-long performance. However, its lyrics and spoken parts are all extremely rude, rustic, and vulgar. Moreover, [their scripts are] uncorroborated with [historical] facts. [Their actors] pay no attention to eye-expression (*kuan mu*) [and hence perform in] insubstantial style. The entire business is a fake. Or else [they] plagiarize from vernacular historical novels names of [familiar] characters in antiquity, [and then] have their deeds altered [for their own ends]. Or else they turn things upside down by copying deeds [from a historical novel], renaming its protagonists; all done in contradiction to [theatrical] principles... When pedlars, commoners, stupid villagers and the unemployed... watch these plays, in which the licentious behaviour of the bad characters is not punished appropriately, instantly in their minds-and-hearts grow improper desires, impropriety, and subversive contempt... At several times in the past during the reigns of Emperors Hsien-fêng and T'ung-chih, edicts have been issued to prohibit this [kind of performance]. But... [things] remain unchanged.[3]

If this author had lived to see the 1920s and the 1930s, he would have been further infuriated by the fact that all these 'bad characteristics' of Cantonese troupes not only persisted, but were magnified. Cantonese opera playwrights continued to borrow loosely from traditional sources of scripts and vernacular novels; stage gimmicks, or innovations depending on one's point of view, were introduced in uncountable numbers. In fact, such repackaging of old scripts was itself a source of attraction because it supplied variants of, and hence alternatives to, this otherwise rigid and strictly conventionalized form of traditional opera.

By the 1920s, although 'modern' Cantonese opera was established as the 'orthodox' regional opera of Kwangtung, criticisms from Western-inspired and foreign-educated intellectuals grew. In the article 'On Cantonese Opera', the disparaging view of its author was typical of how that contemporary intellectual circle saw Cantonese opera. In terms of scripts, it was both socially and culturally worthless:[4]

> Scripts [that are] played by actors in Europe and [North] America... are either adapted from the works of famous literature-writers or artists, or else are commissioned from famous writers... I am afraid that it will be a piece of awe-inspiring news if [there is ever] any [Cantonese opera] company or actor who commissions a university professor or well-known writer to write a script for them [to perform].

In terms of plot development and ending, Cantonese opera was criticized for being unbearably repetitive and predictable: its major protagonists always suffer every kind of injustice and ordeal in the beginning, but survive all odds and difficulties to take revenge eventually on their enemies and marry the one they love. The quality of acting was also condemned: 'With an opium addict playing the role of a scholar, a violent villain playing brave general; a bully playing hero; a prostitute the role of a gracious young lady; these are some characteristics of their casting.' The writer went on to quote a journalist's review of an opera featuring Ma Shih-ts'êng, one of the most popular actors in this period, in which he played the role of a famous Sung general Chao Tzu-lung:

> [Throughout the play, I saw nothing but] actors [that] came and went. They fought chaotically with pennants, flags, spears and swords... [I]n the views of those who understand [opera], it was nothing more than an impression of busy movement, which was so chaotically done that one could hardly tell who was who [on the stage]... Ma Shih-ts'êng... only screamed and jumped wildly like a market-place rascal. If the late General Chao had known about this, he would have felt sad and shed tears... Sao Yün-lan (the leading actress) only knew how to flirt [with her audiences]. Thus, when she played the role of Sun Shang-hsiang, [the image of] this beauty, who [enjoyed a high reputation for] a thousand years, became degraded into that of an unlicensed prostitute and cheap whore.

To the writer Ch'u Chien, the vernacularized lyrics in contemporary opera did not appeal. He criticized actors for their eagerness to bring laughter to audiences by introducing vulgar and smutty phrases into the lyrics and libretto. Anachronistic use of props and costume was also condemned. In the same scene of a play, three characters were said to dress in costumes of three different historical periods: an old man in that of the Ming, his son in Ch'ing, and his daughter-in-law in that of Republican Shanghai. On stage,

> [one can easily find] a few half-naked lower-class workers, standing at both sides of the wings, busy... pulling ropes in a chaotic manner. In [an] old-costume play... the back-drop is, however, painted with numerous electrical lamps. Similarly, in a play set in the T'ang Dynasty, a maid-servant shouts aloud for 'policemen' to catch a thief.

In his view, a 'true form of art' must possess the qualities of ' "truth" as in science, "beauty" as in art, [and] "goodness" as in ethics'. He found none of these in contemporary Cantonese opera. Instead:

> To-day Cantonese opera has become... too decadent to be salvaged... [I]t has been violating the [good] spirit of the [society]... If this [is allowed to] persist for a longer time, it will be just like planting pernicious seeds of decadence into the national character [of the people], into the future of the society, into the evolution of mankind...

The appalling quality of contemporary opera was conveniently ascribed to the uncivic, unpatriotic, and poor educational backgrounds of its audiences (Ch'u Chien 1929: 107–19)[5].

Chinese Communist historians pass similar judgement on the worthlessness of Cantonese opera in this period. One of them, Yü Chia-yen, argues that since most Cantonese opera scripts written in the Republican period were under the 'culturally corruptible' influence of 'imperialistic' Hong Kong and Macao, their contents inevitably 'stink of capitalistic, feudalistic, and imperialistic' vulgarity and absurdity. Historical plays are said to be generally better in artistic quality, because most of them were simply plagiarized from classical scripts or novels. But those that were adapted from Western movies or novels are, due to their 'compadorized, bourgeoisified' nature, denounced by this Marxist historian as 'reactionary, obscene, frivolous, and anachronistic' in content. Some of the scripts are said to be relatively progressive in theme, since they exposed the ugly side of Republican society; their standpoints, however, were too 'capitulationist' and 'compromising' to be classified as 'good' scripts by the Socialist standard (Yü Chia-yen 1983: 430–41).

Ch'u's idealization of Western culture and Yü's of the Chinese past represent two distinct intellectual trends in the two different periods of Chinese history they belong to.[6] Misconceptions of the West had probably led Ch'u to believe that Western theatre was nothing less than the intellectually deep works of Brecht and Ibsen, though this is far from true.[7] Nor it is true that the large repertoire of traditional Chinese opera contains nothing but 'good' scripts. Accusations against the obscenity of popular opera might be mere disdainful remarks made by arrogant scholars who were eager to show off their morally and politically 'superior' outlook. Evaluating the moral quality of an opera is a highly subjective and even idiosyncratic task. As we shall see later in this chapter, contemporary opera scripts were not always 'bad' in quality. Sometimes, they even won acclaim from the intellectual circle.[8] Nonetheless, these 'critical essays' vividly reveal not only how a historical social phenomenon can be interpreted so differently, but also the kind of things that enabled Cantonese opera in its golden age to attract so many audiences.

2. *WHO WANTED SERIOUS OPERA FOR ENTERTAINMENT?*

Criticism of Cantonese opera by the well-educated elite was not something unique to the Republican times, but can be traced at least to mid-Ming. During the late-imperial period, most of the strong-worded condemnations of Cantonese opera (and other forms of local opera such as Ch'ao-chou in the eastern part of the province) were written by either literati or scholar-officials, some of whom were not native Cantonese but had stayed or worked in Kwangtung.[9] The authors of these criticisms never hid their open contempt for the 'poor artistry' and the 'immoral content' of Cantonese opera. Some were also upset by the fact that they could not understand all parts of the libretto since singing was already commonly done in Cantonese or in a mixture of Cantonese and a distorted form of Mandarin. Moreover, since these professed connoisseurs had always judged the quality of Cantonese opera by comparing it with Soochow opera, or *K'un-ch'ü*, which was the most patronized form among the scholar-literati and scholar-official circles from late Ming to late Ch'ing (Mackerras 1988: 92–4), they were naturally disappointed at the failure of Cantonese opera to comply strictly to elements and features found in its Soochow counterpart. *K'un-ch'ü* was appraised by its elitist patrons for its gentility, artistic simplicity and superb techniques; its music was basically smooth and delicate, while it stressed accuracy in enunciation and propriety in delivery in terms of acting and singing (Hu 1988: 70–1)—qualities that were by no means totally absent from Cantonese opera, but hardly its major sources of attraction in the eyes of the common audience whose patronage helped sustain the steady growth and then the eventual boom of this form of opera. Although *K'un-ch'ü* seems to have been liked, though briefly, by some commoners in Kwangtung during the late-Ming period, probably for its novelty. By early Ch'ing, however, in spite of *K'un-ch'ü's* refined taste and elegant artistry, it had lost its attraction in the eyes of the common audience in Canton and elsewhere in Kwangtung,[10] who preferred regional operas for the qualities disapproved by the cultural elite—profanity, unconventionality, sensationalism, impropriety, and vulgarity.[11]

Yang Mou-chien, a scholar from eastern Kwangtung, recorded in the 1840s his disapproving observation of the lack of sophistication and the vulgarity of local opera in the city of Canton:

> There are two types of opera [troupes] performing in Canton: those from other provinces (*wai chiang*), and the local ones. Those *wai-chiang* troupes are all from the outside [of Kwangtung]. The music and the actors [of these *wai-chiang* troupes] are all amusingly selected; the [theatrical] skills and the artistry of their acting are both excellent. To have them invited to entertain guests at a feast is a most delightful and heartfelt audio experience.... They dance respectfully, always with their heads turbaned in beautifully embroidered brocades. Local troupes, however, specialise in acrobatics and martial art; their performances are more focused on man [rather than music and dancing]. The stories their performance [is] based [on] are mostly [casually fabricated and therefore] beyond any close [scholarly] scrutiny. The lyrics [of these plays] are unscholarly and incoherent, while their stories are incoherent and frivolous. Everyday when a play is performed, [so many] firecrackers are burnt that the sky is littered with dust and paper flecks, which poses serious fire hazards to the city. Fortunately, virtuous officials considered this [form of opera] as harmful to the people, and have been trying to ban it strictly. As a result, [local troupes are now] only allowed to perform in the countryside. Blowing horns and beating gongs, its music is so deafening that [it] will make one dizzy. But its costume is so wastefully extravagant and pretty that whenever its actors come on stage, one can hardly resist to have one's eyes set on them, for [their costumes] are just like the seven varieties of gems on display on a grand arena; [similar extravagance] can never be found even in opera theatre in the capital city.[12]

Yang Mou-chien despised Cantonese opera for the things that made it highly attractive to the common audiences: its loud but lively music, its bright and pretty costumes, its unconventional and, in a sense, creative scripts, and its emphasis on acrobatic action. In the light of the 'unrefined' taste of common theatregoers in Canton and its vicinity, the falling popularity of *K'un-ch'ü* was just a matter of course.

The demise of two modern forms of performing art in Canton during the Republican period tells us more about what audiences expected from popular opera, and how much of their preferences still resembled those of their ancestors in the late-imperial times.

In the late-Ch'ing and early-Republican periods, there had been opera troupes that were run and made up of some idealistic young men who vowed to save China by means of the theatre. They styled themselves *chih-shih pan* (patriot troupes). Their popularity and their contribution to the success of the 1911 revolution in Kwangtung are always taken for granted.[13] Since these 'patriot troupes' had established some degree of affiliation with the 'legitimate' T'ung Meng Hui (the Revolutionary Alliance), Chinese Communist historians strongly boost the socio-cultural importance of these theatrical groups and their political contribution to the anti-Manchu Revolution, despite the fact that it was the Constitutionalists who first employed Cantonese folk songs and opera as political weapons against the Ch'ing government.[14]

In the decades before and after the 1911 Revolution, there were about thirty 'patriot troupes' in Canton and Hong Kong (*YCS* 1988: 24). Some of them seem to have been heavily subsidized by the T'ung Meng Hui.[15] These troupes are said to be fond of performing new scripts with highly politicized themes mainly about the misrule of China by the Manchus.[16] 'Whenever they [the patriot troupes] performed', one historian claims, 'they played full-house'; and 'along the aisles in the Pearl River Theatre were always hung congratulatory pennants and inscribed boards presented to these troupes by the masses' (Shih Ping-chou 1983: 264–5).

Cantonese opera historians list at least four major contributions allegedly made by 'patriot troupes' to the maturation of popular opera. First, they pioneered the introduction of highly politicized scripts into Cantonese opera. Secondly, they helped widen the scope of theatrical technique by borrowing extensively from Western drama and silent films. Thirdly, they employed extensively vernacular Cantonese in lyrics and dialogue. Fourthly, they trained and nurtured a large number of actors who later became highly successful in the 1920s and 1930s (*YCS* 1988: 30–1)[17].

These evaluations, however, are only partially true. First, the far-reaching influence of the 'patriot troupes' must not be overstated, for the simple but important reason that some of their most politically critical plays were banned by the local authorities soon after they had been staged; local police was also instructed to pay special vigilance to their performances (*HTJP* 1911, 31 Aug.). Secondly, opera in China had been used for a long time as a means of intellectual expression to criticize the establishment. During the Yüan Dynasty, *tsa-chü* was used as an outlet by scholars to ridicule and challenge the legitimacy of Mongol rule.[18] In the early-Ch'ing period, opera was employed as a political weapon by the Ming Loyalists (Dolby 1976: 114–17). Moreover, scripts with politicized themes were not exclusively performed by the 'patriot troupes'. For example, when the late-Ch'ing authorities were enforcing a ban on gambling in Kwangtung, an 'ordinary' opera company, Ch'ün Kuo Shan Yü, staged a play entitled *Kuang-tung chin-tu chih-lien* (To Commemorate the Ban on Gambling in Kwangtung) to help boost the campaign.[19] Likewise, a troupe called Ch'iung Hua Yü staged a played entitled *Tou-p'i Ch'ing chien pien* (Pockmarked Ch'ing Celebrates the Cutting of Queue), probably to welcome the success of the 1911 Revolution and the birth of a new China.[20] In another instance, two days after the fall of the Manchu administration in Canton in November 1911, most Cantonese opera troupes in Hong Kong (which also performed in Canton) celebrated the occasion by performing additional ritualistic plays heavy with religious symbolical meaning, aiming in all probability to invoke supernatural blessing for the success of the Han rebels.[21] Nor was the use of the vernacular on stage an innovation by 'patriot troupes'. As early as the mid-Ming period, many local troupes (*pên-ti pan*), who performed mainly in the Kwangtung countryside but also in Canton, had already used vernacular Cantonese in singing (*YCS* 1988: 9–10; Lai Po-chiang 2001: 53–8).[22] Hence, one may argue that Cantonese opera has a tradition of vernacularization; and that this tradition was magnified, rather than invented, by the 'patriot troupes'.

No matter how inspiring or important was the role of the 'patriot troupes' in the course of modernizing Cantonese opera, it does not follow that such overtly politicized serious opera was welcomed by common audiences, as is generally alleged by historians. In fact, from the beginning of this theatrical movement, signs of public apathy were discerned. First of all, its distinctiveness from conventional troupes and performance had failed to win the actors membership of the Pai Ho Guild of Cantonese opera. As a result most 'patriot troupes' were blocked from obtaining any performance contracts from local theatres which dealt only with the Pai Ho Guild, and were forced to operate as amateur groups (Shin Pin-ch'ou 1983: 261). And then, none of the troupes was apparently popular enough to achieve any commercial or long-standing success. With the loss of its political orientation after the 'success' of the 1911 Revolution, their already limited popularity suffered a further blow. Even the best-known troupe Yu T'ien Ying Shê earned as little as fifty yüan from one performance, which was a very meagre income for a professional troupe (ibid.); and its popularity was not yet wide enough to allow them playing continuously for any lengthy period of time.[23] The Social Evolution Company, despite its T'ung Meng Hui sponsorship, lasted only for two years (Shih Pin-chou 1983: 265); its closure was a direct result of serious shortage of funds (Feng Tzu-yu 1987: ii. 482).[24] Even the longest-lasting 'patriot troupe', namely Chên Tien Shêng, did not seem to have fared any better. The troupe was founded in Canton in 1906. It had performed there for about ten months before its manager decided to move the company abroad to South-East Asia where it played for about a year. Soon after returning to Hong Kong in 1908, the company was disbanded. It is not known in which year this troupe was regrouped, but it seems that it had performed in the Strait Settlement in 1915. Although this company was said to be 'highly popular' among the Chinese in South-East Asian cities, there is little evidence to indicate it had achieved similar success or popularity in its home city (ibid. 481–3). If choices were available, most audiences in Canton would opt for 'non-serious' popular opera that was less sober in presentation, and less politicized in content.

It must be noted in passing that not all the plays performed by those 'patriot troupes' has to be revolutionary in theme, as is revealed in the reminiscences of

Tou-p'i Yüan (Pockmarked Yüan), a veteran 'patriot' actor. For instance, the story of a play called *T'ou ying mu hsing* (Shadow Stealing, Character Imitating), which was performed by a 'patriot troupe' in 1913, is about the romance between a Miss Li and her boyfriend Mr Liang. A Mr Mou, however, is very jealous of Liang, whom he tries to kill by pushing him into a pit. Liang, however, luckily escapes and goes into hiding. At the end of the story, Mou, who still fails to win the affections of Li, murders his aunt to inherit her wealth; he is subsequently apprehended. Another 'patriot' play, *T'ung ch'u szu ta hai* (To Remove the Four Evils in the Hard Way), seemingly carried a more revolutionary flavour, as its title suggested. A closer look at the outline (the full script was not available at the time of writing), however, reveals a somewhat different picture. The story is about a young wastrel, Sung Hsiang-fu, who is heavily addicted to all four social evils, namely prostitution, opium smoking, gambling, and alcohol. His father-in-law, though concerned, has failed to persuade him to discontinue these bad habits. One day he conceives of another plan that eventually helps his son-in-law rid himself of those addictions once and for all. The plan is simple but harsh: he designs a scam that causes his son-in-law to lose all his money. He becomes so broke that he steals to eke out a living, which subsequently leads to his arrest and being sentenced to sweep the streets, an experience so humiliating that it brings him eventually to his senses, and the 'recovery' of his wealth, which is in the safe custody of his father-in-law. Similarly, the play *Tan chia* (The Cangue) did not reveal any uniquely revolutionary quality though it was performed by a 'patriot troupe'. Its story is about a covetous uncle who tries to appropriate the handsome inheritance of his niece by falsely accusing her of having adulterous relations with a man. When her husband, who is abroad learns about this, he returns quietly to save his wife. Realizing that her uncle is a superstitious man, the husband dresses up as an apparition and begins to haunt him. The plan works so well that her uncle admits his wrongdoing and is eventually arrested and sentenced to wear a cangue in public.[25] The storylines and the structure of the plots of these three examples bore close similarity to many ordinary plays by ordinary commercial troupes. The uniqueness of these 'patriot troupes', both in terms of political commitments and theatrical innovativeness, must not be exaggerated.

One other clue that indicated the lack of success of these 'patriot troupes' was the continuing wide popularity of the opera actor Tsa-chiao Shêng (Bound-feet Shêng). According to the observation of a columnist, despite the heavy propagation by those 'patriot troupes' of the 'evil' of the custom of foot-binding, every show by Tsa-chiao Shêng, who specialized in playing the role of old-fashioned lady with bound feet, continued to enjoy great box-office success (Ch'iao Hua 1911).

After 1910, spoken drama (*wên-ming hsi*, 'civilized play'), probably due to its newness for audiences in Canton, experienced a brief moment of popularity and commercial success there. 'Civilized play' was first introduced into Shanghai in the 1900s as an on-campus amateur art movement, and was closely linked with revolutionary politics (Dolby 1976: 197–208; Ou-yang Yü-ch'ien 1958: 48–108).[26]

In Canton, too, drama was introduced by amateurs, who were mostly intellectuals sympathetic to the cause of reform or revolution, during the last years of the Ch'ing Dynasty.[27] It is not known exactly how many drama companies, both amateur and professional, had existed in Canton. From its inception year in 1902 to the eve of the 1911 Revolution, Fêng Tzu-yu recalled that there had been at least four drama societies (*shê*) in Canton, all of them founded and run by intellectuals with a strong commitment to either revolution or social reform. In spite of the idealistic enthusiasm of their founders, none of these drama companies lasted long. For instance, the first drama troupe in Canton, namely Chên Nan Tien, performed only briefly in Canton before its closure. Another group, which was optimistically called I-fêng Shê (lit. customs reform society), was dissolved by the troupe itself shortly after its formation. The longest-standing spoken drama troupe with a clear national revolutionary stance was Lin-Lang Huan-ching, which was founded in 1907, and performed until at least the late 1920s. This troupe, however, was based in Hong Kong. Shortly after it moved to Canton in 1925, the company gradually lost its original revolutionary fervour and began to show symptoms of commercialization as more and more 'vulgar scripts of demoralizing themes' were played (Fêng Tzu-yu 1987: ii. 481–4; Huang Tê-shen 1987: ii. 2–9). By the 1920s, spoken drama's popularity was apparently low (Tuan Ping 1924: 1). There were commercial drama companies that performed at such low-prestige establishments as roof-top amusement parks and tea-house restaurants. But in the mid-1920s, almost three decades after its introduction into Canton, there was still no theatre largely devoted to drama performance (Kuang-chou-shih shih-chêng-t'ing 1924: 50–1).

The failure of spoken drama to attain commercial success in Canton might be due to its non-musical nature. Kwangtung people were said to be keen lovers of music. Religious festivities were celebrated with opera; birthday parties and formal banquets of well-off families were always conducted amidst music and singing. The large genre of folk songs is said to be indicative of the essential place that music occupied in the life of most Kwangtung people (Li T'iao-yüan 1937: 8–9; Ch'ü Ta-chün 1974: ii. 358–61). Moreover, with its heavy emphasis on issues of serious social and political concern, and its pretentiously intellectualistic, and largely 'humourless', style of presentation, drama alienated itself from the popular taste of general audiences.[28]

In Canton, drama was able to survive in the competitive world of mass entertainment, but only at the cost of giving up its original politicized slant. By the 1930s, professional drama companies were still performing regularly at Canton roof-top amusement parks,[29] but style and script had undergone so many changes to adapt to popular taste that the drama was dissociated more and more from its original form and differed markedly from its predecessors.[30] Even twenty years earlier than this, drama had already quite drifted away from its initial ideal of political realism. A concerned theatregoer expressed his disappointment:

> In Kwangtung . . . [drama] actors are so abundant that they can fill up whole cities. But what are being presented on stage are [only] props made of paper pasted on bamboo-skeletons;

lyrics written [in the language] of the riff-raff... [and] unseemly costume in tawdry colours of red and green. Moreover, in order to... [satisfy] lower-class audiences, overtly vulgar scripts are written and performed... In Japan and the West, the moral character of [drama] actors is sublime. [In contrast], actors in our country show no respect [to their profession]. By doing rapacious, plundering, evil and licentious things [on stage], two or three [of these] rotten creatures [are enough] to inflict serious damage on [the reputation of] this profession... But everywhere in the circle of 'new drama' are these immoral ruffians. The newly budded 'new drama' can no longer escape [the fate of] total failure. [But there is] one thing that I particularly do not understand: [How can audiences] give such ear-deafening applause to those actors who try their best only to act licentiously and preposterously, which has nothing to do with the plots? I [believe] this is [an indication of] the decline of social ethics, and of the poverty of knowledge [of our countrymen]. When I assess the 'new drama' troupes [in Canton] from an artistic point of view, perhaps only one or two of them are worth mentioning... But ordinary audiences may find [them] dry, dull, and boring. (Chin *c.*1918: 5–6, 'Essays')

This popularized form of spoken drama seems to have been without intellectual depth; yet it offered the general audiences what they looked for in and from public entertainment. They were apparently uninterested in watching serious political drama, especially if required to pay for entrance. To enhance its competitiveness, drama had been substantially transformed, or deformed, by inserting 'decadent elements' (which also characterized contemporary opera) to suit the popular taste.

The review of one of the 'best' drama companies, as one contemporary theatre critic put it, provides us with some ideas of what spoken drama was like in Canton in 1923. The title of that drama performance, which was phrased in vernacular Cantonese, was 'Chi-shih pan-ko lao-tou' (lit. Half a Daddy has Died of Anger). It was performed by a female opera company, which also occasionally played spoken drama. The story, according to this critic, was neither original nor novel; it was about a family feud and revenge, which was a rather common theme in opera then. One thing this critic particularly disliked about the play was that there were too many lines for its actresses, and many of these lines were neither necessary nor clear. For example, when a leading player was apprehended by police and taken to the police station, the whole escort party stopped in front of the station, where the actress delivered a lengthy monologue before they walked into the station; this scene was considered as untheatrical by the critic. In another scene, the critic found it unbearable to watch all eight actresses trying to get the limelight in a disorderly manner, which he further remarked was a common weakness of 'new drama'. On costume he was also unimpressed. One character was described as wearing an old fashioned hat, which was used only in bygone-costume plays, a pair of modern gold-framed spectacles, and a pair of yellow leather slippers. Costume as such, he added, was too bad to deserve his comment. This critic was also appalled by how one actress had striven to appease the audience by, first, getting the limelight at will, and, secondly, reciting her lines deliberately with a funny rural accent; she did not have the slightest idea of what acting was about (Fêng Yüan 1923*c*: 14–15). As this was already one of the best, and presumably decent, drama groups in town, the 'problems' of vulgarization and commercialization for other less respectable groups could be a lot worse. To stay alive in the competitive world of commercial entertainment, 'new drama' had, by the 1920s, largely discarded its original politicized and sombre form and content, and looked increasingly to its rival, Cantonese opera, for gimmicks that would help keep it both sustainable and profitable.

Although some young intellectuals continued to pursue their interest in 'serious drama' by organizing themselves into amateur play groups, their influence and popularity should not be exaggerated.[31] 'Popular taste' in public entertainment in this period had become increasingly hard to ignore.

3. *WHY WAS CANTONESE OPERA SO POPULAR?*

Costume

The success of Cantonese opera in this period owed much to its adaptability in meeting the changing demand, and taste, of general audiences. Thus, a number of theatrical innovations were introduced in this period. Some historians suggest that this process of transformation was triggered off in the mid-1920s by the commercial rivalry between two of the then superstars in Cantonese opera business, namely Ma Shih-ts'êng and Hsüeh Chüeh-hsien (*YCS* 1988: 36–7; Liang P'ei-chin 1985: 176–81; Mackerras 1975: 150). This is only partially the cause. It also happened because Cantonese opera had been borrowing extensively from various forms of regional opera for centuries, within a long tradition of change in its history. Moreover, some of those structural and technical changes that were allegedly introduced only in the late 1920s had already been employed decades earlier (Liang P'ei-chin 1985: 176–81; *YCS* 1988: 1–7, 422–56, 57–110, 118–33; Mai Hsiao-hsia 1941: ii. 143–52). Among these was sensational stage costume.

Extant, though sketchy, records from the late-imperial period revealed that a major characteristic, as well as a key attraction, of Cantonese opera, was the 'wastefully extravagant' costume that most of those local troupes adopted.[32] By the twentieth century, stage costume is described as getting even more elaborate, glamorous, and colourful; expensive and glossy embroidery was synonymous with Cantonese opera (Lai Po-ch'iang 2001: 162).

Photographic portraits of two actors in full costume posing from the same play in 1917 give us an idea of how actors in this period sensationalized the stage. The actor playing the knight-errant role dressed in elaborate traditional armour, while the actor who played the lady wore contemporary Western European dress. In order to feminize and perhaps to take the sensational effect further, pads seem to have been used to enhance the shape of 'her' breasts.[33] A magazine article strongly criticized opera actors for their 'heavy make-up and flamboyant clothing and accessories', which are detested as 'a means to appease and flirt' with their lower-class audiences

(I *c.*1918: 3, 'Essays'). One Cantonese opera critic, though welcoming the 'reforms' being taken on stage, was disappointed at the senseless changes in costumes which he had been watching in disgust during the early 1920s:

> In terms of the costumes used on stage, [the recent reform] does not display any substantial, but merely superficial, change. Take a look at those costumes that are being used on stage: [nobody] pays any attention to whether [a particular costume] is appropriate or not for [a play set in the] ancient or modern time. Concerning only with attracting the audiences' attention, [actors] wear traditional and modern costumes [in a same play] confusingly, despite this [being] totally impertinent to the story of the opera. Whenever an actor wants to show off his substantial collection of costumes, he can change several sets of costumes in one single scene about traveling . . . One may ask . . . Is it possible to change [his clothes] in the street? (Fêng Yüan 1923*a*: iv. 7–8, 'Hsi-chü p'ing-lun')

Another critic complained that the 'recent operatic reforms' resulted only in a further deterioration in artistry. He wrote that in northern Chinese opera, the rule of using appropriate costume relevant to the context of a play was well observed. In contrast, Cantonese opera costumes were always wrongly and anachronistically employed with little attention being paid to the context and the story of a play. For example, in a play that was set in ancient China, there suddenly appeared on the stage, in different scenes, three characters who hardly fitted with the plot: a priest clad in a Western-style suit, a woman in a kimono, and a lady in the full outfit (with the emblems of the Red Cross) of a contemporary nurse (Pi Chuan 1924). In another context, actors in ancient warrior costume were found flaunting their golden waist watches, diamond rings, and other glittering jewellery (Fêng-yüan-ch'u-jên 1923: v. 6, 'Hsi-chü p'ing-lun') Anachronistic and sensational (or 'ridiculous' in those critics' language) theatrical costume had become 'alarmingly' common.

In the early 1920s, an all-female troupe took the lead in embroidering colourful, glittering, reflective German-made plastic scales on their costumes, a *tour de force* that produced a spectacular effect under the newly introduced lighting system (Ch'en Fei-nung et al. 1982: 30; *YCS* 1988: 278–9).[34] In order to improve its competitiveness, another all-female troupe fitted multicoloured electrical bulbs on their hats, which caused a sensation at the time (Ch'en Fei-nung and Yu Mu-yün 1982: 55; *YCS* 1988: 259).[35] Advertisements of these all-female troupes showed that their selling point laid not so much on artistry, but on three other qualities that most audiences were apparently looking for: glamorous costumes, uncommon scripts, and splendid scenes.[36] The 'rivalry between Ma and Hsüeh' pushed this trend of glamorous and sensational costume further. For the first time, Western-costume opera was performed; and serious historical research was allegedly carried out before traditional costumes were replicated, though these were mainly reserved for Ma and Hsüeh themselves to wear rather than their casts (*YCS* 1988: 39–40).

In a commercial advertisement, an opera-costume company boasts that it has employed a highly skilful tailor from Shanghai who specializes in making modern round-collar shirts, special safari suits, clothes for ghost roles, costumes of different dynasties, and so on. All products are guaranteed as meeting the company's '[high] standards of [producing] new and wonderful [costumes which] appease those who watch it; [and for being] unconventional [and] newer than any latest [style]' (*Hsi-chü shih-chieh* 3, 1922).[37] In a newspaper advertisement of a forthcoming performance by a well-known troupe, not a word is said about the cast. Instead, the entire advertisement is dominated by the 'newly acquired' sensationally wonderful wardrobes of costumes, designed and made by specially commissioned artists; and sensational scenery, including special visual and audio effects of different weather conditions reconstructed by 'the latest methods imported from the United States' and installed by the Kwangtung School of Art (*KCMKJP* 1926: 10, 20 July). This insatiable quest for spectacular costume was made possible by the existence of about thirty competitive and flexible stage costume companies in Canton in this period (Kuang-chou-shih shih-chêng-fu t'ung-chi ku 1929: 324, 335; Wang Yung-chih 1988: 53).[38]

A historian of Chinese theatre suggests that ordinary audiences enjoyed watching colourful and extravagant costume on stage because in real life most of them could not afford such luxury (Hsü Tao-ching 1985: 46). But this notion may not apply to opera audiences in Canton in this period. Audiences might be fascinated by spectacular costumes, but would not necessarily then dream of possessing them. In real life, anyone who put on, say, colourful Ming-dynasty costume, or fancy garments covered in light bulbs, would be making a fool of himself. Nevertheless, colourful and fancy theatre-costume was seemingly successful in imprinting a visually strong and colourful impression on audiences—an advantage that was denied to talking films which were still in black and white.[39]

Nowadays, although the quest for sensational costume of this sort has died out, most opera audiences in the Canton Delta area continue to assess the 'goodness' of a opera company by (among other factors) whether or not its costumes are beautiful and spectacular enough.[40]

Props and Scenes

Props and scenes, and their uses, were also sensationalized. Traditional Cantonese theatre, like most other forms of Chinese regional theatre before late-Ch'ing times, employed almost no more than tables and chairs as props. For this reason, traditional Chinese theatre is always regarded as a highly symbolic form of art (Brusak 1968: 59–73; Wang Yung-chih 1988: 51–2; Liao Yüan 1922: 3–5, 'Essays').[41] The underuse of props in traditional theatre might be due to the itinerant nature of most troupes (Su Kuo-yung 1984: xiv. 107–13). A practical need to travel light, and to save space on the overcrowded cabins of the Red Boats,[42] apparently discouraged any extensive use of props. However, with the intensification of competition caused by the instant success of all-female opera troupes by the early 1910s,[43] the formation of the city-based Canton-Hong Kong troupes (*Shêng Kang pan*) in the early 1920s, and the increasing commercialization of Cantonese opera, the groundwork for the diversification of stage decoration was laid.

When fresh water was first used on stage for the opera *Shui chin Chin Shan* (To Flood the Golden Hill) in 1898, it caused a sensation in Canton.[44] In 1911, backdrops were first used in Cantonese opera (Mai Hsiao-hsia 1941: 168).[45] A number of what had been unthinkable props and scenes, such as a miniature locomotive, and 'flame-spraying powder', were being used on stage by 1920. Multicolour stage lighting was introduced. Sometimes, in order to recreate a more realistic effect and atmosphere, slides of appropriate climatic or weather conditions were projected onto the backdrop.[46] Gradually, three-dimensional props appeared which subsequently replaced backdrop drawings (Liang P'ei-chin 1985: 193 n. 13; Ou-yang Yü-chien 1957: 131–2). In a contemporary opera smash hit, settings of wheatfields and modern office buildings were so 'faultlessly reconstructed that audience satisfaction is guaranteed'. In the same opera, a real saloon car was also used as prop (T'ang Ti-shêng *c.*1940s). By the mid-1930s, 'mechanical props' (*chi-kuan pu-ching*) became fashionable. In one opera, a 'mechanical living Buddha' tens of Chinese feet high was constructed on stage (*YCS* 1988: 275–6). The ending of one 'prodigious' (*shen kuai*) opera gave a vivid example of how contemporary artists tried to sensationalize stage sets. The scenery of the sea was recreated by 'movable illuminating electrical lamps'. In the final battle between deities and devils, fireworks were set off from the wings, and electric lamps feverishly flashed to create a warlike atmosphere. At the moment when the virtuous monk was near defeat, the prop P'u T'o Hill burst open, and there emerged from it a Thousand-hands Goddess of Mercy who sat on a huge lotus flower. The 'strong light in five colours' that radiated from her body killed all the devils instantly (*Lo chia-shan c.*1920s: 30–1).

A contemporary Japanese ethnographer found the bizarre use of realistic props in Cantonese opera disturbing. In a fight scene in which some characters were slaughtered, realistic models of human brains and intestines were spewed out from the 'dead bodies'—and yet this won a wave of applause from Cantonese audiences (Kōsaka Junichi 1943: 38).

Employment of amazing and sensational scenes and props came to be seen as a major criterion for the commercial success of an opera, and an opera company.[47] By 1920, this trend was already so common that no commercially viable troupe could afford to ignore it. To the dismay of a critic of contemporary opera, sensational and wonderful scenes, above anything else involving the quality of scripts and the artistry of singing and acting, almost guaranteed good box-office returns to any troupe that could deliver them. He supported his argument by citing the example of Yüeh Chien-ch'iu, a troupe that experienced a remarkable turn of fortune from obscurity to fame once it had employed scenes in its plays (Tzu-liu-han 1919). Sometimes failure to conform to this trend could be damaging. For instance, during the early 1930s, the Education Department of Canton sponsored two Cantonese opera troupes as an attempt to reform contemporary opera. Their debut performances, however, were a fiasco because of the appalling lack of acting ability added to unappealing costumes, props, and sets (Wu Yin 1930: 6).

Some scholars voice the criticism that sensational costumes and props were too casually used, being overdone and totally out of place within the opera's content and context. As has been pointed out, a plot set in ancient China was sometimes performed against a Western-setting backdrop (*YCS* 1988: 277); and actors put on so much make-up that they looked as though 'they had been plastering a layer of white-wash on [their] face[s]', which 'causes one to vomit' (Shêng Hua 1926). By the early 1920s, the trend of adopting 'anachronistic props and scenes' had become so common and serious a problem that some contemporary opera critics ridiculed this kind of stage scenery as 'to-draw-a-snake-and-add-feet style of setting' (*shê-chu shih chih pu-ching*), mocking at the superfluous nature of those 'modern innovations' on stage. Many examples they gave, in addition to those already mentioned above, were hilarious indeed: a gravestone was festooned with light bulbs; a magistrate conducted a trial outside his *yamen* (in front of a backdrop depicting the façade of a magistracy); actors in Ming-dynasty costumes appeared in the setting of a modern Western-style building; in a play set in ancient-times were displayed such items of modern novelty as a telephone, an electric bell, rifles, a water tap, and electric light bulbs. In a highly popular play that was set in the famous 'Grand View Garden' (*Ta-kuan Yüan*) from the novel *Dream of the Red Chamber*, the walls of the mansion were spotted with advertisements for a local brand of herbal pills against influenza and the latest products of a tobacco company. To the dismay of one observer, however, most audiences were rarely bothered by these totally inappropriate scenerios, their attention being solely absorbed by the performance of their favourite actors and actresses. Moreover, on many other occasions, audiences seem to have been fascinated and amused, rather than disgusted, by all the sensationalism and many opera companies continued to work hard at satisfying the audience's fondness for a 'new wonder' (*hsin ch'i*) by spending hundreds of dollars on hiring scriptwriters or unqualified amateurs to design those 'excessively extravagant' but 'superfluous' scenes and props which were quite unfitting for the storyline of the play (Fêng Yüan 1923*d*: 3–5, 'Hsi-chü p'ing-lun'; Fêng-yüan-ch'u-jên 1923: 5–8, 'Hsi-chü p'ing-lun').

Music

Traditional stage music was also substantially modified to keep step with the pace of change in contemporary opera. In this period, a number of 'new' musical instruments were introduced. This process of borrowing, however, had been started since the 1880s, albeit at a slower rate, until the 1920s when the pace was accelerated dramatically. It is believed that before the 1870s an ordinary Cantonese opera troupe employed only some seven musicians. By the 1920s, with the adoption of some 'new' Chinese musical instruments, the number of players had grown to about thirteen. Western musical instruments had started to be commonly used by the mid-1920s; all the big opera companies then had a 'Western Music Section' (*hsi-yüeh pu*) that employed six to ten musicians, who sometimes even outnumbered those playing the Chinese instruments.[48] Hence, by the end of that decade, forty-one instruments, both Chinese and Western, were employed in Cantonese opera, in contrast with the fifteen used in other forms of regional opera.

As regards the Chinese musical instruments used in contemporary Cantonese opera, there were more percussion, strings, and brass instruments, giving a sharp and 'noisy' audio effect, compared to that found in the other regional operas. Of the Western musical instruments employed, the banjo, saxophone, guitar, violin, xylophone, and piano were the most common (*YCS* 1988: 111–17; Wang Chien-hsun 1983: 445–6; Mai Hsiao-hsia 1941: 163–4; Mackerras 1975: 150). In *Huan hua-chai* (Repaying the Flower-debt), a big hit in the 1930s, the background music in some acts was for the first time played on entirely Western instruments, which was said to produce a suitably 'soft and easy' effect (Fêng Lan 1931: 4). Such diversification in the use of musical instruments reflects not only the generally favourable popular attitude towards things Western, but also the dominance of popular taste that was partly characterized by an insatiable quest for things new and bizarre, 'bustling and noisy' (*jê-nao*).[49] It must be added, however, that Cantonese opera music, despite its opening up to Western musical instruments, was far from being colonized, so to speak, by the West. Some experimental plays that were conducted with solely Western music were said to have resulted in 'total disaster' in terms of the box offices (Ho Chien-ching 1995: 231).[50] Opera audiences in Canton might be delighted by a mild use of Western music in the plays they enjoyed, but to have the traditional musical arrangement entirely replaced was certainly out of the question. The quest for novelty, however strong, did not extend to uprooting the entire theatrical tradition, which continued to be enjoyed by many of its ticket-buying audiences. It was the mixing of these two types of music that kept the audiences amused. Westernization, though a powerful cultural force in Canton, had not yet succeeded in outdoing traditional drama.

Scripts

Since the early-Republican period, a large number of new scripts had been produced to meet the audience's demand for variety. One historian claims that about 2,600 'titles of opera' (*chü-mu*) had been performed by Cantonese opera troupes between 1870s and 1911; and from 1911 to 1936, there were at least 5,500 opera titles, and scripts, many of them new, performed in Canton and Hong Kong (Liang P'ei-chin 1985: 9).[51] The new generation of actors and opera magnates was quick to realize the commercial potential of new scripts. In the mid-1920s, Ma Shih-ts'êng set up a scriptwriting department in his own opera company at a substantial monthly cost of 30,000 yüan, as a means to enhance its competitiveness. Full-time playwrights were employed; and they were able to produce so many new scripts for the company that its popularity was further reinforced. Soon afterwards, many opera companies followed suit (Shen Chi 1957: 65–6, 71).[52] Gradually, most Canton-based opera companies were required by theatre-owners to perform one 'new', or different, script every weekend (Ch'en Cho-ying 1983: 324–5). Newspaper advertisements of opera performances in the early 1910s had already indicated that a troupe rarely played the same script twice (unless the play was a super hit) at one theatre as long as it stayed there; and many of the plays were, judging by their titles, newly composed scripts targeting the popular taste of the audiences.[53] With the demand for new scripts increasing, the number of professional playwrights also went up, from about eleven in the Ch'ing period to over one hundred by the mid-1930s (Mai Hsiao-hsia 1941: 169–70; Liang Wei 1988: 141–4).[54] New scripts were produced at such a rate that actors were no longer given the necessary time to memorize their lyrics. Henceforth, improvization was often employed on stage, and this, when tactfully and wittily done, was a source of amusement to audiences.[55]

The rapid increase in the number of scripts was also attributable to the changing socio-cultural status of Cantonese opera since the late-Ch'ing period. Although Cantonese opera had been performed in Canton and other major towns in Kwangtung since, at least, late Ming, its popularizing approaches to acting, singing, and script selection were much despised by the ruling elite who generally patronized the arguably more elegant and refined *K'un* opera. The discriminatory attitude of many of these officials resulted in the failure of Cantonese opera troupes to obtain any support from the ruling elite, which could have enabled them to play continuously without interference in Canton; on many occasions Cantonese opera was even banned in this provincial city. For a very long time from the late-Ming period until the 1870s, Cantonese opera, though most of the time allowed to perform cyclically during various temple fairs in Canton, was not able to establish itself permanently in the city, where non-Cantonese troupes specializing in other regional operas dominated firmly with the support of the social and political elites. To survive, all Cantonese opera groups had to travel and perform from place to place throughout the province (Lai Po-ch'iang 2001: 50–1, 56–7, 98, 106–7, 136–8; Hsien Yü-ch'ing 1996: 265–8, 280–4). The itinerant nature of these troupes then enabled them to survive by performing only a small number of scripts; after all, a troupe rarely stayed in one place for more than a week. This situation gradually changed after the 1870s, when this form of local opera was increasingly accepted, or tolerated, by the local authorities in the cities, and the public demand for it was also growing at an unprecedented pace. With the founding of more and more theatres dedicated to the purpose of performance from the 1890s onwards, Cantonese opera began to base permanently in Canton for the first time. By then, a troupe could no longer survive commercially by playing only a handful of scripts. Prompted further by a mass audience that craved novelty, the race to produce new scripts was, as a result, being run at full speed (Liang Wei 1988: 140–1).

Moreover, in order to match the rhythm of modern city life in Canton, the duration of opera performances were substantially shortened to fit with the principle of one script for one performance. In pre-Republican days when Cantonese opera was mainly performed on religious occasions, one performance might last a whole day or, sometimes, over a few consecutive evenings (*P'an-yü hsien hsü chih* 1968: 14–15, ch. 44). By the 1930s, however, performances were divided into day and evening sessions; and the evening performance, instead of being all night, was effectively limited to between eight o'clock and midnight (Fêng Lan 1931: 14; Liu Kuo-hsin 1983: 363).

A combination of commercialization, urbanization, provincialism, and, to an extent, liberalization helped bring about these dramatic changes in the aspects of Cantonese opera during the period in question.

It is wrong, however, to assume that the demand for thematic variety of script was only a Republican phenomenon. During the Southern Sung period, the rapid pace of urbanization and commercialization helped create a boom in opera business. The heated competition among troupes contributed to the production of a large number of new scripts, which kept audiences attracted (Chao Shan-lin 1990: 7–10). During the Ming and Ch'ing periods, it is known that opera audiences were fond of unusual plots. As a result, a large repertoire of 'uncommon scripts', appropriately called *ch'uan ch'i* (uncommon story), was produced (Hsü P'ei-chün et al. 1990: 3, Preface). Similar changes had occurred to Cantonese opera too. Many Cantonese opera historians believe that before the Republican time, Cantonese opera troupes played a limited repertoire of scripts, namely the 'old eighteen classics for all over the country' (*lao chiang-hu shih-pai pên*), and the 'grand-casting eighteen classics' (*ta pai-chang shih-pai pên*) since the 1860s, and most of these scripts were adapted from scripts of other regional operas such as Anhui, Shensi and Kiangsi (Ch'iu Sung-ho 1992: 26–8; Ou-yang Yü-chien 1983: 88–91). This was, however, only partly true. Although these thirty-six classic scripts formed the core repertoire of Cantonese opera and were probably the most performed plays, it did not mean that local opera troupes played no other scripts. Extant records from mid-Ch'ing, especially those written by non-Cantonese literati staying in the areas of Canton and eastern Kwangtung, revealed that many local opera troupes had been performing scripts that were either composed by themselves, or adapted freely from local stories or popular novels.[56] The biographies of a few known amateur playwrights of Cantonese opera during the high- and late-Ch'ing periods indicate the fact that new scripts had already been composed and that this helped enrich the repertoire. Many of those new scripts were original in content and in some cases clearly targeted Cantonese audiences. For instance, Liu Pai, an actor who was famous for playing the jester role, had written a play called 'Kuang chu' (A Successful Civil Examination Candidate from Canton), which was said to have made him into a well-known actor in many parts of the country including Peking. The story is about a successful candidate of the civil examination who, on his way to inaugurate an official appointment in Peking, has stayed a night at a hotel where he is submitted to repeated temptation by a group of prostitutes. In spite of his initial moralizing sermons, he is eventually lured. The promised romance turns out to be a swindle, and all his belongings, including his clothes, are stolen by the prostitutes (Lai Po-ch'iang 2001: 117–18). The operatic works of Liang Ting-nan (1769–1861) were mostly about romance and were sung in Cantonese. One of his plays, 'Yüan hsiang mêng' (Dream of the Fragrant Garden), is about the affection between a scholar and a courtesan. While waiting for his return from the civil examination in Peking, the courtesan protagonist dies of an illness. She then turns into a beautiful spirit in the 'sea of opium' and returns to earth to visit her lover. Determining to reunite with her, the scholar commits suicide at the end of the play (ibid. 118–19). Liang Ting-nan was from a wealthy family and had worked with senior officials including Lin Tse-hsu. His opera scripts, therefore, indicate the popularity of this form of local opera even among the elite, as well as the presence of playwrights who supplied a succession of new scripts to help broaden the repertoire of Cantonese opera as early as the mid-nineteenth century.[57] A modern compilation of old classical plays titles also indicates the existence of a significant number of new scripts that had been performed apart from those standard classics (Ch'iu Sung-ho 1992: 30–8). Hence, what happened to Cantonese opera in this period was ironically both a break from recent theatrical traditions and a revival of an old tradition in Chinese opera.

Some contemporary critics watched this trend of hectic production of 'scripts of novelty' since the early 1910s with apprehension, for they opined that quantity was attained at the expense of quality. As early as 1912, a concerned critic had pinpointed Cantonese opera as the worst form of regional opera in the whole of China in terms of the poor-quality scripts they had been performing. He summarized the major weaknesses of contemporary Cantonese opera scripts as follows: all scholar characters have to be lustful, while the lady characters are promiscuous; all jesters and minor characters peppered their lines with obscene and foul language; maids always behaved like pimps while their young masters were always ready to rape any woman they fell in with; all emperors have to be surrounded by disloyal concubines, while every prime minister was treacherous; armies had to rely on magic in the battlefield, and all vengeances were accomplished with the supernatural assistance of fairies etc. In his view, the storylines and the plots of these plays were so repetitive that they became 'meaningless and exceedingly dull'; they resembled those worthless vernacular novels that were written to titillate the low taste of the inferior sectors of society (Shu Yuan 1912, 170 ct.). A decade later, the 'sinking quality' of Cantonese opera scripts continued to arouse the concern of many critics in Canton. In their view, many of these new plays were incoherent in story, illogical in plot development, and too one-sidedly about romantic affairs between lovers, so much so that 'they ceased promoting the traditional values of loyalty, filial piety, chastity, and righteousness, and the [traditional] aim of promoting virtue and suppressing evil'. Audiences, they argued, rather than the playwrights, should be held responsible for such degeneracy on stage because it was they who demanded this kind of play; and any troupe that refused to play scripts that appealed to their taste, however bad it was, could never survive in the harsh, competitive world of the opera business (Chien Hung 1922: 8–9). Most audiences, however, apparently watched those 'inferior' productions with great delight. One supporter of a promising young female actress wrote to a newspaper to advise her on how to boost her popularity: 'if [her troupe] can compose and play a larger number of new scripts, in order to fulfil what the society wants, she will be naturally successful in the world of theatre' (Fu Shêng 1921).

4. THEATRE TRULY FOR THE PEOPLE

Vernacularization and Humour

Because most 'patriot troupes' employed plain Cantonese on stage in order to let their revolutionary messages spread more effectively, they were believed, despite their short-lived 'popularity', to have left an important legacy of vernacularizing Cantonese opera.

Vernacularization in Cantonese opera, however, had most probably been started already by the mid-Ming period, though it is not known how *exactly* vernacularized it was then. As already pointed out, the reminiscences of a Portuguese missionary Gaspar da Cruz, in 1569, implied that opera in Canton was already being sung in Cantonese dialect (Boxer 1953: 144; Lai Po-ch'iang 2001: 53–4). In the preface of a travelogue ('Yüeh yu chi ch'eng') written in 1712, its non-Kwangtung author (Lu-t'ien-hsien-shêng) recalled his experience of theatregoing in Canton: 'All the rest [of the remaining session] was performed in Cantonese tone (*Kuang ch'iang*). When an actor sang, the rest [of the performers] rhymed [with him] in barbaric tone (*mang yin*)' (cited in *YCS* 1988 9–10) (Lai Po-ch'iang 2001: 73–6). The noisy music and the vernacular language used in lyrics and dialogues, though they disgusted this Northerner visitor, were attractions to local Cantonese audiences.

By the 1900s, the process of vernacularization in Cantonese opera was further helped by the absorption of traditional folk song techniques, especially from 'wooden fish' songs (*mu-yü shu*), Cantonese ballads (*Yüeh-ou*), the 'salt-water songs' (*hsien-shui ko*), and the 'dragon-boat' songs (*lung-chou*) (*YCS* 1988: 77; Liang Wei 1987: 3–4; Li Po-ch'iang 2001: 161–2). These traditional folk items are largely characterized by the heavy use of vernacular and idiomatic Cantonese in lyrics and libretto, and simple but amusing rhyme structure. Apparently, no new opera script could escape from their influence; and thus Cantonese opera was transformed into a musically more amusing form of entertainment with a strong but enjoyable local flavour (Ch'u I-tsun 1986: 247; Ch'ü Ta-chün 1974: ii. 358, ch. 12).

It must be noted that although most opera performances had already been sung in vernacular Cantonese by the 1930s, a few classical, traditional-costume plays were still occasionally being sung in 'stage Mandarin', which was a defected form of Mandarin with a strong local accent that had been commonly used on stage in pre-1900 Canton.[58] Those performances, though loved and praised by some opera critics who were disappointed with 'new opera', were no longer common or particularly successful in box office in this period.[59]

Undoubtedly the 'patriot troupes' did help accelerate the process of 'localization' in Cantonese opera by introducing the 'natural tone' (*p'ing hou*) of singing, in contrast to the traditional style of opera singing that was conventionally in a high pitch, or 'artificial tone' (*chia hou*) as it was generally called (*YCS* 1983: ch. 2; Mai Hsiao-hsia 1941: 166–7).[60] Some of these young men later became commercial opera actors whose natural style of singing gradually became liked by most audiences.[61]

The natural tone of singing had seemingly become dominant by the 1930s (Fêng Lan 1931: 12–13). Actors experimented with different forms of 'natural singing tones' that in some cases helped heighten their idiosyncratic image. Hence, Ma Shih-ts'êng's naturally hoarse singing voice (*sha huo*) earned him tremendous success and popularity as 'Master of the "beggar tone" ' (*ch'i-êrh huo*) which resembled the pitiful singing of a beggar (Shen Chi 1957: 51–7). Since audiences liked this new way of singing, Cantonese opera was further popularized (Tuan Ping 1924: 9). The dominance of natural-tone singing, and the total use of both vernacular and formal Cantonese in lyrics, were expressions of a strong socio-cultural process in which Cantonese opera was consciously moulded into an 'independent' form of regional opera. In the opinion of a contemporary critic, the commercial failure of Peking opera in Canton was attributed partly to its rigid theatrical structure, sober presentation, and Mandarin lyrics. The opposites allegedly accounted for the success and popularity of Cantonese opera (ibid. 5).

Another sign of the popularization of contemporary Cantonese opera was its heavy use of humour. Scripts of this period, both comedy and 'sad' stories (*ai ching*),[62] were packed with humorous lyrics and dialogues. In Peking opera during the Ch'ing period, jesters occupied a crucial position (Chao Ching-shen 1962: 1–9). In traditional Cantonese opera role ranking, however, the jester seemingly held a lower position than that of the other roles.[63] This did not, however, undermine his important function as a source of merriment on stage. Some jesters, for instance, were famous for their incredible stunts and acrobatics (*chüeh chi*), which brought thrills to an audience.[64] Moreover, the role of jester in Cantonese opera had also shown signs of significant change by the late Ch'ing. A Cantonese opera historian notes that when most other regional operas had not yet given their jesters the privilege of singing any lyrics in a performance, jesters in Cantonese opera had been doing so since at least the 1880s. In some plays of that period, jesters were given a lot of opportunities to sing their lines on stage, a privilege that had been hitherto reserved largely to the most important roles of a troupe, such as the knight or the lady (Ho Chien-ch'ing 1995: 216). By early-Republican times, key actors of some 'patriot troupes' such as Ch'iang Hsia-yün and Huang Lu-i, who specialized in playing jester roles themselves, further helped promote the theatrical status of the jester in Cantonese opera by writing witty, sarcastic scripts in which the jester was highlighted as a main character (Ch'en Chiang-fêng 1990: 279). Therefore, regardless of the social or political backgrounds of a troupe, humour had, by the 1910s, become an essential ingredient for success, simply because it was one of the major sources of entertainment, and hence attraction, to the general audiences.

The choice of actors' stage-names was another manifestation of humour. One historian argues that the stage-name was used only after the 1860s, when Cantonese opera had been banned when some actors were found taking part in the T'aip'ing rebellion. Stage-names were then adopted to conceal true identities (*YCS* 1988: 169). It is not known if Cantonese opera actors used stage-names in the pre-T'aip'ing days, but they had already been widely used by actors in the capital cities of the Sung. Actors and actresses then adopted funny stage-names such as Little Gold-fish, Fish Catches Water (*Yu Tê-shui*), and Little Orange Skin (*Hsiao Chu-p'i*) (P'an Kuang-wên 1966: 22–3, 28–30, 35–6). It is likely that stage-names may also have been adopted by Cantonese actors in the pre-1860s period, for a number of plausible reasons. First, since acting was not yet a respectable profession, actors may have adopted stage-names to hide their true identities (Tien Chiang-ch'un 1931*a*: 14–5). Secondly, stage-names could be intended as a means to reinforce the element of humour in opera. This might be corroborated by the fact that by the 1930s, when the days of official discrimination against opera actors were long past and the social position of opera stars had markedly improved, it seems that no actor ever contemplated giving up his stage-name (ibid.).[65]

Probably within the spirit of opera then, which emphasized popularization and sensation, most Cantonese actors adopted stage-names that were downright funny. For instance, there was a 'Footbound Shêng' (*Tsa-chüeh Shêng*), an actor specializing in foot-bound female roles; a 'Yun-lan with a Flirtatious Voice', an actress who was famous for flirtatious acting; a 'New Cabbage' (*Hsin Pai-tsai*); a 'Chi the Broken Tooth' (*P'eng-ya Ch'ao*); a 'One-legged Ying' (*Tu-chüeh Ying*); a 'Puppy from the Country of Barbarians' (*Fan-kou tsai*); a 'Li the Small Snake' (*She-tsai Li*); a 'Yung the Living Ghost' (*Shêng-kuei Yung*); a 'Pockmarked Mei' (*Tou-p'i Mei*), and many more.[66]

Likewise, most 'new' opera scripts were given funny and frolicsome titles: *P'ou fu yen hua* (Cut Open the Belly to Examine the Flower); *Ta-chieh yin-szu lu* (Robbing the Road to Hell); *Ti-yü hsin ch'i* (Searching for a Wife in Hell); *Shen-ching ta-shao* (The Crazy Master); *Ai-ching ch'i chia* (The Price of Love is Rising); *Mo-têng ti-yü* (Modern Hell), *Nai-ma wang* (The King of Wet Nurses), *Fan yün hsiang* (The Fragrant [Lady] that Brings Back the Soul to a Dead Person), are just a few randomly chosen examples (*Kuang-chou nien-chien* 1935: 109–14, ch. 8).[67]

By the 1930s, almost all the new scripts were intended to be humorous in one way or another; and character-roles besides that of the jester were expected to insert a certain number of humorous remarks into their librettos. Quite often, the content of these librettos and lyrics was blatantly out of the scene's historical context. The commercially successful traditional-costume comic opera *Chia ou ping-yung* (The Lovers in War), which was criticized by a contemporary as 'rude, [in] bad-taste, and ridiculous', provides us with an example. In one scene, the hero, a general, is inspecting his troops before setting off to fight the women's army led by the heroine. He sings in the traditional story-telling style (*pai lan*):

> To fight against these women, [we] do not need swords or spears . . . [Instead, we] must bring perfumed tissues . . . [and] make-up powder [with us]. Our movement must be gentle and soft, and we must talk flirtatiously. Dealing with women, the most important thing is to behave femininely. If you act in this way, women will love you. If a woman loves you, you shall be [given the chance] to take advantage [of her]. [Here I am] inviting marriage on the battlefield, turning military activity into seductive affairs. Barracks will be used as quarters for the [would-be] newly wed couple . . .

The courting then proceeds, on and off the battlefield.[68]

The famous dramatist Ou-yang Yü-ch'ien pinpointed the historical opera *Shou Chiang Wei* (To Discipline Chiang Wei) as an example of the 'overuse' of inappropriate humour in lyrics in modern Cantonese opera. The captor of Chiang Wei sang: 'I must arrest and . . . have you butchered. Butcher you and make soup [with your flesh], in which [I shall] pour half a catty of white cooking oil, and four *taels* of raw ginger' (cited in Ou-yang Yü-ch'ien 1983: 128). To common audiences, jocularity and delightfully rhymed vernacular lyrics as such, even if they did not fit the context, were amusing and hence appropriate. Sometimes puns and transliterated English phrases were used to enhance the jocular atmosphere of a scene.[69] Even in the rural context of present-day Kwangtung, Cantonese opera performances are filled with these anachronisms.[70]

A contemporary opera critic aired his concern with the trend of the excessive use of 'thoughtless' humour on stage. He noticed that even some famous opera actresses disarmed their fans by freely making jokes, or chatting to audiences on the floor; ad hoc gestures such as spitting or taking a cup of tea were also frequently employed to inject humour into a scene; most audiences watched these happily (Ch'i Shêng 1921).

Nearly all opera contained vulgar, if not obscene, phrases. Libretto remarks such as 'I give you two pieces of "things" ', with the 'things' taken to mean testes; 'doing all these pimping jobs'; 'to rape your man', are some randomly chosen examples (*Lien hsiang chi-chê* c.1933–4; Ch'en T'ien-tsung n.d.: 44, 51). Even actresses enjoyed titillating their audiences by interpolating libretto that was 'too filthy and obscene to describe', and dirty jokes that were happily received by theatregoers (Hsaio Lou 1922: 3–5, 'Hsi-chü p'ing-lun'). To a certain degree, vulgarity seems not to have angered general audiences; on the contrary, so long as the ribaldry remained funny it delighted them.

Serious-minded critics might be disgusted by these vernacular or anachronistic lyrics and librettos. Comic opera of this sort, however, was never intended to be realistic or historically accurate. Judging by present-day observation, most audiences respond with delight to improvisation on stage, because it brings life, a contemporary feel (which fosters a sense of relevance), timeliness (by means of creating an illusion of timelessness), and, above all, fun to a performance.[71] For them, ribaldry could be very entertaining indeed.

A review of a 1920s smash hit *Hsüan Kung yen shih* (The Love Story at Hsüan Kung) shows that what interested its author, who was seemingly a member of these 'common audiences', as his unpretentious pen-name (Hot Male) suggests, was how well the actors took on the characters, and how funny, though chaotic, some acts and scenes were. Not a word was said about any excessive use of vernacular or vulgar languages, which were 'problems' only in the eyes of intellectual critics (Jê-nan-lang 1931: 34–5).

The extensive use of humour on stage was an expression of the Cantonese love of wit and humour. Traditional Cantonese folk songs were well known for their puns (Ch'u Ta-chün 1974: ii. 358, ch. 12; Chu I-tsun 1923: i. 247). Contemporary popular magazines and newspapers were full of humorous writings whether of ribald or of literary quality.[72] Most Cantonese enjoyed nicknaming people in their social circle, and also writing witty poems or aphorisms on banknotes.[73] Indeed, most Cantonese enjoyed laughter in their daily life as much as in entertainment.

It must be added that a humorous play was not necessarily a farce without any serious meaning. A number of well-received opera pieces featuring the famous jester Liao Hsia-huai were cases in point. Liao was acclaimed as one of the 'four greatest jesters' in modern Cantonese opera. In spite of his humble origin, his plays were sometimes loaded with socially critical messages. For example, the script *Ta-han-shih mai p'ing mi* (The Wailing Brother Number Ten Selling Rice at a Very Low Price) is about a kind-hearted man, Tan-han-shih, who becomes intolerant of the mischievous behaviour of his elder brother, a local bully who gets rich by hoarding rice in a time of food shortage. At the end of the play, the little brother steals all the stockpiled rice from the store and sells it to needy people at a very low price. To further punish and disgrace his elder brother, he plays a number of pranks on him, making a total fool out of him. In the big hit *Kan-ti hui Hsi-shih* (When Gandhi Meets Hsi-shih), Liao played the role of Gandhi who, one evening, meets in his dreams the famous Chinese beauty Hsi-shih. Upon his request, Hsi-shih takes Gandhi on a tour of 'Water-Crystal Palace', the fairy-tale world under the sea, where they come across a number of great Chinese historical characters. Through the lyrics sung by Gandhi, the heroic story of each one of them is narrated, and their patriotic acts glorified. Occasionally they run into one or two bad characters. One of them, a traitor during the Three Kingdoms period, appears on stage in a cangue. When Gandhi sees him, he rushes forward and starts scolding at him. When this guilty official knees down and begs for mercy, Gandhi kicks him to the ground and recites a lengthy libretto:

> You shameless traitor of the Han people. The downfall of the Wu court was attributed to you alone. Although you are still living in this world, you are no longer a [true] human, for

you have sold your own motherland, and sold your own soul! I want to eat your flesh, and to have you skinned. Let's wait and see how a wicked traitor like you will end up eventually... (Ch'en Kiang-fêng 1990: 276–9)

In the words of Liao himself, the play was not intended to bring just laughter to his audiences, but more importantly to be a critique of the dark side of contemporary society, and a call to his countrymen about the importance of loving their own country and the need for their selfless devotion to her construction (Liang Wei 1995: 148–9). The social implications of humour in contemporary Cantonese opera must not be underrated.

The Need for Happy Ending

Most contemporary scripts end happily with either the marriage of the hero and heroine (often after surmounting a series of obstacles); or the reunion of a broken family (usually after a long period of forced separation); or the punishment of the bad and the rewarding of the good characters; or the defeat of foreign invaders in battle.[74] In a way, this resembles the British pantomime, where 'the poor suddenly become rich, the rich are bullied by the intervention of Good and all ends well' (Patrick 1990: 18). Tragedy in the European and Greek sense was very rare, if not non-existent, in the huge repertoire of scripts written in this period. This dislike of tragic opera shows that for most Cantonese the main purpose of entertainment was enjoyment. And this kind of fun-seeking mentality was perhaps best borne out by the casual and easy atmosphere inside contemporary opera houses: audiences were noisy, since chatting with friends was as important as watching a performance; pedlars selling overpriced snacks were buzzing around and shouting at the tops of their voices to compete with the high-pitched Chinese musical instruments; and courting couples were indulging in their 'repulsive act of kissing'.[75] On stage, odd-job men could suddenly emerge from back-stage to remove props or change scenes.[76] Audiences were so often carried away by performances that jeering was commonplace. Sometimes their response was so hostile that actors were forced to retreat before an act was finished.[77]

Happy ending in opera, in the sense of seeing justice done, broken families or separated couples reunited, and reward for the good and punishment for the bad, was seemingly an important source of psychological reassurance, pleasure, and comfort to audiences. This is best illustrated by an anecdote from Peking opera in the late-Ch'ing period. One evening, the opera *T'ien lei pao* (Electrocuted by Retributory Lightning) was staged. By the second to last act, the weather had deteriorated and rain was approaching. The troupe manager then ordered that the final act about the divine punishment of the bad characters should be skipped—the act was so familiar and so short in duration that he supposed that the audience would not mind. However, the audience refused to leave and insisted that this final act of punishment must be performed regardless of the bad weather. After the act was finished, they left in 'high spirits' (Wang Meng-shêng, 'Li-yüan chia hua', cited in Su Kuo-yung 1984: 101–2). An opera seems to have been a symbolic reconstruction of a 'simplified' human world and moral universe in which all actors were conveniently divided into two simple categories of good and bad. The popular need and demand to see the ultimate triumph of good represents a general craving for reassurance of the existence of a just and moral superhuman order, and the validity and inviolability of established mores and values. This source of psychological comfort, which satisfied the illusory feeling of the 'passive mastery of life',[78] appears as particularly important in an age of political turmoil and uncertainty.[79]

This need for a happy ending was perhaps another manifestation of the deep-seated obsession with things auspicious by Cantonese (Potter and Potter 1990: 22–3).[80] Everything with a possible lucky connotation went down exceptionally well with the general public. Hence, it seemed imperative for all opera companies to adopt an auspicious name in the hope not only of appealing to audiences, but also of enjoying the divine blessing it was hoped would be conferred by that lucky name. Almost without exception, successful troupes, such as Jên Shou Nien (literally: man enjoys longevity), Hsin Ching Hsiang (the new era), Ting Ts'ai Wang (plenty of sons and rich in wealth), Yung T'ai P'ing (singing for great peace), Jên T'ien Lo (joyful men and heaven), and many others, took names with auspicious meanings.[81]

Happy ending might also be an expression of the traditional Chinese ideal of family life. To most Chinese, a full and happy family life was one of the ultimate goals. With this ideal ever before one, it became tantamount to imperative not to violate the familial and moral axioms, whether in real or in dramatized life (Su Kuo-yung 1984: 119).

The popular predilection for humour and happy endings in opera was probably the main reason for the commercial failure of the tragic opera *K'o t'u ch'iu hên* (The Bitter Journey of a Sojourner in Autumn). It was adapted from a *nan yin* 'masterpiece',[82] and was played by the then opera superstar Chien Li-ch'ü. The story is about the agony of a frustrated and penniless scholar who does not have the money needed to marry the courtesan whom he loves deeply. The opera ends tragically, with the courtesan committing suicide in order to immortalize her chastity and love for the scholar. The lyrics were mainly lamentations of this frustrated man about his tragic fate (Liang P'ei-chih 1988: 44–5). In spite of the strong cast (Lai Po-ch'iang 1986: 16–41), the audience's response to this tragic opera was so poor that Chien Li-ch'ü experienced the first and only box-office failure in his long opera career (ibid. 41–3).

The opera *Yü Li hun* (The Soul of Jade Peach) suffered the same fate for a similar reason. This opera was adapted from a highly successful eponymous melancholic novel published in Shanghai in the 1910s (Link 1981: 40–54, 56–7). It was scripted by a 'highly regarded' Cantonese journalist, and cast by the well-known dramatist Ou-yang Yü-ch'ien. In spite of all these intellectual efforts, this refined, sombre opera was yet another commercial fiasco (Ch'en Fei-nung and Yu Mu-yün 1982: 8).

It is also interesting to note that the predictable happy ending in Cantonese opera sharply contrasted with the no less predictable sad ending in most highbrow Cantonese literature.[83] An opera that ended happily provided its audience not only with pleasure but also with reassurance and the hope of a better tomorrow.

It must be noted that despite this predictable pattern of the happy ending, the way in which the plots in contemporary opera developed was generally rather unpredictable. The extensive use of intrigue and conspiracies in opera librettos greatly helped enhance the sense of story. It is rather like what happened in the narrative techniques of traditional popular story telling in Kwangtung. Judged by a few extant storytelling texts, what gave structure to this form of oral literature was partly its never-failing happy ending, but also and particularly its lively vernacular language, witty narration, and strong sense of story in terms of unpredictability of plot development:[84] the very same features that contributed to the high success and popularity of Cantonese opera in this period.[85]

'Violence, Sex and Wonder'

Some of the censored scenes of contemporary opera may be of use in showing the bizarre taste of general audiences from another perspective, though it is doubtful how effective censorship of opera was. In 1934, forty-six opera scripts were censored or ordered to be revised, either for containing violent or obscene scenes or lyrics or for promoting superstition. A scene in which a king massages the belly of his concubine was classified as obscene, and banned; the scene of a doctor who takes advantage of a female patient while feeling her pulse was banned for immorality; a scene where the well-known 'bad character' Chin Kuai tortures his maids by slashing them until they bleed, and then having them crucified, was banned; scenes of suicide were censored because of their insensitivity; a scene of mouth-to-mouth feeding with medicated tea was banned for obscenity; and scenes with supernatural beings were ordered to be revised because of 'excessive wonders and absurdity' which helped promote superstition (*Kuang-chou nien-chien* 1935: 109–14, ch. 8). A highly competitive theatre market had also contributed to the release of many scripts with such 'sexy' titles as *Li Su-hsing pi-chien lou nieh-ts'ung* (The Rape of Li Su-hsing and the Bastard to Whom She Gives Birth),[86] and *Yü mo* (The Devil of Lust).

However, it is wrong to jump to the conclusion that commercial opera in this period was only about violence, sex, and miracles, as some contemporary intellectuals or historians allege.[87] These might be merely some of its popular attractions. Nor it is fair to say that only the short-lived, idealistic 'patriot troupes' had performed quality scripts with serious themes.[88] In fact, contemporary Cantonese opera did uphold traditional values and orthodox morality, and was concerned about social and political affairs. Most opera scripts held socially positive, and sometimes overtly patriotic messages and themes. Therefore, instead of being an outlet for escapism, popular opera was in fact a vehicle for positive and responsible attitudes towards life and society.

For example, the opera *Tan pao t'ien* (Fearless) was full of patriotic remarks on contemporary Chinese politics. The main plot is about the invasion of the country Hsi La by Northern barbarians. Most of Hsi La's ministers agree to trade land for peace. But a few of them, led by Lu Tsung-jên, resign in protest. One evening, the frustrated Lu visits his friend Huang Tao-hsiung who is likewise a devout patriot. Dismayed by the court's cowardly act, Huang sings the following lyrics, whose message apparently targeted the audiences:

> Our China has been long stared at by the fierce foreigners. The flesh of the weak is always the feast for the strong. They all want to ruin our country. As a native [and] a citizen, I must therefore cry out aloud this urgent message in the hope of saving my country from a [national] disaster. You people can look around [and count] how many corrupt officials and evil bureaucrats we have in this country. These people bring [so much] suffering to our people . . . I hope that all my fellow countrymen can devote their energy to strengthen [our country] . . . The rise and fall of a country depends on its people. We must learn this by heart. (*Tan pao t'ien c.*1921–8: 11)

Through Huang's introduction, Lu meets Kuan Yin-mei, daughter of the Prime Minister. Yin-mei also deeply resents her father's appeasement policy. They fall in love instantly.

Later, the Prime Minister secretly betrays his country, and forces Yin-mei to marry the barbarian King. On the wedding night, Lu sneaks into the fortified palace and rescues Yin-mei. They return to Hsi La, and disclose the betrayal act of the Prime Minister who is subsequently executed. The barbarians' demand for land is eventually turned down, and there follows a war in which the Hsi La troops crush their enemies. In the highly patriotic final act, the victors sing:

> Imperialism has been knocked down, the revolution has succeeded . . . It is our wish that from now on, every one of us must work hard with one single [goal] in our mind . . . [that is to] support the Republic of China, to keep her from being violated by any foreigners. We shall be glad if we can accomplish that. Long live the Republic of China! Long live the Revolutionary Party! Long live our fellow countrymen! . . . We only wish that the Republic will be prosperous, and its people strong. (Ibid. 44)

This script, like most others in this period, is packed with funny scenes and witticisms in lyric and libretto. The humour does not, however, deflate its sincere patriotism, and its timely socio-political messages.

Many Cantonese operas are not as obscene or fantastic as their highly sensational titles or suggestive script-covers might imply. For instance, the script-cover of a 1930s opera *Ai-ching mo li* (The Magical Power of Love) shows a smiling old man holding a minituarized naked woman in one hand and caressing her nipples. The cover of another script, *Chih-fen lo-han* (The Feminine Arhat), features a meditating Buddhist monk being seduced by a sexy naked woman.

But what actually are these scripts about? *Ai-ching mo li* is a satirical comedy warning about the decline of traditional moral standards among Chinese youngsters. Meng Li is a blind admirer of everything Western. Her obsession with becoming a movie star leads her into the trap of a scoundrel. This, however, helps bring her to her senses. In the end, the scoundrel is arrested and sentenced. The final scene becomes a moral lecture: Meng Li apologizes for her past misdeed in a long confession about her blind faith in Western individual freedom, her fiancé reiterates her advice and also elaborates on the importance of traditional values. The opera ends happily with Meng Li's marriage.

Nor is the opera *Chih-fen lo-han* as licentious as its cover's drawing suggests. It is about a group of bold patriots who try to assassinate a rebel warlord. The entire play is full of dramatic intrigues, including the two male protagonists who impersonate court ladies and penetrate into the enemy's palace. Its ending is archetypical: the heroes and heroines escape from the rebels' captivity and eventually defeat them in a battle. This opera offers its audiences an optimistic message that China will eventually withstand the invasion of her foreign enemies.

It must be noted that there were organizations whose duty it was to safeguard the upright moral standards of Cantonese opera. The powerful Pa Ho Guild of the opera business, being the middleman between opera patrons and member troupes, was one of these regulatory agents. On every performance contract, a patron-client was guaranteed the show's moral quality:

> Although [actors] traverse river and lake [to earn their living], they are the type of men who know and are well content with their position. They have never done anything they should not do. Moreover, [the contents] of all the scripts they perform are [upholding the moral tenets of] loyalty, filial piety, fidelity, and righteousness. Hence, [opera] is a means to release the good element [from one's] character, and cultivate modesty [in one's soul]... [this contract is to guarantee that] all the employees in our [member] troupes are no trouble-makers or criminals; [and] no performances are immoral. If any improper conduct is reported, [this Guild] is determined to take collective action against that [particular troupe] until no similar complaint is heard.[89]

If the Guild, which exercised a wide range of powers over its members,[90] meant what was written on the contract, there was every reason to believe that member-troupes would be very careful to avoid violating this guarantee.

Moreover, journalists and opera critics also performed the function of watchdog over the quality of theatrical performance. Local newspapers such as *Kuo hua pao* and *Kung-p'ing pao* reserved a special column for opera reviews to which readers or specialists were welcome to send in their appraisals or condemnations on specific troupes or performances. From an article published in a highly popular opera magazine, *Hsi-chü shih-chieh* 5 (1923: 1–2), 'Hsi-chü p'ing-lun') (which claimed to have sold 200,000 copies), we are told that this kind of criticism published in the mass media was, at least occasionally, well taken and positively responded to by a criticized troupe. For instance, a highly popular actress in a female troupe had once performed the role of a gentleman in a play. In a scene when 'he' was being forced to concede to an arranged marriage, 'he' improvised a line, which was said to have caused much laughter among her fans, but thoroughly disgusted the critics. Since the line was 'too filthy to be described on paper', there is no way of knowing what the exact words were. Subsequent arguments, however, indicated that the line was about the reason 'he' gave for 'his' refusal to the proposal: that since 'he' was a woman, 'he' could not have sexual intercourse with her. The libretto was said to have caused a wave of strong criticisms in the mass media, so much so that this actress, despite her popularity and fame, subsequently yielded to the pressure of the 'public opinion', and had the problematic line modified to a much milder form: 'Since I cannot perform the duty of that of a man, how can I be [her husband]?' (Hsiao Lou 1922: 3–4) Although her fans did not welcome this modification, the voices of the critics could not be taken lightly either.

In addition, there was the official Municipal Opera Examination Committee, first established in 1926, and thoroughly reorganized in 1929. All the opera scripts were required, in theory, to be examined by this body before they were allowed to be publicly performed. It possessed the authority to censor a script, or provide guidelines for correcting 'problematical' scenes or acts (*Kuang-chou nien-chien* 1935: 89–91, ch. 8).

Explicit and visual forms of obscenity such as nudity or suggestive acting were seemingly not common in contemporary opera. By contrast, some contemporary popular magazines such as *Kuang-chou li-pai-liu* (Canton Saturday) and *Kuang-chou tsa-chih* (Canton Magazine) contain many highly suggestive short stories and articles. In all issues of such pictorials as *Pai man* (White Curtain), *Hsiang hua hua-pao* (Fragrant Flower), and *T'ien ch'ü hua-pao* (Heavenly Joy Magazine), and, in particular, *Chu-kiang shêng-ch'i hua-pao* (The Chu-kong Pictorial), large-size photographic portraits of naked Western and Chinese women, and Western paintings and sculptures of nudes, appeared.[91] A publisher's advertisement tells that a photograph album of nudes went on sale in Canton.[92] Drawings of explicitly sexy girls and suggestive pin-ups appeared in every issue of a popular cartoon weekly.[93] Tabloids and official newspapers in Canton were criticized for publishing too many articles written in 'obscene, low-class, and vulgar language'; photographs of naked girls were used by many commercial products in Canton as logos (*NYSP* 1928: 11, 31 May and 24 July).[94] An advertisement of a brand of medicated oil goes even further: a young lady in modern outfit is drawn half-lowering her dress with one of her breasts exposed. Her lover stands beside her, and applies the advertised medicine to her breast. With eyes half-closed, she looks as if she is enjoying an orgasmic experience (*Kuang-tung shang-yeh nien-chien* 1932). The most perverse and vulgar of all, perhaps, was a bizarre poem about a lady urinating (*Wu-hsien man-hua* 1930: 1/1, 2)!

By contrast, among the twenty randomly chosen contemporary opera scripts we perused, only one scene of just one play could be considered as 'immoral'. In it, two long-separated lovers reunite, and the hero embraces his girlfriend and gives her a long kiss (*Tan pao t'ien c.*1921–8: 38). This is almost insignificant, compared with what has been described above. Moreover, kissing had almost become an acceptable and common 'attraction' in literary works of this period.[95]

In Republican Canton, the use of obscene language in opera performance was seemingly taboo, though a limited quantity of dirty jokes and smutty double-entendres was common and said to be happily accepted by ordinary audiences. For instance, Shui-she Yung was once criticized by his fans for excessive use of 'lower-class' smutty homonyms (Hung-ch'uan-chiu-lü 1931: 58–9). Moreover, not all audiences tolerated obscenity on stage. This is illustrated by an anecdote related to the actor Shê-tsai Ch'iu. In the mid-1920s, mistresses and concubines of the rich and the powerful, as well as ladies from respectable families, were among the regulars at opera in Canton.[96] Since they were rich and careless in spending, their patronage was important to the success of an actor or a troupe. These rich and powerful ladies usually reserved the first three rows of the most expensive seats—*kuei-fei ch'uang* (4-seat box)—in front of the stage. The popularity and success of a particular play was sometimes rated by the number of these seats occupied. Once, the popular actor Shê-tzu Ch'iu performed in Canton the first time after his return from touring South-East Asia. Since he had been quite successful in pleasing the 'rustic and illiterate' Overseas Chinese audiences by occasionally interpolating vulgar phrases into lyrics, he tried to do the same in Canton. But as soon as his foul language reached the ears of these rich Cantonese ladies reclining on the expensive seats, some shouted out words of harsh scolding, while others even left to return only after he had finished his part in the play. After that, Shê's popularity plummeted. He was no longer able to find work in any of the Canton-Hong Kong companies; his tarnished reputation could earn him a place only in the less prestigious 'village troupes' (Li Feng 1986: 62–3). Thus, some Cantonese opera might be vulgar, but not to the extent that foul language could be freely used on stage.[97] Ironically, it was in areas of the contemporary 'serious' literature that a high degree of vulgarity could be seen. For example, Ou-yang Shan was apparently so obsessed with realism and naturalism in portraying the 'lower-class' characters in his pre-1949 novels that foul language was often used in their dialogues. And yet his works were published and distributed by respectable Shanghai publishers, and enjoyed nation-wide circulation and literary appraisal.[98]

5. *CANTONESE OPERA AS A MIRROR OF THE CHANGING SOCIETY*

Western Influence and Its Limits

Unlike Peking opera, or the Nō or Kabuki theatre in modern Japan, Cantonese opera took a course of tremendous changes in this period. As with other aspects of Canton life, the impact of the West was clear and strong.

In addition to Western-style costume, musical instruments, and theatrical techniques that have been discussed earlier, Western films were another source of inspiration in this modernization process. They stimulated the adoption of the natural style of acting;[99] and were tapped as a convenient and important mine of new scripts said to be produced almost at the rate of one per week. In the hope of borrowing new ideas for scripts, famous opera actors along with their playwrights went to Western cinema at least once a day (Ch'en Cho-ying 1983: 325; Ch'i-chui-tou 1931: 2). Commercially successful Western films and literature were unhesitatingly adapted to become opera. Even Shakespearian classics such as *Othello* and *Julius Caesar* found themselves adapted for Cantonese opera (Ou-yang Yü-ch'ien 1983: 126; Huang Ching-ming 1987: 75). In this respect, the cultural challenge of the West seems to have been favourably received.

We must not, however, exaggerate the impact of the West upon Cantonese opera during this period. Total Westernization, anyway an unattainable ideal, was apparently not wanted by either actors or audiences. In contemporary opera, traces of tradition were abundant. The predominance of Chinese music and the conditional use of Western instruments, which has been already discussed above, was a case in point. In addition, traditional costume was still being used, though sometimes anachronistically alongside Western-style costume; many classical pieces from the old traditional repertoire continued to be played and appreciated;[100] some of the 'new' scripts were still partly written in flowery formal Chinese;[101] and traditional 'style of acting' (kung chia) was still commonly adopted even in modern-costume opera (Tu Shao-mu 1971: 142).[102] Traditional themes, plots, music, style of acting and singing, and moral issues survived.

Moreover, not all the 'modern' innovations were borrowings from the West. For instance, the cut in the number of major roles in one troupe from twenty-five during the late-Ch'ing to six in our period was mainly out of the practical concern to reduce the running costs rather than just to provide actors with greater flexibility and the chance to try different character-roles.[103] Moreover, some 'new' techniques were actually borrowed from other regional theatres in China. Hsüeh Chüeh-hsien, for example, introduced the Northern School of martial arts into Cantonese opera with his appointment of a Shanghai martial-arts instructor for his troupe. In respect of artistry, Hsüeh had also travelled to Peking, where he 'learned a great deal' from the famous Mei Lan-fang and Lin Shu-shen (Chang Chieh 1980*b*: 124–5; *YCS* 1988: 38–9).[104] Nonetheless, the cultural ambivalence and anachronism expressed in contemporary opera may reflect complexities in the popular attitude towards things traditional and modern in Republican Canton. A selective synthesis of things new and old, Chinese and Western, apparently helped this form of popular art to adjust to the modern age without being entirely uprooted from its indigenous traditions. This kind of cultural bind may be another expression of the 'formidable inertia of social conventions and modes of thought' that has characterized traditional, and perhaps even modern, China (Balazs 1964: p. xix).

Mass Opera, Mass Society

The evolution of Cantonese opera into an overtly 'mass-oriented' form of entertainment is arguably an illustration of the growth of Canton into a 'mass society' in the late-Ch'ing and the Republican periods.

The decline of the highbrow *K'un ch'ü* and *nan yin* indicated the end of the dominant position enjoyed previously by the old cultural elite in this aspect of urban life. That dominance does not mean, however, that there was no mass-oriented type of theatre in imperial China. Market-place theatre, which was different from the 'refined theatre' preferred by the cultural elite, had been highly popular among the masses in the capital cities of the Southern Sung and Yüan dynasties (Gernet 1962: 222–7; Idema and West 1982: 6, 9).[105] With the Cantonese opera of our period, however, the scale of popularization was unprecedented.

The founding of permanent opera houses gave one of the many indications of its rising popularity. Before the 1840s, troupes that performed in Canton were mostly of non-Kwangtung actors who came from other provinces. They excelled in playing *K'un ch'ü* and *tsa-chü*, theatrical forms that the social and cultural elite, whose residences were venues of performances, keenly patronized.[106] Meanwhile, most Cantonese troupes were forced to be itinerant. They travelled to villages and cities on Red Boats, to perform mainly on occasions of religious fairs in makeshift theatres (Ward 1981; Ch'en Cho-ying 1983: 308–27). It is only after the 1840s that the first permanent theatre in Canton is said to have been established.[107] It is not known, however, if this theatre was open to the public, since there had been rich Cantonese families who had built theatres for their private use (Liu Kuo-hsing 1983: 360). Nor is it known what kind of opera was performed there. In the early 1895, it was known that Cantonese opera was performed in at least three theatres in Canton, which also provided the local government with a modest source of revenue (*HTJP* 1895, 6 Feb.)

By 1920 there were five theatres in Canton that were used exclusively for Cantonese opera performances. 'Non-Kwangtung troupes' (*wai-kiang pan*) had lost much of their previous popularity. Although Peking opera was still being performed at one roof-top amusement park, the disreputable venue suggests that it had gradually lost its former success and glory (Tzu-hang-shih 1919: 5, ch. 4); and its continuous survival seemingly hinged upon the compromises it had made on stage with the popular taste, such as occasionally making suggestive gestures or interpolating extremely vulgar remarks into lines.[108] By 1922 the number of Cantonese opera theatres had increased to seven, the same as that of cinemas (Kuang-chou-shih shih-chêng-t'ing 1924: 43–5, 243). Before overnight performances were banned in 1922, most Cantonese opera troupes performed until dawn. Since then, a performance usually lasted from noon until midnight.[109] By the mid-1930s, at least thirty-two Canton opera companies were performing, only four short of the thirty-six in their heyday after 1910.[110] Performances were held regularly at the city's five opera houses, in addition to the daily shows held at three roof-top amusement parks, not to mention those performances held regularly at local temple fairs throughout the city (*Kuang-chou chi-nan* 1934: 239–40). The 'latest' and the most expensive theatre built in Canton was mainly reserved for opera performance (*Kuang-chou nien-chien* 1935: 86–7, ch. 8).[111]

Some historians suggest that this process of commercialization began only in the 1920s, and that it contributed to the deterioration in the artistic quality of Cantonese opera until this was 'salvaged' by the present Communist government (Li Mên et al. 1983: 407–29; Liang P'ei-chin 1985: 208–23). Commercialization, however, was not unique to this period. Chinese theatre had been a commercially oriented business since at least the Southern Sung, when professional groups performed regularly in 'permanent' theatres and competed with each other by doing all they could to attract audiences (Chao Shan-lin 1990: 1–14, 30–45, 86–94). With modern Cantonese opera, the process of commercialization had already been set into motion at least since the 1900s.

Certain refined qualities of traditional Cantonese opera may have been eroded as a result of commercialization. Modern Cantonese opera, however, was in many respects much closer to the masses. Communist attempts to 'salvage' it by remoulding the genre into a thoroughly politicized and rigid 'People's opera', at the expense of its elements of popular humour and sensational theatrical techniques, ironically resulted in depopularizing this type of performing art. It became increasingly detached from popular taste, and hence alienated from general audiences.[112]

By 'opera of the masses', we are not saying that Cantonese opera must be loved by everyone. Nor is it true that Cantonese opera was a 'class entertainment', that all its audiences had to come from only one particular class of society. Extant Ch'ing sources reveal that even at the time when Cantonese opera occupied a relatively low socio-cultural position in the eyes of the cultural elite, its patrons still included scholar-officials. During the mid-Ch'ing period, these officials' keen patronage of market-place opera contributed to the rise in the wages of actresses.[113] The well-known anecdote of Kou-pi Chang shows that the local Cantonese elite could hire even a low-ranking itinerant troupe to play at a private party.[114] In 1873, when the Nan-hai county magistrate was entertaining guests of high esteem at his residence, the wife of the Grand Secretary grew bored with the performance of a Kiangsi troupe, though it was then the form of regional opera most patronized by the cultural elite. The magistrate then sent in an itinerant Cantonese troupe, which was instantly liked by the lady. The next time when he invited the Grand Secretary and his first lady to a banquet, three itinerant Cantonese troupes were hired to have his important guests entertained.[115]

By the 1930s, the social composition of Cantonese opera audiences had become more diversified. To judge from the common practice of hanging, in front of the stage, couplets written in beautiful calligraphy and presented by scholars to actors and actresses (*YCS* 1988: 313), and of presenting laudatory poems and prose-pieces to actresses, the fans of Cantonese opera also included men of letters. Watching a popular opera show did not necessarily debase one's social status or dignity. Like those upper-class English gentlemen who frequented the popular music halls in Victorian London, the elite seemed to have had their own interpretation and view of what 'popular' meant (Pearsall

1973: 11–15). Moreover, since seats in Cantonese opera houses were hierarchically ranged according to prices, pretentious audiences did not need to worry that their 'superior' identity would not be easily recognized.[116] Furthermore, an arrogant audience might choose to patronize only the prestigious Canton-Hong Kong troupes which performed only in permanent opera houses and charged more for entrance (*YCS* 1988: 286–7; Shih Hsing-pai et al. 1988: 41–3). Contemporary opera was hence, strictly speaking, neither high-class nor classless entertainment.

The changing social position of women in Republican Canton was also reflected in contemporary opera. By the early 1910s, a few all-female troupes had already performed in Canton, which, because of their newness to contemporary viewers, caused a sensation, especially among male audiences. Although these female groups were banned in both Hong Kong and Canton between 1913 and 1918, for a reason that is not clear at the time of this research, their resumption of performance was greeted enthusiastically by loyal fans. By 1920, a popular female troupe charged as much as 500 yüan for one night of performance; three of the most sought-after actresses, namely Lin I-mei, Su-chou Mei, and Li Hsüeh-fang, earned over 10,000 yüan a year at the peak of their careers during the 1920s (Chung 1934; Fêng Yüan 1923*b*: 2–4, 'Hsi-chü p'ing-lun'). Some actresses in those troupes had become so successful and popular that essays about their artistic quality and other personal gossip appeared in nearly every issue of opera magazines and newspaper columns on theatre (e.g. *KHP* 1918–19, 'Hsi-chü ts'ung-t'an' *passim*). By the early 1920s, a local opera critic estimated that no less than 3,000 actresses were working in these all-female troupes in Kwangtung; since a company usually employed about 30 actresses each, there were then at least a hundred female troupes performing in the province in this period (Fêng Yüan 1923*b*: 2–3, 'Hsi-chü p'ing-lun'). The lucrativeness of this trade and the wide popularity of successful actresses were said to have caused many parents to prefer girls to boys; a number of families were also found asking their daughters to learn opera acting and singing, hoping they would emulate the superstars (Chung 1934). At one stage, these female troupes were so popular that the business of many male troupes was said to be badly affected.[117] In order to increase their competitiveness, innovative opera actresses such as Su-chou Mei and Li Hsüeh-fang introduced many technical changes into performances which has helped change the art form of Cantonese opera ever since. These changes included curtains on stage, painted scenery backdrops, colourfully embroidered costumes, and costumes decorated with small colourful electric bulbs (Ch'en Fei-nung and Yu Mu-yün 1982: 55; Fêng Lan 1931: 69–70).

The popularity of all-female troupes had reached its nadir in the late 1920s; after that very few female groups could achieve comparable levels of commercial and artistic success to that of the three divas mentioned above. In spite of this decline in popularity, many all-female troupes continued to perform in Canton, mainly in theatres of lower prestige, well up to the end of our period

(Hsieh Shêng-po et al. 1986: 54–61). Even during the difficult time of the mid-1930s, when many male troupes were forced out of business in Canton because of the Great Depression, female opera companies continued to do well as a result of great demands from audiences in South-East Asia (Chung 1934). The relative decline in popularity had little to do with gender discrimination, as one may suspect. It was, in the observations of contemporary opera critics, the combined outcomes of three factors: the retirement of the three divas by the late 1920s, the lack of artistic quality of those remaining troupes (many actresses were said to be too arrogant and complacent), and the over-supply in a small and highly competitive market (I Hsiao 1922 ii. 9–10, 'Yu-hsi wen-ch'ang'; Fêng Yüan 1923*b*: 2–4, 'Hsi-chü p'ing-lun').

Although female troupes were less commercially successful than their male counterparts, they had shown that they could achieve what men did. The artistry of Li Hsüeh-fang was said to have once captured the unreserved admiration of Liang Ch'i-ch'ao, who compared her with the legendary Mei Lan-fang of Peking opera (*YCS* 1988: 187). After the official ban against mixed troupes was lifted in 1935, more and more actresses of outstanding artistic quality, or from rich and respectable families, joined the profession.[118] Their frequent appearance at official functions and community charity events demonstrated their eagerness to show the public their rising social status, as much as the fact that they were also citizens of the modern Chinese Republic.[119] Their emergence might be understood in the context of a 'women's liberation' movement, however limited in scale, that had been gathering momentum under the half-hearted auspices of the Kuomingtang government in urban Canton.

The emergence of actresses in contemporary opera was, strictly speaking, not a break in tradition in the history of Chinese opera. It should be interpreted more appropriately as the start of a neo-tradition. This is because although all-female opera troupes might not exist until this period, women did play a significant and contributory role in traditional theatre, such as the Yüan Dynastry *tsa-chü*. During the Sung and Yüan periods, mixed troupes were said to be common, even in Kwangtung (Lai Po-ch'iang 2001: 25–7; Dolby 1976: 20–1, 61–2).[120] A sixteenth-century edition of *Kuang-tung t'ung chih* recorded that plenty of actresses worked in theatres in the prefecture of Ch'ao-chou. According to a eighteenth-century travelogue, there were more actresses than actors in Kwangtung, and the former also charged more than the latter (Idema and West 1982: 142–3; Dolby 1976: 61–7; Fêng Yüan-chün 1947: 10–11, 43–8; *YCS* 1988: 6–7, 9–10). By the mid-eighteenth century, when Peking opera had already been completely dominated by actors, mixed troupes were said to be quite popular in Kwangtung.[121] In 1911 there was one mixed troupe that performed in Canton for ten months (*YCS* 1988: 288). Since then, the mixed group had been banned until 1935, when the Hong Kong government lifted the bar to demonstrate its 'modern, progressive, and benevolent' policy—an act that was subsequently copied by the Canton authorities (Ch'en Fei-nung and Yu Mu-yün 1982: 11; *YCS* 1988: 288).[122]

Nor is it true that Chinese women were forbidden to go to the theatre. During the Southern Sung period, theatregoers in market towns and villages included all walks of life (Chao Shan-lin 1990: 23–5). An early-Ming county magistrate in Kwangtung tried to ban Cantonese opera because he realized that most people—rich and poor, young and old, men and women—enjoyed watching the 'obscene' plays performed by local troupes.[123] An early-Ch'ing painting depicting the construction of an embankment in Ch'ao-chou and the celebration of its completion shows that women, among all sorts of people, were also a part of the audience. In 1733, a traveller to Canton noted that performances of local opera were usually stopped during the day, and resumed after dark, because 'most women [there] have to work at day time, but rest and play in the evening' (Lai Po-ch'iang 2001: 71–6). The importance of women as a source of audience to Cantonese opera was vividly obvious. However, by 1921, sex segregation in the opera house was being enforced in Canton. With the exception of the expensive 'reserved box' (*pao hsiang*), and the second- and third-class seats, where audiences of both sexes were allowed to sit together, all seats and standing spaces were segregated by sex and fenced off by barbed wire to place men in the middle and women on both sides. A contemporary writer interpreted this as 'outright discrimination' against women in China (Li Tsung-huang 1922: 212; Wang Yung-chin 1988: 50–1; *YCS* 1988: 318). The lifting of the ban on mixed seating in the 1930s was another sign of improvement in the social position of women in Canton. Nonetheless, the enthusiasm of women in Canton to patronize opera houses was not affected by such seating arrangements. In 1928, a concerned journalist observed that although a seat in the women's section cost 15–30 per cent more than in the men's section, the number of female attendees was always two to five times more than that of the males (Shao Wên 1928). In our period, women were already clearly present in public.

Another expression of the growing power of women in this period comes in the fact that it was common for rich and powerful ladies (including well-off courtesans) to court attractive opera actors openly and ostentatiously. As discussed above, most of the expensive reserved boxes in opera houses were booked year-round by rich female fans of respectable or notorious background.[124] Some of these women—humorously nicknamed 'night owls'—were sometimes so fanatical that they booked the first three rows of the reserved boxes in an opera house in order to demonstrate their support to their idols. Their attendance was taken as a yardstick of the degree of success of an actor (Li Fêng 1986: 62). These city women defy any simple stereotyped image of Cantonese women as objects of manipulation by men. For them, actors—men—were reduced to become objects of desire and manipulation.

From 'Mean People' to Idols

To most Cantonese opera actors, the Republican era was a remarkable time of great improvement in the social image of their profession. Our concept of professional entertainers in imperial China is of course influenced by sources that reflected the prejudices of their authors, who were mainly scholars or officials (Idema and West 1982: 142). It is thus almost impossible to know how ordinary audiences conceived of actors and the acting profession. We are told that by the fifteenth century 'there was no differentiation between actors/actresses and prostitutes in the eyes of the public', because many actresses then also worked as courtesans. Until the mid-Ch'ing, actors had been categorized as 'mean people', and were forbidden to sit for the Civil Examination and wear certain types of clothes. Acting as a profession was officially kept a hereditary business; it was an official punishment to be degraded from the ranks of the officials to an entertainer's status. We are also told that actors were generally believed to be involved in pimping, prostitution, gambling, and theft (ibid. 143).[125]

Although some Cantonese intellectuals continued to despise 'market-place opera' and its actors, by the 1920s the popular attitude towards this profession was apparently positive.[126] In 1922, a Cantonese opera critic quoted an essay by Fu Ssu-nien, the prominent historical philologist, to support his own view that the profession of opera acting, which had been once ostracized, was increasingly regarded as a respectable occupation; and the actors and actresses who were able to attain remarkable artistic achievements were even appraised as 'deified embodiments of aesthetics and literature', or were compared to 'tutors who help nurture the society' (Hsiao Lou 1922: ii. 10). With its increasing popularity, literature specializing in Cantonese opera began to appear. By the mid-1920s, a special column on Cantonese opera appeared regularly in most popular Canton dailies.[127] Official statistics show that through the 1920s and 1930s at least ten magazines wholly or partly about contemporary Cantonese opera were published in Canton.[128] One of these opera magazines, *Hsi-chü shih-chieh (The Theatrical World)*, claimed to have sold an amazing 200,000 copies for the first three issues, despite it being the most expensive magazine of its kind in Canton in the early 1920s (*Hsi-chü shih-chieh* 1923: v. 1–2, 'Hsi-chü p'ing-lun').

By comparing these magazines of different periods, one can see the shift of interest and concern in their editors, and to a large extent their readers, for things to do with Cantonese opera. In those published after 1910 and in the early 1920s,[129] extracts of lyrics from famous actors' 'hits' were a common feature. This may be due to the fact that until the mid-1920s there was still no complete written script in Cantonese opera available in printed form (Ward 1985: 171; Ch'en Shou-jên 1988: 36–7). Moreover, most operas at the time were sung in 'stage Mandarin'—a sort of Mandarin with a strong Kweilin accent (*hsi-pang kuan-hua*), which might be difficult for some Cantonese audiences to comprehend (*YCS* 1988: 64–8). Most of these early magazines also published photographic portraits of famous opera actors in theatrical costume; readers' admiring poems, composed in flowery classical Chinese, about the physical beauty and the bewitching style of various actresses;[130] news about the players; and occasional quizzes on a wide range of subjects to do with contemporary Cantonese opera, which were liked by readers.[131]

A similar magazine published in 1931 suggests that readers' concern and interest had apparently shifted to news, both gossipy and serious, and anecdotes about the life of opera stars. It contained biographies of actors; a brief history of Cantonese opera; reviews of some latest productions; a criticism of the lack of 'work ethics' of a jester; interesting articles such as 'The Real Names of Famous Actors', 'An Investigation into the Agnatic Relatives of Yün Lan the Flirtatious', 'The Unique Hobby of Liang Chung-sheng in Collecting Old Theatre Costume', and 'The Acting Predilection of Handsome Yung'. A 'reader's column' was trailered from the first issue, where readers could elicit personal information concerning their favourite actors.[132] Script extract was no longer published, probably because of the availability of printed complete scripts since the mid-1920s, as well as the increasing vernacularization of contemporary opera (Chang Chieh 1980*b*: 132). Local newspapers were also filled with the latest news about the stars, and the reporting was increasingly focused on trivial personal matters of individual stars (such as who was dating which courtesans, or the recent health of certain actors),[133] a trend that had been already started since at least the early 1910s.[134] This strong curiosity about the public and private life of actors and actresses, rather than just their careers, indicated not only the high popularity of Cantonese opera, but also the rising social position of at least some opera actors. A contemporary writer attributed their enhanced social prestige to the cultural influence of the West. In his view, 'to be able to watch the "slender and graceful deportment" (*fêng fan*) of a [famous] actor is now regarded as a once-in-a-lifetime experience' (Tien Chiang-ch'un 1931: 15).

The personality cult of opera actors had become a new social phenomenon in modern Canton. Whenever famous actors performed, the house was always overcrowded. Additional seats of bamboo folding chairs filled up every available space. Sometimes a three-hundred-seat opera house sold as many as five hundred tickets, and audiences had to scramble for standing room ('Hsi-yüan ti ch'üeh-tien', *KCMKJP* 1926: 4, 10 Aug.).[135] Often, inside an opera house, all the expensive seats at the front were reserved year-round by wealthy or notable patrons.[136] Actors were said to be eager to exchange glances with these rich and lavishly dressed female fans sitting in the front rows (Hung-ch'uan-chiu-lü 1931: 59). Outside, in the case of Macao and probably in Canton too, large crowds of fans always gathered with the hope of glimpsing the 'real faces' of their idols (Wang Yung-chih 1988: 51).

The eagerness of fans to watch performances by their idols may be best illustrated by an anecdote of Ma Shih-ts'êng in the late 1920s. One evening, Ma was late for a show. There was no choice but to have another actor understudy for him. Jeering immediately started in the audience, however, and soon escalated into an uproar when fruit-peel, wooden sandals, and tea-cups were thrown onto the stage. A spokesman from the company tried to calm the audience by lying that Ma was indisposed. But the audience insisted that Ma be carried on stage to 'show' that he was genuinely ill, which was a common practice when a leading actor was declared too ill to perform. At this moment, Ma arrived.

A cheerful atmosphere was restored as soon as he appeared on stage in full costume, and the performance was begun again from the beginning (Shen Chi 1957: 55).

In the early 1920s, Li Hsüeh-fang and Su-chou Mei were probably the most 'chased after' opera actresses in Canton. Many poems and prose pieces glorifying their beauty, voice, deportment, and style of acting were composed and published in opera magazines by their knowledgeable male fans (*Li Ying* 3, *c.*1918: 12–5, 'Miscellany'; 5–7, 'chü p'ing'). At one time their fans organized themselves into a pro-Li and a pro-Su faction, each launching a 'war of the pen' against the other in Canton's dailies (Ch'en Fei-nung and Yu Mu-yün 1982: 3).

By the late 1920s, however, this form of courting game was no longer a men's monopoly. It was said to be highly fashionable among some women opera-patrons as well. These lady fans stopped at nothing to get close to their favourite actors. Since certain famous actors patronized the cinema regularly, some fanatical women fans would dress in flamboyant clothes, put on heavy make-up, and reserve seats as close to their idols as possible in order to seduce them. Outside the cinema, these women would deliberately stand in front of the actors to hail a taxi, 'pretending that they come from a respectable family' (*NYSP* 1928: 24, 29 Oct.).

Sometimes the craze for just gaining an actor's attention was expressed in an almost preposterous manner. For instance, whenever Ma Shih-ts'êng returned to Canton from touring abroad, a large crowd of flamboyantly dressed women usually greeted him at the pier. To please Ma, some of them screwed up Hong Kong banknotes into balls and threw them at him as gifts (Wan Yung 1930: 93). Even small diamonds were sometimes presented to him in greeting.[137] This phenomenon of courting opera actors by wealthy women had become so blatant that it was adopted as the plot of at least one topical opera, which was serialized in a Hong Kong daily in 1927.[138]

During this period, newsreels of special social events related to opera superstars gained wide appeal. Three such newsreels caused a sensation in Canton in 1933. They were documentaries showing the funeral of the mother of a famous jester, Liao Hsia-huai, which 'contain[s] footage of his weeping'; the ceremony of accepting a female student, who was also a well-known actress, by the superstar Hsüeh Chüeh-hsien; and the lavish wedding of Ma Shih-ts'êng and his second wife. Cinemas that ran these three newsreels were jammed with women audiences. A contemporary writer then enviously commented that it was far better to be an actor than a government official, because the former not only enjoyed wide publicity, but also the undue adoration of thousands of ladies (Wu Chun-lin 1933: 8). The private life of a famous actor had become a source of public entertainment; and it won no less attention than a national issue.

The personality cult of opera stars contributed to the publication of Ma Shih-ts'êng's *Chien-li chuang yu chi* (Recollections of the Proud Travelling of the Thousand Li) in 1931. It is an egoistical compilation of biography, photographic portraits, and excerpts from his famous opera scripts. In the perspective of the social position of a Cantonese opera actor, this is a significant piece of work. First, it shows that actors in this period were no longer all illiterates. Ma was a secondary-school graduate (Po Lo 1931: n.p.); Hsüeh Chüeh-hsien graduated from the prestigious St Paul's Boys' School in Hong Kong; Ch'en Fei-nung was a graduate of Lingnan College in Canton; and most impressive of all, Ch'en Hsiao-fêng graduated from the faculty of civil engineering at Kwangtung University (*YCS* 1988: 191–213). Hence by the 1930s it seems that more and more young men and women joined the opera profession not because of poverty or an obligation to follow in a parent's footsteps, though this was still the case with some actors,[139] but out of their genuine interest in Cantonese opera. Most of them even seemed proud of being opera actors. Kuei Ming-yang was a case in point. Growing up in an official's family, Kuei received a high-school education in Canton, where he discovered his interest and talent in opera acting. With the support and encouragement of his mother, he eventually became a professional opera actor (ibid. 200). Li Su-mei, a rising star in the late 1920s, was another example. Born in Canton, Li grew up and received her formal education in South-East Asia where her father was a successful businessman. Under the private tutorship of her father, she learned opera singing and acting at home until the age of 16, when she decided to go professional and joined a local troupe as an apprentice. Her fame grew rapidly because of her excellent singing and performing (*Chu-kiang hsing-ch'i hua-pao* 8, 1927: 7). The story of Ch'en Fei-wo, a successful entrepreneur and the older brother of the famous opera actor Ch'en Fei-nung, was another interesting case. After graduating from a prestigious high school in Canton, Ch'en Fei-wo received his post-secondary education overseas. He later settled in the Strait Settlements where he became a highly successful businessman, with branches of his empire stretching into China and Hong Kong. His interest in Cantonese opera was so strong that he became an amateur actor himself. He performed only for charity. One of these occasions was in Canton in 1926 where he played for noble purposes, to 'help publicise the Party and the country, and to serve the society' (ibid. 4, 1827: 7).

This 300-page work by Ma also reveals the eagerness of a contemporary Cantonese opera actor to seek public recognition of his rising social position. Probably in the hope of presenting him as a learned and refined scholar-gentleman, his book was printed and bound in traditional Chinese style, and most of the essays were written in respectable semi-classical Chinese. He was also unreserved when it came to showing off his self-importance. In two essays about his performance tour in the United States, he proudly describes himself as a 'cultural ambassador' who helped promote cultural understanding between the two countries. In essays giving his views on contemporary theatre, he writes in the tone of an authority; to show off his moral fibre, he quotes Aristotle and advocates bringing higher moral standards to opera. A English essay entitled 'A Brief Biography of Mr Ma Shih-ts'êng' in the same book makes legendary mystique of Ma's hard route to success. Although he was widely known for being forced by economic hardship to start his career in opera, and in private life was also a wastrel (Ch'en Fei-nung and Yu Mu-yün 1982: 73–4) the biography portrays him as a remarkably moral and visionary person:

> [T]o ameliorate the [unjust] conditions of society was his chief object of life. He therefore thought that the best way of bringing this about was through the stage, realizing the powerful hold theatricals had on the minds of the public... There is no one in the theatrical circles in South China today earning more than Mr. Ma, whose income from the stage and [from] singing for gramophone record companies amounts to upwards of several tens of thousands of dollars a year. He does not luxuriously spend the money he makes, nor keeps he [the income] for his own account. According to Confucius' teaching, 'A son should not privately own his fortune while his parents are alive'. Mr. Ma follows his teaching and has practically placed large parts of his earnings at the disposal of his parents. His fund has been used for the education of his brothers and sisters. Moreover, Mr. Ma is a friend of the poor, a helper of the depressed. Any charitable work for the uplife [sic] and [the] betterment of mankind always receives his warm support.

His book was intended to impress his contemporaries, to legitimize his social position, and to boost his social image as the opera star of the 'New Era'.

On the eve of a tour of South-East Asia in 1936, another superstar, Hsüeh Chüeh-hsien, published a volume of collected essays to commemorate the occasion. In one essay, he expounds his vision of transforming Cantonese opera into a 'world opera':

> My ambition is not limited to synthesizing Northern and Southern [Chinese] opera. I particularly want to synthesize Chinese and Western opera into one single body. By removing its shortcomings and retaining its essence, [I intend to] render our country's opera into the world's common opera, so that art of our country will become the highest art of the world. (*Chüeh-hsien chi*, cited in Li Mên 1986: 9)

Dreams or ambitions of such dimension and scope would have been unthinkable from an opera actor before this period. The high social prestige of Hsüeh enabled him to indulge in an egoistical self-perception as a visionary leader of the art world.

On stage, famous actors lost no chance of demonstrating their 'superior' social position. When they performed in summer, their servants were instructed to 'stand at the back of the stage with big electrical fans to keep their masters fresh and cool'. Or, in the midst of a performance, the servants would serve their masters cups of tea as refreshment (*KCHJP* 1933: 10, 17 Feb.).

The growth of the mass-media industry offered the necessary catalyst for promoting the cult of opera stars. Most of them released gramophone records. According to an unofficial estimate, more than ten record companies issued at least two thousand titles of Cantonese opera music in this period (Wang Yung-chih 1988: 49; *YCS* 1988: 109). One of these companies, the Hsin Yüeh kung-ssu (The Crescent Moon Company), sold 46,000 copies of Cantonese opera records in 1928; the total sale figure soared to 61,000 a year later (Yung Shih-ch'êng, forthcoming). While local film companies invited famous opera masters to play leading roles in both silent and talking films (Kuan Wên-ch'ing

1976: 196),[140] some opera superstars set up their own film companies and produced features in which they played the leading roles.[141] Radio broadcasting also helped. In 1929, more than one thousand hours of Cantonese opera music, or nearly half of its total transmission time, was put out by the Canton municipal broadcasting station. From 1930 onwards, the live broadcast of a complete Cantonese opera from one of the opera houses in Canton became a weekly programme.[142] By 1936, the three radio stations in Canton used nearly half their broadcasting time playing albums by famous Cantonese opera stars.[143]

The emotional importance of some popular Cantonese opera actors in the hearts of their fans was best shown by the 1936 funeral of Chien-li Chü, renowned as the 'King of Young Lady Role' (*hua-tan wang*). On the day of his funeral, his coffin was driven on a hearse to the cemetery. Tens of thousands of his fans gathered along the route. They watched solemnly as the hearse passed; many laid wreaths on it, while others even carried out libations and offered sacrificial items on the pavements. In order to give most of his fans a chance to pay their last respects to Chü, the procession route was deliberately spun out for more than ten Chinese miles in length, and passed through most of the main streets in Canton. On the first anniversary of his death, many fans and journalists paid homage at his grave (Lai Po-ch'iang 1986; 149–52).[144] Unlike most opera actors in the imperial times, who died unnoticed, opera celebrities in this period were widely respected by the public, even after their deaths.

If wealth had not been an accurate indicator of the social position of actors in imperial China, it was so now. Wealthy actors were not unheard of in pre-Republican times. In the news report of a lawsuit involving a famous actor in 1911, it was revealed that his annual income was an enviable 6,500 yüan (*HTJP* 1911, 2–5 Oct.), as compared to that of an engineer (300–480 yüan p.a.) in the same period (*YHKPK* 1996: 984). A nineteenth-century gazetteer recorded that some Cantonese opera actors earned as much as several thousand *taels* a year; though its author wrote in a tone of contempt, rather than envy, since he detested Cantonese opera as morally degenerating (*P'an-yü hsien hsü chih* 1931: 14, ch. 44). By the 1920s, however, when writers deal with the enormous income of opera superstars, it is envy rather than contempt that permeates their story. The biographies of Ch'en Fei-nung, Ma Shih-ts'êng, Chien-li Chü, and Hsüeh Chüeh-hsien tell that these actors regarded their enormous income as a source of pride (Shen Chi 1957: 57–67). When Ch'en Fei-nung recalls his record high salary of the mid-1920s, he is carried away by the nostalgia of success and achievement (Ch'en Fei-nung and Yu Mu-yün 1982: 9). In his self-aggrandizing work, Ma Shih-ts'êng writes with great pride that he twice broke the record of highest-paid actor. This was an expression of self-confidence as much as a pompous demand for respect and admiration from the public. It also indicated the changing popular attitude towards wealth. Being rich was no longer one's private secret and something to be humbly 'concealed'. Instead, a rich man would no long be criticized for showing off his wealth, if he did not do so excessively. The general public seemed anxious to know how wealthy these opera stars were, perhaps because they wanted to identify themselves with these successful citizens. Many were humble in origin, and comforted themselves with the illusive dream that one day they might be as rich as their heroes.

One of the implications of the formation of 'Canton-Hong Kong companies' was the lucrativeness of the opera business. Actors already earned so much by performing in these two cities alone that they did not need to take the risk of travelling to the bandit-infested countryside to perform (*HTJP* 1928: 4.4, 30 July). By the 1930s, the income of an actor varied according to his fame. A successful actor, however, could earn enormous sums by local standards. For instance, the transfer fee alone offered by one company to Lien Yung in 1928 was more than 10,000 yüan, though he was going to play a lesser role (ibid. 21 July). An offer of 10,000 yüan each to two 'promising' young actors as annual salary in 1931 was considered 'economical' by an opera journalist (Tien chiang-ch'un 1931*b*: 4; Hu-hua-lang 1931: 68). The salary of 'the master' was substantially higher. For instance, Ch'en Fei-nung earned more than 40,000 yüan a year in the mid-1920s (Ch'en Fei-nung and Yu Mu-yün 1982: 9). Most impressive of all was Ma Shih-ts'êng. He earned as much as 120,000 yüan a year by 1927 as an opera actor alone, in addition to his handsome income from producing records and acting in movies. Moreover, most 'Canton-Hong Kong companies' also performed abroad occasionally, which was another fine source of income to the actors. In Ma's case, a six-month tour of South-East Asia in 1930 brought him 60,000 yüan (Shen Chi 1957: 67, 75, 79, 87). In 1931, he accepted an invitation to perform for the Chinese communities in the United States at a record fee of 150,000 yüan (Ch'i Chui-tou 1931: 2).

The affluence of some actors enabled them to adopt a luxurious and lavish lifestyle. Many actors frittered away their income on, for example, gambling, which led some of them to become heavily indebted and consequently tied to their troupe's owners who, being their creditors and their inducement to further gambling, kept them with the company indefinitely (Ch'en Cho-ying 1983: 320–1). Some patronized sing-song girls or high-class courtesans, or courted the concubines of wealthy men.[145] But not all actors spent their wealth in such a profligate manner. In the 1930s, Hsüeh Chüeh-hsien founded three primary schools for the poor in Hong Kong (Ch'en Fei-nung and Yu Mu-yün 1982: 72; Chang Chieh 1980*b*: 136).

The fame and wealth of successful opera actors rendered them a potential target of extortion by local bullies, both official and civilian alike;[146] a phenomenon that had already become common in the late nineteenth century.[147] Thus, most well-off actors employed armed bodyguards (Ch'en Fei-nung and Yu Mu-yün 1982: 8). With this backing, actors sometimes behaved like bullies. For instance, the well-known actor Lien Shao-fêng once had a squabble with a stranger. Together with his bodyguards, the actor beat the man up badly. Although Shao-fêng was arrested by the police for this, his acquaintance with some high-ranking officials in Canton ensured his quick release after a light fine of 15 yüan (*HTJP* 1927: 3.2, 25 Mar.).

Famous opera actors were usually on good terms with many prominent Canton officials. For instance, the fame of Ma Shih-ts'êng won him the friendship of the Chief Detective of Canton's police force (Ch'en Fei-nung and Yu Mu-yün 1982: 74); Hsüeh Chüeh-hsien's eminence enabled him to establish cordial relations with many social notables in Canton and Hong Kong, including Sir Ho Tung (ibid. 71). General Li Fu-lin, Chou Tien-pang, a prominent local banker and chairman of the Canton Chamber of Commerce, and the editor of a local newspaper, pooled 180,000 yüan to form the Ta Lo T'ien Opera Company in which Ch'en Fei-nung played a leading role (ibid. 2).[148] Such cordiality was essential for the safety of the actors and the opera business. For example, the good relationship enjoyed by Hsüeh Chüeh-hsien with the Chief of Police in Canton not only enabled him to be granted permission to own a pistol, which he carried most of the time, but also gave his troupe the much-needed protection that successfully warded off threats from the local hoodlums (Hu Chên 2000: 85–6).

It was in charity work that the social position of Cantonese opera actors was formally and 'officially' recognized. Capitalizing on the popularity of their opera stars, the Canton authorities invited them to perform on such official occasions as fund-raising performances for the northern expedition of the early Republican army (*HTJP* 1911, 20 and 30 Dec.; 1912, 15 Jan.), for the Northern Expedition of the KMT (*KCMKJP* 1926: 10, 4 and 10 Aug.),[149] and on the Double-Tenth celebration (ibid.: 10, 9 Oct.). In mid-1927, the National Revolutionary Army organized a week-long variety show for the public, with Cantonese opera performances, acted by a number of 'masters', as the highlight of the programmes.[150] A group of the most popular Cantonese opera actresses were invited to take part in a parade celebrating the inauguration of Sun Yat-sen as Extraordinary President in Canton in 1921. In addition, some troupes volunteered to perform free for the new President in the presidential palace (*HTJP* 1921: 1.3, 5–6 May). By taking part in these official functions, actors and actresses seem to have succeeded in elevating their status from ordinary entertainer to that of a citizen of a modern nation.

Some opera stars were increasingly regarded by the public as social notables. Hsüeh Chüeh-hsien became, in 1933, the first opera star invited by a merchandise company to autograph a big wooden signboard, an honour normally reserved for famous scholars or eminent politicians (*KCTC* 21, 1933: 2). Some stars were appointed by invitation as members of the official Theatre Censorship Committee (*KCMKJP* 1926: 10, 4 Aug.). The success of these opera stars helped brighten the image of the profession, and raised their social status into that of celebrities and respectable citizens.

Not all successful actors viewed their profession with the same degree of envy and admiration as their fans did. Some actors were determined not to let their children follow them in their occupation. For instance, Chien-li Chü, despite his huge success, never allowed his children inside an opera house, not even to watch their father.[151] However, the improved social image and the financial promise is said to have attracted many new recruits to the profession.[152] Some actors encouraged, and even trained, their children to become successful opera actors.[153] Opera acting and singing were endorsed as a legitimate means of climbing the social ladder of success; and many actors with poor or humble family backgrounds benefited from this short-cut to wealth and fame.[154] This runs counter to the Chinese Communist historians' view that Cantonese opera actors had been suffering from 'oppression and social discrimination' under the old regime until they were eventually 'liberated' and 'salvaged' by the present government.[155]

It is important to note that although famous actors were the target of publicity, their opera were not always blindly accepted or well received. Biographers of famous Cantonese opera superstars always exaggerate the popularity of their heroes. All their performances are unquestionably assumed to have been well received by audiences. But this was not always the case. For example, a opera critic noted that of all the six new operas performed by the successful company Chüeh Hsien Shêng in 1931, only one enjoyed good public response; the box-office returns for the rest were poor (Tien Chiang-ch'un 1931*b*: 5). Thus opera audiences should not be assumed to be irrational beings incapable of making reasoned choices on what they preferred to watch; and notions of the popularity of Cantonese opera in this period should be approached with caution.

This short excursion into the world of Cantonese opera in the early and mid-Republican periods has shown vividly the different aspects of life, and the complex realities, in the dynamic city of Canton. It has also been an attempt to open up new paths that may lead us to understand the modern history of Cantonese opera in a less intellectually and politically biased way.

REFERENCES

Balazs, Etienne (1964), *Chinese Civilization and Bureaucracy*, trans. H. M. Wright (New Haven: Yale University Press).

Bartke, Wolfgang (1991), *Who's Who in the People's Republic of China*, 3rd edn., 2 vols. (Munich: K. G. Saur).

Boxer, C. R. (1953) (ed.), *South China in the Sixteenth Century: Being the Narratives of Galeote Pereira, Fr. Gaspar de Cruz, O.P., Fr. Martin de Rada, O.E.S.A.* (London: The Hakluyt Society).

Brusak, Karel (1968), 'Signs in Chinese Theater', in Ladislav Matejka and Irwin R. Titunik (eds.), *Semiotics of Art: Prague School Contributions* (Cambridge, Mass.: MIT).

Carr, Edward Hallet (1978), *What is History?* (Harmondsworth: Penguin).

Chang Chieh (1980*a*), 'Chu-ming Yüeh-chü i-jên Ma Shih-ts'êng', *KCWSTL*18.

——(1980*b*), 'Chu-ming Yüeh-chü i-jên Hsüeh Chüeh-hsien', *KCWSTL* 19.

——(1990), '"Hsiao-sheng wang" Pai Chiu-yung', in Kuang-chou-shih chêng-hsieh wên-shih tzu-liao yen-chiu-shih and Yüeh-chü yen-chiu chung-hsin (eds.), *Yüeh-chü ch'un-ch'iu* (Canton: Kuang-tung jên-wên ch'u-pan-shê).

Ch'ang Ch'o (1957), 'Yüeh-yü hua-chü ho i yen-yen-i-hsi?', *NFJP*, 31 May.

Chang Fang-wei (1986), 'San-shih nien-tai Kuang-chou Yüeh-chü shêng shuai', in Kuang-chou-shih chêng-hsieh wên shih tzu-liao yen-chiu wei-yüan-hui et al. (ed.), *Kuang-chou kung shang ching-chi shih liao* (Canton: Kuang-tung jên-min ch'u-pan-shê).
Chao Ching-shen (1962), *Hsi-ch'ü pi t'an* (Shanghai: Chung-hua shu-chü).
Chao Shan-lin (1990), *Chung-kuo hsi-ch'ü kuan-chung-hsüeh* (Shanghai: Hua-tung shih-fan-ta-hsüeh Ch'u-pan-shê).
Ch'en Chiang-fêng (1990), 'Ch'ien-lien hsiao-ch'iang Liao Hsia-huai', in Kuang-chou-shih chêng-hsieh wên shih tzu-liao yen-chiu wei-yüan-hui and Yüeh-chü yen-chiu chung-hsin (eds.), *Yüeh-chü ch'un-chiu* (Canton: Kuang-tung jên-min ch'u-pan-shê).
Ch'en Cho-ying (1983), 'Hung-ch'uan', *YCYCTLH*.
Ch'en Fei-nung and Yu Mu-yün (1982), *Yüeh-chü liu-shih nien* (Hong Kong: Wu hsing chi shu pao shê).
Ch'en Hua-hsin (1983), 'Yüeh-chü yü Hsin-hai kê-ming', *YCYCTLH*.
Ch'en Kiang fêng (1990), 'Chien mian hsiao-hsiang Liao Hsia-huai', in Kuang-chou-shih chêng-hsieh wên shih tzu-liao yen-chiu wei-yüan-hui and Yüeh-chü yen-chiu chung-hsin (eds.), *Yüeh-chü ch'un-chiu* (Canton: Kuang-tung jên-min ch'u-pan-shê).
Ch'en Shou-jên (1988), *Hsiang-kang Yüeh-chü yen-chiu* (Hong Kong: Kuang-chüeh-ching ch'u-pan-shê), i.
Ch'en Tieh-êrh (1984), 'Kuang-tung ta-hsi yü shao-lin wu i', *Kuang-tung wên-hsien chi k'an* 14/3, Sept.
Ch'en T'ien-tsung (*c.*1924–5), *Yü mo* (Canton: Hua hsing shu chü).
Ch'en Ts'ang-ku (*c.*1960s), *Ling-kuan lieh-ch'uan*, 2 vols. (Hong Kong: n.p.).
Chêng Chi-ming (1938), 'Yüeh-chü yü k'ai-fa Kuang-tung min chung', *Nan fêng* 14/1.
Ch'i Chui-tou (1931), 'Ma Shih-ts'êng hsiao shih', *Hsi ch'uan* 1.
Ch'i Shêng (1921), 'Yüeh-chü chih ying kai-liang chê', *HTJP*, 7 April.
Ch'iao Hua (1911), *HTJP*, 11 July.
Chien Hsing-tsun (1936), 'Chang Tzu-p' 'ing ti luan-ai hsiao-shuo', in Shih Ping-hui (ed.), *Chang Tzu-P'ing p'ing ch'uan* (Shanghai: K'ai-ming shu-tien).
Chien Hung (1922), 'Kai chu hsi-chü chih kêng-pên t'an', *Hsi-chü shih-chieh* 1.
Chin (*c.*1918), 'Hsin-chü chih pei-kuan, *Li ying* 3.
Ching Kan (1924), 'Wo tui-yu Kuang-chou ti hsi-wang yü', *KCMKJP*, 27 July.
Ching lei tsui hsiang yün (*c.*1930) (Canton: Ta hsin shu-chü).
Ch'iu Sung-ho (1992) (ed.), *San-tung-wu po-wu-kuan Yüeh-chü tsang p'in* (Hong Kong: Hong Kong Regional Council).
Ch'u Chien (1929), 'Yüeh-chü lun', *Hsi-chü* 1.
Ch'u I-tsun (1986), 'Ming shih tsung', in Hu P'o-an et al. (eds.), *Chung-hua ch'üan kuo fêng-su chih*, 2 vols. (Shanghai: Kuang chi shu-chü). First published 1923 (Shih-chia-chuan: Ho-nan jên-min ch'u-pan-shê).
Chu-kiang hsing-ch'i hua-pao (1927).
Ch'u Pu-chih (1982), 'Chi Hsüeh Chüeh-hsien yü Nan-hai-shih-san-lang', in Ch'en Fei-nung and Yu Mu-yün, *Yüeh-chü liu-shih nien* (Hong Kong: Wu hsing chi shu pao shê).
Chü shêng 1 (1917) (Canton: Chü shêng shê).
Ch'ü Ta-chün (1974), *Kuang-tung hsin yü*, 2 vols. (Hong Kong: Chung-hua shu-chü). First published 1700.
Chung (1934), 'Tun hsien shêng-chi chih nü-yu shêng-huo', *YHP*, 18 Oct.
Chung-kuo hsi-chü-chia hsieh hui, Kuang-tung-shêng wên-hua-chü (1962), *Chung-kuo ti-fang hsu-ch'ü chi ch'êng: Kuang-tung chüan* (Peking: Chung-kuo hsi-chü ch'u-pan-shê).

Chung-kuo jên-min chêng-chih-hsieh-shang-hui-i, Kuang-tung-shêng, and Kuang-chou-shih wei-yüan- hui wên-shih tzu-liao wei-yüan-hui (1960s–) (eds.), *Kuang-chou wên shih tzu liao* (*KCWSTL*) (Canton: Kuang-tung jên-min ch'u-pan-shê).

Docherty, David, Morrison, David, and Tracey, Michael (1987),*The Last Picture Show? Britain's Changing Film Audience* (London: British Film Institute).

Dolby, William (1976), *A History of Chinese Drama* (London: Paul Elek).

——(1988), 'Yüan Drama', in Colin Mackerras (ed.), *Chinese Theatre from its Origins to the Present Day* (Honolulu: University of Hawaii Press).

Fang Tsao (1928), 'Pao-shan chin chiu yu Mei-lung Ch'êng', *KPP*, 28 Mar.

Fêng Lan (1931), 'Yüeh-chü wu-tai pien-ch'ien lu', *Hsi ch'uan* 1.

Fêng Lang (1931), 'Hsüeh Chüeh-hsien yü Ch'en-p'i Mei', *Hsi ch'uan* 1.

Fêng Tzu-yu, 'Kuang-tung hsi-chü-chia yu kê-ming yün-tung', in Hsü Yen-tung et al. (1986–8) (eds.), *Kuang-tung wên-chêng shu pien*, 4 vols. (Hong Kong: Kuang-tung wên-chêng pien-yin wei-yüan-hui).

Fêng Yüan (1923*a*), 'Hsi-chü chih hsing-shih yu shih-chih', *Hsi-chü shih-chieh* 4, 'Hsi-chü p'ing-lun'.

——(1923*b*), 'K'un pan chih yin-kuo t'an', *Hsi-chü shih-chieh* 5, 'Hsi-chü p'ing-lun'.

——(1923*c*), 'P'ing Shêng Shih Chung nü chü-yüan chih i-shu', in *Hsi-chü shih-chieh* 5. 'Hsi-chü p'ing-lun'.

——(1923*d*), 'Shê-chu shih chih pu-ching', *Hsi-chü shih-chieh* 4, 'Hsi-chü p'ing-lun'.

Fêng-yüan-ch'u-jên (1922), 'Fêng yüan tu-ch'ü t'an', *Hsi-chü shih-chieh* 1.

——(1923), 'Fêng yüan tu-ch'ü t'an', *Hsi-chü shih-chieh* 5.

Fêng Yüan-chün (1947), *Ku chü shuo hui* (Shanghai: Shang-wu yin-shu-kuan).

Frith, Simon (1987), 'Towards an Aesthetic of Popular Music', in Richard Leppert and Susan McClary (eds.), *Music and Society: The Politics of Composition, Performance and Reception* (Cambridge: Cambridge University Press).

Fu Shêng (1921), 'P'ing chêng-yin kê nü-chüeh', *KHP*, 30 July.

Gans, Herbert J. (1974), *Popular Culture and High Culture: An Analysis and Evaluation of Taste* (New York: Basic Books).

Gernet, Jacques (1962), *Daily Life in China on the Eve of the Mongol Invasion 1250–1276*, trans. H. W. Wright (Stanford: Stanford University Press).

Hai-chüeh-shih-jên (1931), 'Wu ko ming ling chih ssu', *Hsi ch'uan* 1.

Ho, Kit-yiu Virgil (1994), 'Cantonese Opera in a Rural Setting', in Göran Aijmer and Åsa Boholm (eds.), *Images and Enactments: Possible Worlds in Dramatic Performance* (Gothenburg: Institute for Advanced Studies of Social Anthropology).

Ho Chien-ch'ing (1995), 'Yüeh-chü ch'ang-tzu chü-pên lü-shuo', in Liu Ching-chih and Hsien Yü-i (eds.), *Yüeh-chü yen-tao-hui lun-wen-chi* (Hong Kong: Joint Publishing (HK)).

Hong Kong Regional Council (1988) (ed.), *Cantonese Opera Costumes* (Hong Kong: Regional Council).

Hsi-chü shih-chieh (1922–3), 5 vols. (Canton: Kuang-tung chü hsüeh yen-chiu-shê).

Hsi ch'uan (1931) (Hong Kong: Fêng pai ch'u-pan pu).

'Hsi-yüan chung ti ch'üeh-tien' (1926), *KCMKJP*, 10 Aug.

Hsiao Lou (1922), 'Hsi-chü i chu-chung shuo-p'ai', *Hsi-chü shih-chieh* ii, 'Hsi-chü p'ing-lun'.

Hsiao Lu (1926), 'Ch'ao-p'iao yü', *KCMKJP*, 3–4 Aug.

Hsieh Shêng-p'o and Huang Ho-ming (1990), 'Yüeh-chü ch'üan-nü-pan i-pi', in Kuang-chou-shih chêng-hsieh wên shih tzu-liao yen-chiu wei-yüan-hui and Yüeh-chü yen-chiu chung-hsin (eds.), *Yüeh-chü ch'un-chiu* (Canton: Kuang-tung jên-min ch'u-pan-shê).

Hsien Yü-ch'ing (1996), 'Ch'ing tai liu shêng hsi-pan tsai Kuang-tung', in Fo-shan ta-hsüeh, Fo-shan wên shih yen-chiu shih, and Kuang-tung wên shih kuan (eds.), *Hsien Yü-ch'ing wên chi* (Canton: Chung-shan ta-hsüeh ch'u-pan-shê).

Hsü Fu-chin (1948), *Kuang-tung min-chien wên-hsüeh ti yen-chiu* (Hong Kong: Hai ch'ao ch'u-pan-shê).

Fan Min-shêng Hsü P'ei-chün (1990) (ed.), *Chung-kuo ku-tien ming chü chien-shang tzu-tien* (Shanghai: Shang-hai ku-chieh ch'u-pan-shê).

Hsü Tao-ching (1985), *The Chinese Conception of Theater* (Seattle: University of Washington Press).

Hsü Yen-tung et al. (1986–8) (eds.), *Kuang-tung wên-chêng shu pien*, 4 vols. (Hong Kong: Kuang-tung wên-chêng pien-yin wei-yüan-hui).

Hsüeh Chüeh-hsien tao-nien chi pien-wei-hui (1957) (ed.), *Chüeh-hsien tao-nien chi* (Hong Kong: Hsüeh Chüeh-hsien tao-nien chi pien-wei-hui).

HTJP, see *Hua-tzu jih-pao.*

Hu Chên (2000), *Kuang-tung hsi-chü shih (Hung-ling pien chih erh)* (Hong Kong: Li Yüan shu-pao shê you-hsien kung-ssu).

Hu, John (1983), 'Ming Dynasty Drama', in Colin Mackerras (ed.)., *Chinese Theater from its Origins to the Present Day* (Honolulu: University of Hawaii Press).

Hu-hua-lang (1931), 'I Chiu-shui yü Hsin Ch'un Ch'iu', *Hsi ch'uan* 1.

Hua-tzu jih-pao (*HTJP*) (Hong Kong: Hua-tzu jih-pao shê).

Huang Ching-ming (1987), 'San-shih nien-tai Yüeh-chü ti i-shu tê-chêng', *YCYC* 3, May.

Huang Shao-han (Wong Shiu-hon) (1971), *Yüeh-chü chü-pên* (*A Catalogue of Cantonese Opera Scripts*) (Hong Kong: Centre of Asian Studies, Hong Kong University).

Huang Tê-shen (1987), 'Kuang-tung hua-chü ts'ung Hsin-hai kê-ming chih Chien-fang chien ti fa-chan li-ch'êng', in Chung-kuo hsi-chü-chia chieh-hui, Kuang-tung fên-hui, and Kuang-tung hua-chü yen-chiu hui (eds.), *Kuang-tung hua-chü yün-tung shih-liao chi* (Canton: n.p.), ii.

Hung Chang-tai (1985), *Going to the People: Chinese Intellectuals and Folk Literature, 1918–1937* (Cambridge, Mass.: Harvard University Press).

Hung-ch'uan-chiu-lü (1931), 'Tou-p'i-mei chih ling tê', *Hsi ch'uan* 1.

I (*c.*1918), 'Lun hsi-chü yü shê-hui chih kuan-hsi', *Li yin* 3.

I Hsiao (1922), 'Tan nü-pan ta-yu-ssu san shou', in *Hsi-chü shih-chieh*, ii.

'I nien lai chih kung-tso kai k'uang' (1930), in Kuang-chou-tê-pieh-shih wu-hsien-tien po-yin-t'ai (ed.), *Kuang-chou-tê-pieh-shih wu-hsien-tien po-yin-ta'i chou-nien tê k'an* (Canton: n.p.), 'Report'.

Idema, Wilt, and West, Stephen H. (1982), *Chinese Theater, 1100–1450: A Source Book* (Wiesbaden: Franz Steiner).

Jê-nan-lang (1931), 'Hsüan Kung yen shih' tuan p'ing', *Hsi ch'uan* 1.

Kuang-chou hsin jih-pao (*KCHJP*) (1933) (Canton: Kuang-chou hsin jih-pao shê).

KCLPL, see *Kuang-chou li-pai liu.*

KCMKJP, see *Kuang-chou min-kuo jih-pao.*

KCTC, see *Kuang-chou tsa-chih.*

KCWSTL, *see* Chung-kuo jên-min chêng-chih-hsieh-shang-hui-i et al.

KHP, see *Kuo hua-pao.*

Kōsaka, Junichi (1943), 'Kanton tsushin', *Minzoku Taiwan* 3/12.

KPP, see *Kung-p'ing pao.*

KTHS, *see* Kuang-tung chung-hsüeh hsüeh-shêng tzu-chih-hui.

Kuan Wên-ch'ing (1976), *Chung-kuo yin tan wai shih* (Hong Kong: Kuang-chüeh-ching ch'u-pan-shê).

Kuang-chou chih-nan (1934) (Canton: Kuang-chou shih-chêng-fu).
Kuang-chou li-pai liu (*KCLPL*) (C. 1933–5) (Canton: Kuang-chou li-pai-liu shê).
Kuang-chou min-kuo jih-pao (*KCMKJP*) (Canton: Kuang-chou min-kuo jih-pao shê).
Kuang-chou nien-chien (1935), ed. Kuang-chou nien-chien pien tsuan wei-yüan-hui, 2 vols. (Canton: Kuang-chou nien-chien pien tsuan wei-yüan-hui).
Kuang-chou-shih chêng-hsieh wên shih tzu-liao yen-chiu wei-yüan-hui et al. (1986) (ed.), *Kuang-chou kung shang ching-chi shih liao* (Canton: Kuang-tung jên-min ch'u-pan-shê).
Kuang-chou-shih shih-chêng-t'ing *Kuang-chou-shih shih-chêng pao kao hui k'an* (Canton: 1924).
Kuang-chou-shih shih-chêng-fu t'ung-chi ku, *Kuang-chou-shih shih-chêng-fu t'ung-chi nien-chien. Ti i hui.* Canton: Kuang-chou-shih shih-chêng-fu, 1929.
Kuang-chou tsa-chih (*KCTC*) (1924–30s) (Canton: Kuang-chou tsa-chih shê).
Kuang-chou wên-hsüeh hui (1928) (ed.), *Ying shih* (Canton: Yüeh Kang shou k'uang ch'u-pan pu).
Kuang-tung chung-hsüeh hsüeh-shêng tzu-chih-hui (ed.), *Kuang-tung hsüeh-shêng* (*KTHS*) (Canton: n.p.).
Kuang-tung shang-yeh nien-chien (1932).
Kuang-tung-shêng hsi-chü yen-chiu-shê (1983) (ed.), *Yüeh-chü yen-chiu tzu-liao hsüan* (*YCYCTLH*) (Canton: n.p.)
Kung-p'ing pao (*KPP*) (1924–49) (Canton: Kung-p'ing pao shê).
Kuo hua pao (*KHP*) (1911–50) (Canton: Kuo hua pao-shê).
Kuo Ping-chên (1983), 'Yüeh-chü ti yen-kê yü hsien-chuang', *YCYCTLH.*
Lai Po-ch'iang (1986), *Yüeh-chü hua-tan wang Chien-li-Ch'ü* (Canton: Hua-ch'êng ch'u-pan-shê).
——(2001), *Kuang-tung hsi-ch'ü chien shih* (Canton: Kuang-tung jên-min ch'u-pan-shê).
——and Huang Ching-ming (1988), *Yüeh-chü shih* (*YCS*) (Peking: Chung-kuo hsi-chü ch'u-pan-shê).
Li Fêng (1986), 'Hsüeh Chüeh-hsien ch'uan', *YCYC* 1.
Li Mên (1983), 'Shih lun Yüeh-chü ti ch'uan-t'ung chi ch'i chi-ch'êng fa-chan wen-t'i', *YCYCTLH.*
——(1986), 'Hsüeh Chüeh-hsien ti shêng-p'ing chi ch'i i-shu ch'êng-chiu', in *Hsüeh Chüeh-hsien chi-lien tê k'an* (Canton).
Li T'iao-yüan (1937), 'Nan Yüeh pi chi', in Wang Yün-wu (ed.), *Ts'ung-shu chi-ch'êng* (Shanghai: Shang-wu yin-shu-kuan). First published 1778.
Li Tsung-huang (1922), *Hsin Kuang-tung kuan-ch'a chi* (Shanghai: Shang-wu yin-shu-kuan).
Li Ying 3 (*c.*1918) (Canton: Li ying tsa-chih shê).
Liang P'ei-chih (Leung Pui-chee) (1978), *Hsiang-kang ta-hsüeh so tsang mu-yü-shu hsü lu yü yen-chiu* (*Wooden-Fish Books: Critical Essays and an Annotated Catalogue Based on the Collections in the University of Hong Kong*) (Hong Kong: Centre of Asian Studies, Hong Kong University).
——(1988), *Nan-yin yü Yüeh-ou chih yen-chiu* (*A Study of Nan Yin and Yue Ou*) (San Francisco: Asian American Studies, School of Ethnic Studies, San Francisco State University).
Liang P'ei-chin (1985), *Yüeh-chü chü-mu t'ung chien* (Hong Kong: Joint Publishing).
Liang Wei (1990), 'Yüeh-chü yüan-liu chi ch'i pien-kê chu shu', in Kuang-chou-shih chêng-hsieh wên shih tzu-liao yen-chiu wei-yüan-hui and Yüeh-chü yen-chiu chung-hsin (eds.), *Yüeh-chü ch'un-chiu* (Canton: Kuang-tung jên-min ch'u-pan-she).

——(1995), 'Chien hsi Yüeh-chü chü-pên yu ch'ang-tzu', in Liu Ching-chih and Hsien Yü-i (eds.), *Yüeh-chü yen-tao-hui lun-wên chi* (Hong Kong: Hong Kong University Press).

Liao Yüan (1922), 'Hsi-chü chih la tsa t'an', *Hsi chü shih-chieh* 3.

Lien hsiang chi-chê (*c.*1931–3) (Canton: Hua hsing shu-chü).

Link, Perry (1981), *Mandarin Ducks and Butterflies: Popular Fiction in Early Twentieth-Century Chinese Cities* (Berkeley: University of California Press).

Liu Jung-en (1988) (trans.) *Six Yüan Plays* (London: Penguin).

Liu Kuo-hsing (1983), 'Hsi-pan ho hsi-yüan', *YCYCTLH.*

Liu Ling-yü (1990), *Lo P'in-ch'ao ch'i ch'uan* (Hong Kong: Hsiang-kang chou-k'an ch'u-pan-shê).

Liu Wan-chang (1972), 'Pa-kung ti Kuang-chou kuo nien jih-chi', in Chou K'ang-yen (ed.), *Kuang-tung fêng-su chui lu* (Hong Kong: Ch'ung wên shu-tien).

Lo chia-shan (*c.*1920s) (Canton: Yüeh ch'ü yuen-chiu so).

Mackerras, Colin (1972), *The Rise of the Peking Opera, 1770–1870* (Oxford: Clarendon Press).

——(1975), *The Chinese Theatre in Modern Times: From 1840 to the Present Day* (London: Thames & Hudson).

——(1983) (ed.), *Chinese Theater from its Origins to the Present Day* (Honolulu: University of Hawaii Press).

Mai Hsiao-hsia (1941), 'Kuang-tung hsi-chü shih lüeh', in Kuang-tung wên-wu chan-lan hui (ed.), *Kuang-tung wên-wu*, 3 vols. (Hong Kong: Chung-kuo wên-hua hsieh chin hui).

Ming-pên Ch'ao-chou hsi-wên wu tsung (1985) (Canton: Kuang-tung jên-min ch'u-pan-shê).

Muensterberger, Warner (1951), 'Orality and Dependence: Characteristics of Southern Chinese', *Psychoanalysis and the Social Sciences* 3.

Nan-fang jih-pao (*NFJP*) (1950–) (Canton: Nan-fang jih-pao shê).

Nan-yang shang-pao (*NYSP*) Singapore: Nan-yang shang-pao shê.

Ou-yang Yü-ch'ien (1957), 'Shih t'an Yüeh-chü', in id. (ed.), *Chung-kuo hsi-ch'ü yen-chiu tzu-liao ch'u chi* (Peking: Chung-kuo hsi-chü ch'u-pan-shê).

Ou-yang Yü-ch'ien (1983), 'Shih t'an Yüeh-chü', *YCYCTLH.*

——(1958), 'T'an wên-ming-hsi', *Chung-kuo hua-chü yün-tung wu-shih-nien shih-liao chi* (Peking: Chung-kuo hsi-chü ch'u-pan-shê).

Pan-chiao man-hua (1929–32) (Canton: Pan-chiao man-hua shê).

P'an Kuang-wên (1966), *Chung-kuo ling-jên hsüeh-yüan chih yen-chiu* (Taipei: Shang-wu yin-shu-kuan).

P'an-yü hsien hsü chih (1968) (Taipei: Hsüeh-shêng shu-tien). First published 1931.

Patrick, Tony (1990), 'Going to the Panto? (Oh Yes You Are)', *Sunday Times*, 1 Dec.

Pearsall, Ronald (1973), *Victorian Popular Music* (Newton Abbot: David & Charles).

P'eng Fen (1988), 'Ch'ing-mo Min-ch'u Yüeh-chü shih hua', *YCYC* 7.

Po Lo (1931), Ma shih ch'un-ch'iu', in Ma Shih-ts'êng, *Chien-li chuang yu chi* (Canton: n.p.).

Potter, Jack M., and Potter, Sulamith Heins (1990), *China's Peasants: The Anthropology of A Revolution* (Cambridge: Cambridge University Press).

Scott, A. C. (1965), *Literature and the Arts in Twentieth-Century China* (London: Allen & Unwin).

Shao Pin-ju (1964) (ed.), *Kuang-tung yü hsiao-shuo chi* (Tokyo: Sho ho shoten).

Shao Wên (1928), 'Hsi-yüan tso-chia ho fu-nü', *KCMKJP*, 1 May.

Shen Chi (1957), *Ma Shih-ts'êng ti hsi-chü shêng-yai* (Canton: Kuang-tung jên-min ch'u-pan-shê).

Shêng Hua (1926), 'Kê-ming yü i-shu', *KCMKJP* Suppl. 55, 8 July.

Shih Pin-ch'ou (1983), 'Chin-tai Chung-kuo hsi-chü ti min-chu kê-ming sê-t'sai ho Yüeh-chü ti kai-liang yün-tung', *YCYCTLH*.

Shu Yuan (1912), 'Lun kai-liang hsi-pên chih pieh-yao', *HTJP*, 17 Oct.

Su Kuo-yung (1984), 'Shih lun hsi-ch'ü kuan-chung ti min-chien hsin chi ch'i ying-hsing', *Hsi-ch'ü yen-chiu* 13, Dec.

Sung-hu-chu-jên (*c.*1919), *Ch'ing shan-hu pan pên* (Hong Kong: n.p.).

Tan pao t'ien (*c.*1921–8) (Canton: Hua hsing shu-chü).

T'an Cho-yüan (1965) (ed.), *Kuang-chou ting-ch'i k'an-wu ti tiao-ch'a, 1826–1934* (Hong Kong: Lung mên shu-tien). First published 1935.

T'ang Ti-shêng (*c.*1930s), *Yen Shui-shêng* (Canton: I wên t'ang shu-chü).

Tien Chiang-ch'un (1931*a*), 'Lao-kuan chên hsing-ming k'ao', *Hsi ch'uan* 1.

——(1931*b*), 'Tsui-chin ko pan shêng-i kai k'uang', *Hsi ch'uan* 1.

Tien Han (1958), 'Chung-kuo hua-chü i-shu fa-chan ti lu-ching ho chan-wang' in Ou-yang Yü-ch'ien (ed.), *Chung-kuo hua-chü yün-tung wu-shih-nien shih-liao chi* (Peking: Chung-kuo hsi-chü ch'u- pan-shê).

Tu Shao-mu (1971), 'Man t'an Yüeh-chü', *Kuang-tung wên-hsien chi k'an* 1/1.

Tuan Ping (1924), 'Kuang-chou chih hsi-chü yü chü-p'ing', *KCTC* 1/1.

Tun-chien (1919), 'P'ing Chien-ch'iu pan hsiao-wu Fu Ch'êng chih Sui-chin Ch'i Chün', *KHP*, 9–10 Sept.

Tzu K'uan (1926), 'I mei tsuan-shih', *KCMKJP*, 12 July.

Tzu-liu-han (1919), 'Ku ch'ü t'an', *HTJP*, 9–10 Sept.

Wan Yung (1930), 'Ping hou luan t'u', *Wan jên tsa-chih* 1/3, June.

Wang Chien-hsün (1988), 'Tui yü san-shih-nien-tai Yüeh-chü p'ing-chia ti ch'ien chien', *YCYCTLH.*

Wang Yung-chih (1988), 'Liu-shih-wu nien', *YCYC* 6.

Ward, Barbara (1981), 'The Red Boats of the Canton Delta: A Chapter in the Historical Sociology of Chinese Opera', *Proceedings of the International Conference on Sinology* (Taipei: Academia Sinica).

——(1985), 'Regional Operas and Their Auiences: Evidences from Hong Kong', in David Johnson, Andrew J. Nathan, and Evelyn S. Rawski (eds.), *Popular Culture in Late Imperial China* (Berkeley: University of California Press).

Wu Chên-fang (1936), 'Ling-nan tsa chi', in Wang Yün-wu (ed.), *Ts'ung-shu chi ch'êng* (Shanghai: Shang-wu yin shu kuan).

Wu Chün-lin (1933), 'Kuang-chou ying-pien san-pu-ch'ü', *KCTC* 23.

Wu-hsien man-hua (The Funny Story) (1930–?) (Canton: Nan-fang fu lun shê).

Wu Yin (1930), 'Kuan-yü Min-chung Chü-shê', *Wu hsien man hua* 1.

YCS, see *Lai Po-chiang and Huang Ching-ming (1988).*

YCYC, see *Yüeh-chü yen-chiu.*

YCYCTLH, see Kuang-tung-shêng hsi-chü yen-chiu-shê (1983).

YHP, see *Yüeh hua pao.*

You Lung (1933), 'Hung-mien chiu-chia chih ch'ün-fang yen', *KHP*, 3 June.

Yü Chia-yen (1983), 'Shih lun chieh-fang chien êrh san shih nien ti Yüeh-chü chü-mu chi ch'i chi-ch'êng', *YCYCTLH*.

Yüeh-chü yen-chiu (*YCYC*) (1986–1991) (Canton: Kuang-chou-shih wên-i ch'uang-tso yen-chiu-shuo Yüeh-chü yen-chiu chung-hsin).

Yüeh hua pao (*YHP*) (1927–50) (Canton: Yüeh hua pao-shê).

Yung Shih-ch'êng (forthcoming), 'Chien Kuang-jên chi Hsin Yüeh liu-shêng-chi ch'ang-pien kung-ssu—chien t'an Yüeh-yüeh ch'ang-pien ti shang-pin hsin (1926–1936)', *Journal of Oriental Studies*.

Conclusion

In spite of almost forty years of authoritarian Communist rule, present-day popular perceptions of the various aspects of social reality discussed in this book reveal a remarkable continuity with the values and views of Republican times. The cultural, social, economic, and political position of the city has been elevated to an even higher level. The West, and its symbolic cultural status for local Cantonese, continues to be generally admired. The gradual 'Hong Kongization' of popular culture in Canton, and to some extent in many parts of Kwangtung Province, is a symbolic expression of a somewhat perverted form of the Westernization of society. But most surprising of all is the enduring consistency of popular views of all three forms of the vices that we have studied in the foregoing chapters.

In spite of intensive official campaigns and publicity against the widely re-emerging phenomena of prostitution, gambling, and narcotic drug consumption in present-day Kwangtung, many Cantonese are able to maintain their own private favourable views on these morally and politically sensitive issues. Although most are convinced of the perniciousness of narcotic drugs, many old residents of Canton are sophisticated enough to tell the difference between opium and other more dangerous drugs, such as cocaine, and to know its medicinal value. Many of them continue to defend (privately, of course) the possible physical benefits of consuming opium in moderation.

Although gambling was never completely suppressed even during the radical era of Communist rule, it has been making a rapid reappearance since the inauguration of the 'liberalization' policy in the late 1970s. Today, private gambling, mainly in the forms of *mahjong*, which has been recently recognized and promoted as a form of national sport (*kuo-chia t'i-yu*), and poker, plays an important role in the domestic life of many Cantonese families. As in Republican times, gambling is commonly regarded not only as an acceptable pastime, an agreeable focus for a family or social gathering, but also as a proper way of training one's mental skills and shrewdness. The 'cash-thirst' of the government plays a no less important role in reviving this old Kwangtung tradition of gambling. State-run lotteries attract many keen betters. In some counties, officially run lotteries are held bi-weekly and the drawing of lots is televised. Lotteries organized by the municipal government have become a highly publicized weekly event that attract millions of yüan in bets. This form of state-run gambling is operated under the euphemistic title of 'extending welfare [to the people] and providing relief to [victims of] natural disasters'. It seems that in order to demonstrate its ability to modernize the province, and to catch up with Hong Kong as a modern metropolis in the region, the Canton authorities, after a lapse of more than four decades, have reintroduced horse racing—a seemingly respectable Western pastime and a symbol of its commitment to modernization. These forms of state-run gambling provide the local gamblers, as in Republican times, with invaluable opportunities to pursue their dream of attaining instant wealth, or to realize their preordained fortune with a windfall. There is nothing immoral about such state-run gambling, since a large part of the money staked will—allegedly—be used to finance municipal development projects and, in the latest cliché, 'disaster relief'.

Unlike the former regime, the Communist government is uncompromising on prostitution, to go by official propaganda and literature. Both prostitutes and clients are occasionally arrested and sent off to prison for 'thought re-education'. With the influence of corruption being felt at nearly all levels of society, however, such measures are clearly insufficient to deal with the problem. In Canton, for instance, clandestine prostitutes, both male and female, are easily available in practically all hotels. In hotels owned and managed by the People's Liberation Army, the presence of prostitutes is even more obvious and solicitation more open, not just because the police dare not search Army premises, but also because many senior army officers are said to be major patrons of these women.

Interestingly, popular attitudes towards prostitution today bear a striking resemblance to those that prevailed in the Republican period. Many Canton residents are convinced of the beneficial contribution that prostitution is making to the local economy. Most contemporary Cantonese appear indifferent to the expansion of clandestine prostitution in their city. Local hostility to this 'beautiful merchandise' is unheard of. Instead, many Cantonese hold the view that prostitution in which transactions are conducted fairly and voluntarily is much less harmful to society than heavy gambling, drug addiction, or official corruption.[1]

Our historical journey into the Cantonese society of the Republican period may help us to make sense of present-day social and cultural events in Southern China with better insight and more precision.

This book has not explicitly set out to construct or test any general sociological or cultural theory about the Chinese city in late-imperial and Republican times. What it has demonstrated is how official rhetoric, social perception, or academic fashion can obscure reality and thus block our knowledge and understanding of it. It brings out alternative views and ambiguities, rather than certainty, that could help remind us of the vagueness of socio-cultural reality and historical complexity.

During the 1920s and 1930s, when the history of modern Canton was in its golden age, varied socio-cultural forces were at work in shaping its metropolitan culture.[2] Economic prosperity, urban development, Western cultural influence, and innovative changes in local culture were some of the major sources of impetus behind this change, each interlocked with and hence reinforced by the others. Urbanization, whose pace was markedly accelerated in this period, had turned Canton into a city of over one million inhabitants by the mid-1920s. The expansion of the city, both vertically and horizontally, not only transformed its cityscape but also redefined its cultural position and image. With the rising image of the city as an economic power-house and the agent of modernization, more and more urban residents of Canton began to evaluate themselves with explicit pride as culturally superior to the country 'bumpkins'. This cultural force, however, was not powerful enough to conquer the minds of all citizens, as some continued to romanticize and idealize the countryside and rural culture, while others indulged in criticizing the city and urbanites for rapidly losing their 'Chineseness'. Contrasting views and opinions coexisted; but coexistence as such not only conveyed vagueness, ambiguity, and uncertainty in the mindscape of the people at the time of great socio-cultural change, but also a loss of faith in the idyllic tradition, and the emergent cultic status of the metropolis in the popular imagination.

The gradual 'modernization' of Canton's physical cityscape took place against a backdrop of economic prosperity that the city had been experiencing since the mid 1910s.[3] But the socio-cultural influence of the West was not confined to urban architecture alone. It was in this period that Canton witnessed a rise in the number of Western-style schools, hospitals, and multistorey buildings, automobiles, telephone services and tap-water, and modern infrastructural projects and factories. Western movies, dancing, billiards, and Western-style fashion were also popularly received by residents who increasingly took pride in and sought satisfaction from imitating the fashionable lifestyle in the great cities of Western Europe and the United States. Canton was no longer perceived by its citizens as an ordinary Chinese city, but as a cosmopolitan urban centre whose culture followed closely that of the family of 'advanced nations' which represented 'modern' civilization. Change, and the ability to implement it, were commonly regarded and justified as the means to attain progress and modernization. The belief in change *per se* (but not necessarily iconoclastic changes) had reached an almost cultic intensity.

This popular belief in the necessity of change in one way or another greatly helped transform many facets of life in Canton. It provided a favourable context in which aspects of Western culture were introduced and then syncretically integrated into the indigenous urban culture, as much as facets of the indigenous urban culture were renovated, repopularized and transformed. Western cinema, for example, was one of the most influential agents of change that fostered the cultural process of selective Westernization in Canton. It was through imported movies that the romanticized images of the West were transmitted to, and fascinated, the Cantonese audiences. Fascination as such was not only a source of amusement to the viewers, but also a mine of stimulation and inspiration from which more changes along Western lines were imitated and introduced. Change, like the Western institution of fashion, must be in constant motion for the sake of change itself. Perhaps due to this popular acceptance of change, the urban culture of modern Canton had became more diverse in form and contents. The city was increasingly identified with progressive changes and the transformative power that made these changes possible. And it was this spirit of change that made many Canton residents take pride in their urban identity and despise the village world that was stigmatized more and more as the fortress of backward and so-called 'feudalistic' practices.

The growth of the population, which was buttressed by the improvement in the social and economic conditions of Canton, helped create a general demand for popular leisure. The rising popularity of Cantonese opera was partly a response to that demand. In the context of urban Canton, however, not only traditional Cantonese opera was in great demand, but also the 'modern' kind of Cantonese opera that assumed unprecedented new forms and contents, as well as sensational props and costumes, Western-style music, natural voice production in singing, and so on. The growing popularity of modern Cantonese opera reflected the audiences' demand for new, and sometimes foreign, things in order to satisfy their almost insatiable demand for sensation. It was in the Cantonese opera that the process of cultural hybridization was most vividly seen.

Better economic conditions also fostered the expansion and further self-conscious commercialization of the local restaurant business.[4] Although the history of Cantonese restaurants deserves much more attention and space, it suffices here to point out that 'modern' restaurants in Canton provided another interesting example of how the cultural influence of the West was syncretized with the local culture. The famous Cantonese restaurant T'ao T'ao Chü, for instance, was first open in 1880 on the premises of a defunct academy near the west gate of the walled city. In its early years, the restaurant specialized in Soochow cuisine, which soon became a local attraction. In 1927, this 'old' restaurant was closed down because of bad management. It was soon bought by a syndicate of local restaurant businesses which decided to demolish the old structure and replace it with a Western-style multistorey building in concrete. The new restaurant, which now served Cantonese cuisine, was notorious for its luxurious, traditional style of decoration. The new management also introduced, for the first time in the history of gourmet culture in Canton, the set meal, an idea that is believed to have been borrowed from Western dining culture; and it was popularly received. But sources of change also came from within as more new local dishes were introduced and unconventional advertising gimmicks tried out. Its wide variety of moon-cakes, which was another innovation within the framework of tradition, also brought commercial success and fame to this restaurant (Fêng Pi-ying 1989: 5–7).[5] This experience of T'ao T'ao Chü in many respects reflected the situation of many spheres of urban life and culture in Canton in this period: tradition and change, Western influence and indigenous innovations complementing and interweaving with one another to thread the picture of complex realities.

A purely economic or materialistic approach to history would hamper rather than help us to understand the socio-cultural phenomena of the past. Economic prosperity should not be taken as the predominant or the only factor that governed the course and the process of social and cultural changes in Canton during this period. An economically prosperous environment was certainly important for providing the necessary ingredients for inducing socio-cultural transformations, but it does not follow that cultural changes would have been unattainable without the support of a prosperous economy. Economics provides at most only one of the many possible explanations of the various forms of people's indulgence and cognitive obsession that have been discussed here. Moreover, it is obvious that prosperity did not necessarily produce the kind of change that social reformers—Chinese or Western—would have hoped for. Nor did traditions necessarily have to be torn apart and discarded in this forceful process of change. The West, despite its strong influence on shaping modern Canton's urban culture, was by no means a totally effective iconoclastic agent of change. The history of Canton in this period tells us that old customs and habits coexisted with new ideas and practices. Therefore, for example, traditional Cantonese opera continued to enjoy wide popularity with the audience. Other common forms of old 'pernicious' leisure such as opium smoking, gambling, and brothel-going, despite being attacked occasionally in the name of nationalism and modernity, survived the challenge of change that had been prescribed by the state or the social reformers. The persistence of these facets of tradition should not be understood as an indication of the weakness of this force of change—in many aspects of urban life, remarkable changes were made. It reflected the tension between the public authorities' overt attempts to have them eradicated and the collective capability of individuals in withstanding it. This tension, in turn, provides us with important clues to understanding through a better perspective the complex relations between the state, the society, and the individuals. And only by studying the complexity of this reality can we appreciate the importance of individuals and the element of personal free choice in the historical process.

Economic prosperity, ironically, could also foster the persistence of the past rather than change. Enhanced consumer power allowed many Cantonese to sustain (rather than to reform) their 'pernicious' habits of opium smoking, gambling, and visiting brothels. The cold official ideal of rational citizens was counteracted with a popular instinctive sensuality in which these old habits were not perceived as necessarily pernicious but as enjoyable, acceptable, and even indeed as socio-economically rational. In the mind of the practitioners of these 'deviant' pastimes, the pursuit of these indulgences represented a legitimate quest for individualistic fulfilment that resisted the encroachment of the 'modern', and increasingly collectivistic, nation-state.

Canton in this period was a city full of contrasts and ambiguities. The diversity of individual feelings and social experiences of its people defy any simple generalization. It was a city of discordant views, of contradictory values, and of endless cases of inconsistency between ideals and reality. Examples abound that show this intrinsic complexity and contradiction between life and professed values. Thus, despite Canton's rising socio-cultural position, many urban

Cantonese continued to bask in their dream of an idyllic utopia and idealized the countryside as much as urban proponents did the city. In this period, anti-imperialism was not necessarily expressed in the form of anti-foreignism in the true sense of the term, and the Cantonese pro-foreign mode of thought did not apparently clash with patriotic feeling. Both forces were able to coexist in the same social context and urban milieu, albeit not without occasional tension. On the emotionally charged and morally sensitive subjects of prostitution, opium smoking, and gambling, dissenting favourable perceptions continued to flourish, for all that they were swept under the public carpet by the dominant official ideology. In the case of Cantonese opera, the struggle for dominance between 'popular' and 'aristocratic' taste swung seemingly in favour of the former. However, despite being an unequivocally popular form of performing art, the form and content of Cantonese opera in this period were never totally 'popularized' in any absolute manner. In terms of theatrical characteristics, Cantonese opera remained a strange but wonderful hybrid of things new and traditional, Western and Cantonese, popular and elitist—a true epitome of Cantonese society in this period and, to a large extent, this remains the case even in the present time.[6]

Which brings us to other interesting issues concerning the social and cultural history of modern Canton. In the chapters on prostitution and Cantonese opera, it was noted that many Cantonese tended to idealize the past. The past was thought always to have been better than the present, and they did not seem to care to try to substantiate their cult of it with evidence. The thought in itself, as it were, substantiated the truth; the fact was merely subservient, and substantiation hence unnecessary. However, as the chapter on opera has shown, many Cantonese who idealized or glorified the past, and agitated for the reformation of society and popular culture in the name of Tradition, held highly ambiguous ideas of what tradition really was. Most of them seemed to have had only a very casual, vague, and ill-defined concept of it. Anything from the past could be conveniently deduced to be 'traditional'. The element of change was seemingly given no place in their concept. Tradition, or the past, was mistakenly and self-deceivingly conceived of and taken as something static and hence absolutely unchangeable.

But the history of Cantonese opera tells us that tradition is an ongoing process of creation. Moreover, in this creative process, not only are innovations incorporated, but all-but-forgotten theatrical elements from the past also resurface, and are reinterpreted and reassimilated. Tradition, in this sense, was ironically a source of change that helped transform Cantonese opera into its modern form. Therefore, all the disparaging criticisms about the 'untraditionalness' of Cantonese opera in this period overlook one simple fact: that Cantonese opera had been undergoing a continuous process of change throughout its history. And for that matter, the weakness of the social theory of modernization is also apparent. If Cantonese opera in this period is an illustration of the process of 'modernization' then taking place in Cantonese society, it is by no means a good example of a linear process such as the term 'modernization' implies (Burke 1992: 136–7).[7] Modernity, like tradition, keeps changing.

The fact that dissenting views of the officially labelled 'vices' (i.e. prostitution, opium smoking, and gambling) were able not only to coexist with orthodox ones, but also to influence the action of the people who held these views, demonstrates the limits of the reach of the state. The state remained powerful and culturally dominant only on the official level. On the level of private life, however, individual free will and personal motivation seemingly played a dominant role in the shaping of human actions. The state with its official ideology might have been able to influence some parts of an individual's life and action, but it is doubtful that it was the *only* source of influence, or that it was slavishly accepted by all.

In this study, the stereotyped and misinterpreted images of some marginalized elements in Cantonese society are identified, analysed, and rectified. It is alarming to observe that such stereotypes, despite being misrepresentations of real life, were, and still are, commonly fostered by the learned and readily accepted by the multitudes. These distorted views of reality are often in part preferred because they possess the illusory attraction of being able to reduce the complexity of human life and culture to rigid, simple, and impressive-sounding phrases or sensational models, while actual reality always defies such easy generalizations and presumptions. This love of stereotypes, however, has become such a prevalent and widespread phenomenon that it seriously obstructs our ability to understand the world, its cultures, and even ourselves.

This study has shown the history of Canton in this period to be never the history of one man, one class, or one set of principles. Moreover, no one single social theory suffices to explain and demonstrate the complex nature of social events and cultural phenomena, or the conflicting motivations and contradictory views and values of the actors in the events that constituted this history. The elements of class, social structure and function, economic maximization, emotions, impulses, supernatural beliefs, external influences, and so on, all scramble for their part to play, with differing degrees of success, in shaping an individual one way or another. Human action, as a consequence of this plurality, becomes hardly predictable according to any single pattern or paradigm.

However, this is not to say that social theories have no place in the writing of history. On the contrary, they provide historians with increasingly indispensable tools in the 'craftsmanship' of history—stimulating and insightful concepts that assist us to understand the past from other perspectives and to open new paths into both uncharted and established areas of historical research. But that does not mean that all social theories are faultless as working theory, or that they must be accepted uncritically as laws of history and human culture. A careful eclecticism with regard to history and social theory will go further in making better sense of history, a history that takes into account not only varieties and change, but also multiple patterns and structures.

Based substantially on unofficial reading materials such as vernacular songs, opera scripts, comics, tabloids, popular magazines, and advertisements, as much as on serious or market-place literature, this study has presented the unofficial side of a Chinese city in the Republican era. It offers an alternative way to make sense of and interpret cultural and social phenomena. Due to the very nature of their discipline, which is to interpret past events and human feelings, historians can hardly present a distortion-free view of the past.[8] Hence, alternative approaches are important not only because they allow us to review and reinterpret our past with a variety of perspectives, but also because they help remind us of the importance of understanding, as much as accepting, differences, diversity, and ambiguity in a liberal society. It is only by constantly comparing and analysing different sets of historical materials, historians' interpretations, and contemporary social actors' perceptions of reality that a relatively trustworthy picture of the past could be reconstructed. Having said that, this present piece of historical research work apparently does not share the radical postmodernist view of history that renounces all facts as no more than representations or imagination. Although historical facts are by no means sacred and 'history is the historian's experience' (Carr 1978: ch. 1), it does not follow that all those human events and experiences of the past are nothing but imagined, unreal, and irretrievable. The past, as it is recorded in historical documents or archival materials, is not composed of pristine facts and that are all credible and free of epistemological problems. The existence of problematic historical 'facts', however, should not be casually reduced to a total renouncement of history as verbally constructed fables.[9] There is, I believe, a past 'out there' that is retrievable with a fair degree of accuracy if, and only if, the way of retrieving it is done properly, conscientiously, and critically. Visual images and photographic records of Canton and its residents during the Republican times, writings accounting for the personal feelings and attitudes of many Cantonese and temporary residents towards the city and countryside, the decades of local newspaper reports on all sorts of human activities in this city, popular views of opium smokers, reminiscences of brothel-goers, official campaigns against urban vices, known experiences of prostitutes, magazine and newspaper articles on popular Cantonese opera, and so on—materials on which this present work are based—are all surviving records of facets of contemporary life and human values. The people and their events and activities, their emotions and feelings, are as real as the physical existence of this city and the countless persons who had lived, worked and died there. Their happiness and sufferings, love and hatred, adoration of things new and old, and forms and contents of pleasure, as this book has tried to show, were something more substantive and real than linguistic construction that does not exist in an extra-linguistic experience or realm as it is fashionably claimed by postmodernist theorists. The human world is not an illusory representation as imagined by the people who live in it, just as our historical past is not its narrators' imaginative semiotic reconstruction. After all, I have not yet come across any convincing piece of historical research work by historians who advocate the postmodernist approach to writing history; even they have to rely heavily on conventional historical sources in their own research and writings.[10]

Needless to say, none of the interpretations offered in this piece of work is final. It is to be hoped that they may be able to stimulate further research into the various issues and topics here discussed. This book has shown that there is a past out there that deserves our efforts to retrieve and construe, as well as a past that helps unveil the complexity of human experiences and the problems of historical understanding. To understand the complexity of our world, borrowing the words of wisdom from the late Nobel-laureate physicist Richard Phillips Feynman, is actually making it easier to be understood.

REFERENCES

Brook, Timothy, and Wakabayashi, Bob Tadashi (2000) (eds.), *Opium Regimes: China, Britain and Japan, 1839–1952* (Berkeley: University of California Press).

Burke, Peter (1992), *History and Social Theory* (Cambridge: Polity Press).

Carr, Edward Hallet (1978), *What is History?* (Harmondsworth: Penguin).

Ch'en Shou-jên (1988–90), *Hsiang-kang Yüeh-chü yen-chiu,* 2 vols. (Hong Kong: Kuang-chüeh-ching ch'u-pan-shê).

Ch'êng Hao (1985) (ed.), *Kuang-chou kang shih* (chin-tai pu-fên), (Peking: Hai-yang ch'u-pan- shê).

Arnold, Julian, et al. (1926), *China: A Commercial and Industrial Handbook* (Washington DC: US Dept. of Commerce).

Fêng Ming-ch'üan (1986), 'Man t'an Kuang-chou ch'a-lou yeh', in Kuang-chou-shih chêng-hsieh et al. (eds.), *Kuang-chou kung shang ching-chi shih liao* (Canton: Kuang-tung jên-min ch'u-pan-shê).

Fêng Pi-ying (1989), 'Ming-ch'a mei tien, lo ya t'ao t'ao—T'ao T'ao Ch'ü', in T'an Shao-p'eng et al. (eds.), *Kuang-chou chu-ming lao-tzu-hao* (Canton: Kuang-chou wên-hui ch'u-pan-shê).

Henriot, Christian (1998), Review of *Dangerous Pleasures* by Gail Hershatter, *International Labor and Working-Class* 54, Autumn.

——(2001), *Prostitution and Sexuality in Shanghai: A Social History (1849–1940)* (Cambridge: Cambridge University Press).

Hershatter, Gail (1997), *Dangerous Pleasures: Prostitution and Modernity in Twentieth-Century China* (Berkeley: University of California Press).

Ho, Kit-yiu Virgil (1994), 'Cantonese Opera in a Rural Setting', in Göran Aijmer and Åsa Boholm (eds.), *Images and Enactments: Possible Worlds in Dramatic Performance* (Gothenburg: Institute for Advanced Studies of Social Anthropology).

——(1998), Review of *Dangerous Pleasures* by Gail Hershatter, *China Information* 13/1, Summer.

Hu Chên (2000–2), *Kuang-tung hsi-chü shih (Hung-ling pien chih erh),* 5 vols. (Hong Kong: Li Yüan shu-pao shê you-hsien kung-ssu).

Huang, C. C. Philip (1998), 'Theory and Study of Modern Chinese History: Four Traps and a Question', *Modern China* 24/2, April.

Lee, Bing-shuey Edward (1936), *Modern Canton* (Shanghai: Kelly & Walsh).

Li Chien (1993), *Hsiang-kang Yüeh-chü k'ou-shu shih* (Hong Kong: Joint Publishing (HK)).

Lin Chin-chih (1982), 'Chiu Chung-kuo ti Kuang-tung hua-ch'iao t'ou-tzu chi ch'i tso-yung', *Nan-yang wen-t'i* 2.

Liu Ching-chih and Hsien Yü-i (1995) (eds.), *Yüeh-chü yen-tao-hui lun-wen-chi* (Hong Kong: Hong Kong University Centre of Asian Studies, Joint Publishing (HK)).

Newman, R. K. (1995), 'Opium Smoking in Late Imperial China: A Reconsideration', *Modern Asian Studies* 29/4.

Sha Tung-hsun (1989), *Yüeh hai chin-tai-shih t'an* (Canton: Hua-nan li-kung ta-hsüeh ch'u-pan-shê).

Shang-hai-shih chin-tu kung-tso ling-tao hsiao-tsu pan-kung-shih and Shang-hai-shih tang-an-kuan (1996) (eds.), *Ch'ing-mo Min-ch'u ti chin-yen yün-tung ho Wan-kuo Chin-yen-hui* (Shanghai: Shang-hai ko-hsüeh chi-shu wên-hsien ch'u-pan-shê)

Tsin, Michael Tsang-woon (1999), *Nation, Governance and Modernity in China: Canton, 1900–1927* (Berkeley: University of California Press).

Windschuttle, Keith (1997), *The Killing of History: How Literary Critics and Social Theorists are Murdering our Past* (New York: The Free Press).

Yack, Bernard (1977), *The Fetishism of Modernities* (Notre Dame, Ind.: University of Notre Dame Press).

Endnotes

INTRODUCTION

1. Or, 376,721 *mou* according to Liao Shu-lun (1948: 7).
2. For a brief sociological discussion of this topic, see Tajfel (1972: xi. 567–75).
3. Some of the best examples are Vogel (1969); Ch'êng Hao (1985); Yeung (1998).
4. Zeldin (1979: viii) describes in the Preface 'method is to hold up a multitude of mirrors around the French, so that they may be seen simultaneously from different angles'.
5. This point resembles Levine's (1985: 8–9) critique of the inadequacy of modern social and cultural theory to deal constructively with ambiguity. 'In the quest for precision, social scientists have produced instruments that represent the facts of human life in one-dimensional terms.... For the truth of the matter is that people have mixed feelings and confused opinions, and are subject to contradictory expectations and outcomes, in every sphere of experience.' See also Burke (1986: 443–7).
6. For a valuable critique of the conceptual problems in Weberian thinking on Chinese cities and a lucid reappraisal of the socio-cultural and historical role of such cities, see Rowe (1984: 1–14).
7. The saying reads 'hao p'iao hao tu ching-kuai tzu; hao shih yang-yen ti-i jên.' From the author's interview with Mr Mok Hung, an old Canton resident, in Canton in 1993.

CHAPTER 1

1. This 'bureaucratic' image of the city could be also discerned in traditional cartography. Extant 19th-century maps of Canton indicate that the concept of the city then was solely the city wall, city gates, ramparts, temples, bridges, and important government buildings. In its vicinity, hills and rivers are drawn so as perhaps to reinforce the intended impression of the city as an integral part of nature. No characteristically civic structure was mapped or drawn. Ch'ou Ch'ih-shih (1969), i.
2. Likewise, Mote argues that in Chinese cultural tradition, the city has never represented a distinct style or a higher level of civilization than the countryside. Instead, it was in the 'upper classes' ideals' that 'the rural component of Chinese civilization . . . and not the cities, defined the Chinese way of life'. Chinese 'cultural activities involved both the cities and the countryside' and were 'indistinguishably "urban" and "rural" '. (Mote 1977: 117–18).
3. For examples, see Chang Hsin-tai (1898); Li T'iao-yüan (1937); and Ch'ou Ch'ih-shih (1969).
4. I am indebted to Professor Mark Elvin for this point.
5. Grimm's (1977) argument that the origins of academies reflect a tradition of distinct anti-urban bias is dubious. The mountain retreat ideal for the siting of academies is not necessarily 'anti-urban'. It might be chosen for such practical reasons as the sources of

funding, and the quest for a tranquil atmosphere for studying. Moreover, its shift towards the city did not necessarily mean the loss of such a peaceful environment. Most of the urban academies were so built and located that tranquillity was ensured (ibid. 487–93).

6. For instance, rural popular oral culture is said to be substantially different from its urban counterpart (Johnson 1985: 57).
7. John R. Watt (1977: 353–7) argues that in the Confucianist view, 'the natural order appeared chaotic and destructive'. The function of government was to humanize those men who lived close to nature, or within that 'natural order'. Hence, the separation of administration from rural life was justifiable since cities were regarded as 'humanizing nuclei'. Watt's argument about the 'natural order' is doubtful. The ancient conception was that *t'ien-ching ti-i* (the constant tracks of Heaven, and the generosity/public-spiritedness of Earth) was constant unless disrupted by inappropriate human behaviour.
8. All these urban fascinations, manifested nowhere more cleary and fully in capital cities, were vividly reconstructed by Gernet (1962: 48–55, 219–42). However, these 'lures of the town' predated Southern Sung's Hang-chou. Similar attractions, or 'evils' depending on one's standpoint, had been pointed out by the Legalists during the Warring States period (Chang Chak-yan 1976: 76–8). Archaeological findings and textual records show that trade was booming in many cities during the pre-Ch'in period. For example, see Ch'ü Ying-chieh (1991: 240–4, 282–3). There was seemingly a constant influx of peasants into big urban centres to escape rural poverty, banditry, and wars, though as Mote points out that did not exclude the possibility of urban migration to the countryside. See Chang Chak-yan (1976: 33, 328–31) and Gernet (1962: 91–108). Some of the poems compiled in Chang Ying-ch'ang's *Ch'ing shih* to also indicate that peasants did envy the ease and wealth of city life.
9. *Ch'ao-lien hsiang chih* (1946: ch. 1 p. 54). It should be noted that, although Ch'ao-lien was then a rather large community containing twenty-five family clans, and it is not known if the writer of, and the contributors to, the gazetteer spent much of their life as villagers, they nonetheless consciously perceived, and hence described, Ch'ao-lien as a *hsiang*, or village, throughout the gazetteer.
10. In the Republican period, wealthier landlords were said generally to choose to stay in cities (Ch'en Han-seng 1936: 20). Fei Hsiao-tung (1948: 28–9) was highly critical of the 'exploitative nature' of these landlords who were based and lived in towns and cities.
11. Yang (1959: 17, 20) notes that all the wealthy landlords in Canton's countryside lived in Canton, and preferred their sons to be educated there or in Hong Kong.
12. Although the Canton municipal government also recorded a significant emigration from the city, available data do not show the destinations of these emigrants. Thus, they might not necessarily return to their villages. Many probably emigrate abroad. Nevertheless, the net total of immigration was much higher than emigration. During 1921–9, the number of households and population in Canton had climbed from 170,000 to 190,000, and from 780,000 to about 850,000 respectively (these figures represented the size of population within the boundaries of the city's police jurisdiction; greater Canton was said to accommodate more than 1 million people since the 1880s). It is difficult to tell if all these newcomers were from the countryside, though it was probable. Kuang-chou-shih shih-chêng-fu t'ung-chi ku (1929: 48, 'shê-hui'); *YHKPK* (1996: 877, 1011). On a similar situation of the circulatory flux of

immigration and emigration in 1930s Shanghai, see Mark Elvin's 'Introduction', in Elvin and Skinner (1974: 11). Also Freedman, (1979: 61–5).

13. In the reminiscences of a Kwangtung informant, incessant carnage by the military and pillage by bandits are said to have devastated the countryside throughout the Republican period. Murphey (1974: 37–8). For Shanghai, a 1930s best-selling novel *Jen-hai ch'ao* (Tides in the Human Sea) shows that the idyll has already been ruined by human wickedness and folly; and Shanghai, however full of peril, is perceived as an escape from the absurdity of the countryside; see Elvin (1991). In the case of rural Kwangtung, however, the much-propagated idea of 'bankruptcy of Chinese villages', which was very fashionable and much elaborated especially by leftist Chinese intellectuals during the 1920s and 1930s, might not be verifiable. Data and reports from the Canton Customs in this period showed that the rural sector, despite years of political instability and warfare, did not completely lose its vitality and managed to make signs of progress in some particular commodities such as the silk and tea for export, and cassia barks. *YHKPK*, Decennial Reports nos. 2 to 5 (1892–1931). For a critical review of the problems of verification of this conventional view of the bankruptcy of Chinese rural economy, see Faure (1989).
14. Huang Tsun-shêng (1941: 56–66), attributes the demoralization of Chinese society to the impact of Western culture. The emergence and subsequent predominance of 'Western mercantile culture' (*yang shang wên-hua*) in Cantonese society brought about the disintegration of traditional southern Chinese culture.
15. This perception is seemingly analogous to the views held by a number of intellectuals in late 19th-century and early 20th-century Europe: Lees (1985, esp. chs. 5–7); Edward Turims, 'Unreal City—Theme and Variations', in Turims and Kelley (1985: 1–2). This kind of anti-city attitude also permeated the literary works of some prominent May-Fourth and post-May-Fourth writers. Notable examples, to cite just a few, are Mao Tun's *Midnight*, Li Ta-ch'ao's 'Ching-nien yü nung-tsun', and Kuo Mo-jo's 'Shang-hai ying-hsiang' (Zhang Yingjin 1996: 1–16).
16. According to a contemporary sociologist, although divorce and other marital problems were not unique to the city, the economic deprivation suffered by a large sector of its wage-earner class was believed to be responsible for the increase in the number of divorce cases in urban China (T'an Jen-chiu 1932: 72).
17. Due to the unavailability of a complete run of the magazine in which this story is serialized, it is not clear how the story ends (Ling Hsiao-shêng 1933: 5–12).
18. For a brief summary of Oswald Spengler's view, see Lees (1984: 82–5). Lewis Mumford (1938: 234–9, 250–3) also propagates pessimism about the role of the metropolis in modern civilization.
19. Such an extreme form of hatred against the modern city and its cultures is reflected in an essay entitled 'Tu-shih ti i wan' (One Night in the City; 1935: 39–41) published in the well-known journal of social criticism *Jên chien shih*. Its author, revisiting a city where he had lived for three years, was shocked by how fast and how far life and things were changing in this 'prosperous' city, which was called 'Little Shanghai' (in all likelihood a big city near Shanghai). To catch up with the pace of 'modernization', this boom town now had broad, asphalt-paved avenues, tall and modern buildings, tea houses, cinemas, and even an amusement centre copied from the infamous counterpart, The New World, in Shanghai. But arriving with these artefacts of modernity were also hordes of unwelcome residents, namely prostitutes, tricksters, bullies, sing-song girls, coolies, and so on. This once quiet little town was transformed into a hub

of crime; local newspapers were filled with reports of rape, burglary, kidnapping, suicide, outright poverty, unemployment, homelessness, domestic slavery, and so on. 'On the streets of the city', this writer moaned, 'flourish all the bad institutions and customs other than just prostitution. [There are also] fraudulence, deceit, murders, treacherous conspiracies, exploitation, bullying; all kinds of evil living are first bred in the city and then grow into huge [monsters of] sins and crime.' He ended his admonishment of the modern city by saying that he took great pleasure in noticing that battles and other acts of aggression by foreign imperialists and local warlords were wreaking massive destruction on China, specifically on the cities. He particularly applauded the huge destruction caused by the enemies' air raids on the big cities because all those social evils that were bred and flourished in the city could be exterminated and buried under the rubble. It must be added that anti-urban writing with a similar extreme view was unknown, at least during the course of this research, in the case of Canton.

20. Writings concerned with the 'old native village' (*ku hsiang*) are plentiful in the two student magazines *KTHS*, 2 and 4, and *I-shê ch'i k'an* 2 and 3 (1933).
21. Some Leftist writers in Republican Shanghai also exposed the ugly side of urban life in their works. However, although both the city and countryside were portrayed as hellish places for the poor, it was in the village that social deprivation and destitution were more exigent. Exploitation of all kinds, bankruptcy of the rural economy, and natural calamities turned the countryside into a living hell compared with the city. For a Marxist review of these literary works, see Tien Chung-chi and Sun Chang-hsi (1984: 410–15).
22. For examples see *HTJP* (1927: 2.2), 6 May; (1927: 1.3), 24 May; (1927: 1.3), 10 June; (1927: 1.3), 5 July; (1928: 3.3), 23 May; (1928: 3.3), 5 June.
23. Such an intensity of public obsession with gambling was ridiculed by a contemporary Cantonese historian as a new feature of contemporary Kwangtung culture (Huang Tsun-shêng 1941: 60–1).
24. Such a contemptuous attitude towards the countrypeople was nothing new to Canton. Late-Ch'ing issues of the newspaper *HTJP* had often published articles that ridiculed the ignorance of such 'country bumpkins', in particular their serious lack of knowledge of national and provincial political affairs. Two randomly chosen examples can be read in issues of 15 November 1911 and 25 June 1912. In another context, the presence of an old country gentleman visiting Canton, who was still wearing a pigtail, had reportedly caused great amusement to the onlookers wherever he went. When he was eventually caught by a policeman who demanded to have his braid cut off, he tried to run away, and shouted aloud for help, which afforded the spectators another round of laughter. *HTJP* (1913), 22 April.
25. See Cho Yu (1928: 20). Also 'Ch'ih chih lei' (The Trouble of the Reds), a serialized short story published in *HTJP* (1927: 3.4), 17 August. For a discussion on the traditional ideal of 'gentlemen', see Huang Tsun-shêng (1941: ch. 4); also Murphey (1984: 192).
26. The breakdown of this single-lineage community is not an unusual rural phenomenon in Fukien and Kwangtung since the Republican period. See Freedman (1971: 5–8).
27. This picture seems to be close to survey findings of C. K. Yang on the village of Nanching in the suburb of Canton in the late 1940s. On Nanching, Yang (1959: 61–2, and ch. 5) writes that 'a considerable section [of the local population] lived on minimum subsistence with a precarious margin of safety, and the largest group could not make enough from the farm alone to provide even bare subsistence for the family'.

28. A similar physical picture of 'outward impoverishment' is described by Yang (ibid. 6–7, 78–9) in his study of Nanching Village, which is five miles away from Canton.
29. However, it is not known how 'literacy' was defined in these reports. In Ch'ing and early Republican China, evidence shows that it was not unusual for commoners to read a number of 'basic characters', though their degree of literacy was hardly comparable with that of educated people (Rawski 1979: 1–20).
30. According to the official census of 1931, the illiteracy rate in Canton's suburban area was only slightly higher than the city's. Of the approximately 80,000 people living in suburban Canton, about 55% were said to be illiterate. In the city, about 38% of the population were categorized as 'illiterate', though the census report did not mention how 'illiteracy' was defined. *Kuang-chou-shih êrh-shih-i-nien jên-ko tiao-ch'a pao-kao* (1933).
31. In the entire island of Ho-nan, which had a population of about 50,000 in the early 1930s, there was no hospital or dispensary. All medical services there were run by teams of voluntary doctors and nurses associated with the medical school of Lingnan University (Ma Ya-ko 1934: 1–3). In stark contrast, the municipal government continued to boast about its plans to modernize medical services in the city. For example, see *HCLCCN* (1934: 200–13).
32. These Cantonese scholars, to some extent, resemble in their mentality those 19th-century 'thinkers about human culture and institutions' who regarded their 'advanced' cultural background as granting them the divine right condescendingly to study other cultures, which were all 'primitive' (Beattie 1969: 6–9).
33. They also naively believed that the level of income of all families in the village was more or less equal, and thus that a sampling of 100 households was adequate (Wu and Huang 1935: 109).
34. Most of the families were said to have close relatives working abroad or in Canton, though remittances were never counted as a possible source of income for this village (ibid. 105, 109–13).
35. For a lucid discussion of the 'pessimist school' of argument about the agrarian problem in Republican China and its critique, see Faure (1989: 1–10).
36. An elderly resident in Shun-tê reminisces that 'marriage to an immediately resident spouse would have been not altogether respectable in his eyes', and only women with no status would do that. Sometimes, the great economic and sentimental value of a spinster daughter could be so essential to her natal family that her act of spinsterhood would be welcomed and respected (Stockard 1989: 78–9, 180–3); also Topley (1975: 80, 82).
37. Similar 'superstitious beliefs and practices' were reported as widespread throughout the city in this period. A half-hearted official campaign was launched, without success, to clear away some of these 'feudalistic remnants'. For examples, see *FSKKTK* (1930: 44–84).
38. Comparable experience was also found in many 'rural reconstructors' in Shantung province during the late 1920s and the early 1930s. In the words of one contemporary observer, these intellectuals remained intellectuals and peasants remained peasants because 'the average rural reconstruction worker today is seldom able to effect an integration with the masses'. Moreover, '[a]lthough they advocate going back to the villages, they still want their own wives to enjoy an urban life. Although they go on about the ruralization of education, they want their own children to enjoy privileged education. Or, what is worse, they themselves stay the entire year living in semi-urban style at the hsien town or township and seldom go down into the countryside' (Alitto 1979: 276–7).

39. This seems to echo Rhoads Murphey's (1974: 57–9) idea about the geographic 'confinement' of 'modernization' to the treaty ports in Republican China.
40. Fêng Rui was born and grew up in Canton. In his autobiography, he wrote that since his primary-school years, he had been dreaming of building China into a big country by reforming the villages and their cultures. To pursue his dream, he enrolled in the prestigious Nanking Jinling University where he earned his Bachelor degree in agricultural science. After that, he received a government scholarship to read for his doctoral degree in agricultural economics at Cornell University in the United States. He returned to China in 1925 and became an activist in the rural reconstruction movement in Ting Hsien. From 1931 until his premature death (he was executed on charges of corruption) in 1936, he was Dean of the School of Agriculture of Lingnan University in Canton, as well as Head of the Department of Agriculture and Forestry in the Provincial Government of Kwangtung. 'Fêng Rui tzu-ch'üan' in Ch'en Chao-yü (1937: 1–6); and Kuang-tung shêng Chung-shan tu-shu-kuan and Kuang-tung shêng Chu-hai shih chêng-hsieh (1992: 91).
41. For example, the increase in military activities in the East River region in the summer of 1927 caused a massive inflow of refugees into Canton (*HTJP* 1927: 1.3, 10 June).
42. According to the US Department of Commerce's handbook on China, living expenses in Canton were believed to be higher than most other big cities in China. See US Department of Commerce (1926: 430). In a report on Kwangtung prepared by the Nanking government, Canton was said to be China's most expensive city (*NYSP* 1928: 21, 18 September).
43. Those who slept in front of some important government buildings were dispersed by the police in order to preserve the orderly image of the city (*HTJP* 1927: 1.3, 19 August).
44. A similar contemptuous attitude of the Cantonese today towards rural visitors in the city is still evident. Poor peasants from neighbouring provinces are widely held to be directly responsible for the alarming increase in the city's crime rate. Every night, a number of jobless, homeless, and shabbily dressed countrypeople sleep openly in areas near the bus and train stations. Instead of arousing sympathy from the local Cantonese, the sight generates further hatred and contempt towards them. Locally, these poor rural people are commonly called by a number of highly derogatory names such as *mang liu* (blind wanderer) or *lao hsi* (northern cunt).
45. A lampoon on similar lines called 'Hsiang-hsia-jên k'an tien-ying' can be read in *KCMKJP* 1926: 4, 6 November.
46. Examples can be easily found in both *HTJP* and *KCMKJP*. For a short discussion on how the Canton government tried to bring modernity to the city through a reordering of its urban space during the 1920s and the 1930s, see Tsin (1999: 51–72; 2000: 19–29). In the 1920s, similar efforts to construct modernity, so to speak, in Ch'êng-tu, the provincial city of Szechwan province, were also noted. For more details, see Stapleton (2000: esp. 55–67, 217–42).
47. For a typical official view, see Kuang-chou shih-chêng-fu (1934: 1). For a critical view, see Tzu Yün (1936: 242–3).
48. For more of these monuments, see Lee Bing-shuey (1936: 133–4); Ng Yong-sang (1936: 46–54).
49. An idea of Frederick Law Olmsted, quoted from Hall (1984: 25–6).
50. In the mid-1920s, the radical left-wing authorities were apparently powerless to 'purify' this place. An article in an official daily groaned that the building was still

a place of sin (*KCMKJP* 1926: 4, 25 September). For a leftist writer's view, see Ou-yang Shan (1948: 24).

51. Although the Cantonese 'skyscraper' was admittedly far more modest than its American counterpart, the euphoria and the inflated sense of pride experienced by most citizens of both cities in these modern 'architectural monuments' was the same (Lees 1984: 89–91).
52. Four sets of lifts were installed for customers' service. A generator was installed which supplied electricity exclusively to the building. The circular stairway that ran from the ground to the third floor was praised as a 'rarity' in contemporary architecture (Têng Tuan-pên 1986: 304–5).
53. The Bund, with its line of modern buildings, was certainly the showpiece, and hence the source of pride, of Canton's façade of modernity. To quote a proud Cantonese writer, 'it is the most bustling part of the whole city. Huge skyscrapers have been erected, and hotels and modern office buildings put up. There is all the outward appearance of a modern metropolis' (Ng Yong-sang 1936: 8).
54. Contemporary novels, such as Chang Tzu-p'ing's 'Ch'ang-t'u', tell us that in this period the very well-to-do Cantonese families always occupied the whole block of a two- to three-storey high building. Middle-class families usually lived in a self-contained flat in a multistorey building. To the poor families who can afford only a room in the city, even a room or part of a room is better than living in the 'remote' suburb.
55. The phenomenon was so popular that it became a sub-plot in some contemporary novels. For example, in the short story 'San-shih nien' (Pa Pên, *KTHS* 4: 60), the parents of the protagonist spend all the money he sends them on building a three-storey Western-style residence in the village. In Chang Tzu-p'ing's 'Kung-tsai wei-yüan' (1928), the owner of the Western-style bungalow, built with overseas remittances, falls victim to the protagonist's racketeering.
56. Interestingly, this 'cult' of modern skyscrapers is still very much alive in present-day Canton, and indeed the whole of China. The number of modern skyscrapers is commonly used as an index of a city's—or a region's—prosperity, degree of modernization, and level of culture. For example, see 'Yang-ch'êng, chueh-ch'i kuang hsia wan chien' (*NFJP* 1991: 3, 28 February).
57. For visual examples, see the advertisements in *KCLPL* 9, frontispiece, and 12: 10.
58. On Liang Shou-ming, see Alitto (1979).
59. A contemporary sociological research project on a village in the Swatow area shows that one of the most popular 'wishes' of the villagers was to visit, or move to live in, the county city (Kulp 1925: 45–6).
60. Since the opening of carriageways in Hsi-kuan, land value there rocketed by 90% (Li Tsung-huang 1922: 17).
61. In the mid-1920s, the pull of the city had caused a loss of local rural leadership, which integrated itself into urban communities in the Hai-lu-fêng area (Galbiati 1984: 49–53).
62. By early 1991, it was believed that no fewer than 400,000 such rural economic migrants, derogatorily labelled a 'blind stream' (*mang liu*), loafed about Canton and other prosperous cities in the Canton Delta region. They arrived at the rate of some 30,000 per day at their peak after the Chinese New Year in 1991 (*NFJP* 1991, 23–7 February).
63. The absence of a clear and strong rural–urban continuum in Canton in the 1920s and 1930s shows that the assimilating capacity of urban value and culture was far greater

than the countryside culture in the city. This was also the urban experience of a number of world cities in the early 1970s. See Pahl (1968: 263–305).

64. On the persistence of the rural–urban inequality in pre-1979 China, see Parish and Whyte (1978: 52–4). On Mao's anti-urban ideological stance, see Lewis (1971: 3–5, 10–1).
65. This was still very much so when the first version of this chapter was completed in the winter of 1987.
66. Rural youth has never hidden its preference for working in the city (Chan, Unger, and Madsen 1984: 252–3; Mosher 1983: 163).
67. Some calculating young men from the rural hinterland choose to become apprentice-monks or priests in Taoist or Buddhist monasteries in the city, thus qualifying to have their household transferred to the city. Once this is done, they renounce their priesthood (I Li 1990: 101).
68. An abundance of writings and researches on this subject has been published in Europe and North America since the mid-19th century (Lees 1985: 189–219).
69. For instance, one of these 'self-aggrandizing' works on present-day Canton maps out, meticulously and lucidly, the 'modernized' and superior quality of life of Canton's citizens in virtually all respects. Têng Yên-ch'ao et al. (1988); Huang Nai-ch'ao and Ho Wên-kuang (1987). The city's professional psychiatrists also seem to support the belief in the superiority of city life. In a formal psychiatric report about the situation of mental diseases in sixteen counties in Kwangtung in the early 1990s, the number of cases reported from the villages doubled that of in the city. In a report that analyses the psychology of patients who were charged on superstition-related crimes prepared by specialists from the Canton Psychiatric Hospital, villages are held responsible for breeding and spreading this particular form of unlawful activity. The world of the village and its people is described as culturally backward, lacking in scientific knowledge, incapable of telling what's right or wrong, and so on, simply because illiteracy in these places is commonplace. See Chin Wên-huan et al. (1992) and Huang P'o-yüan et al. (1992: 216–24). In many ways, such works resemble some of the pro-city writings in 19th-century and pre-1914 Europe and America (Lees 1985: 190–209).

CHAPTER 2

1. For examples, Chesneaux (1968) and most Chinese-language literature on Sino-foreign relations, such as Ch'êng Hao (1985).
2. Hughes (1968: 286–7) had noticed in the late 1930s that Chinese had accepted the belief that 'there are friends as well as exploiters' in the Western world. Thus, Western material equipment and implements were accepted as a matter of course.
3. For a more detailed account of the development of various communal facilities on Shameen, see Smith (1939: 19–28).
4. On the red tape relating to the issue of Shameen entry permits to non-Europeans, see Tzu-hang-shih (1919: 3). Lee Bing-shuey (1936: 27–8) said that racial discrimination was a feature of Shameen in the mid-1930s.
5. Except in times of turbulence such as in 1922 (The Seamen Strike), and in 1925–7 (The Canton-Hong Kong strike; the emergence of a radical local KMT government; and the Canton Commune). FO 228/4005, Intelligence Report for Canton Consular District for half-year ending 30 September 1929, p. 342.

6. In Ou-yang Shan's 'Chieh lao-shu', for example, the assault on the protagonist by the Englishmen took place in a residence in Shameen. This short story is edited in Ou-yang Shan (1935).
7. For more detail on how the KMT employed similar tactics to deal with financial crises in Shanghai, see Coble (1980: esp. ch. 2); Bergère (1989: 272–92). For more detail on how the Cantonese merchant community reacted to this extortionate policy of the government during the autumn of 1928, see *NYSP* (1928: 11), 14 February; (1928: 4) 16 March.
8. The story of one of those immigrants from Canton is vividly retold by Elizabeth Johnson in her 'Hakka Women' (1984: 76–91).
9. Collected in Mao Tun's famous compilation of essays are ten pieces of highly critical writings by non-Cantonese writers staying in Hong Kong in the mid-1930s. They felt very strongly about the serious situation of the unequal distribution of wealth in the colony and the common sight of urban poverty. They were disturbed by the willingness of many local Chinese to work for the colonial administration, while many other 'high-class Chinese' cultivated favour with the British to obtain pecuniary and symbolic advantages. Mao Tun (1936: 16, 1–14).
10. The size of the demographic increase from the early 1920s to the end of the 1920s in Hong Kong can be seen by comparing the statistics on population compiled by the Hong Kong government in this period. See e.g. *Administrative Reports*, 1920–30.
11. They included Wang Ching-wei, Ch'en Kung-po, Ch'en Chi-t'ang, Ch'en Ming-shu, Ku Ying-fen, and many other. Ch'en Chi-t'ang apparently bought a lot of properties in Hong Kong when he was the military head of Kwangtung province during the early 1930s. After his downfall in 1936, he and his family sought refuge in Hong Kong where they lived a comfortable life. Prominent Kwangsi 'warlords', namely Li Tsung-jên, Pai Ch'ung-hsi, and Huang Shao-hsiung had also acquired properties in Hong Kong for similar purpose. Among the three, Li and Pai, with their control over the Bank of Kwangsi, had access to enough cash flow for buying up properties in the colony. It was Huang, however, who had bought more properties than Li and Pai. I owe this last point to Mr Wade Ng, a maternal grandson of Huang Shao-hsiung.
12. For instance, in May 1927, when the Finance Department proclaimed the prohibition of export of silver from Canton, and the renaming of the Central Bank notes as the banknotes of the Republic of China (*Chung-hua Min-kuo chih-pi*), it caused a feverish selling of Central Bank notes which consequently dropped by 20 per cent in value (*HTJP* 1927: 1.3, 20 May).
13. For example, this kind of situation had happened during the financial crises of August and September 1927, as well as in the spring of 1928. For detail on the former, see *HTJP*, from 22 August to end of September 1927. For details on the latter, see *NYSP*, from 21 January to May 1928.
14. As we have seen in Chang Tzu-p'ing's 'Ch'ang tu', a male protagonist, Hsiao Szu, is a full-time civil servant whose duty is to dispatch the cheques of his seniors for deposit in the foreign banks in Hong Kong. But that was not fictitious at all.
15. For instance, see *HTJP* (1927: 3.2), 15 May.
16. 'Kuang-chou hsi-yüan', in *KHP* (1935: 2.4), 9 January.
17. The two highly militant rival unions were the Tung-tê and Shang-chiang-ao ch'i lo huo kung-hui. Their clashes, which were usually violent, could be traced at least to 1926 (*HTJP* 1928: 3.2, 26 May).
18. *KHP* (1934), 10 December; *KHP* (1935), 30 January.

19. More details can be found in Ch. 6, on Cantonese Opera. For a short study of the difficulty experienced by an ordinary troupe becoming a Canton-Hong Kong troupe, which always entailed extra capital and additional strong cast members, see *HTJP* (1928: 4.4), 6–7 June. For a brief account of some existing Canton-Hong Kong troupes in 1928, see *HTJP* (1928: 4.4), 13 June.
20. For instance, 'Hsüeh Mei ping tsung k'ou ju' in *KPP* (1928: 8), 7 April; 'T'ang ming-hsing ying Pan chü Pan chih', *KPP* (1928: 8), 20 June. For cases on sing-song girls, *KHP* and *YHP*, issues of 1930s, *passim*.
21. Also see Teng Chung-hsia (1980*b*: 161–4); Chan (1975: 341).
22. A comparable and interesting example was the favourable popular response of the Chinese residents in Weihaiwei towards the arguably 'benevolent rule' of the British, 1898–1930. For a detailed historical survey see Atwell (1985: chs. 2, 3, and 5).
23. Such a shift in 'taste', as pointed out by Mark Elvin, was also reflected in a contemporary Shanghai social novel, *Shanghai: The Living Hell*. See his 'Tales of Shen and Xin', in Feher (1989: esp. 267–315).
24. For instance, *YHP* (1936: 10), 12 August Women's and men's obsession with large breasts is even more intense in present-day Canton, as judged by the large number of advertisements in local official as well as unofficial newspapers every day. Examples are abundant in *Kuang-chou jih pao*, e.g. 6 August 1998.
25. The fashion for short or permed hair had swept through Canton by the mid-1930s. It was so popularly received that at least 70 per cent of women in the cities had reportedly had their hair cut or permed. The business of Western-style hair salons prospered greatly as a result. Hsiao-tzu (1934: 1); Hughes (1968: 270).
26. Examples of these pin-ups can be seen on *Wu-chiao man-hua*, a Cantonese bi-weekly comic published in the 1930s, especially 6/2: 2–5; 6/3: 1; 6/5: 4; 6/9: 6; 6/11: 2; 6/12: 3; 7/3: 4; 7/4: 6; 7/7: 3, 6; 9/4: 6; 9/6: 3–5.
27. 'Cosmetic Surgery in China: A Look West, Straight in the Eyes', *International Herald Tribune* 20 June 1991, p. 1. On the concept of body in the high tide of Communist Chinese emotional extremism, see Elvin (1989: 315–45).
28. *Ch'ün shêng pao hsing-ch'i tsêng-k'an* 1/1 (1935: 14).
29. *Pan-chiao man-hua* (1932) 6/2: 3–4; 6/11: 5. This is perhaps analogous to the wide popularity of the classic 'Rambo' posters in Canton in the 1980s. This kind of Hollywood-style hero, the embodiment of idealized masculine symbols openly envied by thousands of local male youngsters, appear to have replaced the self-sacrificing CCP-made Lei Fêng in the minds of some Cantonese.
30. For visual comparison, a collection of traditional Chinese book-illustrations can be seen in Wood (1985).
31. Contemporary essay and cartoons about dancing vindicated that (Hsü Hsüeh-hang *c*. 1920s: ii. 92–3); and for examples of cartoons, see *Pan-chiao man-hua* quoted above.
32. The number of cinemas in Canton increased from only four in 1922 to twenty in 1934. They had a total capacity of 20,000 seats. Kuang-chou-shih shih chêng-t'ing. 'Ts'ai-chêng shih-su pao-kao' (1924: 48–9); *Kuang-chou nien-chien* (1935: ch. 8).
33. 'Tien-ying ti t'ou-tzu wên-t'i', *HTJP* (1928: 3.4), 7 August.
34. 'Chung-kuo ying-pien kung-szu chih ch'üeh-tien', *KCMKJP* (1926: 4), 19 July.
35. 'Chung-kuo tien-ying yen-yüan chih chi-i wên-t'i', *HTJP* (1928: 4.4), 3 August.
36. *Kuang-tung shêng-chêng-fu kung pao* 329 (1936: 48–50), April.
37. His poignant view was shared by a group of young Cantonese dramatists who condemned contemporary theatre as ribald amusement for '[lewd] students and whores'.

They advocated turning to industrially advanced Western countries to learn modern theatrical forms and techniques (Ch'en Hung 1937: i. 8–9).

38. A similar argument was put forward by another Cantonese dramatist who denounced Cantonese opera outright as 'feudalistic', unaesthetic, and to be reformed immediately along the lines of Western melodrama (Lo Hai-sha 1937).
39. 'Yin-yüeh kan-tung li chih fên-hsi' (1926: 2). Similar pragmatic views on the 'usefulness' of Western music were also shared by some of the first-generation Chinese music-reformers. For instance, Hsiao Yu-mei and Liu T'ien-hua argued that, since Chinese music had been stagnant for nearly one thousand years, European music should be introduced for the 'correction and transformation of Chinese music and musical instrument[s]'. Alexander Tcherepnin, a Russian composer who had performed in North China during the mid-1930s, was worried by the trend towards the 'blind imitation' of European music by Chinese musicians even when playing Chinese music. See Liu Ching-chih (1988: 27–8, 53–4, 79–82).
40. For instance, in the songbook category, only three out of the thirteen were compilations of Chinese songs while the rest were either in English, Japanese, or translations into Chinese from Western languages. As far as the reference texts were concerned, all dealt directly with Western rather than Chinese music. Kuang-tung ts'ai-chêng-t'ing (1930: 276–7).
41. For example, the highly respectable brothers Kao Chien-fu and Kao Ch'i-fêng were both successful businessmen. Both of them had travelled widely abroad and recieved part of their art education in Japan. Kao Chien-fu had also learnt the technique of Western charcoal drawing from a French artist (Li Chien-êrh 1941: 8–13). For a comprehensive analysis of the artistic achievements of the Lingnan School of painting, see Croizier (1988).
42. In 1934, when a humour columnist tried to record what had been increasing most obviously in Canton in recent years, 'modern' buildings were listed among those things that could hardly escape observation. 'I chien jih to' (1934: 55).
43. Author's interview with a senior cadre, who prefers to remain anonymous, from the Kwangtung Navigation Affairs Bureau in 1989, Canton.
44. Such popular acceptance, and cultural idealization, of Western-style interior decoration did not wane even after eight years of war against the Japanese and the rapid growth of Chinese nationalism in these years. In 1946, an advertisement of a furniture and building company in Canton revealed that the 'standard bedroom' in 1934 was still highly influential among those who sought for modernity, taste, and excellence in this respect. The advertisement for the New China Company is in Ho Kuo-hua et al. (1946).
45. This was true at least for the first batch of senior Municipal officials (Huang Yen-pei 1922).
46. In 1934, however, the number of automobiles in Canton had increased to nearly 2,000, and wide roads had become more justifiable. Lee Bing-shuey (1936: App. 8).
47. For a description of the various amenities provided in Central Park, the most renowned of all these parks, see Ng Yong-sang (1936: 51).
48. For instance, in the report on a government education conference, both the group and the individual photographs of the senior officials and the organizers show that nearly all the 273 participants wore Western suits (*Kai-chin ch'üan-shêng chung-têng hsüeh-hsiao chiao-yü fang-an* 1934). In the official book commemorating the inauguration of the new Municipal Offices building in 1934, a group photograph of the departmental staff shows all in *Chung-shan-chuang*, probably in response to the official policy of austerity for civil servants. However, the Mayor and the Governor in

their portraits are dressed in Western suits. It seems to suggest that only the 'elite' were permitted to express themselves in Western outfits, symbolizing their official power and social status (*HCLCCN*: plates).

49. Medicine advertisements with drawings of attractive or inviting girls with a Westernized appearance are plentiful in every issue of *Pan-chiao man-hua*. Those related to children are in 6/1: 4, 6; 6/2: 4.
50. For examples see Yung Shêng (KCMKJP 1924: 7, 15 April); Jên Po (KCMKJP 1925: 9, 8 October).
51. Contemporary novelists such as Chang Tzu-p'ing were quick to reflect this sub-culture. Most of the educated young characters in his novels are fond of sprinkling their conversations with German, French, and English phrases. Many examples can be found in his three-volume *Tzu-p'ing hsiao-shuo hsüan* (1928–30).
52. Such a Eurocentric view of religion was not new. In an article published in a Cantonese magazine in 1925, the author rebutted the arbitrary association of imperialism with Christianity. In his view, China was indebted to Christianity for converting a large number of its superstitious idol-worshippers to the faith (Yüan 1924). By the mid-1930s, Christianity showed 'signs of revival', despite being so 'recently denounced as . . . a disreputable part of western imperialism' (Hughes 1968: 265).
53. A Chinese social scientist argues that because it preaches against idol-worship and other superstitious social customs, the popularity of Christianity helps 'scale down the repercussions of feudal superstitious [beliefs]'. It also helps moralize and harmonize family relations. Cheng K'ai-t'ang (1987: 263–4).
54. Another scholar from Lingnan University published a series of articles in an official daily praising the latest progress achieved by Japan in successfully 'Europeanizing and Prussianizing' (i.e. modernizing) without sacrificing the country's own indigenous culture. In this respect, he argued, China should learn quickly from Japan (Hsieh Fu-ya 1929).
55. The difficulty was indicated by the fact that the ban against the use of the old Chinese Lunar calendar had been reiterated a number of times during this period. For example, see *HTJP* (1927: 3.2), 31 August. In 1929, the Canton KMT office stated that a number of 'bad social customs' (*pu-liang feng-su*) were still prevalent in Cantonese society. A special Social Custom Reform Committee (*feng-su kai-ke wei-yüan-hui*) was set up to monitor a campaign targeted solely at uprooting those bad customs. For details, see *FSKKTK* (1930).
56. *Kuang-tung hsiu-chih-kuan tsu-chih ta-kang*, not paginated.
57. For an interesting discussion on how the KMT had tried to mobilize the masses through its propaganda institutions in Canton and Kwangtung, see Fitzgerald (1996: ch. 7).
58. CO 129/498/3, C.2082, secret memorandum from Clementi to Amery dated 24 December 1925; CO 129/492, C.12714, secret telegraph from Clementi to Amery. For a concise description of the incident and its immediate effect on the city politics, see Tsin (1999: ch. 5).
59. The existence of the problem of the KMT personnel even before the purge of 1927 helps clarify a slightly problematic claim by the late Lloyd Eastman (1974: 8) that the purge filtered out progressive activists and political activism from the Party; the problem with the local KMT in this respect actually predated the purge.
60. A typical example is Huang Ching-hua (1972: ch. 2).
61. For example, open defiance of the imperial edict prohibiting the movement of foreigners outside the Factories area was common. As a sign of appeasement, local

magistrate runners, at the foreigners' request, were quick to disperse local pedlars trading in the Factories area (Hunter 1976: 2–8).

62. According to an American Consulate dispatch cited in Rhoads (1975: 89).
63. FO 228/3695/16453/27/3, Clementi's memorandum to Brenan, British Consulate-General in Canton, dated 1 October 1927.
64. Although this song might be a propaganda work commissioned by the Hong Kong government, many of its allegations were not necessarily unfounded. Indeed, they corroborate Têng Chung-hsia's account of the appalling conditions that most strikers faced (e.g. 1980*a*: 138). The misconduct of the pickets was well documented by both the British Consul in Canton and the Hong Kong Governor, which are compiled in FO 228 and CO 129 files. On the different means of intimidation employed, see Gillingham (1983: 33–42), and Ts'ai Yung-fan (2001: 148–9).
65. FO 228/3581/39, Clementi's memorandum to Amery dated 15 September 1927, enclosures 1 & 2; FO 228/3639/186, Canton Political Report, September 1927.
66. For a full coverage, see FO 228/3729, Canton Consulate-General memorandum to HM's Minister in Peking dated 14 March 1928, pp. 207–12; also *NCH*, March issues, *passim*.
67. In his long story 'Ch'ang t'u' (The Long Way), Chang Tzu-p'ing (1930: esp. 309–10), a contemporary popular novelist, expresses his anger at this unpatriotic act by the Canton administration, which took place so soon after the Shakee Incident.
68. 'Kuang-chou shih hsi-shih chung chung', in *KPP* (1928: 1), 15 March.
69. FO 228/3689/109, Canton Consulate-General Report, July 1927.
70. FO 228/3938/460, Canton Consulate-General Report on the anniversary of the Shakee Incident, 24 June 1929.
71. FO 228/3639/186, Canton Political Report, September 1927.
72. CO 228/3639, British Consulate-General Report, Canton, June 1927; Cavendish (1970: 54–5).
73. *NYSP* and *HTJP*, from May 1928 to early 1929, *passim*.
74. FO 228/2726/129–30, 151–2, memoranda from British Consulate-General in Canton to HM's Minister in Peking, dated 11 September and 4 December 1928.
75. FO 228/3938/278, Hong Kong Governor to Colonial Office memorandum, dated 27 December 1928.
76. Reports of defiance against the boycott by ordinary citizens were abundant and can be read in most issues of *KCHJP* in February 1933.
77. One example is Chung-kuo jên-min chêng-chih-hsieh-shang-hui-i Kuang-tung-shêng (1983: 287–98).
78. On the failure to utilize the frustrated student feelings and to mobilize them against the encroaching Japanese in the early 1930s, Israel (1966) blames the KMT for its over-cautious policy on mass movements.
79. In this exercise, thirty thousand questionnaires were sent out to 'the public'.
80. 'Tsou-ma têng', *HYOC* (*c.*1926: pt. 3, p. 4).

CHAPTER 3

1. *Shu pao*, Chia-shen nien, 15th day of the Ninth Moon.
2. Kuang-chou-shih shih-chêng-t'ing shê-hui-tiao-cha-ku ed., *Ti sze lei: shê-hui pu-liang shih-yeh* (1927: 8).

3. 'Shina chikaiji no ahen mondai', (1931: 50).
4. Kuang-chou-shih chin-yen wei-yüan-hui (1937*a*: 16) 'Pên yüan ch'ou-pei ching-kuo' (1937: 2).
5. *Wên hui pao*, 15 April 1949, cited in Ma Mo-ching et al. (1998: 1504).
6. Kuang-chou-shih shih-chêng-fu t'ung-chi ku (1929: 90).
7. There is seemingly one puzzle in this set of statistics: the number of arrests made and the number of registered addicts added together is still a surprisingly low figure relative to the number of opium/drugs divans suppressed. Perhaps the number of registered addicts represented only a small fraction of the drug-using population. If so, this seems to tally with my argument that many so-called addicts of opium could stop smoking without much trouble, and therefore they escaped the watchful eyes of their local street association and were not reported to the authorities. Another conjecture is that either one of these two sets of figure was misprinted. But it is hard to understand why the Communist government would present such apparently wrong statistics on a social issue that might, otherwise, be ideal for the purpose of anti-KMT publicity. If this latter figure for opium divans is correct, and the number of the addict population wrong, it would then suggest a minimum of 110,000 opium users in this city. This is calculated on the basis that an opium divan handled about thirty clients a day. The total figure is probably twice as large again, since not every client would come every day. But since no other data was available for further analysis during the course of writing this present study, the point remains conjecture.
8. For examples, see Tzu-hang-shih (1919); Liu Tsai-su, (1926).
9. Kuang-tung ch'ing-li-ts'ai-chêng-chü (1910: i. 1–15, Book 6); and Kuang-tung shêng-chêng-fu ts'ai-chêng-t'ing et al. (1934: i. 249–67).
10. Even as recent as the late Ch'ing period, well-educated young gentlemen often congregated at drinks parties, where they amused themselves by smoking opium (Ch'üan Shêng 1924: 7). The addiction rate among Civil Examination candidates was high (Spence 1975: 145). It is not known if opium was commonly used by the literati to stimulate literary thoughts. One Kwangtung poet and scriptwriter did adopt *fu yung* (opium) as the name of his private study, and the title of his literary work (Wang Tsung-hsien 1974: 123–5).
11. Examples are Chu Hsiu-hsia's *Pa-yüeh chien* (1930), and Chang Tzu-p'ing's 'Kung-cha wei-yüan' (1928: i). In the latter, its protagonist is a healthy and industrious young intellectual before he becomes destroyed by his opium addiction and descends to being a wicked tax broker.
12. A 1931 report by the China Anti-Opium Association (Chung-hua min-kuo ch'u-tu hui) shows that in the estimated number of opium addicts in China in terms of professions and occupations, labourers were the highest; and they were followed by businessmen and merchants, politicians, students, and military men. Cited in P'eng Kuo-liang (1981: 194–6).
13. But Yü also remarked that this surprisingly low figure was probably a result of the respondents' reluctance to admit their opium habit.
14. In 1924, the bid for the one-year franchise was 6 million yüan. 'Shina chikaiji no ahen mondai' (1931: 49). An anti-opiumist wrote that the bid for the franchise in 1926 increased to 10 million yüan (Yü En-tê 1934: 181). In 1928, the opium monopoly company in Canton paid 700,000 dollars a month to the Provincial Government, plus 160,000 dollars a month to the military authorities in Kwangtung (FO 415/3466/184/87, enclosure, dated 16 May 1930).

15. During 1927, a total of some 600,000 *taels* of raw opium was imported into Canton each month. In 1930 it was increased to about 750,000 *taels*. 'Information on opium supplied in confidence by the Asiatic Petroleum Company', in FO 228/3678/172, dated 15 October 1927; FO 228/4290/267, Consulate-General Phillips to Sir M. Lampson, dated 16 May 1930.
16. Hong Kong was a favourite destination for smuggled opium, where the drug could be sold at a higher price. In 1928, 'the price of ordinary opium is about $2 an ounce in Wuchow. The same opium costs $10 in Hong Kong' (FO 228/3888/25 Consulate-General Canton to Foreign Office dated 25 June 1928).
17. This was a description of the opium problem in the Swatow area, but it may also apply to the situation in Canton (FO 228/4291/15 Report on Opium Cultivation and Traffic in the Swatow District, dated 22 May 1930).
18. Japan was alleged to have 'enforced' the consumption of addictive narcotic drugs in occupied Manchuria. As a result, one-third of the Chinese population there was believed to have been forced into addiction—a prelude to the Japanese conquest of China by narcotic drugs (Liu Shih-hsin 1937: 8–10). In 1951, the blame was shifted from Japanese to American 'imperialists' (*NFJP*, 1952, leader, 3 June). In this period, the 'drug problem' in China was conceived as being not only about opium, but also about other narcotic drugs. But it should be noted that in nearly all the contemporary Chinese writings on the opium problem, their writers were well aware of the distinction between opium and other narcotic drugs; the latter were commonly conceived to be more harmful than opium not only for being cheaper, but also more powerful and addictive (Lo Yün-yen 1938: 1–11).
19. The International Anti-Opium Association (1922: 135–7) reported that in Tientsin, as in many other places in the Chihli Province, Japanese and Chinese businessmen operated 'medicine shops', selling morphia to the low-class Chinese at a few coppers for a small packet. The spread of narcotic drugs in central Manchuria and Kwantung was already quite serious by the late 1920s. In this area, 'opium has become so expensive to smoke that the habit of doping narcotic drugs, which are much less expensive, has greatly increased among poorer people' (FO 415/7156/184/87, Consul-General Eastes to Mr A. Henderson, enclosure 2, dated 5 December 1930). In Japanese-occupied Peking, 'the occupants of [heroin] drug houses are for the most part made up of lower-class Chinese . . . There is no evidence to show that the drug habit is affecting the better-class Chinese who . . . continue to remain faithful to the opium pipe' (FO 415/10393/27/87, Sir Clark Kerr to Viscount Halifax, enclosure, dated 31 August 1938).
20. FO 415/6622/375/87, enclosure, Consul Paton to Sir J. Tilley dated 20 September 1929; FO 415/10393/27/87, enclosure, Memorandum Respecting the Drug Situation in the Occupied Areas of China dated 1 July and 5 August 1938.
21. Kuang-chou shih shê-hui chü (1941), the section on statistics of commercial activities.
22. The FO 415 files contain a great number of British consular reports that implicate Japanese involvement in the manufacture and smuggling of heroin and morphine into China. But these documents make no mention of any international conspiracy as leading Chinese opinions suggested. For examples, see FO 415/8/8/7, enclosures 1 to 3, 1930. On the British Government's commitment in the International Conferences on the Limitation of the Manufacture of Dangerous Drugs which was convened by the League of Nations, see FO 415/4138/21/87, Sir M. Delevingue to Mr A. Anderson dated 27 July 1931; FO 415/418/225/87, Home Office to Foreign Office dated

23 Dec. 1932. On the quiet situation of narcotic drugs trafficking in the British and French concessions in Canton, see FO 415/1380/7/87, enclosure 5, Consul-General Phillips to Mr Ingram dated 3 November 1932. The signatory countries of the Geneva Opium Convention also succeeded in reducing the volume of the world's illicit narcotic drugs trade (Lo Yün-yen 1938: 118–19).

23. FO 415/10393/27/87, enclosure, Memorandum respecting the Drug Situation in the Occupied Areas of China dated 1 July and 5 August 1938.
24. In 1933, the Kwangtung government outlawed twelve brands of narcotic drugs sold under the description of 'anti-opium medicine'. Of them, only one was manufactured by an American pharmacy; the rest were Chinese-made (*KCHJP* 1933: 5, 18 February). In 1930, for example, the manufacture of morphia by Chinese could be found in Szechwan and Amoy (FO 415/6293/184/87, enclosure 1, dated 14 August 1930; 415/162/2287, enclosure 2, dated 15 December 1930.
25. Although the Ch'ing and the early Republican governments had officially banned morphine, the ban was apparently never seriously enforced (Yü En-tê 1934: 138, 273). For an official version of the situation of morphine use in Canton, see I Chien-ch'uan 'Kuang-chou-shih ch'ing-tu ta hui ch'ou-pei (1937: 25–9). On the failure of the Nanking government in enforcing the prohibition, see FO 415/7610/116/87 Sir A. Cadogan to Sir Samuel Hoare, dated 29 October 1935.
26. FO 228/4292/184–5 Report on the Drug Traffic in the Canton Consular District dated 15 November 1930. A similar situation was also reported by the British Consulate in Swatow in the same period (FO 228/4292/200).
27. Mr Mok Hung, a former resident of Canton during 1925–50, reminisces that narcotic drugs other than opium were not at all popular in Canton. In Japanese-occupied Amoy, notwithstanding the hardship of life, 'the drug evil ... has been confined almost entirely to opium smoking, and there has been little evidence of the heroin and morphia injections which have become so serious a menace in North China' (FO 415/10393/27/87 Sir A. Clark Kerr to Viscount Halifax, enclosure, dated 31 August 1938).
28. For a full version of the will, see *FSKKTK* (1930: 26). Similar anti-opium writings can be easily found in local newspapers in this period. For example, in an official Anti-Opium Day held in June 1930, senior officials and social notables delivered speech after speech on this specific theme in rhetorical language closely resembling that of those compiled in *FSKKTK*. See *YHP* 1930: 5, 4 June).
29. A speech by Chang Chih-kiang cited in Yü En-tê (1934: 8).
30. H. B. Morse believed that as early as the late 1720s, the Chinese had already produced more local opium than that imported into China by foreign traders. Lin Man-hung, however, disputes this view (for details see Lin Man-hung *c.*1980s: 187–8).
31. Quoted from Yü En-tê (1934: 3).
32. Yang Shih-ying's *Chih chih fang*, and Wang Shih's *I chien fang*, as cited in I Wu (1969: 195).
33. Liu Ho's 'Chien-i liang-fang' and other related sources from the Yüan Dynasty, as cited in I Wu (1969: 195–6).
34. Dr McCowan, 'Opium Smoking in China Five Hundred Years Ago', in Sultzberger (1884: 170–1).
35. In a meticulously researched historical monograph, historian Lin Man-hung (*c.*1980s: 174–88, and App. 1) argues that although the Chinese had already been well aware of the medicinal benefits of opium by the late-Ming period, smoking became popular in China only after the early 1700s.

36. This method of consuming opium, however, is more commonly believed to have been first introduced by the natives of South East Asia (Spence 1975: 147–8).
37. In 1683, three *fen* (one fen was equivalent to about a hundredth of a *tael*) of silver was levied on one catty (a little over 1¼ lb.) of opium imported into China. In 1755, the same amount of opium was charged an import tax of five *chien* (one *chien* was equivalent to about one-tenth of a *tael*) of silver (I Wu 1969: 198).
38. For examples, see Yü En-tê (1934: chs. 1 and 2); Lo Yün-yen (1938: ch. 4); Lo Tzu-ch'in (1933: 3–4).
39. The complexity of the subject of the motives of opium consumption is more honestly unfolded by recent studies of present-day opiate addicts (Lindesmith 1968: 16).
40. This argument of Leonard Adam III is quoted from Spence, (1975: 173 n. 222). Similar views was also held by some contemporary Chinese anti-opium writers, such as Lo Yün-yen (1938: 18).
41. The short stories by Ou-yang Shan are examples of this intellectual frustration; see his *Ch'i-nien chi* (1935), *Shêng ti fan-jao* (1937), and *Ch'ing-nien nan-nü* (1937). Most poems compiled in Kuang-chou wên-hsüeh-hui's *Ying shih* (1928), in Li San-pi's *Huan-huo chi* (1930), and in the supplement to *KCMKJP* during the years 1926–30, are gloomy outpourings about the conditions of life and the country.
42. Thomas Szasz (1975: esp. chs. 1–4, 9–12) argues that opiates had been used for centuries as a ceremonial drug on ritualistic occasions. The stigmatization of drug use as 'abuse', and its users as 'mentally sick' or 'addicts' since the twentieth century is the result of the rise of a 'pharmacracy'—modern worship of a combination of pharmacology and psychiatry—a 'therapeutic state' which is voraciously asserting its authority and social controls over individual autonomy and self-control.
43. This view was shared by many other reports such as e.g. Light et al. (1929–30: 13–16).
44. Szasz (1975: 121) states that opiates were commonly used as a panacea in medicine in the United States until the 1950s. In a 'widely accepted and used textbook of pharmacology' published in 1955, opium alkaloids, particularly morphine, were still hailed as 'unequalled as an analgesic and [their] indispensable uses in medicine and surgery are well defined'.
45. This notable medical value of opium is also noted, ironically, in a 1909 anti-opium novel entitled *Heh-chieh yüan yün* by P'eng Yang-ou (1982: 107, 'hsiao-shuo'). The medical use of opiates and opium in 19th-century England and the United States was even more common, and hence recorded in more detail (Berridge and Edwards 1981: ch. 6; Terry and Pellens 1970: 7–28).
46. In the case of the United States by the early 20th century, it was known that 'case histories, clinical notes, and remarks in the medical literature support the view that although opium and morphine were ultimately given for practically everything, even for such unlikely disorders as masturbation, photophobia, nymphomania, and "violent hiccough", it was especially in those who suffering from chronic ailments that use of these drugs led to addiction'. The therapeutic power of opium was widely recognized (Courtwright 2001: 42–8).
47. By 1911, two of the largest charitable associations did provide free medical care to permanent and temporary residents in the city. One of them, the Fang-pien Hospital, even claimed that it had cured more than ten thousand admitted patients in the early years of its existence. This figure, however, was not substantiated. Moreover, on the organization rules of the hospital is a long list of disciplinary regulations targeting the attendants (a sort of nurse) of this institution, apparently trying to stop misbehaviour

such as stealing and taking bribes from patients, mistreating in-patients, and so on. In the eyes of a sick man or woman, the hospital was not necessarily a good place to be unless absolutely necessary. Furthermore, reminiscences of many old residents of Canton inform us that the location of this hospital (on the outskirts of the far north-western part of the old City) was not only too remote but also filled with graves. The location was, therefore, commonly thought of as somewhat spooky and nobody dared to visit unless absolutely essential. Another charitable organization, the Kuang-jên Charitable Hall, boasted a team of five herbal doctors and a pharmacy that sold drugs but provided medical services to the needy at no charge. The three doctors and their entourages were divided into three teams, each moving around in one specific district at a time for consultations. The effectiveness of this service, however, was dubious (*Ch'üan Yüeh shê-hui shih-lu* 1911, and the author's fieldwork in Canton in 1998). In Canton, the first 'free' public clinic was founded in 1933. By 1934, there were three of these clinics in the city of almost one million inhabitants. The biggest of them could treat only seventy out-patients a day, but their budgets were nonetheless cut by the Bureau of Health. Although Canton also had nearly thirty charity halls and other charitable institutions providing free medicine and consultation to the poor, their efficiency was doubtful, otherwise these three government clinics would not have been stretched to their limit in respect of resources and public demand (*Kuang-chou nien-chien* 1935: 93–116, ch. 17).

48. There are at least two slightly different versions of this story. One is collected in Kao Hsiang-li (n.d.: 1), and the other in I Wu (1969: 199–200).
49. The recipients of the opium ashes always expressed their gratitude towards his father by giving him a small sum of money in a red envelope (from the author's interview with Mr Mok Hung who had lived in Canton from 1925 to 1950).
50. There was a close link between working-class self-medication tradition and opium use in 19th-century England (Berridge and Edwards 1981: 21–37, 102–3).
51. A medical article published in 1920 stated that 'some patients have been able to take morphine only when recurrent pain has been present, and, seeking safety by never administering the drug themselves, have managed to go for years without acquiring a habit which they could not break' (Terry and Pellens 1970: 149). A former resident of Canton recalls that one of his old friends, a Mr Wang, had been smoking opium regularly for more than twenty years until the Communist government strictly enforced opium prohibition in 1950. Mr Wang simply replaced opium with tobacco smoking, and did not show any symptom of relapse or withdrawal at all (from the author's interview with Mr Mok Hung).
52. The Preface in Lo-lo-chu-shih's script entitled *Chao yin chü*, collected in Ma Mao-ching et al. (1998: 250–1).
53. Kuang-chou-shih chieh-yen i-yüan (1937: 5–6, 'Statistics'. In a 1897 survey of the opinions of over 100 physicians on the use of opium in China conducted by the Anti-Opium League in China, it was reported that 61% of the opium addicts began to smoke because of illness or for other medical purposes (cited from P'eng Kuo-liang 1981: 11–13).
54. Unfortunately no statistics are given in this advertisement (*HTJP*, 1931: 1.1, 1 April). Nevertheless, tuberculosis was a major fatal disease in Republican China (Lamson 1935: 328–9).
55. An anti-opium Chinese text also indicates that opium helped relieve dysentery incurring from tuberculosis (Kao Hsiang-li n.d.: 15).

56. A contemporary sociological study of opium uses in North China showed that quite a substantial numbers of addicts took the drug as medicine. This phenomenon was even more common in the village communities where doctors were not always available (Yen Ching-yueh 1934: 170–3).
57. The stigmatization of opium and its users in China began on the eve of the Opium War, when pro-prohibitionist scholar-officials and literati publicized the drug as 'poison', rather than a medicine. This process of stigmatization continued well through the Republican era and might have been accelerated by among other factors, the influence of the Western pharmacological 'verdict' on the harmfulness of opiates. At a time when the worship of Western science by the Chinese was high, the acceptance of this piece of apparently scientific evidence was hardly surprising. Hence, most contemporary anti-opium writings supported their argument by citing from Western medical literature on the subject. For examples, Lo Yün-yen (1938: 1–22); Kuang-chou-shih chieh-yen i-yüan (1937: 32–9). The suppression of opium might also be viewed by anti-opiumists as a 'civilizing process' which, in Szasz's (1975: 45) words, 'symbolizes the transformation of a people from a shameful past of "backwardness" to a shining present and future of "modernity" '.
58. *Kuang-tung shêng chin-yen chü chieh-yen liu-i-so ch'êng-li i-chou-nien chi-lien tê-k'an* (1942: 7, 'Chi-lien lün-wên'). It must be added that sometimes this allegation was not totally groundless. For instance, during the late 19th century, opium was popularly known as an effective ointment for treating serious burns. In at least two incidents, the parents of an infant and a young burns victim had nearly intoxicated their children by treating them with a heavy dose of opium applied to the affected parts of the victims' bodies (*Shen pao* 1876, 26 Aug.).
59. Similarly, an official prejudicial view of opium eating was also found in 19th-century England (Berridge and Edwards, 1981: 153–6).
60. In the late 19th century, an English doctor who had served in China testified to the Opium Commission that 'the consumption of opium by the better classes is not condemned as degrading' (Rowntree 1895: 91).
61. Some Chinese historians state in error that this policy was started by the Peiyang warlords (Wu Yü et al. 1988: 287–90). This resembles to some extent the class-biased situation of medical treatment of opium addicts in 19th-century England where 'for the middle-class morphine addict there was medical care and expensive in-patient treatment; working-class addiction was mostly a matter of curtailment of supply' (Berridge and Edwards 1981: 102–3, 158–9).
62. The rich protagonists in P'eng Yang-ou's *Heh-chieh yüan yün* (chs. 2 and 3) smoke opium as a 'playful thing' as well as for its 'spirit-enhancing' function.
63. Evidence presented to the Royal Commission on Opium, and cited from Spence (1975: 145). On the popularity of opium smoking amongst merchants and businessmen in Ch'ing China, see ibid. 144–5; Rowntree (1895: 91–2).
64. Inside the Nan Pei Hang, one of the biggest Chinese grocery import and export company in Hong Kong, opium and smoking tools were always at the service of guests and executives. The prominent status of this firm was also expressed in the fact that the smoking-pipes used there were said to be largely made of gold and silver (Sung Yü 1989: 71). Similar arrangements could be found in many big native banks, trading companies, insurance firms, and even a bookstore (Ch'en Ch'ien 1989: 76–7).
65. For cases in the Ch'ing times, see Spence (1975: 159–61).

66. Newman (1995: 778–9) points out that most 19th-century English-language literature on the opium issue in China indicated that the drug was less widely smoked in the countryside than in the towns. His research tells him that, by the late 19th century, a majority of peasant men and a substantial minority of peasant women took opium occasionally when they felt unwell, but that regular social indulgence in the drug was limited to 5–10% of rural adults.
67. For instance, in Ou-yang Shan's (1948) 'Chu-cha', the third-class cabin of a steamer is portrayed as a pathetic filthy opium and gambling den since nearly all the male passengers, who are mainly poor Kwangtung workers, are addicts of these vices. But this is not fictitious since it fits the description of a contemporary traveller (Champly 1938: 144–5).
68. This system of classifying opium smokers into three categories was probably first started in Shanghai in 1927. There, there were three kinds of opium permits: (1) 'A' class permits for merchants, gentry, and women, which cost 3 dollars per month; (2) 'B' class permits for poorer classes, which cost 1 dollar per month; (3) 'C' class temporary permits for travellers, which cost 30 cents per day (FO415/522/127/87 Confidential Memorandum from Sir M. Lampson to Sir Austen Chamberlain dated 20 December 1927, *The Opium Trade*, vi. pt. XXV, p. 14).
69. *Kuang-tung shêng-chêng-fu min-chêng-ting chin-yen kung-tso pao-kao shu* (1940: 10, 24); *Kuang-tung shêng chin-yen-chü chieh-yen liu-i-so chêng-li i-chou-nien chi-nien tê-k'an* (1942: 18).
70. Kuang-chou-shih chin-yen wei-yüan-hui (1937*a*: 1–2, 'Statistics').
71. The source did not, however, provide us with an actual number of rickshawmen who were using opium (*Kuang-chou nien chien* 1935: 53, ch. 7).
72. For political reasons, this 'morning session' was closed down by the government in 1922.
73. This is perhaps why in these two studies above nothing was mentioned about the devastating effect of opium smoking on rickshawmen in Canton. A resident of London's East End testified that opium helped enhance the stamina of the Chinese seamen who worked long hours there during the early 20th century (Berridge and Edwards 1981: 202).
74. From the lyrics of an anti-opium folk song in Ch'ao-chou (Hu P'o-an et al. 1986: ii. 397). Szasz (1975: 69–73) argues that 19th-century Chinese emigrants to the United States were aided by opium to increase productivity, and subsequently established themselves as one of the country's successful ethnic minorities.
75. For the 19th-century pro-opium views, see Rowntree (1895: 40–4). The massive evidence collected by the Royal Commission on Opium, though by no means unanimous, nonetheless puts the official, 'unquestionable' view on opium smoking in serious doubt.
76. A cryptic phrase used by prisoners, *t'i ta-wang chia* (kicking the king's armour), became in Canton a popular idiom meaning heavy addicts of imported opium. The phrase was usually shouted as a warning by opium-addict inmates when a sudden opium bust was on its way (T'un Huang 1927*b*: 4.4).
77. *KPP* 1933: 3.2, 22 October records a case in which two inmates, who were convicted of murder, were caught smoking opium in cells.
78. *Kuang-chou shê-hui tsa chih* (*c.*1920s: 13, 'Kuang-chou shê-hui chih kuai-hsien-hsiang').
79. Even in official reports, the four prisons in Canton were described as very badly maintained (*HTJP* 1927: 2.2, 22 August).
80. Such honest and favourable views on opium smoking are hard to come by. A few examples can be found in the various prefaces written by scholar-addicts for a late-Ch'ing book entitled *Yen hua* which is included in Ah Ying (1957: 765–6).

81. It was only the poor who patronized opium dens (Turner 1982: 100).
82. In 1919, the price of imported opium from Hong Kong was said to be four times higher than that of Yünnan opium (Yü En-tê 1934: 179).
83. Based on interviews with Mr Liu Chêng and Mr Ferdinand Hoo who lived in Canton until 1949. Similar phenomenon was also found in central China. For an example, see Hung Ching-kiang (1989: 36). For Western medical and psychiatric reports on this particular property of opium, see Terry and Pellens (1970: 505–7).
84. Two of them depict a man copulating with a *yen chi* (opium-brothel beauty) who is preparing opium and a pipe for her partner. Similar erotic graphic images are also carved on the exterior of some elaborate brass opium-boxes (Byron 1987: 68–9, 72–3).
85. In Chang Tzu-p'ing's (1928–30: ii) the male protagonist patronizes one particular opium den because whenever he watches the 'beauty' preparing his opium pipe, he is sexually excited.
86. See the relevant statistics compiled in *YHKPK*. Before the 1900s, imported opium from India could be relatively expensive, especially if its importers chose to declare customs at the various ports under the direct control of the Imperial Maritime Customs, which charged a much higher levy upon the drug than other 'ordinary' Chinese custom stations did. As a result, Chinese importers of Indian opium had already since the mid-19th century avoided calling at Canton to reduce the overhead cost of importation, a practice that had long been noticed and criticized by a helpless Imperial Maritime Customs house in Canton. To those who were daring, smuggling of foreign and local opium was an attractive, lucrative business that persisted throughout the 19th and the first half of the 20th centuries. In short, at the times when importation and retail distribution of opium was under a centralized system of official regulation as it was after 1925, the local price of Indian and Chinese opium was lower than it should be, which might have helped ease the burden on local smokers (*YHKPK* 1996: 182–7, 595, 675).
87. Such supremacy was already noticed by the Imperial Maritime Customs in Canton as early as the mid-1890s (ibid. 358).
88. For a picture of the situation in the larger context of China, see Newman (1995: 769–74). A detailed discussion of how the opium monopoly in Hong Kong helped perpetuate the smuggling of *chandu* into Kwangtung and other parts of China under the full knowledge of the colonial administration there can be read in Miners (1987: chs. 11–12).
89. FO 415/848/238/87 Mr Clive to the Marquess Curzon of Kedleston dated 29 January 1923, enclosure 1, collected in *The Opium Trade*, v., pt. XIX, pp. 39–41.
90. FO 415/1312/229/87 secret memorandum by Sir C. Clementi to Mr Amery dated 12 January 1928, collected in *The Opium Trade*, vi. 42, pt. XXV.
91. FO 415/3466/184/87, enclosure, dated 16 May 1930; FO 228/3678, enclosure 2.
92. FO 415/2609/667/10 Sir B. Alston to the Earl of Balfour dated 29 June 1922, enclosure No. 2, collected in *The Opium Trade*, v. 14, pt. XVIII.
93. When Elizabeth Kendall travelled in the far west of China, there were seventeen coolies in her caravan, of whom only seven smoked, and they limited themselves to one pipe at night (Newman 1995: 783).
94. A British consul in Wu-hu noted that many a opium-den keeper depended for his profits on serving mixtures of ash and extract to his poorer customers, and many customers preferred this, since some varieties of opium were too harsh to the taste when smoked in a pure form (ibid. 773).

95. On the income of rickshawmen in Canton, see Wu Jui-lin (1940: 15–16).
96. *Kuang-tung shêng chin-yen-chü chieh-yen liu-i-so chêng-li i-chou-nien chi-nien tê-k'an* (1942: 19).
97. This tallies with a comment made by J. F. Maddux in 1960 from clinical experience: 'Narcotic addiction seems to occur as a continuum varying in severity from person to person. It may vary from a mild condition from which the person recovers without treatment, to an appalling indefinitely prolonged process in which most of living, working, striving, thinking, and feeling becomes abandoned to narcotization' (*Rehabilitating the Narcotic Addicts* (US Government Print Office, 1966), cited in Maddux and Desmond 1981: 106).
98. For examples of such an argument, which can be easily found in most official anti-opium literature, see *Kuang-tung shêng chin-yen-chü chieh-yen liu-i-so chêng-li i-chou-nien chi-nien tê-k'an* (1942: 8); Kuang-chou-shih chin-yen wei-yüan-hui (1937*b*: 2).
99. A significant percentage of narcotic addicts were found able to discontinue the habit and went through a rather prolonged period of voluntary abstinence (Maddux and Desmond 1981: 99–105). In northern China, Yen Ching-yueh (1934: 170–1) came across a few of these cases. For instance, a 19-year-old woman had formed a habit of smoking opium after she took the drug for curing complaints incurred following a miscarriage. She was able to get rid of the habit one month after she recovered from her illness. In another case, a carriage driver had recovered from his morphine addiction after six months of abstinence from the drug that he could no longer afford. He suffered a relapse eventually because of hard work and the cold weather.
100. If every opium smoker continually increased his or her consumption to maintain the same effect, one cannot explain why a large number of addicts who had been habituated to opium for a long time (in some cases over twenty years) consumed only a very modest dose. For example, see Tu Tsung-ming (1953: 589–90). Although we cannot rule out the existence of addicts who did consume larger doses as time went by (two cases that tallied with this description can be read in Yen Ching-yueh (1934: 170–1)), very few records of such instances exist in contemporary academic or clinical reports from Canton and elsewhere that this research has consulted.
101. *Kuang-tung shêng chin-yen-chü chieh-yen liu-i-so chêng-li i-chou-nien chi-nien tê-k'an* (1942: 19). This tallies with what some economists call the 'theory of rational addiction'. In this theory addictions are no longer seen as an antithesis to rational behaviour. Instead, addicts are seen as rational consumers who 'maximize utility from stable preferences as they try to anticipate the future consequences of their choices'; their 'consumption of addictive goods responds less to temporary changes in prices than to permanent changes' (Becker and Murphy 1988: 675–6). For a more concise and jargon-free exposition of the theory of 'addicts' choice', see Skog (2000: 1309–14).
102. *Kuang-tung shêng chin-yen-chü chieh-yen liu-i-so chêng-li i-chou-nien chi-nien tê-k'an* (1942: 19).
103. In a detailed clinical study on opium addiction conducted in Philadelphia General Hospital, Arthur Light et al. (1929–30: 64–5) made the following interesting observations on withdrawal symptoms: 'Despite the fact that the addicts claim to be so weak as to be scarcely able to move, their response to the staircase climbing test was carried out with the same efficiency as when drugs were administered.... Following the re-administration of the drug, the response was, if anything, poorer.

Such differences as exist in basal blood pressure, heart rate and respiratory rate are too small to indicate any significant change.... The concentration of the blood and loss of weight would indicate some organic disturbance, on the surface, but we believe that these two positive manifestations can be explained on the basis that the addicts will not take food or water and perspire to such an extent that they cannot help showing this loss of weight and the degree of concentration of blood found in our cases.... Further evidence that the picture of withdrawal symptom has as its basis an emotional state is the response on the part of one of our addicts at the end of a thirty-six hour withdrawal period to the hypodermic injection of sterile water. Despite his obvious suffering, he immediately went to sleep and slept for eight hours. Addicts frequently speak about the 'needle habit', in which the single prick of the needle brings about relief.... On the other hand, it has been our experience just as frequently to have the addict know that he was given a hypodermic injection of sterile water and to have him fail to respond to its effect.'

104. Kuang-chou-shih chieh-yen i-yüan (1937: 6–7, 'Statistics'). Medical statistics from Japanese Taiwan provided more clues to the existence of this group of opium users. In the in-patient records of the Government Central Hospital for opium addicts, it is quite interesting to find an opium smoker's assessment of the duration of his habit could be much shorter than the years he spent on using the drug. For instance, a rickshawman called K. Rin was 41 years of age when admitted to the hospital. He claimed that he was 31 years old when addicted, but the 'duration of the habit' was only three years, in all likelihood just prior to his admission to the treatment. Another rickshawman called T. K. Rin was 34 when admitted. He was 23 when addicted, and the 'duration of the habit' was four years. It must be added, however, that the medical history of many other addicts at the same hospital revealed a more expected duration of habit, i.e. they formed a habit once they were addicted to the drug (Tu Tsung-ming 1953: 594–5).
105. Similar horrible images of opium corruption were enthusiastically promoted in anti-opium literature, both official and civilian, from the 1830s and throughout the Republican era.
106. *Kuang-tung shêng chin-yen-chü chieh-yen liu-i-so chêng-li i-chou-nien chi-nien tê-k'an* (1942: 8).
107. Ibid. 20.
108. 'Ya-pien yin', *HYOC c.* 1926: 17–18, 1921 section. A number of humorous vernacular songs written for the similar purpose of warning its readers against opium had already been compiled, published, and sold in Canton, Hong Kong, and probably other big towns in the region from the last years of the Ch'ing Dynasty and throughout the early Republican times. Two examples of this kind of amusing 'morality book' are *Sze yin ch'i* (*c.*1920s), and Ch'i wan hua shê (1910).
109. Official anti-opium literature also anxiously promoted a similar fatalistic image of opium smoking. For instance, see Kuang-chou-shih chin-yen wei-yüan-hui (1937*b*: *passim*).
110. Kuang-chou-shih chieh-yin i-yüan (1937: 9, 'Statistics').
111. This corroborates the finding of a scientific study on the effect of morphine on its addicts conducted in the United States in the early 1930s (Lindesmith 1968: 39). Another study concluded: 'Opium addicts with advanced incurable pulmonary tuberculosis should not be treated for addiction. Treatment adds greatly to their discomfort; it is sometimes dangerous and nothing is gained if the cure is effected.

Addiction is contraindicated, however, in persons with curable pulmonary tuberculosis. It reduces the metabolic rate and lessens the chances of recovery from the tuberculosis' (Kolb, 1928: 181).

112. *Kuang-tung shêng-chêng-fu min-chêng-ting chin-yen kung-tso pao-kao shu*, (1940: 27).
113. Poor diet, prolonged hard work, and the consumption of adulterated opium were said to be detrimental to the physical and mental health of the Chinese coolies in Hong Kong between the Wars (Gillingham 1983: 79). Adulterated opium, a cheaper, though more toxic, alternative for the poor, was accountable for frequent cases of opiate-related poisoning in 19th-century England (Berridge and Edwards 1981: 87–93).
114. The celebrated 19th-century English 'opium eater' Thomas De Quincey was said to be used to an enormous dosage of opium that actually helped prolong his life (Berridge and Edwards 1981: 49–56).
115. Kuang-chou-shih chin-yen wei-yüan-hui (1937*a*: 5–6, 'Statistics').
116. In Canton, relatively reliable demographic records were begun only with the establishment of the municipal government in 1921.
117. *Chia-yin nien hsin t'ung-shu* (1914: 3), 'Ching-yen liang-fang' (Effective Prescriptions Based on Successful Experience).
118. For instance, of the thirty-two suicide cases in September 1930, eleven took their own lives by opium overdoses (Tieh Ma 1931: 21–2). Between the 1880s and 1900s, *Shen pao* (*passim*) did publish a number of reports on such cases of suicide.
119. *Kuang-tung shêng chin-yen-chü chieh-yen liu-i-so chêng-li i-chou-nien chi-nien tè-k'an* (1942: 30–40). Newman (1995: 779–81) notes in his research finding that: 'The safest conclusion seems to be that by the late nineteenth century a majority of peasant men and a substantial minority of peasant women took opium occasionally when they felt unwell, but that regular social indulgence in the drug was limited to between five and ten per cent of rural adults.... Smoking by urban women was much less common; those observers who tried to quantify it usually gave percentage of five or less.' The situation in Japanese Taiwan seems to be somewhat different with the male/female ratio of opium smokers stood at approximately 5: 1 (Tu Tsung-ming 1953: 600 and table 12).
120. Lewin (1964: 61–2) points out that morphine might injure the normal functioning of semen, though it doesn't follow that opiate addiction can be congenitally transmitted by an addicted father. Lindesmith's (1968: 171–2) research shows that there is no scientific evidence to support the assumption that opiate addicts have 'tainted heredities'.
121. According to a popular text for university students in Chinese history entitled *A Daughter of Han*, the husband of its heroine, Ning Lao T'at-t'ai, was an 'opium dreggy' who had ruined his family because of his addiction. In spite of this, none of his offspring had displayed any inclination towards the drug. Moreover, the story ended rather happily with her addictive husband giving up opium smoking completely and rejoining his broken family to start life anew (Pruitt 1967).
122. Full text of this edict can be read in Ma Mo-ching et al. (1998: 43). Spence (1975: 150) has cited this; Chang Hsin-pao (1964: 36).
123. Waley (1958: 176–7) mentioned another incident. During the Opium War, an army officer was held to be responsible for losing a battle because his withdrawal symptoms rendered him unable to command his troops. But even this example did

not show the prevalence of opium smoking among the common soldiers, but the problem of one commanding officer.

124. For example, an uprising of the Yao in Hai-nan island was efficiently and effectively suppressed by a joint force of soldiers and militias (*Shen pao* 1885, 27 June).

125. For an interesting and detailed comparison between the strengths of the British expeditionary force and the Ch'ing army during the Opium War, see Mao Hai-chien (1995: 33–88).

126. *Shen pao* contains a number of these favourable reports on the Chinese soldiers. For instance, 29 May 1885. In another report on the reform of the Eight Banners force in Canton, the author was impressed with the substantial improvement made in the areas of training, morale, provisioning, and the skills of fighting to this once demoralized army (ibid. 12 March 1885). During the Sino-French War, Chinese journalists were quite confident in the military capability of the Chinese forces (ibid. 25 January 1884). None of the above reports mentions anything about opium consumption being detrimental to the military prowess of the Chinese forces. The late-Ch'ing reform gave birth to a new breed of soldiers in China. The new recruits for the New Army were strictly screened for opium use. During the Republican period, the Yünnanese armies were notorious for opium addiction, but not all other armies in China were (Lary 1985: 29, 40, 86). The 'Christian General' Feng Yü-hsiang was well known for imposing strict discipline on his army (Sheridan 1966: 80–7). In a memoir of an army officer in the Nationalist army, it is surprising to find that he mentioned almost nothing about opium smoking in the force, although he writes freely about the problems of prostitution and gambling among the soldiers (Chang Kung-p'ing, 1993).

127. In ancient Greece and Egypt, warriors consumed nepenthe before battle in order to dull their sense of danger and help enhance their fighting spirit on the battlefield (Lewin 1964: 35).

128. Similar observations were made on opium addicts in the United States (Terry and Pellens 1970: 58).

129. In 1935, more than 200,000 people were said to be unemployed (*KCPN*, 1980: ii. 470); Chang Chên-chih (1929: 107–36).

130. In a recent study of a P'ai farming community in Yünnan from the late 1930s to the end of the 1980s, its authors, citing the data from a monograph written by Fei Hsiao-t'ung on the same community in 1939, point out that opium addiction and the soaring in the price of opium, in addition to the 'corrupted rule of the KMT', was held responsible for a general loss of landownership from the native villagers to outsiders, and hence accelerated the process of impoverishment in this village. Their observation, however, seems largely impressionistic and is not supported by enough or pertinent data such as the retail prices of opium in different periods, the amount of opium consumed by addicts, the consumption patterns of opium for these smokers, their income situation and the affordability of indulging in this drug. This negative picture of opium's impact on the local economy seems to be built upon incomplete information mainly in the form of personal reminiscences collected by Fei and these authors in their interviews with local informants (Chien Ch'êng-jun et al. 1995: 48–50).

131. Meanwhile, in some areas of Manchuria, the high land tax being enforced by the soldiers could only be met by the farmers by poppy growing (Lattimore, 1975: 189–90).

132. In 1897, the Imperial Maritime Customs at Canton estimated no more than 50 *piculs* of raw opium was grown in Kwangtung. It predicted that local production of opium would remain insignificantly low in the years to come (*YHKPK* 1996: 358). The 1912 and 1914 *China Year Book* (1920: 676) contain the following statement: 'Kuang-tung—Opium was produced in two *hsiens* near Swatow, but the authorities are now active.' During the early years of the Republic, especially before 1917, the authorities in Kwangtung were apparently quite sincere in their attempt to eliminate poppy planting and opium production in the province. Impressive records of this effort can be read in the official gazette, Kuang-tung shêng hsüan-an-shih kung-ch'u (1912–20s), *Kuang-tung kung pao*, esp. 1914–16, *passim.*
133. Even for Yünnan, Kweichow, and Szechwan, provinces where the problem of poppy growing was most serious, the percentages were, respectively, 17.83, 8.08, and 7.54. Most other provinces were on the low side of between 0.3 and 3% (Lin Man-hung *c.*1980s: 245–52).
134. Despatches nos. 25 and 29 from American Consulate in Swatow to American Minister in Peking, captioned 'Poppy Planting in the Swatow Consular District', dated 20 November 1923 (US Department of State archive).
135. FO 415/3474/184/87 Confidential report from His Majesty's Consul, Swatow, to Mr A. Henderson dated 22 May 1930, compiled in *The Opium Trade* (1974: vi. pt. XXVIII 54).
136. A Japanese source stated that in the area of Swatow, about 25–30% of the population in the cities were addicts; while in the countryside, only about 5% of the population were ('Shina chikaiji no ahen mondai', 1931: 50).
137. In spite of their addiction, the rich merchants appear in a social novel as continuing to be able to make big money (Sung Yü 1989).
138. There was nothing in the whole report on the destructive impact of opium on the working and family lives of the workers surveyed (Yu Ch'i-chung, 1934).
139. *Canton: Its Port, Industries & Trade* (1932: esp. pts. II, III, and V); *YHKPK* 1996 *passim*; Ch'êng Hao (1985: ii, esp. chs. 4–7).
140. As alleged by Kōsaka Junichi (1943: 40–1).
141. In 1930, the fee for a 'smoking den' licence was 4–6 dollars per month; and the tax on each set of smoking paraphernalia in the shop was 0.75 dollar per day (FO 415/3466/184/87, enclosure, dated 16 May 1930).
142. 'Yen-kuan fu' (1910). Late 19th-century descriptions of opium dens in London's 'Chinatown' noted that they were 'something akin to a Chinese social club' (Berridges and Edwards 1981: 196–204).
143. For a brief discussion on the derogatory image, or myth, of the opium den in Victorian England, see Berridge (1999: 195–208). For a glimpse of how a Chinese intellectual perceived these dens in 1930s Peking, see Ah Nan (1997: 367–72). A 19th-century English missionary had written a rare, though sketchy, description of these 'chatting rooms' in Canton (Turner 1982: 47). At times during the late 19th century these smaller establishments were subjected to strict regulation whenever law and order in Canton seemed to be threatened by the outbreak of banditry in the suburb and by rumours of uprisings by the revolutionaries in the city. For instance, in the winter of 1895, public security in the city was ordered to be tightened. As a result, many opium-smoking shops (probably only the smaller shops were affected) were ordered to limit the number of smoking couches to four, and closing hour was set at the second round of the night-watchman's drum. As a silent protest against

such undesirable restrictions, many opium-smoking shops were said to have closed down (*Shen pao* 1895, 3 November).

144. The latter report stated that since business for these low-class dens was so good that many of the owners had their premises tidied up and redecorated, and installed new beds to lure more customers, especially from the less indigent class.
145. *Shu pao*, 11th day of the Ninth Moon, 1884.
146. An extant almanac (*t'ung shu*) printed in Canton in the 1910s contains a section of suggested couplets for different kinds of shops including opium-smoking and opium-retailing shops. For instance, *Chia-yin nien hsin t'ung-shu* contains four pages of such couplets. It is interesting to note that there were a number of similar high-class opium smoking shops, all fabulously decorated, in late-Ch'ing Shanghai. These establishments were so lovely and luxuriously decorated that even non-smokers were reportedly found lingering in them; many of these curious visitors were believed to have subsequently turned to this form of indulgence after several visits (*Shen pao* 1880, 1 December).
147. *Shu pao*, 18th day of the Ninth Moon, 1884.
148. The supplements of many extant Canton newspapers such as *YHP, KPP*, and *Kuo hua pao* published irregularly a number of sketchy reports on these addict actors, see e.g. *KPP* (1934: 3.3, 31 January); *YHP* (1934: 1, 21 October).
149. Although the full script is unavailable to us, it seems improbable that this excerpt carries the moral of the play. It is very likely that the opera would end with the reform of this prodigal and erring husband into someone more orthodox and moral, as symbolized by his wife ('Shih chu ch'i an chih ma ch'i', in Chiu Ho-chin 1924: 122).
150. In 19th-century England, opium was also a subject of humour (Berridge and Edwards 1981: 54).
151. Unfortunately, only Part 1 of this interesting article was available to us (Ch'üan Shêng 1924: 6–9, *Wên-i*). It must be noted that this magazine, despite having the same name as *KCTC* cited throughout this thesis, is entirely unrelated to the latter. The first issue of *KCTC* was published in September 1932.
152. In Manchuria, the high value and low per-unit-weight costs of transport of opium rendered it an important cash crop that played a crucial role in the colonization of this frontier by the Chinese. Poppy-growing communities, despite being geographically disadvantaged in the remote areas of Manchuria, were able to encourage trading in food because of their strong consuming power. This, in turn, helped improve transport and other facilities until these settlements developed into agricultural villages, and to a point that eliminated the importance of opium (Lattimore 1975: 190–7).
153. An elder in the village of Sha-wan (Shun-tê County) laments the passing of the ostentatious celebrations of the local temple fair in pre-Communist days, which lasted for seven days and nights, with non-stop performances of Cantonese opera. That was feasible only with the substantial amount of voluntary contributions donated by, and surcharges imposed on, the village opium and gambling divans (based on the author's fieldwork in 1990).
154. I am grateful to Dr Cheung Siu-woo for drawing my attention to this source.
155. *Shu pao*, 18th day of the Ninth Moon, 1884.
156. A number of such prescriptions are compiled by Kao Hsiang-li in his *Ya-pien*, (n.d.: 15–53). He also provided his readers with detailed suggestions and directions on how to break their opium addiction more easily. Ch'en Kung-min's *Chieh yen*

ch'üan-fa, first published in 1854, also contains a number of prescriptions claimed to be effective in helping opium addicts to get rid of the habit.

157. For a detailed description of one of the charitable organizations supporting opium suppression, see 'Kuang-tung chieh-yen ts'ung-hui', in Têng Yü-shêng (1911).
158. The government institution publication for opium addiction treatment emphasized in the simplicity of terminating one's opium habit under its supervision and encouraged addicts to take a more active role in submitting themselves to this kind of treatment (*Kuang-tung shêng chin-yen chü chieh-yen liu-i-so ch'êng-li i-chou-nien chi-lien tê-k'an*, 1942: 17–18).
159. Such as *Huo-shao Ta-sha-t'ou* (The Fire at Ta-sha-t'ou) and *Yü yen wu yüan* (No Affinity with Opium) (Ch'en Hua-hsin 1983: 299).
160. The popularity of those 'patriot troupes' is also doubtful. The subject will be discussed in more details in the chapter on Cantonese Opera.
161. *YHKPK* 1996: 537–8, 566–7; Kuang-tung shêng hsüan-an-shih kung-ch'u (1912–20s: esp. 1914–16, *passim*).
162. In one exceptional case in 1921, a Chinese gunboat was 'accidentally' caught by the Canton Customs smuggling a 5,000-yüan cache of opium. If the captain of the gunboat had not been so careless as to unload the consignment on to a civilian boat, Customs would have never uncovered the plot. Yielding to strong British diplomatic pressure, the Canton administration was forced to have the captain executed (Tsui-mien-shan-jên *c.*1920s: 6–9). It was stated that by smuggling opium into Canton, an ordinary lieutenant in the army could earn as much as 100,000 yüan a year (Li P'ei-shêng: 1921, 187).
163. Kuang-chou-shih chin-yen wei-yüan-hui (1937*a*: 'photographs'; *Chü-tu yüeh-k'an* 23 (1928: 3).
164. FO 415/4749/4749/87 'Memorandum respecting the Opium Problem in the Far East' dated 10 August 1929, collected in *The Opium Trade* (1974: vi. 37–8, pt. XXVI).
165. 'Shina chikaiji no ahen mondai', (1931: 49).
166. Confidential print no. 18, Foreign Office to Secretary-General, League of Nations (Geneva), in 'Further Correspondence Respecting Opium, 1924', collected in *The Opium Trade* (1974: v. 19–20, pt. XXI).
167. FO 228/3886/344–5 Consulate-General Canton to HM Minister in Peking dated 29 August 1928.
168. FO 415/4749/4749/87 'Memorandum Respecting the Opium Problem in the Far East' dated 10 August 1929, collected in *The Opium Trade* (1974: vi. 38 pt. XXVI).
169. In 1926–7, military expenditure accounted for more than 80% of the provincial budget (Chia Shih-i 1932: 112).
170. Between late 1929 and 1936, gambling revenue brought the Kwangtung government 12–17 million yüan p.a.; and opium revenue 9–12 million p.a. (Fitzgerald 1990: 757); also Kuang-chou-shih chêng-hsieh (1987: 358–60).
171. The importance of opium revenue had long been realized by provincial governments since the late Ch'ing. In some provinces, it was used for filling up deficits in provincial tax quotas and for funding Self-Strengthening Movement projects. Opium tax could also be the main source of local transit duty revenue (Spence 1975: 167–72); Yü En-tê (1934: 96–105).
172. FO 228/3886/344 Consulate-General Canton to HM Minister in Peking, dated 29 August 1928.

173. FO 228/4290/266–7 Consulate-General Canton to Sir M. Lampson, dated 25 June 1930, p. 2.
174. FO 415/3466/184/87 confidential print from Consul-General Phillips to Sir M. Lampson, dated 16 May 1930.
175. For detail of his plan, see *HTJP*, 1927: 3.2, 29 July.
176. FO 228/4290/266–7, p. 3.
177. FO 228/3888/24 Wuchow Custom House to Brenan, dated 12 May 1928.
178. This piece of information is drawn from the testimony of an inspector who was standing trial for causing the death of a suspect during a home search (*HTJP* 1928: 2.2, 26 May). For more information on the reward system in the early years of Republican Kwangtung, see Yü En-tê (1934: 159).
179. Kuang-chou-shih shih-chêng-t'ing, *Kuang-chou-shih shih-chêng pao-kao hui k'an* (Canton: 1924: 277–8), Kuang-chou-shih shih-chêng-fu t'ung-chi ku, *Kuang-chou-shih-chêng-fu t'ung-chi nien-chien. Ti i hui* (1929: 90–1).
180. A well-publicized case happened in the summer of 1928. Two inspectors, in the company of a policeman, searched the house of a Cantonese lawyer. During the search, one of the inspectors planted a small bag of unlicensed opium on the lawyer, and extorted money from him at gun-point. The lawyer dropped dead from a heart-attack (*HTJP* 1928: 3.3, 21 May; 1928: 2.2, 26 May; 1928: 1.3, 2.2, 4 June; 1928: 1.3, 9 June. Chu Hsiu-hsia, *Pa-yüeh chien* (1930) is a satirical novel about the shamefully blatant corruption of a group of Opium Suppression officers.
181. Even when the KMT Left was in power during the mid-1920s, misdeeds by these officers were still noted (*KCMKJP*, 1926: 4, 3 July).
182. *Kuang-tung-shêng-chêng-fu kung-pao* 17 (1929: 7–9, 28 August); 18 (1929: 24–5, 29 August), Kuang-chou-shih chin-yen wei-yüan-hui (1937: 65–7). Another 'Opium Suppression Ordinance' was passed in August 1929, apparently no more sincerely enforced than its numerous predecessors. *Kuang-tung-shêng-chêng-fu kung-pao* 17 (1929: 7–9, 26 August); Yü En-tê 1934: 307–8).
183. Kuang-chou-shih chêng-hsieh (1987: 359–60); *KCPN* 1980: ii. 460; FO 415/7610/116/87 Sir A. Cadogan to Sir Samuel Hoare, dated 29 October 1935; and the author's interview with Mr Mok Hung.
184. Kuang-chou-shih hsin-shêng-huo yün-tung wei-yüan-hui (1937: 65, 69), Kuang-chou-shih chin-yen (1937*b*: 32–5); the author's interview with Mr Mok Hung.
185. 'Pên yüan ch'ou-pei ching-k'uo', in Kuang-chou-shih chieh-yen i-yüan (1937: 2–4).
186. Ibid. 4.

CHAPTER 4

1. 'The Master said: "Hard is the case of him, who will stuff himself with food the whole day, without applying his mind to anything good! Are there not gamesters and chess players? To be one of these would still be better than doing nothing at all." ' Legge (1899: 193). Mencius also held the view that 'if a man fails to take care of his parents [as a result of] gambling or becoming inebriated, he is outright lacking in filial piety'. It seems that gambling was unacceptable only to such an extent. Cited in *Ming-hsin pao chien* (1919: 5).
2. The Legalists of the Chin and Han Dynasties were especially strict in punishing senior officials and princes who were caught gambling. The administrators of the T'ang

Dynasty were also harsh towards gamblers, especially in the main cities. In Southern Sung Hang-chou, gambling was outlawed except briefly for three days during Lunar New Year. Sung Wên (*NFJP* 1990: 3, Weekend Supplement 20 April) Mêng Yüan-lao (1987: 267). For a detailed discussion on anti-gambling tradition in Chinese high-culture, see Kuo Shuang-lin and Hsiao Mei-hua (1995: ch. 1–6).

3. Other examples of anti-gambling treatises of the same period can be read in Kuo Shuang-lin and Hsiao Mei-hua (1995: 240–5).
4. On Confucius's view of wealth and poverty, see Ch'en Li-fu (1987: 303–14).
5. In *fan tan*, the croupier puts a random number of copper coins, or porcelain buttons, inside a cup placed upside down. The gamblers then bet on the number of coins (from one to four) left on the table after extracting four at a time. Due to its ease of play, it was criticized as one of the most devastating forms of gambling. In the 'surnames guessing' game (*wei hsing*), gamblers bet on the surname (all the names were pooled) of the most successful candidates for the forthcoming Civil Examination. It was condemned for generating corruption, and for insulting the dignity of the imperial examination. In the 'pigeon lottery' (*pai-ko p'iao*), the initial eighty characters from the textbook *One-Thousand Characters Essay*, are used as the lots. In the 'flower lottery', one of the thirty-six names of the ancients is drawn as the winning lot. The real identities of these ancients, though unknown, are roughly classified as kings, imperial examination graduates, ordinary women, monks, nuns, doctors, beggars, firewood pedlars, etc. Each character is associated with one element of nature, or with an animal. This mystical element, and its implication of violating the social hierarchical order (e.g. the 'beggar' winning over the other social strata) was criticized as immoral by concerned Confucianists. For the rules of these games, see Chin Hsüeh-shih (1849); Yang Yin-shen (1935); Li Han-ch'ung, *KTFCL*, 112–16; Kuo Shuang-lin and Hsiao Mei-hua (1995: ch. 7); a brief but informative account of gambling in the province can be read in *Nan-hai hsien chih* (1910: 211b–213a, 'Yü-ti lüeh'). Also John Henry Gray (1972: 385–94). On moralist apprehensions about them, see *P'an-yü hsien sü chih* (1968: ch. 42, 2, 15–6); *F'o-shan chung-i hsiang chih* (1923: ch. 11, 17).
6. This echoes what Jan McMillen (1996: 6) says: 'the concept of gambling has no intrinsic meaning; rather, its meaning always depends on the socio-historical context which it occurs'.
7. English news report cited from Edward Rhoads (1975: 170–1). On the same day, all major government *yamen* in Canton were ordered to demonstrate support for this event by hanging up strings of colourful pennants outside their buildings, and huge numbers of firecrackers were set off as one of the celebration. All shops, schools, and guilds were, most probably, ordered to close for the day so that more people were able to take part. Major shops and gates to major streets and neighborhoods (*fang*) were posted with eye-catching banners supporting the official call to suppress gambling. These events were happily enjoyed by thousands of onlookers, among them many women who enjoyed these spectacles, at a fee of 30 cents, on bamboo-made platforms specially built for this occasion. The pageant and other events helped bring a short boom to tourism as all restaurants were said to be fully occupied, as were the ferries plying between Canton, Macao, and Hong Kong. (*Shen pao*, 1911, 4 September).
8. During the early phase of the campaign, the local Party mouthpiece, *KCKMJP*, was unusually enthusiastic about publishing news of the continuing operation of the 'underground', though actually very visually open, gaming establishments in all parts of Canton city. In some issues for July 1925, the daily even printed a proforma to assist its

readers to report cases of violation of the ban on gambling. And the result was an alarming, and embarrassing, discovery of the open breach of the rule. For instance, see *KCMKJP* (1925: 7, 8 July). The ban was apparently enthusiastically enforced by the picket teams of the Canton-Hong Kong boycott. For example, see *KCMKJP* (1925: 7, 23 June).

9. On its inauguration day, a procession was staged in the main business and administrative areas of Canton. All public and private schools in Canton were ordered by the local authorities to take part. Participating students formed street theatre teams to dramatize the evils of gambling. In the evening, a no less boisterous lantern parade was organized in the commercial quarters of the city, to arouse the public awareness of the campaign. Similar publicity campaigns were also orchestrated in other major county cities in the province where the ban on gambling was also described as 'being rigorously enforced'. *CTKL* (1936: 224–5, 235–6); *HTJP* (1936: 2.2, 2.4; 1, 2, 3, 4, 13 September).
10. See the sections on illustrations, speeches, writing competition in *CTKL*. Also refer to the *HTJP* and *YHP*, especially the issues between Sept. and Dec. 1936.
11. Examples are abundant in *CTKL* (1936: 9, 14, 24, 45).
12. In late-Ch'ing Hankow, games of chance were available at a variety of sites; and they 'attracted, and addicted, men and women of all social classes' (William T. Rowe 1989: 193–4). In a preface to *CTKL* (1936: 1), Chiang Kai-shek wrote that it was to the Party's shame that opium and gambling dens could still be seen in Kwangtung. He sided with the notion that these 'social evils' existed in Kwangtung alone.
13. As shown in one of the publicity banners hung in Canton, *CTKL*, photographs section. The same slogan was cited widely in a number of essays collected in the same volume.
14. This idea is more clearly revealed in an essay that tries, albeit unconvincingly, to contrast Kwangtung society before and after the Prohibition of 1936 (*CTKL* 1936: 28–31). Even the commendable separatist KMT regime of Ch'en Chi-t'ang was, after the 1936 takeover, relegated into one of 'the warlords whose long rule of Kwangtung' had caused serious destruction to its people (*YHP* 1936: 2, 7 October).
15. Ironically, the Nanking-backed new administration proclaimed the retention of other 'illegal revenues' that had been formerly designated as national revenues (e.g. the opium tax) by its predecessor (John Fitzgerald 1990: 772).
16. Examples are abundant throughout the pages of *CTKL*. A randomly chosen instance which has been discussed briefly above was a speech delivered by a senior official broadcast through the government radio station. The full text can be read in *CTKL* (1936: 82–6).
17. This aspect resembles one of the main moral arguments upheld by American anti-gambling writings since the 19th century: gambling strikes at the roots of the reward system based upon hard work and rationality (David Weinstein and Lillian Deitch 1974: 142). Downes et al. also state that gambling 'appears to be an *in principle* violation of capitalism'. Quoted from John Dunkley (1985: 14).
18. As discussed earlier, both the Party and the state did try hard to suppress most forms of gambling in Canton proper from late 1928 onwards to protect the reputation of this city as 'cradle of the Nationalist revolution', an image local KMT had been actively promoting since the early 1920s. Kuang-tung-shêng chêng-fu ts'ai-chêng-ting (1934: iii. 973–5).
19. An example of such a view in official proclamations against gambling can be read in *Shen pao* (1922, 2 December), in a statement issued by Ch'en Chiung-ming.

Contemporary journalists' attitudes in this respect, for instance, can be read from *HTJP* (1911, 20 April).

20. This article was originally a leader in a local daily called *Sh'ih-min jih-pao*, which was reprinted in *CTKL* (1936: 164–9).
21. For examples, see Chu Hsi-nung (1965); R. H. Tawney (1932: 69–77); Chou Ku-ch'êng (1930: 338–45).
22. More examples of this derogatory view on the countryside, in connection to the problem of illicit gambling activities there, can be read in *CTKL* (1936: 91–2, 124–5).
23. The author Huang Lin-sheng was also a key figure in the 1936 Anti-Gambling Campaign.
24. As in all the writings by Chinese Communist historians on this subject.
25. The imperial tutor Weng T'ung-ho greatly cherished Chang Yin-heng's insights on current affairs. Hence, he often sent documents and personal notes to Chang for comment. These despatches always arrived in the evening, when Chang was gambling. Chang never read them before a set was finished. As soon as he had commented on them, he would immediately resume the game. Chu Hsiu-hsia (1977: 65–6).
26. The prominent liberal intellectual of Republican China Hu Shih, according to the reminiscences of Chang Ai-ling, was also said to be a player of, probably, *mahjong*. Ma Chia-hui (*Ming pao* 2001, 5 July).
27. Similar views could be found in many other essays compiled in *CTKL* (1936: 95, 144).
28. Throughout the late 19th and early 20th centuries, there were numerous reports on the state's enforcement of the ban on gambling in Canton and other cities in Kwangtung. *Shen pao, HTJP*, and *CSL* v and vi, *passim*.
29. For official records on this unresolved problem, see *CSL*, v and vi. Contemporary newspapers such as *Shen pao*, and *HTJP* since 1894, contained a number of reports about the spread of this social 'problem' in and outside Canton.
30. Examples as such were numerous and can be found easily in *CSL* vi, *Shen pao*, and *HTJP*, 1900–11.
31. The case of Ma P'i-yao has often been cited by writers and historians on this subject because it is commonly believed that his harsh criticism against local officials (Ma was serving as Governor of Kwangtung and Kwangsi) and bookmakers had subsequently cost him his life. Holders of this view, however, never substantiate the point with any concrete evidence. Evidence in *CSL*, moreover, showed no trace of such an allegation, which, if it had had occurred, would not have been able to escape the attention of the imperial court. Tsou Lu was seemingly the first one who wrote about this conspiracy in his much-cited essay on gambling written in 1918 (repr. in *CTKL*). Since then, his view has been taken for granted and appeared in a number of works about gambling in Kwangtung, for examples in the prize essays from a composition competition organized by a Christian association in Canton against gambling during 1922 (reprinted in *CTKL*), and Kuo Shuang-lin and Hsiao Mei-hua (1995: 256).
32. US Department of State, 893.40622, 'Suppression of Gambling in the Province of Canton', from the American Consulate General in Canton to the Secretary of State, Washington DC, dated 12 May 1911.
33. A section about gambling can be read in *Nan-hai hsien chih* 1910: 211b-213a, 'Yü-ti lüeh'.

34. This favourable view was seemingly first introduced by Tsou Lu in his classic essay on gambling, and was then taken up by successive writers and historians on this subject. *CTKL* (1936: 243, 257); Kuo Shuang-lin and Hsiao Mei-hua (1995: 255).
35. Ma has memorialized the throne in 1890 for proposing harsher punishments against violators of the ban on gambling in Kwangsi. I cannot retrieve any other memorials or private papers by him on the issue of gambling in Kwangtung in his collected work compiled by Ma P'i-yao (1969: pt. 2, 140–1).
36. Examples of these common and even open violations of the ban on gambling abound and can be easily read in contemporary dailies such as *Shen pao* and *HTJP* between 1860s and the very last dates of the Manchu regime.
37. For examples, Chang Hsin-tai's *Yüeh yu hsiao chih* and Ch'ü Ta-chün's *Kuang-tung hsin yü*.
38. The accusation against Li Hung-ping for accepting huge bribes from local bookmakers, for instance, was, as already pointed out, hardly substantiated, as the records from *CSL* indicate.
39. The reason was that before Li Hung-chang announcing the lifting of the ban, the Imperial Court had ordered the Governor of Kwangtung to send a prominent Cantonese bookmaker to Li 'for his service' (*CSL* 1995: vi. 380).
40. These illegal gambling dens proliferated beyond control in Canton. Tsou Lu, *CTKL* (1936: 243); Hu Pu-chin, 'Kuang-tung tu-huo shih', *CTKL* (1936: 253).
41. For details on these progressive, though brief 'honeymoon' years, see Edward Rhoads (1975: ch. 10).
42. The magnitude of these natural disasters was truly alarming. For instance, the disastrous flood that inundated a large part of the province during April 1915 destroyed no less than 160,000 houses. Three months later, the provincial administration was still busy with rehabilitation in the affected areas. The extensive scale of destruction had won the sympathy of Western missionaries and the British and the United States consulates in Canton. For further details, see Kuang-tung shêng hsüan-an-shih kung-ch'u, 815 (1915, 13 April); 822 (1915, 12 April); 890 (1915, 1 July); 902 (1915, 15 July). Probably due to some obvious political reasons, contemporary writers or historians write very little about Lung's rule of Canton, let alone about how he actually deployed the gambling revenue. Nonetheless, it is unfair to rule out the possibility that he might have utilized this source of revenue for the relief work. For a brief account of the relief work, see ibid., 822 (1915: 24–8, 12 April).
43. *Kuang-tung kung pao* printed out monthly lists of names and amounts of fines imposed on offenders of gambling suppression ordinances throughout at least 1915. For instances see ibid. 815 (1915: 17–8, 13 April).
44. In December, Ch'en's government passed the 'Provisional Ordinance Against Gambling' which was a harsh one: convicted gambling-house owners were punishable by death, or heavy fine, or imprisonment without term, and so on. For more detail, see Li Tsung-huang (1922: 203–4).
45. Report for the year 1923, London Missionary Society, Canton Station, 4 February 1924.
46. *Shen pao* (1923, 10 February). Some even travelled to Macao, which was described as a 'paradise for gambling' and a popular destination for gamblers from Canton and the Delta area whenever the official ban on gambling in Kwangtung was seriously enforced. Most weekends, the opium dens and gambling houses on this tiny Portuguese colony were tightly packed with customers from Kwangtung and Hong

Kong. As a result, Macao benefited much from Ch'en's anti-gambling policy: her opium and gambling revenues increased by almost 2 million yüan. Li Tsung-huang (1922: 206). This 'function' of Macao certainly predated the 1920s. In 1895, when a ban on *fan tan* and cricket fighting was still being strictly enforced in Canton and most parts of Kwangtung, Macao was reportedly prospering as a consequence: *fan tan* gamblers and cricket fight enthusiasts flocked to this enclave where its guest-houses were fully occupied, and the infamous business of prostitution was also benefiting. *Ching-hai tsung-pao* (2000), repr. of, 28 August 1895.

47. He complained that none of these officers was ever arrested. Li Tsung-huang (1922: 205).
48. For examples, *KCMKJP* 1923: 6, 7 and 10 August; 1925: 7, 22 May; 1925: 7, 1 June; 1925: 6, 5 June; 1923: 7, 27, August; 1925: 7, 11 May; 1925: 7, 19 June. *Shen pao* 1922, 12 August
49. By the winter of 1925, the major business quarter of Canton, the West Gate district, had been reportedly cleared of unlicensed gambling dens that operated variegated games of dices, dominos, and cards (*KCMKJP* 1925: 7, 11 May; 1925: 7, 17 June; 1925: 7, 18 July). This also indicated that the Canton administration did not allow the 'plague of gambling' went unchecked.
50. For more examples, see *HTJP* (1931: 1.3, 3 March); Wu Jui-lin (1934: 110); Yang Yü-shu, 'Kuang-tung tu huo shih' *CTKL* (1936: 267).
51. The *fan tan* woman case was adopted into a current affairs 'dragon-boat song' serialized in *HTJP*, (1927: 2.2, 4.4, 16 June).
52. 'Kuang-tung-shêng-kung-chu fêng ta-yüan-shuai ling chin chueh i-ch'ieh tsa-tu pao-kao', *CTKL* (1936: 227–8). Chinese Marxist historians uphold a likewise view of Sun's innocence. *KCPN* (1980: i. 272, 297); Chung-kuo jên-min chêng-chih-hsieh-shang-hui-i Kuang-tung-shêng Kuang-chou-shih wei-yüan-hui wên-shih tzu-liao wei-yüan-hui (1986: 219–21).
53. One source stated that Liu had informed Sun of the availability of the receipts from the public lottery amounting to several million *taels*. If the plot were successful, Sun could have seized that handsome source of money for buying arms. Harold Schiffrin (1968: 64–5).
54. *KCMKJP*, especially the July issues of 1925. The announcement appeared on 8 July 1925, p. 7.
55. According to Huang Tsun-shêng (1941: 60), 'Ch'ou hsiang' was the euphemism of gambling taxes.
56. In another account the amount totalled more than 17 million, see 'Yüeh-shêng li nien tu-hsiang shou-ju chih tiao-ch'a', *CTKL* (1936: 239).
57. For an eyewitness account of the incident, see Kenneth Rea (1977).
58. Telegrams and petitions condemning the proposal were submitted by many Overseas Chinese chambers of commerce, and *hui kuan*, to the provincial government, *NYSP* (1928, Aug. and Sept.).
59. In spite of the fact that Ch'en Ming-shu, the then Provincial Governor, had earlier outlawed the playing of *mahjong* (*NYSP*, 1928: 11, 13 September). Details on how this specific tax was levied can be read in the municipal gazette. It is interesting to note that in order to avoid abuse, all inspectors were ordered to wear an identification badge bearing a recent photograph. Moreover, this tax apparently targeted mainly the commercial establishments where *mahjong* was played; 'ordinary households and shops where *mahjong* is played occasionally' were exempted. Kuang-chou shih-chêng-fu, *Shih-chêng kung pao* 205 (1928: 44, 14 December).

60. The full text of the 'Three-year Plan' is in *Chêng fêng pan-yüeh k'an*, vol. 3–7 (1935).
61. Kuang-chou-shih chêng-hsieh (1987: 360). Wu Yü (1988: 144); author's interview with Mr Mok Hung.
62. For examples, see *KCHJP* (1933: 15, 25 February); *KPP* (1934: 6, 22 October); *KHP* (1931: 2.3, 21 May).
63. H. P. Burton from the Station of Canton, London Missionary Society Annual Report for the Year 1936, 4.
64. This 'Hang-k'ung kung-lu chien-hsieh chiang-chüan' was sold at ten yüan per ticket, and its first prize was amounted to a handsome 250,000 yüan *YHP* (1936: 12, 3 November). The other was a kind of number lottery called 'Central Saving' (*Chung-yang ch'u-ch'u hui*) which was operated in Shanghai with the full support of the Nationalist government *YHP* (1936: 7, 26 October).
65. A former Canton resident recounts that in the 1930s gambling was never interfered with on this piece of 'special territory'. The main carriageways on the island were lined with licensed opium dens and gambling houses. Hsü Chu-ch'êng (1982: 146).
66. Kuang-chou-shih shih-chêng-t'ing shê-hui-tiao-cha-ku (1927: 9). More than twenty of such establishments prospered there. And beyond occasionally reiterating the official ban, the police force on the island apparently did nothing. *HTJP* (1930: 2.2, 10 March).
67. For instances, see *HTJP* (1927: 4.2, 9 September; 1928: 1.3, 13 February; 1928: 1.3, 24 May).
68. The complexity of this issue is also cogently discussed by Newman (1972: esp. section VI), supported by data collected from his anthropological fieldwork in Britain. Also McMillen (1996: 15–20).
69. A lot of gambling parlours, opium dens, and floating bordellos along the Sino-Vietnamese coast were operated and controlled by pirates. And these gambling dens offered pirates points of contact with local bandits, whose cooperation made plundering easier. Dian H. Murray (1987: 23–4, 83–4).
70. The lack of further historical information on this community hampers us from ascertaining whether illicit or unlicensed gambling houses had ever existed there before 1932. This one founded in 1932 was apparently the first licensed gambling establishment in this settlement.
71. The residents' 'silence' on this issue should not be taken as evidence of the definitive absence of domestic problems caused by gambling activities. On the other hand, if such serious gambling-related domestic misbehaviour in the community had been as common as anti-gambling writings allege, it is unlikely that the whole research team could have failed to notice even one such case.
72. This assumption was widely shared by nearly all the contributors to the anti-gambling campaign journal in Canton in 1936. They believed, or feared, that with the inauguration of the total prohibition of gambling, all gamblers would face the serious problem of having nothing to do for entertainment. Extensive lists of suggested alternatives were proposed. For examples, see *CTKL* (1936: 99–115, 135–7, 146–7).
73. From these findings, from between the 1890s and 1970s, we learn of a strong positive relation between intensity of gambling activities and the degree of urbanization. That is to say, gambling is apparently more common in a city, which is economically prosperous, than in a rural community, for the simple reason that urbanites have more spare money to spend on betting than their rural counterparts. Wen-lang Li and Martin Smith (1976: 191–2).
74. 'Chiu-yüeh-fên ti Kuang-chou shê-hui' (*Chien yen piao* 1931: Vol. 1, no. 1, 22).

75. The earliest newspaper report about that kind of incident known to me at the time of this research, is dated 1885, from a local journal, *Shu pao* (1965: 443). It reported that a fight broke out between a gambler and a divan owner over an argument concerning betting money. The gambler, badly beaten up by the owner, subsequently enlisted the support of his neighbours, some of whom had firearms, and sought revenge on the perpetrator. Outnumbered, the owner of the divan, together with his employees, fled for their lives.
76. US Department of State, 893.40622, 'Suppression of Gambling in the province of Canton', from American Consulate General in Canton to the Secretary of State, Washington DC, 12 May 1911, p. 9.
77. This advertisement and announcement was commissioned by a Li-ch'êng kung-ssu in Canton. *KHP* (1919: 6, 4 September).
78. *Kuang-tung kung pao* 809 (27 March 1915), 22–3; 892 (3 July 1915), 29–31; 931 (18 August 1915), 28–31.
79. *Kuang-chou-shih shih-chêng hui-k'an* (1924: 277–9, 313–4).
80. Kuang-chou-shih shih-chêng-fu t'ung-chi ku (1929: 86–105).
81. Since most forms of gambling had been already legalized by that time, these culprits were probably arrested for running unlicensed gambling dens, or playing some specific kinds of game that were outlawed at the request of the gambling companies, or gambling in illicit houses in the city proper of Canton. For instance, Western-style poker games were outlawed at the request of the company that monopolized the running of *fan tan* dens in Canton. Wu Jui-lin (1934: 111).
82. A British Government study shows that only a small number of prison inmates have committed crimes to support their gambling activities. *Report of the Royal Commission on Betting, Lotteries, and Gambling* (1951), quoted from Weinstein and Deitch (1974: 143).
83. Kuang-chou-shih shih-chêng-t'ing shê-hui-tiao-cha-ku (1927: 9).
84. Kuang-chou-shih shih-chêng-fu t'ung-chi ku (1929: 72–3).
85. The five most favourite pastimes were visiting tea-houses, drinking rice wine, smoking Chinese tobacco, cigarette-smoking, and opium. Yü Chi-chung (1934: 64).
86. A similar situation was noted in British society in the early 1960s (Gorer, 1967: 80–7).
87. For examples, see Scheibe (2000: 145–61); Newman (1972: ch. 3, 172–5).
88. The author's interview with Mr Mok Hung. Mr Mok's reminiscences echo what many Western sociologists have been saying, since the late 19th century, about the positive correlation between economic status and propensity to gamble; gambling is not predominantly a lower-class phenomenon. Wen-lang Li and Martin Smith (1976: 195–9, 204–5).
89. By autumn 1933, for example, all the seven biggest gambling houses in Macao had already been closed down due to poor business, along with a number of high-class brothels. *KPP* (1933: 3.2, 29 November).
90. 'Yü k'o tan tu' (1907: 8–10).
91. For instances *Kuang-tung kung pao* 831 (1915, 22 April) and 931 (1915: 31, 18 August).
92. Although Sha-nan and Chiu Fêng-huang were in many respects rural settlements on the fringes of Canton proper, they fell within the administrative boundary of the city and their data, therefore, may be used as supplementary references to the gambling behaviour of the Cantonese.
93. According to a professional bookmaker who works for a floating casino based in Hong Kong, most gamblers he encounters are not the compulsive type since they are quite

capable of exercising self-control, whether winning or losing. In his experience, most losers would prefer to return another day rather than raise their wagers until they lose everything in a single evening (author's interview with Mr Lo Kuo-chiang).

94. A copy of this book, entitled *Chu Po-lo hsien-sheng chih-chia ko-yen*, which was published in Canton probably during late-Ch'ing or early-Republican times, is kept at the Regional Council Library in Shatin, Hong Kong. Since the late 1950s, an illustrated version of this book has been incorporated into the almanacs for the common people. Some Cantonese informants recall that parents used this book as a character-learning aid for their children. A young Hong Kong informant reminisces that when his father punished him for misconduct, he was sometimes ordered to copy this text with brush and ink.
95. 'Chin pu-huan' (n.d) p. 60.
96. *Hsien ch'i chien fu* (Canton: I wên t'ang). *Tu-tsai ku tan* (Canton: I wên t'ang, n.d.); *ching-chieh-fu ta ma tu-tsai* (Canton: Tsui ching t'ang, n.d.).
97. In a collection of popular folk songs of the Shao-hsing County area, at least three of them preach against gambling. Chiu Chün (1988: 164, 169, 171).
98. At least two scripts were directed at condemning gambling in Canton. *Huo-shao Ta-sha-tou* (The Burning of Ta-sha-tou) and *Tu hsi-chieh* (The Gambling World) were performed in the late 1900s. Ch'en Hua-hsin *YCYCTLH* (1983: 298–9).
99. The period of discontinuation varied, and depended on what kinds of game the violators were caught gambling at. For the 'flower lottery', the punishment was for life; for *fan tan* and 'pigeon lottery', it was ten years; for all other forms of gambling, five years. Ch'iao Kang I Yüan T'ang (1989: 405).
100. It is not known how effective was the ban.
101. However, the ban was said to be completely ignored a few years later. Ku Yü (1936: 268).
102. This seemingly was not something new to the 1920s. In 1895, a group of armed kinsmen under the leadership of a local gentleman vandalized a *fan tan* house that had been opened recently in his neighbourhood in the western part of the walled city of Canton; all the furniture and lamps in this house were destroyed. The bookmakers dared not intervene. (*HTJP*, 8 Feb. 1895).
103. *CTKL*, 1936: 228–30, 233–5, 251–69; Kuang-tung Chi-tu-chiao chu tu hui, *Chu tu hui chêng wên hua chieh hsiao* (Canton: 1925).
104. For a detailed discussion of all these tricks, see 'Chê-pan chê-pan tu-t'u pien-shu', and 'Chuan tu', in *Kuang-chou shê-hui tsa-chih* (*c.*1920s), i; Li Han-ch'ung, 'Hua-hui', *KTFCL* (1988: 116–19); Wu Yü (1988: 113–36). Chinese Marxist historians are keen to unveil the tricks that crooks employed to cheat their customers in the various forms of gambling. Their sensational way of describing the tricks, and their failure to cite their sources, reinforces the feeling that it is done more for ethical and political correctness than in the pursuit of truth.
105. Nevertheless, according to Li, cheating was still possible. But because of the risk and the technical difficulties involved, it is doubtful that cheating was commonplace. Hence, Li's argument may be motivated by his political 'duty' to follow the ideological line set by the CCP on the issue of gambling: that it is condemned as a social evil.
106. 'Chê-pan chê-pan' (*c.*1920s: 7).
107. For examples, see *CTKL* (1936: 56, 62, 64).
108. In Republican Shanghai, some gambling houses were also well known for their luxury decoration and grand services. For detail, see P'ing Chin-ya (1989: 117).

109. There was a group of crooks and loan-sharks who targeted young wastrels from wealthy families. *HTJP* (1927: 3.4, 16 August); Kuan Wên-ch'ing (1976: 114).
110. Most of these illicit gambling places were guarded by armed men who made their presence felt. For instances, see *KCMKJP* (1923: 6, 7 August; 1923: 6, 10 August; 1925: 9, 25 May; 1925: 7, 1 June). Sometimes, these armed guards could be so violent that they even overpowered the local police. A report from 1880 showed that a local crook, who ran a ring of illicit gambling houses in Canton, was so powerful that his illegitimate business could operate publicly without even the need to bribe the local *yamen* runners or officials. A number of times he and his gang succeeded in defeating armed attempts by the local authorities to remove them *Shen pao*, (29 July 1880).
111. Throughout the 1880s and 1900s, there were occasional reports about such serious and open violations of the state's regulation on gambling, and about collusion between unlicensed bookmakers and local officials or *yamen* rank-and-file. For examples, see *Shen pao*, 8 January 1880, 29 July 1880, 3 October 1880, 16 August 1884; *CSL* (1995 vi: 351–2, 453–4).
112. In order to attract customers, their entrances were decorated with gasoline lamps or electric light globes. Yang Yin-shen, *Chung-kuo yu-i*, (1935: 101). During the heyday of uncontrollable gambling in Canton, all gaming dens were guarded enthusiastically by armed soldiers. For example, see *Shen pao*, 1922, 12 August. Many unlicensed gambling houses in Ho-nan also operated with the full knowledge of the local police who apparently could be spotted near these places (*HTJP* 1930: 2.2, 28 February).
113. Harry Franck (1925: 250–1) wrote that 'kidnapping, assassination, unjust punishment, military confiscation, wanton destruction, were the common lot' for the Chinese to suffer in Canton.
114. Reports of violent crimes in Canton were plentiful in *HTJP* for this period.
115. For examples, the drawings of two *fan tan* gambling houses, one in Macao in 1873 and the other in Kowloon, Hong Kong in 1889, can be read in the reprint of a contemporary illustrative magazine, *The Graphic*, in John Warner compiled (1981: 80–2).
116. For examples, see *YHP* (1932: 1, 14 November); *KHP* (1929: 2.3, 6 October); (1931: 1.2, 20 May). There had been attempts to rob a gambling house; but cases of this kind were apparently few and far between. One such case involved a lunatic who, carrying no offensive weapon, rushed into a *fan tan* house and ran away with a few hundred dollars. Staff members later apprehended him. *KHP* (1931: 2.4, 31 January).
117. For example, when three gamblers fought among themselves because of a quarrel over a small amount of stake-money, local policemen were quick to respond to this disruption of public order and had them apprehended (*KHP* 1929: 2.4, 6 October).
118. Kuang-chou-shih shih-chêng-t'ing shê-hui-tiao-cha-ku (1927: 9).
119. Kuang-tung-shêng chêng-fu ts'ai-chêng-ting (1934: 256).
120. In his view, the strict censorship imposed on Cantonese opera music, dancing, and movies, and the closing down of some of the parks in Canton, were alleged to be accountable for the serious shortage of 'proper entertainment' for the citizens who eventually sought entertainment from the 'five vicious' forms of pastime. Yün Shêng *CTKL* (1936: 166).
121. In Hong Kong in the same period, horse racing was commonly seen as a kind of 'cultured gambling' for the Western expatriates and the so-called 'high-class Chinese' in the Colony. With a minimum wager of 5 dollars—enough to cover the

living expenses of an ordinary citizen for a month—it was an expensive form of gambling as well. (Lu Yen 1981: 137–9).

122. In some villages in present-day Shun-tê County, the disappearance of this apparently lucrative source of local income is lamented as one of the main reasons for the failure to revive traditional ostentatious ways of celebrating the birthdays of local patron-deities. (Author's interviews with village elders in 1990.)

123. Kuo Shuang-lin and Hsiao Mei-hua (1995: 195–7); Kuang-tung-shêng chêng-fu ts'ai-chêng-ting (1934: 974).

124. This, however, raised the concern of some anti-gambling supporters. *Sze yin ch'i*, *c.*1920s: 9–10; Li Han-ch'ung 1988 *KTFCL*.

125. *Sze yin ch'i*, *c.*1920s p. 9; 'Kuang-chou tu-po hsüan-k'o shih' (A History of Gambling in Canton) in *KCMKJP* 1925, 2 & 3 June, '*Hsiao Kuang-chou*' column.

126. 'Tu lieh chih tan-kuan' (*c.*1920s: 16–17).

127. For a description on how these forms of 'gambling' were played, see John Henry Gray (391–4).

128. Kuang-chou-shih shih-chêng-t'ing shê-hui-tiao-cha-ku (1927: 9).

129. *Tan-tsao-hsiang tzu-chih-hui pao-kao-shu* (1925: 11). In the social survey on a suburban village in Canton, its author classified gambling and opium smoking under the section entitled 'Entertainment' (*yü-lê*). See Wu Jui-lin (1940: 288).

130. It was noted that in Macao, some Chinese gentlemen visited a gambling-house to enjoy a puff of opium, and gambled a bit for leisure. Rich wastrels with their concubines enjoyed the excitement unleashed by gambling, no matter if they won or lost. (Lilius, *I Sailed*, 1930: 79).

131. *Mahjong* is said to have been the invention of the T'ai-p'ing soldiers in the 1850s. Gradually, the game became widely played in the coastal provinces of Kwangtung and Fukien. (Yang Yin-shen 1935: 98–9). Writing in 1919, Tsou Lu (1936: 243) pointed out that in terms of the nature of the game and the amount of stake usually involved, *mahjong*, compared with other kinds of gambling such as *fan tan*, was less harmful.

132. Kuang-chou-shih shih-chêng-t'ing shê-hui-tiao-cha-ku (1927: 9).

133. To be allowed to gamble at a particular private clubhouse and to join the small, informal, circle of businessmen and merchants identified with that particular club was regarded as a privilege (Sung Yü 1989: 49).

134. 'Chin yu hsu mahjong sung-tsung chê', *YHP*, 1936: 2, 15 September.

135. 'Kuang-chou-shih Chiu-lou ch'a-shih tung-yeh kung-hui cheng', *CTKL* (1936: 186–9); 'Ching-chiu ch'ih-ling Yüeh shêng-fu ch'i-chin mahjong pai', Kuo-shih kuan archive, 055/0246/0788–0792, dated 1 September 1936.

136. The origins of the late-Ch'ing version of *mahjong* were believed to be closely related to a historical anecdote concerning the founder of the Ch'ing Dynasty. For detail, see *Fo-shan chung-i-hsiang chih* (1923: ch. 11, 17–18).

137. From a leader in *Shih-min jih pao*, cited in *CTKL* (1936: 165).

138. 'Sze-fang hsü chi', *Piao tu ch'ui hsin chi* (1910: 7–8) '*hsieh wên*'.

139. According to the author's interviews with villagers in the Canton Delta, and in Canton during 1989–90.

140. These games could be dated to at least the 1860s as they were recorded by Gray (1972: 391–4).

141. Adults also enjoyed playing similar rustic forms of 'gambling'. For details about these games, see Pao, 'Kuang-tung fêng-t'u' (1936: 12). Contemporary Pekingese

also held a similar attitude towards cards and table games. See Sidney Gamble, *Peking: A Social Survey* (New York: 1921), p. 223.

142. The scale of this game varied from place to place, depending on the locality authorities. A small-scale fight could be run inside a family clan hall, see *HTJP* 1929: 4.2, 23 August, while a large and well-organized one, like the one held yearly in Macao, could last 40 days and nights and attracted many enthusiasts and connoisseurs from Canton and other parts of the province. *HTJP* (1936: 2.4, 10 August).

143. An interesting analogy is with 17th-century French nobles who gambled for high stakes and stood ready to lose 'nobly', in order to demonstrate their contempt for money, and their prestige as the ideal 'honnête homme'. Thomas Kavanagh (1993: 44–51).

144. Wu Yü et al. (1988: 103–4). Another animal-related gamble was the pigeon-flying competition, which was highly popular during the mid-Ch'ing (Li T'iao-yüan, *Nan Yüeh pi chi* (1937), pp. 2–3). Quail fights were also common in late-Ch'ing Canton. For detail, see *Nan-hai hsien chih* (1910: ch. 4, 21–2).

145. In Southern Sung Hang-chou, the government lifted the ban on gambling for three days during Chinese New Year in order to satisfy public demand. During these three days, all walks of life gambled with great pleasure, seeing it as part of their New Year celebrations. In some parts of the city, gambling-houses stood side by side with merchandise booths, theatres, restaurants, and cabarets. The whole ambience was gay and festive (Mêng Yüan-lao, 1987: 267). A modern writer also points out that casinos provide their players with many pleasurable experiences, one of them being meeting or making friends there (David Spanier 1987: 129–46).

146. This cult was and is best shown by the almost universal Chinese worship of gods of wealth (Basil Alexéiev 1928: 1–11).

147. A Cantonese writer wrote that many destitute men spent their last coins on gambling mainly because this was the only option that might multiply their meagre resources (Yang Lu, *CTKL* 1936: 234–5).

148. Such a longing for a windfall was certainly not unique to the Chinese; it was, and is, a universal phenomenon. In the United States and Western Europe, gambling, specifically the state lottery, has always been popularly perceived as an affordable source of hope for tens of thousands of betters, as a number of academic monographs on this subject have pointed out. See Otto Newman (1972); William Eadington and Charles Thomas (1976); Karl Scheibe (2000); Edmund Bergler (1957); Charles Clotfelter and Philip Cook (1991).

149. *Hui-t'u tseng-kuang yen-wên* (n.d.: 7). Many old residents of Canton or Hong Kong recall that they had read this book as a text at their traditional private schools during the Republican period. Many of the popular sayings in this book, including the one cited here, are still widely used in the Cantonese-speaking region. The aptitude of this proverb was so widely accepted that it was ridiculed in an anti-gambling folk song. *Kai-liang Ling-nan chi-shih* (n.d.: 60).

150. It should be noted that the Cantonese ways of playing the lottery were markedly different from those of their modern Western counterparts, which are basically lucky draws of numbers. Cantonese lotteries embody more complicated, but also more interesting, rules. For details, see Tsou Lu, *CTKL* (1936: 240–3); Chu Hsiu-hsia (1977: 40–1); Tzu-hang-shih, *Kuang-chou chih-nan* (1919: ch. 4, 7); Liu Tsai-su (1926: 116–8); Wu Yü et al. (1988: 98–111). Another detailed description of how these different forms of lottery were played can be read in Kuo Shuang-lin and Hsiao Mei-hua (1995: 185–99).

151. In order to win the confidence of their clients, these bet-collectors also acted as invigilators at the drawing of lots. Li Han-ch'ung, 'Hua-hui', *KTFCL*, 114.
152. Modern findings in England and Sweden conclude that gamblers are as aware as non-players of the unprofitable nature of gambling. But when they play a lottery, they pursue a hope rather than an expectation of large financial reward. (Weinstein and Deitch (1974: 138); John Dunkley (1985: 15–17)).
153. The drawing of lots has a long history in Western civilization. The word 'lot' is believed to come from a Teutonic root *hleut*, meaning a pebble that was cast to settle arguments arising over the division of property. In Jewish history one finds accounts of selection by lots in order to determine who would kill the survivors of sieges. In Greek mythology the distribution of the world among the gods was decided by lot (Antoine Murphy, 'Is a national lottery just a ticket?' *Financial Times Weekend*, 21–2 May 1994).
154. For examples, see *KPP* (1928: 6, 24 March), the section of advertisements.
155. This popular demand for gambling especially during the New Year times had apparently a long history. In the capital city of Southern Sung, the ban on gambling was lifted for three days during Lunar New Year, Mêng Yüan-lao (1987: 267).
156. According to a contemporary ethnographer, almost everyone in Canton gambled at home on New Year's Day. Liu Wan-chang (1972: 26), also Ana Maria Amaro (1988: 87–9).
157. For examples, see *KCTC* (1934: 17); *KPP* 1928, 24 March, the section of advertisements on page 6.
158. For details on how some gamblers resorted to these mystical means for tips, see Li Han-ch'ung *KTFCL*, 120–2.
159. This source of hope was apparently classless, because the rich were also keen betters on lotteries. Their wagers were far more substantial than were those of their counterparts among the masses. Li Han-ch'ung, 'Hua-hui' *KTFCL*, 116.
160. Some temples in Shun-tê County still retain such paraphernalia donated by winners of 'pigeon lottery' or 'flower lottery' in pre-Communist days.
161. This is also the case in the West (Robert Herman 1967: vii); Geoffrey Gorer (ibid.: 86).
162. For example, in an anti-gambling essay published in a compendium of works dedicated to the cause of eradicating the 'four vices' (namely prostitution, opium smoking, gambling, and alcoholism), its author wrote that the fate of gamblers, though predictable, fell within a diversity of patterns. Although some were 'predictably' doomed and ended up penniless, suicidal, and even resorting to theft, there were also those lucky ones who were able to make handsome fortunes from it and therefore could enjoy all the luxuries of life, or buy themselves a title and join the world of officialdom (*Sze yin ch'i*, 1907: 39). Another anti-gambling essayist warned his readers of the dangers of winning, which did happen to a gambler from time to time, but would inevitably lure him or her to plunge further into the trap of heavy gambling until he or she lost everything (*CTKL*, 1936: 139–40).
163. A Chinese sociologist warned that although poverty had reached crisis level, the government had done very little to alleviate the hardship of the people. Chang Chên-chih (1929: ch. 6). A group of British sociologists has found that gambling offers an outlet for competitiveness and aggression. It can also provide an

opportunity for problem-solving and decision-making on a small scale for people whose lives offer few such opportunities generally (Downes et al., cited in John Dunkley (1985: 14)).

164. In the County of Lung-meng, there was a well-known pool called 'Woman Gambler Pool' (*Tu fu t'an*). For the story about the origin of this name, see Ch'ü Ta-chün (1974: 144).
165. The most sensitive of these words were the homophones of *shu* (to lose) and *kan* (dry and hollow). 'Book' (*shu*, a homophone of the *shu* above) was oftenly deliberately pronounced as *yin* (to win). For more examples, see Liu Wan-chang (1937: 7–8).
166. For examples, see *NFJP* (1953: 2, 13 March; 1954: 2, 27 April; 1957: 3, 26 June; 1990: 2, 16 March; 1991: 2, 24 January; 1991: 2, 15 February).
167. There are abundant newspaper reports on the resurgence of lottery and the fever it has unleashed among the populace. For examples, see *Ming pao* (6 October 2000, 3 November 2001, 28 September 2001); *South China Morning Post* (20 February 1999).

CHAPTER 5

1. For typical Chinese official views on this subject, see Wu Yü et al. (1988: 400–15); also Shang-hai wên-shih tzu-liao (1989: 226–38, 263–4).
2. Biographical accounts of contemporary prostitutes provide us with abundant examples to support this observation. For instance, Ti Ti, a high-class prostitute in Canton, came from a respectable family. She was well educated: in her free time she read Chinese classics and self-improving English textbooks. She entered the business after quarrelling with her parents and running away; the brothel had become her refuge. She was eventually traced by her family and was 'forcibly' taken home, *KPP* (1928: 8, 2 May). Another prostitute, Hui Ching, from a high-class brothel, had reportedly come from a wealthy family. Although her mother was one of the nineteen concubines of a powerful businessman, she had never been mistreated for this reason. She became a prostitute mainly because of her dissipated 'romantic' life, *KPP* (1928: 8, 9 April). For the detailed case of Purple Orchid, another high-class prostitute in Canton in the early 1930s, see Lo Li-ming (1962: iv, 7–71).
3. The Po Leung Kuk in Hong Kong, a semi-official charitable organization since 1878, houses an archive in which biographical records of its inmates, mainly girls and women whom they tried to 'rescue' from this ill-famed business, provide us with a rare picture of the backgrounds of these women. For a detailed study of the Kuk, see Henry Lethbridge (1978), Elizabeth Sinn (1994), and Po Leung Kuk (1978). On the diverse backgrounds of prostitutes and the complex causes of prostitution in Canton and Hong Kong during the late-19th and early-20th centuries, see Virgil Ho (2001: 109–10).
4. It is interesting to note that the relative unimportance of 'poverty' as a genuine cause of prostitution might account for the small number of low-class prostitutes in this part of China. For example, in Swatow, a major port in eastern Kwangtung, low-class whores constituted less than one-third of all prostitutes there. The situation resembled that of Canton in this period, *KPP* (1928: 8, 24 May).

5. The accuracy of the following cited statistics should not be taken for granted. They may, nonetheless, help—especially when better statistics are not available—to give a rough idea of the situation of prostitution in this period. For an interesting discussion on the similar problem with numbers in the scene of Shanghai, see Christian Henriot (2001: 115–21).
6. This ethnic prejudice towards and misconception regarding the Tanka women persisted throughout the Republican period. For more detail about this discriminatory attitude, see Wu Jui-lin (1934*a*: 9); Ch'en Hsü-ching (1946: 124–5).
7. *Kuang-chou-shih êrh-shih-i nien jên-k'ou tiao-cha pao kao* (1933: 'statistics' (n.p.)). According to the statistics provided by the Public Security Bureau, however, there were only 33 licensed floating brothels in Canton in 1932, though the accuracy of this figure is very dubious. Ch'en Hsü-ching (1946: 127).
8. The authors did not spell out clearly the proportions of the two categories of prostitute. Due to the casualness in preparing this set of data, it should be used only as a rough guide rather than as reliable statistics.
9. It is also interesting to note from this document that at least one-third of the licensed brothels did not keep any minors who would be eventually trained into prostitution. This contradicts what many historians claim, that children were commonly raised by madams or procuresses to become prostitutes, and that accounted for a major source in Canton.
10. A recent historical study shows that according to a 1930 survey by the Social Bureau, there were 111 brothels and brothel boats, and 1,172 prostitutes. Elizabeth Remick, 'Taxing Prostitution in Republican Guangzhou' (2002: 10).
11. From a survey by the Social Bureau of Canton Municipal Government in 1926, cited by Wang Shu-nu (1988: 333). An unofficial estimate put the total number of prostitutes in Canton in 1931 at about 5,000. *HTJP* (1931: 1.4, 14 April). Another unofficial estimate in the late 1920s was 10,000. *NYSP* (1928: 24, 20 September).
12. A well-known Cantonese writer, Chiu-chung-fêng-fu, deeply lamented the demise of brothel 'high culture' and the fading of that traditional link between well-educated courtesans and scholars in Imperial China. He recorded, out of nostalgia, the romantic life stories of some of the well-known Cantonese courtesans of the Ch'ing period. *Ling-nan fêng-yüeh shih* (*LNFY*) (*c.*1930s); also 'Chu-kiang hua-shih', *KCLPL* (1934).
13. Comparable descriptions can be read from Yang Chieh-tseng and Ho Yüan-nan (1988). A literary and vivid rendition of this official campaign to reform prostitutes is written by Su T'ung in his *Hung fên* (1992: 5–66).
14. For instance, Chien Ch'iu et al., 'Ch'ang-chi chi heh-mo', (1975: vii, 6236); Sue Gronewold (1985: 67); Liu Fu-ching and Wang Ming-k'un (1992: 144).
15. Reports of unlicensed brothel owners, or inmates, in Hong Kong and Canton being fined for their operation can be found in *HTJP* throughout the 1910s.
16. But the causes of prostitution in this part of South China were apparently much more diverse than that. Virgil Ho's 'To Laugh at a Penniless Man' (2001: 102–4). In fact, this image of prostitution was not invented by Chinese historians committed to the Communist cause; it was those reformist writers of the May Fourth period who took the lead. To make these 'poor girls' look even more pathetic, the prostitute subjects in most of these 'realist' novels almost always end up abandoned by their clients or lovers, or, if they work clandestinely, imprisoned. Tien Chung-chi and Sun Ch'ang-hsi (1987: 166).

17. It should be noted that this short story was written in 1935 and is therefore relevant to the discussion on the perception of prostitutes by the intellectuals at that time.
18. Similar stereotyped views were also commonly held by some Victorian writers. Fraser Harrison (1979: 244–6).
19. Contemporary Chinese movies, such as the 1930s big hits *Ma-liu t'ien-shih* (Street Angel) and *Hsin-nü* (The Prostitute), also depicted low-class prostitutes in this light. Tu Yün-chih (1972: 134); Jay Leyda (1972: 106).
20. This fits well into what Dikötter (1995: 126–37) has said about the medical discourse of disease in Republican cities.
21. The courtesan's guide (1931) contains both photographs and short descriptions of some of these 'fallen angels' in Hong Kong. On contemporary local newspapers such as *HTJP, KPP, YHP*, magazines such as *Chu-kiang hsing-ch'i hua-pao* and *Hsiang hua hua-pao* and so on, articles on this theme can easily be found.
22. A woman prostituting herself to remain filial to her parents is, however, no fiction. Arthur Wolfe's research shows that 'the tolerant treatment accorded former prostitutes reflects a feeling that as filial daughters they deserve sympathy. They may have engaged in an immoral profession, but only for the sake of their parents'. Arthur Wolfe, 'The Women of Hai Shan', in Margery Wolfe and Roxane Witke (1975: 102–4).
23. On a stone plaque recording the identity of donors in Tung Shan T'ang, one of Macao's largest charity hall, names of brothels and individual prostitutes are carved alongside that of respectable citizens. Donations from this particular group of women were, and are, perceived as good as those from the other.
24. Examples of similar deeds committed by prostitutes in Shanghai are mentioned in Henriot (2001: 62–5).
25. This issue also contains reports of similar fund-raising campaign by prostitutes in the Canton Delta city of Kiang-mên.
26. This issue has been discussed in detail elsewhere. Virgil Ho 'To Laugh at a Penniless Man' (2001).
27. This songbook was widely acclaimed by many scholars and prominent officials who composed congratulatory poems and essays as prefaces to it. T'ang Shou-i, a prominent statesman, wrote a prefatory inscription for its title. The views in the book may therefore have been shared by many of his contemporaries. Li Ma-chu, Preface, *HYOC* (*c.* 1926: 1); Clementi (1904: 1); Hsü Fu-chin (1948: 60, 63).
28. For examples, see *HYOC* (*c.*1926: 2–4, 'Hsin Yu kao' (1921 drafts)). For 19th-century examples, see Clementi (1904: 5).
29. 'Tso wo-ti ni-fen lao-chu', *HYOC* (*c.*1926: 11, 'Hsin Yu kao' (1921 drafts)).
30. 'Kuan li tu wu chu tso' (ibid. 10–11, 'Kuei Hai kao' (1923 drafts)).
31. But low-class prostitutes were said to be still pitiable because most of them were physically forced to work in this profession, K'ung Fu-an *KCLPL* (1934: 15–6).
32. A Hong Kong-based Chinese daily also occasionally published poems and prose pieces praising the cultured quality of some of those women. For examples, *HTJP* (1911, 31 October; 1912, 3 February). These instances indicate that such romanticized memories of the past appeared at least since the early 1910s.
33. For a detailed discussion on this favourable popular image, see Virgil Ho's 'To Laugh at a Penniless Man' (2001: 115–27).
34. During the late-Ch'ing period, second-class brothels were usually heavily guarded by 'chicken keepers' (*k'an chi lao*). The girls were not allowed to 'go out onto the street'

without the permission of the madam, or unless 'accompanied' by a maidservant. Wang Shu-nu (1935: 305).

35. If a popular courtesan was seen to be falling in love with a poor scholar, certain money-minded madams might refuse to provide further services to him. If this failed to persuade the girl, a madam might flog her, or even have her moved to another city, and desperate courtesans sometimes resorted to suicide. Liu Ying, 'Chu-kiang ch'i yü chi' *LNFY*, 76–9, 84–5.
36. They traded 'love' for money to prostitutes. Reports of prostitutes who fell victim to these crooks abound in vernacular magazines and local newspapers such as *Chu-kiang hsing-ch'i hua-pao* 1–7 (1927), *HTJP*, and *KPP*. In Republican Shanghai, these swindlers were said to be commonly patronized by famous and well-off prostitutes. Hai-shang-chüeh-wu-shêng (1939: 145–7).
37. Some allegedly common forms of torture imposed by brothel madams on disobedient prostitutes included forcing long candle-sticks into their vaginas, and using a cat to scratch their private parts. Although there is no way to confirm the commonality of these inhuman forms of punishment, writers on this subject take these sensational allegation as true and typical instances. For examples, see Chien Ch'iu et al. (1975: 6228–9, 6238–9); Ts'un Shih, *KTFCL* (1988: 238–43); Wu Yü et al. (1988: 448–63). For more examples of this stereotype image of 'wicked madams', see Ch'en Li-chu et al. (1991: 547, 584–5).
38. In most brothels, an intimate pseudo-family atmosphere was deliberately created, the inmates usually addressing each other with kinship terms. Sue Gronewold 1985: 8–10; Yü Chiao-ch'ing (1909: 21).
39. During this period, many better-off courtesans who dressed fashionably did their daily shopping at expensive department stores, and enjoyed afternoon tea at luxury hotels in the Central district of Hong Kong. Sung Yü (1989: 207, 329–30).
40. A similar description of these luxurious, high-class floating brothels was made by a 19th-century French anthropologist quoted in Fernando Henriques (1962: 256).
41. It should be noted that this source is not dated. But judging by its content, it is probably a work of the mid- or late-Ch'ing.
42. In a late 19th-century popular novel, the bed-chamber of a 'salt-water girl' (low-class Tanka prostitute who served foreign sailors), is described as nicely decorated with a number of Western household objects, which startles the young protagonist who is crazy about things Western. Wu Wu-yao (1986: 388–9).
43. *Kuang-tung ching-ch'a-t'ing chu-t'i chi-kuan chi-t'ing chi ch'ang-chi kuei-tsê* (Caton: n.p. *c.*1920), Clause 29.
44. Photographic portraits of high-class Cantonese courtesans suggest that they took pride in their Western outlook and expensive Western apparel, *Hsiang hua hua-pao* (1929: 2); *Hua ying* (1931).
45. Her obscene remarks were reportedly as follows: 'Who the hell is this mean man who is disturbing my sleep? If you want to find someone to fuck, you can go find some one else [in this brothel]. Or, you can make a left turn to the Fresh Water Fish Market (an area notorious for low-class brothels) where you can pick a whore for fucking...'.
46. A big 'flower banquet' (*k'ai ta-t'ing*) of this kind was expensive. In the early 1920s, when an ordinary worker earned less than 30 yüan a month, such a banquet cost 30–80 yüan a table. Yet an ordinary banquet held at a high-class brothel still cost about 30 yüan for a table. Tzu-hang-shih (1919: chs. 4, 5). A big banquet on a 'flower

boat' was even more expensive and spectacular. It was customary to invite twenty courtesans to serve wine and sing at such a banquet, which usually lasted from the early evening until sunrise (Wang Shu-nu, 306).

47. This was also the case in Shanghai (Hai-shang-chüeh-wu-shêng, 107).
48. Examples of rich brothel-goers in Hong Kong and Canton in this period who spent large amounts of money on pleasing their favourite prostitutes abound in Lo Li-Ming's book. Prominent instances are i. 74–9; iii. 1–36. But this was not exclusively a Cantonese phenomenon. In early Republican Peking, for example, 'it is not uncommon for an official to spend as much as $700 to $800 in gifts, banquets, and forms of entertainment before he can go further than ordinary relations with one of these famous girls'. Gamble (1921: 252).
49. In the latter instance, the disturbance was caused by a row between an off-duty soldier and a group of brothel-goers who wanted to be entertained by a prostitute they all liked. The soldier was outnumbered and beaten up. When he returned with a larger group later, he was dismayed that the party had already gone. He then turned his frustration on the madam and the prostitute by beating them up and destroying some of the furniture. Policemen were called in to settle the dispute. The vengeful soldier, however, was sent away without charge. It should be noted that this soldier did not originally look for trouble in the brothel. The subsequent attack on the inmates was not behaviour to be tolerated from a brothel-goer. More examples of brothel disturbances are provided in the subsection 'Means of Self-Protection' in this chapter.
50. *KPP* contains plenty of reports on the movements of famous sing-song girls and their 'maternal uncle group' fans. These supporters, however, were always disparaged in these reports for being too obsequious and undignified towards their idols.
51. Sometimes, the cheated prostitutes resorted to suicide, *HTJP* (1928: 3.3, 13 June).
52. I have not found any record of how madams and prostitutes in Canton divided the income. Those prostitutes who were pawned to a brothel or brought up by their 'false mothers' might receive very little reward for their work. Hai-shang-chüeh-wu-shêng (1939: 20–1, 25–9). On the situation in Taiwan in the 1960s, see Barnard Wolfe (1980: 36). French archival materials on Shanghai, however, contain vivid records of how the income of a brothel in the French Concession was divided among the different parties. Henriot (2001: ch. 10).
53. Even as late as the late 1930s, most unskilled workers' joint income, if they were married, was generally $14–$30 a month (Gillingham, 79–82).
54. For comparable cases in Shanghai, see Henriot (2001: 154–61).
55. This case aroused considerable interest and, as a result, was adopted as the theme of two pieces of humourous writing published in the same daily. *HTJP* (1911, 4 August and 23 August).
56. The magazine *Hua ying* was mainly sold at the major brothels in Hong Kong.
57. This was mainly because most brothel-goers were reluctant to patronize prostitutes who were known to have fancied Cantonese opera actors: they did not want the money they spent courting these girls to be pocketed by the latter's paramours (*Chu-kiang hsing-ch'i hua-pao* (1927: iii. 5–6; iv. 7; vi. 5–8).
58. K'u Tieh, 'Ling-chi fêng-liu nieh' (The Sin of Dissipation Between an Actor and a Prostitute) was serialized in *HTJP* (1927: 3.4, 21 July and 30 July).
59. This corroborates the recollections of a former resident of Republican Kwangtung, Mr Ferdinand Hoo-an, who was interviewed by the author in 1990. It is, however,

impossible to confirm the general identity of these admirers of Mr Ma. This observation may have been based on the observer's life-experiences, intuitions, and knowledge of popular culture in Canton. The fact is though that these female fans dressed so lavishly, behaved in such 'an uncultured fashion', and spent their money so frivolously that contemporary observers felt certain they knew who they were. A close friend and colleague of Ma's reminisces that the latter was a womanizer and that his girlfriends included the concubines of wealthy men, famous and well-off prostitutes, dancing girls, and so on. The above observation on Ma may, therefore, not be totally groundless. It should also be noted that he was by no means the only opera star who was popular among these types of women. Ch'en Fei-nung (1982: 74–6).

60. For details of these plans and her story, see *Chu-kiang hsing-ch'i hua-pao* (1927: iv. 5).
61. For instance, madams were not allowed to force their girls to solicit customers at brothel gateways; all prostitutes, moreover, had the right to leave the trade any time, or they could seek help from the police (*Kuang-tung ching-ch'a-t'ing chu-t'i chi-kuan chi-t'ing chi ch'ang-chi kuei-tsê c.*1920).
62. Throughout the Republican period and by 1937, there were only two cases of open protest against the prostitution tax by prostitutes and madams in Canton. Elizabeth Remick (2002: 31–4). On the interesting observation of the absence of materials recording any link between local triads and prostitution, both Professor Remick and I shared the same view, and the same surprise, during our archival research on the subject. The situation in Shanghai, however, was very different. Henriot (2001: 159–60).
63. In some contexts, the threat of pollution also applies to women (Göran Aijmer, 'Birth and Death in China' (1984: 8–10)).
64. Collective action by prostitutes was certainly not a uniquely Canton phenomenon: similar known organizations also existed in many major county cities in Kwangtung and Macao. These bodies had staged strikes, or even taken up arms occasionally, to react against unfair treatment of their girls (such as obligatory examination of prostitutes' bodies in Macao), or unreasonable demands for additional taxes by the authorities, throughout the early decades of the Republican period (*HTJP*, 1911, 9 October; 1913, 5 May; 1919: 1.3, 23 April; 1924: 1.3, 14 May; *YHP*, 1934: 1, 27 March). In another case, the arrest of a brothel-owner in Fo-shan sparked off a strike of all brothels in this prosperous commercial city (*KPP* 1928: 6, 24 Apr.).
65. As with most trades in Canton, brothels were concentrated, or segregated, in certain areas. Chou Hsia-min, 'Kuang-chou hsia-chi', *KCTC* (1934: 8–9); Wang Shu-nu (1988: 265–7, 302–4); K'ung Fu-an, 'Chu-kiang', *KCLPL* (1934: 13–7). Similar patterns were seen in Shanghai. Henriot (2001: ch. 9).
66. For instance, on the first Full Moon of the new year, many of them congregated and worshipped at a popular Taoist shrine in Canton. Liu Wan-chang, 'Pa Kung' (1928: 30).
67. The example of Pien Pien, a prostitute who had worked for six different high-class establishments in Canton and county cities in Kwangtung in a short period of six months, was reportedly an unusual one. This report also stated that it was most natural for a prostitute to leave an old brothel to work in another house that offered her better income and working conditions. *KPP* (1928: 8, 4 May).
68. This was best illustrated by the example of four high-class prostitutes in Canton. One of them, Ling Ling, though married to a rich man in the United States, was eager to

maintain their old friendship by travelling a long way back to visit her 'sisters'. *KPP* (1928: 8, 17 April and 20 April).

69. Most courtesans looked forward to being married off to their 'ideal' clients. This was one of the most attractive ways to leave this profession. Chou Yu-liang, 'Chu-kiang' (1935: 87–90).
70. A similar situation existed in traditional India. According to *Kama Sutra*, the first object of a courtesan is to obtain money from her customer. An entire chapter is devoted to 'ways of extracting money from a lover, such as falsely alleging that her property had been lost, or simulating illness and charging the cost of imaginary treatment'. Hilary Evans (1979: 80–1).
71. In this period, modern and expensive department stores in Hong Kong were said to be patronized by many fashionably and lavishly dressed prostitutes who went there every afternoon for strolling or shopping. Sung Yü (1989: 207).
72. 'P'ao kuo tou-fu', *HYOC*, 'Hsin Yu kao' (1921 drafts), 23.
73. 'Mi ku hua wu ken lao tzu', *HYOC*, 'Kuei Hai kao' (1923 drafts), 13.
74. 'Huan hua-chai', *HYOC*, 'Hsin Yu kao' (1921 drafts), 23.
75. *HYOC*, 'Hsin Yu kao' (1921 drafts), 34, 52, 266, 308, 313, 402–6.
76. Some prostitutes apparently made good use of the affluence, relative physical freedom, and free time that the job brought them. For example, one popular courtesan in Canton took up such 'upper-class' hobbies as horse-riding, swimming, and dancing (Hao-chi-shêng, 'Lêng Hung yü nan-hsin' (1928: 2).
77. This is an area that deserves further historical inquiry. At the moment there are at least two opposed views on the issue. The official Chinese view tells us that all these poor prostitutes were happy to see themselves liberated by the present regime, and that they were enthusiastic about the reform programme in which they took part actively and happily, see Yang Chieh-tseng and Ho Wan-nan (1988); Gail Hershatter (1997: ch. 12). This is, no doubt, a retrospective view. Contemporary newspaper reports of the early 1950s, despite state control, somehow hinted at a slightly different picture from that of Yang and Ho. The report notes that many of the rounded-up prostitutes did worry about the life in front of them because they were afraid of the harsh regime of the reform camps: imprisonment, poor food, uncomfortable sleeping quarters, and hard labour. However, the reporter continues, these were all unsubstantiated rumours spreading eagerly by KMT spies. The reports goes on to elaborate on the reasonably good life that these former prostitutes had had at the reform camp in Canton (*NFJP* 1951 17 October). Whether or not this is fact is hard to determine, but it does reveal that many of these prostitutes were not happy with the state which forcibly removed them from a job that many of them did not dislike, rounded them up like criminals, and coerced them into a somewhat strange life of regimentation. The reform camp in Canton might be as good as the newspaper report claimed, but not all the similar camps in the 'new China' shared the same professedly high standard of comfort. Su T'ung (1992), in his short story *Hung fen* reconstructs the lives of a group of prostitutes undergoing harsh reformation at a spartan-style labour camp. This story provides us with a flesh-and-blood account of the physical and psychological difficulties that some of these inmates could have faced under the reform campaign. The story is said to be based on the real experiences of two former prostitutes, and hence not completely fictive but bearing relevance to historical reality. I owe this last point to Miss Mao Chien who is an acquaintance of Su T'ung.

78. A 1960s study of prostitutes in Taiwan states: 'Although a woman who becomes a prostitute often experiences a decline in status, her original status was already very low, and her chances of moving up were minimal, if not non-existent. Prostitution offers her some chance of upward mobility, at least it guarantees that she will have food every day, a roof over her bed, and clothes on her back—all of better quality than she could have at home; it offers her some excitement and the companionship of other women her age' (Barnard Wolfe (1980: 260–1)).
79. Reasons for re-entering the business were multiple. It could be out of economic desperation (e.g. *Chu-kiang hsing-ch'i hua-pao* (1927), vi. 5), or of a sudden loss of emotional dependence as a result of either marriage failure, or the death or departure of partner (e.g. ibid. iii. 5; vii. 5), or sometimes simply because of their 'lewd character' (*KPP* 1927: 8, 29 November).
80. In one case, a well-educated girl had once worked briefly in a high-class brothel in Hong Kong after having serious conflicts with her parents and running away from home. Her mastery of Chinese classics and good command of English had struck many brothel-goers. Before long, her family recovered her and forcibly took her back home (*KPP* 1928: 8, 2 May).
81. *Chu-kiang hsing-ch'i hua-pao* (1927), iv. 3, is an example of a 'decently behaved' sing-song girl in Canton who had been a prostitute. Also *KPP* (1928: 8, 5 May; 1928: 8, 1 June; 1928–9, *passim*).
82. These concubines were believed to lead miserable lives. Herbert Day Lamson (1935: 513–8). For more examples from Shanghai, see Henriot (2001: 130–7).
83. Although the context of the case mentioned in this source is 1930s Hong Kong, it might also reflect a similar situation in Canton in the same period.
84. A favourite concubine could so dominate the first wife that there was even a popular saying—'chih szu ta-p'o' (to tyrannize the first wife)—describing this rather common family phenomenon. *KCMKJP* (1925: 9, 18 September).
85. Frank Dikötter (1995: ch. 5) notes a similar discourse in other metropolitan cities in China.
86. According to the reminiscences of a former resident of Canton, Mr Mok Hung, his father sometimes even took his young daughter to a high-class brothel where young minor members of the staff would play with her while her father was busy socializing with business friends at the dining table. One of the first Japanese-trained Chinese women physicians recalled that when she was a teenager she had twice been taken by her uncles to visit a brothel. On one of these occasions, most of the ladies from her family also accompanied the men to a 'flower boat' on the famous Ch'in-huai River in Nanking. The women guests, who were separated from their husbands and male relatives by a screen, enjoyed the singing and music of the female entertainers. In spite of the author's 'modern' outlook, she recounted these events with nostalgic pleasure rather than disgust. Yang Pu-wei (1967: 32–3).
87. *HYOC*, 'Kuei Hai kao' (1923 drafts), 14.
88. Ching-Ke-Tung [*sic*] (1885), *The Chinese*, cited by Henriques, *Prostitution*, vol.1. (1962), p. 255. In fact, Henriques does not cite the title or the author of this book correctly. The correct citation should be: Tcheng-ki Tong, (1885) *The Chinese: Painted by Themselves* (London: Leaderhall). Tcheng-ki Tong, or Ch'en Ch'i-tung, was a military attaché of China in Paris. His book was first published in French in 1884 and was later translated into English.

89. In imperial Nanking, high-class brothels, until the Ming Dynasty, were located opposite the Examination Hall. This class of brothel was a popular playground for literati, the bureaucrats, and the rich, Tung-kuo-hsien-shêng (1990: 24–8).
90. Most courtesans at high-class brothels were trained as singers and musicians (Ts'un Shih 1988: 234–6).
91. This aspect of the subculture of businessmen is vividly reconstructed in Sung Yü's *T'ang-hsi* (1989).
92. For instance, the advertisements of a Tao-yüan Restaurant printed in *HTJP* (12 Nov. 1911), and of a Yung-ch'ün Restaurant printed in (*Chu-kiang hsing-ch'i hua-pao* (1927: iv. 20)).
93. Food, wine, and singing was an important part of entertainment in Shanghai's bordellos too. Hai-shang-chüeh-wu-shêng (1939: 18–33).
94. With the exception of a few such 'obvious' names as Ming Hua (Famous Flower), Huan Hua (Happy Flower), Têh Hsiang (Captured Fragrance) (Tzu-hang-shih 1919: ch. 4, 5–6).
95. In the 300-page official publication for that campaign, only two short essays denouncing prostitution (of two pages each) are included. *FSKKTK* (1930: 216, 254–6).
96. The section on 'gambling', the editors stated, was deliberately made incomplete and uninformative since it was an activity that 'shatters morality and impairs men'. There was no such moralistic warning in the section on prostitution, however, which suggests that it was considered relatively harmless. Tzu-hang-shih (1919: ch. 4, 5–7); Liu Tsai-su (1926: 111–16).
97. Some of these examples were *Hsiang-hua hua-pao* 1–4 (1928); *Chu-kiang hsing-ch'i hua-pao* 1–8 (1927–8).
98. It is interesting to note that in December 1911, *HTJP* published an announcement released by two guilds related to the brothel-business for at least ten consecutive days. It was a public acknowledgement of those brothels and prostitutes that had responded to a fund-raising campaign in support of a charity in Canton (Virgil Ho, 'To Laugh at a Penniless Man' (2001: 125–6)).
99. 'Jung-mi-i lao', *HYOC*, 'Kuei Hai kao' (1923 drafts), 6–7.
100. This pictorial, like many other locally published pictorial magazines, contains many photographs of and short essays about sing-song girls and courtesans in Canton. The popularity of this form of pastime was vividly reflected by a journal report from the city of Swatow in eastern Kwangtung. The reporter compared the joy and the relief of local patrons of prostitution, after the ban of months on this business had been lifted, to 'thirsty horses which are dashing to a spring' (*HTJP* 1913, 24 April).
101. For details on this aspect of literatus culture, see Tung-kuo hsien-shêng, *Chi-chia fêng-yüeh*; Hsieh Yang Hui-mei, 'Ch'ang-chi ti wen-ti', in the Preface to the Taiwan reprint of Wang Shu-nu (1971: 25–6).
102. A similar 'problem' was noted by Gamble (1921: 256–7) in Republican Peking. Although colleges in Peking 'adopt[ed] very strict rules of discipline concerning it', students were only discouraged, rather than prohibited, from visiting brothels because these 'strict rules' meant a 10 per cent deduction from the final grade marks of any student caught.
103. The source, however, did not say how the incident was eventually ended.

104. In 1928, 600 men and women were arrested on the charge of 'rape and procurement', though it is not known how many of these were arrested purely for rape (Kuang-chou-shih shih-chêng fu t'ung chi ku 1929: 90–1).
105. A demographic imbalance between the sexes seems to have increased the shortage of marriageable women. The 1932 Census shows that there were about 123,000 men, but only about 80,000 women between the ages 13 and 20. In the age-group 21–50 the gap was even bigger, with about 310,000 men to 200,000 women. Of these, some 90,000 men and 40,000 women were unmarried (Kuang-chou-shih jên-k'ou tiao-cha wei-yüan-hui mi-shu ch'u (1932), tables 2 and 3).
106. Lo's books are full of examples of these women, too many to be cited here. The stories of Su Ngo and Tzu Lan-hua are perhaps two representative cases (Lo Li-ming, *hua yüeh hêng*, 1962 iv. 7–88).
107. Selective examples include *Hsiang-hua hua-pao* (1928: i. 22); *chu-kiang-hsing-ch'i hua-pao* (1927: iv. 6); (1927: vi. 6) (1927: vii. 6).
108. I-shih, 'Ch'ang-chi wên-t'i ti yen-chiu', serialized in *HTJP* in May 1924.
109. I-ching-chu-jên, 'Mou-fu hai-tzu ying-yang pao', in Eberhard (1972: 89–171).
110. 'Yu-shih k'ai-tao', *HYOC*, 'Kuei Hai kao' (1923 drafts), 5–6.
111. In a nearly 300-page-long commemorative book published for the campaign, only one short essay of just over a page in length was devoted to the topic of the 'evils' of prostitution in Canton (*FSKKTK* 1930: 25, 216).
112. In the early 1930s there was a 'prostitute-registration campaign' which, however, was concluded without much success (*Kuang-chou nien-chien* 1935: ch. 7, 61).
113. *Kuang-chou-shih shih-chêng pao kao hui k'an* (1923: 197). It is not known what was taught to the inmates. In a similar institution in Peking only sewing was taught. For comparable institutions in other cities, see Gamble (1921: 261); Henriot (2001: ch. 14).
114. In Victorian England, these rescue houses 'were designed as little purgatories... sealed off from the world, the inmates laboured to achieve that state of true penitence which would secure them promotion to the heaven of respectable society' (Fraser Harrison 1979: 254–5).
115. At a similar institution in Peking all inmates were photographed; not only were the pictures displayed in a special room where anyone could inspect them, but many were also posted outside the gate where they could be seen by passers-by. Interested men could propose a meeting with particular inmates. For further details, see Gamble (1921: 262).
116. In one of these scandals the owner of a photography shop had bribed an officer of the refuge, who allowed him to marry one of the inmates under a false name. The woman was taken by him as concubine instead of first wife as the institution stipulated. This misdeed was disclosed by accident when the police investigated another criminal case in which the culprit was implicated (*HTJP* 1920: 1.3, 21 May).
117. *Kuang-tung ch'üan shêng ts'ai-chêng shuo-ming-shu* (1910: i. 38–41), 'Shui-ju pu: Chêng tsa ke chuan'.
118. Similar moves by the tax-farmers in the counties of Fo-shan and Kiang-mên caused strong reactions from the brothel operators in these places who eventually closed down their establishments in protest (*HTJP*, 1911, 28 September; 2 October).
119. Details of the charges can be read in *HTJP* 1914: 3.4, 1 January.

120. *Kuang-chou-shih shih-chêng pao kao hui k'an* (1923: 21, 40–41, 76). Between 1921 and 1923, the total revenue from prostitute-related business increased by almost 20 per cent (Li Tsung-huang 1922: 13).
121. It was said that no official record on this usurped sum had ever been released. But it was estimated that about 100,000 yüan a year had been retained by this 'guest' force (*HTJP* 1924: 1.3, 29 February).
122. The most popular public projects funded by prostitution-related revenues were carriageway construction and vocational education (*Kuang-chou nien-chien* 1935: 74–5). 'Flower tax' was also commonly levied by other city and county authorities of the province. The rate varied markedly from place to place. In order to protect the prostitutes from being overtaxed, the provincial government had announced a plan to standardize the rate. But it was not sure if the plan was ever, or how effectively, implemented (*YHP* 1934: 5, 28 March).
123. In 1933, the standard minimum charge for the same service was increased to 4 yüan, of which 2.6 yüan went to the government in taxes.
124. It must be added that the government was not ruthless or rash in mobilizing this source of revenue. In 1927, for instance, the Finance Department turned down a request by certain tax farmers to raise taxes on brothels (*HTJP* 1927: 2.2, 12 May). A similar lenience had occasionally been shown by the late-Ch'ing administration. The loss of income caused by natural disasters invariably led to a reduction in the taxes levied on brothels (at the latter's request) (*Kuang-tung ch'üan shêng ts'ai-chêng shuo-ming-shu* (1910: 38–41), 'Shui-ju pu: Chêng tsa ke chuan').
125. This point is further highlighted in a recent study on taxing prostitution in Republican Canton (Elizabeth Remick (2002)).
126. In the mid-1910s, all brothels were divided into three classes according to the number of their inmates. The upper-class ones were charged a registration fee of 24 yüan for one-quarter, 12 yüan for the middle-class, and 8 yüan for the lowest ones. Each prostitute was also charged a quarterly registration fee according to the class of the establishment she worked in. Those in the high-class brothels were charged 18 yüan, the middle-class 12 yüan, and the lowest ones 8 yüan. There were also charges on every 'transaction' (*chü*) (including sexual and non-sexual services) that took place in a brothel, ranging from $1\frac{1}{2}$ yüan for a high-class establishment to 50 cents for a low one. In addition, surcharges were imposed on banquets served at, and the number of rooms in, a brothel (*HTJP* 1914: 3.4, 1 January).
127. 'Mei-nü ching-sai yü hua-chieh hsüan-chü' (1930: 2). This is another example of the favourable social perception of some prostitutes, who were comparable to entrants in international beauty contests.
128. In the early 1900s the Hong Kong Government had also used brothels to help foster the 'newly opened' but remote area of West Point (Wu Hao 1989: 11–12).
129. As happened in most Imperial German cities (Lynn Abrams, 'Prostitutes in Imperial Germany', in Richard J. Evans (1988: 191–3)).
130. One of these organizations was the Women's Salvation Society of Canton, whose work was never mentioned in the contemporary official and unofficial literature on the subject of prostitution available to us. The organization is mentioned in the League of Nations' *Report of the Commission of Enquiry into the Traffic of Women and Children in the Far East*, cited by Sue Gronewold (1985: 81).
131. *HYOC*, 'Yen Shu kao' (1922 drafts), 10–12. Like all the *Yüeh-ou* songs in this collection, the narrator was supposed to be a prostitute, though the songs were

composed by a well-educated brothel-goer. It should also be noted that contemporary anti-prostitution writers were well aware of the difficulty in finding enough alternative jobs to resettle all prostitutes in Canton if any serious plan of abolition could be put into practice. Henceforth, the prostitutes' worry about unemployment, as it is depicted in this song, was not far from the truth. Examples of these anti-prostitution writings can be read in *KCMKJP* (1924: 3, 14–15, April). It must be added that materials that contain verbation the voices of prostitutes in Republican Canton are rare indeed. Even in contemporary 'investigative reports' (such as Chou Hsia-min (1934) and Tsui-mien-shan-jên (*c.*1920s) and reminiscences of brothel-goers (such as Lo Li-ming (1962) and Ts'un Shih (1988)) cited in this book, though some voices of prostitutes were reflected, strict autobiographical accounts of such women, and their *ipsissima verba*, are not given. This may not necessarily render any study of the problem of prostitution impossible (for a contrary view, see Hershatter (1997) Introduction). Alternative sources such as contemporary novels, popular songs, cartoons, newspaper reports, and so on provide us with the popular perceptions of, and attitudes towards, prostitutes and prostitution. On the other hand, although the recently published 'autobiographies' of former prostitutes, such as K'ang Su-chên's *Ch'ing-lou hên (hsü chi)*, professedly contain the voices of these women, they seem likely to be exaggerated or distorted to serve the political purpose of anti-prostitution. Even if these voices are authentic, they unveil only the dark side of the situation, which undoubtedly existed. But works such as these apparently do not help us understand the possible alternative views of the public in this matter.

132. For more details, see Wang Shu-nu (1988: 41–3).
133. A contemporary short story adopts this social phenomenon as its opening scene (Chiu-chung-fêng-fu (*c.*1910: 1–2)).
134. An old resident of Canton recalls that most high-class brothels had secret rooms in which army officers could exchange intelligence or make clandestine deals in weaponry or bribes (Ts'un Shih, *KTFCL* 1988: 231–3).
135. They also regularly patronized famous courtesans in Hong Kong (Wu Hao 1989: 17).
136. In 1928, the military commander of the Nationalist Army stationed in the city of Shao-hsing in western Kwangtung ordered the public execution of a prostitute-procuress and her client, who was also recognized as a fugitive. Such extreme measures against prostitutes or their clients were, however, rare (*HTJP* 1928: 3.3, 8 August).
137. Brothels were probably crucial in minimizing the abuse of ordinary women by soldiers in Canton.

CHAPTER 6

1. Undoubtedly, the world of Cantonese opera also reflected the conditions and aspects of life in places other than Canton, such as Hong Kong, in this period. However, since this thesis is mainly concerned with Canton, the situation of Cantonese opera in Hong Kong, though by no means less important, will be mentioned only in places where it is relevant and as supplementary evidence.
2. In imperial Kwangtung, rustic folk songs had been severely criticized as licentious, obscene, and worthless by moralistic scholars (e.g. Wu Chên-fang 1936). Only since

the 1920s had Chinese folklorists started to show unpompous academic interest in folk music (Hung Chang-tai 1985: 58–80; Hsü Fu-chin 1958: 65–8).

3. Yu Hsün-ch'ing, *Ho lang pi-chi*, cited in *P'an-yü hsien hsü chih* (1968: ch. 44, 13–14); and Mackerras (1975: 147).
4. Hu Shih stated that the 'old theatre' should be relegated to the 'category of useless survival' (Scott 1965: 35–6). Among all the well-known intellectual figures in the 1930s, probably only Yü Ta-fu praised the 'progressive achievement' attained by contemporary Cantonese opera, when he compared it with the Min opera (*YCS* 1988: 35).
5. For another disdainful criticism of opera in this period, see Wan Yung (1930).
6. This provides another convincing illustration for E. H. Carr's thesis (1978: ch. 2) that the work of a historian mirrors the society in which he works.
7. The vulgar and ribald popular music and theatre in Victorian London is an example of the contrary case (Ronald Pearsall 1973: 40–59).
8. For instance, after the troupe Hsin Ch'un Ch'iu had performed the opera *Yü Shan Shu* (The Jade Shan Shu) for the occasion of the opening of a theatre in Shanghai in 1932, the chancellor of Chi-nan University strongly recommended it to his students because of its educational value (Ch'en Fei-nung and Yu Mu-yün 1982: 10).
9. For instance, Yu Hsün-ch'ing, *Ho lang pi-chi*, and Yang Mou-chien, *Mêng hua shou po*; both are cited by Lai Po-ch'iang (2001: 105–6, 155–6). In addition, disparaging remarks on Cantonese opera and other forms of local opera abounded in many local gazetteers. Some examples can be read in Lai Po-ch'iang (ibid. 50–2, 97–8, 136–8).
10. The popularity of *Kün-ch'ü* among some commoners was inferred from a poem composed by a late-Ming loyalist Ch'en Tzu-shêng, which is cited by Lai Po-ch'iang (2001: 43–4). On the demise of *Kün-ch'ü* and the growing popularity of Cantonese opera and other forms of local drama in Kwangtung, see ibid. 44–82.
11. These words of criticism were adopted by the editor of a local gazetteer (*Chi-yang hsien chih*) when he attacked the unworthiness of a piece of vernacular local opera that was said to be highly popular in eastern Kwangtung during the late-Ming period. Cited by Lai Po-ch'iang, ibid. 52.
12. Yang Mou-chien, *Mêng hua shou po*, cited by Lai Po-ch'iang, ibid. 105.
13. For instance, Liang P'ei-chin, *Yüeh-chü yen-chiu*, 1985 pp. 172–5; also Ch'en Fei-nung and Yu Mu-yün (1982: 4–5). Neither of them doubts the popularity and the socio-political achievement of these troupes.
14. Examples of this politicized view of the inflated contribution of these troupes are Shih Pin-ch'ou's (1983) and Ch'en Hua-hsin *YCYCTLH* (1983: 226–88); also *YCS* (1988: 21–31).
15. For instance, the T'ien-yen kung-ssu (Social Evolution Company) received a 'substantial amount of money' from the Hsing Chung Hui for running a school of opera and drama between 1905 and 1907, which provided theatrical training and elementary education to about eighty teenagers. Shih Pin-ch'ou *YCYCTLH* (1983: 264–5).
16. Unfortunately, the author could only get hold of one script of this kind at the time of writing this chapter. Its theme and content are strongly politicized. Sung-hu-chu-jên (*c.*1919).
17. It should be noted that although 'patriot troupes'' actors were basically trained for drama, they could have moved into Cantonese opera for two main reasons. First, in order to attract more audiences, some 'patriot troupes' had introduced operatic singing into their production, and therefore also included in their training programme

basic technical skills for conventional Cantonese opera. Secondly, and perhaps more important, after a 'patriot troupe' had closed down, its former actors could start their new careers in some conventional Cantonese opera company, though always as apprentices. As apprentices, they were usually required to go through a very intensive on-the-job training for years depending on their talent. Famous actors such as Pai Chiu-yung and Ch'en Fei-nung, who shifted to conventional Cantonese opera companies in their teens, had spent years of hard training as apprentices before they were eventually given the opportunity to perform major roles on stage. Moreover, these young opera actors, like all actors in this profession, kept perfecting their operatic skills throughout their professional career. The transition, it must be added, was by no means easy. Ch'en Fei-nung vividly recalls how technical mistakes could still have been made in his first Cantonese opera performance notwithstanding years of training as an apprentice after he had left drama. *YCS* (1983: 26–8); Ch'en Fei-nung and Yu Mu-yün (1982: 4–7); Chang Chieh, ''Hsiao-sheng wang' Pai Chiu-yung' (1990: 185–96).

18. 'The Injustice Done to Tou Ngo' by Kuan Han-ch'ing, and Ma Chih-yüan's 'Autumn in Han Palace' are good examples. Liu Jung-en trans. (1988: 12–13, 28–30, 33–4). William Dolby's 'Yüan Drama' in Colin Mackerras (1988: 41–7).
19. See the advertisement for opera shows in *HTJP* 1911, 19 September.
20. See the same, ibid. 2 November.
21. See the advertisement in *HTJP* 1911, 14 November. On the religious symbolisms of those ritualistic plays, see Virgil K.Y. Ho, in Göran Aijmer and Åsa Boholm eds. (1994: 117–24).
29. During the late-Ming period, a few non-Kwangtung scholars and officials had written about their detestation of 'local opera' sung in a local language that they did not understand. Some of these contemporary notes are edited in Liang P'ei-chin (1985: 144–52). Gaspar da Cruz, a Portuguese missionary who had stayed in Canton, wrote in 1569 about theatregoers there: 'Those who do not understand what the actors say are sometimes wearied, but whosoever understandeth them doth delight very much to hear them . . . ' This could well be a sign of vernacularization of Cantonese opera in mid-Ming, for Cantonese dialect might not be understood by everyone, especially non-Kwangtung merchants or officials in Canton. C. R. Boxer (1953: 144).
23. As judged by the irregular appearance of advertisement or performance announcement in *HTJP* during late 1911 and early 1912.
24. It is interesting to note that during its brief years of existence, this company had trained a total of 80 teenage actors. After the disbandment of this troupe, these young actors, in order to earn a living, had all joined old-style opera companies and subsequently, as Fêng Tzu-yu (1987: 482), a contemporary witness, recalled, 'could no longer remember the original [revolutionary] aim of the [disbanded] troupe'.
25. The outlines of these three plays that had been performed by different 'patriot troupes' together with some other supposedly 'progressive' scripts, can be read in Ch'iu Sung-ho (1992: 22–57); the three scripts discussed are on p. 33.
26. Allegedly, drama 'greatly facilitated the success of the 1911 Revolution'. T'ien Han (1958: 4).
27. Ch'en Fei-nung had joined a Min Lo Shê (People's Joy Drama Society) whose members were intellectuals, and whose plays were full of 'revolutionary ideas'. Ch'en Fei-nung, and Yu Mu-yün (1982: 4).
28. Due to its patriotic stance, the popularity of spoken drama is said to have reached its apex during the Second Sino-Japanese War. It fell again, however, with its patriotic

mission soon after the Pacific War. For an 'official' history of spoken drama in Canton, see Ch'ang Ch'o, 'Yüeh-yü hua-chü ho i yen-yen-i-hsi?', *NFJP* (1957: 3, 31 May).

29. As seen from the advertisements for performances shown in Cantonese dailies such as *KCMKJP* and *HTJP*.
30. Unfortunately, very few Cantonese drama scripts of the time are available for perusal. Only extracts from one or two can be read in contemporary magazines related to drama (e.g. *Chü shêng* 1 (1917)). A few magazines that touched on the subject of drama contained articles, reviews, and critical essays which provide an alternative source of information on the general situation of drama in Canton in this period.
31. In 1934 there were five such companies in Canton. *Kuang-chou chih-nan* (1934: 445).
32. This was the opinion of Yang Mou-chien, who wrote about this in *Mêng hua shou po* (*c.*1840s), cited by Lai Po-ch'iang in *Kuang-tung hsi-ch'ü chien shih* (2001: 105). Another scholar, Yang Ên-shou, described in 1865 the costume of a local troupe as 'glittering, bright and fabulous', while its play was 'confusing and gay'. Cited by Liang Wei, 'Yüeh-chü yüan-liu chi ch'i pien-kê chu shu' in Kuang-chou-shih chêng-hsieh wên shih tzu-liao yen-chiu wei-yüan-hui, Yüeh-chü yen-chiu chung-hsin (1990: 4).
33. These photographs of Hsin Li-hsiang and Kuei Tsai were published in *Chü shêng* (1917). For more photographs of contemporary opera stars, see Ch'en Fei-nung and Yu Mu-yün (1982: 17, 18, 25, 40); *Hsi-chü shih-chieh* (1922–3).
34. The 'plastics' mentioned in this source might in fact have been sequins, which were then commonly used by ladies in Western Europe and North America for decorating their formal evening dresses, and by entertainers for their costumes. But it is also likely that these glittering decorative scales were actually made of plastic because plastics research and manufacture in Western Europe and the United States had just begun to grow at considerable rate in the 1920s ('Plastics and Resins', *The New Encyclopaedia Britannica* (Chicago: 1991), xxi. 291).
35. In this aspect, even Shanghai opera companies had to learn from their Cantonese counterparts. (Kuo Ping-chên, 'Yüeh-chü ti yen-kê', *YCYCTLH*, 404).
36. Advertisements of the all-female troupes Chu-kiang Yen-yin, in *HTJP* 1924, 9 April; and of Ching Hau Ying, in *HTJP*, 1919, 11 April.
37. 'Modern' costume had its special attraction to audiences used to watching their favourite opera stars perform only in traditional costume. For instance, when Lien Yung was advertised as appearing, for the first time in his acting career, in 'modern' costume (which included a pair of shorts, and hair styled in the latest American fashion), 'it caused a sensation for some time' during the mid-1920s (Wang Yung-chi, 'Liu-shih-wu nien', *YCYC* (1988: 48).
38. In the 'old days', actors in a troupe always shared theatre-costume with colleagues for nothing. But since 'shared costumes' were usually badly cared for and looked shabby, relatively well-off actors generally kept their own costumes. By the 1930s, their 'private wardrobe [of costumes]' provided famous actors with another means to show off (Ch'en Fei-nung and Yu Mu-yün 1982: 30; Ch'en Cho-ying, 'Hung-ch'uan', *YCYCTLH* 314–15).
39. For illustrations of some colourful opera costume in this period, see Hong Kong Regional Council (1988: 13–51).
40. Based on the author's interviews with villagers and the deputy manager of Kwang-tung Cantonese Opera Company (No. 2 Team) in Shun-tê County, 1990 and 1993.

41. It is dubious that traditional Chinese theatre was always performed without other props. Dolby (1988: 27) points out that props such as 'a flag, a fan, fresh-water chestnuts, a crane, a wine-bottle, and a bowl of hot pigs' trotters' were used in theatre.
42. By the 1920s, most of these itinerant opera troupes travelled from place to place by means of large barges painted red. Among the possible explanations on why the eye-catching colour red was used, the one that emphasizes its symbolic supernatural meanings is, in my view, the most credible (Virgil K. Y. Ho, 1994 'Cantonese Opera in a Rural Setting'; Lai Po-ch'iang 2001: 175–80).
43. This was described by a contemporary opera scriptwriter as the original driving force in 'reforming' stage props and scenes by the commercial rivals of these female troupes (Fêng Yüan 1923*d*: 3).
44. Lai Po-ch'iang (2001: 162) states that this play was first performed in Macao.
45. Ou-yang Yü-ch'ien (1957: 132) stated that this was another innovation of the *chih-shih pan*. According to Fêng Yüan (1923*d*.: 3), a contemporary opera critic, however, it was first used in 1913.
46. For a brief history of the use of props in Cantonese opera after 1910, see *YCS* (1988: 275–6); Ch'en Fei-nung and Yu Mu-yün (1982: 40); Mai Hsiao-hsia (1941: 168); Huang Ching-ming, 'San-shi-nien-tai Yüeh-chü ti i-shu tê-cheng', *YCYC* (1987: 75); Fêng Lan, 'Yüeh-chü wu-tai pien-ch'ien lu', in *Hsi ch'uan* 1 (1931: 11–12).
47. Jên Shou Nien and Chüeh Hsien Shêng were two of these successful troupes in this aspect (Fêng Lan, 'Yüeh-chü wu-tai' (1931: 12)). The massive employment of unconventional props, costume, lighting, and even acting, in the Cantonese version of 'The Thieves of Baghdad' contributed to the remarkable box-office success of Ta Lo T'ien Company in the early 1930s; so much so that it was consequently upgraded into a Canton-Hong Kong troupe (Ch'en Fei-nung and Yu Mu-yün 1982: 9).
48. As shown in an advertisement of Ma Shi-ts'êng's troupe, the number of musicians in the 'Western Music Section' exceeded the 'Chinese Music Section' by four (Liang P'ei-chin 1985: 281).
49. 'Bustling and noisy' served at least two purposes. First, it helped to draw the attention of its audiences. Secondly, it performed the important symbolic and auspicious function of evoking supernatural favour in the theatre and hence had its audiences and venues blessed; Cantonese commonly believed that noise and crowds were more sources of blessing than nuisance (Virgil K. Y. Ho 1994: 113–14). That was perhaps why during the late-Ch'ing period Cantonese opera performances were occasions when a large number of firecrackers were set off (Yang Mou-chien 2001: 105).
50. Ho also states that the play *Huan hua-chai* (Repaying the Flower-Debt) also suffered from a 'disastrous' box office. His point contradicts what other contemporary writers said about this play. He, however, gives no further detail.
51. One source (*YCS* 1988: 142) states that no fewer than 8,000 new scripts were written and performed during the first three decades of the Republican period alone. Mai Hsiao-hsia (1941: 170) estimates that some 5,000 scripts were written in this period. It must be noted that 'title of opera' (*chü-mu*) and script (*chü-pên*) are different things. The former signifies a performed opera which may or may not have any written script. Sometimes the same opera may be performed under different titles. According to a Cantonese opera historian, there had been no less than 12,000 titles performed between the late-Ch'ing period and the modern time (Liang Wei, in Liu Ching-chih and Hsien Yü-i 1995: 140–1).

52. At one stage, the popularity of Ma was threatened by a major replacement of actors in his company. However, he managed to maintain box-office success by producing, and performing, three new scripts a week (Shen chi 1957: 69).
53. As judged by the titles appearing in the advertisement section for opera performance in *HTJP* for 1911. Most of these new scripts were given amusing titles, for instance, 'Huang-liu hsien-shêng i lao-hu' (A Quack Doctor Heals a Tiger), 'Chi-ch'i Nan i ta-tu-p'o' (Nan the Mechanic Heals a Pregnant Woman), 'Ch'in-shih Huang ch'u-shih' (The Birth of Emperor Ch'in), 'Fêng-tsai chung chuang-yüan' (The Crazy Boy Who Passed the Highest-Level Civil Examination), and so on (*HTJP* 1911, 16 June, 20 June, 30 June, and 14 December).
54. For a brief biographical note on some of these playwrights, see *YCS* (1988: 134–41).
55. Some historians believe that a full written script was first introduced by Hsüeh Chüeh-hsien in the mid-1920s. Before then, opera scripts were only brief outlines of the story and cast of each act. (For instance, Ch'ang Chieh 1980*b*: 132). This, however, is not an unproblematic view. Full written scripts had appeared much earlier in at least the early Ming, especially so in the case of Ch'ao-chou opera in the eastern part of Kwangtung. For examples, see *Ming-pên Ch'ao-chou hsi-wên wu tsung* (1985); Lai Po-ch'iang (2001: 31–3, 60–5). There was seemingly also a political reason for the birth of full written scripts. In 1926, the local authorities in Canton imposed a censorship on local opera. Since all performing troupes in Canton were required, at least in theory, to submit a copy of the scripts to be performed for official inspection, a fully written script, therefore, became a necessity (Chang Fang-wei, 'San-shih nien-tai Kuang-chou Yüeh-chü shêng shuai', in Kuang-chou-shih chêng-hsieh wên shih tzu-liao yen-chiu wei-yüan-hui, Yüeh-chü yen-chiu chung-hsin 1986: 81). But this still cannot explain why scripts in similar format had already been published and circulated in Canton in the early 1920s (Ch'iu Sung-ho 1992: 61–3). In present-day Hong Kong, Ch'en Shou-jên (1988: i. 156) states that due to the low educational level of most actors, improvisation is commonly employed as a means to reduce an actor's burden in memorizing lyrics. It must be noted, however, that improvisation had always been a part of Cantonese opera performance, even during the days when most troupes played only a handful of scripts (Ho Chien-ch'ing (1995: 210–11)).
56. At least two pieces of work had pinpointed this 'problem' of local opera, much to the disgust of their authors. They were Lu Tien, who wrote in 1733, and Yang Mou-chien in the 1840s. Both are cited by Lai Po-ch'iang (2001: 73–4, 105–6).
57. For more biographies of other scriptwriters in Kwangtung in the early and mid-Ch'ing periods, see ibid. 114–22.
58. But even 'stage Mandarin' was taken as a product of localization of opera because the local accent in this form of Mandarin was so strong that 'it could be easily understood by local audiences' (Fêng-yüan-ch'u-jên 1923; v. 5–6, 'Hsi-chü p'ing-lun').
59. Two cases were identified during the course of this research. The first instance was noted by Tun-chien (1919). Another example was noted by the famous literary figure Pa Chin, which is cited in Ho Chien-ch'ing (1995: 223).
60. *YCYC*, ii (1987), is a special issue devoted entirely to the study of the transformation of different singing styles in Cantonese opera.
61. The most prominent of them was probably Pai Chiu-yung who was renowned as 'King of the Role of Scholar' (*hsiao-shêng wang*). He was hailed for contributing

much to the change of singing style in Cantonese opera from 'artificial tone' (*chia sang*) to 'natural voice' (*chên sang*) in this period (*YCS*, 1983: 106–7).

62. Unlike European or Greek tragedy, 'tragedy' in the Cantonese opera of this period normally ended happily.
63. In the 'old' ranking order of the twelve categories of role in traditional Cantonese opera as it was shown on most bills, the role of jester always appeared last (*YCS* 1988: 225–6; Mai Hsiao-hsia 1941: 185).
64. For instance, some actors were said to be able to expand and contract the size of their necks; while the famous jester-role actor Shêng She-tsai could lift his hat five inches up from his head, using only 'internal vital energy'. For more examples of similar unbelievable stunts, see Ch'en Tieh-êrh, 'Kuang-tung ta-hsi, Shao-lin wu-i' (1984: 75–8); *YCS* (1988: 244–57).
65. In the 1920s and 1930s, although some young actors preferred to use their real names as stage-names—another indication of improvement in the image of acting as a profession—most 'masters' (*lao kuan*) continued to keep their stage-names.
66. For more examples of stage-names in this period, see *Hsi ch'uan* 1 (1931: 15–18); and advertisements of opera shows in *HTJP*, *KHP*, *KPP*, and *YHP* throughout this period.
67. For more examples, see Ch'iu Sung-ho (1992: 30–8, 60–3); Liang P'ei-chin (1985); Huang Shao-han (1985).
68. On the popularity of this comic opera, see the biography of Ch'en Fei-nung (Ch'en Fei-nung and Yu Mu-yün 1982: 11), who played the heroine. For an extract from the script, and a criticism on it, see Ch'u Chien, 'Yüeh-chü lun' (1929: 112).
69. For a good example of the use of puns, see the printed script of *Ching lei tsui hsiang yün* (*c*.1930: 4). The use of transliterated English words is said to be common in contemporary Cantonese opera, which is interpreted by a Chinese Communist historian as a tag of the 'decadent influence of foreign cultural imperialism' (Kuo Ping-chên, 'Yüeh-chü', *YCYCTLH* 1983: 403). But it is doubtful how 'bad' the situation is, because of all thirty randomly chosen printed scripts we studied, only the aforementioned contains a few English words. Moreover, ordinary audiences might not interpret their use as decadent at all.
70. Short English phrases, such as 'thank you' and 'good-bye', names of contemporary celebrities and places that are by no means pertinent to the opera, are sometimes sung in the course of a traditional-costume opera. Noted in the author's field observations on religious festival opera in rural Shun-tê County in 1990 and 1993; also Ch'en Shou-jên (1988).
71. The author's fieldwork in rural Kwangtung; Ch'en Shou-jên (1988: 25–30, 97, 99–105, 146).
72. Examples can be easily found in *KCLPL*, *KCTC*, and *Wu-hsien man-hua*.
73. Witty humour was apparently expressed by any means to hand. On a banknote, a 'philosopher of life' put forward his view of the place of money in life: '[I] did not bring this [banknote with me] when I was born, [and I] shall not take it [with me] when I die.' An insightful 'lover' wrote his experience on another banknote: 'Who dares to say that this small piece of paper is thin [and hence powerless]? For it can buy the heart of a beauty' (Hsiao Lu 1926: 4).
74. Of all the randomly chosen contemporary scripts read in the course of this research, only one ends unconventionally with the temporary withdrawal of the defensive

forces against the foreign invaders, and the optimistic message that the lost territories will be eventually recovered. This script, *Ts'an hua lo ti hung*, was most probably written during the Japanese invasion.

75. Liu Kuo-hsing (1983: 363); 'Hsi-yüan chung ti ch'üeh-tien', *KCMKJP* (1926: 4, 10 August); also interviews with a Mr Liao and Mr Ferdinand Hoo-an, both of whom were residents in Canton during the 1930s. Relatively less casual manners were noted in Peking theatres in the Ch'ing period (Colin Mackerras 1972: 202).
76. This did not cause any concern to the audiences. *KCHJP* (1933: 10, 7 February).
77. A good example was the initial hostile response of some audiences to the 'beggar tone' of singing of Ma Shih-ts'êng in his debut (Shen Chi 1957: 46). In religious festival opera performances in present-day Kwangtung and Hong Kong, audience manners are very casual (Barbara Ward, 'Regional Operas' (1985: 184)). Ch'en Shou-jên (1988: i. 31) even suggests that one of the functions of libretto in Cantonese opera is to provide its audiences with brief breaks during which they can chat with their companions.
78. This is one of many manifestations of Southern Chinese male passivity seen in North America, as pointed out by a psychoanalyst (Warner Muensterberger, 'Orality and Dependence' (1951: 58–61)).
79. 'Happy ending' was also a common characteristic of other forms of traditional Cantonese popular literature such as 'wooden fish songs', 'dragon-boat songs', storytelling, and, in this period, the highly popular knight-errant novels. These novels were widely read in Republican Shanghai (Perry Link: 20). In Canton, many popular magazines, such as *KCLPL* and *KCTC*, published serialized knight-errant novels.
80. Chinese New Year celebration in rural Kwangtung provides a rich illustration for this auspices-seeking mentality. The events were packed with auspicious symbols of fertility, fortune, longevity, and virility (Liu Wan-chang: 11–31).
81. For more examples, see Huang Shao-han (1971); P'eng Fen (1988: 31–3); Liang P'ei-chin (1985: 347–458).
82. Mainstream *nan yin* songs had been highly popular among scholars and officials in Canton in the late-Imperial and early-Republican period. Their lyrics are elaborate and flowery. Their themes are generally gloomy, mainly lamentation of men's powerlessness to reverse the withering of their youth; eulogies for prematurely dead courtesan-lovers; and the bitterness of separation from one's lover (Liang P'ei-chih 1988: 31–7, and *c*. 3). However, it must be noted that there existed 'market-place' *nan yin* whose humorous and lively lyrics and happy endings resembled those of *mu-yu, lung-chou*, and popular opera. About forty such pieces are kept under the entry *Chi-t'an chin-lan* in SOAS, London.
83. Nearly all the short stories and novels written by Ou-yang Shan in this period ended gloomily or tragically. For examples, see his *Ch'i-nien chi* (1935), *Shêng ti fan jao* (1937), *Ch'ing-nien nan-nü* (1937), and *Shih-pai ti shih-pai-chê* (1948). In the magazine of a Canton literary society, all its collected prose-pieces and 'new' poems carry gloomy or pessimistic themes (Kuang-chou wên-hsüeh hui 1928).
84. Shao Pin-ju (1964) contains some popular storytelling texts written during the Ch'ing period.
85. The opera *Pai-chin lung* (The Platinum Dragon), which was adapted from a Hollywood film and was one of the biggest hits in Canton in the 1930s, is a good example. The

script is reprinted in *Hsi-chü yen-chiu tzu-liao* 10 and 11 (1984). For an intellectualistic critique of this play, see Ou-yang Yü-ch'ien (1983: 126–8).

86. This was even performed by a respectable troupe, Jên Shou Nien (*KHP* 1918, 10 August).
87. An example of this radical view of the 'worthlessness' of contemporary Cantonese opera is Yü Chia-yen (1983: 430–6). For an instance of critical view of an intellectual, see Ching Kan (1924: 27, July).
88. As Ou-yang Yü-ch'ien (1983: 129–30) alleged in 'Shih t'an Yüeh-chü'. He also added that playwrights of Cantonese opera in this period possessed very 'vague and weak' consciousness of their country and people. Thus, all opera ended 'unpatriotically' with compromise reached between the forces of bad and good.
89. Photographic copies of two original contracts are collected in Liang P'ei-chin (1985: 4 and 13).
90. On the organization of the Pa Ho Guild, see *YCS* (1988: 319–25); Ch'en Cho-ying (1983: 318–19).
91. Among these magazines, *T'ien ch'ü hua-pao* contains the most explicit photographs of nude females. See ibid. 2/8 (1928).
92. On the back cover of *Hsi ch'uan* 1 (1931).
93. For examples, see *Pan-chiao man-hua* 60/1–2 (1932).
94. Wood-cut prints of naked girls were used as illustrations for the literary supplement of the official daily *KCMKJP* throughout the 1920s.
95. Impassioned kissing scenes appear in nearly all the early works of Chang Tzu-p'ing, a Cantonese writer who gained national fame for his love stories. For an analysis of the element of sex in Chang's novels, see Chien Hsing-tsun (Shanghai:1936). The youthful obsession with the joy of kissing is best shown by the works of students published in *KTHS*. For example, Ch'en Shih-lung's 'Chui meng', and Chieh's 'Ai chih wei ch'ou' (*KTHS* 1933: ii. 46–50 and 62 respectively), contain fiery scenes of kissing.
96. Among them was the eldest daughter of Kiang K'ung-yin, a prominent member of the Canton local gentry (Ch'u Pu-chih 1982: 69).
97. Although one critic commented that the lyrics of most Cantonese opera pieces were not as beautifully written (*wên-tsai*) as that of other regional operas, he also admitted that they were neither dull nor distasteful. The lyrics of most scripts performed in this period were still largely apt and elegantly written (*pên sè*), though at times vulgar phrases also appeared, mainly as a result of stage improvisation by actors. Vernacularization was not achieved without the least concern for lyrical beauty (Ho Chien-ch'ing, 1995: 211–22.
98. In the Preface to his *Shêng ti fan jao*, Ou-yang Shan (1937) expounds his views on the vernacularization of serious literature, in that he justifies the heavy use of foul language in his literary creative works. Since the 1950s, he has been appointed to a number of senior posts in the Kwangtung Writers' Association, and the CCP Central Committee (Wolfgang Bartke 1991: 447).
99. In 'classical' Cantonese opera, each character-role was rigidly assigned a special style or way of acting that an actor had to follow and strictly observe (*YCS* 1988: 218–27).
100. For a selected list of some of those titles, see Ch'iu Sung-ho (1992: 30–63).
101. It was not uncommon to find that a substantial part of a new script was written in semi-classical Chinese; for example, *Hsüan kung yen-shih* (Canton: 1930s), *Li-hua ya hai-t'ang* (Canton: 1920s), *Hua hu-tieh* (Canton: 1927–8). For a brief discussion on the elegance of lyrics in Cantonese opera, see Ho Chien-ch'ing (1995).

102. It is interesting to note that many contemporary critics and audiences still appreciated this traditional style of acting, as many of them contributed articles to a local newspaper to express their views on how good or bad an actor was, in this aspect of artistry, in a particular play. Examples are abundant in the column 'Yüeh-chü ts'ung-t'an' in *KHP* throughout the late 1910s and the early 1920s.
103. In the late-Ch'ing period, the 'old system' of twenty-five categories of character-role (*hsin tang*) was rigidly structured. Each category of the character-roles could be played only by actors who were specialized in it. An actor who played a 'virtuous' character-role was not allowed to play a 'bad' character-role, or vice versa. Moreover, all character-roles were given a fairly equal chance of playing. For details, see Ch'en Tieh-êrh (1984: 72–3). By the 1930s, only six categories of character-role were upheld as 'foundations' of the prestigious 'Canton-Hong Kong troupes'. With the emergence of such 'all-round' actors as Ma Shih-ts'êng and Hsüeh Chüeh-hsien, the rigid old rule on character-role specialization collapsed (Mai Hsiao-hsia (1941: 180–5); Huang Ching-ming (1987: 74–5); *YCS* (1988: 218–27)).
104. According to Ch'en Fei-nung and Yu Mu-yün (1982: 56), Cantonese opera is also indebted to Peking opera for the use of 'painted face' costume, the Peking style of singing, and other features. Moreover, some of these changes had already been adopted into Cantonese opera by 1900. For details, see Lai Po-ch'iang (2001: 161–3).
105. The condition and situation of theatre in Manchu Peking was better recorded (Mackerras 1972: 197–207).
106. Until mid-Ming times, *K'un-chü* and *tsa-chü* had been very popular among the common people. Since then, they were gradually ennobled because of their popularity among princes, high-ranking officials, and the literati (Dolby 1983 and Hu 1983).
107. The authors of *YCS* (1988: 313) state that this theatre was a sort of tea-house cabaret in which opera was performed occasionally. They 'cite' this from *P'an-yü hsien hsü chih*, which, however, does not contain any such detailed information about it.
108. One example was the performance of a Peking opera troupe in Canton in 1928. The play was an extract from the romance *Dream of the Red Chamber*. In one scene, an actor groped all over the body of the key female character, and shouted aloud that: 'What a big....!' (original words were deleted in the source). The reaction on the floor was mixed: many audiences broke out into hilarious laughter, some jeered and threw fruit peel onto the stage (Fang Tsao, 'Pao-shan chin chiu yu Mei-lung Ch'êng', *KPP* 1928, 28 March).
109. 'Dawn plays' (*t'ien-kuang hsi*) were mainly for the on-stage training of a troupe's inexperienced actors. Since no admission fee was charged for these shows, they were well attended by poor audiences. The 1922 ban was a political decision rather than any reflection of the unpopularity of Cantonese opera. Li Fêng (1986: 59); Wang Yung-chih (1988: 46); *Kuang-chou-shih shih-chêng hui k'an* (1923: 43).
110. *Kuang-chou nien-chien* (1935: ch. 8, 95–108); Ch'en Fei-nung and Yu Mu-yün (1982: 55) recalls that each of these thirty-six troupes employed about 158 employees.
111. For a brief history of theatre in Canton from the late-Ch'ing to the Republican period, see Liu Kuo-hsing (1983: 359–63).
112. Some officially 'acclaimed' examples of these revised scripts are collected in Chung-kuo hsi-chü-chia hsieh hui (1962). In the late 1950s and early 1960s, opera

audiences in Canton continued to show great liking for those Republican-type 'decadent and feudalistic' elements of attraction, which were later conveniently denounced as 'obscene', and censored (*NFJP* 1957: 3, 10 December; 1957: 3, 14 December; 1958: 3, 14 March).

113. Lu-t'ien-hsien-shêng, 'Yüeh yu chi ch'êng', quoted from *YCS* (1988: 10).
114. Due to Kou-pi Chang's resemblance to her prematurely dead daughter, the mother of the Viceroy of Liang-Kwang immediately adopted him as her 'daughter' (since Chang impersonated females in opera) after she saw him during a performance at her birthday party (Liang P'ei-chin 1992: 57–8).
115. Tu Feng-chih, 'Yang-ch'êng chi yu jih-chi', quoted from Kuo Ping-chên (1983: 206–7).
116. Based on author's interview with a 90-year-old Mr Liao who lived in Canton during the 1930s.
117. This led tax-farmers to request a reduction in the tax quota levied on opera houses in Canton (*Kuang-chou shih shih-chêng pao-kao hui k'an* (1924: 44–5)).
118. One of them was Ch'en-p'i Mei. For a brief biography of some opera actresses in this period, see Ch'en Ts'ang-ku (*c.*1960).
119. As early as 1911, shortly after Canton felt into the hands of the revolutionary forces, a female troupe had already volunteered to perform for fund raising for the Republican troops (*HTJP* 1911, 20 December). Throughout the 1920s, female troupes were often invited to perform in official events that propagated the National Revolution (e.g. *HTJP*, 1921: 1.3, 6 May; *KCMKJP*, 1925: 7, 28 May and 11 October).
120. At that time, since acting was mainly a family business, an opera troupe was seemingly always composed of family members and relatives of both sexes. Fêng Yüan-chün (1947: 47–8).
121. Lu-t'ien-hsien-shêng, 'Yüeh yu chi ch'êng' (1733), quoted from *YCS* (1988: 10, 287–8).
122. A similar restrictive policy, however, did not apply to film acting. This reveals the contradiction and confusion in official policy towards public entertainment.
123. From an injunction order issued by the then magistrate of Shun-tê County in 1499, quoted from Liang P'ei-chin (1985: 148). In Ch'ing-dynasty Peking, women were banned from attending the theatre (Mackerras 1972: 214–15).
124. Among them was the eldest daughter of Kiang K'ung-yin, one the most powerful aristocrats in Canton. She admired Hsüeh Chüeh-hsien so much that she had, allegedly, written and presented to Hsüeh a number of scripts to perform (Ch'en Fei-nung and Yu Mu-yün 1982: 69).
125. In spite of a few isolated cases, the lives of most Peking opera actors in the Ch'ing period were 'full of insecurity and hardship' (Colin Mackerras 1972: 40–7).
126. Even some intellectuals argued that Cantonese opera, if refined, could be an indispensable means of educating the common people about patriotism (Ch'eng Chi-ming 1938: 152–3).
127. 'Chü-yüan hsien p'ing', the opera column in *HTJP*, was published regularly. An example of a special opera issue in *KCMKJP* can be read in 1926: 3, 10 August.
128. Going by the entries in T'an Cho-yüan (1965). According to veteran opera actor Ch'en Tieh-êrh, the first specialized magazine on Cantonese opera was published in

1931. This is not true, because *Li ying, Hsi-chü tsa-chih*, and *Hsi-chü shih-chieh*, three of the sources consulted in this research, were published much earlier. Ch'en's view is cited in Liang P'ei-chin (1985: 190–1).

129. Examples are *Li ying* 3 (*c.*1918); *Hsi-chü tsa-chih* 3 (*c.*1922); *Chü shêng* 1 (1917).
130. *Li ying* 3 (*c.*1918): 11–15, 'Miscellany'. This resembles somewhat a literary tradition of Southern Sung scholars, who composed thousands of poems to show their appreciation of certain actress-courtesans.
131. *Hsi-chü shih-chieh* 1–5 (1922–3), 'Yu chieh t'ien-wên-t'ai' and 'Miscellany'; *Chü shêng* 1 (1917: 27), 'Postscript'.
132. *Hsi ch'uan* 1 (1931). *Wu-hsien man-hua* (1929–30s) featured heavily the latest gossip about opera actresses.
133. You Lung, 1933: 1.1, 3 June; 'Nien-shao Fêng chieh-yen chi pien yu wên', *YHP* 1934: 1, 21 Oct. For examples of similar style of reporting in the 1920s and 1930s, see *KPP, YHP, KHP, passim*.
134. For instance, there was a report about the 'love-sickness' suffered by the prominent actor Chien-li Ch'ü (*HTJP* 1913, 16 April) The sensational news of the killing of an Indian police constable by the bodyguard of a famous actor was closely followed and reported in *HTJP* from mid-February to early March 1913.
135. In view of the seriousness of the problem of overcrowding in opera houses, local police were ordered to inspect these premises more frequently, though the effectiveness of this was dubious (*HTJP* 1927: 2.2, 7 July).
136. According to the reminiscences of Mr Ferdinand Hoo-on; Ch'en Fei-nung and Yu Mu-yün (1982: 71); Wang Yung-chih (1988: 50–1).
137. According to Mr Ferdinand Hoo-on. The profligacy of a concubine who gives her idol opera actor a diamond ring, originally a gift from her husband, is the plot of a topical short story (Tzu K'uan 1926: 4).
138. 'Ling chi fêng-liu nieh' (Sin of Dissipation Between an Actor and a Prostitute), *HTJP* 1927, 21–30 July.
139. For brief biographical histories of some of these actors, see *YCS* (1988: 199–201, 207–8).
140. Hsieh Shêng-nung was a successful example in this respect. *KCTC* (1933: 38).
141. Both Ma and Hsüeh had their own film company, though the former's was far less successful. Chang Chieh (1980*b*: 135); (1980*a*: 253–5).
142. 'I nien lai chih kung-tso kai k'uang', in Kuang-chou-tê-pieh-shih wu-hsien-tien po-yin-t'ai (1930: 1–3).
143. For an example of the schedules of the three stations, see *YHP* 1936, 17 November.
144. The funeral of another superstar Hsüeh Chüeh-hsien in 1956 caused a similar sensation in Canton. Many senior government officials from Peking and Shanghai also attended. The Mayor of Canton officiated at the ceremony. Outside the funeral parlour, tens of thousands of men and women gathered to pay their last respects to this celebrity (Hsüeh Chüeh-hsien tao-nien chi pien-wei-hui (1957); Chang Chieh, 'Hsüeh Chüeh-hsien', *KCWSTL* (1980: 144–5)).
145. In order to humiliate the rival patron of a courtesan, Ma Shih-ts'êng paid handsomely for keeping her for one month; this, however, led to an abortive revenge assassination attempt on him Ch'en Fei-nung and Yu Mu-yün (1982: 74). Some other actors were

not so lucky. At least five of them were killed because of their intimate affairs with mistresses of 'powerful' men (Hai-chüeh-shih-jên, 'Wu-ko ming ling chih ssu' (1931: 6–10)).

146. A topical 'dragon-boat song' amusingly recounts a true story about a Police Chief who demanded a bribe of fifty tickets from an opera-house owner for not charging him for having ended a performance earlier than it was advertised (*HTJP* 1927, 23–31 May). The incident itself was reported in *HTJP* 1927, 14 May.

147. In 1884, a 'bad aristocrat' and his bodyguards were beaten up by a group of opera actors after their demand for 'forceful contribution' had been refused by the troupe (*Shen pao*, 1884, 21 January). In 1895, two high-income actors, whose popularity was due to their speciality in performing magic on stage, were kidnapped by a group of local hoodlums after performing in Ho-nan Island. Similar incidents were reportedly very common (*HTJP*, 1895, 7 February).

148. The fact that some opera companies were financed by means of share-holding signified the changing social attitude towards Cantonese opera as a socially worthy business to invest in. Shares were sometimes calculated in terms of the number of seats and their corresponding ticket value in a particular opera house (*HTJP* 1928: 4.4, 5 June).

149. The actors' guild in Ch'ing-dynasty Peking was quite active in organizing charitable work (Mackerras 1972: 228–9).

150. The theme of the variety show was to educate the masses about the importance of the Northern Expedition, and to rally public support to the Kuomintang (*HTJP* 1927: 3.2, 15 July).

151. All three of his sons received a university education, and became professionals (Lai Po-chiang 1986: 150).

152. Most beginners were, however, criticized for joining this profession just for the sake of its financial promise, rather than with a patriotic motive such as 'reforming society via opera' (*KCMKJP* 1926: 4, 27 July).

153. For instance, the two daughters of Pai Chü-yung, the 'King of the Role of Scholar', were trained by their father and become highly esteemed opera actresses (*YCS*, 216–17).

154. One such, Lo P'in-ch'ao, a promising young star in the 1930s, was brought up at an orphanage in Canton (Liu Ling-yü 1990: 2–12). The superstar Pai Chü-yung grew up in a very poor family (*YCS* 1988: 200–1).

155. 'T'i kao Yüeh-chü kung-tso-chê ti chêng-chih ti-wei', *NFJP* (1951: 5, 6 January).

CONCLUSION

1. Information about present-day Canton in this Conclusion was gathered by the author while on anthropological fieldwork in the city and in the Canton Delta between 1989 and 1998. In the past few years, a number of insightful historical studies have been published on these particular aspects of life in mainly other parts of China than Kwangtung. The following are only a few of the best examples. On political governance and social policy, Michael Tsin (1999). On prostitution: Gail Hershatter (1998); Christian Henriot (2001). On opium smoking: R. K. Newman (1995); Shanghai-shih chin-tu kung-tso ling-tao hsiao-tsu pan-kung-shih and Shanghai-shih tang-an-kuan (1996); Timothy Brook and Bob Tadashi Wakabayashi (2000). On Cantonese opera: Liu Ching-chih and Hsien Yü-i (1995); Li Chien (1993); Hu Chên (2000–2).

2. The seven-year rule of Ch'en Chi-t'ang over Kwangtung is retrospectively hailed as the most prosperous and stable period in the province's modern history. For an appraisal of the overall achievements of Ch'en, see Sha Tung-hsun (1989: 193–209). This positive memory of Ch'en's rule is still shared by many old residents of Canton. One of these reminiscences was published in *Yang-ch'êng wan pao*, 1982, 22 September similar comments are given by Mr Li who had worked for a foreign firm in Shamen during the 1930s, and Mr Liu Ch'êng, both of them having been interviewed by the author in Canton between 1989 and 1992.
3. This long period of prosperity was not without occasional interruptions. Labour unrest (1925–7), the outbreak of military confrontation (1929), and the Great Depression (the early 1930s) did leave some negative impact on the economy of Canton. In spite of these unhappy experiences, the overall economic performance of Canton remained reasonably good throughout this period (Ch'êng Hao 1985: 153–257); Arnold (1926) on Canton's economic situation between 1920 to 1925; Lee Bing-shuey (1936: 119–25). Remittances as well as investment from Overseas Chinese, which reached a record high in this period, also helped boost the economic performance of Canton (Lin Chin-chih, 'Chiu Chung-kuo ti Kuang-tung hua-ch'iao t'ou-tzu chi ch'i tso-yung' (1982: 127–47)).
4. For a brief discussion of the development of Cantonese restaurants in this period, see Fêng Ming-ch'üan's 'Man t'an Kuang-chou ch'a-lou yeh' in Kuang-chou-shih chêng-hsieh et al (1986: 186–202).
5. For information on other restaurants in contemporary Canton, see the various articles edited in Fêng Pi-ying (1989: 1–28).
6. This is especially true for religious festival opera (*shen kung hsi*) in Hong Kong and the countryside in the Canton Delta. On the former, see Ch'en Shou-jen (1988 and 1990). On the latter, not much scholarly research has been done. For a somewhat related discussion on this topic, see Virgil Ho's 'Cantonese Opera in a Rural Setting' in Aijmer and Boholm (1994).
7. Yack (1997) has recently written an insightful criticism on the shortcomings of the earlier critics of modernity for their exaggerated views of the power of distinctively modern ideas and institutions.
8. In a lecture delivered in 1961, E. H. Carr has pointed out this intrinsic problem of historical knowledge in his classic work *What is History*? (1978). Nearly forty years later, Carr's perceptive observation is still relevant to describe the predicament of historians of the past and present.
9. On this point, I could not agree more with Professor Philip Huang. In a recent article, he states that 'While . . . we need to be sensitive to and critical of different 'spins' that are put on facts, it does not seem to me to follow that there can therefore be no facts that are reducible to representations. . . . By such a logic, it really no longer matters whether evidence is carefully gathered and texts accurately read, for none has any objective existence outside the discourse in which it is represented. In the end, factual evidence comes to be no different from fabricated evidence, each differing merely by its degree of misrepresentation, each reflecting merely the historian's cultural orientations, and each finally just part of a system of discourse'. Philip C. C. Huang's 'Theory and Study of Modern Chinese History' (1998: 194–5). For another piece of perceptive criticism on the destructive impact of postmodernism on history writing, see Keith Windschuttle (1997).

10. One recent example is Gail Hershatter's meticulous study of the history of prostitution in Shanghai. In this work, Hershatter (1997) begins with a poststructuralistic criticism of the credibility of all textual sources on this subject. However, she writes a long book on prostitution based primarily on all those sources on which she casts serious doubt. For a detailed critical assessment of her book, see my (1998) review and Christian Henriot's (1998) review.

Abbreviations

CKMH	Chih-chi-shêng 支機生, 'Chu-kiang ming hua hsiao ch'uan' 珠江名花小傳 (n.d.). Reprinted in *Pi-chi hsiao-shuo ta kuan* 筆記小說大觀. 5th edn, 10 vols. (Taipei: Hsin hsing shu-ch'ü, 1974), ix.
CO	Colonial Office files. Public Record Office, Kew, London.
CPHH	Lü Hsüeh-hai 呂學海 (ed.), *Ch'üan-pên hsi-hua yen-lun chi* 全盤西化言論集 (Canton: Ling-nan ta-hsüeh hsüeh-shêng tzu-chih hui, 1934), i.
CPHH	Fêng En-yung 馮恩榮 (ed.), *Ch'üan-pên hsi-hua yen-lun su-chi* 全盤西化言論續集 (Canton: Ling-nan ta-hsüeh hsüeh-shêng tzu-chih hui ch'u-pan-shê, 1935) ii.
CSL	Kuang-tung-shêng t'i-fang shih-chih pien-wei-hui pang-kung-shih and Kuang-chou-shih t'i-fang-chih pien-wei-hui pang-kung-shih 廣州地方志編委會辦公室, 廣州地方志編委會辦公室 (eds.), *Ch'ing shih-lu Kuang-tung shih-liao* 清實錄廣東史料, 6 vols. (Canton: Kuang-tung shêng t'i-tu ch'u-pan-shê, 1995).
CTKL	Kuang-tung-shêng chin-tu wei-yüan-hui 廣東省禁賭委員會 (ed.), *Chin-tu kai lan* 禁賭概覽 (Canton: 1936).
FSKKTK	Fêng-su kai-kê wei-yüan-hui 風俗改革委員會 (ed.), *Fêng-su kai-kê ts'ung k'an* 風俗改革叢刊 (Canton: Kuang-chou-tê-pieh-shih tang-pu hsüan-ch'uan-pu, 1930).
FO	Foreign Office files. Public Record Office, Kew, London.
HCLCCN	Kuang-chou shih-chêng-fu 廣州市政府 (ed.), *Kuang-chou shih-chêng-fu hsin chu lo-ch'êng chi-nien tê-k'an* 廣州市政府新署落成紀念特刊 (Canton: 1934).
HTJP	*Hua-tzu jih-pao* 華字日報 (Hong Kong: Hua-tzu jih-pao shê).
HYOC	Chan-ch'i-ho-chu-jên 懺綺盦主人, *Hsin Yüeh-ou chieh hsin* 新粵謳解心 (Canton: n.p., *c.*1926).
HYTS	*Hsiang-yen ts'ung-shu* 香豔叢書 (Shanghai: Kuo-hsüeh fu-lun-shê, 1909–11).
KCHJP	*Kuang-chou hsin jih-pao* 廣州新日報 (Canton: Kuang-chou hsin jih-pao shê, 1933).
KCLPL	*Kuang-chou li-pai-liu* 廣州禮拜六 (Canton: Kuang-chou li-pai-liu shê, *c.*1933–5).
KCMKJP	*Kuang-chou min-kuo jih-pao* 廣州民國日報 (Canton: Kuang-chou min-kuo jih-pao shê).
KCPN	Chung-kuo jên-min chêng-chih-hsieh-shang-hui-i Kuang-tung-shêng Kuang-chou-shih wei-yüan-hui wên-shih tzu-liao wei-yüan-hui 中國人民政治協商會議廣東省廣州市委員會文史資料委員會 (ed.), *Kuang-chou pai-nien ta-shih chi* 廣州百年大事記 2 vols. (Canton: Kuang-tung jên-min ch'u-pan-shê, 1980).
KCTC	*Kuang-chou tsa-chih* 廣州雜誌 (Canton: Kuang-chou tsa-chih shê. 1924–30s).

KCWSTL Chung-kuo jên-min chêng-chih-hsieh-shang-hui-i Kuang-tung-shêng Kuang-chou-shih wei-yüan-hui wên-shih tzu-liao wei-yüan-hui 中國人民政治協商會議廣東省廣州市委員會文史資料委員會 (ed.), *Kuang-chou wên shih tzù liao* 廣州文史資料 (Canton: Kuang-tung jên-min ch'u-pan-she, 1960s–).

KHP *Kuo hua pao* 國華報 (Canton: Kuo hua pao shê, 1911–50).

KPP *Kung-p'ing pao* 公評報 (Canton: Kung-ping pao shê, 1924–49).

KTFCL Kuang-tung shêng chêng-hsieh wên-shih tzu-liao yen-chiu wei-yüan-hui 廣東省政協文史資料研究委員會 (ed.), *Kuang-tung fêng-ching lu* 廣東風情錄 (Canton: Kuang-tung jên-min ch'u-pan-shê, 1988).

KTHS Kuang-tung chung-hsüeh hsüeh-shêng tzu-chih-hui 廣東中學學生自治會 (ed.), *Kuang-tung hsüeh-shêng* 廣東學生 (Canton: vol. 2 (1933), vol. 4 (1934)).

LNFY Chiu-chung-fêng-fu 酒中瘋婦, *Ling-nan fêng-yüeh shih* 嶺南風月史 (Canton: *c.* 1930s).

NCH *North-China Herald*. (Shanghai 1850–1941).

NFJP *Nan-fang jih-pao* 南方日報 (Canton: Nan-fang jih-pao shê. 1950–).

NYSP *Nan-yang shang pao* 南洋商報 (Singapore: Nan-yang shang pao shê).

YCS Lai Po-chiang 賴伯彊，Huang Ching-ming 黃鏡明，*Yüeh-chü shih* 粵劇史 (Peking: Chung-kuo hsi-chü ch'u-pan-shê, 1988).

YCYC *Yüeh-chü yen-chiu* 粵劇研究 (Canton: Kuang-chou-shih wên-i ch'uang-tso yen-chiu-shuo Yüeh-chü yen-chiu chung-hsin, 1986–1991).

YCYCTLH Kuang-tung-shêng hsi-chü yen-chiu-shih 廣東省戲劇研究室 (ed.) *Yüeh-chü yen-chiu tzu-liao hsüan* 粵劇研究資料選 (Canton: n.p., 1983).

YHKPK Kuang-chou-shih ti-fang-chih pien-hsüan wei-yüan-hui pan-kung-shih and Kuang-chou hai-kuan-chih pien-hsüan wei-yüan-hui 廣州市地方志編纂委員會辦公室, 廣州海關志編纂委員會(eds.),*Chin-tai Kuang-chou k'ou-an ching-chi shê-hui kai-k'uang: Yüeh hai-kuan pao-kao hui tsi* 近代廣州口岸經济社會概況：粵海關報告滙集, (Canton: Chi-nan ta-hsüeh ch'u-pan-shê,1996).

YHP *Yüeh hua pao* 越華報 (Canton: Yüeh hua pao shê, 1927–50).

Selected Western and Japanese Language References

Aalst, J. A. van. *Chinese Music*. Shanghai: The Inspector General of Customs, 1884.

Abrams, Lynn. 'Prostitutes in Imperial Germany, 1870–1918: Working Girls or Social Outcasts?' Richard J. Evans (ed.), *The German Underworld: Deviants and Outcasts in German History*. London: Routledge, 1988.

Adams, Leonard P., II. 'China: The Historical Setting of Asia's Profitable Plague'. *The Politics of Heroin in Southeast Asia*. McCay, Alfred W. New York: Harper & Row, 1972.

Agnew, John A., Mercer, John, and Sosher, David E. (eds.), *The City in Cultural Context*. Boston: Allen & Unwin, 1984.

Aijmer, Göran. 'Birth and Death in China: Musings on a Taiwan Groups'. *Ethnos*, 49/1–2 (1984).

——'On Legitimacy in Revolutionary Situations: The Cultural Revolution in the New Territories, Hong Kong'. Edited by Shaw Yu-ming. *Reform and Revolution in Twentieth-Century China*. Taipei: Institute of International Relations of National Cheng-chi University, 1987.

Akimova, Vishnyakova, and Vladimirovna, Vera. *Two Years in Revolutionary China*. Trans. Steven I. Levine. Cambridge, Mass.: Harvard University Press, 1971.

Alexéiev, Basil M. *The Chinese Gods of Wealth*. London: School of Oriental Studies and the China Society, 1928.

Alitto, Guy S. *The Last Confucian: Liang Shou-ming and the Chinese Dilemma of Modernity*. Berkeley: University of California Press, 1979.

Amaro, Ana Maria. 'Fai-vut-lau', in *Review of Culture (Macau: Instituto Cultural de Macau)*, 2/6 (1988).

Anderson, Elam J. 'Music as a Leisure Occupation for College Students'. *The Chinese Social and Political Science Review*, 10/4 (Oct. 1926).

Arnold, Julian, et al. *China: A Commercial and Industrial Handbook*. Washington DC: U.S. Deparment of Commerce Trade Promotion Series 38 (1926).

Atwell, Palmela. *British Mandarins and Chinese Reformers: The British Administration of Weihaiwei (1898–1930) and the Territory's Return to Chinese Rule*. Hong Kong: Oxford University Press, 1985.

Bailey, Peter. *Leisure and Class in Victorian England: Rational Recreation and the Contest for Control, 1830–1885*. London: Methuen, 1987.

Baker, Hugh D. R. *A Chinese Lineage Village: Sheung Shui*. London: Frank Cass, 1968.

——*Ancestral Images: A Hong Kong Album*. Hong Kong: South China Morning Post, 1979.

——*More Ancestral Images: A Second Hong Kong Album*. Hong Kong: South China Morning Post, 1980.

——*Ancestral Images Again: A Third Hong Kong Album*. Hong Kong: South China Morning Post, 1981.

Balazs, Etienne. *Chinese Civilization and Bureaucracy*. Trans. by H. M. Wright. New Haven: Yale University Press, 1964.

Ball, J. Dyer. *Things Chinese*. 4th edn. Hong Kong: Kelly & Walsh, 1903.

Bartke, Wolfgang. *Who's Who in the People's Republic of China*. 2 vols. 3rd edn. Münich: K. G. Saur, 1991.

Beattie, John. *Other Cultures*. London: Routledge & Kegan Paul, 1969.

Becker, Gary S., and Murphy, Kevin M. 'A Theory of Rational Addiction', *Journal of Political Economy* 96/4 (1988).

Bergère, Marie-Claire. *The Golden Age of the Chinese Bourgeoisie, 1911–1937*. Trans. by Janet Lloyd. Cambridge: Cambridge University Press, 1989.

Bergler, Edmund. *The Psychology of Gambling*. New York: Hill & Wang, 1957.

Bernheimer, Charles. *Figures of Ill Repute: Representing Prostitution in Nineteenth-Century France*. Cambridge, Mass.: Harvard University Press, 1989.

Berridge, Virginia. *Opium and the People: Opiate Use and Drug Control Policy in Nineteenth and Early Twentieth Century England*. London: Free Association Books, 1999.

—— and Edwards, Griffith. *Opium and the People: Opiate Use in Nineteenth-Century England*. London: Allen Lane, 1981.

Blunden, Caroline, and Elvin, Mark. *Cultural Atlas of China*. Oxford: Phaidon, 1983.

Borthwick, Sally. 'Changing Concepts of the Role of Women from the Late Ch'ing to the May-Fourth Period'. E. S. K. Fung and David Pong (eds.), *Ideal and Reality*. Lanham, Md.: University Press of America.

Bourdieu, Pierre. *Distinction: A Social Critique of the Judgement of Taste*. Trans. by Richard Nice. London: Routledge & Kegan Paul, 1986.

Boxer, C. R. (ed.). *South China in the Sixteenth Century: Being the Narratives of Galeote Pereira, Fr. Gaspar de Cruz, O.P., Fr. Martin de Rada, O.E.S.A*. London: The Hakluyt Society, 1953.

Bradby, David, James, Louis, and Sharrat, Bernard. *Performance and Politics in Popular Drama*. Cambridge: Cambridge University Press, 1980.

Brandon, James R., Malm, William P., and Shively, Donald H. *Studies in Kabuki: Its Acting, Music, and Historical Context*. Honolulu: The University Press of Hawaii, 1978.

Brook, Timothy, and Wakabayashi, Bob Tadashi (eds.), *Opium Regimes: China, Britain and Japan, 1839–1952*. Berkeley: University of California Press, 2000.

Brusak, Karel. 'Signs in Chinese Theater.' Ladislav Matejka and Irwin R. Titunik (eds.), *Semiotics of Art: Prague School Contributions*. Cambridge, Mass.: The MIT Press, 1968.

Burchard, John, and Handlin, Oscar. *The Historian and the City*. Cambridge, Mass.: The MIT Press and Harvard University Press, 1963.

Burke, Peter. 'Strengths and Weaknesses of the History of Mentalities.' *History of European Ideas*, 7/5 (1986).

Burke, Peter. *History and Social Theory*. Cambridge: Polity Press, 1992.

Byron, John. *Portrait of A Chinese Paradise: Erotica and Sexual Customs of the Late Ch'ing Period*. London: Quartet Books, 1987.

Canton: Its Port, Industries & Trade. Canton: The Canton Advertising & Commission Agency, 1932.

Cantonese Love-songs. 2 vols. Trans. by Cecil Clementi. Oxford: Clarendon Press, 1904.

Carr, Edward Hallet. *What is History?* Harmondsworth: Penguin, 1978.

Champly, Henry. *The Road to Shanghai: White Slave Traffic in Asia*. Trans. by Warre B. Wells. London: John Long, 1934.

Chan, Anita, Unger, Jonathan, and Madsen, Richard. *Chen Village: The Recent History of a Peasant Community in Mao's China*. Berkeley: University of California Press, 1984.

Chan, Ming-kou. 'Labor and Empire: The Chinese Labor Movement in the Canton Delta, 1895–1927'. Unpublished Ph.D. dissertation, Stanford University, 1975.

Chang, Chak-yan. ' "Ruralia" vs "Urbania" in Chinese Political Thought'. Unpublished Ph.D. dissertation, State Univeristy of New York at Binghamton, 1975.

Chang, Ching-sheng. *Sex Histories: China's First Modern Treatise on Sex Education*. Trans. by Howard S. Levy. Yokohama: Pe Yuan Press, 1968.

Chang, Hsin-pao. *Commissioner Lin and the Opium War*. New York: W. W. Norton, 1964.

Ch'ang, Hsin-hsin, and Yeh, Sang. *Chinese Lives: An Oral History*. Trans. by W. J. F. Jenner and Delia Davin. New York: Pantheon Books, 1987.

Chartier, Roger. *Cultural History: Between Practices and Representations*. Trans. by Lydia G. Cochrane. Cambridge: Polity Press; and Oxford: Basil Blackwell, 1988.

Ch'en, Han-seng. *Agrarian Problems in Southernmost China*. Shanghai: Kelly & Walsh, 1936.

Ch'en, Jerome. *China and the West*. London: Hutchison, 1979.

Ch'en, Jerome (ed.), *Studies in the History of China and the Southeast Asia*. Cambridge: Cambridge University Press, 1970.

Ch'en, Li-fu. *The Confucian Way: A New and Systematic Study of 'The Four Books'*. Trans. by Shih-shun Liu. London: Routledge & Kegan Paul, 1986.

Ch'en, Ta. *Emigrant Communities in South China: A Study of Overseas Migration and Its Influence on Standards of Living and Social Change*. Edited by Bruno Lasker. Shanghai: Kelly & Walsh, 1939.

*The China Year Book 1912–1930*s. Edited by H. G. W. Woodhead and H.T. Montague Bell. London: Routledge & Sons.

Choi, Dora. 'Political Participation of Students in Guangdong, 1927–1949'. Unpublished paper, n.d.

Clotfelter, Charles T., and Cook, Philip J. *Selling Hope: State Lotteries in America*. Cambridge, Mass.: Harvard University Press, 1991.

Coble, Parks M., Jr. *The Shanghai Capitalists and the Nationalist Governments, 1927–1937*. Cambridge, Mass.: Harvard University Press, 1980.

Colquhoun, Archibald. *China in Transformation*. 2nd edn. London: Harper & Brothers, 1898.

Comini, Alessandra. *Gustav Klimt*. London: Thames & Hudson, 1975.

Coomber, Ross (ed.). *Drugs and Drug Use in Society: A Critical Reader*. Dartford: Greenwich University Press, 1994.

Corbett, Charles Hodge. *Lingnan University*. New York: 1963.

Courtwright, David T. *Dark Paradise: A History of Opiate Addiction in America*. Cambridge, Mass.: Harvard University Press, 2001.

——*Forces of Habit: Drugs and the Making of the Modern World*. Cambridge, Mass.: Harvard University Press, 2001.

Croizier, Ralph. *Art and Revolution in Modern China: The Lingnan (Cantonese) School of Painting, 1906–1961*. Berkeley: University of California Press, 1988.

Croll, Elizabeth. *Feminism and Socialism in China*. London: Routledge & Kegan Paul, 1978.

De Groots, J. J. M. *The Religious System of China*. 6 vols. Reprinted by Taipei: Ch'eng Wen Publishing, 1972.

Docherty, David, Morrison, David, and Tracey, Michael. *The Last Picture Show? Britain's Changing Film Audience*. London: British Film Institute, 1987.

Dolby, William. *A History of Chinese Drama*. London: Paul Elek, 1976.

Domville-Fife, Charles W. 'A Night on the Pearl River', and 'The Enigma of Teeming Canton'. *World Travels*, v. London: Virtue, *c.*1930s.

Dikötter, Frank. *The Discourse of Race in Modern China*. Hong Kong: Hong Kong University Press, 1992.

——*Sex, Culture and Modernity in China: Medical Science and the Construction of Sexual Identities in the Early Republican Period*. Hong Kong: Hong Kong University Press, 1995.

Dunkley, John. *Gambling: A Social and Moral Problem in France, 1685–1792*. Oxford: The Voltaire Foundation, 1985.

Eadington, William R., and Thomas, Charles C. (eds), *Gambling and Society: Interdisciplinary Studies on the Subject of Gambling*. Springfield, Ill.: Thomas, 1976.

Eastman, Lloyd E. *The Abortive Revolution: China Under Nationalist Rule, 1927–1937*. Cambridge, Mass.: Harvard University Press, 1974.

Eberhard, Wolfram. *Cantonese Ballads: München State Library Collection*. Taipei: Oriental Cultural Service, 1972.

——*Guilt and Sin in Traditional China*. Berkeley: University of California Press, 1967.

——*Moral and Social Values of the Chinese: Collected Essays*. Taipei: Ch'eng Wen Publishing Co., 1971.

Eberstein, Bernd. 'Opera vs Spoken Drama: Some Trends in the Development of Modern Chinese Theater.' Wolfram Kubin and R.G. Wager (eds.), *Essays in Modern Chinese Literature and Literary Criticism: Papers of the Berlin Conference, 1978*. Bochum: n.p., 1982.

Elvin, Mark. *The Pattern of the Chinese Past*. Stanford: Stanford University Press, 1973.

——'Chinese Cities Since the S'ung Dynasty.' P. Abrams and E. Wrigely (eds.), *Towns in Societies*. Cambridge: Cambridge University Press, 1978.

——'The Double Disavowal: The Attitudes of Radical Thinkers to the Chinese Tradition.' Shaw Yu-ming (ed.), *China and Europe in the Twentieth Century*. Taipei: National Cheng-chi University, 1986.

——'Tales of Shen and Xin: Body-person and Heart-mind in China During the Last 150 Years.' Michel Feher (ed.), *Zone: Fragments for A History of the Human Body*, p. II. New York: Urzone, 1989.

——'The Crisis of Absurdity: Reflections on *Tides in the Human Sea*'. Unpublished paper, August 1991.

——and Skinner, G. William edited. *The Chinese City Between Two Worlds*. Stanford: Stanford University Press, 1974.

Esherick, Joseph W. edited. *Remaking The Chinese City: Modernity and National Identity, 1900–1950*. Honolulu: University of Hawaii Press, 2000.

Evans, Hilary. *The Oldest Profession: An Illustrated History of Prostitution*. London: David & Charles, 1979.

Faure, David. *The Rural Economy of Pre-Liberation China: Trade Expansion and Peasant Livelihood in Jiangsu and Guangdong*. Hong Kong: Oxford University Press, 1989.

Fewsmith, Joseph. *Party, State and Local Elites in Republican China*. Honolulu: University of Hawaii Press, 1985.

Fitzgerald, John. 'Increased Disunity: The Politics and Finance of Guangdong Separation, 1926–1936.' *Modern Asian Studies* 24/4 (1990).

Fitzgerald, John. *Awakening China: Politics, Culture, and Class in the Nationalist Revolution*. Stanford: Stanford University Press, 1996.

Franck, Harry A. *Roving Through Southern China*. New York: The Century Co., 1925.

Freedman, Maurice. *Chinese Lineage and Society: Fukien and Kwangtung*. London: The Athlone Press, 1971.

—— *The Study of Chinese Family: Essays by Maurice Freedman*. Selected and Introduced by G. William Skinner. Stanford: Stanford University Press, 1979.

Frith, Simon. 'Towards an Aesthetic of Popular Music.' Richard Leppert, Susan McClary (eds.), *Music and Society*.

Fuma, Susuma. 'Late Ming Urban Reform in Hangzhou'. Linda Cooke Johnson (ed.), *Cities of Jiangnan in Late Imperial China*. Albany: SUNY, 1993.

Fung, S. K. Edmund. 'Nationalist Foreign Policy, 1928–1937.' Edmund S.K. Fung and David Pong (eds.), *Ideal and Reality*. Lanham, Md: University Press of America, 1985.

Furth, Charlotte. 'The Patriarch's Legacy: Household Instructions and the Transmission of Orthodox Values.' Kwang-ching Liu (ed.), *Orthodoxy in Late Imperial China*. Berkeley: University of California Press, 1990.

Galbiati, Fernando. *P'eng P'ai and the Hai-lu-feng Soviet*. Stanford: Stanford University Press, 1984.

Gamble, Sidney D. *Peking: A Social Survey*. New York: George H. Doran, 1921.

Gans, Herbert J. *Popular Culture and High Culture: An Analysis and Evaluation of Taste*. New York: Basic Books, 1974.

Gao, H. S. 'Police Administration in Canton'. *The Chinese Social and Political Science Review*, 10/2–4 (1926).

Geil, William Edgar. *Eighteen Captials of China*. London: Constable, 1911.

Geremek, Bronislaw. *The Margins of Society in Late Medieval Paris*. Cambridge: Cambridge University Press, 1987.

Gernet, Jacques. *Daily Life in China on the Eve of the Mongol Invasion, 1250–1276*. Trans. by H. W. Wright. Stanford: Stanford University Press, 1962.

Gluck, Carol. *Japan's Modern Myth: Ideology in the Late Meiji Period*. Princeton, NJ: Princeton University Press, 1985.

Gillingham, Paul. *At the Peak: Hong Kong Between the Wars*. Hong Kong: Macmillan, 1983.

Gray, John Henry. *Walks in the City of Canton*. Hong Kong: De Souza, 1875.

—— *China. A History of the Laws, Manners and Customs of the People*. 2 vols. Shannon: Irish University Press, 1972. First published 1878.

Great Britain. Colonial Office. *General Correspondence, Hong Kong. Series CO 129*. Public Record Office, London.

Great Britain. Foreign Office. *Confidential Prints, China Series FO 405*. Public Record Office, London.

Great Britain. *Embassy and Consular Archives, Correspondence Series I, FO 228*. Public Record Office, London.

—— *General Correspondence, Political Series FO 371*. Public Record Office, London.

Grimm, Tilemann. 'Academies and Urban Systems in Kwangtung.' G. W. Skinner (ed.), *The City in Late Imperial China.* Stanford: Stanford University Press, 1977.

Gronewold, Sue. *Beautiful Merchandise: Prostitution in China, 1860–1836.* New York: Harrington Park, 1985.

Gulik, Robert Hans van. *Sexual Life in Ancient China: A Preliminary Survey of Chinese Sex and Society from ca. 1500 B.C. till 1644 A.D.* Leiden: E.J. Brill, 1961.

Gunji, Masakatsu, and Yoshida, Chikai. *The Kabuki Theater.* Trans. by Christopher Holmes. Tokyo: Kodansha International, 1987.

Hall, Peter (1984), 'Metropolis 1890–1940: Challenges and Responses.' Anthony Sutcliffe (ed.), *Metropolis*, Chicago; University of Chicago Press.

Hardy, E. J. *John Chinaman at Home.* London: T. Fisher Unwin, 1905.

Harrison, Fraser. *The Dark Angel: Aspects of Victorian Sexuality.* Glasgow: Fontana/Collins, 1979.

Hayes, James. 'Specialists and Written Materials in Late Imperial China.' David Johnson, Andrew J. Nathan, and Evelyn S. Rawski (eds.), *Popular Culture in Late Imperial China.* Berkeley: University of California Press, 1985.

Hayter, Alethea. *Opium and the Romantic Imagination.* London: Faber & Faber, 1968.

Hershatter, Gail. *Dangerous Pleasures: Prostitution and Modernity in Twentieth-Century China.* Berkeley: University of California Press, 1997.

Hegel, Robert E. 'Distinguishing Levels of Audiences for Ming-Ch'ing Local Drama'. David Johnson, Andrew J. Nathan, and Evelyn S. Rawski. (eds.), *Popular Culture in Imperial China.* Berkeley: University of California Press, 1985.

Heinemann, Margot. *Puritanism and Theater: Thomas Middleton and Opposition Drama Under the Early Stuarts.* Cambridge: Cambridge University Press, 1982.

Henriot, Christian. ' "From a Throne of Glory to a Seat of Ignomity": Prostitution in Shanghai Revisited.' *Modern China*, 22/2, April 1996.

——Review on *Dangerous Pleasures* by Gail Hershatter. *International Labor and Working-Class* 54, Fall 1998.

——*Prostitution and Sexuality in Shanghai: A Social History (1849–1940).* Cambridge: Cambridge University Press, 2001.

Henriques, Fernando. *Prostitution and Society: A Survey.* 3 vols. London: Macgibbon & Kee, 1962–8.

Henry, B. C. *Lingnam: or Interior Views of Southern China.* London: S. W. Partridge, 1886.

Herman, Robert D. (ed.), *Gambling.* New York: Harper & Row, 1967.

Hershatter, Gail. 'Prostitution and the Market in Women in Early Twentieth-Century Shanghai.' Rubie S. Watson, and Patricia Buckley Ebery (eds.), *Marriage and Inequality in Chinese Society.* Berkeley: University of California Press, 1991.

——*Dangerous Pleasures: Prostitution and Modernity in Shanghai.* Berkeley: University of California Press, 1997.

Ho, Kit-yiu Virgil. 'Hong Kong Government's Attitude To the Canton-Hong Kong Strike and Boycott of 1925–1926'. Unpublished M.St. dissertation, Oxford University, 1985.

——'Cantonese Opera in a Rural Setting'. Edited by Göran Aijmer and Åsa Boholm. *Images and Enactments: Possible Worlds in Dramatic Performance.* Gothenburg: Institute for Advanced Studies of Social Anthropology, 1994.

——Review on *Dangerous Pleasures* by Gail Hershatter. *China Information*, 13/1, Summer 1998.

——'Whose Bodies? Taming Contemporary Prostitutes' Bodies in Official Chinese Rhetorics', in *China Information*, 13/2–3 (Autumn/Winter 1998–9).

——'Butchering Fish and Executing Criminals: Public Executions and the Meanings of Violence in Late Imperial and Modern China', in Göran Aijmer and Jon Abbink (eds.), *Meanings of Violence: A Cross-Cultural Perspective*. Oxford: Berg, 2000.

——''To Laugh at a Penniless Man Rather Than a Prostitute': The Unofficial Worlds of Prostitution in Late-Qing and Early Republican South China'. *European Journal of East Asian History* 1/1 (2001).

——and Aijmer, Göran. *Cantonese Society in a Time of Change*. Hong Kong: The Chinese University Press, 2000.

Hogshire, Jim. *Opium for the Masses: A Practical Guide to Growing Poppies and Making Opium*. Port Townsend, Wash.: Loompanics Unlimited, 1994.

Hong Kong Regional Council (ed.), *Cantonese Opera Costumes*. Hong Kong: Regional Council, 1988.

Horn, Pierre L., and Pringle, Mary Beth (eds.), *The Image of the Prostitute in Modern Literature*. New York: Frederick Ungar., 1984.

Hsieh, Winston. 'Popular Movement and Mercantile Elite in Canton, 1895–1928.' Unpublished article for the Canton Delta Project, University of Washington, Seattle, n.d.

——'The Ideas and Ideals of a Warlord: Ch'en Chiung-ming (1878–1933)'. *Papers on China*, vol. 16, December 1962.

Hsu, Francis L. K. *Under the Ancestors' Shadow: Kinship, Personality, and Social Mobility in China*. Stanford: Stanford University Press, 1967.

Hsü, Tao-ching. *The Chinese Conception of Theater*. Seattle: University of Washington Press, 1985.

Huang, C. C. Philip. 'Theory and Study of Modern Chinese History: Four Traps and a Question'. *Modern China*, 24/2, April 1998.

Hughes, E. R. *The Invasion of China by the Western World*. 2nd edn. London: Adam & Charles Black, 1968.

Hung, Chang-tai. *Going to the People: Chinese Intellectuals and Folk Literature, 1918–1937*. Cambridge, Mass.: Harvard University Press, 1985.

Hunter, William C. *Bits of Old China*. London: Kegan Paul, Trench, 1855.

——*The 'Fankwae' at Canton Before Treaty Days. 1825–1844*. Reprinted by Taipei: Ch'eng Wen Publishing, 1976.

Idema, Wilt, and West, Stephen H. *Chinese Theater, 1100–1450: A Source Book*. Wiesbaden: Franz Steiner, 1982.

The International Anti-Opium Association: Peking. *The War Against Opium*. Tientsin: Tientsin Press, 1922.

The International Anti-opium Association: Peking. *Opium Cultivation and Traffic in China: An Investigation in 1923–1924*. Peking: The International Anti-opium Association Peking, 1924.

Israel, John. *Student Nationalism in Republican China, 1927–1937*. Stanford: Stanford University Press, 1966.

Joardar, Biswanath. *Prostitution: A Bibliographical Synthesis*. New Delhi: Inter-India Publications, 1984.

Joardar, Biswanath. *Prostitution in Historical and Modern Perspectives*. New Delhi: Inter-India Publications, 1984.

Johnson, David. 'Communication, Class, and Consciousness in Late Imperial China.' David Johnson, Andrew J. Nathan, and Evelyn S. Rawski (eds.), *Popular Culture in Late Imperial China*. Berkeley: University of California Press, 1985.

—— 'The City-God Cults of T'ang and Sung China.' *Harvard Journal of Asiastic Studies* 45/2, December 1985.

Jordan, R. Furneaux. *A Concise History of Western Architecture*. London: Thames & Hudson, 1979.

Juan, Fang-fu. *Sex in China: Studies in Sexology in Chinese Culture*. New York: Plenum Press, 1991.

Jusêk, Karin J. 'Sexual Morality and the Meaning of Prostitution in fin-de-siècle Vienna.' *From Sappho to De Sade: Moments in the History of Sexuality*. London: Routledge, 1989.

Kavanagh, Thomas M. *Enlightenment and the Shadows of Chance: The Novel and the Culture of Gambling in Eighteenth-Century France*. Baltimore: Johns Hopkins University Press, 1993.

Kazantzakis, Nikos. *Japan, China: A Journal of Two Voyages to the Far East*. Trans. by George C. Pappageotes. Berkeley: Creative Arts Book Co., 1982.

Kennedy, Emmet. *A Cultural History of the French Revolution*. New Haven: Yale University Press, 1989.

Kōain Seimubu. *Kanton no sembai jigyō*. N.p., 1939.

Kolb, Lawrence. 'Drug Addiction', in *Archives of Neurology and Psychiatry* 20 (1928).

Kōsaka, Junichi. 'Ingo yori mitaru Kanton sha kai so.' *Minzoku Taiwan* 3/4–5, 1943.

—— 'Kanton tsushin.' pts. 1 and 2. *Minzoku Taiwan*, 3/9 and 12, May and Dec. 1943.

Krejci, Jaroslav. 'From the Margins to Centre Stage.' *The Times Higher Education Supplement*, 15 Feb. 1991.

Kristof, Nicholas D. 'Cosmetic Surgery in China: A Look West, Straight in the Eyes.' *International Herald Tribune*, 20 June 1991.

Kulp, Daniel Harrison, II. *Country Life in South China: The Sociology of Familism. i. Phenix Village, Kwangtung, China*. New York: Teacher College of Columbia University, 1925.

Kuo, Wên-fang. *Modern Canton Illustrated*. 2nd edn. Canton: The China Photo-Engraving Co., 1924.

La Motte, Ellen N. *The Opium Monopoly*. New York: Macmillan, 1920.

Lai, T. C. *To the Yellow Springs: The Chinese View of Death*. Hong Kong: Joint Publishing Co. and Kelly & Walsh, 1983.

Lamson, Herbert Day. *Social Pathology in China*. 2nd. edn. Shanghai: The Commercial Press, 1935.

Lattimore, Owen. *Manchuria: Cradle of Conflict*. Revised edn. New York: AMS Press, 1975. First published 1935.

Larsen, Jeanne (trans. and introd.). *Brocade River Poems: Selected Works of the T'ang Dynasty Courtesan Xue Tao*. Princeton, NJ: Princeton University Press, 1987.

Lary, Diana. *Region and Nation: The Kwangsi Clique in Chinese Politics, 1925–1937*. Cambridge: Cambridge University Press, 1974.

—— *Warlord Soldiers: Chinese Common Soldiers, 1911–1937*. Cambridge: Cambridge University Press, 1985.

League of Nations Advisory Committee on Social Questions. *Enquiry Into Measures of Rehabilitation of Prostitutes*. 3 vols. Geneva: 1938.

Lee, Bing-shuey Edward. *Modern Canton*. Shanghai: Kelly & Walsh, 1936.

Lee, Leo Ou-fan. *The Romantic Generation of Modern Chinese Writers*. Cambridge, Mass.: Harvard University Press, 1973.

Lees, Andrew. 'The Metropolis and the Intellectual.' Anthony Sutcliffe (ed.), *Metropolis: 1890–1940*. (Chicago: University of Chicago Press).

—— *Cities Perceived: Urban Societies in European and American Thought, 1820–1940*. Manchester: Manchester University Press, 1985.

Leeuw, Hendrik de. *Cities of Sin*. London: Neville Spearman, 1953.

Legges, James. *Confucian Analects*. Shanghai: Shang-hai shu-chü, 1899.

Leong, S. T. 'The Hakka Chinese of Lingnan: Ethnicity and Social Change in Modern Times.' David Pong, and Edmund S. K. Fung (eds.), *Ideal and Reality*. Lanham, Md.: University Press of America, 1985.

Leppert, Richard, and McClary, Susan. *Music and Society: The Politics of Composition, Performance and Reception*. Cambridge: Cambridge University Press, 1987.

Lethaby, W. R. *Form in Civilization*. Oxford: Clarendon Press, 1922.

Lethbridge, Henry J. 'The Evolution of a Chinese Voluntary Association in Hong Kong: Po Leung Kuk'. Henry J. Lethbridge (ed.), *Hong Kong: Stability and Change*. Hong Kong: Oxford University Press, 1978.

Leung, Pui-chee. *A Study of Nan Yin and Yue Ou*. San Francisco: San Francisco State University, 1988.

Leung, Pui-chee. *Wooden-Fish Books: Critical Essays and An Annoted Catalogue Based on the Collections in the University of Hong Kong*. Hong Kong: Centre of Asian Studies, University of Hong Kong, 1978.

Levine, Donald N. *The Flight From Ambiguity: Essays in Social and Cultural Theory*. Chicago: University of Chicago Press, 1985.

Levy, Howard S. *Chinese Footbinding: The History of a Curious Erotic Custom*. London: Neville Spearman, n.d.

Lewin, Louis. *Phantastica: Narcotic and Stimulating Drugs*. Reprinted by London: Routledge & Kegan Paul, 1964.

Lewis, John Wilson edited. *The City in Communist China*. Stanford: Stanford University Press, 1971.

Leyda, Jay. *Dianying: Electric Shadows: An Account of Films and Film Audience in China*. Cambridge, Mass.: The MIT Press, 1972.

Li, Chien-nung. *The Political History of China, 1840–1928*. Trans. and ed. by Teng Ssu-yu and Jeremy Ingalls. Stanford: Stanford University Press, 1967.

Liao, Kuang-sheng. *Antiforeignism and Modernization in China, 1860–1980*. Hong Kong: The Chinese University Press, 1986.

Light, Arthur B., and Torrance, Edward G. *Opium Addiction*. Chicago: American Medical Association, [1929/30].

Lilius, Aleko E. *I Sailed with Chinese Pirates*. London: J. W. Arrowsmith, 1930.

Lindesmith, Alfred R. *Addiction and Opiates*. 2nd. edn. Chicago: Aldine, 1968.

Link, Perry. *Mandarin Ducks and Butterflies: Popular Fiction in Early Twentieth-Century Chinese Cities*. Berkeley: University of California Press, 1981.

Liu, James J.Y. *The Chinese Knight Errant*. London: Routledge & Kegan Paul, 1967.

London Missionary Society. Reports from South China District Committee, 1920s–1930s. London, The School of Oriental and African Studies Library.

Lynch, Kevin. *The Image of the City*. Cambridge, Mass.: The MIT Press, 1985.

Liu, Jung-en (trans.) *Six Yüan Plays*. London: Penguin Books, 1988.

Mackerras, Colin. 'Education in the Guomindang Period, 1928–1949.' Edited by D. Pong and Edmund S. K. Fung (eds.), *Ideal and Reality*. Lanham, Md.: University of America Press, 1985.

——*The Chinese Theatre in Modern Times: From 1840 to the Present Day*. London: Thames & Hudson, 1975.

——(ed.), *Chinese Theater From its Origins to the Present Day*. Honolulu: University of Hawaii Press, 1983.

——*The Rise of the Peking Opera 1770–1870: Social Aspects of the Theater in Manchu China*. Oxford: Clarendon Press, 1972.

Maddux, James F., and Desmond, David P. *Careers of Opioid Users*. New York: Praeger, 1981.

Merriam, Alan P. *The Anthropology of Music*. Evanston, Ill.: Northwestern University Press, 1964.

Metcalf, Thomas R. *An Imperial Vision: Indian Architecture and Britain's Raj*. Berkeley: University of California Press, 1989.

McMillen, Jan edited. *Gambling Cultures: Studies in History and Interpretation*. London: Routledge, 1996.

Miners, Norman. *Hong Kong under Imperial Rule, 1912–1941*. Hong Kong: Oxford University Press, 1987.

Mosher, Steven W. *Broken Earth: The Rural Chinese*. New York: The Free Press, 1983.

Mote, F. W. 'The Transformation of Nanking, 1350–1400.', in G. William Skinner (ed.). *The City in Late Imperial China*. Stanford: Stanford University Press, 1977.

Muchembled, Robert. *Popular and Elite Culture in France, 1400–1750*. Trans. by Lydia Cochrane. Baton Rouge: Louisiana State University Press, 1985.

Muensterberger, Warner. 'Orality and Dependence: Characteristics of Southern Chinese.' *Psychoanalysis and the Social Sciences* 3, 1951.

Mumford, Lewis. *The City in History: Its Origins, its Transformations, and its Prospects*. London: Penguin Books, 1961.

——*The Culture of Cities*. New York: Harcourt Brace Jovanovich, 1938.

Murayama Shigeru. *Kanton sa da*. Osaka: Ki bunku, 1941.

Murphy, Antoine. 'Is a national lottery just the ticket?' *Financial Times Weekend*, May 21/22, 1994.

Murphey, Rhoads. 'The Treaty Ports and China's Modernization,' in Mark Elvin and G. William Skinner (eds.), *The Chinese City Between Two Worlds*. Stanford: Stanford University Press, 1974.

——'City as A Mirror of Society: China, Tradition and Transformation.' J. A. Agnew, J. Mercer, and D. E. Sosher (eds.), *The City in Cultural Context*. Boston: Allen & Unwin, 1984.

Murray, Dian H. *Pirates of the South China Coast, 1790–1810*. Stanford: Stanford University Press, 1987.

Newman, Otto. *Gambling: Hazard and Reward*. London: The Athlone Press of the University of London, 1972.

Newman, R. K. 'Opium Smoking in Late Imperial China: A Reconsideration'. *Modern Asian Studies* 29/4 (1995).

Ng, Yong-sang (Wu Yang-shêng). *Canton: City of the Rams*. Canton: M. S. Cheung, 1936.

The Opium Trade. 6 vols. Wilmington, Del.: Scholarly Resources, 1974.

Pahl, R. E. 'The Rural–Urban Continuum.' R. E. Pahl (ed.), *Readings in Urban Sociology*. Oxford: Pergamon Press, 1974.

Parish, William L., and Whyte, Martin King. *Village and Family in Communist China*. Chicago: University of Chicago Press, 1978.

Pearsall, Ronald. *Victorian Popular Music*. Newton Abbot: David & Charles, 1973.

Philippine Commission, Opium Investigation Committee. *Report of the Committee appointed by the Philippine Commission to investigate the use of opium and the traffic therein and the rules, ordinances and laws regulating such use and traffic in Japan, Formosa, Shanghai, Hong Kong, Saigon, Singapore, Burma, Java and the Philippine Islands/Bureau of Insular Affairs, War Department*. Washington: Government Print Office, 1905.

'Plastics and Resins'. *The New Encyclopaedia Brittannica*, xxi. 290–304. Chicago: Encyclopaedia Brittannica, 1991.

Po Leung Kuk. *Centenary History of the Po Leung Kuk* (in Chinese). Hong Kong: Board of Directors of Po Leung Kuk, 1978.

Polachek, James. *The Inner Opium War*. Cambridge, Mass.: Harvard University Press, 1992.

Potter, Jack M., and Potter, Sulamith Heins. *China's Peasants: The Anthropology of A Revolution*. Cambridge: Cambridge University Press, 1990.

Pruitt, Ida. *A Daughter of Han: The Autobiography of a Chinese Working Woman*. Stanford: Stanford University Press, 1967.

Rainbow, Paul (ed.), *The Focault Reader*. Harmondsworth: Peregrine, 1987.

Rapport, Amos. 'Culture and the Urban Order.' John A. Agnew, John Mercer, and David E. Sopher (eds.), *The City in Cultural Context*. Boston: Allen & Unwin, 1984.

Rawski, Evelyn S. 'Economic and Social Foundations of Late Imperial Culture.' David Johnson, Andrew J. Nathan, and Evelyn S. Rawski (eds.), *Popular Culture in Late Imperial China*. Berkeley: University of California Press, 1985.

—— *Education and Popular Literacy in Ch'ing China*. Ann Arbor: The University of Michigan Press, 1979.

Raychaudhuri, Tapan. *Europe Reconsidered: Perceptions of the West in Nineteenth-Century Bengal*. Delhi: Oxford University Press, 1988.

Raz, Jacob. *Audience and Actors: A Study of their Interaction in the Japanese Traditional Theatre*. Leiden: E. J. Brill, 1983.

Rea, Kenneth edited. *Canton in Revolution: The Collected Papers of Earl Swisher, 1925–1928*. San Francisco: Westview Press, 1977.

Redfield, Robert, and Singer, Milton. 'The Cultural Role of Cities.' Richard Sennett (ed.), *Classic Essays on the Culture of Cities*. New York: Prentice-Hall, 1969.

Remick, Elizabeth. 'Taxing Prostitution in Republican Guangzhou'. Unpublished paper presented at Association for Asian Studies Annual Meeting, 4 April 2002.

Rhoads, Edward J. M. *China's Republican Revolution: The Case of Kwangtung, 1895–1913*. Cambridge, Mass.: Harvard University Press, 1975.

—— 'Lingnan's Response to the Rise of Chinese Nationalism: The Shakee Incident (1925).' *Papers on China* 15, 1961.

—— 'Nationalism and Xenophobia in Kwangtung (1905–1906): The Canton Anti-American Boycott and the Lienchow Anti-Missionary Uprising.' *Papers on China* 16, Dec. 1962.

Rojek, Chris (ed.), *Leisure for Leisure*. London: Macmillan, 1989.

Rowe, William T. *Hankow: Conflict and Community in a Chinese City, 1796–1895*. Stanford: Stanford University Press, 1989.

Rowe, William T. 'The Public Sphere in Modern China.' *Modern China* 16/3, July 1990.

Rowntree, Joshua. *The Opium Habit in the East: A Study of the Evidence and Report of the Royal Commission on Opium, 1893–5*. Westminster: P. S. King & Son, and E. T. W. Dennis, 1895.

Karl E. Scheibe, *The Drama of Everyday Life*. Cambridge, Mass.: Harvard University Press, 2000.

Schiffrin, Harold. *Sun Yat-sen and the Origins of the Chinese Revolution*. Berkeley: University of California Press, 1968.

Schlegel, Gustav. *A Canton Flower-Boat*. Leiden: E. J. Brill, 1894.

Scott, A. C. *Literature and the Arts in Twentieth-Century China*. London: Allen & Unwin, 1965.

Scott, George Ryley. *Far Eastern Sex Life*. London: Gerald G. Swan, 1943.

Seton, Grace Thompson. *Chinese Lanterns*. New York: Dodd, Mead, 1924.

Sheridan, James E. *Chinese Warlord: The Career of Feng Yü-hsiang*. Stanford: Stanford University Press, 1966.

Sheridan, Mary, and Salaff, Janet W. (eds.), *Lives: Chinese Working Women*. Bloomington: Indiana University Press, 1983.

Shiach, Morag. *Discourse on Popular Culture: Class, Gender and History in Cultural Analysis, 1730 to the Present*. Stanford: Stanford University Press, 1989.

'Shina chikaji no ahen ondai.' *Shina* 22/1–4 , 1931.

Silbergeld, Jerome. 'Chinese Painting Studies in the West: A State-of-the-Field Article'. *The Journal of Asian Studies* 46/4, Nov. 1987.

Sinn, Elizabeth. 'The Protection of Women in 19th-Century Hong Kong'. Maria Jaschok and Suzanne Miers (eds.), *Women and Chinese Patriarchy: Submission, Servitude and Escape*. Hong Kong: Hong Kong University Press, 1994.

Siu, Helen F. *Agents and Victims in South China*. New Haven: Yale University Press, 1989.

Skinner, G. William (ed.), *The City in Late Imperial China*. Stanford: Stanford University Press, 1977.

Skog, Ole-Jørgen. 'Addicts' Choice', *Addiction* 95/9 (2000).

Smith. H. S. *Diary of Events and the Progress on Shameen, 1859–1938*. Hong Kong: Ye Olde Printerie, 1939.

Spanier, David. *Easy Money: Inside the Gamblers' Mind*. London: Sphere Books, 1987.

Spence, Jonathan. 'Opium Smoking in Ch'ing China.' Frederic Wakeman Jr. and Carolyn Grant (eds.), *Conflict and Control in Late Imperial China*. Berkeley: University of California Press, 1975.

Stapleton, Kristin. *Civilizing Chengdu: Chinese Urban Reform, 1895–1937*. Cambridge, Mass.: Harvard University Press, 2000.

Sultzberger, Hartman (ed.), *All About Opium*. London: Wertheimer, Lea & Co., 1884.

Sutton-Smith, Brian, Roberts, John M., and Kozelka, Robert M. 'Game Involvement in Adults.' *The Journal of Social Psychology* 60, 1963.

Stockard, Janice E. *Daughters of the Canton Delta: Marriage Patterns and Economic Strategies in South China, 1860–1930*. Stanford: Stanford University Press, 1989.

Sutcliffe, Anthony edited. *Metropolis: 1890–1940*. Chicago: The University of Chicago Press, 1984.

Szasz, Thomas. *Ceremonial Chemistry: The Ritual Persecution of Drugs, Addicts, and Pushers*. New York: Anchor Press, and Doubleday, 1975.

Tajfel, Henri. 'Social Perception', in David. L. Sills (ed.), *International Encyclopedia of the Social Sciences*, New York: Macmillan, 1972, xi.

Tanaka, Issei. 'The Social and Historical Context of Ming-Ch'ing Local Drama.' David Johnson, Andrew J. Nathan, and Evelyn S. Rawski (eds.), *Popular Culture in Late Imperial China*. Berkeley: University of California Press, 1985.

Tawney, R. H. *Land and Labour in China*. London: George Allen & Unwin, 1932.

Terahiro, Teruo. 'Kanton ni okeru ko Ei undo.' *Memoirs of the Osaka University of the Liberal Arts and Education* 2, 1954.

Terry, Charles E. and Pellens, Mildred. *The Opium Problem*. New Jersey: Patterson Smith, 1970. First published in 1928.

The Canton Advertising & Commission Agency compiled. *Canton: Its Port, Industries & Trade*. Canton: The Canton Advertising & Commission Agency, 1932.

Thomas, S. Bernard. *'Proletarian Hegemony' in the Chinese Revolution and the Canton Commune of 1927*. Michigan Papers in Chinese Studies 23. Ann Arbor: The University of Michigan, 1975.

Ting, Hsu Lee-hsia. *Government Control of the Press in Modern China, 1900–1949*. Cambridge, Mass.: Harvard University Press, 1974.

Trocki, Carl A. *Opium and Empire: Chinese Society in Colonial Singapore, 1800–1910*. Ithaca: Cornell University Press, 1990.

Tsin, Michael Tsang-woon. *Nation, Governance and Modernity in China: Canton, 1900–1927*. Berkeley: University of California Press, 1999.

Turims, Edward and Kelly, David (ed.), *Unreal City*. Manchester: Manchester University Press, 1985.

Turner, J. A. *Kwangtung or Five Years in South China*. Hong Kong: Oxford University Press, 1982. Originally published in 1894.

Umeda Ikuzō. 'Kanton no iji oyobi eisei.' *Shina* 4/9, May 1913.

Vaidya, K. B. *Reflections on the Recent Canton Revolt and After*. 2nd edn. Canton: National Publishers, 1936.

Vogel, Ezra. *Canton Under Communism: Programs and Politics in a Provincial City, 1948–1968*. Cambridge, Mass.: Harvard University Press, 1969.

Wakeman, Frederic, Jr. *Strangers at the Gate: Social Disorder in South China, 1839–1861*. Berkeley: University of California Press, 1966.

Waley, Arthur. *The Opium War Through Chinese Eyes*. London: George Allen & Unwin, 1960.

Waln, Nora. *The House of Exile*. London: Cresset Press, 1933.

Ward, Barbara. 'Not Merely Players: Drama, Art, and Ritual in Traditional China.' *Man*, NS 14, 1979.

—— 'The Red Boats of the Canton Delta: A Chapter in the Historical Sociology of Chinese Opera.' *Proceedings of the International Conference on Sinology*. Taipei: 1981.

—— 'Regional Operas and Their Audiences: Evidences from Hong Kong.' David Johnson, Andrew J. Nathan, and Evelyn S. Rawski (eds.), *Popular Culture in Late Imperial China*. Berkeley: University of California Press, 1985.

Warner, John (comp). *Hong Kong Illustrated: Views and News 1840–1890*. Hong Kong: John Warner, 1981.

Warren, James Francis. 'Chinese Prostitution in Singapore: Recruitment and Brothel Organization'. Maria Jaschok and Suzanne Miers (eds.), *Women and Chinese Patriarchy: Submission, Servitude and Escape*. Hong Kong: Hong Kong University Press, 1994.

Watson, James L. 'Of Flesh and Bones: The Management of Death Pollution in Cantonese Society.' Maurice Bloch and Jonathan Parry (eds.), *Death and the Regeneration of Life*. Cambridge: Cambridge University Press, 1982.

Watt, John R. 'The Yamen and Urban Administration.' G. William Skinner (ed.), *The City in Late Imperial China*, Stanford: Stanford University Press, 1977.

Weiner, Annette B., and Schneider, Jane (eds.), *Cloth and Human Experience*. Washington: Smithsonian Institution Press, 1989.

Weinstein, David, and Deitch, Lillian. *The Impact of Legalized Gambling: The Socioeconomic Consequences of Lotteries and Off-Track Betting*. New York: Praeger, 1974.

Westermeyer, Joseph. *Poppies, Pipes, and People: Opium and Its Use in Laos*. Berkeley: University of California Press, 1983.

Who's Who in China. 5th edn. Shanghai: The China Weekly Review, 1936.

Willets, William. *Chinese Arts*. 2 vols. Harmondsworth: Penguin, 1958.

Williams, Raymond. *The Country and the City*. London: The Hogarth Press, 1985.

Wilson, John. *Politics and Leisure*. Boston: Unwin Hyman, 1988.

Windschuttle, Keith. *The Killing of History: How Literary Critics and Social Theorists are Murdering our Past*. New York: The Free Press, 1997.

Wittgenstein, Ludwig. *Culture and Value*. Trans. by Peter Winch. Oxford: Basil Blackwell, 1988.

Wolfe, Arthur. 'The Women of Hai Shan.' Margery Wolfe, Roxane Witke (eds.), *Women in Chinese Society*. Stanford: Stanford University Press, 1975.

Wolfe, Barnard. *The Daily Life of A Chinese Courtesan Climbing Up a Tricky Ladder*. Hong Kong: Learner's Bookstore, 1980.

Wood, Frances. *Chinese Illustration*. London: The British Library, 1985.

Woodfield, James. *English Theatre in Transition, 1881–1914*. London: Croom Helm 1984.

Woon, Yuen-fong. *Social Organization in South China, 1911–1949*. Ann Arbor: The University of Michigan, 1984.

Yack, Bernard. *The Fetishism of Modernities*. Notre Dame, Indiana: University of Notre Dame Press, 1977.

Yang, C. K. *A Chinese Village in Early Communist Transition*. Cambridge, Mass.: The M.I.T. Press, 1959.

Yeh, Wen-hsin. *Alienated Academy: Politics and Culture in Republican China, 1919–1937*. Cambridge, Mass.: Harvard University Press, 1991.

Yen Ching-yueh, 'Crime in Relation to Social Change in China'. Unpublished Ph.D. dissertation. University of Chicago, Chicago, Ill, 1934.

Yeung, Wing-yu Hans. 'Guangzhou, 1800–1925: The Urban Evolution of a Chinese Provincial Capital'. Unpublished Ph.D. dissertation. The University of Hong Kong, 1998.

Yung, Bell. *Cantonese Opera*. Cambridge: Cambridge University Press, 1989.

Zeldin, Theodore. *France, 1848–1945. Ambition and Love*. Oxford: Oxford University Press, 1979.

Zhang, Yingjin. *The City in Modern Chinese Literature and Film*. Stanford: Stanford University Press, 1996.

Selected Chinese Language References

Ah Mên 阿悶. 'Shih-t'ang yü fêng shên.' 石塘與封神 *Hsiang hai hua-pao* 香海畫報, 1, 1928.

Ah Nan 阿難, 'Pei-p'ing ti pai-mien fang-tzu' 北平的白麵房子 in K'o Ling 柯灵 edited, *Erh-shih shih-chi Chung-kuo chi-shih wên-hsüeh wên-k'u, 1900–1949: Tien-t'ang yü ti-yü* 二十世紀中國紀實文學文庫:天堂與地獄. Shanghai: Wên-hui ch'u-pan-shê, 1997.

Ah Ying 阿英. *Ya-pien chan-chêng wên-hsüeh chi* 鴉片戰爭文學集. 2 vols. Peking: Ku-chi ch'u-pan-shê, 1957.

Ai-ching mo-li 愛情魔力. Canton: Hsing hua shu-chü, *c.*1931–1933.

An Nien 安年. 'Yüeh-chü ta-shih Hsüeh Chüeh-hsien' 粵劇大師薛覺先 , *Kuang-chou shih chih* 1/1, Jan. 1987.

Ao Hsiang 翺翔. 'Tu-shih ti i wan' 都市的一晚, in *Jên chien shih* 人間世, Vol. 35, Sept. 1935.

Aoki Masaru 青木正兒 . *Chung-kuo chin-shih hsi-chü shih* 中國近世戲曲史. Trans. by Wang Ku-lu. Changsha: Shang-wu yin-shu-kuan, 1938.

Chan Tê-lung (Tsim Tak-lung 詹德隆) compiled. *Hsiang-kang Chung-kuo hsi-chü hsien-ku'ang yen-t'ao hui-i lu*. Chinese Theatre in Hong Kong: Proceedings of A Symposium, 22–23 November, 1968. Hong Kong: Centre of Asian Studies, University of Hong Kong, 1968.

Chan-ch'i-ho-chu-jên 懺綺盦主人. *Hsin Yüeh-ou chieh hsin* 新粵謳解心. Canton: 1926.

Chang Chên-chih 張振之. *Mu-chien Chung-kuo shê-hui ti ping-tai* 目前中國社會的病態. Shanghai: Min-chih shu-chü, 1929.

Chang Chên-chin 張振金. *Ling-nan hsien-tai wên-hsüeh shih* 嶺南現代文學史. Canton: Kuang-tung kao-têng chiao-yü ch'u-pan-shê, 1989.

Chang Chieh 張洁. 'Chu-ming Yüeh-chü i-jên Hsüeh Chüeh-hsien.' 著名粵劇藝人薛覺先. *KCWSTL*, vol. 19, 1980.

Chang Chieh 張洁. 'Chu-ming Yüeh-chü i-jên Ma Shih-ts'êng.' 著名粵劇藝人馬師曾. *KCWSTL*, vol. 18, 1980.

Chang Chieh 張洁. '"Hsiao-sheng wang" Pai Chiu-yung' '小生王白駒榮'. *Yüeh-chü ch'un-ch'iu* 粵劇春秋. Edited by Kuang-chou-shih chêng-hsieh wên-shih tzu-liao yen-chiu-shih Yüeh-chü yen-chiu chung-hsin. Canton: Kuang-tung jên-wên ch'u-pan-shê, 1990.

Chang Chieh-fêng 張結鳳. 'Chiu-ch'i tien-yin shih-tsai tai shao! Hsiang-kang tao-yen chi t'an chêng-chih.' 九七電影實在太少！香港導演忌談政治. *Pai hsing* (Hong Kong) 百姓, no.162, Feb. 1988.

Chang Ching-shêng 張競生. 'Hsing mei' 性美, in *Hsin wên-hua* 新文化 (Shanghai), Vol. 1, no.6, 1927.

Chang Chüeh-ch'u 張覺初. *Wang shih* 往事. Hong Kong: Tzu-yu ch'u-pan-shê, 1955.

Chang Hsiao-mei 張肖梅. *Kuei-chou ching-chi* 貴州經濟. Cited in *Kuei-chou chin-tai ching-chi shih tzu-liao hsüan chi* 貴州近代經濟史資料選輯. Vol.1. Edited by Kuei-chou shê-hui k'o-hsüeh pien-chi pu, et al. Ch'êng-tu: Sze-chuan-shêng shê-hui k'o-hsüeh yüan, 1987.

Chang Hsin-tai 張心泰. 'Yüeh yu hsiao chih.' 粵游小志 *Hsiao-fang-hu-chai yü-ti ts'ung ch'ao* 小方壺齋輿地叢抄, vol. 9. Edited by Wang Hsi-pu. Shanghai: Chu i t'ang, 1898.

Chang Kung-p'ing 張贛萍. *Têng-yü yü-shêng shu* 彈雨餘生述. 3 Vols. Taipei: Lung-wên chu-pan-shê ku-fên yu-hsien kung-ssu, 1993.

Chang Mêng-chêng 張夢徵, Chu Yüan-liang 朱元亮 edited. *Ch'ing-lou yün yü* 青樓韻語. 2 vols. Shanghai: Chung-yang shu-tien, 1935.

Chang Tzu-ch'iang 張自強. *Kuang-tung nung-min yün-tung* 廣東農民運動. Canton: Ling-nan ta-hsüeh, 1927.

Chang Tzu-p'ing 張資平. *Ai chih chiao-tien* 愛之焦點. Shanghai: Tai tung t'u-shu-tien, 1927.

——*Luan-ai ts'o-tsung* 戀愛錯綜. Kumming: Chung-hua shu-chü, 1939.

——*T'o-liao kuei-tao ti hsing-ch'iu* 脫了軌道的星球. Shanghai: Hsien-tai shu-chü, 1933.

——*Tzu-p'ing hsiao-shuo hsüan* 資平小說選. Shanghai: Hsien-tai shu-chü, 1928 vol. 1, 1930 vol. 2 and vol. 3, 2nd edn. Shanghai: Lo ch'ün shu-tien, 1930.

——*Tzu-p'ing tzu-ch'uan* 資平自傳. Taipei: Lung wên ch'u-pan-shê ku-fên yu-hsien kung-ssu, 1989. Originally published in 1932.

Chang Tzu-chih 張子次 edited. *Ch'ing-tai Yen-tu li-yüan shih-liao* 清代燕都梨園史料. Peking: Ya chai shu-tien, 1934.

Chang Yen-fêng 張燕風. *Lao yüeh-fêng-pai kuang-kao hua* 老月份牌廣告畫. 2 vols. Taipei: Han-shêng chu-pan shê, 1994.

Chang Ying-ch'ang 張應昌 edited. *Ch'ing shih to* 清詩鐸. 2 vols. Reprinted by Peking: Chung-hua shu-chü, 1960. Originally printed in 1869.

Chang Yüan-tsi jih-chi 張元濟日記. 2 vols. Peking: Shang-wu yin-shu-kuan, 1981.

Chao Ching-shen 趙景深. *Hsi-ch'ü pi t'an* 戲曲筆談. Shanghai: Chung-hua shu-chü, 1962.

Chao (I) Ou-pei 趙甌北. 'Yen pao tsa chi.' 簷曝雜記. *Pi-chi hsiao-shuo ta kuan*. 5th edn, vii no. 4. Taipei: Hsin hsing shu-chü, 1975.

Chao Shan-lin 趙山林. *Chung-kuo hsi-ch'ü kuan-chung-hsüeh* 中國戲曲觀眾學. Shanghai: Hua-tung shih-fan-ta-hsüeh ch'u-pan-shê, 1990.

Chao-tai ts'ung-shu 昭代叢書. Edited by Chang ch'ao 張潮, Yang Fu-chi 楊復吉, Shen Mou-te 沈楙德. 11 vols. Shih chai t'ang, 1849.

Chao-tai ts'ung-shu pieh chi 昭代叢書別集. N.p.: Shih chai t'ang, 1849.

Ch'ao-lien hsiang chih 潮蓮鄉志. Edited by Lo Tzu-chün. Hong Kong: n.p., 1946.

Ch'ên 臣. 'Tzu-sha chih yüan-yin chi ch'i chiu-chi fang-fa.' 自殺之原因及其救濟方法. *Chung shê*, vol. 3, June 1930. Canton: Kuang-chou ssu-li Ling-nan ta hsüeh Chung shê.

Ch'en Chao-yü 陳昭宇. *Kuang-tung t'ang-yeh yü Fêng Rui* 廣東糖業與馮銳. N.p., n.p., 1937.

Ch'en Ch'i-hui 陳啓輝. 'Kuang-tung t'u-ti li-yung yü liang-shih chan hsiao.' 廣東土地利用與糧食產銷. 2 vols. *Ming-kuo erh-shih nien-tai Chung-kuo ta-lu t'u-ti wen-t'i tzu-liao*. Edited by Hsiao Ch'êng. Taipei: Chêng wên ch'u-pan-shê, and Chinese Research Materials Centre, 1977.

Ch'en Chi-t'ung 陳季同. *Chung-kuo jên tzu-hua hsiang* 中國人自画像 (Original English title: *The Chinese Painted by Themselves*). Trans. by Huang Hsing-t'ao et al. Kuei-yang: Kuei-chou jên-min ch'u-pan-shê, 1997.

Ch'en Ch'ien 陳謙. *Hsiang-kang chiu-shih chien-wên lu*. 香港舊事見聞錄. Kuang-tung jên-min ch'u-pan-shê, 1989.

Ch'en Cho-ying 陳卓瑩. 'Hung ch'uan shih-tai ti Yüeh pan kai ku'ang.' 紅船時代的粵班概況. *YCYCTLH.*

Ch'en Fei-nung 陳非儂, Yu Mu-yün 余慕雲. *Yüeh-chü liu-shih nien* 粵劇六十年. Hong Kong: Wu hsing chi shu pao shê, 1982.

Ch'en Hsi-ch'i 陳錫棋. *Kuang-tung San-yüan-li jên-min ti k'ang-Ying tou-chêng* 廣東三元里人民的抗英斗爭. Canton: Kuang-tung jên-min ch'u-pan-shê, 1956.

Ch'en Hsiao-lin 陳曉林. 'Min-su wên-hsüeh ti yüan-liu yü wu-hsia hsiao-shuo ti ting wei.' 民俗文學的源流與武俠小說的定位. *Chin-tai Chung-kuo wu-hsia hsiao-shuo ta hsi*, vol. 1. Taipei: Lien ching ch'u-pan-shê, 1985.

Ch'en Hsü-ching 陳序經. *Chung-kuo nan pei wên-hua kuan* 中國南北文化觀. Taipei: Wu t'ung ch'u-pan-shê, 1976. Originally published in 1934.

—— *Chung-kuo wên-hua ti ch'u lu* 中國文化的出路. Shanghai: Shang-wu yin-shu-kuan, 1934.

—— 'Sun Chung-shan yü K'ung Fu-tzu.' 孫中山與孔夫子. *Ling-nan hsüeh pao*, vol. 1, no. 2, May 1930.

—— *Tan-min ti yen-chiu* 蛋民的研究 Shanghai: Shang-wu yin-shu-kuan, 1946.

—— 'Tung hsi wên-hua kuan.' 東西文化觀. *Ling-nan hsüeh pao*, vol. 5, no. 1–4 July, Sept. and Dec. 1936.

Ch'en Hua-hsin 陳華新. 'Yüeh-chü yü Hsin-hai kê-ming.' 粵劇與辛亥革命. *YCYCTLH.*

Ch'en Hui-ts'ang 沈惠蒼. 'Ching-chü tsai Hsiang-kang.' 京劇在香港. Chan Tê-lung (ed.), *Hsiang-kang Chung-kuo hsi-chü hsien-ku'ang yen-t'ao hui-i lu.*

Ch'en Hung 陳洪. 'Chung-kuo hsin-ko-chü ti chuan-tso.' 中國新歌劇的創造. *Hsi-chü i-shu*, vol. 1, 1937.

Ch'en Hung 陳洪. 'Tsu-chih Kuang-chou kuang-hsien-yüeh-tuan chi-hua.' 組織廣州管絃樂團計劃. *Hsi-chü i-shu*, vol. 1, 1937.

Ch'en Kung-min 陳恭敏. *Chieh yen ch'üan fa* 戒烟全法. Originally printed in *c.*1854. Reprinted by Peking: Chung-kuo shu-tien, 1998.

Ch'en Li-chu, Huang Hsiu-hua and Kuan Li-chen 陳麗珠, 黃秀華, 官麗珍 edited by Kuang-tung fu-nu yun-tung li-shih tzu-liao 廣東婦女運動歷史資料. 8 vols. Canton: Kuang-tung-sheng fu-nu lien-ho-hui, Kuang-tung-sheng tang-an kuan, 1991.

Ch'en Nien-ti 陳念棣, 'Hung wan' 紅丸, in *Jên-chien shih* 人間世, vol. 20 (1935), pp. 12–13.

Ch'en Pei-ying 陳佩英. 'Hsiang-kang lü-hsing chih.' 香港旅行記. *KTHS*, vol. 4, 1934.

Ch'en Ping-han 陳炳瀚. 'Kuang-chou nü-ling i tang nien' 廣州女伶憶當年, in Kuang-chou shih jên-min chêng-fu ts'an-i shih 廣州人民政府參議室 edited, *Sui ts'an wên shih tzu-liao* 穗参文史資料 (Canton), vol. 2 (1996).

Ch'en Po-nan hsien-shêng nien-pu 陳伯南先生年譜. Taipei: Ssu-li Tê-ming hsing-chêng kuan-li chuan-k'o hsüeh-hsiao, 1972.

Ch'en Shou-i 陳受頤. 'Ho Ch'iu Ch'uan chih tsui tsao ti Ou i.' 好逑傳之最早的歐譯. *Ling-nan hsüeh pao*, vol. 1, no. 4, Sept. 1930.

—— 'Lu Pin-sun ti Chung-kuo wên-hua kuan.' 魯賓孫的中國文化觀. *Ling-nan hsüeh pao*, vol. 1, no. 3 June, 1930.

—— 'Shih-pa hsi-chi Ou-chou wên-hsüeh lü ti Chao-shih Ku-êrh.' 十八世紀歐洲文學裏的「趙氏孤兒」. *Ling-nan hsüeh pao*, vol. 1, no. 1, Dec. 1929.

Ch'en Shou-jên 陳守仁. *Hsiang-kang Yüeh-chü yen-chiu.* Part I. 香港粵劇研究. Hong Kong: Kuang-chüeh-ching ch'u-pan-shê, 1988.

—— *Hsiang-kang Yüeh-chü yen-chiu*. Part II. 香港粵劇研究. Hong Kong: Chung-kuo hsi-ch'ü yen-chiu ch'i-hau, 1990.

Ch'en Ta 陳達. 'Chin pa nien lai kuo nei pa-kung ti fen-hsi.' 近八年來國內罷工的分析. *Ch'ing hua hsüeh pao*, vol. 3, no. 1, June 1926.

Ch'en Tieh-êrh 陳鐵兒. 'Kuang-tung ta-hsi yü shao-lin wu i.' 廣東大戲與少林武藝. *Kuang-tung wên-hsien chi k'an*, vol. 14, no. 3, Sept. 1984.

—— 'Yüeh-chü ko yüeh chin pai nien lai ti ch'ien pien.' 粵劇歌樂近百年來的遷變. *Kuang-tung wên-hsien chi k'an*, vol. 14, no. 2, June 1984.

—— 'Yüeh-chü ko yüeh wên-hsien ch'u t'an.' 粵劇歌樂文獻初探. *Kuang-tung wên-hsien chi k'an*, vol. 11, no. 3, Sept. 1981.

—— 'Yüeh-chü ts'ang-sang ku chin t'ung k'ai.' 粵劇滄桑古今同概. *Kuang-tung wên-hsien chi k'an*, vol. 12, no. 3 Sept. 1982.

Ch'en Tieh-hsiang 陳鐵香, Kiang Chung-ya 江仲雅, and P'eng Ch'u-li 彭楚立 (ed.), *Kuang-tung shang-yeh nien chien* 廣東商業年鑑 . Canton: Kunag-chou Shih-shang-hui, 1931.

Ch'en T'ien-tsung 陳天縱, Lu You-yung 盧有容, Mai Hsiao-hsia 麥嘯霞. *Hua hu-tieh* 花蝴蝶. Canton: Hua ku'ang shu-chü, 1927–8.

Ch'en T'ien-tsung 陳天縱. *Yü mo* 慾魔 . Canton: Hua hsing shu-chü, circa 1924–1925.

Ch'en Ting-shan 陳定山. 'Ch'un Shên chiu wên.' 春申舊聞. *Pi-chi hsiao-shuo ta kuan*. 7th Edition, vol. 10. Taipei: Hsin hsing shu-chü, 1975.

Ch'en Ting-yen 陳定炎 edited. *Ch'en Chiung-ming hsien-shêng nien-pu* 陳炯明先生年譜. 2 vols. Taipei: Li Ao ch'u-pan-shê, 1995.

Ch'en Ts'ang-ku 陳倉穀. *Ling-kuan lieh-ch'uan* 伶倌列傳. 2 vols. Hong Kong: n.p., *c.*1960s.

Chêng Ch'ên 鄭塵. 'Fu-nü chieh-fang ti wo chien.' 婦女解放的我見. *Ch'ün shêng*, vol. 1, no. 1, Nov. 1922.

Chêng Chi-ming 鄭智明. 'Yüeh-chü yü k'ai-fa Kuang-tung min chung.' 粵劇與開發廣東民眾. *Nan fêng*, vol. 14, no. 1, 1938.

Ch'êng Chi-hua 程季華, Li Shao-pai 李少白, and Hsing Tsu-wên 邢祖文. *Chung-kuo tien-ying fa-chan shih* 中國電影發展史. 2 vols. Peking: Chung-kuo tien-ying ch'u-pan-shê, 1981.

Ch'êng Hao 程浩 edited. *Kuang-chou kang shih* 廣州港史. 2 vols. Peking: Hai-yang ch'u-pan-shê, 1985.

Ch'êng T'ien-ku 程天固. *Ch'êng T'ien-ku hui-i-lu* 程天固回憶錄. Hong Kong: Lung mên shu-tien, 1978.

Chi-hsien-hsiao-yin 寄閒小隱. *Kai-liang Ling-nan chi shih* 改良嶺南即事. Canton: Ta hsin shu-chü, n.d.

Chi-lien chu-ming Yüeh-chü i-shu-chia Hsüeh Chüeh-hsien shih-shih san-shih chou-nien ch'ou-pei wei-yüan-hui 紀念著名粵劇藝術家薛覺先逝世三十週年籌備委員會 edited. *Hsüeh Chüeh-hsien chi-lian tê k'an* 薛覺先紀念特刊. Canton: 1986.

Chi t'an chin-lan 寄探金蘭. Canton: P'an kuei t'ang, n.d.

Ch'i Chih-t'ang 祁植棠. 'Kuang-chou shih ti tai chien-chu' 廣州市的大建築, in *Shêng-li I-chung hsüeh-shêng jih-chi hsüan* 省立一中學生日記選. Canton: Kuang-tung Shêng-li I-chung, 1934.

Ch'i-chui-tou 七搥頭. 'Ma Shih-ts'êng hsiao shih.' 馬師曾小史. *Hsi ch'uan*, vol. 1, 1931.

Ch'i Tzu 楔子. 'Kuang-chou-shih Tung-shan liu-shih nien nai fa-chan kai shu.' 廣州市東山六 十年來發展概述. *KCWSTL*, vol. 14, no. 1, 1965.

Ch'i wan hua-shê 啓頑畫社 (ed.), *Chung-kuo shih ta hai* 中國十大害. Canton: Shêng ch'ün shu-chü, 1910.

Chia fêng hsi chên huang 假鳳戲真皇. Canton: Hua hsing shu-chü, n.d.

Chia Shih-i 賈士毅. *Min-kuo hsü ts'ai-chêng shih* 民國續財政史. Shanghai: Shang-wu yin-shu-kuan, 1932.

Chia-yin nien hsin t'ung-shu 甲寅年新通書. Canton: n.p., 1914.

Ch'iao Kang I Yüan T'ang 僑港詒遠堂. *Liang-shih chia-pu* 梁氏家譜. Hong Kong: Ch'iao Kang I Yüan T'ang, 1989.

Chien 傑 'Ai Chin wei ch'ou shen hsu kuo' 哀志未籌身許國 *Kuang-tung hsüeh-shêng* (*KTHS*) 2, 1933.

Chien Ch'êng-jun et al. 錢成潤. *Fei Hsiao-t'ung Lu Tsun nung-t'ien wu-shih-nien* 費孝通祿村 農田五十年. Ku-ming: Yün-nan jên-min ch'u-pan shê, 1995.

Chien Ch'iu 劍秋. 'Ch'ang-chi chih heh-mo.' 娼妓之黑幕. *Pi chi hsiao-shuo ta kuan*. 7th edn. vol. 7. Taipei: Hsin hsing shu-chü, 1975.

Chien yen piao tsa-chih 千巖表雜誌, vol. 1, no. 1. Canton: 1931.

Chien Yu-wên 簡又文. 'Ho Tan-yü ti yu-mo' 何淡如的幽默, in *Kuang-tung wên-hsien chi k'an* 廣東文獻季刊, vol. 3, no. 3, Sept. 1973.

Chih-fen lo-han 脂粉羅漢. Canton: Hua hsing shu-chü, n.d.

Chin Hsüeh-shih 金學詩. 'Mu-chu hsien hua.' 牧豬閒話. *Chao-tai ts'ung-shu pieh-chi*. Edited by Chang Ch'ao, Yang Fu-chi, and Shen Mou-tê. n.p.: Shin k'ai t'ang, 1849.

Chin Mang-ch'êng 金滿成. *Yung-hu kê-ming ti ching-jên chih* 擁護革命的情人制. Shanghai: Mei ti shu-tien, 1928.

Chin Wên-huan 金文煥 et al., 'Kuang-tung shêng 16 hsien shih chih-li tsan-chi tiao-cha ti tzu-liao fên-hsi chi fang-tsan chien-i' 廣東省 16 縣市智力殘疾調查的資料分析及防殘建議, in Kuang-tung hsin-li hsüeh-hui 廣東心理學會 edited, *Kuang-tung hsin-li hsüeh tsung-hêng* 廣東心理學縱横. Canton: Hua-nan li-kung ta-hsüeh ch'u-pan-shê, 1992.

Ch'in Ch'in 秦琴. 'Yüeh-chü chih chin hsi kuan.' 粵劇之今昔觀. *Hsi ch'uan*, vol.1, 1931.

Ching-chieh-fu ta ma tu-tsai 貞節婦大罵賭仔. Canton: Tsui ching t'ang, n.d.

Ching Fo 情佛. 'Mai shên chê yen.' 賣身者言. *KCTC*, vol. 20, 1934.

Ching-hai tsung-pao 鏡海叢報. July 1893 to December 1895. Reprinted by Shanghai: Shanghai shê-hui ko-hsüeh yüan and Ao-men chi-chin hui, 2000.

Ching Hsiao 擎霄. 'Ch'ing-tai Yüeh-tung hsieh-tou shih shih.' 清代粵東械鬥史實. *Ling-nan hsüeh pao*, vol. 4, no. 2, June 1935.

Ching lei tsui hsiang yün 情淚醉霜魂. Canton: Ta hsin shu-chü, *c*.1930.

Ch'ing-ch'un 青春. Vol. 1, no. 2–3, April 1932. Canton: Ch'ing-ch'un ch'u-pan-shê.

Ch'ing Shui 清水. 'Kuang-chou-jên ti chiu-li hsin-nien fêng-su.' 廣州人的舊曆新年風俗. *Ko yao*, vol. 2, no. 37, 1937.

Chiu Chün 丘均 edited. *Shao-hsing min-chien ko-yao* 肇慶民間歌謠. Canton: Kuang-tung jên-min ch'u-pan-shê, 1988.

Chiu-chung-fêng-fu 酒中馮婦. 'Ch'ih fan-ts'ai chih.' 吃香菜記. *KCTC*, vol. 25, 1934.

—— 酒中馮婦 'Kung-kai yen yin' 公開驗孕. *KCTC*, vol. 33, 1934.

—— 'Ping ssu chih k'u.' 兵死之苦. *Kuang-chou shê-hui tsa chih*, vol. 1, c. 1910.

Ch'iu Ho-chin 丘鶴琴 edited. *Yüeh tung ming yu ch'ü pên* 粵東名優曲本. Canton: Ta hsin shu-chü, 1924.

Ch'iu Sung-ho 邱松鶴 edited. *San-tung-wu po-wu-kuan Yüeh-chü tsang p'in* 三棟屋博民館粵劇藏品. Hong Kong: Hong Kong Regional Council, 1992.

Cho Yu 卓如. 'Shang-hai ti lai hsin', 上海的來信, in Kuang-chou wên-hsüeh hui (ed.), *Ying sh'ih*. Canton: Yüeh Kang shou k'uang ch'u-pan pu, 1928.

Ch'ou Ch'ih-shih (1969) 仇池石. 'Yang-ch'êng ku ch'ao' 羊城古鈔. 2 vols. Reprinted in *Chin-tai Chung-kuo shih liao ts'ung k'an*. Edited by Shen Yün-lung. Taipei: Wên hai shu-chü, 1969. Originally printed in 1806.

Chou Chung 舟中. 'Shui ti tsui-kuo.' 誰的罪過. *KTHS*, vol. 4, 1934.

Chou Hsia-min 周俠民. 'Kuang-chou hsia-chi chi-nü chih ta hsieh chên.' 廣州下級妓女之大 寫真 *KCTC*, vol. 33, Dec. 1934.

Chou Hsien-wên 周憲文. 'Chung-kuo chih yen huo chi ch'i chiu-chi ts'ê.' 中國之煙禍及其救濟策. *Tung-fang tsa-chih*, vol. 23, no. 20, Oct. 1926.

Chou Hsing 周行. 'Huo-yen shan.' 火焰山. *KTHS*, vol. 4.

Chou I-po 周貽白. *Chung-kuo hsi-ch'ü fa-chan shih kang-yao* 中國戲曲發展史綱要. Shanghai: Ku-ch'i ch'u-pan-shê, 1979.

—— *Chung-kuo hsi-ch'ü lun chi* 中國戲曲論集. Peking: Chung-kuo hsi-chü ch'u-pan-shê, 1960.

—— *Chung-kuo hsi-chü shih* 中國戲劇史. Shanghai: Chung-hua shu-chü, 1953.

Chou K'ang-yen 周康燮 edited. *Kuang-tung fêng-su chui lu* 廣東風俗綴錄. Hong Kong: Ch'ung wên shu-tien, 1972.

Chou Ku-ch'êng 周谷城. *Chung-kuo shê-hui chih chieh-kou* 中國社會之結構. Shanghai: Hsin shêng-min shu-chü, 1930.

Chou Kuo-hsiung 周國雄. 'Lüeh lun Chung-kuo ku-tien hsi-chü ti pên-chih tê-chêng.' 略論中國古典喜劇的本質特徵. *Hua-nan shih-fan ta-hsüeh shê-hui-k'o-hsüeh hsüeh pao* 華南師範大學社會科學學報, no. 3, 1987.

Ch'ou Wêng 儔翁. 'I pan-shih-chi chien ti Yüeh-chü.' 憶半世紀前的粵劇. *Kuang-tung wên-hsien chi k'an*, vol. 4, no. 3, 1974.

Chou Yu-liang 周友良. 'Chu-kiang Mei Liu chi.' 珠江梅柳記. Reprinted in *Ch'ing-lou yün yü*. Edited by Chang Mêng-chêng, Chu Yüan-liang. Shanghai: Chung yang shu-tien, 1935.

Chü Hsiang 拒霜. 'Ts'un-chü sou chih' 村居璅志 in *Hsien-tai shêng-chan tsa-chih* 現代生產雜誌 (Canton), vol. 1, nos. 5 and 6 (1935).

Chu Hsi-nung (1965), 'Shih-nien lai ti Chung-kuo nung-yeh', in Chung-kuo wên-hua chien-shê, *K'ang-chan chien shih-nien chih Chung-kuo* (Hong Kong: Lung-mên shu-tien).

Chu Hsiu-hsia 祝秀俠. *Man-t'an Kuang-cho*u 漫談廣州. Taipei: Hai wai wên k'u ch'u-pan-shê, 1955.

—— *Pa-yüeh chien* 八月間. Shanghai: Hsien-tai shu-chü, 1930.

—— *Yüeh hai chiu wên lu* 粵海舊聞錄. 2 vols. Taipei: Chung wai wên k'u, 1977.

Chu-kiang hsing-ch'i hua-pao 珠江星期畫報 (Canton: n.p., 1927–8.).

Chu Po-lo hsien-sheng chih-chia ko-yen 朱柏廬先生治家格言. Canton: Chao chin shu-wu, n.d.

Chü shêng 噱聲, no. 1, 1917. Canton: Chü shêng shê.

Chu Tao-nan 朱道南. *Tsai ta-kê-ming ti hung liu chung* 在大革命的洪流中. Shanghai: Jên-min ch'u-pan-shê, 1977.

Chü-tu yüeh-k'an 拒毒月刊. Shanghai Chung-hua kuo-min chü-tu hui.上海中華國民拒毒會.

Chu Tzu-ch'ing 朱自清. *Chu Tzu-ch'ing san-wên hsüan* 朱自清散文選. Hong Kong: Ta t'ung shu-chü, n.d.

Chu Yang 朱洋. 'Kuang-tung ti ya-pien' 廣東的鴉片, in *Jên-chien shih* 人間世, vol. 30, Oct. 1935.

Chu Yung-ch'un 朱用純. *Chu-tzu chih-chia ko yen* 朱子治家格言. n.p.: n.d.

Ch'u Chien 驅 漸. 'Yüeh-chü lun.' 粵劇論. *Hsi-chü*, vol. 1, 1929.

Ch'u-nü lo fu 處女羅敷. Canton: Yüeh-ch'ü yen-chiu shê, *c*.1931–3.

Ch'ü Ta-chün 屈大均. *Kuang-tung hsin yü* 廣東新語. 2 vols. Reprinted by Hong Kong: Chung-hua shu-chü, 1974. Originally printed in 1700.

Ch'u Ying-chieh 曲英杰. Shêng-Ch'in tu-chêng fu-yüan yen-chiu 先秦都城復元研究. Harbin: Hêh-long-kiang jên-min ch'u-pan-shê, 1991.

Ch'üan Han-shêng 全漢昇. 'Ch'ing-mo ti hsi-hsüeh-yüan-chu-Chung-kuo shuo.' 清末的「西學源出中國」說. *Ling-nan hsüeh pao*, vol. 4, no. 2, June 1935.

Ch'üan Shêng 雋生. 'T'an-hua-ch'u su chi.' 談話處速記. *KCTC*, vol. 1, no. 1, Dec. 1924.

Ch'üan Yüeh shê-hui shih-lu 全粵社會實錄. Canton: Tiao-cha ch'üan Yüeh shê-hui chü, 1911.

Ch'ün shêng 群聲. vol. 1, 1922. Canton: Ch'ün shêng shê.

Ch'ün shêng pao hsing-ch'i tsêng k'an 群聲報星期增刊, vol. 1, no. 1, 1935.

Chung Ching-wên 鍾敬文. *Li-chih hsiao p'in* 荔枝小品. Shanghai: Pei hsin shu-chü, 1927.

Chung Ching-wên 鍾敬文. *Lu Hsün tsai Kuang-tung* 魯迅在廣東. Shanghai: Pei hsin shu-chü, 1927.

Chung-kuo jên-min chêng-chih-hsieh-shang-hui-i Kuang-tung-shêng Kuang-chou-shih wei-yüan-hui wên-shih tzú-liao wei-yüan-hui 中國人民政治協商會議廣東省廣州市委員會文史資料委員會 edited. *Kuang-chou chin pai nien chiao-yü shih liao* 廣州近百年教育史料. Canton: Kuang-tung jên-min ch'u-pan-shê, 1983.

Chung-kuo jên-min chêng-chih-hsieh-shang-hui-i Kuang-tung-shêng Kuang-chou-shih wei-yüan-hui wên-shih tzú-liao wei-yüan-hui 中國人民政治協商會議廣東省廣州市委員會文史資料委員會 (ed.), *Sun Chung-shan san-tzu tsai Kuang-tung chien-li chêng-ch'üan* 孫中山三次在廣東建立政權. Peking: Chung-kuo wên-shih ch'u-pan-shê, 1986

Chung-kuo hsi-chü-chia hsieh hui, Kuang-tung-shêng wên-hua-chü 中國地 廣東省文化局, 廣東省文化局. *Chung-kuo ti-fang hsi-ch'ü chi ch'êng: Kuang-tung chüan* 中國地方戲曲集成：廣東省卷. Peking: Chung-kuo hsi-chü ch'u-pan-shê, 1962.

Chung-kuo shê-hui k'o-hsüeh-yüan Shang-hai ching-chi yen-chiu so 中國社會科學院上海經濟研究所 (ed.), *Nan-yang hsiung-ti yen-ts'ao kung-ssu shih liao* 南洋兄弟煙草公司史料. Shanghai: Shang-hai jên-min ch'u-pan-shê, 1958.

Chung shê 中社 . vol. 1, no. 1, June 1930. Canton: Kuang-chou ssu-li Ling-nan ta hsüeh Chung Shê.

Dai Kan-Wa jiten 大漢和辭典, edited by Morohashi Taksuke 諸橋轍次. 14 vols. Tokyo: Taishukan Shoten, 1989.

Drilzo, Salomon Abramovich 羅佐夫斯基. *Kuang-chou kung-shê* 廣州公社. Canton: Wu-ch'an chieh-chi shu-tien, 1930.

En Jên 甄人, T'an Shao-p'êng 譚紹鵬. *Kuang-chou chu-ming lao-tzu-hao* 廣州著名老字號. Canton: Kuang-chou wên-hua ch'u-pan-shê, 1989.

Fang hai yüeh-k'an 方海月刊. Canton: Kuang-chou P'ei Ying chung hsüeh i-chiu-san-liu nien chi Fang Shê, 1928–1936.

Fei Fei 非非. 'Pieh liao, wo ti ku-hsiang.' 別了，我的故鄉. *I-shê ch'i k'an*, vol. 2, 1933.

Fei Hsiao-tung 費孝通. *Hsiang-tu chung-chien* 鄉土重建. Shanghai: Kuan-cha shê, 1948.

Fêng Lan 馮蘭. 'Yüeh-chü wu-tai pien-ch'ien lu.' 粵劇舞台變遷錄. *Hsi ch'uan*, vol. 1, 1931.

Fêng Ming-ch'üan 馮明泉. 'Man t'an Kuang-chou ch'a-lou yeh' 漫談廣州茶樓業 in Kuang-chou-shih chêng-hsieh et al. (eds.), *Kuang-chou kung shang ching-chi shih liao*. Canton: Kuang-tung jên-min ch'u-pan-shê, 1986.

Fêng Pi-ying 馮碧英. 'Ming-ch'a mei tien, lo ya t'ao t'ao—T'ao T'ao Ch'ü' 明茶美點, 樂也陶---陶陶陶居. T'an Shao-p'eng et al. (eds.), *Kuang-chou chu-ming lao-tzu-hao*. Canton: Kuang-chou wên-hua chù-pan-shê, 1989.

Fêng Rui 馮銳. 'Hsiang-tsun shê-hui hsin-li chih fen-hsi' 鄉村社會心理之分析, in *Shê-hui-hsüeh chieh* 社會學界 (Peking), vol. 1, no. 2, June 1928.

Fêng Tzu-yu 馮自由. 'Kuang-tung hsi-chü-chia yu kê-ming yün-tung' 廣東戲劇家與革命運動, in Hsü Yen-tung et al. (eds.), *Kuang-tung wên-chêng shu pien* 廣東文徵續編, vol. 2. Hong Kong: Kuang-tung wên-chêng pien-yin wei-yüan-hui, 1987.

Fêng Yüan-chün 馮沅君. *Ku chü shuo hui* 古劇說彙. Shanghai: Shang-wu yin-shu-kuan, 1947.

Fo-shan chung-i hsiang chih 佛山忠義鄉志. 1923 edn.

Hai-chüeh-shih-jên 海角詩人. 'Wu ko ming ling chih ssu.' 五個名伶之死. *Hsi ch'uan*, vol. 1, 1931.

Hai-shang-chüeh-wu-shêng 海上覺悟生. *Chi-nü ti shêng-huo* 妓女的生活. Shanghai: Ch'un ming shu-tien, 1939.

Han Ta-ch'êng 韓大成. *Ming-tai ch'êng-shih yen-chiu*. 明代城市研究. Peking: Chung-kuo jên-min ta-hsüeh ch'u-pan-shê, 1991.

Hao-chi-shêng 好寄生. 'Lêng Hung yü nan-hsin.' 冷紅與男性. *Hsiang hai hua-pao*, vol. 1 1928.

Hao yüeh ch'i ts'an hung 皓月泣殘紅. Canton: Ta hsin shu-chü, 1930.

Hêng mei yüeh pao 恆美月報. Canton: Hêng mei yüeh pao shê, 1920s–30s.

Ho Ch'i-t'ang 何季鏜. 'Kuang-chou Shih-chung-shê shih ling.' 廣州詩鐘社拾零. *KCWSTL*, vol. 19, June 1980.

Ho Chien-ch'ing 何建青. 'T'i Yüeh-chü suan ming.' 替粵劇算命. *YCYCTLH*.

Ho Chin-hsing 何錦卿. 'Nung-ts'un fu-nü yü ch'êng-shih fu-nü.' 農村婦女與城市婦女. *I-shê ch'i k'an*, vols. 2–3, 1934.

Ho Kuo-hua 何國華 et al. (eds.), *Kuang-chou shih san-shi-wu nien-tu shang-yêh nien-chien* 廣州市三十五年度商業年鑑. Canton: Kuang-chou Shih Shang Hui shang-yêh nien-chien ch'u-pan hui-yüan-hui, 1946.

Hsi-chü 戲劇. vol. 1, 1929. Canton: Kuang-tung hsi-chü yen-chiu-so.

Hsi-chü i-shu 戲劇藝術. vol. 1, no.1, Mar. 1937. Canton: Kuang-chou chien-fêng chü shê.

Hsi-chü shih-chieh 戲劇世界. 5 vols. Canton: Kuang-tung chü hsüeh yen-chiu-shê, 1922–23.

Hsi ch'uan 戲船. Hong Kong: Fêng pai ch'u-pan pu, 1931.

Hsiang hai hua-pao 香海畫報. vol. 1, 1928. Canton: Hsiang hai hua-pao shê.

Hsiang hua hua-pao 香花畫報. no. 1–4, 1928–29. Canton: Hsiang hua hua-pao shê.

Hsiao Ling 小鈴. 'Mi mang chung.' 迷茫中. *Wan jên tsa-chih*, vol. 1, no. 1, April 1930.

Hsiao-tian-shih 簫天氏 (ed.). *Sze yin ch'i* 四淫齊. Hong Kong: Kuang mou hao, 1907.

Hsiao-yün Liu 銷魂柳. Canton: Hua hsing shu-chü, *c.*1931–1933.

Hsieh Hsing-po 謝醒伯, Li Shao-cho 李少卓. 'Ch'ing-mo Min-ch'u Yüeh-chü shih hua.' 清末民初粵劇史話. *YCYC*, vol. 7, June 1988.

Hsieh Pin-ch'ou 謝彬籌. 'Chin-tai Chung-kuo hsi-chü ti min-chu kê-ming sê ts'ai ho Yüeh-chü ti kai liang yün-tung.' 近代中國戲曲的民主革命色彩和粵劇的改良運動. *YCYCTLH*.

Hsien ch'i chien fu 賢妻諫夫. Canton: I wên táng (n.d.).

Hsien-shui-ko 鹹水歌. 2 vols. Canton: n.p., n.d.

Hsien-tai ch'ing-nien 現代青年. Kuang-chou min-kuo jih-pao fu-k'an 廣州民國日報副刊, Oct. 1929–Apr. 1930. Canton: Kuang-chou min-kuo jih-pao shê.

Hsien Tzu-lung 冼子龍. 'Kuang-chou Hsin-ya chiu-tien.' 廣州新亞酒店. *Kuang-chou kung shang ching-chi shih liao*. Ed, by Chung-kuo min-chu chien kuo hui Kuang-chou-shih wei-yüan-hui. Canton: Kuang-tung jên-min ch'u-pan-shê, 1986.

Hsien Yü-ch'ing 冼玉清. 'Ch'ing tai liu shêng hsi-pan tsai Kuang-tung' 清代六省戲班在廣東, in Fo-shan ta-hsüeh Fo-shan wên shih yen-chiu shih 佛山大學佛山文史研究室, Kuang-tung wên shih kuan 廣東文史館 (ed.). *Hsien Yü-ch'ing wên chi* 冼玉清文集. Canton: Chung-shan ta-hsüeh ch'u-pan shê, 1996.

Hsin ch'u lung-chou-ko: Kung-jên tan wu kêng 新出龍舟歌：工人嘆五更. Hong Kong: 1925.

Hsing Chuang 杏莊. 'Hsiang ku-liang.' 香姑娘. *KCLPL*, vol. 4, 1933.

Hsiung Fo-hsi 熊佛西. *Hsi-chü ta-chung-hua chih shih-yen* 戲劇大眾化之實驗. Nanking: Chêng chung shu-chü, 1937.

Hsü Ch'ang-lin 徐昌霖. 'Tsao-ch'i Chung-kuo yin-mo shang ti min-tsu tê-sê.' 早期中國銀幕上的民族特色. In *Dianying: An Interdisciplinary Journal of Chinese Film Studies*, vol. 1, Dec. 1983. Hong Kong: Hong Kong Chinese Film Association.

Hsü Ching-yüan 徐景元. 'Kuang-chou tsui chin chih chü tu yün-tung lun.' 廣州最近之拒毒運動論. *Kuang-chou tsa-chih*, vol. 1, no. 1, 1924.

Hsü Chu-ch'êng 徐鑄成. *Chiu wên tsa i* 舊聞雜憶. Hong Kong: San lien shu-tien, 1982.

Hsü Fu-chin 許復琴. *Kuang-tung min-chien wên-hsüeh ti yen-chiu* 廣東民間文學的研究. Hong Kong: Hai ch'ao ch'u-pan-shê, 1948.

Hsü Hsu 徐訏. *Hsi liu chi* 西流集. 7th edn. Shanghai: Yeh ch'uang shu-wu, 1946.

Hsü Hsüeh-hang 許雪航 (ed.), *Hsin-pien Kuang-tung shêng-ch'êng pai-hua* 新編廣東省城白話. 3 Vols. Rangoon: Wen-hua chu-tzu kung-ssu, *c.*1920s.

Hsü P'ei-chün 徐培均, Fan Min-shêng 范民聲 (ed.), *Chung-kuo ku-tien ming chü chien-shang tzu-tie*n 中國古典名劇鑑賞辭典. Shanghai: Shang-hai ku-chi ch'u-pan-shê, 1990.

Hsü Wei-nan 徐蔚南. *Tu-shih ti nan nü* 都市的男女. Shanghai: Chên mei shan shu-tien, 1929.

Hsü Yen-tung 許衍董 et al. (eds.), *Kuang-tung wên-chêng shu pien* 廣東文徵續編. 4 vols. Hong Kong: Kuang-tung wên-chêng pien-yin wei-yüan-hui, 1986–8.

Hsüeh Chüeh-hsien tao-nien chi pien-wei-hui 薛覺先悼念集編委會 (ed.), *Chüeh-hsien tao-nien chi* 覺先悼念集. Hong Kong: Hsüeh Chüeh-hsien tao-nien chi pien-wei-hui, 1957.

Hu Chên 胡振. *Kuang-tung hsi-chü shih (Hung-ling pien chih erh)* 廣東戲劇史 (紅伶篇之二). Hong Kong: Li Yüan shu-pao shê yu-hsien kung-ssu, 2000.

Hu-hua-lang 護花郎. 'I ch'iu-shui yü Hsin Ch'un Ch'iu.' 伊秋水與新春秋. *Hsi ch'uan*, vol. 1, 1931.

Hu P'o-an 胡樸安 et al (eds.), *Chung-hua ch'üan kuo fêng-su chih* 中華全國風俗志 2 vols. Shanghai: Kuang chi shu-chü, 1923. Reprinted by Shih-chia-chuan: Ho-nan jên-min ch'u-pan-shê, 1986.

Hua-ts'ung-fên-tieh 花叢粉蝶. 'Ta-hsüeh shêng k'o-wai.' 大學生課外. *KCTC*, vol.20, 1933.

Hua-tzu jih-pao pien-chi pu 華字日報編輯部 (ed.), *Hua-tzu jih-pao ch'i-shih-i chou-nien chi-nien k'an* 華字日報七十一周年紀念刋. Hong Kong: Hua-jih jih-pao yin-yeh pu, 1934.

Hua ying 花影, vol. 1, 1931. Hong Kong: Published privately by Ching-shao-êrh-lang.

Huan hua-chai 還花債. Canton: Hua hsing shu-chü, *c.*1931–3.

Huang Ching-hua 黃敬華. *Chung-kuo chin-tai shih chang-shih* 中國近代史常識. Hong Kong: Chao yang chu-pan-shê, 1972.

Huang Ching-ming 黄鏡明. 'San-shih nien-tai Yüeh-chü ti i-shu tê-chêng.' 三十年代粵劇的藝術特徵. *YCYC*, vol. 3, May 1987.

Huang Ho-ming 黄鶴鳴. 'Shih lun Hsiang-kang Yüeh-chü ch'ao-liu.' 試論香港粵劇潮流. *YCYC*, vol. 8, Aug. 1988.

Huang Hsin 黄粲. 'Lun hsiao-hsüeh ti yin-yüeh chiao-yü' 論小學的音樂教育. *Kuang-chou yin-yueh*, vol. 3, no. 67, 1935.

Huang Ming-hui 黄明慧. *Kuang-chou chi Hsiang-kang* 廣州及香港. Shanghai: Hsin shêng-ming shu-chü, 1936.

Huang Nai-ch'ao 黄乃釗, Ho Wên-kuang 何文光. *Kuang-chou jên: tso-jih yü chin-jih* 廣州人：昨日與今日. Canton: Kuang-chou wên-hua ch'u-pan-shê, 1987.

Huang P'o-yüan 黄柏元 et al. 'Mi-hsin fan-tsui chih hsin-li p'ou-hsi' 迷信犯罪之心理剖析, in Kuang-tung hsin-li hsüeh-hui 廣東心理學會 (ed.), *Kuang-tung hsin-li-hsüeh tsung-hêng* 廣東心理學縱橫. Canton: Hua-nan li-kung ta-hsüeh ch'u-pan-shê, 1992.

Huang Shao-han (Wong Shiu-hon) 黄兆漢. *A Catalogue of Cantonese Opera Scripts* 粵劇劇本目錄. Hong Kong: Centre of Asian Studies, Hong Kong University, 1971.

Huang Tê-shen 黄德深. 'Kuang-tung hua-chü ts'ung Hsin-hai kê-ming chih Chien-fang chien ti fa-chan li-ch'êng' 廣東話劇從辛亥革命至解放前的發展歷程, in Chung-kuo hsi-chü-chia chieh-hui Kuang-tung fên-hui, Kuang-tung hua-chü yen-chiu hui 中國戲劇家協會廣東分會, 廣東話劇研究會 (eds.), *Kuang-tung hua-chü yün-tung shih-liao chi*, 廣東話劇運動史料集 vol. 2. Canton: n.p., 1987.

Huang Tsun-shêng 黄尊生. *Ling-nan min hsin yü Ling-nan wên-hua* 嶺南民性與嶺南文化. Canton: Min-tsu wên-hua ch'u-pan-shê, 1941.

Huang Wên-to 黄文鐸. 'Kuang-chou-shih jên-li-chê shih-yeh ti tiao-ch'a.' 廣州市人力車事業的調查. *Nan-ta ching-chi*, vol. 2, no. 1, Jan. 1933.

Huang Yên-p'ei 黄炎培 (ed.), *I-sui chih Kuang-chou-shih* 一歲之廣州市. 4th edn. Shanghai: Shang-wu yin-shu-kuan, 1927.

Huang Yin-p'u 黄蔭普 et al. (eds.), *Kuang-chou p'i-fa wu-chia chih-shu hui k'an, 1927–1933* 廣州批發物價指數彙刊 民國十六 年至二十二年. Canton: Kuo-li Chung-shan ta hsüeh ching-chi tiao-ch'a ch'u, 1934.

—— *Kuang-chou kung-jên chia-t'ing chih yen-chiu*. 廣州工人家庭之研究. Canton: Kuo-li Chung-shan ta hsüeh ching-chi tiao-ch'a ch'u, 1934.

Hui-t'u tseng-kuang yen-wên. 繪圖增廣賢文. Hong Kong: Ch'en-hsiang-chi shu-chü, n.d.

Hung-ch'uan-chiu-lü 紅船舊侶. 'Tou-p'i-mei chih ling tê.' 豆皮梅之伶德. *Hsi ch'uan*, vol. 1, 1931.

I Ch'iu-shuang 易秋霜. 'Tui yü Yüeh-chü li ti yin-yüeh chih yen-chiu.' 對於粵劇裏音樂之研究. *Hsi chü*, vol. 1, 1929.

I Hsaio 異笑 (*c.*1922), 'So-yeh fu' 索野賦, *Hsi-chü shih-chieh* 1/3, Section of, 'Yu-hsi wên-chang', vol. 1, no. 3.

I Li 伊妮. *Yü hai yü shên-ên* 慾海與神恩. Changsha: Hu-nan wên-i ch'u-pan-shê, 1990.

I P'ing 一平. 'Hu Shih "Hu Shih"? Nan-fang wên-hua chung-hsin yü? Pei-fang wên-hua chung-hsin yü?' 胡適「胡適」？南方文化中心歟？北方文化中心歟？ *Hsin hsin*, vol. 1, no. 2, Jan. 1935.

I shê ch'i-k'an 一社季刊 , vol. 2–3, Dec. 1933. Canton: Kuang-tung shêng-li ti-i nü-tzu chu-chung ai pan.

I Wu 抑吾. 'Ying-shu' 罌粟. *Chung-ho yüeh-k'an shih-liao hsüan-chi* 中和月刊史料選集. Taipei: Wên hai chu-pan-shê, 1969 reprint.

—— 'Yen ku' 烟蠱. *Chung ho yüeh-k'an shih-liao hsüan-chi.* vol. 2 中和月刊史料選集. Taipei: Wên hai chu-pan-shê, 1970 reprint.

Jê-nan-lang 熱男郎. '"Hsüan kung yen shih" tuan p'ing.' 璇宮艷史短評. *Hsi ch'uan*, vol. 1, 1931.

Kai-liang Ling-nan chi-shih 改良嶺南即事. Ed, by Ling-nan shih-shih shê 嶺南時事社. N.p., n.d.

K'ang Su-chên 康素珍. *Ch'ing-lou hên hsü chi* 青樓恨（續集）. Ch'ang-ch'un: Chi-lin wên shih ch'u-pan-shê, 1990.

Kao Hsiang-li 高象麗. *Ya-pien liu-tu shih* 鴉片流毒史. n.p.: n.d.

Kao Yü-han 高語罕. *Kuang-chou chi yu* 廣州紀游. Shanghai: Ya tung t'u-shu kuan, 1922.

Kiang Lin 江陵. 'Hsiang-kang i-ch'iu-szu-ch'iu nien i lai ti Yüeh-chü.' 香港一九四九年以來的粵劇. Chan Tê-lung (ed.), *Hsiang-kang Chung-kuo hsi-chü hsien-ku'ang yen-t'ao hui-i lu.*

Ko Lin 柯靈. 'Shih wei Wu-szu yü tien-ying hua i lun-kuo.' 試爲五四與電影畫一輪廓. *Dianying: An Interdisciplinary Journal of Chinese Film Studies*, vol. 1, Dec. 1983.

Ko-lin kung-ssu chueh hsin ch'i-shih-szu ch'i ch'ang-pien ch'ü pu mu-lu 歌林公司最新七十四期唱片曲譜目錄. Canton: Ko-lin kung-ssu, *c.*1940s.

Ko-yao 歌謠. Peking: Pei-ta ko-yao yen-chiu hui.

Ku Chieh-kang 顧頡剛, Liu Wan-chang 劉萬章. *Su Yüeh ti hun sang* 蘇粵的婚喪. Taipei: Folklore Books Co. Ltd., 1969. Originally published in 1928.

Kuan Chien-êrh 關健兒. 'Yün hsing chih kuang: Chi Yüeh-chü chu-ming yen-yüan Liang Yin-t'ang.' 殞星之光：記粵劇著名演員梁蔭棠. *YCYC*, no. 5, Dec. 1987.

Kuan Wên-ch'ing 關文清. *Chung-kuo yin tan wai shih* 中國銀壇外史. Hong Kong: Kuang-chüeh-ching ch'u-pan-shê, 1976.

Kuang-chou chih-nan 廣州指南. Canton: Kuang-chou shih-chêng-fu, 1934.

Kuang-chou hsin jih-pao 廣州新日報. Canton: Kuang-chou hsin jih-pao shê, 1933.

Kuang-chou kung shang ling-hsiu jên-wu chih 廣州工商領袖人物誌. Canton: Kuang-chou wên-hua ch'u-pan-shê, 1948.

Kuang-chou min-kuo jih-pao chiao-yü lan. 1934–5. 廣州民國日報教育欄. 2 vols. Canton: Kuang-chou min-kuo jih-pao.

Kuang-chou nien-chien pien tsuan wei-yüan-hui 廣州年鑑編纂委員會 (ed.), *Kuang-chou nien-chien* 廣州年鑑. 2 vols. Canton: Kuang-chou nien-chien pien tsuan wei-yüan-hui, 1935.

Kuang-chou Po-chi i-yüan 廣州博濟醫院 (ed.), *Po-chi nien pao 1918* 博濟年報 1918. Canton: n.p., 1919.

Kuang-chou shê-hui tsa-chih 廣州社會雜誌 , vol. 1, *c.*1920s. Canton: Kuang-chou shê-hui tsa-chih shê.

Kuang-chou shih-chêng-fu 廣州市政府. *Kuang-chou shih chih po-yin-t'ai* 廣州市之播音台. Canton: 1934.

Kuang-chou shih-chêng-fu 廣州市政府. *Kuang-chou shih-chêng-fu liang-nien lai shih-chêng pao kao shu* 廣州市政府兩年來施政報告書. Canton: 1933.

Kuang-chou-shih chêng-hsieh wên shih tzu-liao yen-chiu wei-yüan-hui 廣州市政協文史資料研究委員會 (ed.), *Nan t'ien sui yüeh: Ch'en Chi-t'ang chu Yüeh shih-ch'i chien wên shih lu* 南天歲月：陳濟棠主粵時期見聞實錄. Canton: Kuang-tung jên-min ch'u-pan-shê, 1987.

Kuang-chou-shih chêng-hsieh wên shih tzu-liao yen-chiu wei-yüan-hui 廣州市政協文史資料研究委員會 et al. (eds.), *Kuang-chou kung shang ching-chi shih liao* 廣州公商經濟史料. Canton: Kuang-tung jên-min ch'u-pan-shê, 1986.

Kuang-chou-shih chêng-hsieh wên shih tzu-liao yen-chiu wei-yüan-hui 廣州市政協文史資料研究委員會, Yüeh-chü yen-chiu chung-hsin 粵劇研究中心 (ed.), *Yüeh-chü ch'un-chiu* 粵劇春秋. Canton: Kuang-tung jên-min ch'u-pan-shê, 1990.

Kuang-chou-shih chieh-yen i-yüan 廣州市戒煙醫院 (ed.). *Kuang-chou-shih chieh-yen i-yüan nien pao* 廣州市戒煙醫院年報. Canton: 1937.

Kuang-chou shih chih 廣州史志. Canton: Kuang-chou shih chih pien-chi shih, 1987–.

Kuang-chou-shih chin-yen wei-yüan-hui 廣州市禁煙委員會 (ed.), *Kuang-chou shih chin-yen wei-yüan-hui kung-tso chi-yao*. 廣州市禁煙委員會工作紀要 Canton: n.p., 1937.

Kuang-chou-shih chin-yen wei-yüan-hui 廣州市禁煙委員會 (ed.), *Kuang-chou shih ch'ing tu yün-tung tê k'an* 廣州市清毒運動特刊. Canton: 1937.

Kuang-chou-shih ching-ch'a-chü kung-an shih-heng pao kao, 1922–1923. 廣州市警察局公安事項報告 1922–1923. Canton: 1924.

Kuang-chou-shih hsin-shêng-huo yün-tung wei-yüan-hui 廣州市新生活運動委員會 (ed.). *Kuang-chou-shih hsin-shêng-huo yün-tung chi-yao ti i chi* 廣州市新生活運動輯要第一輯. Canton: 1937, n.p.

Kuang-chou-shih jên-k'ou tiao-ch'a wei-yüan-hui mi-shu ch'u 廣州市人口調查委員會祕書處 (ed.). *Kuang-chou-shih êrh-shih-i-nien jên-k'ou tiao-ch'a pao kao* 廣州市廿一年人口調查報告. Canton: Kunag-chou-shih jên-k'ou tiao-ch'a wei-yüan-hui, 1933.

Kuang-chou-shih jên-min chêng-fu pan-kung tien 廣州市人民政府辦公廳 (ed.). *Kuang-chou ching-ku'ang tiao-cha* 廣州情況調查. Canton: n.p., 1951.

Kuang-chou shih-shang-hui 廣州市商會 (ed.), *Kuang-chou shang-yeh nien-chien* 廣州商業年鑑. Canton: 1932.

Kuang-chou-shih shê-hui-chü 廣州市社會局 (ed.), *Kuang-chou-shih shê-hui-chü kuei-ch'êng hui pien* 廣州市社會局規程彙編. 2nd. edn. Canton: 1932.

Kuang-chou shih shê-hui chü 廣州市社會局 (ed.), *Shê-hui tê k'an* 社會特刊. Canton: Kuang-chou shih shê-hui chü, 1941.

Kuang-chou-shih shih-chêng-fu tsung-wu k'o 廣州市市政廳總務科 (ed.), *Kuang-chou-shih shih-chêng kung pao* 廣州市市政公報. Canton: 1921–36.

Kuang-chou-shih shih-chêng-fu t'ung-chi ku 廣州市市政府統計股. *Kuang-chou-shih shih-chêng-fu t'ung-chi nien-chien. Ti i hui* 廣州市市政府統計年鑑.第一回. Canton: Kuang-chou-shih shih-chêng-fu, 1929.

Kuang-chou-shih shih-chêng-t'ing 廣州市市政廳. *Kuang-chou-shih shih-chêng kai yao* 廣州市市政概要. Canton: 1922.

Kuang-chou-shih shih-chêng-t'ing 廣州市市政廳. *Kuang-chou-shih shih-chêng pao kao hui k'an* 廣州市市政報告彙刊. Canton: 1924.

Kuang-chou-shih shih-chêng ting tsung-wu k'o 廣州市市政廳社會調查股 (ed.), *Kuang-chou-shih shih-chêng kung pao*. 廣州市市政公報. Canton: 1921–36.

Kuang-chou-shih shih-chêng-t'ing shê-hui-tiao-cha-ku 廣州市市政廳社會調查股 (ed.), *Ti sze lei: shê-hui pu-liang shih-yeh* 第四類: 社會不良事業. Canton: 1927.

Kuang-chou-shih shih-li i-yüan 廣州市市立醫院 (ed.). *Kuang-chou shih shih-li i-yüan nien pao (1936)* 廣州市市立醫院年報 (1936). Canton: n.p., 1937.

Kuang-chou shih tzu-tung tien-hua kuan-li wei-yüan-hui 廣州市市政廳社會調查股 edited. *Kuang-chou shih tzu-tung tien-hua hao-ma pu* 廣州市自動電話號碼薄. Canton: Kuang-chou shih tzu-tung tien-hua kuan-li wei-yüan-hui, 1936.

Kuang-chou ta kuan lu 廣州大觀錄. vol. 2, no. 2, 1919.

Kuang-chou-tê-pieh-shih-chêng-fu t'ung-chi ku 廣州特別市政府統計股. *Kuang-chou shih chin liang nien lai tzu-sha t'ung-chi* 廣州市近兩年來自殺統計. Canton: 1930.

Kuang-chou-tê-pieh-shih wu-hsien-tien po-yin-t'ai 廣州特別市無線電播音台. *Kuang-chou tê-pieh-shih wu-hsien-tien po-yin-t'ai chou-nien tê k'an* 廣州特別市無線電播音台周年特刊. Canton: 1930.

Kuang-chou wên-hsüeh hui 廣州文學會 (ed.), *Ying shih* 嬰屍. Canton: Yüeh Kang shou k'uang ch'u-pan pu, 1928.

Kuang-chou yin-yüeh 廣州音樂 , vol. 3, nos. 6–7, 1935. Canton: Kuang-chou yin-yüeh yüan.

Kuang-tung Ch'i-tu-chiao chu-tu hui 廣東基督教拒賭會. *Chu-tu hui chêng wên hua chieh-hsiao* 拒賭會徵文畫揭曉. Canton: 1925.

Kuang-tung ching-ch'a-t'ing chu-t'i chi-kuan chi-t'ing chi ch'ang-chi kuei tsê 廣東警察廳取締妓館妓艇及娼妓規則. Canton: n.p., *c.*1920.

Kuang-tung ch'ing-li-ts'ai-chêng-chü 廣東清理財政局. *Kuang-tung ch'üan shêng ts'ai-chêng shuo-ming shu* 廣東全省財政說明書. 2 vols. Tientsin: Ching-chi hsüeh hui, 1910.

Kuang-tung Kuang-chou tsung-shang-hui 廣東廣州總商會. *Kuang-tung shang-yeh nien-chien* 廣東商業年鑑. Canton: Kuang-chou shih-shang-hui, 1931.

Kuang-tung shêng-chêng-fu 廣東省政府 (ed.), *Kuang-tung shêng-chêng-fu kung-pao* 廣東省政府公佈. Canton: 1920s–30s.

Kuang-tung shêng-chêng-fu min-chêng-ting chin-yen kung-tso pao-kao shu 廣東省政府民政廳禁煙工作報告書. Canton: n.p., 1940.

Kuang-tung shêng-chêng-fu ts'ai-chêng-t'ing 廣東省政府財政廳 and Kuang-tung ts'ai-chêng tê-pai-yüan kung-chü 廣東財政特派員公署 (ed.), *Kuang-tung shêng ts'ai-chêng chi shih* 廣東財政紀實. 3 vols. Canton: Kuang-tung-shêng chêng-fu ts'ai-chêng-t'ing, 1934.

Kuang-tung shêng chin-yen chü chieh-yen liu-i-so ch'êng-li i-chou-nien chi-lien tê-k'an 廣東省禁烟局戒烟留醫所成立一周年紀念特. Canton: n.p., 1942.

Kuang-tung shêng Chung-shan t'u-shu-kuan 廣東省中山圖書館 and Kuang-tung shêng Chu-hai shih chêng-hsieh 廣東省珠海市政協 (ed.), *Kuang-tung chin-hsien-tai jên-wu t'zu-tien* 廣東近現代人物詞典. Canton: Kuang-tung k'o-chi chu-pan-shê, 1992.

Kuang-tung shêng hsüan-an-shih kung-ch'u 廣東省巡按使公署 (ed.), *Kuang-tung kung-pao* 廣東公報. Canton: 1912–1920s.

Kuang-tung shêng-li ti-i chung-hsüeh-hsiao 廣東省立第一中學校 (ed.), *Shêng-li i-chung hsüeh-shêng jih-chi hsüan* 省立一中學生日記選. 3 vols. Canton: Kuang-tung shêng-li ti-i chung-hsüeh-hsiao, 1932/4.

Kuang-tung ts'ai-chêng-t'ing 廣東財政廳. *Kai-chin ch'üan shêng chung-têng hsüeh-hsiao chiao-yü fang-an* 改進全省中等學校教育方案. Canton: 1930.

Kuang-tung wên-hsien chi-k'an 廣東文獻季刊. Taipei: Kuang-tung wên-hsien chi-k'an wei-yüan-hui.

Kuang-tung wên-wu chan-lan hui 廣東文物展覽會 (ed.), *Kuang-tung wên-wu* 廣東文物. 3 vols. Hong Kong: Chung-kuo wên-hua hsieh chin hui, 1941.

Kung-ho shih-yung fu ju san szu wu tzu shu 共和適用婦孺三四五字書. Canton: Lin shu ko, 1911.

Kung-p'ing pao 公評報. Canton: Kung-p'ing pao shê, 1929–49.

Kuo-fu ch'üan chi 國父全集 6 vols. Taipei: Chung-yang wên-hua kung-ying shê, 1961.

Kuo hua pao (Kwok Wa Po) 國華報. Canton: Kuang-chou Kuo hua pao shê, 1911–50.

Kuo Ping-chên 郭秉箴. 'Kuang-tung hsi-ch'ü kai-kê san-shih nien.' 廣東戲曲改革三十年. *YCYCTLH.*

Kuo Ping-chên 郭秉箴. 'Yüeh-chü ku chin t'an.' 粵劇古今談. *YCYCTLH.*

Kuo Ping-chên 郭秉箴. 'Yüeh-chü ti yen-kê yü hsien-chuang.' 粵劇的沿革與現狀. *YCYCTLH*.

Kuo Shuang-lin 郭雙林 and Hsiao Mei-hua 肖梅花. *Chung-hua tu-po shih* 中華賭博史. Peking: Chung-hua shu-ch'ü, 1995.

Lai Po-ch'iang 賴伯彊. *Kuang-tung hsi-ch'ü chien shih* 廣東戲曲簡史. Canton: Kuang-tung jên-min ch'u-pan-shê, 2001.

—— *Yüeh-chü hua-tan wang Chien-li-ch'ü* 粵劇"花旦王"千里駒. Canton: Hua-ch'êng ch'u-pan-shê, 1986.

Lee Tai-cho 李泰初. *Hsiang-kang chih-pi yu Kuang-chou wu-chia chih ch'u-pu yen-chiu* 香港紙幣與廣州物價之初步研究. Canton: Kuang-tung shêng-li Hsiang-chin ta-hsüeh shang-hsüeh yüan, 1936.

Lei To 雷鐸. 'Ling-nan jên ti wu hsin.' 嶺南人的悟性. *NFJP*, 1990: 6 Oct..

—— 'Shih chüeh chiang han ti Nan-fang.' 失卻強悍的南方. *NFJP*, 1991: 9 Sept..

Li Che-hou 李澤厚. *Chung-kuo hsien-tai ssu-hsiang shih lun* 中國現代思想史論. Peking: Tung-fang ch'u-pan-shê, 1987.

Li Chien 黎鍵. *Hsiang-kang Yüeh-chü k'ou-shu shih* 香港粵劇口述史. Hong Kong: Joint Publishing (HK) Co. Ltd., 1993.

Li Chien-êrh 李健兒. *Kuang-tung hsien-tai hua-jên ch'uan* 廣東現代畫人傳. n.p.: 1941.

Li Fêng 李峰. 'Hsüeh Chüeh-hsien ch'uan.' 薛覺先傳. *YCYC*, vol. 1–3, Apr. 1986–Apr. 1987.

Li Fu-lin 李福林. *Li Fu-lin ko-ming shih-liao: Li Fu-lin chiang-ch'ün ts'an-chia kê-ming ching-kuo tzu-shu* 李福林革命史料：李福林將軍參加革命經過自述. Hong Kong: Wên-hua chiao-yu, 1995.

Li Han-chang 李翰章 *Ho-fei Li Ching-lo kung (Han-chang) chêng-shu* 合肥李勤恪公(瀚章)政書. Edited by Li Ching-yü (Reprinted by Taipei: Wên hai ch'u-pan-shê, 1969).

Li Han-ch'iao 厲厂樵. *T'ui ch'uang chi* 推窗集. Canton: Tai-shan shu-tien, 1930.

Li Han-ch'ung 李漢沖. 'Hua-hui tu-po chung chung.' 花會賭博種種. *KTFCL*.

Li Hsiang-yung 李向榮. 'Tu-shih yü tê-mo-kê-la-hsi.' 都市與德模克拉西. *Chung shê*, vol. 1, no. 1, June 1930.

Li Hsun-huan 李煦寰. 'Chin-tu yü fan-yung kuo-min ching-chi.' 禁賭與繁榮國民經濟. *CTKL*.

Li Hsüeh-ying 李雪英. 'Chung-kuo fu-nü tsen yang tsai nêng t'i kao ti-wei.' 中國婦女怎樣才能提高地位. *Hsin hsin*, vol. 1, no. 1, Jan. 1935.

Li I-chi 李奕棋. *Yen-hai hsiang tu shih* 海宴鄉土史. Hong Kong: Published privately by Yü Chung-hüan, 1960.

Li Mên 李門 et al. 'Shih lun Yüeh-chü ti ch'uan-t'ung chi ch'i chi-ch'êng fa-chan wen-t'i.' 試論粵劇的傳統及其繼承發展問題. *YCYCTLH*.

Li P'ei-shêng 李培生. *Kuei-hsi chü Yüeh chih yu-lai chi ch'i ching-kuo* 桂系據粵之由來及其經過. Canton: n.p., 1921.

Li Po-yüan 李伯元, Jen Kung-t'an 任公坦. *Kuang-tung chi-ch'i kung-jên fen-tou shih* 廣東機械工人奮鬥史. Taipei: Chung-kuo lao-kung fu-li ch'u-pan-shê, 1955.

Li San-pi 李散碧. *Huan huo chi* 幻火集. Canton: Chin ch'üeh shu-chü, 1930.

Li T'iao-yüan 李調元, 'Nan Yüeh pi chi.' 南越筆記. *Ts'ung-shu chi-ch'êng*. Edited by Wang Yün-wu. Shanghai: Shang-wu yin-shu-kuan, 1937. First printed in 1778.

Li Tsung-huang 李宗黃. *Hsin Kuang-tung kuan-ch'a chi* 新廣東觀察記. Shanghai: Shang-wu yin-shu-kuan, 1922.

Li Ying 梨影. vol. 3, *c.*1918. Canton: Li ying tsa chih shê.

Liang Kung-ch'ên 梁恭辰. 'Kuang-tung huo chieh chi.' 廣東火劫記. *HYTS*, vol. 10.

Liang Ch'i-ch'ao 梁啓超. *Li Hung-chang chüan* 李鴻章傳. Tientsin: P'ai-hua wên-i ch'u-pan-shê, 2001.

Liang P'ei-chih (Leung Pui-chee) 梁培熾. *Nan-yin yü Yüeh-ou chih yen-chiu* A Study of Nan Yin and Yue Ou. San Francisco: Asian American Studies, School of Ethnic Studies, San Francisco State University, 1988.

—— *Hsiang-kang ta-hsüeh so tsang mu-yü-shu hsü lu yü yen-chiu* Wooden-fish Books: Critical Essays and An Annotated Catalogue Based on the Collections in the University of Hong Kong. Hong Kong: Centre of Asian Studies, Hong Kong University, 1978.

Liang P'ei-chin 梁培錦 *Liu-kuo ta fêng hsiang* 六國大封相. Hong Kong: Urban Council, 1992.

—— *Yüeh-chü chü-mu t'ung chien* 粵劇劇目通檢. Hong Kong: Joint Publishing Co. Ltd., 1985.

—— *Yüeh-chü yen-chiu t'ung lun* 粵劇研究通論. Hong Kong: Lung mên shu-tien, 1982.

Liang Tê-so 梁得所. *Tê-so sui pi* 得所隨筆. 2nd edn. Shanghai: Liang yü t'u-shu yin-shua kung-ssu, 1932.

Liang Yüan-san 梁垣三 *Lo chia-shan* 落伽山. Canton: Yüeh-ch'ü yen-chiu so, *c.*1921–8.

Liang Yün-chiao 梁雲蛟. 'Ai wo ku-hsiang.' 哀我故鄉. *KTHS*, vol. 4, 1934.

Liao Shu-lun 廖淑倫 (ed.), *Kuang-chou ta kuan* 廣州大觀. Canton: T'ien nan ch'u-pan-shê, 1948.

Liao Yüan 了緣. 'Hsi-chü chih la tsa t'an.' 戲劇之拉雜談. *Hsi chü shih-chieh*, vol. 1, no. 3, Oct. 1922.

Lien hsiang chi-chê 憐香記者. Canton: Hua hsing shu-chü, *c.*1931–3.

Lin Chin-chih 林金枝, Ts'ang Wei-chi 庄衛璣 (eds.), *Chin-tai hua-ch'iao t'ou-tzu kuo nei chieh-yeh shih tzu-liao hsüan chi* 近代華僑投資國內企業史資料選輯. Hsia-mên: Fu-chien jên-min ch'u-pan-shê, 1989.

Lin Chin-chih 林金枝. 'Chiu Chung-kuo ti Kuang-tung hua-ch'iao t'ou-tzu chi ch'i tso-yung' 舊中國的廣東華僑投資及其作用 in *Nan-yang wen-t'i* 南洋問題, no. 2, 1982.

Lin lao ju hua ts'ung 臨老入花叢. Canton: Ta hsin shu-chü, n.d.

Lin Man-hung 林滿紅. *Ch'ing-mo shê-hui liu-hsing hsi-shih ya-pien yen-chiu: kung-chi-mien fên-hsi, 1773–1906* 清末社會流行吸食鴉片研究：供給面分析, 1773–1906 (Taipei: n.p., *c.*1980s).

Ling Hsiao-shêng 靈簫生. 'Chih-fên yü shêng.' 脂粉餘生. *KCLPL*, vol. 4, 1933.

Liu Ching-chih 劉靖之, (ed.). *Chung-kuo hsin yin-yüeh shih lun chi* 中國新音樂史論集. Hong Kong: Centre of Asian Studies, Hong Kong University, 1988.

Liu Ching-chih 劉靖之, Hsien Yü-i 冼玉儀 (ed.), *Yüeh-chü yen-tao-hui lun-wen-chi* 粵劇研討會論文集. Hong Kong: Hong Kong University Centre of Asian Studies, Joint Publishing (HK) Co. Ltd., 1995.

Liu Fu-ching 劉付靖, Wang Ming-k'un 王明坤. *Chiu Kuang-tung yen tu ch'ang* 舊廣東煙賭娼. Hong Kong: Chung-hua shu-chü, 1992.

Liu Kuo-hsing 劉國興. 'Hsi-pan ho hsi-yüan.' 戲班和戲院. *YCYCTLH*.

Liu Ling-yü 劉伶玉. *Lo P'in-ch'ao ch'i ch'uan* 羅品超奇傳. Hong Kong: Hsiang-kang chou-k'an ch'u-pan-shê, 1990.

Liu Shu-fên 劉淑芬. *Liu-chao ti ch'êng-shih yü shê-hui* 六朝的城市與社會. Taipei: Hsüeh-shêng shu-chü, 1992.

Liu Tsai-su 劉再蘇. *Kuang-chou kuai lan* 廣州快覽. Shanghai: Shih-chieh shu-chü, 1926.

Liu Wan-chang 劉萬章. 'Pa-kung ti Kuang-chou kuo nien jih-chi.' 巴公的廣州過年日記. Chou K'ang-yen (ed.), *Kuang-tung fêng-su chui lu*.

Liu Wan-chang 劉萬章. 'Kuang-chou ti chiu sang su.' 廣州的舊喪俗. *Su Yüeh ti hun sang* 蘇粵的婚喪. Canton: Chung-kuo min-su hsüeh hui, 1928.

Liu Yao-hsin 劉瑤信. 'Chung-kuo tu-shih shê-hui ti wei-chi.' 中國都市社會的位置. *Shê-hui yen-chiu ch'i k'an* 社會研究期刊. Canton: vol. 1, no. 1, 1935.

Liu Ying 劉瀛. 'Chu-kiang ch'i yü chi.' 珠江奇遇記. Chang Mêng-chêng (ed.), *Ch'ing-lou yün yü*. Shanghai: Chung-yang shu-tien, 1935, ii.

Liu Yüeh-shêng 劉粵聲. *Kuang-chou Chi-tu chiao kai ku'ang* 廣州基督教概況. Canton: Kuang-chou Chi-tu chiao lien hui, 1937.

Lo Chia-lun and Huang Chi-lu 羅家倫、黃季陸 (ed.). *Wu Chih-hui hsien-shêng ch'üan chi* 吳稚輝先生全集 18 vols. Taipei: Chung-kuo Kuo-min-tang chung-yang wei-yüan-hui tang-shih shih-liao pien-hsüan wei-yüan-hui, 1969.

Lo Chu-fêng 羅竹風. *Chung-kuo shê-hui-chu-i shih-ch'i ti tsung-chiao wen-t'i* 中國社會主義時期的宗教問題. Shanghai: Shang-hai shê-hui k'o-hsüeh yüan, 1987.

Lo Li-ming 羅澧銘. *T'ang-hsi hua-yüeh hêng* 塘西花月痕. 4 vols. Hong Kong: n.p., 1962.

Lo Hai-sha 羅海莎. 'Min-tsu fu-hsing yün-tung chung hsin-hsi-chü i-shu ti chien-li.' 民族復興運動中新戲劇藝術的建立. *Hsi-chü i-shu*, vol. 1, 1937.

Lo I-ch'ün 羅翼群. 'Sun Chung-shan hui Yüeh chung-chien chêng-ch'üan hou ti Kuang-tung chêng-chü.' 孫中山回粵重建政權後的廣東政局. *SCSST*, pp. 212–19.

Lo Ming-yu 羅明佑. 'Kuang-tung jên yü Chung-kuo tien-ying.' 廣東人與中國電影. Kuang-tung wên-wu chan-lan hui (ed.), *Kuang-tung wên-wu*, vol. 2.

Lo Tzu-ch'in 盧子芩. 'Chung-kuo ya-pien wen-t'i ho tui yu nung-ts'un ti yin-hsiang.' 中國鴉片問題和對於農村的影響. *Nan-ta ching-chi*, vol. 2, no. 2, May 1933.

Lo Yün-yen 羅運炎. *Tu-p'in wen-t'i* 毒品問題. 2nd edn. Changsha: Shang-wu yin-shu-kuan, 1938.

Lu Hsün 魯迅. *Lu Hsün shou ts'ê* 魯迅手冊. Edited. by Têng Ou-yün. Shanghai: P'o lan shu-chü, 1938.

Lu Yen 魯言. *Hsiang-kang chang-ku* 香港掌故. vol. 2. Hong Kong: Kuang-chüeh-ching ch'u-pan-shê, 1981.

Lung Ch'en Jo-lan 龍陳若蘭. 'T'an hsi-chü yü Hsiang-kang hua-chü.' 談戲劇與香港話劇. Chan Tê-lung (ed.), *Hsiang-kang Chung-kuo hsi-chü hsien-ku'ang yen-t'ao hui-i lu*.

Ma Ch'ao-chün 馬超俊. *Chung-kuo lao-kung wen-t'i* 中國勞工問題. Shanghai: Min-chih shu-chü, 1927.

Ma P'i-yao 馬丕瑶 *Ma Chung-chêng (p'i-yao) i-chi* 馬中丞丕瑶遺集. Edited by Ma Ch'i-shen and Ma Ch'i-chang. Reprinted by Taipei: Wên hai ch'u-pan-shê, 1969.

Ma Shih-ts'êng 馬師曾. *Chien-li chuang yu chi* 千里壯遊集. Canton: 1931. Privately published by Ma Shih-ts'êng.

Ma Ya-ko 馬雅各 (James Laidlaw Maxwell). *Kuang-chou Ho-nan wei-shêng kung-tso chi-hua* (Honan Island Health Scheme). Canton: Kuang-tung chia-ting wei-shêng ts'u-chin hui, 1934.

Mai Hsiao-hsia 麥嘯霞. 'Kuang-tung hsi-chü shih lüeh.' 廣東戲劇史略. Kuang-tung wên-wu chan-lan hui, *Kuang-tung wên-wu*, vol. 2.

Mao Hai-chien 茅海建. *Tien-chou ti pêng-k'uei* 天朝的崩潰. Peking: San-lien shu-tien, 1995.

Mao Tun 茅盾 et al (eds.). *Chung-kuo ti i jih* 中國的一日. Shanghai: Shêng-huo shu-tien, 1936.

Mei Ch'i 梅綺. *Hsi-chü ti jên-shêng* 戲劇的人生. Hong Kong: Wên-tsung ch'u-pan-shê, 1956.

'Mei-nü ching-sai yü hua-chieh hsüan-chü.' 美女競賽與花界選舉. *Wu-hsien man-hua*, vol. 1, no. 7, 1930.

Mêng Yüan-lao 孟元老. *Tung-ching mêng hua lu* 東京夢華錄. Vernacularized and abriged by Sun Ming-sun. Taipei: Shih pao wên-hua ch'u-pan ch'i-yeh yu-hsien-kung-ssu, 1987.

Ma Mo-ching et al. 馬模貞等 *1729 nien–1949 nien Chung-kuo chin-tu shih tzu-liao* 1729 年–1949 年中國禁毒史資料. Tientsin: Tientsin jêm-min ch'u-pan-shê.

Min-su t'ung-shu, wan-nien-li 民俗通書、萬年曆. Hai-k'ou: Hai-nan jên-min ch'u-pan-shê, 1990.

Ming-ch'ü ta-chüan 名曲大全. Shanghai: Pai tai kung-ssu, *c.*1920s.

Ming-hsin pao chien 明心寶鑑. Canton: Tsui ching t'ang. 1919.

Ming-pên Ch'iao-chou hsi-wên wu tsung 明本潮州戲文五種. Canton: Kuang-tung jên-min ch'u-pan-shê, 1985.

Mo-têng ti-yü 摩登地獄. Canton: Hua hsing shu-chü, n.d.

Nan-fang jih-pao. 南方日報. Canton: Nan-fang jih-pao shê, 1950– .

Nan-hai hsien chih 南海縣志. 1910 edn.

Nieh Chên-pin 聶振斌. 'Chung-kuo chin-tai pei-chü lun.' 中國近代悲劇論. *Hua-nan ssu-fan ta-hsüeh hsüeh pao*, no. 3, 1986.

Niu Chih 牛志. *Hun-yin ta kê-ming* 婚姻大革命. Canton: Hsin hua shu-tien, 1951.

No Chih 諾志. 'Liu-yüeh ti tien-yeh.' 六月的田野. *KTHS*, vol. 4, 1934.

Ou An-nien 歐安年, et al. *Ling-nan chang ku* 嶺南掌故. Canton: Kuang-tung lü-yu ch'u-pan-shê, 1987.

Ou Chi-liang 歐季鸞. *Kuang-chou chih yin-yeh* 廣州之銀業. Canton: Kuo-li Chung-shan ta-hsüeh fa-hsüeh-yüan ching-chi tiao-ch'a ch'u, 1932.

Ou Man-lang 歐漫郎. 'Chung-kuo ch'ing-nien hsü yao shih-mo yin-yüeh.' 中國青年需要甚麼音樂. *Kuang-chou yin-yüeh*, vol. 3, nos. 6–7, 1935.

Ou-yang Shan 歐陽山. *Ch'i-nien chi* 七年忌. Shanghai: Shêng-huo shu-tien, 1935.

—— *Ch'ing-nien nan nü* 青年男女. Shanghai: Hsiao-hsing wên-k'u, 1937.

—— *Shêng ti fan jao* 生底煩擾. Shanghai: Wên-hua shêng-huo ch'u-pan-shê, 1937.

—— *Shih-pai ti shih-pai-chê* 失敗的失敗者. Shanghai: Ch'iao-fêng ch'u-pan-shê, 1948.

—— 'Tsai shen ching li' 在滲井裏. in *Shih-pai ti shih-pai-chê* . Shanghai, Ch'iao-fêng ch'u-pan-shê, 1948.

Ou-yang Yü-ch'ien 歐陽予倩. 'Hsi-chü kai-kê chih li-lun yü shih-chi.' 戲劇改革之理論與實際. *Hsi-chü*, vol. 1, 1929.

—— 'Shih t'an Yüeh-chü.' 試談粵劇. Ou-yang Yü-ch'ien (ed.), *Chung-kuo hsi-ch'ü yen-chiu tzu-liao ch'u chi* 中國戲曲研究資料初輯. Peking: Chung-kuo hsi-chü ch'u-pan-shê, 1957.

—— 'T'an wên-ming-hsi.' 談文明戲. *Chung-kuo hua-chü yün-tung wu-shih-nien shih-liao chi* 中國話劇運動五十年史料集. Peking: Chung-kuo hsi-chü ch'u-pan-shê, 1958.

—— *Tzu wo yen hsi i lai*. 自我演戲以來. 2nd edn. Shanghai: Shen-chou kuo kuang shê, 1939.

—— 'Yüeh-chü Peh-chü hua ti yen-chiu.' 粵劇北劇化的研究; and 'Yung Yüeh-yü yen hua-chü.' 用粵語演話劇. *Hsi-chü*, vol. 1, 1929.

Pai Ch'ü-yung 白駒榮. 'Szu-shih nien lai Yüeh-chü piao-yen i-shu ti p'ien-hua.' 四十年來粵劇表演藝術的變化. *Hsi-ch'ü yen-chiu chi-k'an*, vol. 1, Jan. 1958.

Pai man tien-ying yüeh-k'an 白幔電影月刊, no. 6, 1931. Canton: Pai man tien-ying yüeh-k'an shê.

Pai-ngo-t'an hua-pao 白鵝潭畫報, vol. 1, Jan. 1929. Canton: Pai-ngo-t'an hua-pao shê.

Pai-chin lung. 白金龍 Reprinted in *Hsi-chü yen-chiu tzu-liao*, vol. 10, 1984. Canton: Kuang-chou wên-i yen-chiu shê.

Pan-chiao man-hua 半角漫畫. Canton: Pan-chiao man-hua shê, 1929–32.

P'an Kuang-wên 潘光文. *Chung-kuo ling-jên hsüeh-yüan chih yen-chiu* 中國伶人血緣之研究. Taipei: Shang-wu yin-shu-kuan, 1966.

P'an-yü hsien hsü chih 番禺縣續志. 1931 edition. Reprinted by Taipei: Hsüeh-shêng shu-tien, 1968.

P'ang Tê-hsin 龐德新. *Ts'ung hua-pên chi i-hua-pên so chien chih Sung-tai liang ching shi-min shêng-huo* 從話本及擬話本所見之宋代兩京市民生活. Hong Kong: Lung-mên shu-tien, 1974.

Pao 包. 'Kuang-tung fêng-su pien pien t'an.' 廣東風俗翩翩談. *Yüeh fêng*, vol. 2, no. 3, 1936.

P'eng Kuo-liang 彭國亮. *Hsi-nan san shêng Ch'uan Tien Ch'ien chin-tu yü chin-yen chih yen-chiu, 1911–1940* 西南三省(川滇黔)煙毒與禁煙之研究 (1911–40). Kuo-li Chêng-chih ta-hsüeh li-shih hsi shuo-shih lun-wên, 1981.

P'eng Yang-ou 彭養鷗. *Hêh-chieh yüan-yün* 黑藉冤魂. Originally published in 1909. Compiled in *Wan-Ch'ing wên-hsüeh ts'ung-ch'ao. Hsiao-shuo, vol. 3*. Edited. by Ah Ying. Peking: Hsin-hua shu-chü, 1982.

P'iao p'iao 飄飄, vol. 1, 1929. Canton: P'ing shê.

Piao tu ch'ui hsin chi 嫖賭吹新集. Canton: Shêng-ch'êng Liu yüeh chin kuan, 1910.

P'ing Chin-ya 平襟亞. 'Chiu Shang-hai ti tu-po' 舊上海的賭博. Shang-hai wên-shih yen-chiu kuan (ed.). *Chiu Shang-hai ti yen tu ch'ang.*

P'u Liang-chu 蒲良柱. 'I-nien lai chi Kuang-chou tang-chêng' 一年來之廣州黨政 in *Kuang-tung Kuang-chou tang-chêng kung-tso kai-ku'ang pao-kao* 廣東廣州黨政工作概況報告. Canton: n.p., 1929.

Sha Tung-hsun 沙東迅. *Yüeh hai chin-tai-shih t'an* 粵海近代史譚. Canton: Hua-nan li-kung ta-hsüeh ch'u-pan-shê, 1989.

Shang-hai shih chin-tu kung-tso ling-tao hsiao-tsu pan-kung-shih 上海市禁毒工作領導小组辦公室, and Shang-hai shih tang-an-kuan 上海市檔案館 (eds.), Ch'ing-mo Min-ch'u ti chin-yen yün-tung ho Wan-kuo Chin-yen-hui 清末民初的禁煙運動和萬國禁煙會. Shanghai: Shang-hai ko-hsüeh chi-shu wên-hsien ch'u-pan-she, 1996.

Shang-hai wên-shih yen-chiu kuan 上海文史研究館 (ed.), *Chiu Shang-hai ti yen tu ch'ang* 舊上海的煙賭娼. Hong Kong: Chung yüan ch'u-pan-shê, 1989.

Shao Pin-ju 邵彬儒 (ed.), *Kuang-tung yü hsiao-shuo chi* 廣東語小説集. Tokyo: Sho ho shoten, 1964.

Shê-hui heh-mo 社會黑幕, vol. 14, June 1934. Canton: Shê-hui heh-mo tsa-chih shê.

Shen Chi 沈紀. *Ma Shih-ts'êng ti hsi-chü shêng-yai*. 馬師曾的戲劇生涯. Canton: Kuang-tung jên-min ch'u-pan-shê, 1957.

Shen Chiang-lung 沈祥龍. 'Li-an heh-mo.' 尼庵黑幕. *KTFCL*.

Shen pao 申報 (Shanghai), The Shun Pao Chinese daily news, 1842–1949.

Shêng hsin 聖心, no. 2, July 1933. Canton: Shêng-hsin chung-hsüeh-hsiao.

Shih Ch'ih 詩癡. 'Mai p'iao yin.' 買票吟. *KCLPL*, vol. 20, Aug. 1934.

Shih-jih t'an hsün-k'an shê 十日談旬刊社. *Shih-jih t'an hao wai tsêng k'an hsüeh-shêng shêng-huo tê chi* 十日談號外增刊學生生活特輯. Shanghai: T'i-i ch'u-pan-shê, 1934.

Shih Ping-hui 史秉慧 (ed.), *Chang Tzu-p'ing p'ing ch'uan* 張資平評傳. Shanghai: K'ai-ming shu-tien, 1936.

Shu pao 述報. Originally published in Canton by Kuang-chou Shu-pao shê between 18 April, 1884 to 4 April, 1885. Reprinted by Taipei: Tai-wan hsüeh-shêng shu-tien, 1965.

Shun-tê hsien chih 順德縣志. 1929 edn. Reprinted by Taipei: Chêng wên ch'u-pan-shê, 1965.

Ssu hsü 思絮, vol. 1, no. 1, Apr. 1931. Canton: Kuang-tung shêng-li ti-êrh chung-hsüeh-hsiao Ssu shê.

Su Kuo-yung 蘇國榮. 'Shih lun hsi-ch'ü kuan-chung ti min-chien hsin chi ch'i ying-hsing.' 試論戲曲觀眾的民間性及其影響. *Hsi-ch'ü yen-chiu*, vol. 13, Dec. 1984.

Su T'ung 蘇童. *Hung fên* 紅粉. Hong Kong: Tian-t'i tu-shu yu-hsien kung-ssu, 1992

Su Yü-tê 蘇裕德. *Kuang-tung hsien-tai jên-wu chih* 廣東現代人物誌. Canton: Hua-nan hsin-wên shê, 1949.

Sun Lung-chi 孫隆基. *Chung-kuo wên-hua ti shên-tsêng chieh-kou* 中國文化的深層結構. Hong Kong: I shan shu-wu, 1983.

Sung-hu-chu-jên 宋湖主人. *Ch'ing shan-hu pan pên* 青珊瑚班本. Hong Kong: n.p., *c.*1919.

Sung Yü 宋玉. *T'ang-hsi chin-fên* 塘西金粉. Hong Kong: I yüan ch'u-pan-shê, 1989.

Sze yin ch'i 四淫齊. Hong Kong: Kuang-mou hao, 1907.

Ta Fu 大夫. 'Tou lung chuan fêng yü tu-tu kuan-hsi.' 偷龍轉鳳與賭徒關係. *Tien-têng-tan*, vol. 12, *c.*1930s.

Tan pao t'ien 膽包天. Canton: Hua hsing shu-chü, *c.*1921–8.

Tan-tsao hsiang tzu-chih-hui pao kao shu 丹灶鄉自治會報告書. Canton: n.p., 1926.

T'an Cho-yüan 譚卓垣. *Kuang-chou ting-ch'i k'an-wu ti tiao-ch'a, 1826–1934* 廣州定期刊物的調查 1826–1934. Reprinted by Hong Kong: Lung mên shu-tien, 1965. Originally published in 1935.

T'an Jen-chiu 譚紉就. *Chung-kuo li-hun ti yen-chiu* 中國離婚的研究. Shanghai: Chung-hua Chi-tu chiao nü ch'ing-nien hui ch'üan kuo hsieh hui, 1932.

T'an Shao-p'eng 譚紹鵬 et al (eds.), *Kuang-chou chu-ming lao-tzu-hao* 廣州著名老字號. Canton: Kuang-chou wên-hua ch'u-pan-shê, 1989.

T'an Yü-chien 譚汝儉. 'Sze-shih-ch'i nien lai Kuang-tung pao-yeh shih k'ai lü' 四十七年來廣東報業史概略, in Hua-tzu jih-pao pien-chi pu 華字日報編輯部 ed., *Hua-tzu jih-pao ch'i-shih-i chou-nien chi-nien k'an* 華字日報七十一周年紀念刊. Hong Kong: Hua-jih jih-pao yin-yeh pu, 1934.

T'ang Hsüeh-hsing 唐雪卿 . *Chi-hun yüan shih chêng-hun-jên* 結婚原是證婚人. Canton: Yüeh-ch'ü yen-chiu shê, *c.*1931–3.

T'ang Kê 唐克. 'Lun nü-jên ti mei yü ch'ou.' 論女人的美與醜 ; and 'Wo ti chêng-hu nü-jên fa.' 我的稱呼女人法 . *KCTC*, vol. 33, Dec. 1934.

T'ang Ti-shêng 唐滌生. *Yen Shui-shêng* 閻瑞生. Canton: I wên t'ang shu-chü, *c.*1930s.

Têng Chên-tê 鄧真德. *Kuang-chou shih wei-shêng hsing-chêng chih chien-t'ao* (A Review and Forecast of Public Health Administration in Canton). Canton: Kuang-chou shih-chêng-fu wei-shêng-chü, 1934.

Têng Fei-p'eng 鄧飛鵬. 'Yang-ch'êng hua-hsü.' 羊城花絮 . *Kuang-tung wên-hsien chi k'an*, vol. 8, no.1, 1978.

Têng Ping-ch'üan 鄧炳權. *Kuang-chou kê-ming shêng ti shih hua* 廣州革命勝地史話. Canton: Kuang-tung jên-min ch'u-pan-shê, 1984.

Têng Tuan-pên 鄧端本. *Ling-nan chang-ku* 嶺南掌故. Canton: Kuang-tung lü-yu ch'u-pan-shê, 1986.

Têng Yen-ch'ao 鄧演超 et al. *Kuang-chou-jên ti shêng-huo fang-shih* 廣州人的生活方式. Hai-k'ou: Hai-nan jên-min ch'u-pan-shê, 1988.

Têng Yü-shêng 鄧雨生 (ed.). *Ch'üan Yüeh shê-hui shih-lu ch'ü-pien* 全粵社會實錄初編. Canton: T'i-cha ch'üan Yüeh shê-hui chü, 1911.

Ti-i-tzu kuo-nei kê-ming chan-chêng shih-ch'i ti kung-jên yün-tung 第一次國內革命戰爭時期的工人運動. Peking: Jên-min ch'u-pan-shê, 1980.

Tieh Ma 鐵馬. 'Jui-yüeh-fen chi Kuang-chou shê-hui.' 九月份之廣州社會. *Chien yen piao*, vol. 1, no. 1, 1931.

Tien Chiang-ch'un 點絳唇. 'Lao-kuan chên hsing-ming k'ao.' 老倌真姓名攷. *Hsi ch'uan*, vol. 1, 1931.

—— 'Tsui chin ko pan shêng-i kai ku'ang.' 最近各班生意概況. *Hsi ch'uan*, vol. 1, 1931.

T'ien ch'ü hua-pao 天趣畫報, vol. 1, 1928. Canton: T'ien ch'ü hua-pao shê.

Tien Chung-chi 田仲濟, and Sun Chang-hsi 孫昌熙. *Chung-kuo hsien-tai hsiao-shuo shih* 中國現代小說史. Chi-nan: Shan-tung wên-i ch'u-pan-shê, 1984.

Tien-têng-tan 電燈膽. Canton: *c.*1930.

Tien Han 田漢. 'Chung-kuo hua-chü i-shu fa-chan ti lu-ching ho chan-wang.' 中國話劇藝術發展的路程和展望. Ou-yang Yü-ch'ien (ed.), *Chung-kuo hua-chü yün-tung wu-shih-nien shih-liao chi.*

Ts'ai Ch'ien 蔡謙. *Yüeh-shêng tui wai mou-i tiao-ch'a pao kao* 粵省對外貿易調查報告 Shanghai: Shang-wu yin-shu-kuan, 1939.

Ts'ai Hsien-fên 蔡衍棻. *Nan-yin lung-chou ho mu-yü ti pien hsieh* 南音龍舟和木魚的編寫. Canton: Kuang-tung jên-min ch'u-pan-shê, 1978.

Ts'ai Jên-chien 蔡仁堅 (ed.). *Tien-kung k'ai-wu* 天工開物. Taipei: Shih-pao wên-hua ch'u-pan ch'i-yeh yu-hsien kung-ssu, 1987.

Tsai Liang 才良. 'Wo ti kuo-ch'ü.' 我的過去. *KTHS*, vol. 4, 1934.

Ts'ai Yung-fang 蔡榮芳. *Hsiang-kang jên chih Hsiang-kang shih* 香港人之香港史. Hong. Kong: Oxford University Press, 2001.

Ts'an hua lo ti hung 殘花落地紅. Canton: Ta hsin shu-chü, *c.*1935–6.

Tsê An 策安, Wei Chih 爲之. 'T'ien-hai sui-pi.' 天海隨筆. *KTHS*, vol. 2, 1933.

Ts'êng Min-chih 曾敏之. *Ling-nan sui pi* 嶺南隨筆. Canton: Kuang-tung jên-min ch'u-pan-shê, 1957.

Ts'êng Chung-pi 曾仲璧: 'Tui yü i-pan ch'ing-nien ti fên-hsi ho i-chien.' 對於一般青年的分析和意見. *Hsin hsin*, vol. 1, no. 3, Jan. 1935.

Tsou Lu 鄒魯. *Tsou Lu hsien-shêng wên-chi* 鄒魯先生文集. Ed, by Chung-kuo Kuo-min-t'ang Chung-yang hui-yüan-hui t'ang-shih wei-yüan-hui. Taipei: Chung-yang wên-chien kung-ying-shê, 1984.

Tsou Lu 鄒魯. 'Tu huo.' 賭禍. *CTKL.*

Tsui-mien-shan-jên 醉眠山人. *Kuang-tung heh-mo ta kuan* 廣東黑幕大觀. Canton: n.p., circa 1920s.

Ts'un Shih 存實. 'Yen-hua hsüeh lei hua Ch'en-t'ang.' 煙花血淚話陳塘. *KTFCL.*

Tu Chuan 杜撰. 'Pien ti wen-t'i' 辮的問題. *KTHS*, vol. 4, 1934.

Tu-po ming lun liao chiang 賭博明論瞭講. Ning-po: Hua hua shêng-ching shu fang, 1847.

Tu Shao-mu 杜少牧. 'Yüeh-chü ao t'an.' 粵劇贅譚. *Kuang-tung wên-hsien chi k'an*, vol. 3, no. 2, 1973.

—— 'Man t'an Yüeh-chü.' 漫談粵劇. *Kuang-tung wên-hsien chi k'an*, vol. 1, no. 1, 1971.

Tu-tsai ku tan 賭仔哭攤. Canton: I wên t'ang, n.d.

Tu Tsung-ming 杜聰明. 'Statistical Studies on Opium Addiction in Formosa, Eight Report' 臺灣阿片癮者之统計的調查，第8報告 in *Tu Tsung-ming yen-lun chi* 杜聰明言論集. vol. 2. Taipei: Tu Tsung-ming p'o-shih huan-li chi-nien chiang-hsüeh chih-chin kuan-li wei-yüan-hui, 1953.

Tu Yü-ming 杜如明 . 'Mu-yü shu.' 木魚書. *Kuang-tung wên-hsien chi k'an*, vol. 4, no. 3, 1974.

Tu Yün-chih 杜雲之. *Chung-kuo tien-ying shih* 中國電影史. 2 vols. Taipei: Shang-wu yin-shu-kuan, 1972.

Tuan Ping 短兵. 'Kuang-chou chih hsi-chü chi chü-p'ing.' 廣州之戲劇及劇評. *KCTC*, vol. 1, no. 1, Dec. 1924.

Tung-kuo-hsien-shêng 東郭先生. *Chi chia fêng yüeh* 妓家風月. Shih-chia-chuang: Peh-yüeh wên-i ch'u-pan-shê, 1990.

Tung Shao-pi 佟紹弼, Yang Shao-ch'üan 楊紹權. 'Nü-ling hsüeh lei shih.' 女伶血淚史. *KTFCL*.

Tung Tso-pin 董作賓. 'Min-su wên-hsüeh chung ti ya-pien-yen. 民俗文學中的鴉片煙'. *Ko-yao*, no. 67, Nov. 1924.

Tzu-hang-shih 慈航氏. *Kuang-chou chih-nan* 廣州指南. Canton: Hsin hua shu-tien, 1919.

Tzu Yün 紫雲. 'Kê-ming t'sê-yüan ti.' 革命策源地. *Ta-chung shêng-huo*, vol. 1, no. 10, Jan. 1936.

Wan jên tsa-chih 萬人雜誌. Canton: Wan jên tsa-chih shê.

Wan Yung 婉嵘. 'Ping hou luan t'u.' 病後亂塗. *Wan jên tsa-chih*, vol. 1, no. 3, June 1930.

—— 'T'an tao chiang-chien.' 談到強姦. *Wan jên tsa-chih*, vol. 1, no. 5, Aug. 1930.

Wang Chien-hsün 王建勛. 'Tui yü san-shih-nien-tai Yüeh-chü p'ing-chia ti ch'ien chien.' 對於三十年代粵劇評價的淺見. *YCYCTLH*.

Wang Chiu-hsing 王就興. 'Hsin-fêng-huang tsun kai-k'uang tiao-cha' 新鳳凰村概況調查, in *Nan fêng* 南風 (Canton), vol. 1, nos. 4/5 (1937).

Wang fu hua shih 望夫化石. Canton: Hua hsing shu-chü, n.d.

Wang Hsien-ch'ien 王先謙 (ed.), *Kuo (Shih-lang) Sung-t'ao tsou-kao* 郭（侍郎）嵩燾奏稿. 3 vols. Taipei: Wên hai ch'u-pan-shê, 1969 reprinted.

Wang Po-chih 王博之. 'Ch'ung-pai k'o-hsüeh wên-ming ti i p'ieh.' 崇拜科學文明之一瞥. *Ling-nan hsüeh pao*, vol. 1, no. 3, June 1930.

Wang Shu-nu 王書奴. *Chung-kuo ch'ang-chi shih* 中國娼妓史. Reprinted by Shanghai: San-lien shu-tien, 1988.

Wang Sun-chia 王孫賈. 'Mai lien-pang.' 買聯榜. *KCTC*, vol. 26, 1934.

Wang T'ang 王棠. 'Peh-ching-lu hua chiu.' 北京路話舊. *Kuang-chou shih chih*, vol. 1, no. 1, Jan. 1987.

Wang Tsung-yen 汪宗衍. *Kuang-tung wên-wu ts'ung t'an* 廣東文物叢談. Hong Kong: Chung-hua shu-chü, 1974.

Wang Yung-chih 汪容之. 'Liu-shih-wu nien Yüeh-chü hsi-mi tsa i.' 六十五年粵劇戲迷雜憶. *YCYC*, vol. 6, 1988.

Wei Fu-min 韋輔民 et al. *Kuang-tung ta-hsi k'ao* 廣東大戲考. Shanghai: Kuang-tung po-yin-chieh lien-i shê ch'u-pan-chu, 1947.

Wu Chên-fang 吳震方. 'Ling-nan tsa chi.' 嶺南雜記. Reprinted in *Ts'ung-shu chi ch'êng*. Edited by Wang Yün-wu. Shanghai: Shang-wu yin-shu-kuan, 1936.

Wu chia pao 無價寶, vol. 1, Nov. 1931. Canton: Kuang-chou wu chia pao tsa-chih shê.

Wu Chün-lin 吳俊林. 'Kuang-chou ying-pien san-pu-ch'ü.' 廣州影片三部曲. *KCTC*, vol. 23, 1933.

Wu Hao 吳昊. *Fêng yüeh T'ang-hsi* 風月塘西. Hong Kong: Po i ch'u-pan-shê, 1989.

Wu-hsien man-hua (The Funny Story) 五仙漫話. Canton: Nan-fang fu lun shê, 1929–30s.

Wu Ju-chou 吳汝洲. 'Hsin-nien sui pi.' 新年隨筆. *KTHS*, vol. 2, 1933.

Wu Jui-lin 伍銳麟. 'Kuang-chou-shih Ho-nan tao Hsia Tu ts'un ch'i-shih-liu chia tiao-ch'a' 廣州市河南島下渡村七十六家調查. *Ling-nan hsüeh pao*, vol. 6, no. 4, June 1941.

—— *Kuang-chou-shih liu-pai jên-li-chê-fu shêng-huo ts'ang-ku'ang chih tiao-ch'a* 廣州市六百人力車伕生活狀況之調查. Canton: Ling-nan ta-hsüeh shê-hui-hsüeh hsi shê-hui tiao-ch'a-so, 1940.

—— *San-shui tan-min tiao-ch'a* 三水蛋民調查. Canton: Ling-nan ta-hsüeh shê-hui yen-chiu-so, 1934. Reprinted in Lou Tsu-K'uang (ed.), *Folklore and Folk Literature*. Taipei: The Orient Cultural Service, 1971.

—— 'Sha-nan tan-min tiao-ch'a pao kao.' 沙南蛋民調查報告. *Ling-nan hsüeh pao*, vol. 3, no. 1, 1934.

—— and Huang En-lin 黃恩憐. 'Chiu Fêng-huang ts'un tiao-ch'a pao kao.' 舊鳳凰村調查報告. *Ling-nan hsüeh pao*, vol. 4, no. 3, 1935.

Wu tzu shu 無字書. Canton: Yüeh-ch'ü yen-chiu shê, *c.*1921–1928.

Wu Wu-yao 吳沃堯. *Wu Yen-jên hsiao-shuo hsüan* 吳研人小說選. Edited by Chung Hsien-p'ei. Chêng-chou: Chung chou shu hua shê, 1986.

Wu Yin 無因. 'Kuan-yü Min-chung Chü-shê.' 關於民眾劇社. *Wu-hsien man-hua*, vol. 1, 1930.

Wu Yü 吳雨, Liang Li-ch'êng 梁立成, Wang Tao-chi 王道智. *Min-kuo heh-shê-hui* 民國黑社會. Nanking: Kiang-su ku-chi ch'u-pan-shê, 1988.

Yeh T'ao 也淘. 'Chung-kuo min-tsu-hsin ti hsiao ch'ên yü wu-hsia tu-wu.' 中國民族性的消沉與武俠讀物. *Ch'ün shêng pao hsing-ch'i tsêng k'an*, 31 Jan. 1937.

Yang-ch'êng wan-pao 羊城晚報. Canton: Yang-ch'êng wan-pao shê, 1950-.

Yang Chieh-tseng 楊潔曾 and Ho Yüan-nan 賀宛男, *Shang-hai ch'ang-chi kai-tso shih hua* 上海娼妓改造史話. Shanghai: Shang-hai san-lian shu-tien, 1988.

Yang Pu-wei 楊步偉. *I-ko nü-jên ti tzu-chüan* 一个女人的自傳. Taipei: Chüan-chi wên-hsüeh ch'u-pan shê, 1967.

Yang Yin-shen 楊蔭深. *Chung-kuo yu-i yen-chiu* 中國遊藝研究. Shanghai: Shih-chieh shu-chü, 1935.

Yao Hsin-nung 姚莘農. 'Chan-hou Hsiang-kang hua-chü.' 戰後香港話劇, Chan Tê-lung (ed.). *Hsiang-kang Chung-kuo hsi-chü hsien-k'uang yen-t'ao hui-i lu.*

Yao T'ung 尤侗. 'Chieh tu wên.' 戒賭文. *Chao-tai ts'ung-shu pieh chi.*

Yeh Fang-pu 葉芳圃. 'Wu hu Kuang-tung ti chiao-yü.' 嗚呼廣東教育. *KCTC*, vol. 1, no. 1, Dec. 1924.

Yeh Yün-shêng 葉雲笙, Yeh Pai-heng 葉柏恆 (ed.). *Kuang-tung shih-jên chih* 廣東時人誌. 2 vols. Canton: Kai-t'ung ch'u-pan-shê, 1946.

Yen Fu-sun 嚴芙孫. *Ch'ieh huo* 妾禍. Hong Kong: Hsiang-kang ta kuang pao, 1924.

Yin Hai-kuang 殷海光. *Chung-kuo wên-hua ti chan-wang* 中國文化的展望. 2 vols. Hong Kong: Wên hsing shu-tien, 1965.

Ying tê ch'ing-lou po hsing ming 贏得青樓薄倖名. Canton: Yüeh-ch'ü yen-chiu shê, *c.*1924–5.

Yu Ch'i-chung 余啓中. *Kuang-chou kung-jên chia-t'ing chih yen-chiu* 廣州工人家庭之研究. Canton: Kuo-li Chung-shan ta-hsüeh ching-chi tiao-ch'a ch'u, 1934.

—— *Kuang-tung yen chiu shui yen kê* 廣東煙酒稅沿革. Canton: Kuo-li Chung-shan ta-hsüeh ch'u-pan pu, 1933.

—— *Min-kuo shih-êrh-nien chih Min-kuo êrh-shih-êrh nien Kuang-chou lao tzu chêng-i ti fên-hsi* 民國十二年至民國二十二年廣州勞資爭議底分析. Canton: Kuo-li Chung-shan ta-hsüeh ching-chi tiao-ch'a-ch'u, 1934.

Yü Chia-yen 于家言. 'Shih lun chieh-fang chien êrh san shih nien ti Yüeh-chü chü-mu chi ch'i chi-ch'êng.' 試論解放前二、三十年的粵劇劇目及其繼承. *YCYCTLH.*

Yü Chiao-ch'ing 俞蛟清. 'Ch'ao Chia fêng yüeh chi.' 潮嘉風月記. *HYTS*, vol. 1.

Yü En-tê 于恩德. *Chung-kuo chin yen fa-ling pien ch'ien shih* 中國禁煙法令變遷史. Shanghai: Chung-hua shu-chü, 1934.

Yu-hsi-chu-jên 游戲主人. *Hsiao lin kuang chi* 笑林廣記. Hong Kong: Wu kuei t'ang shu-chü, n.d.

Yu Yang 游揚. *Chün-hsiao shêng-huo ti hui-i* 軍校生活的回憶. Hong Kong: Shih-chi ch'u-pan-shê, 1950.

Yü Yu-kuo 余憂國. 'Hsing-ping chêng tsai Ta-lu man-yen.' 性病正在大陸蔓延. *Chêng ming* (Hong Kong) 爭鳴, no. 124, Feb. 1988.

Yüan 元. 'Fan-tui Chi-tu chiao ho fan-tui ti-kuo-chu-i.' 反對基督教和反對帝國主義, *KCTC*, vol. 1, no. 1, Dec. 1924.

Yüan Shu-i 苑書義 et al. edited. *Chang Chih-t'ung ch'üan chi* 張之洞全集. 6 vols. Shi-chia-chuang: Ho-pei jên-min ch'u-pan-shê, 1998.

Yüeh fêng yüeh k'an 粵風月刊. Shanghai: Yüeh fêng yüeh k'an shê, 1935–?

Yüeh hua pao 越華報 Canton: Yüeh hua pao shê, 1927–50.

Yün An 雲菴. 'Ch'ün pien jên yü.' 裙邊人語. *KCLPL*, vol. 4, 1933.

Yung I-yin 容宜燕. 'I-chiu-szu-chiu-nien i lai Hsiang-kang hua-chü ti fa-chan.' 一九四九年以來香港話劇的發展. Chan Tê-lung (ed.). *Hsiang-kang Chung-kuo hsi-chü hsien-k'uang yen-t'ao hui-i lu.*

Yung Shih-ch'êng 容世成. 'Chien Kuang-jên chi Hsin Yüeh liu-shêng-chi ch'ang-pien kung-ssu—chien t'an Yüeh-yüeh ch'ang-pien ti shang-pin hsin (1926–1936) 錢廣仁及新月留聲機唱片公司---兼談粵樂唱片的商品性. *Journal of Oriental Studies*, forthcoming.

Glossary

Ah Po ssu lao-t'ou 阿波死老豆
ai ch'ing 哀情
Ai-ch'ing ch'i chia 愛情起價
Ai-ch'ün (Building) 愛群
Chang Chih-tung 張之洞
Chang Ching-shêng 張競生
Chang Hsüeh-liang 張學良
Chang Yin-heng 張蔭桓
chang tu 長賭
Chao Tzu-lung 趙子龍
Ch'ao-chou 潮州
Chên Nan Tien 振南天
chên sang 真嗓
Chên Tien shêng 振天聲
chêng pên 正本
chêng-tang 正當
Ch'en Chi-t'ang 陳濟棠
Ch'en Chiung-ming 陳炯明
Ch'en Fei-nung 陳非儂
Ch'en Hsiao-fêng 陳笑風
Ch'en Hsü-ching 陳序經
Ch'en Ming-shu 陳銘樞
chi-kuan pu-ching 機關佈景
Chi-liang-so 濟良所
ch'i 氣
ch'i-êrh hou 乞兒喉
ch'i kung 氣功
chia hou 假喉
chia hsun 家訓
Chia ou ping-yung 佳偶兵戎
chia sang 假嗓
chia-tzu 架子
Chian Kai-shek 蔣介石
chien 儉
Chien Li-ch'ü 千里駒
chien-ting 監碇
Ch'ien tzu wên 千字文
chih-shih pan 志士班
chih szu ta-p'o 治死大婆
ch'ih hsi-ts'ai 吃西菜
ching 景
Chin Kuai 秦檜
Chin Man-chêng 金滿成
ch'ing 情
Ch'ing-ming shang-ho t'u 清明上河圖
Chiu-fêng-huang ts'un 舊鳳凰村
Chiu-kiang 九江
Chou Tien-pang 鄒殿邦
Ch'ou hsi so 售吸所
ch'ou hsiang 籌餉
Chu Chia-hua 朱家樺
Chu Hui-jih 朱暉日
chü lo pu 俱樂部
chü-mu 劇目
chü-pên 劇本
Chuang-yüan-fu-jên 狀元夫人
chüeh chi 絕技
Chüeh Hsien Shêng 覺先聲
chün tzu 君子
chui-chi-k'o 追雞客
Chung-shan 中山
Chung-shan-chuang 中山裝
ch'ü-hsien-mei 曲線美
Ch'ü Ch'iu-pai 瞿秋白
ch'uan ch'i 傳奇
fa ch'iung mi 發窮迷
fa hêng-ts'ai 發橫財
Fan-kou Tsai 番狗仔
fan tan 番攤
Fei ch'ang 廢娼
fei chih 非智
fêng fan 豐範
fêng-shui 風水
Fêng Tsai 鳳釆
fu 賦
Fu-nü chien-tê hui 婦女儉德會
fu yung 芙蓉
hao-ch'ing 豪情

hao p'iao hao tu ching-kuai tsai, hao shih yan-yen ti-i jên 好嫖好賭精乖仔, 好食洋煙第一人
heh mi 黑米
hêng-ts'ai shun-li 橫財順利
Ho lang pi-chi 荷廊筆記
Ho-nan 河南
Ho Tung 何東
Hsi-kuan 西關
hsi-peng kuan-hua 戲棚官話
hsi tu 吸毒
hsi-yüeh pu 西樂部
hsiang-ts'un ching-shen 鄉村精神
hsiang-hsia lao 鄉下佬
hsiang-hsia lao chu ch'êng, ku-ling ching-kuai 鄉下佬出城, 古靈精怪
Hsiao Chu-p'i 小橘皮
hsiao hsien 消遣
hsiao-kuei 小鬼
Hsiao-pei 小北
hsiao p'in pu-hsiao ch'ang 笑貧不笑娼
hsiao-shêng wang 小生王
hsin ch'i 新奇
Hsing Ching Hsiang 新景象
Hsin Ch'un Ch'iu 新春秋
hsin li 心理
Hsin Pai-tsai 新白菜
hsin tang 行檔
Hsing Chung Hui 興中會
Hsüan Kung yen shih 宮豔史
Hsüeh Chüeh-hsien 薛覺先
hsüeh-shêng kuo-huo nien 學生國貨年
Hua-chieh kung-hui 花界公會
hua-liu fang-chuan 花樓房捐
hua-pang hsuan-chu 花榜選舉
hua-shih 花事
hua-tan wang 花旦王
Huan hua-chai 還花債
Huang Shao-hsiung 黃紹雄
hung wan 紅丸
Huo Chi-ting 翟芝庭
I-fêng Shê 移風社
jê-nao 熱鬧
Jên-hai Ch'ao 人海潮
Jên Shou Nien 人壽年
Jên T'ien Lo 人天樂
jên wu hêng-ts'ai pu-fu 人無橫財不富
k'ai ta-t'ing 開大廳
k'an-chi-lao 看雞佬
Kan-ti hui Hsi-shih 甘地會西施
kan-tung-li 感動力
Kao Chien-fu 高劍父
Kao Ch'i-fêng 高奇峰
kê-ming t'sê-yüan-ti 革命策源地
Kiang K'ung-yin 江孔殷
k'o-hsüeh yü 科學慾
K'o t'u ch'iu hên 客途秋恨
Kou-pi Chang 勾鼻章
ku hsiang 故鄉
ku-p'o wu 姑婆屋
kuan-mu 關目
Kuang ch'iang 廣腔
Kuang-tung hsi-chü yen-chiu-so 廣東戲劇研究所
Kuang-tung t'ung chih 廣東通志
kuei-fei ch'uang 貴妃床
kuei-ma 鬼馬
Kuei Ming-yang 桂名揚
kung-chia 工架
Kung-wu-yüan chin-yen k'ao-chêng t'iao-li 公務員禁煙考証條例
K'un chü 崑劇
kuo-min 國民
Kuo-min hua-yüan 國民花園
lan li 懶理
lan-yung 濫用
lao chiang-hu shih-pai pên 老江湖十八本
Li Chêng-i 李承翼
Li-chi (Bay) 荔枝(灣)
Li Chi-shen 李濟深
Li Fu-lin 李福林
Li Hsüeh-fang 李雪芳
Li Hung-chang 李鴻章
Li Shih-chên 李時珍
Liang Ch'i-ch'ao 梁啓超
Liang Shou-ming 梁漱溟
Liang Ting-nan 梁廷枏
Liao Hsia-huai 廖俠懷
lien-ai tzu-yu 戀愛自由
Lien Shao-fêng 靚少風
Lien Yung 靚容
Lin Lang Huan Ching 琳瑯幻景
Lin Shu-shen 林樹森
liu ch'ang 流娼

Liu I 劉毅
Liu Pai 劉八
lo-hsiang pan 落鄉班
Lo-shan 廬山
Lu Hsün 魯迅
Lung Chi-kuang 龍濟光
lung-chou ko 龍舟歌
Lung-meng 龍門
Ma Shih-ts'êng 馬師曾
ma tiao (dominoes) 馬吊
mahjong 麻將
mai-hsiao shêng-ya 賣笑生涯
mang liu 盲流
mang yin 蠻音
Mei Lan-fang 梅蘭花
mi-ssu 蜜絲脫
mi-ssu-shih 蜜絲仕
mi-ssu-t'o 蜜絲脫
mien-hua chien-chiang 眠花健將
Min Lo Shê 民樂社
mo-tan i-wai chih ts'ai 莫貪意外之財
mo-têng nan 摩登男
mu-yü shu 木魚書
mui-tsai (mei-tzu) 妹仔
Nan-hai 南海
Nan Pei Hang 南北行
nan-yin 南音
nung-ts'un p'o-chan 農村破產
Ou Mi p'ai 歐美派
Ou-yang Shan 歐陽山
Ou-yang Yü-ch'ien 歐陽予倩
Pai-chin Lung 白金龍
Pai Ho (Guild) 八和(會館)
pai-ko p'iao 白鴿票
pai lan 白欖
pai mi 白米
pai shui 白水
Pai Yü-mei 白玉梅
P'an Chih-chung 潘至中
pao hsiang 包廂
pei-chih 北芷
p'ei-yang shê-hui ti shêng-ch'i 培養社會的生氣
pên-ti pan 本地班
P'eng-ya Ch'ao 崩牙超
pien tai 變態
p'i-p'a 琵琶
p'ing hou 平喉
Po tan 卜攤
P'ou fu yen hua 破腹驗花
pu-i 不義
pu-jên 不仁
pu-liang fêng-su 不良風俗
pu tao ching-ch'êng chung chien ku 不到京城終賤骨
p'u p'iao 舖票
P'u To (Hill) 普陀(山)
San-yüan-li 三元里
Sao Yün-lan 騷韻蘭
Sha-chi ts'an an 沙基慘案
sha hou 沙喉
Sha-nan 沙南
Sha-pei 沙北
Sha-wan 沙灣
Shakee (Sha-chi) 沙基
Shameen (Sha-mien) 沙面
shan-k'u 衫褲
shan p'iao 山票
Shao-hsing 肇慶
shao-ya pao 燒鴨包
shê-chu shih chih pu-ching 蛇足式之佈景
Shê-Tsai Ch'iu 蛇仔秋
Shê-Tsai Li 蛇仔李
Shen-chen 深圳
Shen-ching ta-shao 神經大少
shen kuai 神怪
shen shu 神衰
Shêng Kang pan 省港班
shêng kua 勝瓜
Shêng-kuei Yung 生鬼客
Shêng Shê-tsai 生蛇仔
shih heh-mi 食黑米
shih kua 絲瓜
shih tu chiu pien 十賭九騙
Shou Chiang Wei 收姜維
shou-chiu p'ai 守舊派
shou-pên hsi 首本戲
shu 輸
shu-yüan 書院
shui-chi t'ing 水雞艇
Shui-chin chin shan 水浸金山
Shui-shê Yung 水蛇容
shui-tsai shan-hou yu-chiang i-hui 水災善後有獎義會

Shun-tê 順德
Su-chou Mei 蘇州妹
Su Tung-p'o 蘇東坡
Sun K'o 孫科
Sun Shang-hsiang 孫尚香
Sung Tzu-min 宋子民
Ta An 大奀
Ta-chieh yin-ssu lu 打劫陰司路
Ta-hsin kung-ssu 大新公司
Ta-kuan Yüan 大觀園
ta lao-hu 打老虎
Ta Lo T'ien 大羅天
ta pai-chang shih-pai pên 大排場十八本
ta shou 打手
tai-tzu chang 太子賬
T'ai-shan 台山
tan (unit) 擔
tan chia 擔枷
t'an-hua shih/ch'u 談話室、處
Tanka 蛋家
tao 道
tê-chung yü-lo shui 特種娛樂稅
t'i ta-wang chia 跌大王甲
Ti-yü hsin ch'i 地獄尋妻
t'ien-ching ti-i 天經地義
t'ien-ju 天乳
t'ien-kuang hsi 天光戲
T'ien lei pao 天雷報
T'ien-yen kung-ssu 天演公司
Ting-ts'ai Wang 丁財旺
Tou-p'i Mei 豆皮梅
Tou-p'i Yüan 豆皮元
T'ou ying mu hsing 偷影摹形
tsa chü 雜劇
Tsa-chiao Shêng 扎腳勝
tsou-ma têng 走馬燈
tu chieh tou kan 賭蔗鬥柑
tu chü chih yen 獨具隻眼
tu chü hui yen 獨具慧眼
Tu-Chüeh Ying 獨腳英
Tu-fu T'an 賭婦潭
tu-hua 毒化
tu p'in 毒品
T'ung ch'u szu ta hai 痛除四大害
T'ung Ming Hui 同盟會
Tung-shan 東山
tzu hua 字花
tzu-yu shen 自由身
wai-kiang pan 外江班
wai shêng 外省
wai-shêng jên 外省人
wan nung 玩弄
wei hsing 圍姓
Wen Chi-fêng 溫祺鳳
wên-ming hsi 文明戲
Weng T'ung-ho 翁同龢
Wu Chao-shu 伍朝樞
wu fen-chung jê-tu 五分鐘熱度
Wu Sung 武松
Wu Tieh-ch'êng 吳鐵城
Wu Tsao 烏曹
wu yin chê 無癮者
yamen 衙門
Yang Mou-chien 楊懋建
yang-shang wên-hua 洋商文化
yao-ch'ien shu 搖錢樹
yen chi 煙妓
yen hua 煙花
yen kuei 煙鬼
yin-yüeh-hua 音樂化
yu 柔
yu-chin yü-chêng 寓禁於徵
Yü-li Hun 玉梨魂
Yu Liang 玉娘
Yu Tê-shui 魚得水
Yu T'ien Ying Shê 優天影社
Yüeh Chien Ch'iu 樂千秋
Yüeh-ou 粵謳
yung shêng 榮生
Yung T'ai P'ing 詠太平

Index

abduction 227, 233, 262
absurdity 303, 327
abuse 232, 233, 234–5, 246, 254, 261
  hard evidence of 247
  not all prostitutes would quietly endure 263
  paternal 17
  prostitutes seen as sufferers of 239
  protection against 255, 263
  psychological deterrent to 245
  rarity of cases in high-class brothel world 251
  regular 241
  subhuman blood-suckers who resorted to 242
  verbal 185, 266
academies 11
acculturation 59
address forms 75
advertisements:
  coolie recruitment 82
  dining 63, 280
  eye-catching 236–7, 282
  fashion 60, 62, 70, 72
  fortune-tellers 215
  gimmicks in 215
  lottery 181, 216
  medicine 38, 73, 283, 315, 330
  newly developed land 289
  opera troupes 312, 313, 317
  tobacco 315
  troop-station 200
affluence 344
  famous courtesans 258
  only available short-cut to 213
  relative 260
Africa 78
agitation 84
agriculture 23, 130
  commercialization of 12
  fall in output 129
  large-scale projects 180
  sidelines 130
Ah Hung 251
Ah Lung 247
Ah Mên 253
Ah Po ssu lao-t'ou 204
Ah Ying 116
Ai Ai 250
Ai-Ch'ün Building 69
alchemy 105, 137
alcohol 164, 189, 206
  excessive indulgence in 283
All-China Seamen Union 57
ambivalence:
  cultural 332
  'official' causes 291–5
  pecuniary causes 285–91
American Consulate 168, 187
American Medical Association 108
American products 80
Americanization 39
Amoy 130
amusement parks 38, 164, 181, 289
  roof-top 36, 309, 333
amusements 212–18, 317
  Chinese chess competitions 199
  favourable image of gambling as 207
  favourite 279
  highly cultured 68
  illegal 157
  mahjong widely regarded as 188
  popular 58
  respectable, for classy people 210
  serious shortage of facilities 164–5
  unleashed by gambling 208
  Western-style 71
An Tuan 168
anachronisms 303, 315, 323, 332
analgesics 108, 109
Angel 257
Anhui 318
anomie 107
anti-drugs literature 107
anti-foreignism 4, 49–50, 53
  political 78–89
anti-gambling campaigns 159, 202
  compendium of essays devoted to 167
  large-scale 161, 195, 215
  relatively sincere 180
  short-lived 175
  whole-hearted 190
Anti-Gambling Committee 162, 180
anti-gambling treatises 156, 158, 201
  moral 161, 193–4

anti-gambling treatises (*cont.*)
  much-cited assumption in nearly all 183
  prize-winning essays 208
  targeting only certain forms of gambling 157
anti-imperialism 4, 33, 34, 49, 54, 88
  political campaigns 81
  propaganda 56, 78, 85
Anti-Japanese Movement 84–5
anti-Japanese resistance campaign (1932) 236
Anti-Opium Association of Kwangtung 141
Anti-Opium Bureau of Kwangtung Province 113
Anti-Opium Society 141
Anti-Poisonous Drugs Convention 147
anti-prostitution literature/discourse 230, 231, 235, 237, 254, 263
  madam usually depicted as incorrigible devil 247
  official treatises 227
  one of the most often used images 241
  reformers 234
  short story 273
anti-urban bias 13
apathy 78, 83, 84, 86, 88
aphorisms 324
aphrodisiacs 73, 106, 107, 116
appeasement 84, 328
architecture:
  changing values expressed through 37
  distinctive forms 11
  modern 36, 37, 38
  Western 69–70
Aristotle 341
armed guards/bodyguards 101, 344
army:
  bribing
  errant officers 173
  gratitude to 237
  places under open protection of 199
  see also People's Liberation Army
arranged marriage 26, 262, 329
arrests 57, 122, 129, 145–6, 186, 263, 264, 265, 344
  army officers and bureaucrats 294
  assassin 292
  blind sing-song girls 268
  bookmakers 172, 174
  gambling/opium violations 97, 141, 172, 187–8
  unlicensed prostitutes 231, 232
arsenic 100
artificial-tone singing 321
asphalt roads 1
Association of Canton Women Consoling the Anti-Communist Armed Comrades 203
asthma 109, 110
attitudes 2, 4, 6, 23, 212
  aloof 256
  ambiguous 205, 253
  ambivalent 279, 285
  anti-rural 164
  anti-urban 10
  belligerent 177
  biased 186
  caring 243
  contemptuous 31
  discriminatory 317
  disrespectful 277
  fatalistic 215
  haughty 257
  impudent 256
  morally upright 181
  permissive 226
  positive and responsible 327
  practical 238
  pragmatic 274
  preferential 42
  pro-Western 201
  social 7
  tolerant 230
  uncompromising 173
  worship 26
  see also favourable attitudes; popular attitudes
authoritarianism 61
  parental/familial 22, 23, 284
  pickets 82
automobiles 1, 35
autonomy 204, 212

Baber, Colbourne 115
backdrops 314, 315, 335
background music 316
backwardness 23–30, 32, 165
  cultural 41
  socio-political 34
  stigma of 35
  technological 129
  traditional theatre 67
bad habits 162, 187, 193, 205, 308
  sustaining 186, 194
  villagers' persistence in practising 184
Baker, Hugh D. R. 194, 212, 215
Balazs, Etienne 9, 11, 179, 332
Ball, J. Dyer 101, 106, 116
ballads 320
banditry 87, 122, 158, 159, 160
  gambling held to be a major cause of 161

bandits 21, 31, 102, 157, 158, 165, 344
  main source of recruits for 128
  river 56
  roving 170
Bank of Commerce 56
Bank of Kwangtung 69
bankers 51
banknotes 55, 56, 85
  screwed up into balls as gifts 340
  value plummeted 180
  writing witty poems or aphorisms on 324
bankruptcy 5, 102, 160, 278, 279, 285
  gamblers doomed to 157, 193
  rural 25, 28, 129, 165
banquets 252, 253, 255, 257, 259, 278
  formal 309
  ritualistic farewell 275
  sumptuous 280
beauty 51–2, 240
  actresses 338
  aesthetic sense of 70
  changing concept of 59
  classical music 67
  inner 61
  official standards of 61
  politics and 61
beauty contests 288–9
bedrooms 70
beggars 31, 131, 157
  crippled 159
beliefs:
  improper 29
  religious 26, 29, 157, 245
  superstitious 76
Bengali intelligentsia 75
beri-beri 24, 110
Berridge, Virginia 108, 110, 114, 124
betrothal money 40
betting 168, 171, 182, 190–3 *passim* 196, 197, 199, 204, 214
  failure to obtain money from wife for 184
  fatalistic attitude towards 215
  legalised 218
  maid's fondness in 186
  size of 212
  unlicensed 164
Bird, Isabella 115
'black rice' 133
'blind marriage' 26
blockade 171
blood 108
  menstrual 265
boat-people community 99, 121, 122, 194
  women from 228, 274
Bogue 103
bondage 26
  'feudalistic' 60
bone-related illness 105
bookmakers 165, 167, 168, 178, 182, 185, 203, 206
  arrests of 172, 174
  bet collectors working for 171
  bribery 169, 202
  bullying swindlers 195–8
  collection of lottery bets for 214
  companies operating legalized lotteries 188
  dishonest 196
  fan tan companies 215
  gimmicks from 202
  infamous 173
  legitimate means to acquire wealth 206
  plunge in income 190
  poor business 191
  proposal to build racecourse 201
  prosperous 181
  stake taken away by 207
  Sun's long record of seeking help from 175
  temple fees 202
  unlicensed 200
  wealthy 173, 180
bordellos, *see* brothels
boredom 107
  entertainment to drive away 201
  most comfortable way of alleviating 134
  prison 115
bourgeoisie 9, 72, 304
  cultural idioms 76
  modern 37
Boxer, C. R. 320
Boxer Uprising (1900) 171
box-office returns 314, 316, 346
  failure 326
  success 308, 321
boycotts:
  anti-American (1905) 80
  anti-British (1927) 83
  anti-Japanese (1926–35) 51, 82, 85, 87
  see also Canton-Hong Kong strike/boycott
bravery 3–4
brawls 200, 267
breasts:
  bigger 61
  exaggeratedly large 60
  exposed 330
  flattened 59, 60
  pads used to enhance the shape of 311
Brecht, Bertolt 304
bribed officials 99
bribery 167, 179, 199
  bookmakers 169, 202

bribery (*cont.*)
officers more or less tolerated for taking 181
police accepting 174, 200, 202, 263
soldiers allegedly receiving 197
violation of ban on 187
Britain 100
Christian values and faith 157
law/lawyers 57, 265
opium 140, 143
pantomime 325
British Consulate-General 101, 120, 131, 167, 206
British Customs 173
British Intelligence 82
British invasion (1925) 33, 79–80
brothels 6, 147, 205, 235
business badly hit 229
closed down 248
dress manual for 75
family decision to sell to 227
girls sold to 255
inspectors' unexpected visits to 263
middle-class 228
number of 227, 228, 229
opium served in 106–7, 116, 117
playing *mahjong* at 209
popular perception of 279
popularity of large breasts 59
'privilege' seemingly denied to 133
prospering 202
specific names and addresses for 98
superior 240
unlicensed 231
see also floating brothels; high-class brothels; low-class brothels; madams
Brusak, Karel 313
'Buddha porridge' 104–5
Buddhism 77, 213, 258, 328
nuns 199
personification of Buddha 137, 314
priests 213
scriptures 258
buildings:
brick 11
commercial 69
dominant 54
high-rise 36, 37, 38, 69
impressive 37
modern residential 52
multi-storey 37, 69, 70
office, palatial 34
prestigious 37
Western-style 37, 69, 250, 289, 315
bullies 164, 169, 199, 247, 251
bribing 200
potential target of extortion by 344
prostitutes as 258
protection from 294
shooting 185
Bund 37, 181, 259, 289
East 291
burglars 157, 158, 259
Burma 63
business relations 209
businessmen 51, 81
opium-using 113, 129, 131
buttocks 59, 60

cafés 63
caffeine 100
calendar posters 210
California 275
camaraderie 115
Campbell 211
cangue 159, 260
Canton Advertising 228
Canton District Attorney Office 187, 192
Canton-Hong Kong troupes 313–14, 331, 335, 344
Canton-Hong Kong strike/boycott (1925–6) 50, 51, 54, 58, 79, 81–2, 86, 160, 243, 259
blow to brothel business 259
Canton Hospital 127
Canton Industry Association 180
Canton Opium Addiction Termination Hospital 121, 125, 148
admission records 110, 111, 122, 127, 128
Canton Opium Suppression Committee 97, 98, 102
Canton Republican News 177
Canton Sing-song Girls Union 117
Canton Uprising (1927) 54, 81, 177
Canton Yearbook (1935) 281
Cantonese language 63, 64
Cantonese singing 304
capital punishment 165
card games 182, 191, 201
Western 215
carnal desires 137, 242
carnal pleasure 253, 266
carnal problems 27
carriageways 35
concrete 36
wide 37
cartoons 159
casting 303
Catholicism 77
celebrities 343
Celestials 52

censorship 57, 67
opera scenes/scripts 328, 330
part-time 82
Central Asian opium 139
Central Bank 55
crises (1927/1928) 51, 56
rapidly depreciating notes 113
Central China 129, 184, 258, 287
Central Park 74
Central Political Council (Canton Division) 178
Chambers of Commerce 55–6, 113, 345
Champly, Henry 75
chance:
anarchic rule of 157
gamblers obsessed with 163
games of 157, 202, 213, 216
psychological dependence on 29
Chang Chak-yan 9, 10
Chang Ch'ang-chia 137–8
Chang Chieh 332, 339, 344
Chang Chih-tung 170, 171
Chang Ching-shêng ('Dr Sex') 60, 62, 282
Chang Hsiao-mei 139
Chang Hsin-pao 112
Chang Hsin-tai 227
Chang Hsuëh-liang 166
Chang Kung-p'ing 193, 196
Chang-lao-yeh 250
Ch'ang-liao su-yü 278
Chang Lo-chih 86
Chang Meng-chêng 107
Chang Ming-ch'i 158, 168
Chang Shu-shêng 168, 169
Chang Tzu-p'ing 17, 36, 54, 64, 192, 214
Chang Yen-fêng 210
Chang Ying-Ch'ang 157
Chang Ying-chin, *see* Zhang Yingjin
Chang Yin-heng 166
Chang Yüan-tsi jih-chi 57
Chao (I) 228
Chao Ching-shen 321
Ch'ao-chou 304, 337
Chao Shan-lin 318, 334, 337
Chao Tzu-lung 303
Ch'ao-yang 131
chaos 53, 163, 165, 199
socio-political 161
charities 236, 237
charity halls 141
charm 59, 61, 73
Chartier, Roger 2
chatting rooms/places 132
cheating 163, 195–8
Chekiang 104
chemicals 85
Ch'en (prostitute's lover) 278
Ch'en Chiang-fêng 322
Ch'en Ch'i-hui 130
Ch'en Chi-t'ang 63, 66, 72, 78, 145, 147, 148, 163, 179, 180
ambitious Three-year Plan 201
overthrow/fall of 161, 287
Ch'en Chiung-ming 131, 142, 143, 159, 160, 162, 191, 291, 292
coup d'état against Sun Yat-sen (1922) 173
repeated warnings against brothel-going by military men 293
Ch'en Cho-ying 114, 134, 317, 332, 333, 344
Ch'en Fei-nung 335, 336, 312, 326, 340, 342, 343, 344
Ch'en Fei-wo 341
Ch'en Han-hua 137
Ch'en Han-seng 130
Ch'en Hsiao-fêng 341
Ch'en Hsü-ching 41, 76, 77
Ch'en Hung 68
Chen, Jerome 77
Ch'en Kiang fêng 325
Ch'en Li-chu 227, 228, 229, 231, 235, 240, 250, 278
Ch'en Ming-shu 71, 145, 178, 179, 209
Chên Nan Tien 309
Ch'en Nien-t'i 101, 118
Ch'en Pei-ying 15
Chen Ping-han 58
Ch'en Shih 78
Ch'en Shou-jên 338
Ch'en Ta 37
Ch'en-t'ang 237, 291
Chên Tien shêng 307
Ch'en T'ien-tsung 323
Ch'en Ting-yen 160
Ch'en Tsê 144
Ch'en Yü-hsing 145
Cheng (old resident of Canton) 119, 120
Chêng Ch'ên 63
Ch'eng Hao 58, 180
Ch'êng wai 31
Ch'i-chui-tou 332, 344
Chi-hsien-hsiao-yin 256, 266, 280
Chi-liang So 271
Ch'i Mei 278
Ch'i Shêng 323
Ch'i Tzu 53
Ch'i wan hua she 235
Chia Shih-i 145, 177
Ch'iang Hsia-yün 322

Chiang Kai-shek 53, 55, 145, 160, 162, 175, 177, 181, 294
celebration of 50th birthday 237
fiftieth birthday 294
Chiang-men County 275
Ch'iao Hua 308
Chicago 108
'chicken chasers' 257
Chieh 22
Chieh-yang 131
Chi'en 276
Chien Hung 320
Chien Li-ch'ü 326, 343, 345
Ch'ien-lung period (1736–95) 108
Ch'ien tzu wên 214
Chien yen piao tsa chih 72
Chien Yu-wên 135
Chih-chi-shêng 236
Ch'ih hsi-ts'ai 63, 66
Chih-shih pan 306
children:
characters-learning text for 193
charitable refuge for 262
folk songs sung by mothers to 194
fondness for shop lottery 182
gambling 212
games for 182–3
healthy and well clad 210
intellectual differences between 39
lost 286
medicine for 73–4
no apparent tendency to steal 81
selling 160, 165
spectators inside *fan-tan* houses 200
Chin 310
Ch'in Ch'in 39
Chin Hsüeh-shih 207
Chin Lan 241–2
Chin Man-ch'êng 282
Chin Tsai 267
Chin Tsê-ching 158
'Chin-tu chih kung-tan' 207
Chin Wei 51
China Music Association 65
Chinese New Year 20, 65, 215
Chinese Revolution (cradle of) 3, 7, 98, 177, 178
Ch'ing Bell of Poesy 157
Ching-chieh-fu ta ma tu-tsai 194
Ch'ing Dynasty (1644–1912) 50, 61, 79
gambling 157, 158–9, 160, 166–72, 187, 191–4 *passim* 207, 211, 215, 216
opera 302, 304, 305, 306, 309, 317, 318, 321, 325, 332, 334, 337, 338
opium 95, 96, 98, 106, 107, 110, 115, 116–17, 127, 128, 132, 135, 137, 139, 140, 141, 142
prostitution 227, 228, 229, 235, 240, 242, 246, 248, 250, 255, 258, 269, 275, 288, 292
Veritable Records of 169
Ching Fo 239
Ching Hsiao 200
Ch'ing-ming Shang-ho t'u 11
Ch'ing Shui 215
Chiu, Aunt (brothel madam) 245
Chiu-chung-fêng-fu 56, 236, 240, 246, 248
Chiu-fêng-huang 23–4, 25, 26–7, 99, 120, 138, 182, 192, 202
Ch'iu Sung-ho 318, 319
Ch'iung Hua Yü 306–7
Cho Yu 62
cholera 108, 115
Chou Chung 20
Chou Dynasty (1050–256 BC) 1, 10
Chou Hsia-min 249, 270
Chou Hsing 21
Chou Hsüeh-ying 265
Chou Sui-ying 246
Chou Tien-pang 345
Chou Yu-liang 107, 235
Christian communities 160
Chü (*fan tan* trickster) 198
Chü (lineage organization) 195
Chü Ch'i 61
Chu Chia-hua 146
Ch'u Chien 67, 303, 304
Ch'ü Ch'iu-pai 127
Chu Hsia-min 258
Chü Hsiang (pseud.) 17–18
Chu Hsiu-hsia 166, 216
Chu Hui-jih 71
Chu I-tsun 320, 324
Chu-kiang hsing-ch'i hua pao 39, 238, 240, 246, 248, 277, 330, 341
Ch'ü Ta-chün 23, 37, 212, 309, 320, 324
Chu Ting-ho 121
Chü-tu yüeh-k'an 131
Chu Yang 121, 132, 133
Chu Yung-ch'un, Maxims for Family Management 193
Ch'üan Shêng 117, 126, 137
Chüeh-hsien chi 342
Chüeh Hsien Shêng 346
Ch'ün-fang-p'u 106
Ch'ün Kuo Shan Yü 306
Chün T'ien 269
Chung 174, 335, 336
Chung Chiao 170, 191, 214

Chung Ching-wên 66
Chung-shan 138
churches 52
cigarettes 189, 208, 282
  imported 75
cinemas 56, 164, 333, 340
cityscapes 36
  'breeze from the West' in 69–71
  spectacular 54
civic order 53
civil engineering 56
'civilized play' 308
CKMH (Chu-kiang ming hua hsiao ch'uan) 246, 249, 250
clandestine prostitution 230–2, 240, 250, 268
  affluent 258
  increase in number 239
  popularity among students 283
  serious problem of 289
class 5, 6, 12, 112
  humble background 213
  lower 122, 209, 310, 311, 331
  middle 116, 209
  strong bias 111
  upper 37, 116, 157, 158, 209, 334
  urban, absence of 9
cleanliness 39, 52, 70
  restaurant 63
Clementi, Cecil 79, 84, 236
clothes/clothing 24, 31, 61, 71–6, 86
  expensive 250, 261, 271
  flamboyant 311, 340
  lavish 250
  see also costume
coal 85
cocaine 100, 147
'cock' board game 183
comic opera 323–4
commemoration events 215
commercial activities 12
Commercial Press, The 57
'commercial quarter' 147
'commercial war' 139
commercialization 309, 311, 314, 318, 334
Communism/Communists 5, 20, 42
  artistic quality of opera 'salvaged' by 334
  authoritarian and xenophobic rule 61
  country being poisoned by bad influence of 87
  deliberate act of arson by 57
  early authorities 230
  gradual re-emergence of *mahjong* (1970s) 212
  impact of uprisings 281
  misconception still held by 77
  purgation of 177
  radicals 79
  rhetoric 4
  totalitarian 218
  view of gambling 218
Communist historians 52, 303, 306, 346
  description of prostitutes as victims 232–3
  history books 4, 96, 142
compensation 57, 267
compulsory 'lending'/'borrowing' 51, 56
concubines 6, 61, 216, 217, 259, 261, 284, 331
  accidental poisoning by 276–7
  courted by wealthy actors 344
  dislike of husband's interference 262
  disloyal 319
  persistence of the system 226
  prostitutes turned 276
  selling 159
condemnation 285
Confucius/Confucianism 10, 163, 342
  ambiguous attitude towards gambling 156
  classics teaching 33, 78
  concept of wealth 157
  dismantling of ideological foundation 13
  ethical system potentially threatened 157
  orthodox 156
  priests 213
congenital addiction 127
conservatism/conservatives 41, 77
Constitutionalists 306
construction work 36
consumer class 12
consumer culture 36
consumption capacity 63
coolies 53, 97, 111, 138, 174, 217
  advertisement for recruiting 82
  sedan-chair 115
corner-shops 214
corruption 57, 102, 286
  criticisms on 170
  hotbed of 145
  KMT 96
  melodrama of 85
  prostitution a symbol of 233
  soldiers 171
  spiritual and physical 17, 36
  see also official corruption
costume 159, 310, 311–13
  anachronistic use of 303
  sensational 315
  traditional 320–1, 323, 332
  unseemly 310
  Western-style 331, 332

coughing 105, 108
subduing 110
country bumpkins 31–3
stupidity of 40
'countryside spirit' 41
courtesans 58
beautiful 209, 216, 269–70, 279, 288
biographies of 235
buxom 59
devotion and sincerity towards lover-clients 238
familiarization between client and 253
famous 240, 246, 248, 258, 269–70, 275
frustrated 246
high-class 75, 229, 240, 242, 245, 250, 251, 252, 255, 272, 344
intellectual female companionship 280
motive for killing 194
opera stars dating 339, 344
poet 244
popular 249, 253, 255, 257, 258, 260
reticent and sad-looking 241
rich 261
talkative 279
traditional literati patronizing 283
virtuous 240
well-off 337
young 243
'courtesy names' 1
courtship 61, 241, 251, 325
established pattern of 252
expensive 257, 275
financially exhausting 253
long 253, 257, 276
covetousness 21
CPHH (*Chüan-pên hsi-hua yen-lun su-chi*) 41
cricket fighting 157, 207, 212
crime 8, 111, 129, 132, 160, 187
admitted 186
economic 206
gamblers more prone to commit 188
gambling-houses the seed beds of 198
petty 259, 260
serious, totally unheard of 183
uncontrollable spread of 5
unforgivable 160
violent 21, 200
criminalization 111, 112, 162
criminals 31, 107–12, 111, 146
in cangue 159, 260
opportunities to mingle with 186
crooks 199, 242, 262
crop disease 130
crowds 202
Cruz, Gaspar da 320
CSL (*Ch'ing shi-lu*) 169
CTKL (*Chin-tu kai lan*) 38, 159, 160, 162, 164, 165, 167, 168, 175, 179, 180, 181, 202, 203, 208, 213
cuisine 86
flower boats, superior 280
foreign 72
Western 63, 64, 199
cultural hobbies 61
cultural identity 3, 28
strong sense of 49
cultural invasion 68, 74, 78
currency 55, 180
curves 60
customs 30, 63
'backward' 25
'bad' 234, 281, 285
brothel 244
courting 252
'feudalistic' 230
foot-binding 308
inviolable 38
music's capacity to transform 67
New Year 215
persistence of 1, 77
stage 302
tightly bound breasts 60
unquestioned observance of 30
unwritten 251
customs duty 106
see also Imperial Maritime Customs
Czechoslovakia 75

Dai Kan-Wajiten 193
dance halls 257
dance parties 65
debauchery 239
debt 21
decadence 233
decorated floats 159
defloration 262, 271
degree graduates 12
deities 26, 215, 217
thanksgiving offerings to 216
democracy 77
demographic imbalance 27
demoralization 28, 86, 100, 101, 113, 184
effective antidote to growing problem of 33
means to reform 141
opera themes 309
dental caries 124
depopulation 28
depreciation 55

depression (economic) 63, 191
worldwide 129, 190, 229, 336
depression (psychological) 107, 123
destiny:
control over 204
one of the commonest ways to realize 214
diabetes 108
dialect 63, 251, 320
dialogues:
foul language 331
humorous 321
vernacular language 306, 320
diarrhoea 106, 108, 136, 138
dice games 182, 195, 196, 208
dictatorships 77
military 172
diffusion 49
Dikötter, Frank 235
dinner 63–4
dirty jokes 323, 330–1
disapproval 285
diseases 24, 27, 106, 125
acute 109
chronic 109, 110
cured 108, 109
effectiveness of opium in treating 140
incurable 235
psychological 163
see also venereal diseases
disorder 157, 165
social 282
disorderliness 53
divination 204–5, 214
lottery tips through 215
division of labour 10
Docherty, David 301
documentaries 340
dog-racing 178
Dolby, William 306, 308, 336
dominoes 182, 191, 193, 201, 208
ma tiao 157
ox 188
'doomed prisoners' 256
'dope fiends' 124
Dosing 83
double-entendres 330–1
Double-Tenth celebration (1926) 33, 65, 345
dowry-lists 116
dragon-boat races 202
drama 67
'new' 311
political 310
professional companies 309
substantially transformed 310
Western, borrowing extensively from 306
see also spoken drama
dreams 216, 217
dress, *see* clothes; fashion
drinkers 244, 247, 249, 251
drinking parties 257, 269
dross opium 98, 121, 138
drug addicts 95, 99, 102, 114
cheap Chinese opium welcomed by 119
compulsory treatment to 129
congenital 127
consumption of 96, 120
criminalized 112
cured 148
demoralization of 101
detoxicating 96
economic burden shouldered by 140
justification for 117
low-class 101, 122
low-income 114
making ashamed 116
military troops 128
motive for using opium 110
negatively stereotyped 123
numbers 21, 97, 100, 122
occupational group with highest concentration of 100
opera actors/musicians 114
physical characteristics and physical fitness 124
physiological dependence 121–2
poor 120–1, 126
registered 97, 98
relapse rate 148
richer 120
rise of addiction attributed to actions of quack doctors 109
stigmatization of 111, 116
studies on the subject 107–8
unhygienic and impoverished life of 125
Dunkley, John 182
dysentery 105, 108, 109

Eberhard, Wolfram 59, 265
economic dependence 58
economic need 227
education 8, 28, 61
equal opportunity for 76
funding 171
higher 180
knowledge of foreign language perceived as yardstick of 75
modern 99, 281
music 68

education (*cont.*)
  not considered essential for women 26
  parental indifference to 24
  physical 64
  poor facilities 24
  quality of 33
  school, effects of 195
  subsidies on 142
  Western 64
'Education and Culture' category 202
Education Department of Canton 314
Edwards, Griffith 108, 110, 114, 124
élites 11, 80, 319
  academic 169
  cultural 7, 305, 333, 334
  herbal doctors 105
  out-migration of 12
  political 12
  prominent 173
  ruling 317
  sport/spectacle widely enjoyed as high-class pastime by 202
  urban 10
  well-educated 304
Elvin, Mark 9
emaciation 102, 123–4, 125
  gamblers 161, 164
embezzlement 169, 172, 179
emotion 11, 67
En Jên 69
English language 75
entertainment 58, 86, 209, 238, 276
  agreeable 278–84, 285, 290
  commercial 311
  decent, serious shortage of 38
  discerning the right or wrong of a particular form of 165
  finest available 201–2
  free 202, 212
  highly enjoyable 207
  improper 288
  legitimate 208
  main purpose of 325
  mass 309, 332
  musically more amusing 320
  noble form of 211
  non-gambling 199
  normal 209
  popular 301, 311
  proper 26
  public, private life as 340
  real 208
  'righteous' 26, 27
  serious opera for 304–11
  superior 27
entrepôts 58, 100
enunciation 305
erogenous zones 59
ethics 67
  social 310
euphoric experiences 115, 116, 136, 137
Europe 78, 86, 279
  gambling behaviours 184
  horse racing 201
  scripts played by actors in 302
  urban planning 35
Europeanization 39, 50, 51
Evans, Hilary 279
Examination Hall 203
execution 57
  on the spot 175
exodus 54, 55
exploitation 13–14, 232, 241, 242, 243, 248
  financial, ruthless 258
  forced sex 252
  landlord 21
  outright 250
  'poor' brothel-goers 253
  protection from 271
  quiet, by authorities 268
  sufferings and 239, 254
expulsion 74
extortion 13, 113, 146–7, 185
  potential target of 344
extradition 145
eye-expression 302
eyes:
  diseased 24
  irritation in 125
  large, deep-set 60
  pupils contracted 123, 124
  rounder, surgery to achieve 60

Fa-ti 188
face-reading 215
family tragedies 161
  breakup 5
  ruin 190
  squandered/depleted fortune 192, 193
fan tan 157, 166, 167, 173, 181, 182, 183, 188, 189, 208
  attraction of 209
  bookmaking companies 215
  cheating in 195
  children present as spectators inside houses 200
  divine betting tips 204–5
  dying business, partly resuscitated 202

financial and social 'destructiveness' of 191
gambler refused admittance to dens 198
government tax 202
legal houses guarded by soldiers 200
mahjong fans too proud to stoop to play 211
pernicious social effects of 193
played with great fairness 207
prohibited 176, 195
punishment for playing 194
strongly criticized by anti-gambling politicians 207
threat of lottery much worse than threat of 191
unlicensed houses 205
Fang hai yüeh k'an 72
fang li 11
Fang-ts'un 188
farmers 24, 208
farmers compelled to cultivate poppies 131
see also tax farmers
fascism 77
fashion 71–6, 86
dining 63
hair 62, 63
high 260
keeping mistresses 61
tight-fitting 60
Western 250
'Fat Woman Number Four' 245
fatigue relief 105
favourable attitudes:
towards bookmaking 205
towards gambling 206, 207, 208
towards opium 132
Fei Fei 14
female body parts 59
feminist movement 62–3
Fêng Lan 316, 318, 321, 335
Fêng Rui 28–9, 30
Fêng Shan 277–8
feng-shui 26, 215
Fêng-shun 131
Fêng T'sai 246
Feng Tzu-yü 175–6, 307, 309
Feng Yü-hsiang 127
Fêng Yüan 310, 312, 315, 335, 336
Fêng yüan ch'u-jên 312, 315
Fêng Yüan-chün 336
ferry-boats 181
festivals 212
annual 269
civic 252
religious 26, 138, 199, 202, 252, 269, 309
temple 215
feudal practices 28
Filipino musicians 63
film stars 281
films 276
silent 306, 342
to promote nationalism 67
Western 331
Finance Department 178
fines 147, 231, 236, 271
light 344
monthly table of 187
fire 57, 140
brothels 229, 291
Fitzgerald, John 145, 163, 177
'five-minute enthusiasm' 87
flags 76, 81, 84, 293, 303
floating brothels 113, 227, 228, 250
clean and lavishly decorated 248, 249
decent image defended 279
estimate of prostitutes working on 229
high-class 291
superior cuisine 280
floating pageants 199
floods 172
flour 80, 100
flower boats, *see* floating brothels
flower feasts 256, 268, 279
flower lottery 157, 174, 181, 184, 185, 197, 208
cheating possible but difficult 196
easily used to defraud 207
fondness in betting on 186
popularity of 213
punishment for playing 194
'flower tax' 287
'flowery badge' 295
Fo-shan 291
Fo-shan chung-i hsiang chih 167
folk songs 123, 193–4, 205, 207, 213, 235
absorption of opera into traditional techniques 320
employed as political weapons against Ch'ing government 306
large genre of 309
well known for puns 324
food:
good 261
largest item of expense for average family 184
offered to deity 215
shortages 102
significant role in brothel culture 280
foot-binding 308

foreign goods 82
foreign imperialism:
  incessant official rhetoric against 75
  rabid nationalism against 235
  trend that survived waves of political campaigns against 76
foreign languages 75
'foreign mud' 118
foreign nationality 61
foreign trade 55
Formosa 100, 120
'fornication-related' misfortunes 285
fortune-tellers 215
Foucault, M. 28
foul language 319, 331
France 140, 292
  ambassador to 292
  war with 171
franchise 100
Franck, Harry A. 1, 52, 71, 76, 81, 143, 174, 176, 181, 200, 273, 286, 293
fraternity 14
fraud 186, 187, 260
free love 282
freedoms 22, 56, 238, 262, 283
  moral 240
  payment in return for 246
  personal and social, symbol of 212
fresh water 314
Frith, Simon 301
fruit growing 130
FSKKTK (*Fêng-su kai-kê ts'ung k'an*) 26, 102
fu 11
Fu Shêng 320
Fu Ssu-nien 338
Fukien 104, 119, 208, 243
Fuma, Susuma 12
funerals 76
Fung (theatre owner) 244
furniture:
  brothel 248, 249, 250, 254, 260, 263, 275
  Western-style 70, 210
Furth, Charlotte 194

Gamble, Sidney D. 252, 275
gambling 4, 5–6, 10, 27, 87, 156–225, 292, 293
  analysing the causes of 38
  arrests for violations 97
  booths for 138
  daily surcharge to village organizations 138
  debt incurred by 21
  guide-books on 98
  inherited fortune squandered on 262
  insincerity of authorities in suppressing 99
  licensed houses 147
  many actors frittered away their income on 344
  plan to ban 146
  prison 115
  'private' houses 147
  'privilege' seemingly denied to gaming houses 133
  revenues from 143, 145
  short-lived prohibition against 147
  suppression of 142
  unlicensed houses 144
gangsters 31
Gans, Herbert J. 301
garrisons 174
gastric trouble 108
Gazetteer of Nan-hai County 169
Geil, William Edgar 69
genealogy 194
gentry 194
  hypocritical 160
  'mischievous' 164
geomancy 105
German language 75
Gernet, Jacques 333
ghosts 26
Gillingham, Paul 54
gimmicks 202, 215, 259
  stage 302
girls:
  attractive 60, 247, 250
  country, idealized 16
  explicitly sexy, drawings of 330
  marriage and 26, 27
  naked, photographs of 330
  pin-up 60, 70
  'procured' 286
  prohibited from working in brothels 286
  scantily clothed and alluring 73
  sold to brothels 255
  young, illegal employment as maids in brothels 281
  see also sing-song girls
go-betweens 40
'Golden Pills' 106
goodness 23
gossip 27, 30, 281, 339
Governor-Generals 142
gramophone records 342
Gramsci, Antonio 7
Gray, John Henry 194, 200
Greece 279
greed 21, 162, 239

  gambler's 205
  insatiable, for money 194
Gregorian calendar 77
Grimm, Tilemann 11
Gronewold, Sue 75, 226, 233
guessing games 207–8
  see also sugar-cane; surnames
guest houses 283, 292
  unlicensed prostitution at 293
'guest soldiers' 97, 174, 175, 176
guidebooks 208, 249–50, 281
guilds 237
Gulik, Robert Hans van 265, 268, 280
gunboats 56, 142, 144

Hague, The 96
Hai-fêng 281
Hai Lung 121, 125
Hai-shang-chüeh-wu-shêng 75, 240, 252, 255, 261, 265, 270, 279
hair salons 260
hairpins 250
hairstyles 60, 74, 75, 86
Han Dynasty (206 BC–221 AD) 11
Han Pi 198
Han Ping 129, 139
Han rebels 307
Han Ta-ch'êng 12
Hang 65
Hankow 201
Hankow-Canton railroad 131
Hao-chi-sheng 256
hard labour 230
hardships 82, 236, 240
harmony 157, 159
Harrison, Fraser 250
Hayes, James 193
HCLCCN (*Kuang-chou shih-chêng-fu hsin shu lo-ch'êng chi-nien tê-k'an*) 24, 31, 34, 35, 36, 71, 126, 201
health 73, 109, 201
  'apparently very good' 183
  corrosive influence on 278
  far from satisfactory 24, 125
  feminine 59
  mental 71
  poor 126
  psychological and physiological 60
  spiritual 68, 73
health inspectors 286
hedonistic culture 66
hegemony 7
Henriques, Fernando 279, 280
herbalists 105, 106, 109
Herman, Robert D. 192
heroin 98, 100, 147
  awareness of danger of addiction 102
  irritating diluents used with 124
Hershatter, Gail 226, 243, 271, 273
hetaerai 279
high-class brothels 58, 240–5 *passim* 249, 253, 259, 262, 284
  affected by recession 229
  clean and lavishly decorated 248
  client taken to court for beating 264
  crowded with inebriated senior army officers 291
  donations solicited by 236, 237
  inspections conducted by local health authority 250
  lives in 272
  low-class compared with 272
  maltreatment of prostitutes by customers 251
  manners of customers and prostitutes 252
  number of 227–8
  officials in Revolutionary government often patrons 293
  quasi-restaurants 280
  rules of respect 254
  standard minimum charge 287
  'ten commandments' governing behaviour of clients 252
  theft from prostitutes in 260
high society 112
hips 60
Ho Chien-ch'ing 316, 321
Ho Chin-hsing 38
Ho lang pi-chi 302
'Ho-pei' 178, 188
Ho T'an-yü 135
Ho Tung, Sir 345
Ho, Virgil Kit-yiu 54, 202
hoarding 26
Hogshire, Jim 122
Hollywood movies 36, 66
Ho-nan 23, 81, 197
  houses specializing in card and domino games 201
  fan tan houses 188
  gambling dens 158, 180, 181, 200
  legal gambling houses 188
  opium retailers/dens 95, 97, 147, 148
  well-lit and lavishly decorated gambling establishments 198
Hong Kong 31, 53–9, 83, 147, 168, 179
  bookmakers based in 171
  brothels/prostitution 58, 229, 236–7, 240, 245, 247, 249, 252–60 *passim* 264, 274, 275, 292

Hong Kong (*cont.*)
'imperialistic' 303
newspapers 236–7, 239, 277–8, 282, 340
opera troupes 39, 306, 307, 309, 316, 335, 336
opium 100, 101, 119
primary schools for the poor 344
ruffian sentenced to hard labour for robbery 260
St Paul's Boys' School 341
secret trading link between Shameen and 82
sing-song girls 117, 274
social notables 345
social novel set in 243–4
see also Canton-Hong Kong strike/boycott; Clementi; Kowloon; New Territories; Victoria Peak; Whampoa
Hong Kong and Shanghai Banking Corporation 54
Hong Kong University 57, 275
hoodlums 267, 345
hope 213, 214, 216, 218
Horlicks 74
horse-racing 201–2, 218
hospitals 52
charitable 237
construction of 202
see also Canton Hospital; Canton Opium Addiction; Municipal Hospital
hotels 65, 257, 271, 274
expensive 265
game extensively and intensively played in 210–11
special task force to inspect all classes of 231
unlicensed prostitutes able to operate freely at 232
Hsaio Lou 323
Hsi-chü 67
'Hsi-chü p'ing-lun' 312, 315, 335, 336, 338
Hsi-chü shih-chieh 313, 329, 338
'Hsi-chü ts'ung-t'an' 335
Hsi Hua 65
Hsi-kuan 37, 132, 204
Hsia Kuan-pu 116
Hsia-tu 130, 183
Hsiang Chün 247
Hsiang-hsia lao 31
Hsiang hua 330
Hsiang-hua hua-pao 70, 282
Hsiao Chi 262
Hsiao Fêng 259
Hsiao Lou 330, 338
Hsiao Mei-hua 158, 167
Hsiao-pei 37
Hsiao-tian shih 235
hsiao-kuei 261
Hsieh Shêng-po 336
Hsien ch'i chien tu 193–4
Hsien-fêng 302
Hsien Tzu-lung 69
Hsien Yü-ch'ing 317
Hsin Ching Hsiang 326
Hsin-fêng 130
Hsin-fêng-huang 27, 28
Hsin-tung-fang-shuo 257
Hsin Yin 34
Hsin Yüeh kung-ssu 342
Hsing Chuang 16
Hsing Tsai 275
Hsü cha-ch'êng 181
Hsü Ching-Yüan 103
Hsü Chu-ch'êng 198, 214, 217
Hsü chung ch'ing 78
Hsü Hsu 60, 70
Hsü-Hsueh-hang 64
Hsü Nai-ch'i 139
Hsü P'ei-chün 318
Hsü Tao-ching 313
Hsüeh Chüeh-hsien 311, 312, 332, 340, 341, 342, 343, 344, 345
Hsüeh Ch'ün 256–7
HTJP (*Hua-tzu jih-pao*) 31, 41, 53–7 *passim*, 71–4 *passim*, 81, 84, 100, 102, 115, 135, 138, 145–8 *passim*, 163, 168, 180, 184, 189, 202, 227, 229, 231, 232, 235, 236, 237, 239, 242, 243, 246, 247, 249, 253, 259, 260, 263, 264, 265, 268, 276, 278, 283, 287, 290–4 *passim*, 306, 333, 343, 344, 345
Hu Chên 345
Hu Han-min 292
Hu-hua-lang 344
Hu, John 305
Hu P'o-an 63, 249, 255
Hu Pu-Chin 172, 176
Hua Lin ('thermos jug') 255–6
Hua-ts'ung-fên-tieh 256, 283
Hua-tzu jih pao 179, 282
Hua ying 260
Huai-ping-tzu 279
huan hua-chai 236
Huan Tsun 104
Huang (disgruntled lottery patron) 197
Huang (lottery cheat) 196
Huang (prostitute's client) 278
Huang (shop-owner) 266
Huang Ch'ao-yu 86
Huang Ching-ming 332
Huang Chüeh-tzu 139

Huang En-lin 24, 25, 26, 27, 100, 120, 125, 138, 182, 202
Huang Kang-pu 167
Huang Lin-shêng 202
Huang Lu-i 322
Huang Ming-hui 52, 57
Huang Shao-hsiung 72, 145
Huang Tê-shen 309
Huang Wên-to 113, 131
Huang Yin-p'u 25
Hui You 61
humiliation 32, 53, 73, 102, 128, 193, 263
  national 52, 83
  ultimate 285
humour 328
  heavy use of 321
  popular 326, 334
  social implications in contemporary opera 325
  stage-names a manifestation of 322
  'thoughtless' 323
Hunan 128, 160, 242
Hundred Days Reform 166
Hung-ch'uan-chiu-lü 331, 339
Hung Lang 114, 121
hunger strikes 246
Hunter, William 79
Huo Chi-ting 180
Hupeh Ting Hsien 29
hygiene 59
  brothel 250
  brothels 286
  clear identification with 64
  poor 24
  public, growing concerns over 235
  restaurant 63
hypodermic needles 102, 124

'I-chiu-erh-liu nien tung-fang-ling' 31
I-fêng Shê 309
I Hsaio 36, 336
I Wu 104, 105, 106, 140
Ibsen, Henrik 304
idealization 6, 18
  country girls 16
  cultural 70
  male body 62
  village life 14
  Western feminine beauty 62
Idema, Wilt 333, 336, 338
identity:
  actors hiding 322
  geo-cultural 13
  superior 3, 11, 335
  rural 22, 32
  vocational 267
  see also cultural identity; urban identity
ideology
  egalitarian 10
  indoctrination 230
  Legalist 9
  moralistic orthodox 218
  national revolution 51
  traditional 3
idols 337–45
idyll 11, 12, 13, 19
ignorance 113, 181
  rural 40, 165
illicit dealers 131
illicit gaming 164
illiteracy 24, 25
  women above 20 years of age 26
immorality 117, 163, 206, 281, 304
  opera scene banned for 327
Imperial Maritime Customs 80, 82, 95, 96, 118, 119, 129
  annual and decennial reports 131
  not allowed to search Chinese warship 142
  seizures of smuggled narcotics 101
'imperial rice' 105
imperialism 50, 59, 77
  not always hated by general public 86–7
  official campaigns against 81
  opium and 104–7
  religious wing of 52
  symbol of 51
  Western, evils of 65
  see also anti-imperialism; foreign imperialism
imports 55, 80, 82
  essential 85
  liquor 75
  luxury goods 36
  opium 95, 96, 106, 112, 119, 140
  wine 63
impoverishment 25, 28, 102, 105, 118, 125, 131, 163
  general 230
  prostitution a symbol of 233
  widespread 21
imprisonment 260
improper behaviour/impropriety 29, 305
improvization 317, 324
incense 258
income 145, 163, 171, 180
  addicts' families 129
  average 25, 182
  bookmakers' plunge in 190
  courtesan 248
  exhausted 165

income (*cont.*)
handsome 247, 344
illegitimate 115
important source for local government 142
loss of 203
lucrative sources of 101, 140
major source of 171
municipal government 202, 287
opium and gambling revenues 143
professional opera troupe 307
provincial treasury 158
reaped by madams 258
'special' 272
substantial 259
superstars 343
village office deprived of major source of 183
Indian opium 96, 117–18, 119, 130, 139, 140
confiscation and destruction of 103
individualism 62
indulgence 74–5, 116, 120, 129, 137
costly 121
excessive 215, 283
mass 157
inebriation 137
infanticide 27
infantrymen 232
inferiority 38, 50, 77
Chinese attire 73
deep-seated awareness of 58
entertainment 58
low-class whores 254
socio-cultural 53
information blackout 98
insightfulness 73
Institute for Educating the Poor 203
insurance companies 57
intellect 211
intellectuals 4, 11, 19, 40, 77, 135, 241, 327, 338
anti-prostitution 234
contemptuous 38–9
criticisms by 157, 302
criticisms of 290
drama societies founded and run by 309
foreign-educated 302
nationalistic 33, 84, 278
prostitutes seen in somewhat different light 239
sympathetic to reform or revolution 309
Western-inspired 302
young 107, 311
International Anti-opium Association 130, 142
International Conference on Opium Suppression 96
interrogation 185, 186, 254
intoxication 103, 107
chronic opium 127
death as a result of 122
opiates, symptoms of 108
irrationality 157
Israel, John 86
itinerant opera troupes 334

Jacobus, J. 279
Japan 31, 71, 175, 314
attitude of scholars towards 77
bank loan from 143
colonial period 110
essential imports from 85
fear and hatred of 101
goods from 86
Japanese in Formosa 100
moral character of actors 310
occupation authorities 181
theatre in 331
see also boycotts
Japanese Boycott Committee 85
Japanese goods 85
smuggling 51
Japanese invasion (1938) 131, 237, 294
Jê-nan-lang 324
Jên Shou Nien 326
Jên T'ien Lo 326
jesters 318, 319, 321–2, 339
famous 324, 340
jingoist fanatics 78
journalist reports 161, 185, 199, 201–2, 216–17, 227, 229
Ju Shih 33
junk crews 115
justice 213, 245

K'ang shu-chên 233
Kang Tou 202
Kao Hsiang-li 108
Kao Yu-yün 87
karma 285
Kazantzakis, Nikos 114
KCHJP (*Kuang-chou hsin jih-pao*) 75, 85, 146, 246, 342
KCMKJP (*Kuang-chou min-kuo jih-pao*) 33, 39, 65, 79, 82, 99, 115, 144, 160, 173, 175, 184, 185, 186, 197, 199, 203, 205, 208, 209, 214, 258, 271, 274, 278, 288, 293, 274, 313, 339, 345
KCPN (*Kuang-chou pai-nien ta-shih chi*) 142, 143, 148, 159, 172, 180, 291, 292
KCTC (*Kuang-chou tsa chih*) 60, 72, 74, 345
Kendall, Elizabeth 115

KHP (*Kuo hua pao*) 63, 184, 186, 201, 237, 294, 335
Kiang household 197
Kiang-men 294
Kiangsi 318, 334
Kiangsu 137, 262
kidnappers 56, 81
kidneys 105, 283
kinship 29, 30, 194
kissing 325, 330
KMT (Kuomintang) 34, 72, 83, 98, 142, 294
  belligerent attitude towards Left government 177
  Canton Branch headquarters 69
  corruption of 96
  extortionate financial policies 54
  financing military expeditions 176
  historians 175
  modernity projects 288
  National government 145
  newly reorganized 230
  newspapers 177, 205
  official anti-gambling publications 172
  opinion poll on performance 86–7
  political technique 161
  predicament on the opium question 99
  prominent officials 237, 292
  Propaganda Bureau 165, 166
  racketeering expedient often used by 51
  reorganized, Canton under control of 160
  women's liberation movement gathering momentum under 336
  see also Northern Expedition
Kōain, Seimubu 134
Kōsaka, Junichi 106, 115, 117, 133, 134, 314
Kou-pi Chang 334
Kowloon 15, 56
  robbery in middle-range brothel 260
KPP (*Kung-p'ing pao*) 32, 121, 131, 192, 205, 217, 227, 229, 239, 242, 244, 245, 251, 254, 256, 257, 259, 260, 262, 264, 266, 267, 268, 270, 274–7 *passim*, 284, 288, 289
Krejci, Jaroslav 75
KTFCL (*Kuang-tung feng-ching lu*) 233
K'u Tieh 271
Ku Yü 184
Kuan Wên-ch'ing 65, 66, 342–3
Kuang-chou chih-nan 25, 34, 37, 333
Kuang-chou li-pai-liu 330
Kuang-chou min-kuo jih-pao 99
Kuang-chou nien-chien 24, 41, 58, 63, 66, 129, 172, 188, 189, 228, 229, 281, 286, 287, 327, 330, 333
Kuang-chou shê-hui tsa chih 198
Kuang-chou-shih chêng-fu 68, 71, 74, 201, 202, 288
Kuang-chou-shih chêng-hsieh 71, 72, 78, 177, 180, 181, 289, 291
Kuang-chou-shih chieh-yen i-yüan 111
Kuang-chou-shih chin-yen wei-yüan-hui 133, 148
Kuang-chou-shih je ên-min chêng-fu pan-kung tien 230
Kuang-chou-shih shê-hui chü 228, 229, 272
Kuang-chou-shih shih chên-king 288
Kuang-chou-shih shih-chêng-fu 203, 228
Kuang-chou-shih shih-chêng-fu t'ung chi ku 129
Kuang-chou-shih shih-chêng hui k'an 333
Kuang-chou-shih shih-chêng pao-kao hui k'an 229, 231–2, 309
Kuang-chou-shih shih-chêng t'ung-chi hui k'an 286, 287, 313
Kuang-chou-shih shih-li i-yüan 127, 128
Kuang-chou-shih tzu-tung tien-hua 133
Kuang-chou tsa chih 330
Kuang Lao-chiu 209
Kuang-tung ch'ing-li-ts'ai-chêng-chü 118, 142, 171
Kuang-tung ch'üan shêng ts'ai-chêng shuo-ming shu 289
Kuang-tung kung-pao 159, 268
Kuang-tung shang-yeh nien-chien 330
Kuang-tung-shêng chêng-fu ts'ai-chêng-t'ing 145, 176, 177, 179, 180, 192
Kuang-tung shêng chin-an-shih kung-chü 289
Kuang-tung shêng-fu kung-pao 203
Kuang-tung ts'ai-cheng-ting 64
Kuang-tung t'ung-chih 77, 336
Kublai Khan 105
Kuei Ming-yang 341
K'un-ch'ü 304–5, 333
K'ung Fu-an 239–40, 256, 280, 289, 291
Kung-ho shih-yun fu 193
K'ung pa-an 205
Kung-p'ing pao 281, 329
Kuo-fu ch'üan-tsi 144, 174, 175, 176
Kuo-hua pao 281, 329
Kuo-min hua-yüan (restaurant) 63
Kuo Shuang-lin 158, 167
Kuo Sung-t'ao 170–1
Kuo Wên-fang 70
Kwangsi 104, 142, 160
  Ch'en ousted by joint force from Yünnan, Kwangtung and 173
  Government Chairman 145

Kwangsi (*cont.*)
lifting of ban on gambling dictated by unruly army officers from 175
reinforcing the coastal defence 171
Kwangsi militarists 159, 172, 173
gambling legalized by 195
Kwangtung All-Occupations' Anti-Japanese Association 85
Kwangtung Central Committee for the Severance of Economic Relations with Great Britain 83
Kwangtung Christian Church 195
Kwangtung School of Art 313
Kwangtung University 341
Kweichow 104, 119, 130, 139, 160
military forces invade Kwangtung (1912) 165
Kweilin accent 338

labour camps 273
labour politics 56
labour unionists, *see* trade-unionists
Lai Po-ch'iang 307, 311, 317, 318, 319, 320, 326, 336, 337, 343
lampoons 159
Lamson, Herbert Day 110
landlords 12, 21
landscape painting 11
Larsen, Jeanne 280
Lary, Diana 127
laughter 303, 324
law 57
law and order 239
lawsuits 212–13, 217
layabouts 129
League of Nations 100, 143
Lee, Edward Bing-shuey 24, 25, 71, 280, 286, 288
Lee, Leo Ou-fan 62
Lee Tai-cho 53, 55
Leeuw, Hendrik de 249
Leftists 55, 123, 287, 288
legal credibility 57
Legalist ideology 9
Lei Li-pin 234
Lei P'ei-chin 316
leisure 27, 100, 189, 207, 210, 238
fashionable form of 209
healthy 164
opium smoking an agreeable form of 132
popular activities 183
unquestioned pursuits 208
Leng Hung ('Cold Red') 256
Leng Yen 117
Lethaby, W. R. 36
Lewin, Louis 124, 126
Li (businessman/lottery trickster) 197–8
Li Chêng-i 145–6
Li Chi-shên 83, 179, 294
Li Chien-êrh 69
Li Chien-lou 110
Li Feng 331, 337
Li Fu-lin 178, 181, 345
Li Han-chang 168, 169
Li Han-ch'iao 85, 86
Li Han-ch'ung 196, 218
Li Hsiao-cheng 262–3
Li Hsüeh-fang 335, 336, 340
Li Hsüeh-ying 61
Li Hsun-huan 201
Li Hung-chang 139, 160, 167, 171, 176
Li Hung-ping 170
Li I-chi 217
Li Lin 186
Li Mên 334, 342
Li Min 17
Li P'ei-shêng 142
Li Shih-chên 106
Li Su-mei 341
Li T'i 186
Li T'iao-yüan 309
Li Tsung-huang 34, 35, 52, 142, 286, 287, 337
Li Ying 340
Liang Ch'i-ch'ao 171, 336
Liang-Kuang 168
Liang Kwang Company 145
Liang lineage 194
Liang P'ei-chin 311, 314, 334
Liang Shou-ming 41
Liang Ting-nan 319
Liang Wei 317, 320, 325
Liang Yen-hsien 75
Liang Yün-chiao 22
Liao Chung-kai 293
Liao Hsia-huai 324, 340
Liao Kuang-sheng 49
Liao Yüan 313
libel 56
'liberal era' 42
liberalization 318
librettos 304
filthy and obscene 323
funny scenes and witticisms 328
humorous remarks in 323
idiomatic 320
intrigue and conspiracies in 327
strong criticisms in mass media 330
vulgar and smutty phrases 303
licences 142, 143, 229, 230, 232
application for 203

Li-chi Bay 209
Lien Ch'êng 137
Lien-chou Incident (1905) 80
Lien hsiang chi-chê 323
Lien Shao-fêng 344
Lien Yung 344
lighting systems 312
Light, Arthur B. 108, 125
Lilius, Aleko E. 200, 217
Lin Chin-Chih 69
Lin I-mei 335
Lin-Lang Huan-ching 309
Lin Man-hung 104
Lin Shu-shen 332
Lin Tsê-hsü 98, 103, 139, 141, 143, 170, 319
Lindesmith, Alfred R. 109, 123, 124, 148
lineage membership 194–5
Ling Hsiao-shêng 15–16
Ling Ling 275–6
Lingnan College 341
Lingnan University 24, 27, 39, 72, 76, 81, 114, 125
  Department of Sociology 182, 189
Link, Perry 18, 19, 326
lion-dance teams 15
lips 60, 123
liquor 75
literacy 24
literati 280, 283, 302, 304, 318
literature:
  classical, most commonly adopted motif in 11
  contemporary 'serious' 331
  highbrow 327
  oral 193
  specializing in Cantonese opera 338
  vernacular 11
  Western 332
  see also poems; prose; scripts
Liu Hsüeh-hsün 173, 175, 176
Liu I 211
Liu Kuo-hsing 318, 333
Liu Pai 318–19
Liu Po-wên 105
Liu Shu-fên 11
Liu Tsai-su 35, 52, 208, 214, 250, 269, 280
Liu Wan-chang 215, 252
Liu Wei-chi 72
Liu Yao-hsin 40
Liu Yu-lun 60
living conditions:
  appalling 125
  brothels, comfortable 273
  deterioration in 23
  harsh 13
  materially inferior 23
  scarcity of living-space 37
LNFY (*Ling-nan fêng-yüeh shih*) 240, 246, 248
Lo chia-lun 292
Lo chia-shan 314
Lo I-ch'ün 176
Lo Kuan-wei 76–7
Lo Li-ming 240, 241, 245, 252, 253, 254, 259, 274, 275, 280, 284
Lo-lo Chu-shih 110
Lo Shan 104
Lo-ti-jên 250
Lo-ting 130
Lo Tzu-ch'in 108, 112, 116, 126, 128, 129
Lo Yün-yen 100, 101, 106, 109, 122, 123
loan-sharks 184, 199
loans 56, 113
  foreign 142, 143
local newspapers 33, 80, 83, 148, 177, 185, 235, 277
  accounts of misbehaviour towards girls 251
  advertising in 60, 181, 215, 282
  beauty contest favourably reported in 289
  favourable reception of prostitution 281–2
  latest news about stars 339
  massage business report 276
  moralistic reports 184
  popular 38, 72
  readers write to 62, 73, 76, 84, 250
  reports of interesting phenomenon 210
  special column for opera reviews 329
longevity 139, 140
looting of villages 20
lotteries 167, 171, 172, 175, 181, 185, 189, 216
  cheating in 195–8
  conspicuous celebration by winners 217–18
  damaging impact of 168–9
  danger of being obsessed with 191
  first legal 203
  main attraction of 214
  mahjong fans too proud to stoop to 211
  means to raise funds 170
  popularity of 192, 213, 214, 215, 218
  troop-protected 200
  unlucky winners 217
  see also flower lottery; horse-racing; mountain lottery; pigeon lottery; shop lottery; soccer; sports lottery; surnames
love 63, 246, 257
  attitudes towards 226, 238
  idea of freedom in 62
  strong commitment to 235

'lover-slaves' 261
low-class brothels 236, 254, 262, 263, 280
  conditions of 249, 270
  experience of a regular to 253
  high-class compared with 272
  inspections conducted by local health authority 250
  lives in 272
  madam arranging deal to sell girl to 242
  number of 228
  strike against surcharge on 268
low-income groups 97
loyalty 29, 240
  civic 37
  national 117
Lü Hsüch-hai 77
Lu Hsün 127
Lu Wên-lung 135
Lu Yen 268
luck 29, 157, 211, 213, 217
  bad 265, 266
  best time of year to test 215
  gamblers obsessed with 163
  wishing 215
Lunar New Year 215
Lung Chi-kuang 160, 172
luxury 313
  consumer businesses 202
luxury goods 36, 112, 116, 260
Lynch, Kevin 36
lyrics 302
  funny scenes and witticisms in 328
  humorous 321, 323
  Mandarin 321
  vernacular 193, 303, 306
  violent or obscene 327
  vulgar and smutty phrases in 303, 331
  written in the language of the riff-raff 310

M-isms 65
Ma (addictive gambler) 184
Ma Huan-huan 286
Ma Mo-ching 139, 141
Ma P'i-yao 168, 169
Ma Shih-ts'êng 261, 303, 311, 312, 316, 321, 339–42, 343, 344, 345
Macao 106, 120
  gambling 171, 199, 200, 217
  'imperialistic' 303
  opera fans 339
  prostitution 236, 246, 276, 277
Mackerras, Colin 304, 311, 316
madams 233, 255
  abusive 262, 264
  aggressive 6, 243, 245
  alleged maltreatment by 281
  brave 264
  call for police intervention 254
  caring 243
  coercion exercised by 245–6
  considerate 244–5
  ensuring proper treatment by 263
  evil 243
  exercise of power by 247
  income reaped by 258
  inflicting punishment on girls 265
  inhumane 246
  interference in love affairs 242, 246
  mischief-making 246
  mistreatment by 6, 243, 265, 270
  negotiating a price with 252
  outraged 264
  relationship between prostitutes and 244, 269
  retired 262
  robbed 259
  ruthless financial exploitation by 258
  severe exploitation by 241
  share of charge 288
  stabbed during row 268
  surprisingly weak 247–8
  temperamental 262
  vindictive 234
  vulnerability of 247
  wicked 242, 243, 246
magazines 281, 335, 338–9, 340
  popular 324, 329, 330
mahjong 158, 166, 182, 183, 193, 201, 207, 208–12, 256, 283
  popularity of 188
  returning rapidly and widely played in private 218
  suicide after loss on 184
  taxing the playing of 178
Mai (young courtesan) 243
Mai Hsiao-hsia 311, 314, 316, 317, 321
make-up 75
  heavy 311, 340
malaria 109
malnutrition 114, 125
malpractices 196
maltreatment 248, 250, 251, 257, 261, 263, 286
  alleged 281
  helpless and silent victims of 254
Manchu regime 184–5
  collapse/fall of 158, 159, 291, 307
  corruption 162
  last days of rule 292
  monarchs 167
  stigmatized image of 166–7
  words to underline the guilt of 170

Manchuria 166
Mandarin:
  lyrics 321
  singing 304
  'stage' 321, 338
mandarin oranges 212
mandarins 168
mansions 11, 37, 132, 205, 258
  luxurious 210
  Western-style 216
manual work 14
Mao Hai-chien 79, 128
Mao Tse-tung 19
marketing tactics 74
marriage 39–40, 63, 241, 286
  arranged 26, 262, 329
  'blind' 62
  courtesans redeemed by 275
  girls at early age of puberty 27
  modern 65, 70
  perceived as the ideal way of quitting prostitution 277
  virginity of the bride 56
  young girls pledged to stay together to avoid 26
martial arts 332
martyrdom 83
Marxist historians 5, 79, 175, 304
mass media 342
  criticism published in 329
  effective use of 161
  libretto strongly criticized in 330
  officially controlled 81
mass rallies 81
massage business 276
material progress 38, 50, 76
materialism 36, 66, 261
'maternal uncle teams' 257
May Thirtieth Movement 84, 86
Mê (affluent businessman) 276
meanings 9–48
  auspicious 326
  constructed into social phenomena and historical events 2
  cultural 73
  symbolic 3, 51, 59, 69, 73, 77, 307
medical treatment 5
medicines 38, 73–4
  anti-opium 144, 145
  benefits/value of opium 104–11, 115, 140
  herbal 136, 138, 140–1
  traditional 283
Mei Lan-fang 332, 336
menstruation 265
mental retardation 126
mentalities 7
  capitulating 82
  fun-seeking 325
  gambling 162, 163
  peasant 29
  popular 42, 274
  pro-Western 4, 61, 76
merchant associations 115
merchants 51, 56, 81
  anti-opium 125
  'Big Fire' victims 57
  grave economic despair 160
  hypocritical 160
  immoral 206
  moralistic 160
  non-Kwangtungese, and American trade 80
  opium-using 118, 129, 131
  opulent 55
  Portuguese 106
  scheming 206
  surcharge on goods held by 85
  well-to-do/wealthy 190, 132
Merchants' Anti-Japanese Organization 85
merits 245
Metcalf, Thomas R. 69
migration, *see* rural migration
militarism/militarists:
  accused 160
  corrupt 162
  physiocratic 9
  provincial 119
  Yünnanese 287
  see also Kwangsi militarists
military administration 232
military defence 66
military service 20
Miners, Norman 118, 119
Ming Dynasty (1368–1644) 12, 105–6, 107, 116, 167, 227, 235, 304, 305, 306, 313, 317, 318, 320
Ming-hsin pao chien 193
Ministry of Finance 293
misconduct 20, 169, 254
  pledge eschewing 264
  soldierly 160, 232, 239
  warlords' 238
missionaries 52, 95, 125, 131, 132, 194, 200
mistreatment 6, 27, 32, 40, 243, 265, 268
  pretended 270
mistresses 61, 277, 331
mixed opera troupes 336
Mo-têng-nü 257
Mo Yin-chih 33
mobile prostitutes 229
mockery 32

model carriageways 35
modernity 9, 34–8
  belief that imported goods stood for 86
  city closely identified with 19
  critique of 235
  dress identified with/a symbol of 71, 74
  KMT projects 288
  promise of 41
  struggle for 76
  upper-class prostitutes 'titillating with' 75
modernization 22, 24
  beachhead of 41
  cultural 7
  effective Western means of 201
  financing projects 5
  ideology believed to be conducive to 218
  immediately achieving 41
  military 128
  not appreciated by everyone 61
  successful model of 53
molestation 247, 251
Mongols 105, 107
  outlet to ridicule and challenge legitimacy of rule 306
monocles 73
moon-cakes 135
moral preachers 290
moral ruin 161
morality 35
  acts damaging 26, 289
  Confucian codes of conduct 156
  corrosive influence on character 278
  fall in 163
  gambling detrimental to 159
  gradual shattering of traditional mores 6
  gradually collapsed and disappeared 167
  loose morals 17
  opera 304
  opium issue 141
  orthodox 327
  social 289
  standards plunged 160
  strong commitment to 29
  teachings on righteous behaviour 193
  validity and inviolability of established mores 326
morphine 98, 100, 123
  addiction not characterized by physical deterioration 108
  awareness of danger of addiction 102
  injection of 101, 140, 142
  irritating diluents used with 124
mortality 110, 127
  female, premature 27
  infant 126
Mote, F. W. 9, 10
mountain lottery 180, 188
  fairly played 207
  minimum wager 214
  popularity of 213–14
movies 36, 65–7, 74, 281
  Western, plays adapted from 303–4
Mukden Incident (1931) 85
Municipal Government 71, 78, 188
  concern for conditions of low-class establishments 281
  first and nascent, reforming spirit of 231
  major source of income for 287
  Social Bureau 208, 228, 229, 272
  Social Investigation Unit 188
Municipal Hospital of Canton 127
Municipal Opera Examination Committee 330
Municipal Radio 68, 161
Murayama, Shigeru 1
Murphey, Rhoads 10, 12, 13, 42, 49, 50, 55, 80, 141, 171
music 63, 67–8, 114, 134, 229, 315–16
  keen lovers of 309
  noisy 320
  smooth and delicate 304
musical instruments 325
  Western 316, 331, 332

Namhoi and Pan-Yu magistrates 200
Nan-hai County 169, 190–1, 334
  Liang lineage 194
Nanking 87, 135, 145, 147, 148, 161, 162–3, 166, 177, 180, 183, 203, 288
  anti-gambling campaign 190
  Ming-dynasty 227
Nanking University 29
narcotic drugs, *see* cocaine; heroin; morphine; red pills
nation-building 163
National Anti-Opium Day 103
National Products Association 78
National Revolution (mid-1920s) 4, 32–3, 51, 142
  birthplace and base of 34
National Revolutionary Army 345
nationalism 104
  commemorative events related to 86
  films to promote 67
  modern 34
  rabid 235
  revolutionary 56
  source of inspiration to champion of 58
Nationals' Sports Hall 65
natural phenomena 29

natural-tone singing 321
nature 11, 14
NCH (*North-China Herald*) 54, 55, 56, 83, 84
Neo-Confucian ideals 194
neon-lit signboards 181
New Asia Hotel 69, 72
'New China' 62
'New Era' 342
New Life Movement 53, 74, 147, 163
New Territories 198
Newman, Otto 157, 192, 204, 211
Newman, R. K. 115
newspapers 56–7, 128, 140, 164, 176, 179, 205, 229, 231
  actress writing to 320
  advertisements 187, 236–7, 313, 317
  columns on theatre 335
  gossip column news 275
  news related to prostitution 264
  official 208
  official, criticized 330
  popular 324
  pro-Nationalist 99
  reports of disturbances or rows at brothels 254
  respectable 277–8
  sensational headline 186
  unlicensed prostitution reports 232
  see also local newspapers
newsreels 340
NFJP (*Nan-fang jih-pao*) 98, 100, 233
Ng, Yong-sang 1, 34, 36, 37, 52
nicknames 324
Nien rebels 128
Nineteenth Route Army 215
norms 30
North America 184, 302
North China 100, 101, 184
North-eastern China 131
Northern Expedition 145, 160, 165, 177, 288
  fund-raising performances for 345
  preparing for 173
Northern Expeditionary Army 82
Northern School of martial arts 332
noses:
  higher-bridged 60, 61
  shrunk 123
nouveaux riches 69–70
novelty 305, 315, 317, 319
  quest for 316
nudity 330
NYSP (*Nan-yang shang-pao*) 54, 56, 57, 72, 85, 98, 178, 201, 209, 258, 269, 288, 294, 330, 340
obscene language 251, 319, 330
obscenity 67, 83, 304, 323, 327, 337
  explicit and visual forms of 330
  not all audiences tolerated 331
Occidentalism 61
occupational backgrounds 111
odour 253
official corruption 142, 162, 166, 167, 168, 170
  fertile ground for 113
  major cause of 159
  prevalence of 85
  rampant and uncontrollable 169
  widespread 179
official promotion games 157, 182
official propaganda 7, 99, 102, 103, 178
  gambling in 204, 218
oil 80
old people's homes 52
opera 7–8, 70, 281, 289, 301–53
  all-female troupes 36, 202, 312, 313, 335–6
  ambitious goal for companies 58
  Americanization of troupes 39
  apprentices of the art 276
  commercially successful 194
  countryside troupes 39
  delight in chasing famous stars 261
  free performances 22, 212
  fund-raising performance 138
  girls' reputation for keeping singers as paramours 247, 248
  opium-addicted actors/musicians 114, 116, 134
  performed nightly 199
  popular actor with serious financial problem 121
  popularity of 3
  progressive troupes 141, 194
  social implications 3
  see also music; patriot troupes; plays; scripts
Opium Prohibition Bureau 131
opium smoking 3, 4–5, 6–7, 34, 87, 95–155, 186, 205, 206, 292
  bad effects of 193
  brief campaign against 160
  contemporary debate on 163
  debt incurred by 21
  gamblers' money spent lavishly on 164
  inherited fortune squandered on 262
  obsession with 162
  quality 199
  rooms for 27

opium smoking (*cont.*)
  widespread 21
  see also drug addicts; poppies
Opium Suppression Bureau 96, 143, 144, 146, 148
  abolition of 145
Opium Suppression Office 145, 146–7
  paralysed 146
Opium Suppression Ordinance 111, 113
Opium Termination Institutions 96
Opium Wars:
  (1839–42) 79, 98, 112
  (1856) 50
oppression 38
order 157
  public 160, 185
  see also social order
orderliness 14, 51, 54, 70
  brothels 252, 254
  clear identification with 64
'Ordinance on the Scanning of Opium Addicted Civil Servants' (1929) 147
orphanages 52, 271
ostentatious exhibition 70
Ou An-nien 69
Ou-yang Hsi 145
Ou-yang Hui-tsung 103
Ou-yang Shan 85, 88, 123, 233–4, 236, 249, 273, 275, 283, 331
Ou-yang Yü-ch'ien 67, 308, 314, 318, 323, 326, 332
ovary trouble 27
overdoses 111, 126–7, 136
overindulgence 205, 281
overnight performances 333
overseas audiences 331

Pa Ho Guild 329
Pa Ku 244–5
Pai Ho Guild 307
Pai man 330
Pai Yü-mei 117
pain relief 108, 114
painting 68–9, 116
  innovations in 11
  nudes 330
palliatives 110
Pan-chiao man-hua 38, 73, 210, 250
P'an Chih-chung 68–9
P'an Kuang-wên 322
P'an-yü hsien hsü chih 343
Pang Tê-hsin 11
Pao 212
parades 158–9, 199
parasites 130
parks 35, 164
  prestigious 34
  see also amusement parks
parochialism 23
patriarchalism 22
Patrick, Tony 325
patriot troupes 306, 307–8, 320
  key actors of 321–2
  'localization' process 321
  short-lived, idealistic 327
patriotism 3–4, 5, 51, 52, 65, 83
  active, of the masses 88
  anti-opium 143
  boosting the sale of licensed opium 117
  countryfolk assumed to be innately weak in 33
  cultivating feelings of 86
  failure of 86
  fanatical 58
  intimidation into 82
  journalists 80
  lack of commitment ridiculed 87
  sincere 328
  veneer of 85
pauperization 226
pavements 35
Pearl River 23, 69, 178
  attempt to drown in 243
  Bridge 181
  delta 229
  floating brothels 228, 280, 291
  north/south banks 188
Pearl River Theatre 306
Pearsall, Ronald 334–5
'peasant consciousness' 19
'peasant rebellions' 9–10
pedlars 13, 325
Pei (prostitute/concubine) 276
Peking 96, 110, 159, 332
  Grand Council 168
  highly acclaimed brothels 252
  horse-racing 201
  Peking opera 321, 325, 333, 336
Pellens, Mildred 108, 114, 121, 124, 127, 128
penalties 74
P'eng Kuo-liang 119
P'eng Yong-ou 112
pennants 293, 303
  congratulatory 306
People's Liberation Army 230
perception-construction 38
perfume 86
personality cult 165, 166, 339, 340
pharmacology 108, 110, 135

Philadelphia General Hospital 108
Philippine Commission 122, 125
photographs 71, 72
physical attraction 59, 216
physical fitness 61, 125
Pi Chuan 312
P'iao-p'iao hua-pao 69
picketing teams 85
pickpockets 198, 200
pictorials 330
Pien Ying 293
pigeon lottery 157, 168, 183, 188, 191, 192, 208, 217
  easily used to defraud 207
  illicit ring 200
  minimum stake 214
  popularity of 213
  punishment for playing 194
  tax levied on prize money of 203
pimps 245, 319
pin-ups 60, 70
  suggestive 330
P'ing Chin-ya 162, 226, 254
Ping Lan 256, 266
Ping-shi 275
plagiarism 302, 303
plagues 130, 236
plain-clothes detectives 292
plays:
  adapted from Western movies 303–4
  classical, traditional-costume 320–1
  experimental 316
  humorous 324
  'obscene' 337
  old classical, modern compilation of 319–20
  popularity and success rated 331
  ritualistic 307
pleasure 281, 282
  carnal 253, 266
  drugs 106
pleasure boats 199
Po Leung Kuk 255, 276
Po Lo 341
poems/poetry 116
  anti-gambling 157
  bizarre 330
  classical, pre-Han 11
  euphoric experiences immortalized in 115
  innovations in 11
  laudatory/glorifying, actresses 334, 340
  vernacular 280
  witty 324
poker 188, 195–6
Polachek, J. 79
police 30, 32, 65, 84, 147, 180, 270–1
  armed 197
  armed conflict between unruly soldiers and 263
  arrests of unlicensed prostitutes 231, 232
  attacked 185
  blind eye on ban on gambling 215
  bribing 174, 200, 202
  chiefs of 145, 174, 345
  complaint against 185–6
  complaint to 197
  drugs violations 97, 98, 111
  Indian 236
  instructed to pay special vigilance to opera performances 306
  intervention of 254, 266, 268
  madam reported to 247
  maintaining a modern force 171
  off-duty, popular hang-outs for 201
  places under open protection of 199
  prostitute clients 257
  prostitute shot and seriously wounded by 278
  protection from 263, 263
  records on gambling-related charges 187, 188
  reprimanded 263
  shops forced by 83
  streets full of 200
policy insincerity 85
political instability 173, 282
  revenues crucial at time of 177
political rituals 86
political turmoil 6, 51, 53, 54, 259, 326
  devastating impact of decades of 107
  perfect refuge in times of 55
polytheism 26
poorer classes:
  marriageable women available to 284
  opium smoking among 100, 113, 114, 117, 120–1, 122, 131
poppies 104–5, 106, 130
  authorities tough on eradicating farms 142
  ban on growing/planting 139, 140
  disease-curing 108
  farmers compelled against their will to cultivate 131
  meanings of life completely shattered by 123
  medical records about 107
  'narcotic quality' 140
  processing of 139
  quality of soil and climate not ideal for growing 131
  widespread cultivation of 119

popular attitudes:
- towards city 164
- towards gambling 204
- towards opera profession 338
- towards opium smoking 141
- towards prostitutes 238, 260
- towards traditional and modern things 332
- towards wealth 343
- towards West 49–94, 316

popular culture 7
population 1, 37
- falling 25

Portuguese 106, 171, 217, 320
Potter, J. M. and S. H. 42, 326
poverty 13–14, 17, 24, 129
- delusion of discarding 215
- devastated China plagued by 231
- dire 6, 214
- factor in causing and intensifying disease 110
- lucrative alternative to 273
- mass 40
- migration induced by 17
- opium smoking associated with 113
- permanent 6
- prostitution and 226, 227, 230, 233
- 'repose in' 157
- rural, preconceived ideas about 28
- tension generated by 218
- unwelcoming physical signs of 114

prayers 215, 217
preferential treatment 73
pregnancy 127
prejudice 26, 27, 28–9, 31, 32, 40, 169
- official, against gambling 206
- social, armour against 75

prestige 86, 211, 212, 258, 274–5
- social 70, 216, 342

pride 49, 61, 257
- civic 35, 37
- lost 261
- moral 238
- national 77

prison inmates 115, 187–8
privatization 146
privilege 42, 258, 321
- political 61

productivity 129, 131
- pernicious effect of gambling on 163
- suffering 158

profanity 305
profiteering 206
'profligate' pastimes 4
pro-foreignism 59–78, 84
progress 28
prohibition:
- gambling 147, 167, 173, 179, 189, 194, 203
- opium 100, 139, 183

Prohibition of Gambling (1936) 162
promiscuity 243–4, 319
propaganda 84, 101, 148, 161
- anti-gambling 204
- anti-imperialist 56, 78, 85
- anti-opium 100, 132, 141
- anti-prostitution 231
- *see also* official propaganda

props 325
- anachronistic use of 303, 315
- paper pasted on bamboo-skeletons 309
- scenes and 313–15

prose:
- euphoric experiences immortalized in 115
- humorous 239
- pieces glorifying beauty of actresses 340
- presenting laudatory pieces to actresses 334

prosperity 129, 131, 202
- commercial 289
- floating-brothel business 227
- indicator of 203
- materialistic 54
- restaurant and other trades 211

Prostitution Control Regulations 250
prostitution/prostitutes 4, 10, 36, 137, 157, 189, 206, 226–300
- beautiful 216, 257
- contradictory social perceptions of 3
- covert 31
- depiction of sallow addict 123
- differentiation between actors/actresses and 338
- gamblers' money spent lavishly on 164
- guide-books on 98
- man persuades wife to work in 194
- mistreatment by madams 6, 243
- opium smoking closely linked with 116
- patronized by soldiers 143
- retiring 39, 244, 276
- upper-class 75
- worn-out 85–6
- *see also* brothels; courtesans; unlicensed prostitutes

protection 200
- armed 173
- brothels, from harassment by bullies 294
- much-needed 345
- unlicensed prostitutes' bribes to military officers in return for 232
- *see also* self-protection

protection fees 56, 145, 160, 199
Protestant Christianity 77

proverbs 31
Provincial Assembly 69, 158
Provincial Examination Hall 170, 203
Provincial Finance Department 69
Provincial Government 71, 72, 203, 209
Provincial Treasury 178, 179
provincialism 318
psychological issues:
  comfort 326
  escape 107
  pressure 253
  traits 29, 30
  treatment 5
psychology 29, 60, 205
  social 30
Pu Hsiao-ku 258
P'u Liang-chu 87, 99
Pu, Miss ('Chuang-yuan fu-jên') 269–70
public health utilities 25
public opinion 158, 177, 178, 213, 330
  moralistic 201
  organized, lack of 290
Public Safety Bureau/Department 30, 71
public security 8, 28, 289
  escalated 292
  unaffected by popular interest in gambling 183
Public Security Bureau 186, 201, 230, 231
public-works projects 201
publicity 99, 182, 195, 340
  famous actors the target of 346
  texts 161
punishment 42
  capital 165
  harsh 169
  madams inflicting 265
  official 338
  predestined 285
  retributive 245, 285
  symbolic 194
Punjab 27
Purple Orchid 244–5
pyorrhea 124

quack doctors 109–10
quail fighting 207
Quaker Oats 74
qualities of life 13
quality control 129
quasi-captivity 242
quasi-restaurants 280
quinine 100

racecourses 71, 201, 202
racketeering 20, 51
radicalism:
  activism 33
  mass movement 160
  peasant movements 130
  political, anti-foreign 86
  revolutionary 230
  unionists 177
radio broadcasting 343
Rainbow, Paul 28
ransoms 56, 243
rape 284, 319
Raychaudhuri, Tapan 75
Rea, Kenneth 81
real estate 52, 69
realism 11
recession 82, 130, 191, 230
  deep 202
  serious 229
reconstruction 29, 172
recreation 27, 102
  addictive 137
  gambling activities existing the guise of 181
  healthy 35
  one of the few affordable types of 114
  opium use 116
Red Boats 333
Red Flower 257
red pills 98, 100, 101, 102, 118
Red Rose 260
Redfield, Robert 49–50
'Reds' 56
re-education 230, 273
reform shelters 286
refuge shelters 271
regional consciousness 7
relaxation 115
Relief Bureau 172
religion 29, 77, 245
  popular 26, 157
religious fairs 333
religious paraphernalia 216
remittances 25, 37
repentance statement 74
Republican Daily News 33
Republican Provincial Assembly 141
Research Institute of Performing Arts of Kwangtung 67
resentment 49
resistance to change:
  obstinate 23, 41
  strong 30
respect 75
  rules of 251–5
respiratory diseases 27

restaurants 35, 36, 237, 257, 266, 269, 271, 292, 295
  advertisements for 280
  business badly hit 229
  exclusive 259
  'flower' 252
  game extensively and intensively played in 210–11
  high-class 260
  opium in 113
  special task force to inspect all classes of 231
  tea-house 309
  Western-style 63, 65, 73, 260
Restaurants and Tea-Houses Guild 211
revenue:
  gambling 143, 145, 160, 162, 169, 173, 175–9 *passim* 192, 211
  local, lucrative source of 119
  lottery 168, 171, 172, 175
  military 144
  opera 333
  opium 5, 95, 100, 117, 142–6 *passim* 148, 173
  pocketed by high-ranking officials 170
  prostitution-related 232, 286–7, 288, 294
  'sacrificing' of 'immoral source of' 163
Revenue Raising Bureau 176
Revolution (1911) 54, 141, 142, 168, 236, 286, 307, 309
  operatic contribution to success of 306
'Rewards-giving Lotteries for Flood Relief' 172
rheumatism 110, 114
rhyme structure 320, 323
ribaldry 323, 324
rice 130
rice-balls 100
rich people 54–5, 116, 260–1
  gambling activities 208
  opera patrons 331, 333
  promotion to the rank of 218
  wastrels 190
rickshawmen:
  gambling 189, 190
  lawsuit by 212–13
  opium smoking 97, 100, 110, 111, 113–14, 121, 125, 129, 138, 139
ridicule 32, 87, 159, 251
'ridiculous occurrences' 15
riff-raff 246, 247, 258, 310
Rightists 55, 287
river bridges 34
River Police Department 286
roadways 35
robbery 260
rural culture 164
rural migration 12–13
  call for special attention to 31
  induced by poverty and paternal abuses 17
  trend of 42
'rural peril' 31
Rural Reform School 41
ruralism 9
Russian language 75
rustics 31–2

safety 81
salt 139
sampans 188
San-shui 121, 274
San-yüan-li Incident (1840) 50, 79
Sansui 284
Sao Yün-lan 303
satirical comedy 328–9
scenery (landscape) 14, 15, 52
  balance between human emotion and 11
  world-famous 54
scenery (stage) 314
  painted 335
  ridiculed 315
  sensational 313
Scheibe, Karl E. 211
Schiffin, Harold 175–6
Schlegel, Gustav 248, 251, 280
schools 52, 161
  anti-opium publicity in 99
  building of 286
  Confucian classics reintroduced as compulsory subject 78
  cultural invasion of 74
  government 11
  middle 19, 68, 86, 87, 159, 228
  prestigious 37
  primary 24, 28, 68, 283–4, 344
  run only by voluntary agencies 25
  village 28, 33
scouts 267
scripts 302, 316–20, 339
  anti-opium 141
  censored 327
  'culturally corruptible' 303
  examined before allowed to be publicly performed 330
  funny 322, 328
  'good' 304
  happy ending 325–7
  highly politicized 306
  humorous 321, 322–3
  'immoral' 330
  new ideas for 331–2

  overtly patriotic messages and
    themes 327–8
  politicized 306
  quality of 314, 327
  serialized 271
  'sexy' titles 327
  vulgar 309, 310
  witty, sarcastic 322
scriptures 199
sculptures 330
secret lovers 261
secret societies 80
security 200
  national 107
  potential threat to 171
  see also public security
segregation 30
  sex 337
self-control 192, 193, 213
  lost 271
self-destruction 182
self-medication tradition 108, 109, 110
  manuals 140
self-protection 261–9
self-reliance 204
selfishness 21, 30
  triumph of 86
sensationalism 159, 305, 311, 313, 314
  theatrical techniques 334
sensual orientation/pleasure 59, 65, 231, 279
sericulture industry 229
sex 61, 136
  attitudes towards 59, 226
  casual 253, 254
  demand to examine whore's genitalia
    before 263
  depression of activity 124
  enjoyed thoroughly 272–3
  excessive indulgence in 283
  forced 242, 252
  general suppression of 60
  insertion of odorous material into vagina 251
  lowering of moral standards in relation to 226
  penniless customer begging for 264
  psychological pressure 253
  'raw' 253
  unambiguous 283
sex-idols 257
sexual demands:
  refusing 240, 251, 265, 266
  repeated 262–3
  unreasonable and excessive 268
sexual desire:
  abnormal development of 60
  fulfilled instantly 253
sexual impulses:
  excessive, soothing 116
  relief of 284
sexual liberation 282
sexual services 261
sexuality 235
Sha-nan 23–6 *passim*, 99, 120, 130, 134, 138,
    182, 192
  children especially fond of gambling 212
  elders able to stop villagers from
    gambling at poker 195
  folk songs locally sung 194
  most adult males said to be fond of
    gambling 183
  most pleasurable form of gambling 209
  Western card games 215
Sha-pei 202
Sha Tung-hsu 180
Shakee 281
  see also Shameen Incident
Shakespearian classics 332
shamans 215
Shameen 80, 81, 83
  Legation Quarter 291
  secret trading link between foreign
    communities in Hong Kong and 82
Shameen (Shakee) Incident (1925) 33, 50–3,
    59, 83, 84, 88
Shang-yeh yin-hang 56
Shanghai 1, 18, 31, 60–1, 79, 303
  brothels serving opium to customers 116
  cityscape considered even more lovely
    than 54
  'civilized play' 308
  highly skilful tailor from 312–13
  horse racing 201
  martial arts 332
  melancholic novel published in 326
  movie world 276
  organized gambling 162
  prostitutes 240, 251–2, 255, 259,
    261, 270, 273, 276
  vulgar works published and distributed by
    respectable publishers 331
  see also *Shen pao*
Shanghai Incident (1932) 87, 289
Shantung 85
Shao-chou 255
Shao-hsing (city) 229
Shao-hsing (county) 268
Shao Hsing (prostitute) 267
Shao-kuan 241
Shao Wên 337
Shao Ya 259
Shao Ying 266

Shê-tsai Ch'iu 331
Shê-tzu Ch'iu 331
Shen-chen 147, 180
  well-organized gambling places 198–9
Shen Chi 317, 321, 340, 343, 344
Shen pao 80, 96, 115, 140, 159, 160, 169, 173, 176, 206
Shêng Hua 315
Shêng Kang pan 39, 313–14
Shêng Kuei-yung 134
Shensi 318
Shih Ch'ih 216
Shih Hsing-pai 335
Shih-jih t'an hsün k'an shê 86
Shih Ping-chou 306
Shih-yu Shih-jên 215
Shin Pin-ch'ou 307
shop lottery 182, 192, 203
  fairly played 207
  popularity of 213
shops 56, 76, 228
  closure of 185, 194
  clothing, Western-style 260
  forced by police 83
  opium 95, 96, 100, 101, 113, 132–5, 138–9
shrines 269
Shu-ssu chieh 194
Shu Yuan 319
Shui-she Yung 331
Shun-tê hsien chi 194–5
'sick cats' 256
side-effects 108, 140
  pernicious 107
  unwanted 105
silk 129, 250, 271
sing-song girls 58, 199, 266, 274, 276, 282
  blind 236, 268
  famous, report about 205
  forced into 'transaction' 251
  highly popular 246
  professedly patriotic 117
  unlicensed prostitution and 276
  wealthy actors patronized 344
Singapore 178, 233
Singer, Milton 49–50
Siu, Helen F. 12
skin trouble 24
Skinner, G. William 11
skyscrapers 1, 54, 69, 86
slogans 159
  eye-catching 103
  most frequently quoted 162
  nationalistic 86
slovenliness 23
sly prostitutes 229
small-mindedness 22
smiles 255–8
Smith, H. S. 50
Smith, Martin 192, 204, 211
smoking pipes 98, 106, 116
smuggling:
  Japanese goods 51
  opium/narcotics 96, 101, 104, 118, 119, 142
soccer lottery 218
social Darwinism 163
Social Evolution Company 307
social language 31
social order 182, 235
  acts disrupting 26
  destructive force undermining 40
social position:
  wealth an accurate indicator of 343
  women 7, 25–6, 61, 226, 335, 337
social reality/realism 3, 19
  dissatisfaction with 107
social reform:
  official campaign for 286
  radical and intrusive 235
  strong commitment to 309
social rehabilitation 177
social security 218
social status 37, 334
  accepted symbol of 63
  chance to establish 211
  dress identified with 71
  knowledge of foreign language perceived as yardstick of 75
  low 265
  opera troupes 39
  rising 336
  superior 75
social transformation 12
social vices 35, 36
  brief official campaign against 289
socialites 260
socio-cultural functions 3, 40, 48, 77, 84
  implications of gambling for the nation 165
  inferiority 53
  more favourable circumstances 39
  opera 321, 334
  role 9
  significance and importance of the city 42
socio-political order 157
socio-political rights 194
soldiers:
  analogy between prostitutes and 239
  bullying 264

legal *fan tan* houses guarded by 200
unruly 254, 263, 268
unscrupulous, protection from harassment by 258
violent clashes between local bullies and 199
songs:
anti-gambling 194, 205
brothel 251
dragon-boat 31, 193, 207, 320
love 238, 285
lung-chou 194
moralistic 205
popular, anti-opium 110
salt-water 320
vernacular 205, 238, 265
'wooden-fish' 82, 193, 320
see also folk songs; *Yüeh-ou*
Soochow 105, 304
South East Asia 78
opera in 307, 331, 336, 342, 342, 344
opium legally imported from 106
South-western China 142, 173, 176
Soviet Union 75
special effects 313
Special Entertainment Taxation 180
specialization 10
Spence, Jonathan 114, 116, 127
Spengler, Oswald 18, 40
sperm 106, 136, 138
spinsterhood 26
spirit-mediums 215
spiritual pollution 66
'spiritual training' 112
spoken drama 308, 309
popularized form of 310
sports 61, 201
Western-style 64
sports lottery 218
Ssu-ma I 134
stage lighting 314
stage-names 322
standard of living 24, 25
starvation 273, 284
statues 34
status symbols 61, 116
stereotypes 182, 195
low-class whore 255
negative 123
stigmatization 5, 6, 12, 49, 51
backwardness 35
countryside 164
gambling 161, 187
Manchu regime 166–7
modern urban lifestyle 36
opium users 111, 116, 132
stimulants 114, 117
euphoric 116
luxurious 112
stimulation 120
insatiable demand for 122
opium 134
storytelling texts 327
Strait Settlements 307, 341
streets:
back- or side-, gaming houses in 194
narrow 35
strikes, *see* boycotts
student culture 8
'Students' Year of National Products' 86
stupidity 20, 26, 29, 31, 32, 40
Su (better-turned-businessman) 217
Su-chou 12
Su-chou Mei 335, 340
Su Kuo-yung 313, 326
Su T'ung-p'o 18, 104, 106
sugar cane 129, 212
sugar-cane guessing game 157, 208
suggestive gestures 333
suggestive short stories/articles 330
suicide 126, 158, 160
attempted 243, 246
caused by losses in gambling 184–5
gambling held to be a major cause of 161
official statistics on 189
opera scenes of 327
popular means of 127
threat to commit 246, 270
Sun Company Building 36, 69
Sun Fan-wên 137
Sun K'o 65, 79
Sun Mo-han 292
Sun Tzu 239
Sun Yat-sen 57, 58, 65, 71, 102, 162, 173, 232, 239, 287
Ch'en's *coup d'état* against (1922) 173
death of 160
denunciatory writings against opium smoking 143, 144
enemies of 160, 161
'Father of the Nation' 165, 174–81
loyal follower of 292
military interventions of regional forces 239
parade celebrating inauguration as Extraordinary President 345
personality cult 165, 166
success in winning nomination for president 292
Three People's Principles 112
Sun Yat-sen Memorial Hall 34, 161
Sun Yat-sen University 25

Sung Dynasty (960–1279) 11, 104, 105, 106, 249, 303, 318, 322, 333, 334, 336, 337
Sung Tzu-min 79
Sung Yü 59, 209, 243, 256, 275, 276
'superior hobbies' 189
superiority 13, 19, 50
  belief that imported goods stood for 86
  city 32, 34
  cultural 3, 38, 39
  firearms and military tactics 128
  materialistic 28
  modern applied technology 56
  symbolic 41
  things Western 201
  total, publications asserting 42
supernatural issues 242, 245, 307, 327
superstars 311, 326, 340
  income of 343
superstition 26, 30, 76
  fostered 29
  promoting 327
surcharges 288
  'flowery business' 294
  'flower-feast' 287
  gambling 138
  goods held by merchants 85
  low-class brothels 268
surnames guessing games 157, 158, 168–71 *passim* 175, 203
  legalization of 206
Swatow 130, 178
Sweet Peach 257
swindlers 40, 157, 206, 258
  bullying 195–8
  danger of 207
  professional 247
  prostitute 238–9, 279
Swisher, Earl 81
symbolism 14, 16, 17, 22, 84, 313
  cultural 73
  destroyed 71
  intellect and perceptiveness 72
  material progress 41
  modernity 38
  political 34, 35
  religious 307
  urban 35
  visual identity 36
  Western 62, 64, 69, 71, 73
symphony orchestras 68
symptoms 108
  effective agent in treating 110
  help to alleviate 110
  physiological emaciation 123
  withdrawal 122, 128, 148
syphilis 235, 236, 240
Sze Mei 267
Szechwan 104, 119, 130, 139

Ta An 245–6
ta cha-wei 254
Ta Fu 213
Ta Lo T'ien Opera Company 345
Ta-sha-tou 147
Ta Yin-lien 205
table manners 63, 64
taboos 59, 218
  obscene language in opera 330
T'ai-shan 217
T'ai Tsai 255
Taipei 122
  Government Central Hospital 110
  Protestant Episcopal Church 122
T'aip'ing rebels 80, 128, 158, 170
  actors found taking part 322
Taiwan 110, 120, 121, 122, 126, 129
  see also Formosa
Tan Chung-lin 169
Tan pao t'ien 328, 330
T'an Shao-pêng 69
T'an Yü-chien 57
T'ang Dynasty (618–906) 11, 104, 303
T'ang-hsi chin-fen 243, 272
T'ang Kê 59, 75
T'ang Ti-shêng 70, 194
Tanka women 228, 249, 256, 267
T'ao Ching-chieh 18
Taoism 77
  alchemists 137
  priests 213, 245
tap-water 24
tapeworm 24
tax 13, 161, 172
  gambling-related 163, 179, 180
  opium 98, 112, 134, 142, 144, 145
  prostitution-related 227, 229, 231, 264, 286
tax brokerage 95, 229, 251, 268–9, 287
  brothel-taxes 274
  rights 229
tax-farmers 100, 144, 145, 237, 288, 295
  actively involved 286
Tê 157–8
tea 23, 130
  deliciously perfumed 279
tea-houses 58, 64, 132, 237, 276, 295, 309
  chatting with friends in 183
tea parties 254, 255
  expensive 252
Tec, Nechama 182

teenagers 279
teeth 123, 124
temple fairs 138, 202, 317
temples 216, 287
Têng Feip'eng 279
Têng T'ing-chêng 139
Terada, Revd 122
Terry, Charles E. 108, 114, 121, 124, 127
textile products 82
thanksgiving 216
theatre:
  market-place 333
  traditional, criticized 67
  Western/Western-style 304, 331
Theatre Censorship Committee 345
theft 122, 129, 160, 186, 231
  brothel 259–60
  gambling held as a major cause of 159
  violation of ban on 187
therapeutic treatment 110, 113, 114, 115
thieves 165
Thirteen Factories 79
throat conditions 124
thyroid 124
Tien Chiang-ch'un 322, 339, 344
T'ien ch'ü hua-pao 330
Tientsin 201, 292
Ting Ts'ai Wang 326
Ting Yu Kung 58
tips 265, 272
tobacco 135, 282, 315
  promoted 208
Tou-p'i Yüan 308
tourist sites 281
towns 9, 202, 229
trade associations 268
trade-unionists 79, 161, 269
  intimidation by 82
  militant 56
  radical 83
trading 12
tragic opera 325, 326
traitors 79
tranquillity 14
traps 206
treaty-ports 4, 12, 49, 250
triads 264
tricksters/trickery 39, 195–6, 197–8, 235, 253
Trocki, Carl A. 5
truancy 24
Tsa-chiao Shêng 308
tsa-chü 306, 333
Ts'ai Ch'ien 55
Tsai Hung 244
Tsai Liang 14
T'sai Yung-fan 54
Ts'ang Wei-chi 69
Tsê An 65, 74, 75
Tseng Kuo-fan 139
Tsinan Incident (1928) 294
Tsou Lu 158, 170, 172, 195, 292
Tsui-mien-shan-jên 258
Ts'un shih 249, 252, 257, 265, 266
Tu Chuan 22–3
Tu Fu 18
Tu Shao-mu 332
Tu Tsung-ming 110, 120, 121, 126, 129, 140
Tuan Ping 309, 321
tuberculosis 27, 108, 110, 114, 125
'Tuchuns' 76
T'un Huang 116
T'ung-chih 302
Tung-kuan 130, 277
T'ung Meng Hui 172, 306, 307
Tung-shan 37, 52, 53, 70
Turner, Revd John 95, 96, 125
Twenty-one Guilds of Swatow 178
Tzu-hang-shih 208, 333
Tzu-liu-han 314

Umeda, Ikuzō 116, 141, 227
'uncommon scripts' 318
unconventionality 305
undernourishment 125
unemployment 129
unhygienic lifestyle 125
uniforms 74, 82
United States 78, 125
  brothels 252
  clinical studies on opium addiction 121
  Committee on Drug Addictions 127
  goods from 86
  modern research on gambling 192
  opera performance tours 341, 344
  opiate addiction studies 124
  Social Hygiene Bureau 124
  urban planning 35
  weather conditions reconstructed by methods imported from 313
universities 37
unlicensed prostitutes 199, 229, 233, 244, 267
  arrests of 231, 232
  'emergence' of 240
  head of government department twice spotted patronizing 293
  number of 230, 232, 291
  occupation popularly perceived as 236
  perfectly decent workplace of 250

unlicensed prostitutes (*cont.*)
primary school principal patronizing 283–4
protecting the operation of 293
sing-song girls said to have taken to 276
unsophisticatedness 32, 40
urban identity 14–48, 36
absence of 9–13
consolidation of 38
urbanization 318

values:
aesthetic 7
alternative 3
'backward' 25
changing 37
Christian 157
countryside 19, 42
cultural 2, 7, 62, 65
established, validity and inviolability of 326
ethical 157
idyllic 3, 18, 19, 41
politicized 132
popular 7
positive 210
rural 10, 13, 18, 23
social 7
traditional 6, 319, 327, 329
urban 9, 13, 23
Western 4, 59, 62, 65
venereal diseases 267, 285
students found to have 283
transmission to spouse and offspring 278
see also syphilis
vernacular language 7, 63, 218, 310, 339
dialogue 306, 320
humour and 320–5
lively 327
lyrics 193, 303, 306, 320, 321, 323
novels 302, 319
poems 280
songs 205, 238, 265, 307
viceroys 158, 168, 169, 171, 200
vices 4
ardent crusader against 131
government report (1927) 208–9
popular perception of 7
rural places reportedly full of 31
social respectability of 6
see also social vices
Victoria Peak 54
Victorian London 250
music halls 334
villages 13–14
culture of 41
illegal imposition of surtaxes upon 20–1
serious shortage of amusement facilities 164–5
socio-political rights and lineage membership 194
violence 67, 263, 327
anti-foreign 79
British gunboat 83
clashes between rival groups of soldiers or local bullies 199
collective 21, 29, 79
commonplace 200
death as a result of 122
women prepared for 197
virginity 56, 271, 275
lost 244
Vogel, Ezra 230
voluntary associations 159
vomiting 108
vulgarity 305, 311, 323, 324, 330
extreme 333
high degree of 331
'imperialistic' 303

wai-chiang troupes 305
wai shêng 31
Waichow Uprising (1900) 175
waitresses 266
attractive 199
Wakeman, F. 79, 80
Waley, Arthur 79, 128
Waln, Nora 51, 52, 65, 82
Wan-yi 144
Wan Yung 258, 261, 283, 284, 294, 340
Wang Chien-hsun 316
Wang Chiu-hsing 27
Wang Hsiang-chin 106
Wang Hsien-ch'ien 171
Wang Shih 106
Wang Shu-nu 116, 227, 228, 229, 250, 254, 258, 265, 288, 290
Wang Sun-chia 218
Wang Yung-chih 313, 337, 339, 342
Ward, Barbara 202, 333, 338
ward system 11
warlords/warlordism 52, 57, 87, 172–4, 178, 238
corrupt regimes 162
indelible link between opium revenue and 104
narcotic drugs policy 100
partitioning by 102
rise of 96
Warren, James Francis 226
'Warring States' period (403–221 BC) 9

Washington, DC 187
'water-chicken' 249
wealth 12, 51, 52, 55, 116, 175, 241
  changing popular attitude towards 343
  earned by exploiting others 285
  'improper' access to 157
  instant, dream of 163–4
  irrepressible human desire for 213
  legitimate means to acquire 206
  lost in gambling 184
  means to express 70
  outright and fervent believers in cult of 213
  power and 258–61
  relative, of some prostitutes 259
  short-cut to 346
  spent on lawsuit 217
  successful opera actors 344
  waste of 156
Wei Chih 65, 74, 75
Wei Dynasty (386–535) 11
Wei Feng-chin 265
Wei Yüan 106
Wen Chi-fêng 85
Wen-lang Li 192, 204, 211
Wêng-yüan 130
West, Stephen H. 333, 336, 338
West Point 264
West River region 172
Western culture:
  idealization of 304
  influence in opera 331–46
'Western Music Sections' 316
Western opium 139
Western Powers 100
Westernization 1, 4, 7, 63–78, 316
  advocated 41
  physical appearance 60–1, 62
  residences 52, 53
  students under the bad influence of 33
  total, apparently not wanted 332
  wholesale 41
Whampoa 56, 58
wife-selling 159, 160
'wild chickens' 267
wild pigeon fighting 207
Wiley, James 271
Williams's shaving cream 73
'win-a-roasted duck' game 182–3
windfalls 196, 197, 213, 214, 216, 217
  best time of year to test luck in 215
wine 63, 138, 140, 199
  mixed with vinegar 264
  murky 253
wit 324
'Wo ti kuo-ch'ü' ' (prose-piece) 13–14
women:
  abandoned 216–17
  attractive 16
  badly beaten and killed 184
  beautiful 205, 207
  characters-learning text for 193
  charitable refuge for 262
  cheated in lottery 196–7
  country 33
  disabled 32
  fanatical 340
  flirtatious 266
  folk songs mainly sung by 194
  fondness for shop lottery 182
  hairstyles for 60
  homeless 286
  ideal 59
  ignorant 181
  job opportunities for 284
  lack of economic independence 284
  lion-dance teams 15
  lotteries very popular among 214
  mistreatment of 27, 32
  modes of address 75
  naked 330
  'nosy' 214
  opium users 127
  popularity of gambling among 174
  respectable form of amusement for 210
  rich 260
  selling of 262
  social position of 7, 25–6, 61, 226, 335, 337
  suffering of 38
  suicide by swallowing opium 184
  surgery to enlarge eyes 60
  urban and rural, compared 38
  virtuous wives 193, 194
  young 60, 266
  see also girls; prostitution
women's associations 78, 275, 288
women's liberation movement 38, 60, 336
  failure of 61
working class 99, 189
  opium consumption 111
working conditions:
  hellish 272
  inferior 254
writing competitions 161
Wu Chao-shu 65
Wu Ch'i 239
Wu Chih-hui 292
Wu Chun-lin 340
Wu hsien man hua 330
Wu Ju-chou 66

Wu Jui-lin 24–7 *passim* 100, 110, 114, 120, 121, 122, 125, 129, 130, 131, 134, 138, 182, 183, 184, 189, 190, 194, 195, 202, 209, 212, 214, 215, 274
Wu K'o 277
Wu Sung 115
Wu Tieh-ch'êng 65, 166
Wu Tsao 211
Wu Yin 315
Wu Yü 114, 117, 181, 233, 253, 268
Wuhan 177

xenophobia 50, 61, 80

yamens 167, 200, 206, 268, 277
Yang Mei 264
Yang Mou-chien 305
yang yao 106
Yao rebels 128
YCS (*Yüeh-chü shih*) 306, 307, 311, 312, 314, 315, 316, 320, 321, 322, 332, 334, 335, 336, 337, 338, 341, 342
Yeh Pai-heng 166
Yeh Yün-shêng 166
yen chi 117
Yen Hua 116, 117
Yen Jui-shêng 194
Yenan 19
YHKPK (*Chin-tai Kuang-chou k'ou-an ching-chi shê-hui kai-k'uang*) 80, 82, 96, 118, 119, 130, 131, 142, 167, 173, 206, 343
YHP (*Yüeh hua pao*) 55, 65, 68, 70, 73, 76, 97, 103, 116, 119, 132, 148, 163, 165, 177, 178, 181, 191, 197, 199, 202, 205, 208–11 *passim* 14, 216, 229, 235, 237, 259, 260, 262, 263, 266, 276, 282, 284, 295
Yin Tsai 254, 255
youth culture 36
Yü Ch'i-chung 99, 120, 189
Yü Chia-yen 303, 304
Yü Chiao-ch'ing 116, 236, 246, 250, 258, 269, 270
Yü En-tê 95, 106, 116, 119
'Yu-hsi wen-ch'ang' 336
Yu-K'u-style cauldron 249
Yü Liang 246
Yu Mu-yün 336
Yu T'ien Ying Shê 307
Yüan (merchant) 267
Yüan Dynasty (1279–1368) 105, 306, 333, 336
Yuan Shih-k'ai 142, 143, 159
Yüan shu-I 171
Yüeh Chien-ch'iu 314
Yüeh-hua pao 282
Yüeh-ou songs 235, 238, 272, 279, 282, 285, 290
  1920s version of 285
Yün An 14–15
Yung Ch'i 229
Yung Shih-ch'êng 342
Yung T'ai P'ing 326
Yung Tao 104
Yünnan 104, 119, 130, 142, 160
  Ch'en ousted by joint force from Kwangsi, Kwangtung and 173
  lifting of ban on gambling dictated by unruly army officers from 175
  militarists 287
  military forces invade Kwangtung (1912) 165
Yünnan hui-kuan 55

Zeldin, Theodore 2
Zhang Xinxin 273
Zhang Yingjin 19